GOVERNOR THOMAS McKEAN

THE KEYSTONE
IN THE
DEMOCRATIC ARCH:
Pennsylvania Politics
1800-1816

•

By SANFORD W. HIGGINBOTHAM

•

COMMONWEALTH OF PENNSYLVANIA
PENNSYLVANIA HISTORICAL AND
MUSEUM COMMISSION
HARRISBURG
1952

PENNSYLVANIA HISTORICAL AND MUSEUM COMMISSION

•

CHARLES J. BIDDLE, *Chairman*

LEROY E. CHAPMAN*	JOHN W. OLIVER
FRANCES DORRANCE	ISRAEL STIEFEL*
JOHN R. HAUDENSHIELD*	EDGAR T. STEVENSON
A. ATWATER KENT, JR.	CHARLES G. WEBB
THOMAS MURPHY	RICHARD NORRIS WILLIAMS, 2D

NORMAN WOOD*

FRANCIS B. HAAS, *ex officio*
Superintendent of Public Instruction

DONALD A. CADZOW
Executive Director

SYLVESTER K. STEVENS
State Historian

TRUSTEES—EX OFFICIO

JOHN S. FINE
Governor of the Commonwealth

WELDON B. HEYBURN
Auditor General

CHARLES R. BARBER
State Treasurer

---

* Members representing the General Assembly.

PREFACE

Few Americans stop to consider that the fact of their self-government constitutes one of the most amazing phenomena of modern history. Less than 170 years ago, thirteen British colonies scattered along a thousand miles of the Atlantic Coast and bound together loosely in a weak confederation received recognition as an independent nation. Severe as had been the trials of the revolution in which the colonies had achieved their independence, they were no greater than those which faced the new country in the succeeding years. Despite the magnitude of these problems, there emerged a government and a nation sufficiently virile and enduring to master a territory of continental extent, to weather a civil war of titanic proportions, and to achieve a position of economic and political leadership in the world today.

The elements, internal and external, which operated to bring about this astonishing change were many and exceedingly complex; and each may be studied with great profit. One of the most important was the development of political techniques capable of making an intricate federal system based upon an ambiguous written instrument function effectively in a wide area and under the most diverse circumstances. National political parties, with their peculiarly American incongruities, furnished the chief device for the accomplishment of this task. The story of party politics in the United States therefore illuminates the process through which broad democratic principles, written frames of government, and the conflicting desires of antagonistic groups were translated into practicable popular rule.

The first national parties appeared soon after the establishment of government under the Constitution. The Federalists, founded by Alexander Hamilton and directing the administration in the formative years, sought to create a strong central government devoted to the protection of life and property and to the maintenance of conditions favorable to commercial prosperity. Conservative by nature and distrustful of the masses, they were firmly convinced that government was the prerogative of men of birth, wealth, and education. It was natural that they should violently oppose the French Revolution and should favor the British in the wars which flowed from it.

Their Republican opponents, marshalled under the astute leadership of Thomas Jefferson and to a large extent sharing his agrarian outlook, emphasized the doctrine of popular rule and wished to restrict the powers of the central government to bare essentials. The French Revolution as a popular revolt against tyranny enlisted their sympathies; and this feeling combined with the traditional antipathy toward Great Britain to determine their attitude toward the European wars.

Enjoying the benefit of such popular principles and aided by Federalist blunders in the administration of John Adams, the Republicans developed political machinery which transformed a potential into an actual majority and swept the Federalists out of power in 1800.

Although their opponents were never able to threaten seriously the predominance thus established, the Republicans found that the fruits of victory were not all sweet. The absence of a strong opposition weakened the compulsion for unity which had been so important a factor in their triumph; and the responsibilities of office resulted in modifications of their principles. By the beginning of Jefferson's second administration there were signs of the disintegration of the victorious party and of the inception of new political alignments.

The principal factor inhibiting this development was the renewal of serious problems of neutrality occasioned by the resumption of the European wars. The Federalists saw new hopes of victory in opposing Jefferson's policies, particularly that of the embargo, and they began to make strenuous efforts to regain power. The revival of opposition restored Republican unity; and Madison was chosen as Jefferson's successor in 1808.

From this time until news was received of the Treaty of Ghent, the issue of foreign policy served to maintain Republican cohesiveness, although centrifugal forces within the party gained strength. With the end of the war the last obstacles to a realignment were removed; and the Jeffersonian Republicans began to disintegrate as a party. The old organization, nevertheless, retained sufficient momentum to carry Monroe to victory in 1816.

A realignment of parties was evidently in the making as Monroe took office, but its exact form was to be uncertain for many years. A political vacuum, sometimes inappropriately described as the "Era of Good Feeling," existed until the situation was clarified. This amorphous condition resulted from the complex combination of political, social, and economic changes which had taken place since Jefferson's first election.

Pure Federalism had proved politically impossible; and the bulk of the party had come to modify their aristocratic outlook. Many Republicans of a conservative bent had begun to feel that popular rule required the restraints of wisdom in its own best interests. Members of both parties had modified their attitudes on national policies as they lost or gained control of the central government. Commercial changes attendant upon the restoration of peace in Europe, the growth of manufacturing, the resumption of heavy European immigration, westward expansion, and the development of new modes of transport and travel created new forces and brought new issues to politics. Adding to the confusion were the factional and personal quarrels of politicians seeking the perquisites of office for themselves.

In the sixteen years between the first election of Jefferson and that of Monroe, it was the proud boast of the Republicans in Pennsylvania that they formed the "key stone in the democratic arch"; and the presidential elections of 1808 and 1812 amply justified their claim. The State maintained an undeviating loyalty to the national administration throughout the period; and its staunchness was a vital factor in giving to Jeffersonian Republicanism a national basis and in preventing the consummation of sectional projects sponsored by the New England Federalists.

The pages which follow present a study of the politics of Pennsylvania in these years, when Henry Adams considered it to be the "ideal American State" and the "only true democratic community then existing in the eastern states." Though concerned primarily with the course of politics within the State, it attempts to show the interaction between national and State politics and to evaluate the effect of one upon the other. Considerable attention has been given to methods of political organization and to the effect of personalities upon events. While there is some consideration of social and economic trends, discussion of these matters has been subordinated to the presentation of the actions and techniques of the outstanding political figures. It is hoped that the study will contribute to a better understanding of the role of American political parties in the self-government of the American people.

A word may be added on the use of the terms, Democrat and Republican. All Jeffersonians in Pennsylvania considered themselves

Republicans. They also referred to themselves as Democrats or Democratic Republicans. Though not completely consistent in the matter, by 1805 they seem to have formed the habit of using Republican in a generic sense or when referring to national politics and of using Democrat with reference to State politics. This study has generally followed such a distinction.

The author wishes to acknowledge a heavy obligation of gratitude to the many who have assisted him in his research and writing. In gathering material he received many courtesies from the following: R. Norris Williams, II, director, and the staff of the Historical Society of Pennsylvania; the staff of the University of Pennsylvania Library; the Trustees, President Merle M. Odgers, and Miss Hazel Erchinger, librarian, of Girard College; the staff of the Bryn Mawr College Library; R. W. G. Vail, director, and Miss Dorothy C. Barck, librarian, of the New-York Historical Society; St. George L. Sioussat, late chief, and the staff of the Division of Manuscripts of the Library of Congress; Alfred D. Keator, director, and Miss Nellie B. Stevens, assistant general librarian, of the Pennsylvania State Library; A. L. Robinson, librarian, and Professor Leland D. Baldwin of the University of Pittsburgh; the staff of the Carnegie Library of Pittsburgh; and Franklin F. Holbrook, director of the Historical Society of Western Pennsylvania.

The printing of the book was made possible through the generous policy of the Pennsylvania Historical and Museum Commission. To the members of the Commission, to Dr. S. K. Stevens, State Historian, who read the manuscript and recommended its publication, and to Donald H. Kent, Associate State Historian, who has performed a careful and much appreciated job of editing, the author is most grateful. He also wishes to thank Gordon Alderfer for reading the proof.

At the University of Mississippi the author is indebted to James W. Silver, chairman of the department of history, for furnishing material aids to his research and writing, and to his colleagues, Harris G. Warren and George A. Carbone, for reading the manuscript and offering suggestions as to its improvement.

Throughout the course of his work the author has benefited from the encouragement and sound criticisms of his friend and professor, Roy F. Nichols of the University of Pennsylvania, who has directed this study.

The author also wishes to express his gratitude to John Thomas McCants of the Rice Institute and to Lynn Marshall Case of the University of Pennsylvania, who prompted and assisted him in embarking upon his graduate studies.

Finally, the author owes much to his wife, Evangeline M. Higginbotham, for her long patience, her heartening faith, and her assistance in multifarious ways.

TABLE OF CONTENTS

		PAGE
	Preface	iii
I.	The Keystone in the Democratic Arch	1
II.	Unity and Local Quarrels: 1799-1802	25
III.	Judicial Reform and the Tertium Quids: 1803-1804	49
IV.	Constitutional Reform and the Election of 1805	77
V.	Quid Problems and the Emergence of National Issues: 1806	103
VI.	A Year of Confusion: 1807	121
VII.	The Election of 1808	147
VIII.	The Olmsted Affair: State Rights and Factional Politics: 1809	177
IX.	Snyder Honeymoon: 1810-1811	205
X.	Foreign Affairs, War, and the Presidential Election: 1809-1812	237
XI.	War, Politics, and Schism: 1813-1814	271
XII.	Peace and Democratic Disintegration: 1815-1816	303
XIII.	Pennsylvania Politics in Retrospect: 1800-1816	325
	Footnotes	337
	Bibliography	383
	Index	389

ILLUSTRATIONS

GOVERNOR THOMAS MCKEAN. Copy by James R. Lambdin from an original by Gilbert Stuart. From the Collections of The Historical Society of Pennsylvania .... *frontispiece*

GOVERNOR SIMON SNYDER. Copy by James R. Lambdin from an original by Thomas Sully. From the Collections of The Historical Society of Pennsylvania .... *opposite page* 205

CHAPTER I

THE KEYSTONE IN THE DEMOCRATIC ARCH

THE JEFFERSONIAN REPUBLICANS in Pennsylvania were firmly convinced that they had been largely responsible for the triumph of Thomas Jefferson and his party over the Federalists in 1800. Proud of their exploits, they boasted that their State was the *"key stone in the democratic arch,"* unmoved by all attempts to dislodge it.[1] In the national political crises of the sixteen years which followed, events were amply to justify this claim.

The emphasis of these exultant Republicans was upon Pennsylvania's position in party politics; but in a broader sense the State itself was the real keystone of American democracy and of the Union. It best realized in many respects Jefferson's ideal polity, and it exhibited in microcosm much of the diversity that characterized the United States as a whole.

In his *Notes on Virginia* Jefferson set down his ideas for the creation of a superior commonwealth. It is interesting to note in how many particulars Pennsylvania conformed to these views. To Jefferson's mind a vigorous republic could only be sustained by a people whose manners and spirit were uncorrupted. Such a people, generally speaking, was to be found only among the cultivators of the soil whom God had made the repository of virtue. They should also be free from the taint of slavery, which corrupted the masters and contributed an element of weakness to society as a whole.[2]

With its mass of farmers and with slavery verging toward extinction, Pennsylvania certainly harmonized with the Jeffersonian pattern in these respects. In the matter of religion, the diversity of its sects and the prevailing toleration were cited by Jefferson as an example for his own state of Virginia to follow. In like manner, the Constitution of Pennsylvania lacked the basic defects of restricted suffrage, unequal apportionment, and an overpowerful legislature which vitiated the constitution of the Old Dominion.[3]

Similarly, Pennsylvania possessed in its multiformity a goodly portion of the varied attributes of the nation at large. Her western sections reflected the spirit of the frontier, while the mercantile classes of Philadelphia shared the interests and ideals of the eastern states. Her racial stocks and religions matched those of all other sections of the country. Her economy was extended over a broad base which comprehended agriculture, commerce, and manufacturing. It was little wonder that Henry Adams described her as the "ideal American State," whose interests became more and more those of the nation. The same keen observer further characterized her as the "only true democratic community then existing in the eastern states."[4]

In a very real sense Pennsylvania was the keystone in the democratic arch.

I

Physically, Pennsylvania covers an area of 45,000 square miles and measures some 280 miles from east to west and slightly over 150 miles from north to south. In 1800 Pennsylvania formed the land link between South and North and between the Northeast and the Northwest. New York and New Jersey formed its northern and eastern boundaries, except for the extreme northwestern tip which touched Lake Erie. On the west were the Northwest Territory and the panhandle region of Virginia. In that part of the State which lay west of the Allegheny Mountains, the Ohio River was formed by the junction of the Monongahela and the Allegheny and began its long journey south and west to the Mississippi. Geographically, ethnically, and economically, western Pennsylvania was a part of the Ohio Valley region and the Old Northwest.

The southern border of the State touched Virginia in the west, Maryland for its entire breadth, and Delaware in its eastern corner. Across this boundary passed the series of mountainous ridges, which, after entering the State, swing sharply eastward in such fashion that if a diagonal line were drawn from the northeastern to the southwestern corner of the State all the principal mountains, with negligible exceptions, would lie below the line. Thus, the greater part of the mountainous portions of the State are to be found in its south-central and east-central sections.

The southeastern corner of the State lies almost wholly in the Piedmont Plateau. It is bounded on the west and north by South Mountain and Blue Mountain, which are extensions of the Virginia Blue Ridge. Beyond this is the fertile Great Valley of Pennsylvania, which corresponds to the Shenandoah Valley of Virginia, and a series of valleys and ridges until the Allegheny Mountains are reached. Apart from Laurel and Chestnut ridges, the remainder of the region north and west of the Allegheny Front consists of rugged plateau lands.

In addition to the Ohio River system already mentioned, the principal rivers of Pennsylvania are the Delaware and the Susquehanna. The former flows along the entire eastern boundary of the State and empties into Delaware Bay. It is the State's only direct avenue of foreign trade. The Susquehanna served as an important artery of commerce in the early history of the State. Its North Branch rises in southeastern New York and after wide meanders reaches a junction at Northumberland with the West Branch, whose source lies in central Pennsylvania. From there it flows in a southerly and easterly direction through the State, emptying into Chesapeake Bay at Havre de Grace, Maryland. Its course made a great portion of Pennsylvania a commercial tributary of Baltimore rather than Philadelphia in the early years of the 19th Century.[5]

The population of the Commonwealth was marked by diversity of both distribution and origin. In 1800 it reached a total of 602,365.[6] By 1810, in the middle of the period now under consideration, there were 810,091 inhabitants, of which 795 were slaves and 22,493 free Negroes. Thirteen counties in the southeast, covering the Piedmont area and a portion of the Great Valley and eastern ridges, contained nearly 61 per cent of the population, though occupying less than a quarter of the area of the State.

The five counties in the southwestern corner, together with the southern border counties of Somerset and Bedford, constituted the next most populous region with 152,286 people, or nearly 19 per cent of the whole. The large central section of ten counties accounted for perhaps a third of the land surface of the State and had 100,434 inhabitants, a little more than 12 per cent of the aggregate. Population in this region was very unequally distributed. Northumberland County in the Susquehanna Valley boasted 36,327, but Indiana County in the mountainous western section numbered only 161.

The least settled areas lay in the North. Luzerne and Wayne counties in the northeast corner had 22,434 people; the seven counties which lay north and west of the Ohio and Allegheny rivers had 41,614; but McKean, Potter, and Tioga, which lay along the middle portion of the New York boundary, accounted for only 1,858 among them. The frontier regions of Pennsylvania were to be found principally in its interior and northern sections.[7]

The overwhelming majority of the inhabitants lived in rural areas. In 1810 only Philadelphia, Lancaster, Pittsburgh, Reading, and York claimed more than 2,500 inhabitants, though Carlisle had nearly reached that level. Of these, only Pittsburgh, at the junction of the Allegheny and Monongahela rivers, lay outside the older southeastern counties. The city and county of Philadelphia numbered 111,210 people, amounting to nearly 14 per cent of the total population. Of these, 53,722 were residents of the city.[8]

Three main racial stocks lived in the State—the English, the Scotch-Irish, and the Germans. In 1790 it was estimated that the English comprised nearly half of the inhabitants. They were scattered over the entire State, but constituted a majority only in the three original counties of Philadelphia, Chester, and Bucks, and in the Wyoming Valley in Luzerne. The settlers of the last were Yankee immigrants from New England who had migrated on the strength of Connecticut's claim to the northern portion of the State. Another area of sizable English population was southwestern Pennsylvania where Virginians made up the chief element of the population until outnumbered by the Scotch-Irish in the late 1780's.[9]

The next most numerous racial group was the German, which included somewhat less than a third of the people of the State in 1790. The earliest German immigrants were members of the pietistic sects who came in search of religious freedom. They were followed by a mass migration of "church people," communicants of the Lutheran and German Reformed faiths, a considerable number of whom paid for their passage by indentured servitude. The Germans settled principally in Northampton, Berks, Lancaster, and York counties, where they were in the majority, but they also formed sizable minorities in many of the other counties of the Commonwealth.[10]

The large Scotch-Irish immigration of the 18th Century flowed most heavily into Pennsylvania, where many of the immigrants remained, though others moved down the Great Valley to people the back country of the South. In 1790 they constituted perhaps a fifth of the population, settling thickly in the Cumberland Valley and in southwestern Pennsylvania where they were the most numerous element.

Like the English, however, they were to be found in all parts of the State.[11]

A few minor stocks were also present in the population. The Welsh, who had formed a considerable body of the earliest immigrants to the proprietary colony, had been largely absorbed by the English. A similar amalgamation was eliminating the Scotch and Swedish migrants as distinct elements. A few people of French, Dutch, and Irish descent added variety to an already heterogeneous mixture.[12]

Economically, Pennsylvania exhibited a similar versatility. No direct figures can be cited to show the extent of her agriculture, but the relatively heavy population in an overwhelmingly rural area is indicative of its importance. A further evidence of the significance of farming is found in the extent of the State's domestic exports. Adam Seybert calculated in 1818 that the average annual value of these shipments from 1803 to 1812 amounted to $4,155,151, giving to the Commonwealth fourth rank in that category. To this figure should be added an indeterminate amount of agricultural products which found their way down the Susquehanna to Baltimore and helped to raise the small state of Maryland to sixth position in the amount of domestic exports.[13]

In spite of the competition of Baltimore and the inconveniences of navigating the Delaware, foreign commerce as a whole flourished in Pennsylvania. During the same ten-year period, the State ranked third in re-exports of foreign goods and in the amount of registered tonnage engaged in foreign trade. It likewise held the same rank in customs receipts from foreign imports for the decade from 1800 to 1809.[14]

Contributing to the success of Pennsylvania commercial enterprises was the position of Philadelphia as the financial center of the country in the first part of the 19th Century. The chief factor in this pre-eminence was the presence of the first Bank of the United States, located there from 1791 to 1811. Other strong institutions were the Bank of North America, the Bank of Pennsylvania, and the Philadelphia Bank, all operating under State charters, and the private bank of Stephen Girard, which opened in 1812.[15]

Holding a high rank in agriculture, commerce, and finance, Pennsylvania enjoyed an overwhelming superiority over its sister states in the field of manufactures. It stood first in the value of manufactured goods as reported by the returns of the Federal marshals in 1810; and its total production amounted to $32,089,130, nearly equal to the combined output of Massachusetts and New York, which ranked second and third respectively.[16]

The variety of the State's population and economic activities was matched by the numerous religious groups which flourished in the traditional freedom established by William Penn. Presbyterians were by far the most numerous. They were found in all parts of the State, but predominated in the Scotch-Irish regions of central and western Pennsylvania. Lutherans and German Reformed congregations ministered to the bulk of the Germans, though the minor sects—Schwenkfelders, Mennonites, Moravians, and Dunkers—were prominent in the German counties. The Society of Friends centered largely around Philadelphia, but it had long since ceased to be the most numerous and influential group. Even smaller numerically were the Episcopalians, who suffered from the effects of toryism during the Revolution. Among their communicants, however, was a significant number of wealthy leaders of Philadelphia business, professional, and social life. Less important in 1800 than they later became, the Baptists, Methodists, and Roman Catholics maintained congregations among the people.[17]

Free from trammels in the exercise of religion, the citizens of Pennsylvania were also blessed in possessing a liberal constitution. In the hectic days of 1776, an extra-legal convention had met and drawn up a Constitution distinguished by many unusual features. With the typical colonial aversion to a strong executive, it created a government based on a unicameral legislature and gave to the latter all the real power. The executive duties were vested in a President and a Supreme Executive Council. Their functions were almost purely administrative, and they lacked even the weakest check on legislation. Another strange feature of this instrument was the Council of Censors, an elected body required to meet every seven years to review the conduct of the government. It was to determine what alterations in the Constitution were required and had the sole power of calling a convention to make such changes.[18]

Conservative reaction to this unique frame of government was bitter; and for the next fifteen years the touchstone of politics in the Commonwealth was one's attitude toward the Constitution. Its opponents were labeled Anti-Constitutionalists or Republicans; and its supporters were appropriately denoted Constitutionalists. By the end of the period the former had wrested the initiative from their adversaries; and a new Constitution was adopted in September, 1790.[19]

Although the new Constitution gave evidence both of its origin as the product of conservative triumph and of the influence of the recently adopted Federal Constitution, it still gave to the Commonwealth one of the most liberal state governments of the time. The major differences from its predecessor appeared in the abolition of the Council of Censors, the creation of a bicameral legislature, and the substitution of a Governor with a suspensive veto for the ineffective President and Executive Council.

The legislature was called the General Assembly and consisted of a House of Representatives and a Senate. Representatives were chosen annually by the eligible voters; State Senators served four-year terms, one-quarter of them being elected each year. Representation in both houses was apportioned on the basis of taxable population, with redistributions to be made according to censuses taken in 1793 and every seven years thereafter.

The Governor was also popularly elected for a term of three years and might serve nine years in any twelve. He was given a qualified veto over all legislation, and a two-thirds majority in each house was required to override it. In addition, he had an unusually broad appointive power, choosing all officials whose mode of selection was not otherwise specified in the Constitution.

Members of the judiciary held office during good behavior and could only be removed by impeachment or by address of two-thirds of the members of each branch of the legislature.

Suffrage was exercised by all freemen of the age of twenty-one and over who had lived in the State for two years previous to the election and who had paid a State or county tax assessed at least six months prior thereto. The tax payment was waived in the case of sons of qualified electors during the first year of their majority. All elections were by ballot. No qualifications other than age, citizenship, and residence were required of officeholders or members of the legislature. The Constitution also contained a bill of rights which, among other things, gave categorical recognition to the people's right to reform, alter, or abolish the government, but it established no procedure whereby this might be exercised.[20]

Pennsylvania thus had a government which guaranteed the liberties of the people and gave to them an effective voice in the election of their rulers. It did not establish manhood suffrage; but in 1800 this was not considered a serious deficiency. At that time, only New Hampshire, Vermont, Kentucky, and Tennessee had provided this feature, while seven of the fifteen states still placed property restrictions on the exercise of the ballot. Furthermore, the difference between the Pennsylvania system and universal manhood suffrage amounted to very little. One authority has estimated that the ratable male population above the age of twenty-one amounted to only five per cent less than the entire male population of the same age group.[21]

The Pennsylvania voter in 1800 was called upon to make frequent use of his franchise. State Representatives were chosen annually; Congressmen were elected biennially; sheriffs, coroners, and the Governor were voted on every three years; and State Senators came up for election every fourth year. The choice of these officials involved the holding of two annual elections, since the inspectors of the general election on the second Tuesday in October were chosen in a preliminary election held ten days earlier. Every fourth year there was still a third election since the electors of the President and Vice President were selected on the fifth Friday preceding the first Wednesday in December. As if this were not enough to make the voter politically conscious, borough and township elections were held annually in the spring; and the legislature was in session for three months or more each winter.[22]

The politics of such a State in such an era were certain to be furious, complex, and interesting.

II

As one of the United States, Pennsylvania found itself vitally interested in the international situation of the country. The waning years of the 18th Century had been momentous ones for Europe and for the new government in the western hemisphere. In France, revolutionary excesses, reactionary corruption, and the pressure of never-ending war had resulted in the *coup d'état* of the 18th Brumaire. Napoleon Bonaparte, First Consul and archetype of the man on horseback, had placed himself in the saddle, and for the next decade and a half all of western civilization was to experience the manifestations of his unscrupulous genius. Not least among those drawn into conflict was the fledgling republic in the New World.

The exigencies of European conflict were not new to the United States in 1800. The Federal government had scarcely been organized and set into operation when the French declaration of war on Great Britain in 1793 had given it the difficult choice of remaining neutral in its own best interests or of taking up arms against its recent foe alongside its Revolutionary ally and sister republic of France. In the years that followed the people had been torn with dissension over successive crises arising out of the war and foreign relations generally. The affair of Citizen Genêt, Jay's treaty with Great Britain, British and French commercial depredations, the XYZ Affair, and an undeclared naval war with France had been severe trials for the country; yet in the succeeding years still greater perils were to threaten its security and even its continued existence.

The twenty years of European war also had a profound effect on the economic life of the nation. The development of a strong central government with its aid to commerce in the forms of tariff and tonnage duties, the negotiation of commercial treaties, the establishment of a navy, and the provision of better credit facilities through the creation of the first Bank of the United States, had stimulated foreign trade greatly, but the European wars contributed another factor which made this period unique in American commercial development.[23]

The years from 1790 to 1815 showed a complete cycle in our trade abroad. A competent authority has described the era of growth up to 1807 as "unique in that there has never been since, in the history of the United States, a period of such length in which the foreign trade so completely absorbed the attention of a large portion of the people and exercised so vital an influence on industry in general." Capital flowed into shipping; and the building of vessels on a large scale was resumed. The great markets for foodstuffs abroad led to higher prices for farm products and channeled capital and labor into agriculture. Manufacturing alone received no important stimulus. It suffered from lack of capital and still more from the heavy imports of European manufactured goods. However, the period from 1807 to 1815 saw foreign trade fall sharply through the effects of commercial restrictions and war; and during these years American manufactures received their first great impetus.[24]

Americans were keenly interested in the course of the wars in Europe and were sharply divided in their sympathies; but there was for them a still greater absorption in their domestic affairs where there was much to be done. In 1800 the people had before them the conquest of the continent. Population had resumed its westward march following the Revolution; and the states of Kentucky and Tennessee had extended the sisterhood of the Union to the Mississippi. North of the Ohio River lay the vast Northwest Territory, while to the south of Tennessee was the new Mississippi Territory. By 1816 this great western region, whose settlement had been seen as the work of a thousand generations by Jefferson in 1801, had been dwarfed by the acquisition of Louisiana and further extended along the Gulf of Mexico by the annexation of West Florida. Ohio and Louisiana had already become full members of the Union; and by 1819 all of what had been the West in 1800, with the exception of the Michigan Territory, had been formed into states.

No less pressing than the matter of occupying and populating the extended lands of the West was the problem of government. The framework had been drafted in the convention held in Philadelphia during the hot summer months of 1787, and its machinery had been set in operation in New York two years later. Still to be determined, however, was the matter of its survival and progress.

There had been great accomplishments in the early years. A functioning organization had been created; national credit had been restored and finances placed on a sound basis; the centrifugal tendencies of the period of the Confederation had been reversed; and a threat to the national authority had been convincingly crushed in the instance of the Whiskey Insurrection. Foreign nations had witnessed the phenomenon and had accorded a grudging recognition to the power of the new government—England had withdrawn her troops from the Northwest, and Spain had settled the disputed southern boundary and granted navigation of the Mississippi.

Yet all was not smooth sailing. Particularism among the states had not died; and under the lash of economic and social differences, local jealousies, and political conflict, it was to reappear in a form more threatening than it had yet shown. So, too, there were questions to be answered respecting the control of government and the extent and nature of its powers.

Government under the Constitution had been created principally through the efforts of the commercial and moneyed classes supported by those who sought a stable society and favored a strong, effective government. Its early policies were naturally tailored largely to fit their interests. The farming population and the laborers, mechanics, and small tradesmen of the cities received less obvious benefits, although they formed much the greater proportion of the citizens. As one Hamiltonian measure followed another, their discontent grew and under the aegis of skillful political leaders found expression in the creation of a party of opposition. The new party not only denounced control of the government by the dominant minority but also the growing expansion of Federal power at the expense of both liberty and the reserved rights of the states.[25]

The bitterness of this basic clash of economic interests for power was augmented by divergences over foreign policy occasioned by the incidents of the European conflict. Sympathies in the struggle tended to divide along the same lines and to give added vigor to the nascent party struggle for the control of the government.

American attachment to France and the self-conscious pride of the new republic had united in causing an almost unanimous acclaim of the opening stages of the French Revolution. The mounting violence, disorder, and radicalism which accompanied the overthrow of the monarchy in France, however, gave pause to the more conservative elements in the United States. Their alarmed fancies descried among the masses of their own countrymen the same sans-culottism which had destroyed order in France, confiscated property, and sent its erstwhile owners to the guillotine. The devout were shocked by the revolutionary attack on Christianity and viewed Jefferson's deism as the omen of similar assaults in America.

The conflict between France and Great Britain brought added strains. By and large, the commercial and capitalistic interests reaped great profits from trade with the British, despite losses occasioned by the latter's seizure of a number of American ships. Economic motives thus furnished them with further reasons for opposition to the French Republic. To their antagonists, this leaning toward England smacked of toryism; and the hatred of the French Revolution appeared as a desire for monarchy and a hostility to the liberties and well-being of the people as a whole. Each group by its reactions to foreign affairs confirmed in the mind of its opponent the suspicions and distrusts which had first developed over purely domestic concerns.

The party struggles between the Federalists, led by Alexander Hamilton and representing the interests of the conservative and moneyed groups, and the Republicans, led by Thomas Jefferson and reflecting the views of the agrarian and laboring elements, centered around these two main issues of domestic and foreign politics—the extent of the powers of the central government, and the attitude to be adopted toward the great belligerents in Europe.

Pennsylvania played an important part in the acrimonious combats of the Federalists and Republicans. Her capital city of Philadelphia had served as the national capital for a period of ten years; and she had known at first hand the triumphs of the dominant Federalist party of the 1790's. It was in the Quaker City that Citizen Edmond Genêt had brought to a climax his efforts to circumvent American neutrality and had been dismissed for his pains; it was in Pennsylvania that the first major exercise of Federal power had subdued the Whiskey Insurrection; here had burst the passionate protest which greeted the disclosure of the terms of Jay's Treaty; here, too, an unreasoning Federalism had taken advantage of a threatened war with France to pass measures of almost unparalleled political stupidity; and here, finally, had come the harbinger of national Republican triumph in Thomas McKean's election as Governor in 1799.

These things and many others Pennsylvania had witnessed, and her own political behavior had been crystallized in patterns formed largely by these questions of national import.[26] In Philadelphia were found the great party organs which set the tone for the press of the entire country. John Fenno's *Gazette of the United States* disseminated the views of Hamiltonian Federalism; Philip Freneau's *National Gazette* served as the Jeffersonian oracle; William Cobbett poured abuse on the Republicans through the columns of *Peter Porcupine's Gazette;* and, pre-eminent among the Republican journals, the *Aurora,* edited by Benjamin Franklin Bache and his successor, William Duane, thundered forth denunciations of Federalism and all its works.

In the midst of this continuous verbal barrage, astute Republican leaders organized their forces and developed a disciplined political machine which seized upon the Alien and Sedition Acts, direct taxes, and other Federalist legislation to achieve a complete, if narrow, victory in 1799.[27] This was shortly followed by the Republican success in the presidential election of 1800, and to the exulting Jeffersonians of Pennsylvania it seemed that their labors had been the major factor in that achievement.

III

Politics in Pennsylvania were a source of continuous bewilderment to the Republicans of other states and of despair to the Federalists of New England who hoped for a revival of their power. Hence, those who had some knowledge of the subject were often called upon to explain the nature of the parties in the State and the forces which acted upon them.

The basic phenomenon of Pennsylvania politics in the Jeffersonian era was its overwhelming and undeviating Republicanism. Albert Gallatin and William Duane, who differed widely on many issues, were united in their explanation of this matter. Gallatin summed it up neatly by asserting that "Republicanism rests there on principle pretty generally, and it rests on the people at large. . . ." Duane was more diffuse in explaining that political strength lay with the great mass of the people, but he avowed flatly "that upon a question of *principle*, Pennsylvania is always to be relied on." John Binns in an analysis of the State's politics in 1812 reached similar conclusions.[28]

The fundamental Republican tenet was insistence upon popular rule. This received expression in varied forms, but it was frequently reiterated in Republican addresses and in the press. A meeting at Northumberland in 1808 declared that the foundation of Republicanism was the belief *"that the people are capable of self government"*; while Binns, in delivering the "long talk" before the Tammany Society of Philadelphia in the previous year, had gone further in describing the means through which popular control was exercised. "Few and simple," he asserted, "are the principles of democracy. *Universal suffrage —frequent elections—rotation of, and responsibility in, office.*" These were the "pillars of democracy" which would sustain the supremacy of the people against all who would question it.[29]

The remaining articles of Republican faith were erected upon this foundation, and they were supported because they were believed to contribute to the realization of this popular rule. One of these minor principles was opposition to the creation of privileged orders, which were considered dangerous to the public liberties. This explained the perennial Republican antagonism to the establishment of banks and other chartered monopolies. In like manner, the party regarded a permanent national debt, standing armies, and a large navy as steps toward despotism, while it looked upon a strong militia as the true bulwark of defense for a republic. The Republicans also detected great dangers to liberty in the tendency toward expansion of the powers of the Federal government, especially of the judiciary with its independence of popular control. To combat this, they laid great emphasis on the federative nature of the union and the maintenance of state rights. Finally, the Republicans placed great stress upon the constitutional rights of trial by jury, freedom of opinion in both civil and religious matters, and freedom of the press.[30]

The negative character of these derivative principles arose to some extent from Republican experience as a party out of office. It resulted even more, however, from the watchful jealousy which was felt essential to prevent public officials from usurping undelegated powers. Likewise, the Republican sympathy for the French Revolution, while based to some degree on the feeling that the French were following the American example in creating a republic, stemmed mainly from the belief that the primary issue in the struggle was one of liberty and popular rule against tyranny and monarchy.[31]

By inference, if the Pennsylvania Republicans were supporters of liberty and popular government, it might be supposed that the Federalists were believers in monarchy and aristocracy and were opposed to the constitutional freedoms so loudly insisted upon by their opponents. Such an opinion was often expressed by the Republicans,[32] and it found some justification in the writings of the more extreme Federalists. One of the latter asserted in 1813, "that few patriots, genuine, resolute, and firm, have ever risen to power, in *elective* governments."[33] Nevertheless, the true picture was somewhat different.

The Federalists bitterly denied such charges and even disputed with their opponents the appellation of Republican. They held that the latter were more properly to be called Democrats, or Democratic Republicans. The Federalists, on the other hand, did not persevere in calling themselves Republicans, though they did make frequent use of the label, Federal Republican.[34]

The Federalists were, for the most part, genuine republicans, whatever may have been their vagaries in the matter of party names; and this truth was recognized even by William Duane in his more candid moments.[35] They differed from their adversaries chiefly in giving greater emphasis to the rights of property and the preservation of order than to the rights of man and the maintenance of liberty.

One of the best definitions of their beliefs was given by the *Gazette of the United States* at the time of Jefferson's first inauguration. The paper wrote:

> Federalism is not favouriteism[*sic*]: it is not a blind attachment to particular men, founded upon ambitious hopes. It is an attachment to good order secured by good government, by respect to the rights of person and property, by religion, morality, and law, and manifested by the *peaceable* fruits of righteousness—an attachment which never will and never can be subdued in the breasts of honest men. . . . if the measures of the government should tend to the ruin of our commerce and the consequent decay of industry and agriculture, to the destruction of public credit, to the corruption of morals and to the discouragement of literary and religious institutions, we shall never shrink from the duty, however unpleasant, of lifting up our voice against such an abandonment of our dearest and most important interests.[36]

The basic tenet of Federalism, therefore, was an insistence upon sound government with adequate guarantees for the security of life and property. Such government could in their opinion be expected only from "the wealthy, the well informed and the well principled."[37] To them what the Democrats called rule of the people was pure Jacobinism with no kinship to true liberty and justice.

The corollaries to this major principle of Federalism were support of a strong central government and abhorrence of the French Revolution. The first originated to some extent from the circumstance of Federalist control of the government in its formative years, but it also arose from the conviction that the interests of property could be best promoted and protected by that agency. The second sprang from their natural tendency to abhor all that savored of anarchy and disorder; and they viewed the conditions in France as a confirmation of their worst fears of popular rule and as omens of what might be expected in this country under Republican auspices.[38]

Duane, Gallatin, and Binns also agreed that the Republicans in Pennsylvania had no great party leaders. Binns stated that the party had "never yet been remarkable for its prominent characters"; Gallatin, that not a single person had enough influence to carry even one county; and Duane, more flatly, that there were no leaders because "the great body of the people will not submit to be led."[39] Though these judgments were in the main true, there were, nevertheless, Pennsylvania Republicans in 1800 who were in some degree leaders; and a knowledge of the more important of them is essential to any understanding of the political behavior of the State.

The nominal head of the party was the Governor, Thomas McKean. A native of Pennsylvania descended from Scotch-Irish parents, he was sixty-five years of age when first inaugurated in 1799. Holding public office almost continuously from the time he was eighteen, he had a distinguished record. A signer of the Declaration of Independence and one-time president of Congress, he had helped draft the Delaware Constitution of 1776 and the Pennsylvania Constitution of 1790; and he had for twenty-two years served as the Chief Justice of Pennsylvania. Essentially a conservative and renowned for his irascibility, his choice as the Republican candidate for Governor was probably due more to the influence of Alexander J. Dallas than to his own popularity. However, he had previously identified himself with the party through his opposition to Jay's Treaty and to the Alien and Sedition Acts. His intemperate statements before taking office and his removals afterward had earned for him the bitter hatred of the Federalists; and though this served in some measure to raise his standing with the Republicans, he still had little political influence outside a narrow circle of officeholders.[40]

McKean's Secretary of the Commonwealth in 1800 was Alexander James Dallas, Jamaican-born British subject of Scotch descent, who had come to Philadelphia in 1783 at the age of twenty-four. Admitted to the bar two years later, he soon achieved some prominence by the publication of his reports of judicial cases in the Pennsylvania and Federal courts. His great energy and ability led to his appointment as Secretary of the Commonwealth by Thomas Mifflin in 1791; and he served in that capacity until Mifflin left office in 1799. Dallas had taken an active part in Republican party affairs; but his greatest abilities lay in the preparation of addresses and the organization of political machinery behind the scenes rather than in popular leadership. Politically ambitious, he was handicapped by his own aristocratic tastes and by his desire for social prominence in a society dominated by Federalists. After Jefferson's inauguration he resigned his position with the State government to become United States Attorney for the District of Pennsylvania.[41]

High in the circles of Republican leadership was William Duane, editor of the *Aurora*. A storm center during the days of John Adams's "terror," he had caused a riot by an attempt to circulate a petition against the Alien Act and had received a merciless beating at the hands of a group of volunteer officers whose actions in the suppression of Fries's Rebellion had been criticized in his journal. His strictures against a presidential election bill under consideration by the United State Senate in 1800 had led to his indictment under the Sedition Act, and he was constantly assailed by libel suits instituted by aggrieved individuals.

The tempestuous events of these years were matched by the vicissitudes of his early life. Born in New York in 1760 of Irish parents, he was taken to Ireland upon the death of his father five years later. Here he acquired a passionate devotion to Irish freedom and a dislike of the British government which was to color all his subsequent career. His antipathy toward Great Britain was not lessened by his experiences in India.

He was engaged to go to Calcutta in 1787 for the purpose of editing the *India Gazette* for a term of three years. His contract being broken after his arrival, he subsequently established three other papers in that country and also held minor positions in the government of Bengal. In 1792, while editing the *Bengal Journal,* he was arrested on the orders of Lord Cornwallis and imprisoned, because, according to his story, he had exposed an attempt by speculators, including the acting governor, to create an artificial scarcity of rice.

Suffering great losses from this incident, Duane in the same year established the *India World* and was again prospering when a new disaster overtook him. On December 27, 1794, after he had already announced his intention of selling his holding on January 1 and returning to America, he was placed under arrest by Sir John Shore and two days later was sent to England. His offense in this case was a criticism of government favoritism to officers of the regular army at the expense of the veterans of the East India Company. He was unable to obtain restitution for his property losses; and the remainder of his brief residence in England is notable principally because he presided at a large public meeting in November, 1795, sponsored by the London Corresponding Society to protest parliamentary infringements on the Bill of Rights.

He departed for America not long afterward and upon arriving in Philadelphia was associated for a few months with the *Philadelphia Gazette* before joining Benjamin Franklin Bache on the *Aurora.* When the latter died in the yellow fever epidemic of 1798, Duane succeeded him as editor, and through marriage to Bache's widow in 1800, he became proprietor of the paper as well.

As a party editor Duane had few peers. His trenchant style combined with audacious courage and a sincere conviction of the righteousness of the causes he sponsored made the *Aurora* the most influential Republican press in the country and the most hated by the Federalists. In spite of his very real abilities, however, Duane's influence steadily declined in the years of Jeffersonian ascendancy. To some extent this was the result of the removal of the capital from Philadelphia to Washington, but it was due even more to Duane's own limitations.

Forthright and dogmatic, Duane regarded himself as a guardian of the true Republican faith, and he was not disposed to show leniency to those who departed therefrom. The dangers of this attitude were not lessened by his vanity and by a propensity to sublimate personal grievances into questions of principle. Like John Randolph of Roanoke, he was by temperament a person who thrived best when in opposition; and, as in the case of Randolph, this penchant was to be the occasion of party feuds and schisms.[42]

One of Duane's closest friends and political allies was Dr. Michael Leib, Congressman from Philadelphia County. The son of a German immigrant, he was born in the county in 1760 and studied medicine at the University of Pennsylvania. He served as surgeon to a militia battalion during the Revolution; but his real medium was politics rather than medicine, and he abandoned practice as he became more deeply involved in political affairs. Taking an active part in the work of the Democratic and German Republican societies, he was chosen to three successive terms in the legislature, where his abilities attracted notice from Jefferson. He was then elected to Congress in 1798 and re-elected in 1800.

An able writer of polemical matter, Leib was still more forceful in debate, where his sneering manner and withering invective silenced even the stoutest opponent. He was a master politician in his own district of Northern Liberties in Philadelphia County; but his insatiable lust for power gave play to a natural talent for intrigue; and his cruelty and vindictiveness toward those who crossed him was one of the fundamental causes of Republican division in Pennsylvania in the years which followed.[43]

A number of other leaders were also of some significance. Tench Coxe and Dr. George Logan were high in the party councils in Philadelphia. Joseph Hiester of Berks County and Peter Muhlenberg of Montgomery County were the most influential leaders of the Germans in the State. William Maclay, former United States Senator, was a power in Dauphin County, while his brother Samuel played a similar role in Northumberland. William Findley, John Smilie, Albert Gallatin, and Hugh Henry Brackenridge were prominent in party affairs in the western counties; although the last two became less important after 1800, since Gallatin became Secretary of the Treasury and Brackenridge a Justice of the Pennsylvania Supreme Court. The list of leaders might be greatly enlarged as nearly every county had its quota of those who wielded or wished to wield political power.

It is even more difficult to single out the leaders of the Federalists. In many ways their organization was so casual and their strength so unco-ordinated as to make it a real question whether they constituted a party or a state of mind. Duane asserted that they had leaders whom they followed implicitly and that they were always systematic in their actions. Binns, on the other hand, described the party as being "made up of nearly all leaders, but with few followers"; and he seems to have come nearer the truth.[44] Certainly, it is impossible to discover any two or three men who controlled the party.

The best-known personality was probably James Ross of Pittsburgh. Born in York County in 1762 of Scotch parents, he went to Canonsburg when eighteen years of age to teach in a Presbyterian academy. Intending to enter the ministry, he was persuaded by Brackenridge to become a lawyer. Studying in Philadelphia, he practiced in Washington County until he moved to Pittsburgh in 1795. He soon became involved in politics, helping to frame the State Constitution of 1790 and acting as one of Washington's commissioners to negotiate with the insurgents in the Whiskey Insurrection. Chosen as United States Senator in 1794, he served until 1803. His unsuccessful campaign as Federalist candidate for Governor against McKean in 1799 made him at least the nominal leader of his party. Yet he probably had no more influence in western Pennsylvania than Alexander Addison, John Wilkins, James O'Hara, John and Presley Neville, and a number of others.[45]

It is no easier to select the outstanding Federalist leaders in other parts of the State. Charles Smith, a lawyer, and William Hamilton, editor of the *Lancaster Journal,* were prominent in their county; but they were not a whit more powerful than numerous others. Joseph Hopkinson, James Milnor, Charles Willing Hare, William Lewis, and William Rawle were Philadelphia lawyers who participated actively in party affairs; but they did not overshadow the merchants, Levi Hollingsworth and George Latimer. There were many more of equal significance who might be named.

On the whole, it seems probable that in most cases the Federalists conducted their politics through agreements arrived at through social contacts. Apparently, their solidarity was due more to mutual opposition to Republican policies than to disciplined following of recognized leaders.

In the matter of political machinery Federalism was deficient almost by necessity. It had developed at Lancaster a system of nominations by a county committee composed of delegates chosen by township and borough meetings; but elsewhere in the State the selection of candidates was left to haphazardly organized meetings in which a ticket was drawn up by an appointed committee and adopted by the whole group. To co-ordinate the activities of different localities, the Federalists made use of corresponding committees.

The party supported a large number of substantial newspapers. In Philadelphia there were four daily papers disseminating its views— *Poulson's American Daily Advertiser,* the *True American,* the *Philadelphia Gazette,* and the *Gazette of the United States.* The last two devoted the most attention to politics. The most prominent Federalist weeklies were the *Lancaster Journal* and the *Pittsburgh Gazette,* but every important town had one of its own.

These papers usually prospered because of the extensive patronage they received from the commercial classes in their communities; but their effectiveness as political instruments is questionable. The ingrained Federalist belief that government was properly the function of "the wealthy, the wise, and the good" made it almost impossible to present a program calculated to appeal to the mass of the people. It is reasonable, therefore, to suppose that these papers circulated principally among those holding such convictions and that they did little to add new recruits to the party.

In like manner, the stiff-necked Federalist sense of propriety restrained its followers from pandering to the public for the sake of its votes. Alexander Hamilton recognized the party's deficiencies in this respect and proposed to remedy the situation by establishing a program of charitable societies under Federalist patronage. His suggestions, which have been described as an attempt to preach fraternity as a substitute for equality, were unheeded in Pennsylvania until 1813.[46]

The Republicans experienced none of the misgivings which hampered the Federalists in their political efforts. The uphill fight to overthrow Federalist control of the State had emphasized the necessity of unity; and it was achieved through the development of political machinery. This was principally a matter of concentrating their efforts in support of a single ticket so that their opponents might not profit from Republican divisions. Thus the crux of party organization lay in the question of nominations.

The problem was made somewhat simpler by the prevailing antipathy to self-announced candidacies. They did not exist in Pennsylvania at this time except for the offices of sheriff and county commissioner; and the practice was frowned upon even in these cases. In general, it was held that the office should seek the man. A public official was regarded as a public servant; and it was expected that the people should choose their own agents. Although this might be circumvented in various ways, it was too firmly believed to be the object of direct attack.

In the making of nominations, both Republican principles and expediency dictated that popular participation should be as broad as possible. While a general meeting open to all members of the party was in theory the most democratic method, it was subject to the practical objections that in large districts an equitable representation was impossible and that the people of the community in which the meeting was held had a disproportionate voice in selecting the candidates. For these reasons, the Republicans turned to the district delegate system in which the townships or other electoral divisions chose representatives to serve on a county committee which was authorized to make nominations. With local variations, this plan had been adopted in several counties of the State prior to 1800, and it became virtually standard procedure in all counties in the next few years.

Apart from establishing a method for the selection of candidates, the county machinery usually provided for the creation of a standing or permanent committee which carried on correspondence, exercised a general supervision over the conduct of campaigns, and guarded the

Republican interests in the intervals between elections. Vigilance committees were usually established in each township to distribute literature, see that the voters got to the polls, and perform any other necessary tasks.

Above the county level, organization was not quite so well developed. In senatorial and congressional districts which covered more than one county, nominations were made by committees of conference composed of delegates chosen by the county organizations. Their nominations were usually accepted without question. However, no fixed or satisfactory system of nominations had been developed for the statewide elections of Governor and presidential electors.

A rather haphazard State convention had been held in Harrisburg in 1788 to nominate an Anti-Federalist ticket for Congress; but the State nominating convention, although a matter of dispute in 1792, was unsatisfactory both because of the difficulties and expense of travel and the lack of well-organized local machinery to insure its representative character. The pure legislative nominating caucus had not been adopted by 1800; and gubernatorial candidacies and electoral tickets were, for the most part, determined by meetings composed of legislators and the Republican leaders of Philadelphia. The same group also chose the State corresponding committee and gave it the duties of publishing addresses and co-ordinating the efforts of the party units in the counties.[47]

The work of these semi-official party committees was aided by the Republican papers in the State. Duane's *Aurora*, published daily in Philadelphia, was the most influential, while the Lancaster *Intelligencer* and the Pittsburgh *Tree of Liberty* were the most important of the weeklies printed outside the city. The Tammany Society of Philadelphia was also active in party affairs and was regarded by the *Aurora* as "the principal rallying point of republicanism."[48] Its efforts were supported by the celebrations of the Republican militia and volunteer companies on the Fourth of July and other suitable occasions.

Possessing the advantages of a well-conducted press and efficient political machinery based on democratic principles and bolstered by a traditional acquiescence in majority rule, the Republicans were also fortunate in the broad electorate to which they appealed. Duane asserted that the party was "composed of the great body of the cultivators who are themselves the actual tillers of their lands, [and] of the manufacturing classes in the city and principal towns." On the other hand, Binns reported that the Federalist party was made up of "nearly all the lawyers, nearly all the merchants, most of the persons [parsons], many of the physicians, everything that considers itself a part of the natural aristocracy."[49]

Under such circumstances, it is not surprising that Pennsylvania maintained itself as the Democratic keystone in the sixteen years after 1800.

CHAPTER II
UNITY AND LOCAL QUARRELS: 1799-1802

A STRONG AND AGGRESSIVE Federalist Party had contributed much to the Republican victory in Pennsylvania in 1799. It had forged Republican unity and, by its excesses, had added large numbers to the ranks of its opponents. After the election of 1800 Federalism in the State declined precipitately; and within two years John Quincy Adams was to describe it as "so completely palsied, that scarcely a trace of it is to be discovered except in here and there a newspaper edited by New England men."[1] Gratifying as such a metamorphosis must have been to the Republicans, it was not without its cost. The virtual disappearance of Federalism weakened the compulsion for unity and gave play to Republican differences on measures and men which by 1802 had resulted in a number of local divisions in the party.

I

The Federalist decline in Pennsylvania began with the momentous gubernatorial election of 1799, and the party's downfall in that year was due in large measure to its own actions.

The subdued Federalism of 1802 was a far cry from the arrogant party of 1798. In the spring of 1798 a Federalist Congress had responded with enthusiasm to John Adams's request for additional military and naval preparations against France and had levied a direct tax on slaves and dwellings to help pay for them. Unpopular as these measures were with the Republicans, they could be justified by the threatening state of foreign relations. However, the Federalists went even further and used the anticipated war as an excuse for the passage of the Alien and Sedition Acts. Federalist officials enforced these laws in a partisan manner, and individual members of the party committed other outrages as they sought to stigmatize the Republicans as traitors to the country.

In Pennsylvania this intemperance was best shown in the incidents growing out of Fries's Rebellion. John Fries, in March, 1799, had led a body of armed German farmers of Northampton, Berks, Bucks, and

Montgomery counties to Bethlehem to free a number of prisoners arrested for opposing the assessment of the dwelling tax. This action led to the proclamation of a state of rebellion; and several Federalist volunteer military units were sent into the region.

The conduct of these troops was such as to create an enduring hatred of Federalism. The editor of a German newspaper at Reading was flogged; the prisoners taken in the disaffected areas were treated with callous and unnecessary harshness; and William Duane was given a severe beating by a group of Philadelphia officers, who were incensed by his criticisms of their actions. These and other instances of Federalist violence in 1798 and 1799 gave substance to the Republican charges that the Federalists had instituted a reign of terror.[2]

It was under such conditions that the Pennsylvania gubernatorial campaign was fought in 1799. At its conclusion in October, Thomas McKean had polled 37,255 votes to 32,643 for James Ross, his Federalist opponent. The latter had carried the city of Philadelphia and thirteen counties, including Allegheny in the west, Huntingdon in the central section, Bucks and Luzerne in the east, and all nine of those that lay along the southern border. McKean received majorities in twelve counties, with 46 per cent of his total vote coming from the eastern counties of Philadelphia, Montgomery, Northampton, Berks, Dauphin, and Northumberland. He also carried Washington, Westmoreland, Lycoming, Mifflin, and Wayne, while he had a substantial vote in a number of counties which furnished majorities for Ross.[3]

The Federalists were inclined to blame their defeat on the German vote. Alexander Graydon thought that the explanation lay chiefly in the program of taxation which touched the German farmers in their highly sensitive pocketbooks. He was inclined to regard Fries's Rebellion almost in the light of a Republican campaign maneuver intended to exploit this antipathy to taxation.[4]

John Adams also considered the Germans responsible for McKean's triumph, but he explained it differently. He believed that the chief factor had been the great influence of Peter and Frederick A. Muhlenberg, who had led their people against the administration out of personal pique—Peter, because Washington had refused the tender of his services in the Provisional Army; and Frederick, because of Adams's own unwillingness to appoint him to office.[5]

The views of Graydon and Adams do not suffice to explain the Republican victory. While it was true that the German counties of Berks and Northampton gave McKean a majority of 5,700 votes; Lancaster, also a German county, gave Ross a margin of 1,000 votes. In general, the Republican triumph appears to have been the result of good organization and leadership which capitalized on Federalist taxes, the Alien and Sedition Acts, Fries's Rebellion, and the "terror" to give actuality to what had previously been only a potential majority. The Federalists were almost inevitably in the minority, but they were not overthrown so long as their rule was satisfactory. The arbitrary measures of 1798 and 1799 aroused the latent power of Pennsylvania Republicanism and ended Federalist control of the State forever.[6]

II

There was scarcely a respite in politics after the Republican victory in the gubernatorial election. The attention of both parties was directed to the presidential contest in 1800, and excitement continued high until Jefferson's election was finally decided upon by Congress in February, 1801.

Part of the bitterness which continued after the campaign of 1799 arose from the acrimonious disputes of McKean with his Federalist opponents. Their personal attacks on his character caused him to retaliate with the assertion that the opposition to his election included "Traitors, Refugees, Tories, French aristocrats, British agents, and British subjects, and their corrupt dependants [sic], together with not a few apostate Whigs."[7] Infuriated by these epithets, the Federalists were still further enraged by McKean's energetic removal of Federalist officeholders in the State.

When the Federalist Senate referred to these matters in an insulting reply to his inaugural address, McKean answered with characteristic asperity. He pointed out that his remarks on his opponents had been made prior to his inauguration and could be of no concern to an official body. Furthermore, they had reference to only a part and not all of the Federalists. He defended his removals vigorously, asserting that they deserved approbation rather than censure. Some officials had been removed from a conviction of their unfitness, others because of the "prostitution of official influence to party purposes . . . [and] the defamation of the Executive Magistrate," but many had had their commissions renewed even though they had been among his "most decisive and influential opponents." However true McKean's analysis may have been, the Federalists were unimpressed and continued to denounce him with fury.[8]

Of greater importance was the dispute over the presidential election law. In 1796 presidential electors had been chosen on a general ticket voted on by the whole State. This law had expired, and a new one was necessary for the election in 1800. In the light of McKean's majority in 1799, it was virtually certain that a renewal of the old act would give the entire electoral vote of the State to the Republican candidates, Thomas Jefferson and Aaron Burr.

Federalist control of the State Senate gave them the means of preventing such an unfavorable result. When in December, 1799, the Republican-controlled House of Representatives passed a measure for the use of a general ticket, the Senate ignored the bill and passed one of its own. This provided for dividing the State into districts so arranged that the Federalists would carry six out of the total of eleven and gain nine of the State's fifteen electors, if the popular vote were the same as it had been in 1799. Neither house would recede from its position; the session ended without adopting any legislation on the subject.[9]

McKean was much irritated by this deadlock. At first he considered calling a special session in August, 1800, intending to issue a proclamation directing the manner of the election if the two houses again disagreed. Later he discarded this plan and decided to await the results of the October elections, hoping that a new legislature might prove more co-operative.[10]

His hopes seemed well-founded when the results began to come in. The Federalist decline was spectacular. The party carried only seven counties—Yankee-populated Luzerne; the southeastern triumvirate of Delaware, Chester, and Lancaster; Adams, newly created out of York; and Somerset and Huntingdon, the last of which has been called the "Tory center of the West."[11] The Federalists even lost one of the six representatives from the city of Philadelphia.

Overall, the Republicans won 55 out of 78 seats in the House, six out of seven State Senators, and ten out of thirteen Congressmen. They nevertheless fell short of their objective, since the Federalists retained control of the State Senate by a slim majority of two votes.

Despite his disappointment, McKean issued a proclamation convening the General Assembly on November 5, 1800.[12]

Party spirit immediately focused on the impending contest in the legislature. A public meeting at the State House in Philadelphia drew up a memorial to the Senate and the House. It protested the failure to revive the old law for the use of the general ticket and prayed that the legislators would in this instance choose the electors by a joint ballot of the two houses. A similar meeting was also held in Montgomery County.[13]

The *Aurora* meanwhile declaimed passionately against those who belittled the presidential election as a mere contest of parties. On the contrary, it would decide the questions of peace or war; extravagance or economy; increased or reduced taxes; speculation with, or honest management of, the public funds; and, finally, the renewal of proscription and terror or the establishment of "a moderate and liberal spirit."[14]

The Federalists were equally active. Their hopes rested on the firmness of the thirteen Senators who formed their majority in that branch of the legislature. In a special edition on the opening day of the session, the *Lancaster Journal* addressed an appeal "To Honest Men of All Parties." In its view, the Federalist Senators had made an honorable proposal in the previous session which the Republicans had rejected, and they could not now agree to any terms without surrendering the rights of themselves and their constituents forever. To agree to a joint ballot would mean the election of Jefferson and would make the Federalists "hewers of wood and drawers of water" to a party which sought to engross all Federal as well as State offices. Furthermore, a joint ballot would infringe upon the spirit of the Constitution. If the Senators would remain steadfast, they would be "protected, honored and respected by the people, when the revolutionary projects of the present day" were buried.[15]

A Federalist meeting at Dunwoody's Tavern in Philadelphia on the same day provided legalistic support for this attitude. Waiving the question of the constitutional power of the legislature to choose electors under any circumstances, they categorically denied its right to select them by joint ballot of the two houses. They held that the superior numbers of the House of Representatives so outweighed the power of the Senate under such circumstances that it made a mockery of the latter's status as an independent branch of the legislature. Thus, unless a joint ballot was specifically provided for in the Constitution, it was illegal. It was not so provided in this case; and, therefore, it was "only by concurrent voice [of the two houses] that the sense of the people in the choice of electors can be constitutionally conveyed."[16]

Such glib subterfuges did not pass without challenge. Alexander J. Dallas replied to the constitutional objections in a public letter, while Republican meetings were quick to point out that the Federalist United States Senators, James Ross and William Bingham, had no right to their seats if joint ballots of the legislature were unconstitutional except where specifically provided for.[17]

The Federalists, however, refused to be disturbed by such trifling inconsistencies and persisted in their tactics. The House of Representatives drew up a bill for election by joint ballot; the Senate amended it to provide that the House should choose eight and the Senate seven electors; the House refused to concur in the amendment; and the Senate would not recede. Matters were thus stalemated. The thirteen Federalist Senators stood firm; and the delighted editor of the *Gazette of the United States* was lavish in praise of their "Spartan Virtue," hailing them as the "SAVIOURS OF THEIR COUNTRY."[18]

The Republicans were forced to give way. With the support of McKean, a bill was introduced which provided for the choice of fifteen electors by joint ballot, with each house making eight nominations. It passed and was signed by the Governor on December 1, 1800. In the election on the following day, eight Republican and seven Federalist electors were chosen, and they cast their votes for their respective party candidates.[19]

McKean was much annoyed by the situation and blamed Federalist officeholders for the recalcitrance of the thirteen Senators; but he wrote Jefferson that he had supported the compromise because a single vote might be decisive in such a close contest and because he felt that it would be a bad precedent for any state to fail to participate in a presidential election.[20]

The election was not so close as McKean had expected. It was soon known that Jefferson and Burr were assured of election by the votes of South Carolina. Thus, the efforts of Pennsylvania's Federalist Senators had been in vain. Most of the party accepted the results with reasonable equanimity. Jasper Yeates, an Associate Justice of the State Supreme Court, thought that there would be little essential change in the measures of the government, but he hoped to profit by the purchase of the government stock which he expected alarmed investors in England to sell.[21]

The *Pittsburgh Gazette* also found some redeeming aspects of the situation: the *Aurora* would no longer be filled with lies and slander; the Federalists could demonstrate by decent behavior how a minority should act toward the constituted authorities; and, finally, the Republicans would learn the great difference between "directing and abusing" the conduct of government.[22]

Although the Republicans were overjoyed by their electoral triumph, they were soon dismayed by a new complication. Jefferson and Burr had an equal number of votes; and by the terms of the Constitution the choice between them lay with the House of Representatives voting by states. The more extreme Federalists saw an opportunity to defeat Jefferson and to destroy Republican unity by supporting Burr; and some even hoped to prevent an election altogether before the expiration of Adams's term. The balloting began in the House of Representatives on February 11, 1801; and on the first trial Jefferson was supported by eight states, Burr by six, and the votes of Vermont and Maryland were divided. Further polls resulted in the same deadlock until the thirty-sixth ballot on February 17, when enough Federalists abstained from voting to give Jefferson ten states and the necessary majority.[23]

The Republicans in Pennsylvania were necessarily helpless pending the result of the contest. The *Aurora* had given warning of the Federalist scheme as early as January 10, 1801, but it had not been able to suggest a practical method of combating it. Governor McKean, however, thought he had found a solution for the problem. He proposed that Jefferson and Burr should themselves decide which was to be president in case Congress failed to make a choice. If this were done, he intended to recognize their authority by a proclamation and to call out the militia for their support. He likewise planned to arrest the members of Congress who were responsible for the situation and to try them for treason. He was pleased, however, that it had been unnecessary to carry out these projects.[24]

The Republicans had thus triumphed over the Federalists in national as well as State politics, but they soon found that their difficulties were far from ended.

III

It has always been easier to unite people in opposition to something than to obtain their agreement on a program of positive action. Federalist supremacy had been overthrown by a diverse combination of those whom it had alienated. Individual differences among the Republicans had been subordinated until victory was secured; but once the party was safely ensconced in power, divergences of belief and temperament, and, above all, personal jealousies began to shatter its one-time unity. The first ominous sign of division appeared in the senatorial election of February 18, 1801, in the legislature.

The facts were simple. In joint session, the two houses of the General Assembly had met and balloted for a United States Senator to succeed William Bingham, whose term expired on March 3, 1801. On the first ballot, there had been no choice. Peter Muhlenberg and Dr. George Logan were tied with 45 votes each; and one vote had been given to William Jones, Republican Congressman-elect from the city of Philadelphia. On the second ballot, John Bleakley, a Federalist Representative from the city, voted for Muhlenberg instead of Jones and broke the tie.[25]

The Republican reaction was violent. Jonathan Roberts, Jr., a young Representative from Montgomery County, had become somewhat disillusioned with his party in December; but he now felt that it was "in an hand g[a]llop to destruction." The *Aurora* also condemned those who had supported Muhlenberg and expressed the hope that none of them would be re-elected.[26]

Such disapproval did not arise from any lack of party orthodoxy in either candidate. Logan was a descendant of one of the most prominent Quaker families of the Commonwealth. Educated abroad, he had practiced medicine briefly in Philadelphia and had then retired to manage his family estate of "Stenton." A friend of Benjamin Franklin and an admirer of Jefferson, he had become a Republican during the 1790's. His most noted exploit was the self-appointed mission to France in 1798, when he attempted to solve the dispute which was bringing the United States and France to the verge of war. The Federalists were enraged by his effrontery and responded by passing the Logan Act which forbade private citizens to meddle in such matters; but the Republicans acclaimed him and sent him to the legislature, where he was serving at the time of the senatorial election.[27]

Muhlenberg had had a more spectacular career. Born in Montgomery County, he was descended from two of the outstanding German families in the State. Sent to Germany, where he was apprenticed to a grocer, he ran away and returned to America as a soldier in a British infantry regiment. Following his discharge, he studied for the ministry and became pastor of a German congregation in Virginia's Shenandoah Valley. Taking an active part in the events leading up to the Revolution, he entered military service in 1776, was commissioned a brigadier general in the Continental Army the following year, and was breveted a major general in 1783.

After the war he returned to Pennsylvania and became active in politics, serving in the Supreme Executive Council, the Constitutional Convention of 1789-1790, and the first, third, and sixth Congresses. He had great influence with the Germans and had been a strong contender for the Republican nomination for Governor in 1799. In 1801 he was serving his third term in Congress and had been elected for another. It was generally understood that he would succeed to the Governorship when McKean retired.[28]

The Republican outcry, however, was not concerned with the question of the candidates. It was rather the alarming fact that fifteen Republicans had sided with 31 Federalists to defeat Logan, who had 45 Republican votes. What had happened to the tradition of unanimity and majority rule? While it was true that the Federalists had not elected a candidate of their own, they had triumphed in the defeat of a man whom they hated only less than Jefferson. The friends of General Muhlenberg had done him and the Republican cause a great disservice. So went the refrain in the *Aurora,* accompanied by more or less open threats of reprisals against those who had thus sinned.[29]

These strictures were soon answered. An anonymous correspondent, described as a member of the Assembly who had voted for Muhlenberg, published a long letter in the *Lancaster Journal,* taking umbrage at Duane's attempt to set the standards of Republican conduct and sneering at his threats. He went on to belittle the accomplishments of Logan and to praise highly the merits of his opponent.[30]

The opinions of this writer were contested in the *Aurora* by "Senex," who asserted that the paper had not unduly praised Logan and certainly had not disparaged the abilities of Muhlenberg. The objections were wholly to the manner of the election. "Senex" then accused his opponent of being involved in a plot to overthrow McKean as Governor.[31]

There seems to have been some substance to this charge of political intrigue; but its extent and nature are hard to determine. Not all who voted for Muhlenberg were animated by a desire to unseat McKean. William Findley, Senator from Westmoreland County, defended his vote on the grounds of consistency and personal preference. He had placed Muhlenberg's name in nomination, and he believed him to be the better qualified of the two candidates.[32]

Duane was insistent that there had been underhand maneuvers, but he was most inconsistent in explaining what they were. In June, 1801, he wrote Jefferson that Frederick A. Muhlenberg, then an officeholder under McKean, had been mainly responsible for the division and that he was being considered by the Federalists as a candidate for Governor. This appears to clarify the innuendoes of "Senex" and to identify Frederick Muhlenberg as the author of the letter in the *Lancaster Journal*.[33]

However, Duane did not stick with this explanation. In October, 1802, the *Aurora* published an article which laid the blame on Frederick Conrad, a Representative from Montgomery County. He was accused of having engineered Muhlenberg's election to the Senate in order to create an opportunity to obtain a seat in Congress for himself. A year later Duane had again changed his story. This time he gave Dr. Michael Leib the chief credit for Logan's defeat.[34]

Governor McKean was an interested spectator of these events. According to Findley, he had been active in the support of Logan, and he had certainly entertained hopes that Muhlenberg would not accept the office. When Muhlenberg did so, McKean proposed that Jefferson give Muhlenberg the office of Supervisor of Revenue so that Logan might be appointed to the senatorial vacancy. Although the suggestion was made ostensibly for the purpose of restoring harmony, McKean had probably given some consideration to the desirability of removing Muhlenberg as a possible rival for the governorship. In any case, the proposal was acted on; and Logan was commissioned in July to act as United States Senator pending the meeting of the legislature.[35]

Whatever the true explanation of these intricate political maneuvers, the senatorial election had disclosed divisions in the Republican ranks. The party had begun a new era in its history.

IV

The campaign of 1801 was rather quiet in contrast to those of the two preceding years. The Federalists made very little effort to combat their victorious opponents, and the most noteworthy aspect of the election was the appearance of a number of Republican local schisms.

In his conciliatory inaugural address Jefferson had sought to play down the bitter party animosities which had been so prevalent. The Federalist *Lancaster Journal* hailed his words as the "Downfall of Anarchy and Jacobinism," contrasted Jefferson's conduct with that of McKean, and called for a "union of good men" to combat disorganizers and Jacobins. It even adopted as its motto and published at its masthead the following sentence from the inaugural address: "We are all Republicans—we are all Federalists: We have gained little if we countenance a political intolerance, as despotic as wicked, and capable of bitter and bloody persecutions."[36]

Other Federalist papers professed similar gratification; but this "era of good feeling" was soon ended. As Jefferson began to remove some of the Federalist officeholders and replace them with Republicans, the Federalist editors became more and more critical. By midsummer most of them were in full cry against the administration. Their attacks gained added venom when they learned that Jefferson had invited the "obscene old sinner," Tom Paine, to return to the United States aboard a public vessel.[37]

The *Aurora* replied to these attacks with its usual vigor; but Duane was pretty thoroughly occupied with judicial matters. In April and May a number of the officers who had beaten him in 1799 were tried and fined. Almost immediately afterward the first session of the Federal circuit court established in Philadelphia by the Judiciary Act of 1801 was held, with William Tilghman presiding. Duane was arraigned before it on May 12, 1801, under the Sedition Act for his publication of an attack on the United States Senate; but the case was postponed until the next session to permit him to gather further evidence for his defense.

The following week he was tried before the same court for a libel against Levi Hollingsworth, a Federalist merchant of Philadelphia. Duane protested the jurisdiction of the court, claiming that he was an

American citizen and that the cause should have been tried before the State courts. The judges, however, ruled that he was a British subject.

To a person of Duane's background, no epithet could have been more galling; and he was moved to publish a bitter denunciation of the decision. As a result of this imprudent conduct, he was once more called before the court and sentenced to thirty days in prison for contempt of court. Smarting from the experience, Duane gained an increased hatred of the new judiciary act and of the doctrine of constructive contempts.[38]

The Republicans in Philadelphia had begun to organize for the fall elections by the time Duane was released from confinement. In the city the year was chiefly notable for the introduction of the party's ward committee system.

The plan had its inception at an adjourned meeting of the city Republicans at the State House on July 6, 1801. After selecting a conference committee of fifteen members to confer with similar representatives from Philadelphia and Delaware counties on a nominee for the State Senate, the meeting adopted a resolution directed to the city members of the party. It requested the citizens of the various wards to meet and to choose committees of five persons "for the purpose of consulting together and promoting the general interest of the republic, and to make a report of their proceedings at the next town-meeting."[39]

Responding to this appeal, the Republicans in the various wards met in August, 1801, nominated election inspectors and assessors, and chose the committees in the manner recommended. The ward representatives then met together, forming the "general ward committee," which was charged with the duty of making nominations for members of the city councils and the House of Representatives. The ticket thus prepared was then presented to a town meeting on September 21, 1801. Since there was some dissatisfaction with certain nominees, the nominations were revised at a second town meeting a week later.[40] With certain additions and modifications in 1802, this machinery became virtually standardized for the Republicans in the city.

A similar procedure was followed by the party in Philadelphia County. A general county meeting held at the Northern Liberties townhouse on June 20, 1801, selected fifteen conferees on the senatorial nomination and recommended that another general meeting be held on September 5 to determine what method should be used in drawing up an assembly ticket. The September meeting voted to leave the nomination of the representatives to a committee of 23 delegates to be chosen in a fixed ratio by the different election districts in the county. The delegates were elected according to plan and presented their ticket on September 19, 1801.[41] Unfortunately, the county Republicans did not continue to follow this "district delegate" system, and their failure to do so was to be the source of many future disputes within the party.

The Federalists showed little spirit in the face of this Republican energy. Their first meeting was held on September 29, 1801, only four days prior to the "ward" elections in which inspectors of the general election and assessors were chosen. The meeting adopted a ticket and appointed a committee of one member from each ward which was charged with the responsibility of organizing preparations for the election within the wards. However, the party appeared unable to throw off its lethargy.[42]

The Republicans won a convincing victory in the ward elections on October 3, 1801, and did equally well in the general election ten days later. They carried every office and put an end to the city's consistent record of Federalism.[43] Although the Federalist newspapers claimed that the election had been conducted improperly by the Republican judges, they contented themselves with abuse and made no effort to contest the results.[44]

The Federalists did little better elsewhere in the State. In Lancaster County they lost five out of six seats in the House of Representatives; and in Chester County their majority of more than a thousand votes in 1799 was cut to an average of less than a hundred. They carried only Luzerne, Delaware, Chester, Adams, Huntingdon, and Somerset counties. In the legislature their representation was reduced from 23 to fifteen in the House and from thirteen to seven in the Senate.[45]

More significant than the decline of Federalist strength was the appearance of local schisms among the Republicans. One of the most bitter took place in Pittsburgh over the introduction of the district delegate system of nominations. The plan had been devised by a number of persons at the March term of court. They had agreed among themselves that the townships of Allegheny, Beaver, and Butler counties, which formed a district for the choice of Representatives and

Senators, should hold meetings and elect delegates who should meet together in Pittsburgh at the June session of the court.[46]

No announcement of this arrangement appeared in any of the newspapers nor were the proceedings of the township meetings published. Nevertheless, the delegates met and prepared a ticket for Senator, Representatives, and the various local offices. They also sent representatives to a conference at Washington on August 3, 1801, where William Hoge of Washington County was agreed upon as a candidate for the Congressional seat vacated by the resignation of Albert Gallatin.[47]

Opposition to this procedure appeared almost immediately. A Republican meeting at Pittsburgh on August 19, 1801, denounced the delegate meetings as dictatorial and drew up an opposition ticket headed by General Alexander Fowler and Dr. Andrew Richardson as candidates for Congressman and State Senator respectively.[48]

With the lines thus drawn, the newspapers began to be filled with vituperation. Richardson, Fowler, and their adherents made savage attacks on the "Clapboard Row junto," claiming that it had sponsored the new system for the purpose of fixing its control upon the party. They made particularly vicious assaults upon William Gazzam, an Irish merchant of Clapboard Row, and upon John B. C. Lucas, an associate judge, whom they charged with seeking the nomination to Congress.[49]

Gazzam and Lucas replied in kind, asserting that Fowler had taken part in the March meeting at which the plan was broached and then had broken away because of his own disappointed ambitions. John Israel, editor of the *Tree of Liberty,* also joined in the fray. He pointed out that the Federalists were not offering a ticket of their own and accused them of instigating the Republican schism with the hope of profiting at the next gubernatorial election.[50]

It is impossible to evaluate justly these charges and countercharges, but there appears to have been truth on both sides. Those who fostered the delegate system had certainly given the matter little publicity and were open to criticism on that score. On the other hand, Richardson and Fowler had long been aware of the matter, and their decision to oppose the regular ticket was almost certainly made with a view to Federalist support. Whatever their calculations, the delegate candidates won easily in every contest.[51]

A somewhat different situation existed in Bucks County. Here the Republican county committee based on the delegate system had been established for two years, and the manner of its choice was not open to the same criticisms as at Pittsburgh. The controversy in this instance arose over the selection of a candidate to succeed Peter Muhlenberg in Congress.

The district was comprised of the counties of Bucks, Montgomery, Northampton, Wayne, and Luzerne; but since the latter was hopelessly Federalist, the choice of Republican candidates was made by a conference committee composed of fifteen delegates—five from Bucks, five from Montgomery, and five from Northampton and Wayne. It was customary in selecting the nominees to rotate them among the counties of the district; and in 1801 the candidate was due to be taken from Bucks.

Following the usual practice, the Bucks County Republican committee met and sent its delegates to the conference, and the conference chose Isaac Van Horne of that county as the candidate. The decision had hardly been announced before it was attacked in the *Aurora* by a series of communications, most of them signed, "A Citizen of Bucks." The substance of the charges was that the Bucks County conferees had been instructed to support Joseph Clunn rather than Van Horne and that intrigue had been used to thwart the will of the people. Van Horne was also accused of being a trimmer whose Republicanism was open to suspicion.

The matter was taken up by the county committee; and when it appeared that nearly a third of the townships represented were opposed to the nomination, the committee directed that new township elections be held in September and that the new committee chosen at that time meet and decide the question. The second committee unanimously supported Van Horne, and he was successful in the election.[52]

Of themselves, these local divisions were not of much significance; but, like the senatorial election in the previous February, they were ominous signs of the beginning of Republican disunity.

V

Although a Governor was to be chosen in the election of 1802, political affairs in Pennsylvania were relatively quiet except for quarrels among the Republicans. McKean received a somewhat perfunctory endorsement for re-election; but there were signs that many were becoming dissatisfied with his administration. In Philadelphia differences of opinion within the party appeared over the repeal of the judiciary act and the question of Federal patronage. The Republicans were also forced to cope with the Rising Sun group which opposed Leib's nomination as Congressman. Nevertheless, the party remained united and won a convincing triumph at the polls.

The members of the legislature were annoyed when they convened in December, 1801, by McKean's failure to give them immediate notice of his appointment of Logan as United States Senator. He had likewise omitted to inform them of the elevation of his nephew, Thomas McKean Thompson, to the office of Secretary of the Commonwealth to succeed Dallas, who had resigned in April. Nettled by these things, the two houses refused to receive any communications from Thompson until this oversight had been remedied.[53]

The senatorial question was settled by an election held on December 16, 1801. Logan was chosen with 68 votes; but Joseph Hiester received the ballots of thirty members, including nineteen Federalists and eight of the Republicans who had voted for Muhlenberg in February. Nine additional votes were cast for Isaac Weaver, Samuel Maclay, Nathaniel B. Boileau, and John Kean. More Republicans had voted against Logan than in the preceding election, and they had had Federalist support; but this time they were not criticized.[54]

The most interesting event of the session, apart from the legislation on the judiciary and the impeachment of Alexander Addison,[55] was the passage of the Incompatibility Act over the Governor's veto. The matter had arisen because McKean had appointed Dallas as recorder of the city of Philadelphia despite the fact that he already held the Federal office of United States Attorney for the District of Pennsylvania. A Federalist attempt to remove the latter by court action had failed in September.[56]

The question was brought before the House of Representatives by Nathaniel B. Boileau, a Republican of Montgomery County, and a bill was passed which made the holding of both offices illegal. In the Senate the measure was amended so that it affected Leib, who held the office of physician at the Philadelphia Lazaretto in addition to being a member of Congress. The provisions of the bill were also made retroactive. The Governor returned the measure disapproved on February 3, 1802; but the House overrode the veto by a 76-4 majority, and the Senate by 18-7.[57]

This was the first in a series of vetoes by McKean which were in time to contribute to a complete division among the Republicans. Party tradition stressed legislative supremacy; and some of the more extreme Republicans regarded the executive veto as an instrument of aristocracy since it defeated the will of the people as expressed through their representatives.[58] The possibilities of friction were increased by the Governor's dogmatic temperament and his bristling resentment of criticism in any form. In this instance he was astute enough to recognize that better than half the legislators had voted for the bill because they believed that they were giving proof of consistent adherence to principle, but he was not shrewd enough politically to humor them in a matter where little of real consequence was at stake.[59]

Such incidents were not calculated to improve the Governor's chances for renomination. Some members of the legislature were much dissatisfied with him; and there were rumors that the Comptroller General, Samuel Bryan, was seeking the nomination for himself.[60] A more serious possibility was that Peter Muhlenberg might be chosen by the Republicans or that he might run in opposition to McKean with Federalist support.[61] The Governor was naturally aware of these things and, according to the *Lancaster Journal,* sought to quell the opposition by giving sumptuous dinners to the legislators and by making effective use of the patronage to mollify them.[62]

Responding to such treatment, 51 or 52 Republican members of the legislature held a caucus in Lancaster "a few evenings previous to their adjournment" on April 6, 1802. They voted to support McKean for re-election, but they did not publish any formal proceedings or issue an address. While this informality may have resulted in part from a lack of enthusiasm for the nominee, it was principally due to the fact that the caucus system of nominations had not been fully developed and accepted by the party in Pennsylvania.[63]

The threatened opposition of Muhlenberg was eliminated through the co-operation of Jefferson. This was accomplished by appointing him Collector of the Port of Philadelphia to replace George Latimer, a Federalist, who was removed in August, 1802. The Federalists were much angered both because Latimer had been dismissed and because Muhlenberg had been made unavailable as a gubernatorial candidate.

They claimed that this amounted virtually to a denial of suffrage since no other person had a chance to defeat McKean.[64]

Meanwhile, the Republicans in Philadelphia had begun to divide over the repeal of the Judiciary Act of 1801 and the question of Federal patronage. Jefferson and his followers charged that the new courts created in 1801 had been designed primarily to afford offices for Federalists where they would be secure from removal and at the same time be in a position to thwart the will of the people. They also asserted that the new system of courts was both unnecessary and extravagant. The repeal of the measure was, therefore, one of the first objectives of the Republican Congress which convened in December, 1801.[65]

No one was more bitterly opposed to the new courts than William Duane, who had been ruled a British subject and then imprisoned for contempt by the circuit court sitting in Philadelphia. He had attacked the judiciary act intermittently during the year and was in Washington to observe the fight over its repeal. He and other Pennsylvania Republicans were much dismayed when the actions of Vice President Burr seemed to threaten the failure of the project, and they took steps to bring additional pressure on Congress. Public meetings in Philadelphia on January 30 and February 2, 1802, began work on a memorial; while the Pennsylvania legislature adopted a joint resolution instructing the Senators and requesting the Representatives in Congress to work for repeal.[66]

Most of the Pennsylvania Republicans were therefore greatly shocked when a memorial from the Philadelphia bar was presented in the United States Senate. Waiving the question of the constitutionality of destroying the new system of courts, the memorialists requested that it be retained because of its efficiency. A number of prominent Republican lawyers were among the signers—Sampson and Moses Levy, Peter Stephen DuPonceau, Alexander J. Dallas, and Joseph B. McKean, son of the Governor and State Attorney General. The Federalist press made good use of this circumstance and twitted Duane because members of his party had approved a court which declared him a foreigner and sent him to prison.[67]

The *Aurora* was much disgruntled by the new turn of affairs, and, though avoiding an open attack on Dallas and the others concerned, it chided them for placing their names where they could be used as a means of dividing the party. It also hinted broadly that, as lawyers interested in fees and the multiplication of courts and litigation, their views could not be considered disinterested.[68]

The final repeal of the act in March put an end to the controversy; but it was the occasion of mutual suspicions among the Republicans, and it drew from Duane a severe castigation of lawyers as a class which foreshadowed the later attack on the Pennsylvania judiciary.[69]

Dallas and Duane were also on opposite sides in the matter of Federal patronage. The Federalists understandably opposed any and all removals from office; but no such consistency of view existed among the Republicans. Duane and a number of others wished a thorough sweep made of the Federalists, particularly of those in the Philadelphia customhouse. The *Aurora* declared that the Republicans would "think themselves persecuted if every man of them is not discharged"; and Duane reiterated this sentiment in a letter to Pierce Butler.[70]

Jefferson, on the other hand, hoped to pursue a relatively mild policy in the expectation of winning many of the moderate Federalists to the support of the administration.[71] Gallatin favored this program as did Dallas, who may have been motivated to some extent by his social contacts and ambitions. Their opinions had little effect on Duane, who wished revenge for former sufferings and who believed Federalist officeholders in Philadelphia were using their power to persecute him in his business ventures.[72] These grievances were probably enhanced by his failure to receive what he considered to be a proper share of the public printing and stationery contracts at Washington.[73]

These differences over patronage were not publicized at this time. Duane did not openly criticize Gallatin and Dallas, but he continued in the *Aurora* to demand the removal of the customs officials. Privately, however, he and other Republicans were asserting that Jefferson was too much under the influence of Gallatin and that the latter followed the advice of Dallas and William Jones.[74]

The election of 1802 took place against this background of conflicting views and interests; and that election was to bring into prominence yet another element of Republican discord in the Rising Sun split in Philadelphia County.

In July the "democratic citizens" of the county had met in the Northern Liberties and adopted resolutions in support of McKean for Governor and Leib for Congressman. They had also chosen conferees to meet with those of the city and Delaware County to prepare the congressional ticket. In August these delegates had assembled and nominated Leib as one of the three congressional candidates. Their action had been ratified by another general county meeting on September 4, 1802, which also chose the nominees for the State House of Representatives.[75]

No evidence of opposition to Leib was reported at that time. However, his personal character was open to attack on the charge that he had sought to deprive certain orphans of a portion of their inheritance and that he had made restitution only when forced by judicial action to do so. The *Aurora* defended his conduct, asserting that nothing would have been heard of the matter if Leib had not been a target for political opponents. The circumstances were, nevertheless, peculiar, and they made Leib vulnerable to criticisms on the score of personal honesty.[76]

Opposition appeared when 30 "Democratic Republicans" met on September 15, 1802, at Martin Ludie's Rising Sun Tavern on the Germantown road and issued an address which referred to divisions "arising from the improper character nominated to represent this county in the congress of the United States, and some improper characters to the legislature." To remedy this situation, they issued a call for a general county meeting to be held at the same place on September 21.[77]

Their schemes were doomed to failure. The *Aurora*, which had for some time been printing hints of Federalist intrigues among the Republicans in the county, now began a savage denunciation of those involved, while it lavished praise on Leib's record and character. At the same time the paper exhorted Leib's supporters to attend the meeting and prevent any change in the settled ticket.[78]

These efforts were successful. The second meeting at the Rising Sun adopted a set of mild resolutions declaring that the committee of conference had been duly authorized to select the candidate for Congress and that it was improper, inexpedient, and harmful to the interests of the party to alter its decision. The assembly ticket was also approved. A resolution denouncing the first Rising Sun meeting was withdrawn for the sake of harmony.[79]

Most of those who had sponsored the meeting accepted its decision, although a few held a third meeting and drew up a ticket in opposition to Leib and to certain of the nominees for the House of Representatives.

The principal leaders of this group were Samuel McFerran, Nathan Jones, and Michael Freytag. The *Aurora* castigated them without mercy and professed to believe that they were acting under the direction of Levi Hollingsworth for the benefit of the Federalists. The paper asserted that the latter were seeking to create a Republican split in the hope of rebuking Jefferson by the election to Congress of George Latimer, whom the President had removed as Collector of the Port.[80]

Behind the scenes, however, there was another story. George Logan was the real instigator of the Rising Sun movement as Duane well knew. Leib and Logan cordially hated one another, and the latter had refused to serve on the Republican state correspondence committee in 1802 because it included the former. Leib, according to Thomas Leiper, believed that Logan wished to become Governor and that he sought to destroy the influence of Leib and Muhlenberg because they stood in his way. The apparent harmony of the second Rising Sun meeting had been due principally to the work of William Jones and Dallas, the latter having drafted the resolutions adopted at the meeting. Jones later wrote that the accord had been based to some extent on Leib's declarations that he would not again be a candidate.[81]

Meanwhile, the Republicans in the city had made their preparations with a minimum of friction and had perfected the ward committee system begun the previous year. The citizens of the wards met in June, 1802, and selected their representatives who formed the general ward committee. This body chose the congressional conferees and prepared a ticket which was adopted at a town meeting in August. A second round of ward meetings was held in August and September which made nominations for assessors and election inspectors. In these meetings the practice arose of appointing ward vigilance committees, which were charged with the duties of getting out the vote, supplying ballots, and performing other tasks of that nature. At the same time, a general committee of superintendence was created by the town meeting to manage the conduct of the elections in the city as a whole.[82]

Steps were also taken to support McKean's campaign for Governor. A meeting, apparently called by the participants, was held at Germantown on September 6, 1802, with Thomas Leiper as chairman and Mathew Carey as secretary. It selected a committee, composed of Muhlenberg, Dallas, Jones, Leiper, Leib, and three others, and assigned it the duty of corresponding with other Republicans in the State on the election. An address, prepared by Dallas, was issued by this committee and published both in newspapers and pamphlets. Rather general in nature, it devoted most of its attention to contrasting the happy conditions under Jefferson to the terrors and abuses which had existed under Adams.[83]

Although the *Gazette of the United States* replied to this address at great length and made harsh attacks on Dallas and Leib, the Federalists as a whole did little to oppose McKean's re-election. Ross was unwilling to be a candidate, and even he would not have had the slightest chance of success. The *Lancaster Journal* sought to make the best of the situation. Believing the election of a Democrat inevitable, it preferred McKean to any other member of the party. He could do no more harm to the Federalists, while his temperament assured his opposition to the "silly and destructive measures" of his constituents.[84]

Some Federalists saw things differently. A writer in the *Gazette of the United States* felt that a nomination should be made in order to give the party a rallying point. A number of others shared his views; and a meeting of the city Federalists on August 25, 1802, nominated Ross to oppose McKean.[85]

Nevertheless, no serious campaign was made for Ross either in the city or elsewhere. The Federalist strategy seemed rather to be the exploitation of Republican splits for the purpose of electing a few key Congressmen. At any rate, this appears to have been their hope in Philadelphia, where they encouraged, if they did not originate, the revolt against Leib. Also in Pittsburgh, where the schism of the previous year reappeared, the Federalists co-operated with the rebels on a ticket which was headed by McKean for Governor, but which included John Wilkins, Jr., a Federalist, as a candidate for Congress.[86] Similarly, in the congressional district of Bucks, Montgomery, Northampton, Wayne, and Luzerne counties, the Federalists were accused of having prompted Nathaniel B. Boileau to oppose Frederick Conrad in the hope that they might be able to elect Samuel Sitgreaves.[87]

The election returns showed an overwhelming Republican victory. McKean polled 47,879 votes to Ross's 17,037 and carried every county except Luzerne, Adams, and Delaware. The Federalists failed to elect a single Congressman or State Senator and won only nine out of 86 seats in the House of Representatives. On the other hand, the Republicans had triumphed over their own schismatics as well as the Federalists.[88]

In the three years from 1799 to 1802 the Republican majority in Pennsylvania had climbed from less than 5,000 to more than 30,000 votes. Federalism was almost completely demoralized and, except in a few scattered counties, had ceased to offer any effective opposition. At the same time there had appeared a few minor rifts in Republican unity, but none of them had made any serious impression on the party. On the whole, Republicanism in the State had never enjoyed brighter prospects than in October, 1802.

CHAPTER III
JUDICIAL REFORM AND THE TERTIUM QUIDS: 1803-1804

THE COMPARATIVE CALM of McKean's first administration was succeeded by years of growing bitterness. Prior to the election of 1802 there had been minor divisions based largely upon personal jealousies and the quest for offices; and a vague dissatisfaction with the Governor had developed. A new cause of dissension became prominent in 1803 and and 1804 as the legislature began to attempt modifications in the judicial system and to use its powers of impeachment against the judges of the State courts. McKean's opposition to most of these measures alienated many Republicans; and some of his supporters sought Federalist aid to redress the political balance.

Simultaneously, the Philadelphia quarrels over patronage and the power of Leib became more and more violent. A group avowedly opposed to Leib and Duane established its own newspaper and began an open contest for control of the party in the city and county. This crumbling of party unity at first resulted in a confused pattern with many contradictory relationships; but by the end of 1804 a new alignment was emerging, which, while it still rested principally on the conflict of personal ambitions and the desire for offices, was also founded upon an essential difference in attitudes—the agelong conflict between the supporters of the *status quo* and the advocates of change.

I

The legislative session of 1802-1803 was marked by a growing struggle between the legislators and the Governor over the question of judicial reform. It also witnessed the impeachment of Alexander Addison and the introduction of the Passmore memorial complaining of the conduct of three judges of the Supreme Court. The ground was being prepared for a major break within the Republican Party.

When the legislature convened in December, 1802, one of the matters of greatest interest was the choice of a United States Senator to succeed James Ross, whose term expired in March, 1803. In the election held on December 14, Samuel Maclay received 66 votes; and his Republican opponents, Isaac Weaver, Jr., and William Maclay, got 28 and eleven votes respectively.[1] This victory not only replaced the last Federalist to represent Pennsylvania in the national Senate, but it also raised to high office a man whose political ambitions were great and whose prospects were bright.

Sixty-one years of age in 1802, Maclay was State Senator from the Republican stronghold of Northumberland County. A brother of William Maclay, Pennsylvania's Senator and disapproving diarist in the First Congress, he was born of Scotch-Irish parents in Franklin County and spent much of his early youth assisting his brother as a surveyor. Using the opportunities thus afforded him, he became a resident and one of the largest landholders of Buffalo Valley in Northumberland County (now in Union County).

An officer of the Pennsylvania militia during the Revolution, he had an active political career after its close. Prior to his election to Congress in 1794, he served four terms in the General Assembly and two years as an associate judge for his home county. After leaving Congress, he was chosen a State Representative in 1797 and in the following year was elected State Senator, being re-elected to that station in 1802. A man of some means and considerable talents, Maclay was considered by Duane in 1803 to have the best chance of succeeding McKean as Governor.[2]

The same session of the legislature witnessed another election which indirectly brought prominence to the man who in fact succeeded McKean. Jacob Carpenter, the State Treasurer, died in February, 1803; and a joint session of the two houses was held to choose his successor. Nathaniel B. Boileau, who had unsuccessfully opposed Frederick Conrad for Congress, had some faint hopes of election; but the real choice lay between the ambitious Speaker of the House, Isaac Weaver, Jr., and Jacob Martin of Lancaster, who offered to perform the duties and turn over the salary to Carpenter's widow and child. Weaver was elected by a vote of 59-44, but he was sharply criticized by the Republican Lancaster *Intelligencer* for his cupidity and oppression of the helpless.[3] Apparently unimpressed by such reproaches, Weaver resigned as Speaker on March 1; and the House chose Simon Snyder of Northumberland County as its new leader.

There was little in Snyder's previous career to warrant anticipations of his future election as Governor. Born forty-three years earlier in Lancaster, he was the son of a mechanic who had emigrated from the Palatinate. Apprenticed to a currier and tanner at York when seventeen he had attended night school and received a basic education. Soon after the Revolution he moved to Selinsgrove in Northumberland County, where he attained a modest prosperity as a storekeeper and owner of a mill. He acted as a scrivener for the people of his community and served for a number of years as justice of the peace; and it was a matter of great pride to him that none of his decisions in that capacity was ever appealed to the courts. He represented his county in the convention which drafted Pennsylvania's second Constitution, and then in 1797 he began an almost unbroken public career as a member of the State House of Representatives. His greatest interests were the extension of the jurisdiction of the justices of the peace and the establishment of a permanent system of arbitration as a part of the Pennsylvania judicial procedure.[4]

It was this question of judicial reform which overshadowed all others during the legislative session of 1802-1803. The matter had been under discussion for a number of years, and everyone was agreed that the existing system was unsatisfactory. With the experience of more than twenty years as Chief Justice, McKean, in his annual address to the legislature in December, 1800, asserted that the judicial arrangements were "no longer adequate to the regular and efficient administration of justice." To remedy this situation, he recommended increasing the number of Supreme Court judges and the number of circuits which they served. When he failed to get legislation in that session, he reiterated his proposals to the next.[5]

The reforms suggested by McKean were embodied in bills introduced in both the House and the Senate; but none of these reached final action. Instead, the members prepared certain measures of their own which they felt would achieve the desired objectives. It seemed almost axiomatic to the average Republican in Pennsylvania that if the people were capable of ruling themselves, they were also able to administer justice. In his opinion, the long delays and heavy expenses of litigation arose not out of a shortage of judges but from the existence of a legal system operated for the benefit of lawyers, who fattened their purses with fees. All that was required to rectify matters was the restoration to the people of the administration of justice and the elimination of the legal paraphernalia which caused all the trouble.

As a step in this direction, the legislators proposed to widen the powers of the justices of the peace. A temporary act of this nature had been passed in 1799, giving jurisdiction to the justices and aldermen in actions for damages up to $20 and in cases of rent up to $53.33. The act expired by limitation in 1802; and the House then prepared a new bill making permanent the original act and further extending its scope. This was adopted and sent to the Senate on March 26, 1802, where it died without consideration.[6]

However, the Senate incorporated many of its provisions in a still more sweeping measure of its own—"An Act for the Recovery of Debts not exceeding Sixty Dollars, and to Direct the Manner of Choosing Constables within this Commonwealth." Sent to the House on March 20, it was amended there so as to raise the limit from sixty to one hundred dollars. The Senate accepted the change; and the measure went to the Governor on April 3, the day before adjournment.[7]

Under the provisions of the Constitution, the bill would have become law unless vetoed by McKean within three days after the opening of the next session of the General Assembly. Thus, one of the first matters to come before the legislature was the Governor's message of December 9, 1802, expressing his dissent to what was popularly called the Hundred Dollar Act.

McKean objected to the bill on four main grounds. In the first place, by giving the justices jurisdiction over virtually all causes of controversy among the poor, it left the latter at the mercy of men unskilled in law and unrestrained by a jury in matters of fact. The self-interest of the justices would be unfettered, and they would become instruments of oppression. Secondly, because of the unsatisfactory situation thus created, appeals would be more numerous than ever; and the cost of litigation would be increased rather than decreased. Thirdly, by removing many cases from the jurisdiction of the courts of common pleas where a jury was used, the act tended to elude if it did not violate the constitutional injunction that the right of trial by jury should remain as it had previously been. In McKean's opinion, it was unwise "to indulge the spirit of innovation" on such a question because in worse times it might result in the abolition of jury trial in criminal causes. Finally, the bill was objectionable because it failed to provide for the use of counsel, which would have prevented justice from being warped because of the unequal talents of the various suitors before the justices.[8]

As the bill had originated in the Senate, that body voted first on its passage over the veto. The vote was delayed until December 30, 1802, when the Governor was sustained by eighteen votes, while only seven were cast in favor of the bill.[9]

However, McKean's fight was far from won. The next day a bill was introduced in the Senate for the settlement of disputes by arbitration. After discussion and amendment by both houses, it was passed and sent to the Governor on March 16. Five days later McKean returned it disapproved, stating that he found it even more objectionable than the Hundred Dollar Act and for much the same reasons. On the same day he also returned with his veto a general act providing for the erection of private dams on streams designated as public highways. In this instance, he objected to the third section of the measure because it gave justices of the peace jurisdiction up to fifty dollars in actions for damages caused by such dams. The Senate sustained the veto of the arbitration bill with thirteen favoring passage and eleven opposed, but it overrode the Governor's negative on the so-called Wing Dam Bill; and the House followed suit.[10]

With the defeat of the arbitration bill, the House once more took up the Hundred Dollar Act. However, this was finally postponed until the next session. But the House did consider a measure to revive the act of 1799 extending the powers of the justices of the peace. Though this bill had failed in the previous session, it now passed both houses within three days and was sent to the Governor on April 2, 1803, two days prior to the adjournment of the legislature.[11]

While the Governor and the legislature were unable to agree on judicial reform, they had no quarrels over the impeachment of Alexander Addison, whom McKean described as the "transmontane Golia[t]h of federalism" in Pennsylvania.[12] Addison was born in Scotland and educated for the ministry at Aberdeen University. Arriving in Washington County in 1785, he studied law, was admitted to the bar, and became president judge of the fifth judicial district after the adoption of the new Constitution which he had helped to frame. A violent Federalist, he took a leading role in politics and frequently made use of his position to criticize democracy in addresses to grand juries.[13] His political activities made him an object of attack by the Republicans in general and particularly by Hugh Henry Brackenridge, their leader in Pittsburgh and a lately appointed judge of the Supreme Court.

Irritating as Addison's diatribes were, they offered no direct method of redress; but an indirect way presented itself. One of the associate judges of Allegheny County was John B. C. Lucas, born in Normandy and a graduate in law from the University of Caen. He had emigrated to western Pennsylvania shortly after the Revolution and had become a close friend and supporter of Brackenridge.[14] Probably at the instance of the latter, he attempted in December, 1800, to address the grand jury in answer to Addison, but the latter refused to permit him to speak.

The Pittsburgh *Tree of Liberty* immediately called for Addison's impeachment, but Lucas preferred to take the matter through legal channels. Accordingly, Joseph B. McKean, Attorney General for the Commonwealth, appeared before the Supreme Court in April, 1801, and asked for permission to file an information against Addison for misconduct. The court held that there had been no indictable offense, but it unanimously declared that every judge had a right and the duty to express his opinion on matters before a court. The members of the court added that "It would be indecent and improper in any presiding Judge, to attempt to prevent his associates from the exercise of this right; from the performance of this duty."[15]

Addison chose to ignore this severe rebuke from the State Supreme Court and stubbornly persevered in his actions. On June 22, 1801, he once more refused to permit Lucas to address the grand jury and thus opened the way for his own impeachment.[16]

A House committee made an investigation of the affair in the session of 1801-1802, and it recommended that articles of impeachment be drawn up. They were accordingly prepared and were approved by the House on March 18 and 19, 1802. The only recorded vote on the matter showed 65 members in favor of impeachment with eight Federalists opposed. The Senate decided to postpone the trial to the second Tuesday in the following December.[17]

Nevertheless, when the legislature convened in December, the House did not immediately proceed with the trial, but referred the matter to a committee which made a long report on December 15, 1802, recommending that the House refrain from prosecuting the charges and that it appoint another committee to give further study to the question. The committee believed that Addison's actions gave sufficient justification for his removal by address of two thirds of each branch of the legislature, but it doubted that they were impeachable. It also thought that in this case the penalties prescribed for conviction on an impeachment were too severe. Two days later the House rejected the report without a record vote and proceeded to make arrangements for the trial.[18]

The trial began on January 17, 1803, with Alexander J. Dallas acting as prosecutor for the House and Addison conducting his own defense. When the Senate balloted nine days later, eighteen Republicans declared him guilty, and four Federalists voted for acquittal. On the following day Addison was sentenced to removal from office and was disqualified to act as a judge in any Pennsylvania court.[19]

Addison's impeachment has received severe criticism as a mere partisan action designed to injure a political opponent and to give another office to the Republicans. Such a contention is supported by the vote for conviction; and, in the light of the political situation then existing, it would be foolish to deny that such motives were probably important. McKean was evidently delighted that the removal of such an obnoxious judge would probably result in the downfall of Federalism in the western counties; but it seems unlikely that even this prospect would have overcome his hypersensitiveness toward judicial prerogatives had there not been reasonable grounds of impeachment. The same considerations would appear to apply to Dallas. Furthermore, the Federalist papers and leaders were abnormally quiet if they regarded the conviction as unjust. McKean noted that neither Ross nor any other political ally of Addison had taken his part; and the party press contented itself with the mildest of criticisms.[20]

Toward all these things the *Aurora* maintained a remarkably passive attitude. It seldom offered any comment on McKean's vetoes and in general seemed more favorable to the Governor's position than sympathetic with the ideas of the legislators.[21] The Philadelphia delegation in the House displayed a similar lack of interest in the new judicial schemes. In the vote taken on April 1, 1802, to amend the Senate bill so as to raise the jurisdiction of the justices of the peace from sixty to one hundred dollars, the five members from the city were unanimously opposed and four county members (two were absent) divided evenly on the question. In a vote on the arbitration bill on March 4, 1803, three city members were favorable and one opposed; but the county delegation stood five to one against the measure.[22] The question of judicial reform up to this point was not a matter of difference between the Governor and the Duane group in Philadelphia.

No such diffidence marked Duane's reactions to the Passmore memorial. In 1801 Thomas Passmore, a merchant of Philadelphia, had insured a vessel which later sprang a leak and was abandoned by him.

He then entered claim against the underwriters, and the matter was referred to arbitrators who made an award to Passmore. A few weeks later Andrew Pettit and Andrew Bayard, two of the insurers, filed exceptions to the judgment. This action enraged Passmore, and on September 8, 1802, he wrote and posted a notice on the bulletin board at the exchange room of the City Tavern, assailing this new delay and denouncing Bayard as "a liar a rascal and a coward."

Dallas, as attorney for Pettit and Bayard, asked the Supreme Court, before which the cause was depending, for an attachment against Passmore for contempt. The court then made certain interrogatories, which Passmore answered at great length. He avowed that he had no knowledge that a suit was depending since he thought the judgment of the arbitrators final; that he had not intended to reflect upon the court; and that the writing in question had been posted in a fit of anger and had been removed within a few minutes.

In the view of the court, this did not purge Passmore of contempt since he had admitted writing the notice in question. However, the court recognized that he meant no disrespect to it and would probably have dropped the matter had Passmore followed the suggestion that an apology be made to Bayard. This he refused to do, and he was accordingly sentenced on December 28, 1802, to pay a fine of fifty dollars and to serve thirty days in prison.[23]

Convinced that he had been treated unjustly and desiring retribution, Passmore prepared a memorial protesting against the conduct of Chief Justice Edward Shippen and Associate Justices Jasper Yeates and Thomas Smith. Brackenridge, the fourth and only Republican member of the court, had not taken part in the proceedings.

The memorial was presented to the House on February 28, 1803, by Hugh Ferguson, a member from the city. It was referred to a committee which reported that while a summary punishment of contempts might be necessary where there was a direct insult to the court or resistance to its authority, it saw no such necessity "where the contempts are only consequential or constructive, and not committed within the hearing of the court, nor by treating with disrespect the rules and process, thereof." In such cases the matter should be decided by a jury, and it was therefore recommended that a committee be appointed to draft a bill defining the powers of a court in questions of contempt.

The memorial was then referred to a second committee which reported on March 18, 1803, that a bill defining contempts should be prepared and that an inquiry into the conduct of the judges should be recommended to the next legislature. No action was taken on this report; but three days later David Mitchell of Cumberland County introduced a bill entitled "An Act concerning Contempts of Court." The measure was amended in committee of the whole and approved on its second reading, but it was lost by a tie vote of 36-36 on the final reading.[24]

In 1801 Duane had spent thirty days in prison on the charge of contempt;[25] his experience thus gave added force to whatever theoretical objections he may have had to the methods of the common law. In following the actions of the House on the Passmore memorial, the neutrality shown by the *Aurora* toward other measures of judicial reform completely disappeared; and the paper not only supported punishment of the judges and legislation on contempts, but it also began to attack the theory of judicial independence:

> The frequent abuse of power by judges of the courts and justices of the peace will one day render a total revision of the received maxims concerning the tenure of judicial office necessary. It will one day be a subject of enquiry, why judges and justices of the peace should be more independent of the control of a free people, than those who have the formation and the execution of the laws entrusted to them. It will become a subject of enquiry, whether there is any analogy between what is called the *independence of the judges in England,* and the *independence of the judges* in America—and whether making the former independent of the *king* justifies the making of the latter independent of the people.[26]

When the bill on contempts was lost, the *Aurora* castigated the legislators harshly, declaring that they had sat too long and done too little, that they had done some things which they should not have done and had failed to do some which should have been done. They were trifling with the security and happiness of their fellow citizens; and the *Aurora* felt it a matter of duty to expose them to their constituents.[27]

Such strictures, however, did not apply to the Philadelphia members of the House. Whether from conviction or the pressure of Duane, nine of the city and county members unanimously supported the bill on contempts. One member from each delegation was absent.[28]

The Passmore affair was destined to become increasingly important in the next two years; but, from a political point of view, its chief significance at this time lay in the fact that it offered a method of uniting Duane and the Philadelphia Republicans with the country members in a joint attack on the judicial system. Such an alliance was not yet formed, but its feasibility was beginning to be apparent.

II

The election of 1803 found the Republican splits becoming deeper and more widespread. The quarrel over Federal patronage in Philadelphia nearly reached the point of an open breach, while the Rising Sun movement against Leib gained added strength in Philadelphia County. In Lancaster some of the State officeholders made an unsuccessful attempt to organize a third party movement in support of McKean. The Federalists for the most part abandoned active politics, although the dissident Republican factions courted their aid.

In the winter and spring of 1803 Republican differences over Federal patronage reached the boiling point in Philadelphia. The *Aurora* began to renew its demands for getting rid of the Federalist officeholders in December, 1802; and in the same month Michael Leib wrote Mathew Carey from Congress, proposing that Carey organize a popular movement which would prove to Jefferson by memorials that the people demanded these removals. Leib also hoped that such a demonstration would show the President "how to appreciate the opinions of such characters as advise him to act in opposition to the sentiments of the people."[29]

One of these "characters" was William Jones, Congressman from the city and a close friend of Dallas. To counteract the efforts of those seeking removals, Jones, in February, 1803, along with Andrew Gregg, Robert Brown, John Smilie, John A. Hanna, Isaac Van Horne, and John Stewart, all Congressmen from Pennsylvania, drew up a letter to Jefferson indignantly denying that the Pennsylvania delegation was dissatisfied with him because he had not removed all Federalists from office. Such was far from true; and the agitation arose, they believed, from a "small minority" and particularly from "interested individuals."

The letter was shown to Leib and other Congressmen from the State who suggested certain modifications, especially the omission of the phrases just given. A second draft was accordingly drawn up which Leib promised to sign; but after Jones left Washington he not only refused to sign it but took a copy of the original letter and spread word of it around Philadelphia. The signers of the first letter then decided not to send either but to make their expressions of confidence to Jefferson in person.[30]

The disclosure of Jones's letter aroused an immediate storm. A meeting of the Democratic Republicans of South Ward on March 9, 1803, adopted resolutions demanding removal of the Federalists and calling on the other wards to hold meetings to nominate committeemen to draw up a memorial removing any impressions which might have been given to Jefferson that the people opposed such a course. In the next two months these meetings were held and the committee appointed. However, the movement lost its momentum, possibly because of the character of some of the leaders; and though a memorial was eventually prepared and sent to Jefferson, it was never published, and it received no answer. Dissatisfaction over the patronage was partially allayed by the appointment of Tench Coxe to succeed Israel Whelen as Purveyor of Public Supplies; but the two remaining Federalists with important offices continued to hold them.[31]

The whole affair by its sudden subsidence seemed to be a tempest in a teapot; but the appearance was deceptive. Duane and his group were angry at Jones's opposition and were convinced that it was the work of Dallas and Gallatin. On the other hand, Jones and his friends were embittered by what they regarded as Leib's treachery, and they were becoming increasingly resentful of the domination of the party by the Germans and the Irish led by Leib and Duane. They were at the point of fighting to restore control to those Jones termed "real american republicans."[32] Thus, the dispute over Federal patronage was further widening the rifts in Republicanism in Philadelphia.

One reason for the quieting of the patronage question may have been the *Aurora's* absorption in a dispute with the Philadelphia board of health over the enforcement of quarantine regulations. The city had long been subject to periodic visitations of yellow fever, with the worst epidemic occurring in 1798 when more than 3,400 died. Among the victims was Benjamin Franklin Bache, Duane's predecessor as editor of the *Aurora*.[33]

Under such circumstances, it was not surprising that a person of Duane's temperament should have been almost violent on the subject. In the previous year there had been a renewed outbreak of the disease; and the *Aurora's* clamorous warnings had irritated many merchants who felt that Duane was disturbing business by causing an unnecessary panic. Nevertheless, the epidemic had been serious enough to cause a considerable number of deaths and to induce the removal of newspaper offices from the infected areas.[34]

On May 24, 1803, the *Aurora* began to attack the board of health because it had ordered the lifting of the quarantine on a vessel at the Lazaretto prior to the expiration of the legal time. The articles against the board continued; and a town meeting on June 6 appointed a committee headed by Charles Biddle, a Federalist, to investigate the conduct of the board and report to the Governor. The meeting was the scene of considerable disturbance when Enos Bronson, editor of the *Gazette of the United States,* and a number of other young Federalists opposed its actions on the ground that they were motivated by partisan purposes.

In truth, there was good reason to suspect that politics was involved. The president of the board of health was William T. Donaldson, one of the 30 Republicans who had attended the first Rising Sun meeting in the previous September. Donaldson had also announced his candidacy for the lucrative office of sheriff; and his leading opponent was Frederick Wolbert, one of Leib's closest allies and political lieutenants in the Northern Liberties.

While the *Aurora* strenuously denied that political questions entered into the matter and disdained to notice charges of the *Gazette of the United States* that the attacks were made on Donaldson because McKean had appointed him over the opposition of Duane and Leib, it nevertheless accused Donaldson of apostasy and asserted that his refusal to observe quarantine regulations was due to his hope of getting the support of Federalist merchants for his candidacy. The controversy slackened by the end of June, but it was renewed with vigor in September when a few cases of yellow fever made their appearance in the city.[35]

Using the agitation over the yellow fever as an excuse, "Civis," in the *Aurora,* suggested that a call for ward meetings be issued immediately. Despite some opposition, the meetings were held in June. The machinery worked smoothly in the city; and the town meeting on August 20, 1803, adopted the ticket presented by the general ward committee without change.[36]

No such harmony prevailed in Philadelphia County. There the opponents of Leib, led by those who had taken part in the Rising Sun movement, made a determined effort to overthrow what they termed his dictatorship of the county. Trouble appeared at the first county meeting held on July 7 at Wray's Tavern in the Northern Liberties. The two factions disputed over who was to preside at the meeting. Leib was placed in the chair by his adherents, but the opposing group withdrew and organized separately under Manuel Eyre. When the Leib supporters refused to adjourn and attend a second meeting on July 23, the seceders then issued a call of their own for this meeting.

Meanwhile, the original meeting had drawn up resolutions providing for the holding of district elections on August 1, 1803, to choose nineteen delegates authorized to serve as conferees on the Senatorial and sheriff's nominations and to prepare the assembly ticket. Among the resolutions was one providing that no person might participate in the election of delegates who was not a Democrat and empowering the general committee to vacate the seat of any delegate chosen in violation of this clause.[37]

In the interval between the meetings, "Mower" and "Reaper," in *Poulson's American Daily Advertiser*, savagely attacked the first county meeting and the dictatorship of Leib. They charged that the meeting had deliberately been called at a time when the farmers were in the midst of the harvest and could not attend. One article denounced the exclusion of Federalists from the district meetings. "Franklin," in the *Aurora*, pointed out that the meeting had done nothing more than provide for district elections which were to be held after the harvest was complete, and he went on to ask how Democrats could consider dictatorial a provision restricting party meetings to Democrats.[38]

Despite their earlier refusal, Leib's supporters attended the meeting on July 23, 1803; and when Manuel Eyre attempted to proceed as chairman, they upset the table on which he was seated and installed their own man. Once again the meeting divided into two sections. But at this juncture the Republicans of the city intervened. They had been considerably alarmed by the dissensions in the county and appointed a committee to attend the meeting. The mediators persuaded both factions to appoint representatives to meet with them; and five days later these men reached a compromise which, with a slightly less belligerent phrasing, provided for virtually the same plan adopted by the meeting on July 7.[39]

Hopes of harmony proved delusive; and the factions soon split over the matter of political machinery—a question which was to be a source of controversy in the county for more than a decade. The district delegate system had been used there in 1801 and abandoned in the following year. In 1803 the system had once more been established with the full approval of the Leib group.

However, as the district elections took place, it began to be apparent that Leib's opponents, whom the *Aurora* called the "Rising Sun men," had taken advantage of the system to gain control of the county. They had achieved this by permitting Federalists to take part in the district elections. The anti-Leib faction captured eleven of the nineteen delegates, with the other eight being chosen in the Northern Liberties where Leib's strength was concentrated. However, they overreached themselves when they permitted each district meeting to nominate its proportion of the ticket instead of leaving the matter to all the delegates of the county.[40]

The Leibites were quick to seize their advantage. Meeting in the Northern Liberties on September 2 with Frederick Wolbert in the chair, they denounced district nominations and, in blithe disregard of their own proceedings on July 7, 1803, likewise denounced the delegate system as a whole. Furthermore, they called a general county meeting for the following day. This meeting convened, renominated the county representatives of the previous year, and appointed a committee to draft an address.[41]

The reasons for this action are apparent from an analysis of the political situation in the county. There were 7,919 taxables in the county as a whole, of which 3,522, or 44 per cent, lived in the Northern Liberties. An even larger proportion of the Republican vote was located there.[42] When the system of general county meetings was used for nominations, the assemblages were held in the Northern Liberties, which meant that that district would normally dominate by reason of its heavy population and the distances (up to fifteen miles) which citizens from other parts of the county had to travel to attend. Within the Northern Liberties Leib had a perfectly functioning political machine, and he was thus able to command the politics of the entire county so long as a general meeting remained the accepted mode of making nominations. Use of the district system, which allowed the Northern Liberties less than a majority of the delegates, threatened this control and, of course, Leib's wider political ambitions.

These facts apparently were first recognized by Leib's opponents in 1803; but they failed to use them properly, making the errors of appealing for Federalist support and of attempting to make nominations in the district meetings rather than in the full committee of delegates. Their opposition was also hampered by the superior polemical skill of the Leib group and by the necessity of using the Federalist papers to publish their articles and proceedings.

The Federalists held no meetings in either the city or the county, though there were members of the party running for sheriff and commissioner, offices for which the practice of self-nomination prevailed. When the election was held, few of the city Federalists bothered to vote except for these two offices; and the majority of their votes for sheriff was cast for Donaldson rather than the Federalist candidate. In the county, they also supported Donaldson and the Rising Sun ticket for assembly. With this aid, Donaldson came within 271 votes of defeating John Barker, a bibulous but harmless veteran of the Revolution, whom the conferees had nominated in preference to Wolbert in the hope of appeasing the anti-Leib faction. The Rising Sun group also came within 150 votes of electing their candidates for assembly.[43]

Confronted by these divisions, the *Aurora* was by no means silent. As early as April it had sought to link the Rising Sun men with Burr and his famous toast to "The union of all honest men," made before a Federalist dinner in Washington in 1802.[44] In the opinion of the *Aurora*, there were too many men who preached this doctrine, and the party could survive only by casting them from its ranks. One writer, afterward identified as Tench Coxe, in exploiting this theme, coined the phrase "Tertium Quid," which later came into general usage in both national and State politics. Referring to those who preached moderation in partisan matters, he wrote:

> Moderation in the sense used by certain men is .... a *half-way-house* between virtue and vice, between truth and falsehood, where souls devoid of energy, and minds twisted with corruption may repose. ... What an hermaphrodite thing, partaking of two characters, and yet having neither! A *tertium quid* from the combination of good and evil, of the *mule kind*, incapable of propagating itself![45]

Burr's paper, the *New York Morning Chronicle*, took notice of these articles and asserted that the *Aurora* had begun to attack McKean and the union of honest men. The *Aurora* denied this so far as it applied to

McKean; but there was developing in Lancaster a movement which was to draw the paper's attention to some close friends of the Governor.[46]

At Lancaster a small group headed by James Hopkins, a lawyer, William Barton, county prothonotary, and Andrew Ellicott, mathematician and Secretary of the Land Office, began to take organized measures to create a third party in support of McKean. In their eyes, the wild projects and personal intrigues in the last legislature threatened to destroy all the benefits of Republicanism. To prevent this, they proposed to work in every place where there was any prospect of success for the election of men pledged to uphold the Governor. They accordingly prepared pamphlets, wrote letters, and sent emissaries to various places to achieve their objectives. Among those solicited for support was Dallas, who had a letter from Hopkins and was visited by Ellicott and Barton; but there is no evidence to show that he gave them any encouragement.[47]

Even at Lancaster they achieved only meager results. With much stealth they published pseudonymous articles calling for a "union of honest men"; but the Lancaster *Intelligencer* soon identified the men involved and asserted that they were working in close collaboration with Charles Smith, a lawyer and leader of the Federalists in the borough. Late in September the third party issued an anonymous pamphlet which set forth their objects, attacked the last legislature and the Republican county committee, and offered a mixed ticket of Federalists and Republicans for support by the voters. A number of the Republicans so nominated publicly repudiated the address and refused to be considered candidates. When the election was held, the Governor's supporters were soundly defeated. The regular Republican ticket lost between 200 and 300 votes as compared with the previous election; but the Federalists did not turn out in strength to support the dissenting candidates.[48]

In all these quarrels of the Republicans, the Federalists generally showed little interest. In most parts of the State they did not bother to hold meetings and to nominate candidates of their own, and they made no really concerted efforts in Philadelphia, Chester, Lancaster, and Allegheny counties where their votes were courted by dissident factions among the Republicans.[49] Though they approved McKean's vetoes and welcomed the growing factionalism of their opponents, they were not yet willing to co-operate wholeheartedly with men so recently their bitter enemies. Instead, if their papers be a true guide, they devoted most of their attention to national affairs, attacking administration policy on the closing of the Mississippi and the purchase of Louisiana, taking a pro-British view of the renewed war in Europe, and continuing to make slanderous attacks on Jefferson.[50]

The election returns indicated the extent of their inactivity. They were reduced to a single State Senator, and they elected but five out of the 86 members of the House of Representatives. Only Huntingdon County was completely Federalist; while their strongholds in Delaware, Adams, and Luzerne counties gave equal representation to the Republicans.[51]

On the other hand, Republican splits were becoming deeper and more irreconcilable. The *Aurora* had not yet come to the point of openly assaulting the Governor and Dallas; but Duane personally was convinced that both, along with "seventeen twentieths" of the officeholders in the State, were involved in the third party schemes; and he believed that McKean had hopes of becoming President in place of Jefferson.[52] A full-scale schism was inevitable; and the events of 1804 served only to define more clearly the lines of division.

III

The year 1804 was one of political ferment among the Pennsylvania Republicans. The rift between the Governor and the legislature over judicial reform grew wider, and the impeachment of the Supreme Court judges made matters even worse. At the same time dissident Republicans in Philadelphia established their own newspaper and made a concerted effort to destroy the influence of Duane and Leib over the party in that area. Local divisions were likewise prevalent elsewhere in the State. The demoralized Federalists were unable to profit from the situation, however, and the Republican ticket of presidential electors had no really significant opposition.

The legislative session of 1803-1804 was to a great extent a repetition of the previous one. McKean's address reiterated the urgent necessity for judicial reform and again proposed an increase in the membership of the Supreme Court, while it warned the legislators against mistaking "innovation for reform."[53]

Neither his advice nor his warning were very palatable to the members. Their discontent was shown to some extent by the failure of the Senate to return a reply to his address,[54] but it was displayed more strongly by overriding his veto of the bill reviving the act of 1799 extending the powers of the justices of the peace. McKean had returned this bill with his veto on December 8, 1803, objecting to it for the same reasons he had given in opposing the Hundred Dollar Act. The House reconsidered the measure on December 22 and gave it a thumping 75-4 majority; the Senate passed it by an equally decisive 20-2 margin on January 5, 1804.[55]

This veto, though perfectly consistent, demonstrated McKean's obstinacy and lack of political astuteness. To denounce as unreservedly bad and unconstitutional a measure which only revived an act signed by his predecessor and enforced for three years without opposition was to court criticism; and severe strictures on his conduct were printed in the Republican papers.[56]

He showed a similar lack of political wisdom in failing to sign the Hundred Dollar Act. This measure was again introduced in the House in January and passed its third reading on February 29 by a vote of 68-14. The Senate made some minor amendments but approved the bill by a majority of 18-3. The two houses reached an agreement on their differences and sent the bill to the Governor, who, seeing the futility of a veto, permitted it to become law without his signature. Even the *Aurora*, which had manifested little interest in the bill, noted that it was only a temporary measure and felt that it should be given a trial in view of the widespread sentiment in its favor.[57]

Though the *Aurora* was at best tepid in the support of the judicial measures passed by the legislature, it was thoroughgoing in its demands for action against the Supreme Court justices in the Passmore case. The House had referred the question to its committee on grievances in January; and on March 13, 1804, that body recommended impeachment on the ground that the judges had exceeded their powers and acted in an arbitrary and unconstitutional manner in imprisoning and fining Passmore. A week later the report was adopted by a vote of 57-24, with nineteen Republicans joining the five Federalists in opposition. The entire representation from the city and county of Philadelphia voted; and all except Samuel Carver, a member from the city, voted yea. Articles of impeachment were then drafted and sent to the

Senate where, after much discussion, it was decided to postpone the trial to the first Monday in January, 1805. The judges had requested an immediate trial, but their petition was denied.[58]

The affair was given a new turn and McKean's disapproval of the proceedings made manifest as a result of a letter received by the Speaker of the House on March 24, 1804, from Hugh Henry Brackenridge. The latter was the only Republican judge on the Supreme Court, but he had not been included in the impeachment since he had not participated in the decision on the Passmore contempt. This omission gave the appearance of partisan motives to the arraignment of the other justices; and in his letter Brackenridge requested that he be impeached along with them because he approved of their official conduct in the Passmore case and also because "the interest of the republican administration" required that he be included.

The House was highly incensed and regarded the letter as a "premeditated insult" since it insinuated that the members were actuated by party feelings in their proceedings. An address for Brackenridge's removal was prepared and adopted by a vote of 53-22 on March 31. The Senate concurred by a majority of 17-2, and the address was sent to the Governor.[59]

However, McKean, without bothering to give formal notice to the General Assembly, refused to remove him. He later defended his conduct by saying that the Constitution used the word "may" rather than "shall" with respect to the Governor's action on addresses for removal and that he was not therefore bound to follow the wishes of the legislature. He also pointed out that the address had not received the approval of two-thirds of the entire membership of the House and hence that it was not legal.[60]

The end of the session found McKean and the majority of the legislature more than ever estranged, and it also saw a growing coolness manifested toward the Governor by the *Aurora*. In following the Passmore affair, the paper had been drawn into controversies which led it to attack lawyers as a class because of their alleged subservience to the judges. After adjournment, the *Aurora* made a strong criticism of McKean's refusal to remove Brackenridge, although it professed to believe that the Governor had not in fact flouted the will of the people in this fashion.[61] It was increasingly evident that common opposition to McKean and the judiciary was to be the means of uniting the country Republicans with the Duane group in Philadelphia.

An important step toward further crystallization of the Republicans into two main factions was the launching of the *Philadelphia Evening Post* on February 20, 1804. The printer was William McCorkle, formerly associated with John M. Snowden in the publication of the Greensburg *Farmers Register;* and he announced his intention of considering public men without reference to party, though confessing friendship for the existing State and Federal administrations.[62] Answering the accusation that it was a "McKean paper," the *Post* observed smugly "that every good man must advocate the administration of so meritorious an officer."[63]

Despite such quibblings, it was perfectly obvious that the new paper was the organ of the Governor's supporters and that it was also intended to give to the Rising Sun men and other opponents of Leib and Duane an instrument in their fight to gain control of the party in Philadelphia.

It was not slow in beginning its work. The earliest numbers were filled with articles in defense of the existing judicial system and attacks on the proposed arbitration law. More important from a political point of view, the *Post* was soon engaged in assailing Duane and Leib. A pseudonymous article appeared in March which bitterly decried the subjection of native-born citizens to foreign printers. The following month another article attacked Leib as "First Consul" because of his alleged intrigues in a county militia election. These sniping tactics were only the prelude to open and rancorous warfare.[64]

The first real breach came on the occasion of the celebration of the Louisiana Purchase on May 12, 1804. In the dinners which followed the procession and oration, the toasts of the Tammany Society and the Republican Greens were remarkable for their failure to include the Governor. Since Duane and Leib dominated the Tammany Society and the former captained the Republican Greens, it was obvious that a direct provocation was intended. The *Philadelphia Evening Post* announced that the Governor's friends would remember this slur, and the *Aurora* replied with a diatribe against courtiers and special friends of the executive. It added that it was quite willing to be included among the enemies of the Governor if he was capable of aligning himself with such men.[65]

From this beginning developed one of the most slanderous and malignant campaigns Philadelphia had ever known. The original differences over the Governor soon dropped out of sight, and the whole matter became a fight to oust Leib and Duane from their control of the Republican Party in the city and the county. The *Post,* which became the *Freeman's Journal* on June 12, 1804,[66] was soon engaged in vicious and incessant onslaughts against Leib, denouncing him for political intrigue and republishing the pamphlet accusing him of attempting to defraud the Penrose orphans. Duane received similar attentions as the putative dictator of Philadelphia politics.[67]

The *Aurora* immediately replied by defending Leib and Duane and by assailing the third party, which it began to call the "Tertium Quid" or, more familiarly, the "Quids."[68] Its task was made easier and its diatribes gained effectiveness through the emergence of Tench Coxe as an active champion of the third party.

Coxe, once described by the *Aurora* as a "man of brilliant talents," was one of the outstanding American political economists of his time and wielded a trenchant pen in party warfare.[69] Vitiating his acknowledged accomplishments was his avid seeking of public office and an almost incredible record of political inconstancy. Descended from two of the most distinguished colonial families of the Commonwealth, Coxe studied law and then entered his father's countinghouse. He joined with enthusiasm in the preliminary stages of the Revolution and even became a member of a volunteer military company, but in 1776 he left Philadelphia to join the British in New York. Thus began a career which, as Alexander Graydon remarked, gave Coxe "the singular fortune to behold with equal eye, the carting of the tories in Philadelphia in the year 1775; the sad havoc of the whigs in New-York, in the year 1776; the discomfiture of the anti-federalists in the years 1790 and 1794; then the overthrow and persecution of the federalists in the year 1800."

Coxe returned to Philadelphia with General Howe but became a Whig after the departure of the British. Taking an important part in the Annapolis Convention in 1786, he supported the adoption of the Constitution and was rewarded by the office of Assistant Secretary of the Treasury in 1789. Three years later he was made Commissioner of Revenue. Removed by Adams in 1797, he became a Republican and after McKean's victory was appointed Secretary of the Land Office of the Commonwealth. He resigned this position in 1801 to become Collector of Internal Revenue at Philadelphia under Jefferson, and two years later he succeeded Israel Whelen as Purveyor of Public Supplies. An object of contemptuous scorn by the Federalists, he had been defended by the *Aurora* as a man who had repented of the errors of his youth.[70]

Such a charitable view quickly disappeared when Coxe was found to be a writer for the *Freeman's Journal* and an important organizer for the Quids. Then the *Aurora*, to the malicious glee of the Federalists, reviewed Coxe's career in its entirety with a veritable torrent of abuse, which was maintained, with brief intervals, until the election in October.[71]

The assaults on Coxe began when it was discovered that he had participated in a caucus at the Harp and Eagle Tavern on May 14, 1804, which set on foot a call for immediate meetings of the wards. The *Aurora* protested that there was no occasion for such early meetings and asserted that some of the Rising Sun men and others were attempting to capture control of the general ward committee. Nevertheless, the meetings were held, but the adherents of Duane upset the Quid plans by obtaining a majority of the committeemen.

Taking advantage of their control, the Duane faction forced through a recommendation of Joseph Clay, Jacob Richards, and Michael Leib as candidates for Congress.[72] Normally, the general ward committee would have recommended only one man; Philadelphia and Delaware counties would have indicated their preferences for the other two positions; and the final ticket would have been drafted by the conferees from the three units. Thus, the city committee by this action had virtually pre-empted the functions of the entire congressional district.

The Quids likewise sought to gain the initiative in the county by issuing a call for the election of district delegates on June 23, 1804. Before these elections could be held, the Leibites hurriedly convened a general county meeting on June 21, which chose conferees instructed to support Leib for Congress and renominated the assembly ticket of the previous year. On the same day the Leib conferees presented themselves to the general ward committee. The Quid district delegates assembled on June 27 and appointed a committee to announce their proceedings to the Republicans of the city.[73]

Faced with this dilemma, the general ward committee adopted a resolution to recognize both sets of conferees from the county and to even up the representation by appointing double the usual number of delegates from the city. This solution was indignantly spurned by the Quids in the county, and they withdrew and made a separate nomination of William Penrose as the county candidate for Congress. The action of the general ward committee was also criticized by Tench Coxe and 21 other committeemen who signed and published a protest against it.[74]

Meanwhile, the quarrel spread into Delaware County, which constituted a part of the senatorial and congressional districts. At a meeting held on August 4, 1804, the Republicans in that county selected their local candidates and recommended Jacob Richards for Congress and John Pearson for the State Senate, but, contrary to custom, they chose no conferees. The proceedings of the meeting as they first appeared in the *Aurora* and the *Freeman's Journal* soon became the occasion of bitter controversy. Duane and Major William Brooke of Delaware County were accused of having mutilated the proceedings by omitting a resolution proclaiming neutrality as between Leib and Penrose. The charges were denied, though the secretary of the meeting averred them to be true with respect to Brooke.

Under pressure from the city and county conferees, another meeting was held in Delaware County which chose conferees and instructed them to support Pearson for Senator. The latter by this time was suspected of complicity with the Quids; and the committee of conference forced the Republicans in Delaware County to hold a third meeting on September 28, 1804, which dropped Pearson and recommended William Pennell in his stead. Another meeting on the same date upheld Pearson, and the *Aurora* began to denounce him publicly.[75]

Prior to the selection of the conferees of Delaware County, those of the city and county had met on August 15, 1804, and proceeded to nominate a congressional ticket for the district. At this time they gave consideration to a letter from Leib in which he requested that he not be considered as a candidate as he wished to make a "peace offering" of himself in the interests of party harmony. Written in the tone of selfless martyrdom, it was perfectly apparent that the offer of withdrawal was a mere gesture; and the conferees played their role to perfection, rejecting the sacrifice in a laudatory resolution and directing that the letter be published along with the proceedings of the meeting.[76]

These strong-arm tactics combined with the unrivaled technique of the *Aurora* in political propaganda had their effect. The weakness of the Quids was exposed when they refused to attend a town meeting which they themselves had called after the Duane faction exhorted its adherents to be present.[77] The third party was thus outmaneuvered and overpowered in the city and county of Philadelphia as well as in Delaware County; and the Federalist support which it received was not in sufficient volume to overcome the regular Republican vote.

In the city the Quid candidates for assembly and the city councils ran from 100 to 200 votes behind their opponents, although Leib was only eighteen votes ahead of Penrose. In Delaware County Leib polled 433 votes less than Penrose; but Philadelphia County gave him a majority of 722 votes, enough to give him a total of 3,992 to Penrose's 3,685. Much of the narrowness of Leib's margin must be attributed to his own unpopularity, since William Pennell, the regular nominee for State Senator, had a majority of more than a thousand votes over Pearson in the same district. The rest of the Republican ticket was also victorious, except that the Federalists in Delaware County elected their candidates for the assembly.[78]

An interesting shift in emphasis was shown during the conduct of the campaign. In its early stages, it appeared that the split was over the support of Governor McKean and his conduct with respect to the legislature; but by September the *Aurora,* which was seeking to damn the Quids by linking them with an alleged national Federalist plot, was asserting confidently that McKean's character was invulnerable to such schemes.[79] Similarly, though the Quids were referring to the regular Republicans as "Jacobins," the reference was to the dictatorial tactics of the general ward committee and the conferees rather than to any schemes of judicial reform.[80]

At bottom the fight was almost wholly based upon local issues, particularly the personality and political influence of Leib; and it widened further the gap between the Republican factions in Philadelphia. Dallas broke with Duane in August because the *Aurora* published a statement that Dallas had publicly denounced Coxe as a liar; and by October the paper was accusing Dallas of being the author of a Quid address and the active leader of the party behind the scenes. While it seems certain that Dallas was opposed to Leib, his own statement and the testimony of William Jones indicate that he remained passive during the contest.[81]

The election also brought Duane to the point of making thinly veiled public attacks on Gallatin. As early as 1802 Duane had written Gallatin stating that it was reported that Gallatin was his enemy and was seeking to prevent him from obtaining stationery and printing contracts. Gallatin had endorsed on the letter that the statements were untrue and had added that he suspected Leib to be at the bottom of the affair.[82] Other such incidents were probably responsible for his seeking to warn Duane sometime during the 1803-1804 session of Congress that he would be ruined if he persisted in his attachment to Leib. Duane, in his obstinate fashion, seized upon this as an insult and broke permanently with Gallatin, whom he decided had been motivated by personal hatred of Leib.[83]

As the Philadelphia elections drew near in October, 1804, a writer in the *Aurora* made unspecified charges of Washington interference in the campaign. By the end of the month the attacks on Gallatin were becoming more open. A victory celebration featured toasts which denounced treasury interference in elections and castigated the heads of departments who mistook "interest for duty and themselves for the nation."[84]

There were also local quarrels in the rest of the State. In Chester and Lancaster counties, unsuccessful efforts were made to elect combined Quid and Federalist tickets; and in Northampton County a Quid intrigue to replace Congressman Robert Brown by John Ross also failed.[85]

In Washington County, William Hoge was superseded by John Hamilton as Congressman, ostensibly because he had opposed the administration measure which later became the Twelfth Amendment to the Constitution. Commenting on this contest, the *Aurora* later accused John Israel, editor of the Washington *Herald of Liberty* and the Pittsburgh *Tree of Liberty*, of machinations to obtain the nomination for himself. Israel denied the charges, and it is uncertain whether they were true or whether the *Aurora* was motivated by the fact that Israel's father, Israel Israel, ran on the Quid city ticket for assembly.[86]

The Federalists made minor gains as a result of these Republican divisions. The most important was the choice of James Kelly to succeed John Stewart as Congressman from York and Adams counties.[87] Overall, the Federalists elected one out of eighteen Congressmen and eight out of 86 Representatives; but the Senate became wholly Republican as they lost their sole remaining member of that body.[88]

Almost unnoticed in the hubbub over local politics was the presidential election of 1804. Despite the importunities of Timothy Pickering and Uriah Tracy, Federalist Senators from Massachusetts and Connecticut, McKean concurred with the legislature in supporting the adoption of the Twelfth Amendment, which required the electors to designate the respective persons voted for as President and Vice President and thus prevented the re-occurrence of anything like the Jefferson-Burr contest of 1801.[89]

Another notable feature of the presidential election of this year was that it led to the first well-organized use of the legislative nominating caucus in Pennsylvania. In a caucus on March 22, 1804, the Republican members of the legislature drew up a ticket of electors for President and Vice President. They also appointed a committee to prepare an address, which was approved at a subsequent meeting and published in the *Aurora*. The address reviewed the ancient struggle between tyranny and liberty and spoke of the terrors of the Federalist rule which had been overcome. It then emphasized the necessity of Republican unity and made this the apology for the caucus selection of an electoral ticket. It concluded with a warning against a third party, describing it as an engine of Federalist intrigue.[90] The Philadelphia Quids protested indignantly against the charge of co-operation with the Federalists, but they gave hearty support to the caucus electoral ticket.[91]

The Federalists were disorganized both nationally and in Pennsylvania. The Republican ticket, consisting of Jefferson and George Clinton of New York, had been adopted at an open caucus of the Republican members of Congress on February 25, 1804; but no public choice of the Federalist candidates was made. They were generally understood to be Charles Cotesworth Pinckney of South Carolina for President and Rufus King of New York for Vice President; but the *Aurora* in November professed not to know who were the real candidates.[92]

In Pennsylvania, the party ignored the presidential election until October 15, 1804, when a meeting of Adams County Federalists at Gettysburg took the responsibility of drawing up a ticket of electors. The party papers published this; but the *Lancaster Journal* remarked that it did so only because requested and called it "an unavailing, useless thing." Though the *Aurora* professed alarm and characteristically tried to connect the Philadelphia Quids with the formation of the Gettysburg ticket, the returns of the election on November 2, 1804, demonstrated the accuracy of the *Journal's* evaluation. Out of a very light vote, the Republican electors polled 22,081 ballots to 1,239 for the Federalists, with only Adams County giving a majority to the latter.[93] Whatever may have been their local disagreements, the Pennsylvania Republicans were united behind Jefferson; Federalism could not prevail against this unity.

In the two years since the re-election of McKean, Republican quarrels had grown to serious proportions. In Philadelphia, disputes over Federal patronage and the influence of Leib and Duane had reached the stage where neutrality was impossible. In the legislature, the relations between the majority of the members and the Governor were approaching an open rupture due to their differences over reform of the judiciary. A union between the Duane-Leib group and the legislative opposition was becoming almost inevitable because of Duane's insistence upon impeachment of the Supreme Court judges and because the *Freeman's Journal* acted not only as the organ of the Philadelphia Quids but proclaimed itself the champion of the Governor. Jefferson, viewing the situation from Monticello, astutely observed: "Pennsylvania seems to have in its' [*sic*] bowels a good deal of volcanic matter, & some explosion may be expected."[94] It came in 1805.

CHAPTER IV

CONSTITUTIONAL REFORM AND THE ELECTION OF 1805

THE GUBERNATORIAL ELECTION of 1805 brought to a climax the Republican divisions of the preceding years. Beginning with the impeachment trial of the Supreme Court justices, the year witnessed a movement for constitutional reform, the caucus nomination of Simon Snyder for Governor, the development of the Constitutional Republicans to support McKean's re-election, and the resurgence of Federalism as a political force holding the balance of power between warring Republican factions. Though the election was to a great extent a struggle between conservatives and radicals—between those opposing and those seeking change—it reflected as well the old personal feuds over patronage and political power, and it foreshadowed the passing of political hegemony in the State from Philadelphia to the country regions. A new era had begun.

I

The legislative session of 1804-1805 set the stage for the succeeding gubernatorial campaign. The chief events were the failure of the attempt to impeach the Supreme Court judges, the fight over the revision of the Constitution, and the final break between the Governor and the majority of the Republicans in the legislature. These developments resulted in the Republican caucus nomination of Snyder for Governor and in the renomination of McKean by a number of Federalist and Republican members.

The House of Representatives on December 10, 1804, indicated its intention of proceeding with the impeachment trial of the Supreme Court judges. At that time 64 Republicans and one Federalist, over the opposition of nine Republicans and seven Federalists, adopted a resolution to appoint a committee to manage the impeachment and to authorize it to employ counsel. Nathaniel B. Boileau, Jacob Bucher, Abner Lacock, Hugh Ferguson, and James Engle were speedily chosen as the committee of managers; but the matter of counsel offered a more difficult problem.[1]

It soon became apparent that there was little hope of obtaining competent legal assistance from the lawyers of the State. Dallas, who had conducted the prosecution of Addison, had been retained as counsel for the judges along with Jared Ingersoll, former Attorney General for the Commonwealth. Other leading Republican lawyers joined their Federalist colleagues in refusing to assist in the prosecution. The *United States' Gazette* was highly pleased at this turn of affairs, while the *Aurora* regarded it as another evidence of the arrogance of the lawyers and recommended that the legislature do without legal assistance.[2] The embarrassment of the House was relieved, however, when it succeeded in obtaining the services of Caesar A. Rodney, Congressman from Delaware and one of the managers of the approaching impeachment trial of Justice Samuel Chase before the United States Senate.[3]

The article of impeachment adopted by the House charged that the conduct of the judges in fining and imprisoning Passmore was "arbitrary and unconstitutional and a high misdemeanor" for five reasons— because the notice published in the City Tavern did not reflect upon the judges either in their personal or judicial capacities; because it did not directly allude to any cause then pending in the court; because Passmore was warranted in concluding that the suit between him and Pettit and Bayard was ended; because it appeared that the judges were satisfied with Passmore's answers to the interrogatories so far as they concerned them; and, finally, "Because it appears that the punishment was inflicted not because he had committed a contempt of court but because he would not apologize or make atonement to Mr. Andrew Bayard as the court had expected."[4]

To the average man untrained in law, the charges of the House must have seemed clear and reasonable. To be sure, the judges must have the power to punish contempts of court, but here was a case where a man had made no reference to the court but only to an individual. Even if he had thereby been guilty of a technical violation of the law, it had been done through honest error, and it had been alleviated by a full atonement so far as it respected the court. To attempt to force an apology to Bayard was a completely arbitrary proceeding beyond the bounds of reason, and it indicated a contempt for the rights of free citizens not to be tolerated.

During the trial, which lasted from January 7 to January 28, 1805, the counsel for the defense sought to show that the judges had adhered to the law in their conduct and that even though they might have erred, it was an honest error and was not willful misconduct which would justify their removal by impeachment.

When the arguments were concluded, Dallas was confident of victory; and from a legal point of view he and Ingersoll had had the best of the argument. The actual vote, however, was close. After postponing its decision from Saturday to Monday, the Senate voted 13-11 for conviction; but as a two-thirds majority was necessary, the judges were acquitted.[5]

Duane had attended the sessions of the trial and had sent somewhat prejudiced accounts of the proceedings to the *Aurora* as it progressed. He seems to have expected the conviction of the judges; and when their acquittal was voted, the *Aurora* trumpeted forth a bitter denunciation of the decision. In its opinion, the actual issue of the trial had been "whether the constitution established upon the principles of the revolution of 1776 should remain—or, the dark, arbitrary, unwritten, incoherent, cruel, inconsistent, and contradictory maxims, of the *common law* of England, should supercede them." If the acquittal were correct, the State Constitution was "no better than a *blank sheet of paper*," the Revolution was but "a speculative theory," and liberty was "a mere sound dependent on the *mercy*—the *discretion*—the *caprice*—the *malice*—or the *family interests* of any men vested with judicial authority."

However, since the decision had been rendered, it must be respected as fully "as if it accorded with the most scrupulous reverence for the rights of the citizen and the constitution." Nevertheless, the *Aurora* felt it a duty to warn its readers to be circumspect in speaking and writing of causes depending in any courts or of persons having suits pending. Otherwise, they might become victims to "the combined force of the whole bench and bar—an interest too visibly more powerful than the people or the constitution."[6]

The conviction that the people were sufferers under a tyranny of lawyers and judges was not new. Duane in 1802 had written that "The present age is as much in danger from lawyers as the three last have been the victims of priests."[7] In December, 1804, an article in the *Aurora* had proclaimed that the excellence of American government arose from "having *destroyed* the *established monarchy, aristocracy,* and *hierarchy* of England, and leaving the people free to govern themselves." The lawyers were "the *only remaining ancient imposture.*" If they could be eliminated by restoring the administration of justice to the people, then the Americans could well boast that they had "the best government on earth."[8]

After the acquittal of the judges, another writer in the *Aurora* rejoiced that the people would now be brought to a realization of the true state of affairs. They would see that the Constitution was so worded as to defeat their will, and they would recognize the necessity of altering it.[9]

Such a suggestion did not pass without response. Without any previous reference to the matter, the *Aurora* suddenly published on February 28, 1805, a long memorial to the legislature and exhorted the people to sign copies and send them in as rapidly as possible. The memorial began by reciting the constitutional right of the people to "alter, reform or abolish their government" as they saw fit. The present Constitution had been in existence for fifteen years, and experience had shown the necessity for amendment in several particulars.

In the legislature, the four-year term of the Senators had proved contrary to the interests of the people and should be eliminated. Many states provided for an annual election of the Governor, and there was no good reason why the Pennsylvania Senators should not be chosen on the same basis.

As for the executive, while the memorialists did not mean to imply that their statements referred to the present Governor and legislature of Pennsylvania, it was nevertheless true that the extensive patronage of the Governor combined with his veto power made it possible for him "efficiently to controul the acts of the legislature, to the utter subversion of the principle that the majority shall govern." Patronage might lead to favoritism, favoritism to partiality, partiality to injustice; and where injustice existed, there was injury and oppression. The danger was very great in Pennsylvania where the Governor had a patronage as extensive as that of the King of England.

The situation in the judiciary was still more alarming. Here was a body of men even further removed from responsibility to the people and, "by a late decision," possessing enormous powers of common law jurisdiction "incompatible with and hostile to our republican system and the very idea of civil liberty." Moreover, the judges claimed the additional right of deciding on the constitutionality of acts of the legislature. These were more than imaginary dangers as the numerous petitions against judicial abuses showed. A "radical error" had been made in the establishment of the judicial department, and it could be obviated only by bringing the judges periodically "to the tribunal of an election, or re-appointment." The memoralists also requested a "simplification of court proceedings" to insure *"justice* without *sale, denial* or *delay."*

In brief, the memorial sought amendment of the Constitution so as to provide for annual elections of Senators, a reduction in executive patronage, the election or appointment of judges for specified terms, and a reform of judicial procedure. It also insinuated that the Governor's veto power should be abolished or greatly limited.[10]

The appearance of this memorial aroused a storm of protest from the Federalists and Quids. The *Freeman's Journal* immediately accused Duane of being the author of the memorial and the instigator of the movement for a convention; but this was denied by the *Aurora*. William J. Duane asserted flatly that his father had never seen or known of the existence of the memorial since he was in Washington attending the impeachment trial of Justice Samuel Chase. In the face of such a positive contradiction, the *Freeman's Journal* retreated and asked plaintively who had fathered the memorial if it had not been Duane.[11]

The real mover of the convention and author of the memorial was almost certainly Nathaniel B. Boileau, representative from Montgomery County. Born of Huguenot parents in 1763, he had graduated from Princeton and had then become a prosperous farmer. Despite his good education and material success, Boileau experienced an unusual frustration in his private life. He was engaged successively to three sisters: the first died before marriage; the second died two years after they were married; and the third, although she lived for many years after their marriage, never bore him any children.

His political life was to prove little more satisfactory. Elected to the legislature in 1797, he had served in that body continuously except for the session of 1802-1803, when he had been eliminated because of his unsuccessful campaign for Congress against Frederick Conrad, the regularly nominated Republican candidate. In the legislature Boileau had been one of the most radical of the Republicans, sponsoring legislation to prevent the reading of British cases and precedents in the

Pennsylvania courts and seeking to weaken the Governor's appointive power by requiring legislative election of the Comptroller General and the Register General. He had also been responsible for the introduction of the Incompatibility Act in 1802. As one of the House managers in the impeachment of the Supreme Court judges, he had made violent attacks on the legal profession, the common law, and the judiciary. Aside from this radicalism, Boileau, like Leib, was unfortunately distinguished by an inordinate ambition, a jealous spirit, and an inherent propensity for intrigue. These traits were to become more evident in 1805 and succeeding years than they had previously been.[12]

The opponents of the convention always maintained that there was no real demand for one and that the flood of memorials was inspired by members of the legislature. The conduct of Boileau gave proof that they were right. On March 1, 1805, he wrote a hurried note to Jonathan Roberts, Jr., sending him copies of the memorial and asking him to put them in circulation. Rather cynically, he added: "I think there would be an impropriety for members of the Legislature to commence the business— It ought to originate with the people— You are one of the Sovereign people."[13] Similar letters were presumably sent by Boileau and other legislators to correspondents throughout the State; and on March 12 the first memorials were presented in the House.[14]

Meanwhile, the opponents of a convention had not been idle. Dallas had written Gallatin in January, 1805, deploring the tendency toward anarchy and the servility of the party to such men as Duane and Leib. The "tyranny of the printers" must be resisted; and he felt that "Perhaps, the crisis is arrived, when some attempt should be made to rally the genuine Republicans, round the standard of reason, order, and law."[15] Whatever doubts Dallas may have had, the attempt to amend the Constitution apparently convinced him that the crisis was at hand; and he began to take active measures to oppose it.

The first evidence of this appeared in reports of a dinner of the "Democratic Constitutional Republicans" held at the White Horse Tavern in Philadelphia on March 4, 1805, to celebrate Jefferson's second inauguration. A few days later the *Freeman's Journal* printed a proposal, dated March 14, for forming "The Society of Constitutional Republicans." This document recognized the sovereignty of the people, the principle of majority rule, and the right of the people, to alter and abolish their government as they saw fit. However, it described the Pennsylvania Constitution, along with the Federal Constitution, as "the noblest invention of human wisdom, for the self-government of man" and avowed that it should be changed only when the motives and causes were "obvious, cogent, general, and conclusive." Great political blessings were enjoyed under the Constitution, and it required no alteration. The list of the society's principles closed with an assertion of loyalty to the existing State and Federal administrations.

The proposal then went on to provide for the creation of a general society to be located in Philadelphia with branches in each county. A committee of fourteen members, including Dallas, George Logan, William Jones, and Peter Muhlenberg, was to circulate the paper over the State; and it was also instructed to prepare a memorial to the legislature against the proposed convention, using only such language as could be subscribed to by all opponents of the convention regardless of party.[16]

A memorial and remonstrance conforming to these specifications was printed in the *Freeman's Journal* on March 18, 1805. Three days later, it was read by Dallas to a meeting of the Constitutional Republican Society, which approved it and made arrangements for its circulation throughout the State in both English and German. The remonstrance opposed the holding of a convention because there was nothing wrong with the Constitution; because the "ostensible" reforms contemplated would destroy the balance between the various branches of the government and give all real power to the General Assembly; and, finally, because there was no way of being certain that a convention, motivated by a spirit of innovation, would not go beyond the stated objects and make changes leading to anarchy and tyranny. Confining itself to the sole question of amendment of the Constitution, the remonstrance received the warm approbation of the *United States' Gazette,* which recommended it to the Federalists.[17]

With the lines thus drawn, the two groups began a warm contest to get the greatest number of memorials before the legislature. When the first memorial had been received on March 12, 1805, it had been referred to a "grand committee," composed of one representative from the city and one from each county in the State. Additional memorials and remonstrances were referred to the same committee. By the time its report was submitted on April 1, it was apparent that Dallas and the Constitutional Republicans had won at least a partial victory.

The report had a rhetorical preamble which lauded the American system of government and the sovereign right of the people to alter it as they saw fit. It scoffed at those who feared a new convention of the people. They were certainly as "wise, prudent, virtuous, and patriotic" as those of fifteen years before, and they might as safely be trusted to manage their own concerns. However, because there had not been sufficient time to get the opinions of a majority of the people, the committee offered a resolution to the effect that, though they considered the Constitution defective, there had not been sufficient petitions to justify calling a convention at this time, and they therefore referred the matter to the people who might make their wishes clear to the next legislature.

Such bombast deceived no one. When the report came up for consideration two days later, its opponents immediately offered a substitute resolution. Arguing that there was no justification for the expression of a legislative opinion on the Constitution and pointing out that 5,590 had signed memorials against a convention while only 4,944 had petitioned in its favor, they moved that no action be taken on the subject. The substitute was defeated by a majority of 54-22; and the committee's report was adopted by a vote of 51-25, with eight Federalists voting with the minority in each case.[18] The matter of constitutional reform was thus left to the electorate.

While the question of the convention was being settled, the already strained relations between McKean and the legislature had been snapped. Dallas in January had observed and tried to allay the "ferment" which existed. Knowing the choleric disposition of McKean, he had written him in terms as diplomatic as he could muster of the necessity of preventing the misconduct of his enemies "from producing any warmth, or asperity, on your part." Overcome them, he counseled, "not only by the preeminence of your character, your station, your wisdom, and your worth, but, also, by your indulgence and forbearance."[19] To a person of McKean's temperament such admonitions were wasted, and the eventualities Dallas had foreseen were realized with a vengeance.

On March 21, 1805, McKean indulged in a passionate outburst against his opponents under such circumstances as to give them exactly the opportunity they sought. Abraham McKinney, Representative from Northumberland County, along with Simon Snyder, his colleague and Speaker of the House, visited the Governor on that day to urge the appointment of Henry Latscha as a justice of the peace. The Governor demurred and indicated that he intended to appoint another person who had been well recommended. McKinney protested that this man was not a Republican, but McKean replied that he had appointed too many people whose sole recommendation had been their Republicanism.

From this matter, McKean passed on to discuss a letter published by John Stewart, a retiring Congressman, to his constituents in York and Adams counties. In this letter Stewart had blamed lawyers and "men of talents" for the delays in legislation and had expressed his intention of opposing the election of any such people to office. Commenting on this, McKean, according to his own account of the affair, said:

> "I suppose we shall have him, and other such clodpoles (or, if they please, clodhoppers) of the same pernicious sentiments, returned as delegates to the projected convention! Can such men be qualified to legislate, or to form systems of government for so great a state as Pennsylvania? The memorial (I continued) for calling a convention, was a palpable libel, and the men, now attempting to destroy our happy form of government, were weak, mischievous, and wicked. How (I asked) besides, can any man who has a regard for truth, and is not grossly ignorant, sign his name to one, at least, of the assertions in the memorial; *'that the governor of Pennsylvania had as great patronage as the king of England?'* ["] . . . .
>
> The present constitution, likewise, I described to be the production of as patriotic learned and enlightened men, as, perhaps, ever assembled for a similar purpose; and delivered my opinion, that it approached as near to perfection as any that ever did, or now does, exist in the world. I exclaimed, indeed, "shall a set of clodpoles, and ignoramuses, overthrow it! No: it cannot be! I will firmly resist it: I will use my utmost exertions, to prevent the danger and the mischief: and I fear not the want of aid and assistance, from all wise and good men."[20]

The first version of the affair, however, appeared in an anonymous letter published in the *Aurora* on March 29, 1805. Differing in detail, it was more highly colored and was fashioned to suit the needs of McKean's opponents. It read in part as follows:

> the speaker . . . called on the governor to recommend a respectable neighbor of his for the magistracy in his county;

when the governor, in a strain of indecent and intemperate invective told him that he had already appointed too many ignoramuses; that the republicans were a set of clodhoppers, who had no more understanding than Geese, and wondered at their impudence in talking of calling a convention, to alter the constitution, which they never did and never could understand; that he would not allow it &c. . . . Their astonishment and indignation is more easily conceived than described; such treatment unusual among decent men, was perhaps never shewn by an executive officer towards the speaker, or towards the members of a legislature. Their astonishment at this treatment was such that they cannot precisely determine whether his insolent abuse was levelled at the members alone, or extended to the people at large.—You may suppose what are the feelings of the legislature on this indignity to their speaker, whom every man must respect from his personal merits and integrity, as well as towards the representatives and those very people to whom the governor owes his elevation.[21]

The legislative ire was not allayed by the renewal of McKean's vetoes which almost immediately followed this incident. On March 25, 1805, he returned with his negative an act providing for the legislative election of the Comptroller General and Registrar General rather than for their appointment by the Governor as had previously been the case. McKean objected to the measure in the first place because be considered it an unconstitutional encroachment of the legislature on the powers and rights of the executive. Furthermore, he regarded it as inexpedient, since election by the legislature would result in intrigue among the members and since "a large public body is not so well qualified to select the best characters for subordinate Officers, as a single person, responsible, unfettered, and independent."

The message closed with what amounted to a direct challenge to the legislature on the project of constitutional reform. McKean disclaimed any desire for personal power but affirmed that it was his duty to "transmit the Constitution, (which approaches as near to perfection, as any that ever did, or does now exist in the world) to my successor, unimpaired by any act of mine."[22] The House responded by passing the measure over his veto; but the Senate sustained it by failing to muster the required two-thirds majority.[23]

Four days later McKean returned another bill entitled "An Act Regulating the Administration of Justice within this Commonwealth." The measure was in fact a general arbitration bill, which provided that all suits must first be referred to arbitrators for settlement before going to court. In his veto the Governor called attention to his previous messages on similar bills and then added sarcastically that if the suitors were to be burdened with the expenses of a trial by referees before the matter could come to court it would have been better "for Suitors in our Courts, to pay a certain stipulated sum of money to the State, for an allowance to have a trial by Jury in the first instance." The message also declared unconstitutional certain provisions relating to changing the salaries of the judges in the State courts. The House vote of 50-26 fell short of the necessary two-thirds majority, and the bill was lost.[24]

The means of revenge lay easy to hand for the legislators, and they proceeded to use it. A caucus of fifty Republican members of the legislature, presided over by John Steele, Senator from Lancaster County, met on April 3, 1805, and chose Simon Snyder as the Republican candidate for Governor. Snyder received 42 votes, with McKean getting seven, and Samuel Maclay one. The basis of Snyder's choice was reported to be "that the selection should be from among the German interest, that the candidate should not be a lawyer, and that a clod hopper should be preferred."[25]

Behind this selection lay a great deal of political maneuvering. Even before the clodpole affair and the vetoes by the Governor, a movement was on foot to replace McKean. Duane was accused early in March of having sent a list of suitable candidates to Lancaster; and both he and Leib had visited there in the latter part of the month, either to influence the choice of a candidate or to forward the convention movement or both.[26] Duane in 1803 had listed Samuel Maclay, Joseph Hiester, and Peter Muhlenberg as the most likely successors of McKean; and, with the addition of Simon Snyder, these men were the leading candidates in 1805.[27] Maclay, however, seems to have been dropped because of the mutual understanding that a German should be chosen.

Hiester, retiring Congressman from Berks County, was a man of great prestige among the Germans and was described by Duane in 1803 as "the most wealthy man in the commonwealth." Fifty-three years of age in 1805, he had a distinguished public record, having fought in the Revolution and suffered as a captive aboard one of the British prison ships at New York. He had spent fourteen years as a State Representative and Senator and eight years as a member of Congress besides taking part in the conventions which ratified the Federal Constitution and drew up the Pennsylvania Constitution of 1790. He was later to serve as Governor of the State. In 1805 he was certainly a logical candidate for the office. However, when approached by a Berks County Representative on the subject, he declined to let his name be used, asking how he could consistently oppose McKean whom he had recommended so warmly to the people on two previous occasions.[28]

Muhlenberg seems to have wanted the nomination, but his chances were ruined by his election as president of the Society of Constitutional Republicans. Whether he had any prior knowledge of this event or whether, as the *Aurora* charged, it was a clever maneuver by Dallas to destroy his availability is uncertain. In any case, Muhlenberg refused to serve as president of the society and wrote a letter to a friend in Lancaster stating that he had done so. At the same time he expressed his opinions on the reform of the Constitution. He would not oppose a convention if the people desired one, but he objected to legislative action without a popular mandate. The publication of the letter would indicate that Muhlenberg was not unreceptive to the nomination; but the members were apparently unconvinced of his soundness on revision of the Constitution, and he was not taken up.[29]

Snyder's nomination seems to have resulted principally from his German descent and from the elimination of Hiester and Muhlenberg as prospective candidates. Furthermore, as Speaker of the House and a principal in the clodpole affair, he served as a symbol of legislative prerogatives against a domineering executive. However, his nomination meant even more than this. It marked the passing of Republican political hegemony from the city to the country.

Duane and Leib were both cool to the choice; and the *Aurora* later charged that it had been engineered by the intrigues of Boileau with the understanding that Snyder would appoint him Secretary of the Commonwealth.[30] Leib did not want Snyder and was reported to have pursued a most erratic course in seeking to prevent his nomination. At first he opposed the plan for dropping McKean, and then he attempted to obtain the nomination for Muhlenberg, being credited with having persuaded the latter to refuse the presidency of the Constitutional Republican Society. In all these things, according to his enemies, Leib was seeking only his personal advantage. He had wanted to retain McKean in the hope of succeeding him in 1808, and he had supported Muhlenberg in the expectation of dominating him.[31] Whatever were the actual facts on this matter, it was certain that the country members had overridden the desires of Leib and Duane in choosing Snyder.

All opposition to the nomination did not immediately disappear. A Republican meeting at Lancaster on May 15, 1805, issued a call for a nominating convention to be held at Carlisle on August 6 "to consider and determine on the propriety of the aforementioned call of a [constitutional] convention, and the recommendation of SIMON SNYDER, Esq. and, if they approve of these measures, to devise the most efficient means of obtaining those ends." The principal mover of this project seems to have been Samuel Bryan, the Comptroller General, who had some idea of obtaining the nomination for himself. However, the scheme was doomed from the start. The *Aurora* disapproved of the idea even before it had been openly broached at Lancaster. A few counties chose delegates to the convention; but only three persons attended the meeting, and they disbanded without taking any action.[32]

While their opponents were going ahead with the nomination of Snyder, the supporters of McKean did not remain idle. On the day of the Snyder caucus, 34 members of the legislature, including all eight of the Federalists, signed a paper recommending the election of McKean. It was later claimed that seventeen additional members had declared their intention of supporting his re-election.[33]

The long-expected Republican schism was now a reality, and the gubernatorial contest in 1805 was to be waged between the factions of that party.

II

The gubernatorial campaign began even before the adjournment of the legislature, and it continued with increasing bitterness until the election in October. Political societies, newspapers, and numerous meetings organized the forces on both sides and issued a mass of propaganda to influence the voters. Amid this clamor, the campaign was finally decided by the issue of constitutional reform, by Federalist co-operation with the Constitutional Republicans, and by the German voters in Berks and Northampton counties.

After issuing its initial proposal, the Society of Constitutional Republicans proceeded with great activity to organize the opposition to a constitutional convention. At a meeting on March 21 the society chose Peter Muhlenberg as president, George Logan as vice president and treasurer, Samuel Wetherill as secretary, and Dallas, Isaac Worrell, and Jonathan B. Smith as a corresponding committee. When Muhlenberg declined to serve on the ground of ill health, Logan was made president; and Israel Israel was selected to succeed him as vice president.[34]

Despite the embarrassment occasioned by Muhlenberg's defection, the society continued to work effectively toward its objectives. A new circular letter was sent out by the corresponding committee urging that the remonstrance be forwarded to the legislature as quickly as possible and calling on the counties to form branches of the society. It deplored that any division should arise among the Republicans, but asserted that as the object of the party had always been "to preserve and perpetuate free, Republican institutions, the moral, social, and political principles, of our country," the Constitutional Republicans intended to repel all attacks upon these institutions and principles whether "under the mask of Federalism, artfully employed to disguise monarchy; or in the garb of Democracy, unworthily employed as a cover for anarchy."[35]

After the nomination of Snyder, the society decided on April 13, 1805, to extend its program to include the election of "Democratic Republican" legislators opposed to a convention and the support of McKean's re-election as Governor. In furthering these aims, the corresponding committee was directed to prepare an address favorable to McKean.[36]

The establishment of the Constitutional Republican Society had elicited sneering comments on Dallas's *"club legislation"* from the *Aurora;* but the success of its operations produced that sincerest form of flattery—imitation. At a meeting in John Miller's Green Tree Tavern on March 27, 1805, presided over by Thomas Leiper, the constitution of "The Society of Friends of the People" was presented and adopted. A subsequent meeting on April 1, 1805, chose the following provisional officers: Matthew Lawler, president; Thomas Leiper and Frederick Wolbert, vice presidents; George Bartram and James Carson, secretaries; and William Duane, Michael Leib, Joseph Clay, Paul Cox, and John Barker, members of the corresponding committee.

The purpose of the society was proclaimed to be the maintenance of the principles that all power was vested in the people; that governments were established for their benefit; and that they might alter, reform, or abolish their government as they saw fit. The preamble then gave as a sort of creed the "self-evident" truths of the Declaration of Independence. The society was to cover the State; but there were to be separate units in the city of Philadelphia and in each county.[37] The organization was formed too late to affect the outcome of the struggle in the legislature; but it was to be a useful instrument in the campaign which followed.

Continuing the practice of the preceding year, the *Aurora* referred to the Constitutional Republicans as Quids. The latter professed to find the title an honorable one. A writer in the *Freeman's Journal* asserted that a "tertium quid" was a substance used in pharmacy to transform a poison into a medicine and avowed that there was a great need for such an element in politics. A third party would determine whether there would be *"liberty or despotism."*[38] Both factions claimed to be "Democratic Republicans," but it will be convenient hereafter to use the term "Democrats" when alluding to the Republicans in opposition to McKean.

Scurrility and denunciation were prominent features of the campaign on both sides. The *Aurora* had begun to make more or less open attacks on McKean as early as February, 1805. By April all pretenses had disappeared, and he was assailed without reserve. His nepotism and vanity, his aristocratic ways, his arbitrary actions as a judge and as Governor were all attacked. He was accused of having opposed the Louisiana Purchase and of having violated the law of nations by imprisoning Joseph Cabrera, secretary of the Spanish legation—both because of the influence of his son-in-law, Don Carlos Martinez Yrujo, the Spanish minister.[39]

Vying with McKean for the first place in the attentions of the *Aurora* was Dallas. Dubbed "His Super Excellency" by the paper in token of his supposed domination of McKean, he was depicted in lurid colors as a form of evil genius who, behind the scenes, had been responsible for every bit of intrigue and third partyism in the State. He was even blamed for the legislative deadlock in 1800 which split the State's electoral votes; though, as in most other instances, there was only the assertion of this charge and no proof.[40] Dallas and McKean were by far the most favored objects of attack; but attention was given to many other Quid leaders as well.

The Quid papers also continued harsh assaults on their opponents; but they were neither as frequent nor as effectively written. Generally, they centered their attention on Leib and Duane or concentrated on blanket denunciations of Jacobin violence and the dangers of anarchy. The *Freeman's Journal* seized upon a figurative allusion to the scaffold in the *Aurora* to compare Duane and his cohorts with Danton and Robespierre and to cry melodramatically:

> Oh, People of Pennsylvania! People of America! will you take no warning; will you rest in false security, till your streets also may run with blood, your best citizens be butchered, and your wives and children become outcasts and wanderers.[41]

The Quids pictured their opponents as revolutionists who sought not only to destroy the Constitution but also to overthrow property rights and religion. See their toasts to an equal division of property! See in their ranks Leib, the defrauder of orphans; Duane, the enemy of religion; and Joseph Clay, who blasphemously wrote a check payable to Jesus Christ or bearer![42] Such were the writings in the Quid papers.

Accompanying these newspaper articles and editorial comments was a plethora of addresses from political meetings and organizations. The most outstanding on the Democratic side was that published in the *Aurora* on May 20, 1805, purporting to be an address adopted in April by the legislative caucus which nominated Snyder. It was almost wholly devoted to attacks on McKean, assailing him for his disrespect toward the legislature, his long series of vetoes, his refusal to remove Brackenridge, and his opposition to the will of the people with respect to judicial reform and the calling of a convention. It also accused him of active sponsorship of the third party in 1803 and of using official pressure to obtain the acquittal of the Supreme Court judges. Appended were statements by Daniel Montgomery and Abraham McKinney detailing their versions of the clodpole incident.[43]

The Society of Constitutional Republicans on June 10, 1805, adopted a long address prepared by Dallas and ordered 5,000 copies to be printed as pamphlets and distributed throughout the State. The address, which nearly filled three pages of the *Freeman's Journal,* was skillfully written. Blaming the Republican divisions on a group of malcontents seeking office and power, it exposed the visionary and vicious nature of the schemes for judicial reform and charged that the project of constitutional revision was fostered by legislative conspirators. Arguments were also advanced to show that the Constitution needed no changes. The malcontents were likewise credited with responsibility for the opposition to McKean and accused of making a deliberate attempt to provoke an outburst from him which would excuse the nomination of another person. Finally, consideration was given to the purported address of the legislative caucus. Denying that the caucus had adopted any address, it denounced the contents of the address printed in the *Aurora* as perversions of the truth and labeled certain statements, particularly that charging the Governor with using his influence for the acquittal of the judges, as lies and vicious libels.[44]

The Quid charge that the caucus had adopted no address was later supported by statements from members of the legislature who had attended; and in 1807 it was verified by articles in the *Aurora*. The true story seems to have been that an address was prepared by Boileau but was rejected by the meeting. This production was later sent to Duane and, after being revised by him and Leib so as to make it *"a very different thing"* from the original, was published in the *Aurora* over the signatures of John Steele and David Mitchell, who had served as chairman and secretary of the caucus. It was prefaced by an introduction which indicated that it had been unanimously agreed to by the caucus on the evening following the nomination of Snyder.[45] The incident is significant as a demonstration of the campaign methods of the time and also as an evidence of Duane's unscrupulousness in political matters and his propensity for altering material published in the *Aurora* to suit his own views.

Mutually engaged in such fierce assaults, both factions claimed to be acting upon the original Republican principles and denounced their opponents as apostates. It was only natural that each should seek the approval of Jefferson as a means of proving its orthodoxy beyond dispute. Such attempts were made in vain. Jefferson had correspondence with both Logan and Leib, and to both he emphasized his regret over the Republican dissensions; but he positively refused to indicate approval or disapproval of either faction.[46] Neither was able to use the influence of Jefferson to advance its cause.

Eventually, the result of the election turned upon three principal things: the question of a constitutional convention, Federalist support of the Quids, and the German vote, especially in Berks and Northampton counties.

From April to September the *Aurora* was filled with articles assailing lawyers and judges and calling for the holding of a constitutional convention to restore rule to the people and overthrow the last vestiges of tyranny. Its efforts had been seconded by the Democratic political meetings which almost always provided for the circulation of memorials favoring a convention.[47] The Quids responded with long articles denying the necessity of constitutional revision and warning of the dangers to be apprehended from such revolutionary procedures; and their meetings made arrangements for the circulation of petitions against a convention.[48]

The emphasis on the constitutional question was welcome to the Constitutional Republicans, and they refused to let it be subordinated. As early as July, 1805, the *Freeman's Journal* noted that some were saying that the "Revolutionists" had erred in attacking both McKean and the Constitution, but it insisted that the two were so intimately connected that they must stand or fall together. After all, the *Journal* said, the chief objection to McKean had been his strong fight in behalf of the principles of the Constitution.[49]

A conviction of error was beginning to dawn on the Democrats; and their meetings in August and September adopted resolutions strenuously denying that there had been any intention or desire to alter or destroy the fundamental principles of the Constitution. They also tried desperately to break down the conviction that Snyder's election meant the calling of a convention and McKean's, the retention of the Constitution as it was.[50]

The clearest indication of the effectiveness of the Quid propaganda was shown in the hasty resolutions adopted by the Philadelphia Society of Friends of the People at a special meeting on September 26, 1805. The first of these denied that the society had sought to forestall the opinion of the people on constitutional reform and recommended that all efforts to promote a convention be suspended. The second asserted that Snyder's nomination had not been made with any view to the calling of a convention, but solely to advance the interests of the people *"and to reduce to a private station the man who has cast opprobrium on the people, exercised an unjustifiable tyranny; and who has arrogated to himself a power to render the laws and the constitution subservient to his private and personal views."*[51] Thus the Democrats made a last frantic effort to change the issue from McKean and the Constitution to McKean alone; but it was too late.

The constitutional question was also significant because it offered a plausible basis for close co-operation between the Federalists and the Quids. As early as April, 1805, Jasper Yeates had warned that the Federalists deserved all the evils of a disorganized society if they failed to support the re-election of McKean; and the Federalists in the legislature on April 4 had signed the paper recommending him to the voters.[52] The warm manner in which the party had supported the remonstrance against the convention also seemed to assure their aid for the Governor's campaign. However, all was not to be so simple.

Dallas, as the moving spirit of the Constitutional Society, had included in its principles a statement of approval of both national and State administrations; and the early circulars of the society had mentioned the old dangers of Federalism and had specifically avowed the objects of the society to be the election of McKean and "Democratic Republican" legislators in addition to the preservation of the Constitution. Nor had the June address done more than welcome the support of "honest men."[53]

Apparently, Dallas was determined that no opening should be given for Democratic charges of apostasy. While he probably expected and desired the aid of the Federalists, he wanted it only in the form of their support of Constitutional Republican nominees. Such a prospect was not likely to appeal to the Federalists; and by May the *United States' Gazette* was denouncing the Quids roundly as mere officeseekers and proclaiming its neutrality in a petty contest of Republican factions.[54]

The *Lancaster Journal* adopted a radically different view. It reprinted from the Wilkes-Barre *Luzerne Federalist* on July 19, 1805, an article which, though highly critical of McKean, advocated his support by the Federalists as a means of saving the Constitution. To this, William Hamilton, editor of the *Journal,* appended some able remarks of his own. Some Federalists, he wrote, had avowed their neutrality, doubting that Snyder's election would be more injurious than McKean's. Some had even carried their hatred of McKean to the extent of supporting Snyder. Still others had felt that the crisis of Jacobinism had to be endured sooner or later, and the quicker it destroyed the government the sooner the people would be forced to return to the virtuous principles and administration of Federalism. To these last he recommended a study of the course of events in France.

Hamilton then went on to argue for Federalist aid to McKean. Though it might be true that Dallas and his group had been "haughty and supercilious" toward the Federalists in Philadelphia, no such attitude marked the conduct of the Constitutionalists in Lancaster. They were willing to co-operate fully. McKean's re-election was necessary to stem the tide of Jacobinism; and the Federalists might well consider what would be their fate as a party if they permitted personal antipathies to prevent them from doing what was necessary for the good of the Commonwealth. Such advice was closely heeded in Lancaster, where the Constitutional Republicans and Federalists met together to form a joint ticket.[55]

Meanwhile, a change was taking place in Philadelphia. The *United States' Gazette* reported in August that there were rumors of a Quid attempt to bargain for Federalist support of McKean in return for Quid votes for Federalists for the city councils.[56] The price was not to be so cheap.

On September 16, 1805, a Quid town meeting assembled to receive the report of a previously appointed nominating committee. The report was prefaced with a long preamble which stated that the times were too serious for quibbling; that "an union of honest men" was necessary; and that the committee had therefore disregarded "shades of difference in political opinion" and had selected candidates with a view to giving representation to all interests in the district. With this statement, it then presented a ticket including both Federalists and Quids.[57]

A few days later William Lewis, a leading Federalist lawyer, published a long appeal to the party to support McKean and all opponents of the "Jacobins" as the only way to preserve the Constitution and a government of law. Some Federalists immediately accused him of seeking office and denounced him as "Pope Lewis" for his attempted dictation to other members of the party. He denied the accusations and reiterated his statements that a crisis had arrived which demanded the best efforts of all Federalists in order to defeat the "Jacobins."[58]

These events showed that the Quids by September had been forced to abandon their attempt at independence and to seek Federalist co-operation on the best terms that they could get. On the other hand, the Federalists had given up their pretense of neutrality and had openly avowed their support of the Governor's re-election.

Another incident of great significance in the campaign was Peter Muhlenberg's public declaration in favor of McKean. This would have been important regardless of the circumstances, but it was announced in a manner calculated to have the greatest effect on the German vote. At a large public meeting at Reading on August 24, Joseph Hiester addressed the gathering in both English and German. He read to his audience the letters he had received from two of the Berks County legislators asking him to be a candidate for Governor and denounced the two men as intriguers. At the same time he read a letter from Peter Muhlenberg, dated August 3, 1805.

Popularly known as the "trout letter" because it opened with a reference to Hiester's fishing in the Blue Mountains, it was evidently written with a view to publication and was skillfully drafted to appeal to the German farmers. Muhlenberg began by saying that he had intended to play a passive role in the election since he felt that to be the proper course for a public officer. However, he was much concerned at seeing the Germans so misled. Did they realize the dangers which might attend an alteration of the Constitution under which they had so abundantly prospered? He was convinced that any changes at this time would bring great troubles to the farmers. There were many who hoped to profit from upsetting the old order. "For Heaven's sake only read that shameless toast drank publicly on the 4th of July last, 'Equal distribution of property.' Woe, therefore, unto him who has a large farm, particularly when others possess none."

In his opinion, the question of a convention and the election of a Governor could not be separated. While it was natural that the Germans would like to have a German Governor, "he ought to be a man qualified for the task, who would do honor to himself & the Germans; not one who would bring ridicule on them as well as himself." Snyder might be an "honest good man," but much more was required to be a good Governor. McKean could serve only three more years; and the Germans could then "look around for a man qualified to fill the governmental cha[i]r with honor and dignity." McKean had made a good Governor and had always had German support. How could they consistently oppose him now? The letter closed with the assertion that the "violent Federalists" in Philadelphia were inclined to support Snyder.[59]

Here was political propaganda of an almost perfect sort, and the Quids were not slow to take advantage of it. While the Democratic charge that more than a half million copies of the letter were printed and distributed seems much exaggerated,[60] there is no doubt that it was circulated in huge quantities in the German counties and elsewhere.[61] Its effectiveness could hardly be doubted. No German farmer could think of supporting Snyder when solemnly assured by two of his most trusted leaders that Snyder's success meant the destruction of the Constitution and a division of his laboriously acquired property. The potency of the appeal was demonstrated in the election returns.

The letter seems to have caught the Democrats by surprise; but after a two-weeks silence the *Aurora* began a savage attack on Muhlenberg. His vacillating conduct at the time of the legislative caucus was recalled; and his "trout letter" was attributed to a desire to ruin Snyder in order to obtain the nomination for himself in 1808. He was accused of having listened to Federalist proposals that he run against McKean in 1802 and of having refused them only after he had received the appointment as Collector of the Port. Furthermore, he was charged with a willful perversion of the truth in publishing as genuine a toast to the "equal distribution of property," when he knew that the true toast was to the "equal distribution of justice."[62] Such attacks, however, could not repair the damage done by the letter.

In the midst of this propaganda, the two groups organized for the election in October. In the city of Philadelphia the Democrats held their ward meetings in May; and the general ward committee subsequently prepared a ticket; but it was not submitted to a town meeting as had been customary. The Democrats in the county held a general meeting in June, adopted resolutions for Snyder and against McKean, appointed a committee to circulate petitions for a constitutional convention, and chose conferees. Another meeting in September nominated the assembly ticket.[63]

Meanwhile, the Society of Constitutional Republicans recommended that the Quids use the district delegate system in the county and a general town meeting in the city. Their suggestions were followed. A city meeting on August 19, 1805, appointed a nominating committee to draw up a ticket and authorized its members to act as conferees on nominations for State Senator, County Commissioner, and Coroner. The county delegates, elected by the district meetings, nominated an assembly ticket and conferred with the city and Delaware County conferees on other candidates. As previously noted, the city nominating committee made a report on September 16 calling for close cooperation with the Federalists and offered a ticket including men from both parties. This was adopted; but the Federalists were dissatisfied and backed a ticket which gave to them a larger share of the offices.[64]

In almost every county of the State there were bitter struggles as the Republicans split and began to align themselves for and against McKean. Leading Republicans in Bucks, Chester, and Montgomery counties quickly broke away from their old comrades and allied with the Federalists to advance the re-election of the Governor.[65] Joseph Hiester led the Constitutionalists in Berks County and was opposed by his cousin, State Senator Gabriel Hiester, who sought to win the voters for Snyder.[66] In western Pennsylvania, William Findley, longtime Republican leader and Congressman of Westmoreland County, threw his very considerable influence behind McKean and wrote numerous articles in his behalf.[67] In the perennially Democratic stronghold of Washington County, McKean's friends were accused of making an open and vicious use of the patronage to buy off the Governor's opponents.[68]

Nowhere was the fight hotter than in Pittsburgh, where Tarleton Bates, Prothonotary of Allegheny County, and a number of other officeholders broke away from the Democrats after the committee of delegates had supported Snyder by a 2-1 majority. Co-operating with the Federalists and enjoying the aid of the Pittsburgh *Tree of Liberty* and the *Pittsburgh Gazette,* they made considerable headway. To combat them, Duane and other Philadelphians helped to establish the Pittsburgh *Commonwealth,* which began publication on July 24, 1805, under the editorship of Ephraim Pentland, a young Philadelphian.[69] This paper and John Binns's Northumberland *Republican Argus* received high praise from the *Aurora* for their "original thinking—and bold and correct discussion."[70]

The election took place on October 8, 1805; and the closeness of the returns showed how severely contested the campaign had been. The official count gave McKean 43,644 votes to Snyder's 38,483; although the latter was justly entitled to 395 additional votes from Bucks County which, by a clerical error, were listed as being for "Samuel Snyder." McKean was therefore credited with a majority of 5,161, but he actually polled only 4,766 votes more than Snyder. The Governor won in seventeen counties and the city of Philadelphia; Snyder carried seventeen counties.

With few exceptions, the most important being Westmoreland, Berks, and Northampton counties, McKean was victorious in the same counties which had returned Federalist majorities for Ross in 1799. From the areas favorable to Ross the Governor had received 13,492 votes, or 36.2 per cent of his total vote in 1799; but in 1805 he received from them 24,294 votes, or 55.6 per cent of his total vote. In the German counties of Northampton and Berks McKean polled 6,772 votes to Snyder's 3,216. Had these figures been reversed, as they might easily have been but for the efforts of Hiester and Muhlenberg, Snyder would have been elected. McKean's success was unquestionably due to Federalist and German votes.[71]

The Federalists and Quids also won 53 out of 86 seats in the House of Representatives and elected three out of seven State Senators.[72]

The most impressive fact about the election results is how poorly McKean did with the many advantages he possessed. Snyder, his opponent, was virtually unknown outside the legislature and his home county; and many Republicans were at best only lukewarm in his support. On the other hand, McKean had been a prominent and distinguished person in national and State affairs for a generation. He had the active aid of the bench and the bar and of a large body of officeholders whom he had appointed. The attack on the Constitution had brought many moderate Republicans and the majority of the Federalists to his assistance. The most influential German leaders had done their utmost to give him the votes of their people. The Society of Constitutional Republicans had flooded the State with circulars and pamphlets; and 30 of the State's 40 newspapers had been devoted to his cause.[73] Yet he had won by only 5,000 votes out of more than 82,000 cast. In Gallatin's opinion, the election had been a victory for the Duane group since they had carried at least two-thirds and probably three-quarters of the Republican vote.[74]

The year 1805 had been a crucial one in the politics of Pennsylvania. Republican unity, which had been shaken by the many local quarrels over patronage and political power and by the disputes between the legislature and the Governor over judicial reform, was now completely shattered. The supporters of McKean and the opponents of Leib and Duane had organized themselves behind the Governor and the Constitution and had sought to gain control of the party. In this they were defeated, but by an alliance with the Federalists they had managed to win the election. On the other side, mutual opposition to McKean, Dallas, and the judiciary had brought a coalition between the Leib-Duane faction in Philadelphia and the bulk of the country Republicans in the legislature. The next few years were to demonstrate the instability of these coalitions.

CHAPTER V

QUID PROBLEMS AND THE EMERGENCE OF NATIONAL ISSUES: 1806

THE YEAR WHICH FOLLOWED the election of 1805 was a turbulent one in the politics of the Commonwealth. McKean had been re-elected by a combination of Federalists and Constitutional Republicans formed to defeat the movement for constitutional revision. This alliance was subjected to heavy strains. To the natural conflict for control between the two elements was added an even stronger divisive force. National issues, which had been largely subordinated during Jefferson's first administration, once more became of primary importance. The threatening state of foreign affairs compelled Federalists and Republicans to rally along traditional lines on the question of supporting Jefferson's foreign policy. The Democrats united behind the administration on foreign affairs; but in domestic matters a segment of the party was greatly attracted to John Randolph and gave some evidence of following him in his break with Jefferson. There were further complexities arising from personal jealousies of the Democratic leaders and the bitter feud between Duane and the Governor.

I

Observing Pennsylvania affairs from Washington in October, 1805, Gallatin wrote that he did not think a reconciliation of the Republicans probable although he ardently wished it. "McKean and Duane will be both implacable and immovable, and the acts of the first and the continued proscriptions of the last will most probably and unfortunately defeat every attempt to reconcile."[1] Time was to prove the soundness of his views as it was also to demonstrate the tenuousness of the Constitutionalist coalition of Federalists and Quids.

The election returns were barely in before McKean began a policy of removals certain to alienate his opponents still further. His enemies in office were forced out and replaced by his supporters, whether Federalists or Republicans. The first to be superseded was Samuel Bryan, Comptroller General, and others followed him in speedy succession. The policy drew bitter denunciations and charges of corruption from the *Aurora;* but the Governor gave no heed to those who abused him.[2]

McKean's course was highly pleasing to some of the Quids. William Barton, Prothonotary of Lancaster County and one of the original promoters of the third party in 1803, wrote to Dallas in November, beseeching him to use his influence with the Governor for the appointment of Federalists to office. In Barton's opinion, this would make it possible to replace "two *nominal* and *inefficient* Parties" by a single effective one. There should then be "no political distinctions, but *Constitutionalists* and *Jacobins*"; and Barton had only contempt for "illiberal and contracted souls" who could not see the benefits of such an eventuality.[3]

It is highly unlikely that Dallas welcomed these effusions of Barton, since he must have assuredly numbered himself among the "illiberal and contracted souls" who had no desire for close co-operation with the Federalists. He had sought to avoid any such alliance in the preceding campaign, and the events then transpiring in Philadelphia proved that he had not changed his views. Among the first of the appointments made by the Governor after the election was that of James Gamble, State Senator from Philadelphia, as auctioneer.[4] Gamble's resignation as Senator necessitated the election of a successor and precipitated an open quarrel among the Quids.

The Federalists of the city met on November 18, 1805, and nominated John Hallowell for the vacancy. They also attended in force a Constitutionalist meeting held two days later. Both factions agreed on the choice of a Quid chairman for the meeting; but a loud dispute broke out when the Federalists nominated one of their own number for secretary. Dallas opposed this on the ground that it was a meeting of Constitutional Republicans, who were dedicated not only to the support of the Constitution but also to friendship with the State and national administrations. James Milnor, a Federalist lawyer, denounced Dallas for attempted dictation and refused to accept his views on the nature of the meeting.

The Federalist success in electing their secretary led Dallas and his supporters to withdraw from the meeting. Subsequently holding one of their own, they chose as their candidate, Samuel Wetherill, Sr.; but he declined the nomination for personal reasons. A number of Quids refused to leave the original meeting, but remained and co-operated with the Federalists in supporting Hallowell.[5]

Such an event could not be accepted lightly by Dallas. As one of the leading Federal officeholders of the State he could hardly afford to be put into a position of supporting the enemies of the national administration. He had apparently intended and desired a reconciliation with the Democrats immediately after the October election; but this was impossible so long as Duane and Leib controlled the party.[6] However, he must and could avoid aiding in the election of a Federalist.

His attitude probably had much to do with a meeting of the Society of Constitutional Republicans a few days later. It published an address stating that the society had achieved the object of its founding and would soon cease to exist. The members were warned not to be misled because they had received Federalist aid and had been opposed to other Republicans. They were urged to avoid apostasy and to rejoin their Republican brothers who had been deceived by a faction. This was followed on December 12, 1805, by the formal dissolution of the society.[7]

The Democrats were delighted by these evidences of dissension and made the most of the equivocal position of the Quids. They nominated John Dorsey to succeed Gamble and conducted an active campaign in his behalf. The supporters of Hallowell worked equally hard; but he lost by 200 votes in what McKean believed to be the most vigorous contest over the election of a single member of the legislature that he had ever seen.[8]

The incident highlighted one aspect of the dilemma which faced the Pennsylvania Quids so long as they existed—how to avoid becoming a tail to the Federalist kite when the Democratic leaders would not permit them to rejoin their old party.

II

The legislative session of 1805-1806 was marked by much political maneuvering. The Democrats seized upon the question of foreign relations to disrupt the Federalist-Quid coalition and were momentarily successful; but they were unable to prevent the enactment of a legislative program of judicial reform drafted to meet the views of the

Governor. A good portion of the session was devoted to political feuding between the supporters of McKean and those who opposed him.

The growing seriousness of American foreign relations made the position of the Constitutional Republicans even more difficult. One of the key issues dividing the Federalists and Republicans in the 1790's had been their divergent attitudes toward the European belligerents in the wars growing out of the French Revolution. Impelled by their hatred of Jacobin excesses in France and by the lucrative returns of trade with the British, the Federalists had been violently anti-French and at least mildly pro-British.

The Republicans had regretted Jacobin violence, but they viewed the French Revolution generally as a movement of the people against tyranny and oppression, and they tended to be sympathetic to France. The traditions of the American Revolution gave additional support to this attitude. France had been the ally, and Great Britain had been the enemy and oppressor. Furthermore, the mass of the Republicans were not affected by the commercial interests which influenced the Federalists.

During Jefferson's first administration foreign affairs had not been of major concern. The difficulties with France had been settled prior to his inauguration; and the Peace of Amiens in March, 1802, had ended the wars in Europe. The only serious international question had been settled by the Louisiana Purchase, and the Federalists were able to interest but few in their criticisms of that settlement.

The renewal of the European wars in May, 1803, was to have a profound effect on the American people. The old party attitudes showed themselves almost immediately. The *Aurora* proclaimed that a strict neutrality was the only true policy for the country, but it insisted that the resumption of the war was not solely the fault of France and Napoleon. Rather, it was basically a commercial war begun by the British to maintain their supremacy in trade and colonial dominion.[9]

The *Gazette of the United States* regarded Great Britain as "the only barrier to restrain the mad ambition of Bonaparte, and to stop his ascention [*sic*] to universal empire." It admitted that the Republicans were giving little praise to Napoleon at that time but predicted that when he desired it the "jacobin presses" would respond with alacrity.[10] Soon afterward the two papers were debating over

British seizures of American ships and impressment of American seamen.[11]

Despite this early clamor, the war did not become a matter of great public interest until the latter part of 1805. The virtual British blockade of American ports had been tightened; their impressments had become more frequent; and the decision of Sir William Scott in the case of the *Essex* had struck a heavy blow at the American carrying trade. Neutral rights were once more of primary concern.[12]

The *Aurora* in December, 1805, demanded that an embargo be laid on British vessels, that British property be sequestered, and that British subjects be seized as hostages for the impressed seamen until Great Britain made amends for her wrongs.[13]

The Federalists were inclined to blame matters on the policy of the administration and demanded that the government furnish protection for commerce. The *United States' Gazette* warned the government that the merchants could hardly be expected to continue the payment of heavy duties on their trade when they saw all their rights abandoned and no efforts made to protect them. At the same time the merchants of Philadelphia drew up a memorial stating their grievances and calling for strong measures of defense.[14]

When the legislature convened in December, 1805, the Democrats seized upon this issue to embarrass the Quids and Federalists. The House committee appointed to draft an answer to the Governor's address reported one which ignored foreign affairs. In the committee of the whole a paragraph was added referring to the aggressions on American commerce and expressing complete confidence in "the collected wisdom and patriotism of the executive and legislative branches of the federal government." When the paragraph came up for consideration, the Federalists moved to strike out this expression of confidence in the national administration. The Democrats called for a record vote, and the Federalists were defeated 70-13.[15]

The incident was not of great importance in itself, but it indicated that the Constitutional Republicans and the Federalists had not been amalgamated into a new party, and it foreshadowed the destruction of their alliance as national questions gradually became the most important political issues.

The Constitutionalists co-operated somewhat better on other matters. They pushed through a bill for judicial reform, which, though not completely satisfactory to the Governor, was certainly far from the radical alterations desired by the Democrats. The High Court of Errors and Appeals was abolished as were trials *en banc* by the Supreme Court. The original jurisdiction of the latter in civil suits was greatly restricted, and provision was made for the Supreme Court to hold one term of court annually in Pittsburgh as well as two in Philadelphia. Circuit courts presided over by one Supreme Court judge were to be held at least once a year in each county. Finally, four additional judicial districts were created for courts of quarter sessions and common pleas.[16]

The Democrats aided by fourteen Quids in the House were able to get passed an act regulating arbitrations; but it was not one which conformed to their ideas on the subject. It merely provided a procedure for the use of arbitration when desired by both parties to a suit and made the decision binding only when neither objected. Furthermore, it was a temporary act limited to a period of three years.[17]

The session was also taken up with much political skirmishing. During the preceding summer the Quids had established the Lancaster *Constitutional Democrat*, whose editor, John R. Mathews, was later appointed printer of bills for the House. On December 17, 1805, the paper published an article which aimed at jocularity on the theme of the equal distribution of property. It went far beyond the bounds of propriety, however, in statements such as the following:

> Bar well your doors, Citizens; for there are Schneiderites among us; lock fast your strong boxes—lock every drawer—turn every key. Mind your pockets, Cits; guard well your purses, watches, &c. *An equal distribution of property* is their Motto. . . . Let them once raise a standard, every Highwayman, Footpad, Pickpocket, Thief, Pilferer, &c. will rally around. . . .[18]

The Democrats immediately introduced a resolution to revoke Mathews's appointment as printer of the House bills; and the resolution was adopted with the aid of 24 Quids despite Mathews' letter of apology.[19]

The Democrats were less fortunate in their attempts to defend Samuel Bryan. When McKean had removed the latter as Comptroller General in October, both Bryan and the Democratic papers had protested loudly against the removal of a competent public servant for his political beliefs. With the apparent intention of discrediting Bryan and justifying the Governor, the Quids in the House on January 1,

1806, appointed a committee to investigate Bryan's conduct in carrying out the provisions of an act adopted in the previous session for payment of county taxes on certain lands claimed by the State.

The investigation resulted in personal violence on January 9, 1806, when Bryan was testifying before the committee. Thomas McKean Thompson, nephew of the Governor and Secretary of the Commonwealth, interrupted him several times with *"very opprobrious epithets,"* and after the session was adjourned Thompson followed Bryan outside and began to beat him. The Democrats in the House tried to pass a resolution censuring Thompson, but they could not prevail against the Federalist-Quid majority.

The committee made its report in February, 1806, and it was well calculated to serve the Quid purposes. On the specific matter in question, Bryan was proved to have made little attempt to follow the provisions of the act and, as a result of his failure to do so, to have paid $4,658 in taxes to Luzerne County when the actual claims amounted to only $333. While there were some extenuating circumstances, Bryan's own testimony was contradictory, and his excuses were feeble. He was shown to be a petty intriguer, highly suspicious of those about him and given to recording trivial incidents which might later be used against them. Of this nature were certain charges made by him against the Governor which bordered on the ridiculous. The committee concluded its report by offering resolutions which specifically condemned Bryan's conduct and made him liable for any losses sustained in attempting to recover the overpayments.

The Democrats introduced substitute resolutions excusing Bryan's failure to follow the terms of the act and relieving him from liability. The substitution was defeated, and the whole affair was concluded by referring it to a select committee instructed to take measures for the return of the money by the counties.[20]

One other incident of the session created a great stir. In the Senate the Democrats had control by the narrow margin of thirteen to twelve. On January 30, 1806, an election was held by it to choose three of the State's six directors on the board of the Bank of Pennsylvania. The Democratic candidates were Thomas Leiper, John Harrison, and William Duane; but the latter failed of election because Henry Wertz, Democratic Senator from Bedford County, refused to vote for him.

Hardly anything could have pleased the Governor more than the defeat of Duane, and the *Aurora* began to accuse the Governor's officials of having used improper means to accomplish it. It alleged that Thomas McKean Thompson, the Secretary of the Commonwealth, and John Hastings, the Governor's private secretary, had offered Wertz the appointment as Prothonotary of Bedford County if he would vote against Duane.

The charges were denied by Thompson; and the *Aurora* and the Lancaster *Intelligencer* began to denounce Wertz for failing to answer these denials, since Wertz's own statements were the basis of the accusations against Thompson and Hastings. Wertz maintained silence; but the Governor instituted libel proceedings against William Dickson, the editor of the *Intelligencer*. Wertz did not testify during the trial; and the testimony of other witnesses, while it showed that Wertz had discussed appointments with Hastings, did not give proof that Wertz had been promised an office for opposing Duane.

Dickson was fined and sent to prison for three months, and the Democrats acclaimed him the first martyr in the new reign of terror. He was appointed treasurer of Lancaster County while in prison; subscriptions were taken for the payment of his fine; and a big Democratic celebration was held on his release after serving his sentence. Political differences and personal feuds were thus inextricably mixed in the politics of the times.[21]

The legislative session gave ample proof that the warfare between the Constitutionalists and the Democrats had only begun.

III

While the Quids had been forced on the defensive to prove their Republicanism, Duane's impulsiveness in supporting John Randolph of Roanoke in Congress came very near to giving them the opportunity of reversing their role.

Since September, 1804, the *Aurora* had claimed that the Yazoo land speculation lay at the bottom of third partyism in Philadelphia and the country at large. It had subsequently published a mass of material on the matter, making much of Gideon Granger's attempt to gain congressional votes for the compromise settlement and charging that Dallas and Gallatin were financially interested in the affair. Although no evidence was given, the *Aurora* strongly inferred that these two had sponsored the opposition to Leib and Duane because they refused to support the Yazoo bill pending before Congress. These articles continued at short intervals all through the year 1805; and on November 11 the paper asserted pontifically that "the *Yazoo question* . . . is to determine the relations, the principles, the characters, and the strength of parties in the next session of Congress."[22]

Acting on this assumption, Duane was naturally inclined to follow the leadership of John Randolph who had been the outstanding opponent of the Yazoo claims in Congress.[23] Unfortunately for him, it was at this session that Randolph broke completely with the administration. Still more unluckily, a great deal of the business of Congress at this time was done in secret, so that Duane had no way of knowing what was really taking place.

When Congress had met in December, 1805, Jefferson's message had displayed a very bellicose tone toward Spain and had given the impression that the administration intended to take military measures against her. However, a secret message on the subject was much milder in tone; and it was learned that Jefferson proposed to attempt to purchase Florida by negotiating at Paris to gain Napoleon's aid in forcing Spain to sell the territory.

Randolph refused to be a party to this and fought viciously against the proposal during the secret consideration of the matter in the early part of January, 1806. He was defeated; but during the remainder of the session he continually denounced the administration as dishonorable and corrupt, accused it of using "back-stairs influence" to govern Congress, and opposed almost every important measure that it supported. He was largely responsible for the defeat of resolutions for strengthening the harbor defenses and building six ships of the line. Furthermore, he ridiculed nonimportation as a measure of retaliation against Great Britain and asserted that France, not England, was America's real enemy.[24]

Duane in January knew nothing of what was actually going on; but, responding to hints of a Republican division published in the Federalist papers, the *Aurora* began to denounce those who opposed Randolph as enemies of the President and attributed their opposition to the baleful influence of the *"Yazoo league"* led by Granger. Learning that there was talk of replacing Randolph as Republican leader of the House, the paper on February 5, 1806, asserted:

> Now if some members of Congress are to be *bribed with post office contracts* to obtain their votes for a nefarious speculation on one hand, and if a member of congress superior to all corruption and all collusion or dishonor is to be *pulled down*—and the offices of government are to be employed to such ends—it is vain to pretend that republican government can stand, if such corruption and such corrupt men are suffered to retain the power which they prostitute—and if men of virtue, honor, talents and integrity are to be made the victims of intrigue bottomed on such corruption.[25]

In this diatribe Duane was unwittingly attacking Jefferson and the Republicans who were supporting his measures. The damaging effect of such a course was not lost on Leib, who wrote plaintively from Washington to Caesar A. Rodney, beseeching him to prevent Duane from making "any further random animadversions." Leib was bound to secrecy and could not inform him of his errors, but he assured Rodney that Duane was dealing blows to his friends and to staunch supporters of the administration and that the measures adopted in secret were in accordance with Democratic principles and would be approved by the party and the nation. If such ill-timed articles continued to appear, the public would "be led to infer, that we must be as wrong in respect to Pennsylvania affairs, as we are in respect to those of the union"; and the Quids would gain ground.[26]

Leib's warning seems to have been conveyed to Duane because the *Aurora* ceased its violent assaults on those who opposed Randolph, and it gave full approval to the Florida purchase bill when it was made public. Nevertheless, Duane and his followers continued to be sympathetic to Randolph and wavered in their allegiance to Jefferson. As the quarrels in Congress progressed, the *Aurora* gave full publicity to Randolph's views and never directly attacked him. Even his opinions on France and Great Britain did not call forth the denunciation which might have been expected from Duane's past conduct and his confirmed Anglophobia.[27]

In Congress Leib was fascinated by Randolph's savage tirades and spoke regretfully of the violence which drove many from acting with him. Leib felt that Jefferson's conduct had a "suspicious aspect" and that the foundation of a serious schism had been laid. Almost sorrowfully, he concluded that the Pennsylvania Democrats had best be neutral in the conflict since the Quids might otherwise be revived in strength.[28] Joseph Clay, Congressman from the city and a close ally of Leib and Duane, disdained such opportunistic counsels and gave wholehearted support to Randolph.[29]

The *Freeman's Journal* took note of the situation and declared that Duane was being neutral until he could determine whether Jefferson or Randolph was the stronger.[30] Its observations were justified; but so long as the Quids were allied with the Federalists they could hardly expect to profit from the situation unless Leib and Duane went into open opposition to the administration. Nevertheless, the equivocal position of the Philadelphia Democrats added a further complication to the muddled political alignments of the State.

IV

Political tensions continued high in the election of 1806. While Duane was busily engaged in a personal quarrel with the Governor, he and Leib were acting in such a highhanded fashion in Democratic affairs as to lay the basis for a new split in the party. The Quids united with the Federalists once more; but again the two were unable to reach a complete agreement on the candidates in the Philadelphia area. Politics were also extremely bitter in the Pittsburgh section. The election returns showed substantial gains for the Democrats in the State; but they won control of the legislature by an exceedingly narrow margin.

Despite the great attention bestowed on national affairs, the *Aurora* did not neglect State politics. Duane's feud with the Governor was steadily maintained. McKean was attacked for attending a banquet of the Society of the Sons of St. George at which William Pitt was toasted; his nepotism was assailed; and a list of the "patronage, honors, and profits" of "The Royal Family and the Titularies of the Grand Dignitaries" was published. The appointment of McKean's son-in-law, Dr. George Buchanan, as Lazaretto physician was declared to be illegal because the latter was a citizen of Maryland. The Governor was reported to be using a facsimile stamp for signing public documents, and the *Aurora* questioned the legality of instruments thus signed. He was also accused of having made proposals to discontinue certain Commonwealth prosecutions pending against Duane if the latter would withdraw his suits against Joseph B. McKean and the other volunteer officers who had beaten him in 1799.[31] This unceasing vituperation and the growing number of charges of official misconduct soon made it clear that Duane had begun to lay the foundation for an impeachment against the Governor.[32]

McKean did not accept the situation without response. In August certain of the *Aurora* publications were made the basis of libel charges against Duane; and the latter was called before the mayor to make bond for his appearance and also to *"keep the peace and be of good behavior."* The hearing before the mayor was delayed for a day due to the absence of witnesses; and Duane in the meantime made bond to an alderman of the city but without the injunction to keep the peace.

Two days later Duane was arrested and imprisoned on libel charges brought before the mayor by the Spanish minister Yrujo, McKean's son-in-law. He was freed on a writ of habeas corpus issued by William Tilghman, who had succeeded Edward Shippen as Chief Justice of the State Supreme Court. Joseph B. McKean argued against the issuance of the writ; but Tilghman ruled that Duane was justified in refusing to make a bond with the provision to keep the peace and that there was no reason for imprisoning him since he had already made bond for his appearance.

The decision was an important one because it severely limited the Governor's ability to control publications in the press. As Chief Justice, McKean in 1797 had bound William Cobbett under such a recognizance and then had sued him for forfeiture of the recognizance for later publications on the ground that they tended to break the peace. A similar procedure had been used by Joseph B. McKean to counter Duane's suit against him in 1799.

Had the procedure been upheld by Tilghman, the Governor and his friends could have harassed Duane with lawsuits for libel without any decision by a jury as to whether the publications complained of were in fact libelous. Even though such suits might later have been dismissed, the editor would have been burdened with almost prohibitive legal fees for several years, while his credit would have been impaired if not destroyed.[33]

Meanwhile, Duane enforced his will on the Democrats in the city ruthlessly, castigating those who opposed him and pushing through the renomination of Joseph Clay for Congress despite the latter's support of John Randolph in the previous session.[34]

In the county the Leib group completely controlled the situation, and they acted with equal arbitrariness. The conferees were nominated at a meeting in August and instructed to support Leib for Congress, although he had requested that he not be nominated. Leib sent a similar letter to the committee of conference, which acceded to his request and chose Dr. John Porter as candidate in his stead. At a second county meeting in September three of the county representatives in the last session of the legislature were dropped, and Leib was chosen to fill one of the vacancies.[35]

These changes caused a new rift among the county Democrats. One of the representatives dropped from the ticket was Jacob Holgate of Germantown who had served in the assembly since 1801. On the day of the second county meeting an article in the *Aurora* accused Holgate of approving John R. Mathews' libel on the House of Representatives because he had voted to reimburse Mathews for some of his losses.[36] Apparently this charge was used at the meeting as the excuse for omitting him from the ticket.

Holgate's friends in Germantown met and asserted their intention of supporting his re-election since he had done nothing to merit distrust. The *Aurora* countered with a furious onslaught against Holgate as a trimmer and made much of the fact that he had been taken up on the Quid ticket. It also spoke menacingly of interference in the county affairs by Nathaniel B. Boileau, who was described as Holgate's friend "*in an adjoining county.*"[37]

The tremendous uproar over such a trivial matter was explained by the *Freeman's Journal*. Leib hoped to be elected United States Senator to succeed Logan whose term expired in the following March. It was for this reason that he had sought election to the assembly. Holgate, the paper said, had been laid aside because he was believed to favor Boileau rather than Leib as Logan's successor.[38]

The Federalists and Quids also had their disagreements. In contrast to the procedure adopted in 1805, the two groups held joint ward meetings and selected delegates to a general ward committee. In the county the district delegate system was continued. When the conferees of the city and county met with those of Delaware County, they agreed to support a Federalist candidate for State Senator, a Federalist from

Delaware County for Congress, and a Quid from Philadelphia County for Congress; but no agreement was reached on the city congressional candidate because the Federalists and Quids were disputing the question. The Federalists wanted Joseph Hemphill, and the Quids were backing John Sergeant. Neither would give way so each nominated its own man and organized an independent corresponding committee in his behalf.[39]

Enjoying the Quid dilemma hugely, the *Aurora* listed all the Federalists on the coalition ticket and asked how the Quids could be friends to Jefferson when they were supporting his avowed enemies for office and particularly as members of Congress. It renewed its attacks on Dallas and accused him of backing Sergeant for Congress with the knowledge that Sergeant would decline to run just before the election. Dallas would thus be able to avoid an open break with the administration while satisfying his dislike of Jefferson by voting for a Federalist. Sergeant, of course, did not withdraw; and the accusation was probably nothing more than an attempt to discredit Dallas with no foundation in fact.[40]

At the same time the *Aurora* was assailing Granger and Gallatin, claiming that the Yazoo speculators were interfering with the election. It also sought to link Dallas and Granger with the movements of Aaron Burr which were beginning to arouse suspicion.[41]

The Quids attempted to prove their orthodoxy by strongly reaffirming their attachment to Jefferson. A meeting in October appointed a committee to draft an address expressing their confidence in his administration and their willingness to support him so long as he might desire to continue as President. In taking this action, the Quids were only offsetting a projected Democratic address for the same purpose.[42]

The Philadelphia campaign in 1806 was still further complicated by a sheriff's election. In 1803 the Republican split in Philadelphia had centered around the opposing candidacies of Frederick Wolbert and William T. Donaldson for sheriff. The Republican conferees had chosen John Barker as a compromise candidate; but Donaldson had refused to withdraw and had run on the Rising Sun ticket. In 1806 Wolbert was selected as the Democratic candidate, and Donaldson was backed by the Federalists and Quids. The *Aurora* attacked Donaldson for alleged mishandling of public funds and also for holding a barbecue. The last was rather extravagantly described as "one of the grossest and most presumptuous attempt[s] to gain votes by bribery ever practised in this state."[43] The *Freeman's Journal* defended Donaldson and assailed Wolbert for defaults in his accounts as a tax collector.[44]

At the election on October 14, 1806, the vote was even heavier than in 1805. The Federalists and Quids carried the city by approximately 200 votes out of nearly 3,900 cast. The Democrats rolled up a majority of more than a thousand votes in the county, and they elected their candidates for Congress, the State Senate, and the office of sheriff. In the congressional election Sergeant, the Quid candidate, polled only 1,578 votes to 2,922 for Hemphill who was supported by the Federalists.

Although the Democratic congressional candidates had an average majority of nearly 700 votes in the city and county of Philadelphia, the returns for sheriff were much closer. Wolbert received 3,905 votes, Matthew Lawler 3,847, and Donaldson 3,811. Lawler was not really a candidate for the office but was run by the Democrats because the Constitution permitted the Governor to commission either of the two highest candidates as sheriff; and they did not wish to give McKean the option of choosing between Donaldson and Wolbert.[45]

Politics were also hotly contested in Pittsburgh in 1806. Tarleton Bates and Henry Baldwin, the most prominent Quid leaders at that place, had purchased the *Tree of Liberty* and installed Walter Forward as its editor. Through its columns they conducted a bitter exchange of personalities with Ephraim Pentland, editor of the *Commonwealth*. The abuse became so great that Bates, accompanied by several friends, seized Pentland one evening in January, 1806, and administered a beating to him with a cowskin. Pentland demanded satisfaction; but Bates refused on the ground that Pentland was a coward and also because he claimed the challenge was a trick—that if he accepted Pentland would go to court and seek to have him removed from his office as Prothonotary for breaking the law against duelling. Pentland's message had been carried to Bates by Thomas Stewart, a merchant, who regarded Bates's explanation as a personal reflection upon him. He therefore sent a challenge; and Bates was killed in the duel held on January 8.[46]

There was no further violence; but the election campaign was very bitter and centered chiefly about the congressional contest. The Constitutionalists had prepared a ticket headed by John Wilkins, Jr., a

Federalist of Pittsburgh, as candidate for Congress. The Democrats backed Samuel Smith of Erie County, who had been elected the previous year to fill the unexpired term of John B. C. Lucas.

The *Commonwealth* was filled with charges against Wilkins and the Quids who supported him. Wilkins was denounced as an aristocrat and an associate of land speculators. He was also accused of being over a half million dollars delinquent in the settlement of his accounts as the former Quartermaster General of the army; and it was alleged that Gallatin would find a way to clear the books if Wilkins were chosen to Congress.

The *Commonwealth* during the campaign also laid much stress on the struggle between the "actual settlers" of the lands north and west of the Ohio and Allegheny rivers and the Population and Holland land companies who held warrants for much of the land in the region. Smith's vote against the Yazoo compromise was recalled, and he was pictured as the friend of the people and the enemy of land speculators.[47]

The election returns differed little from those of the preceding year. Allegheny County had a Federalist-Quid majority of about 170 votes; but the Democratic majorities in Beaver and Butler, which were in the same electoral district for State Representatives, overbalanced it. In the congressional district, which comprised Erie, Crawford, Mercer, Venango, and Warren counties, in addition to the three already mentioned, Smith polled 3,339 votes to 2,621 for Wilkins. Despite the Democratic attempts to woo back the Quids, the relative strength of the two groups was practically the same as in 1805.[48]

In the State as a whole the Democrats did much better than in the previous year. In 1805 the Constitutionalists had elected 53 Representatives to 33 by the Democrats. In 1806 even the Federalist papers claimed only 44 seats to 42 for the Democrats. The *Aurora* credited the Democrats with a majority of 51-35, but this was certainly excessive. The Northumberland *Republican Argus* set the figures at 46 Democrats and 40 Constitutionalists; this estimate seems to have been fairly accurate.[49] These variant estimates reflected the muddled political situation of the State. Local disputes in the counties blurred sharp party distinctions; while the Constitutional Republicans were made up of men with diverse views, who could be listed on one side or the other depending on the particular standard used by the writer. Some were primarily supporters of the Governor; others were conservatives in all matters of constitutional and judicial reform; and still others, though opposing constitutional revision, favored many of the Democratic plans for altering the judicial system.

Using the Federalist claims as the basis, the Democrats still showed substantial gains. Fayette, Somerset, Cambria, Lycoming, and Montgomery counties changed to the Democratic column; and York divided its representation equally. The Democrats lost ground only in Franklin County, where they elected but one of the three Representatives, thus losing two seats. Even here the Federalist-Quid margin was only eight votes.[50] The Democrats also elected four out of six State Senators.[51]

The Constitutionalists elected six out of eighteen Congressmen; but this meant little since the Quids would not follow the Federalist lead in national affairs. Of the six Congressmen, only James Kelly, who was re-elected from York and Adams counties, was definitely a Federalist. Robert Jenkins, William Milnor, William Findley, Matthias Richards, and John Hiester were all Republicans, although the first two were inclined to wander from the party line. The Federalists, therefore, had benefited little in national affairs by the Pennsylvania schism.[52]

The first year of the Republican split in Pennsylvania had not been a happy one for the Constitutional Republicans. They lacked leadership and were embarrassed by McKean's arbitrary actions. Not really forming a party themselves, they had little desire to unite with the Federalists in a coalition certain to be dominated by the latter. Their embarrassment had been increased by the necessity of taking a positive stand in support of Jefferson's foreign policy. Yet they saw no desirable alternative. The Democrats were still determined on a radical program of judicial reform, and they were still largely under the control of Duane whom most Quid leaders hated and feared.[53] The lot of a third party was hard.

CHAPTER VI
A YEAR OF CONFUSION: 1807

THE ELECTION of 1806 was followed by a year of political confusion. A turbulent legislative session witnessed the renewal of the struggle over judicial reform, a nearly successful attempt to impeach the Governor, and the development of a bitter split between the city and country Democrats destined to have a lasting effect on State politics. All these issues were important in the campaign of 1807; and their significance was increased by the approaching gubernatorial election of 1808. At the same time American relations with the European belligerents became more critical and began to overshadow local questions in politics.

I

The vindictive feud of McKean with Duane and Leib became even more rancorous after the election in October, 1806. On the day of the election the *United States' Gazette* had taken note of the clandestine circulation of a pamphlet called the *Quid Mirror,* which included scurrilous sketches of the Governor, Dallas, Joseph B. McKean, and a dozen other Quid leaders. The *Gazette* described it as the most severe thing of the kind that it had ever seen and hinted broadly that Duane and Leib were probably the authors. The *Aurora* reprinted the statements of the *Gazette* but otherwise ignored the matter.[1] Thomas McKean, Jr. was convinced that Leib was the author and sent him a challenge, but Leib denied authorship and refused the duel.[2]

Interest in the *Quid Mirror* was soon overshadowed by the dispute over the Philadelphia sheriff's election. Under the Constitution the Governor commissioned as sheriff one of the two persons having the greatest number of votes; and by the 19th section of the general election law of 1799 he was made a competent judge of the validity of the election of any sheriff.[3] In the Philadelphia election Frederick Wolbert, Leib's political henchman, had polled 3,905 votes; Matthew Lawler, also a political ally of Leib and Duane, had been second with 3,847 votes; and the Quid candidate, William T. Donaldson, had been third with 3,811 votes.[4] Since a number of Donaldson's supporters had petitioned the Governor to set the election aside on the ground that legal votes had been rejected and illegal votes received, McKean on October 28, 1806, appointed a commission to investigate the matter and to report the findings to him.[5]

Leib and Duane had anticipated that there might be some difficulty; and they prevailed upon John Barker, the incumbent sheriff and a friend to both McKean and Wolbert, to accompany the latter to Lancaster and seek to have his commission issued by the Governor. According to Barker's story, Leib and Duane visited him; and Leib told him that if the Governor would appoint Wolbert "they would bury the hatchet—they would present the olive branch, and that they would cease any further to persecute the governor or his family." Duane was generally silent but acquiesced in what Leib had said. At a subsequent interview Leib also suggested to Barker that McKean be reminded that his term would soon expire and that he would be succeeded by a Democrat who would determine whether members of McKean's family should be continued in office.[6]

When Barker went to Lancaster with Wolbert in October, the Governor refused to see them together or to see Wolbert at all. Barker later returned alone and, after some hesitation informed McKean of the propositions of Leib and Duane, though he did not state the source. The Governor flew into a rage and refused to hear him. He denounced Leib and Duane for attempting to threaten him, said that he could not be frightened, and avowed that he would do his duty even though he was certain that his enemies carried daggers. He added that he could not constitutionally commission Wolbert until the validity of the election had been determined. If it were set aside, Barker was to remain in office until a successor was chosen at the next general election in October, 1807.[7]

Barker's trip soon became public knowledge. On November 7, 1806, "A Republican" addressed him in the *Freeman's Journal* and insisted that he had a public duty to make the facts known. This appeal, accompanied by much flattery, was several times repeated. Then on November 27 "Another Republican" detailed the substance of the story together with the assertion that the Governor had been threatened with assassination.[8]

Barker became restive under such treatment and requested Duane to publish his version of the affair in the *Aurora*. Duane refused to do so on the ground that Barker had been misled and did not understand what he was doing. Whereupon Barker had his statement published in *Poulson's American Daily Advertiser.* Though the *Aurora* ignored the incident altogether, Duane answered Barker by a public letter in Poulson's paper. He explained his reasons for failing either to print or return Barker's letter and asserted that Barker had written it because of his greed for another year of profit in the sheriff's office. He also charged that the real purposes of the letter were to keep Wolbert from becoming sheriff and to assure the election of a United States Senator favorable to McKean.[9]

The fight was now transferred to the legislature where Leib made good his threat of unceasing war on the Governor if Wolbert were not commissioned. McKean's address to the legislature in December gave him his first opportunity. It had reiterated the need for increasing the number of Supreme Court judges and had made a number of other recommendations on the selection of juries, internal improvements, education, and the militia. The most important part, however, dealt with the matter of libels.

In the Governor's opinion, libeling had become the "crying sin of the nation and the times." The licentiousness of the press had destroyed its usefulness. "Citizens of the same community are pledged to mutual hatred and persecution. All respect for the magistracy and the laws is falling into derision." The very stability of republican government was threatened. To remedy this, McKean proposed that editors and printers should be forced to register as evidence of the fact of publication; that they be made to give bond for their future good behavior whenever their presses were presented as nuisances by a grand jury; and that the courts be authorized to suppress them for a limited time under such circumstances.[10]

As was customary, the House appointed a committee to draft an answer; and on December 9, 1806, the committee reported an innocuous reply. When the answer came up for its second reading, Leib moved to postpone for the introduction of a substitute.

His substitute was written in a tone of insolent mockery. Beginning with strictures on McKean's continued use of the unrepublican practice of addressing the legislature in person, it professed a willingness to sacrifice etiquette to avoid "every imputation of a want of decorum." Quoting the Governor's reference to the prevailing prosperity, it expressed surprise that a system productive of such beneficence should be changed merely to gratify a desire for novelty and a spirit of innovation. It then assailed the proposed restrictions on the press as more objectionable than the infamous Sedition Act and quoted Jefferson's views on the benefits of a free press. It closed with a declaration of confidence in the national administration. The House deferred consideration of both Leib's and the committee's answers until January 5, 1807, when both were postponed generally by a vote of 44-40. Leib voted with the majority.[11]

Another opportunity to strike at the Governor's address was afforded Leib by his appointment to head a committee to study the question of libels. The committee's report was submitted on January 13 and was even more vitriolic than the proposed answer to the address. It accused the Governor of lack of respect for the General Assembly in submitting to them such a degrading recommendation. The legislature had no constitutional right to legislate on the subject of the press. Furthermore, though the Governor had so often declaimed loudly in support of jury trial and the Constitution, his proposals would deprive a printer of his property without trial by jury; and, by forcing the printer to register as evidence of the fact of publication, they would unconstitutionally compel him to testify against himself. Paraphrasing one of McKean's veto messages in 1805, the report recommended that the House "hold it a sacred duty to transmit the Constitution to their successors, unimpaired and unshackled by any act of theirs."

The committee felt that the laws on libel were already "tyrannically severe." Under the common law governing such cases, "words, not actionable in themselves, and not admitting of civil action, if published in writing, and tend[ing] only to the discredit of an individual or of public characters, are held to be libels"; and the one who circulated them was held to be equally as guilty as the printer. The Governor was well aware of these things and had instituted damage suits for libels totaling more than $200,000. Furthermore, Duane in November, 1806, had been three times indicted for libels because his publications were alleged to have a tendency to break the peace. Were they any more disturbing to the peace than calling men "refugees, old tories, apostate whigs, and rascals, villains, geese, ignoramuses and clodpoles?"

The report concluded by offering a resolution to appoint a committee to bring in a bill barring criminal prosecutions for libel and restricting actions for libels upon public men and public conduct to the authors and printers concerned. The House ordered the report printed as a pamphlet but took no further action on its recommendations.[12]

McKean's libel suits were also responsible for Leib's introduction of a bill to debar lawyers from serving as Recorder of the city of Philadelphia. This was intended to force the removal of Moses Levy, an active Quid leader, who was an attorney for Joseph B. McKean in suits against Duane. If permitted to continue as Recorder he would preside in the mayor's court on the trial of other actions against Duane. Leib's bill passed the legislature; but the House was unable to muster enough votes to pass it over the Governor's veto.[13]

The main issue, however, was the Philadelphia sheriff's election. On December 10, 1806, Leib introduced a bill to amend the provision of the general election law regarding the settlement of disputed elections of sheriffs and coroners. The bill provided that such disputes should be referred to a commission of five men—two to be selected by each candidate and the fifth member to be chosen by the other four. Any illegal votes discovered in the investigation were to be deducted from the votes of the candidate for whom they were cast if that were known and otherwise should be deducted from the votes of each candidate proportionately. If the commission's report was unfavorable to the returned candidate, the Governor was to be required to call a special election immediately.

This bill was studied in committee of the whole on January 8 and 22, 1807, and was considered by the House on January 26. It passed its second reading at that time but was considerably modified. Leib thereupon dropped this bill and on the same day introduced a new one which provided simply for the repeal of the 19th section of the general election law which made the Governor the sole judge of the validity of elections of sheriffs and coroners. The second bill passed the legislature and became law without the Governor's signature; but it was too late to affect the situation in Philadelphia.[14]

Leib apparently abandoned his original bill because the Governor had received on January 19, 1807, the report of the commission appointed to investigate Wolbert's election. The report indicated that 91 illegal votes had been received and seven legal votes for Donaldson had been rejected. Declaring that there was no way to determine for whom the illegal votes had been cast, McKean issued a proclamation on February 16, 1807, which set aside the election, called for a new one to be held in the following October, and continued Barker as sheriff until his successor should qualify.[15]

Duane and Leib now began a determined effort to impeach the Governor. The *Aurora* on January 12, 1807, demanded that the legislature should impeach McKean; and on January 27 Leib interrupted the reading of the House Journal to assert that the Governor had not signed certain bills as had been stated therein but had used a facsimile stamp. For this reason Leib gave notice of his intention to submit a resolution to inquire into McKean's official conduct. Such a resolution was introduced on January 30; but it was laid on the table by a tie vote when Boileau and others objected to making an investigation while the Governor was so ill. At the end of February the *Aurora* reported that McKean had recovered; and on March 3 the House voted 43-38 to have a committee headed by Leib make an inquiry into the Governor's actions.[16]

Leib reported for the committee on March 30, 1807, and recommended that the Governor be impeached on six counts. The first of these was his setting aside of the sheriff's election in Philadelphia. It was asserted that the Governor's commission designating the men to investigate the election had been issued in blank and that the names were later filled in by Joseph B. McKean, who also served as Donaldson's counsel during the investigation. Denying the Governor's statement that 91 illegal votes had been cast and that seven legal votes for Donaldson had been rejected, the committee asserted that only 42 illegal votes were received and three legal votes rejected. It therefore charged that the Governor had willfully deprived Wolbert of his election despite the fact that he had a majority of 49 votes even after deducting all illegal ballots.

The second charge was that the Governor had usurped judicial authority in imprisoning Joseph Cabrera in 1805 and had then broken the law by changing Cabrera's punishment. The third charge was that McKean had violated the Constitution in appointing Dr. George Buchanan, his son-in-law, to the position of Lazaretto physician. Buchanan was a citizen of Maryland; and the Constitution specified that any person appointed to an office within a county should have been a resident therein for at least a year. The committee claimed that the Lazaretto physician was a Delaware County official and not a State officer.

The fourth charge asserted that the Governor had flaunted the express terms of the Constitution in using a facsimile stamp on public documents, "a precedent, acknowledged to be derived from the king of Great-Britain." The fifth charge was that Dr. James Reynolds had been illegally removed from the Philadelphia board of health before the expiration of the year designated by law as his term. The final charge was that McKean had unconstitutionally made overtures to Duane and his surety (Leib) to discontinue actions of the Commonwealth against them for forfeiture of their recognizances if Duane would withdraw civil actions against Joseph B. McKean and others for the assault made on him in 1799.[17]

The committee's recommendations were reported favorably on April 8, 1807, after being debated for two days in committee of the whole. Boileau then moved that the matter be referred to the next legislature. The following day, Rosewell Welles, a Federalist member from Luzerne County, moved to kill the impeachment by a general postponement. His motion was defeated by a vote of 44-40; and the House then adopted Boileau's proposal by a vote of 43-41.[18]

During the course of the investigation McKean's family was guilty of exceedingly stupid behavior. Joseph B. McKean on March 19, 1807, sought a warrant from the Supreme Court for the arrest of Leib on the charge that he and Duane had conspired to intimidate the Governor into appointing Wolbert as sheriff. Joseph Hopkinson, a prominent Federalist, served as Leib's counsel and argued that the latter was privileged from arrest as a legislator and even if he had not been so privileged there was "a delicacy in this case that ought to have prevented the application for a warrant." He pointed out that the application was one made on behalf of the Governor to arrest a member of the assembly who was chairman of a committee to investigate his conduct. Whatever the real motives of the request, it would have the effect of stopping the inquiry and would give the appearance of having been intended to do so. The rest of the committee might be prevented from proceeding by like means and the investigation thus be completely halted. The court made no decision on the matter; but the request for a warrant was withdrawn.[19]

In Lancaster Thomas McKean, Jr., was reported to have tried to intimidate witnesses and members of the General Assembly by walking in the street outside the legislature carrying a heavy bludgeon. On the day that the committee's report was approved by the committee of the whole he sought unsuccessfully to pick a fight with Leib and with John Thompson, another member from Philadelphia County.[20]

Apart from the feud with Leib the Governor had many other unpleasant experiences during the legislative session. In February the Senate and House approved a resolution making it the function of a joint legislative committee to determine what laws should be published and to designate the particular papers in which they were to be printed. This was, of course, an attack upon McKean's patronage; and he responded with a veto which the Senate was unable to override. However, the legislature circumvented the veto by adopting a second resolution prohibiting the publication at state expense of any laws unless so specified by the legislature. McKean permitted this to become law without his signature.[21]

The Governor and the legislature also disputed the question of the jurisdiction of the Federal courts on land litigation in Pennsylvania. For many years there had been conflicts in northwestern Pennsylvania over the respective rights of "actual settlers" and "warrantees" in their claims to land under the ambiguously phrased land act of April 3, 1792. The decisions in the Pennsylvania courts had generally adopted an interpretation of the act favorable to the settlers rather than to the land companies and other speculators who held by warrant; but the Holland Land Company, being owned by foreigners, was able to bring the matter before the Federal courts. In February, 1805, Chief Justice John Marshall had delivered an opinion in the case of *Huidekoper's Lessee* v. *Douglass* highly favorable to the warrantees.[22]

This decision had been exceedingly unpopular in the western section of the State; and a committee of the House headed by Abner Lacock of Beaver County had prepared a lengthy report which closed by stating that the interests of the Commonwealth were directly involved in such suits and denying "the right of any court of the United States to take cognizance, or exercise any jurisdiction," in any actions brought under the act of 1792. The resolution was accepted by the Senate and went to the Governor who vetoed it. McKean held that it was an encroachment of the legislature upon judicial functions and of a State upon Federal powers; that the Federal courts unquestionably had jurisdiction in such suits; and that the resolution was "in itself so extraordinary either as an instrument of advice or intimidation" and its consequences so injurious or abortive that he felt it a duty to himself and to the peace and happiness of the country to return it. The House failed to pass it over the veto.[23]

The Governor likewise returned disapproved an act giving the right of peremptory challenge of jurors to defendants in trials for misdemeanors. In his message McKean irritably observed that it did not accord with his ideas of justice "that the assassin of public character, or private reputation, should have rights conferred on him, which are withheld from the injured and innocent victim, of his malice and revenge." This veto was also sustained.[24]

The legislature had better success with its other measures of judicial reform. The Hundred Dollar Act was amended slightly and made perpetual by an overwhelming majority. Another act further increased the jurisdiction of aldermen and justices of the peace. In both instances McKean permitted the bills to become law without his signature.[25]

More serious was the attack on the common law. Boileau, acting on the principle "that the laws should be so simple, plain, and extensively promulgated that every citizen may have it in his powers [sic] to know the laws by which his conduct and property are to be regulated," introduced a resolution in the House for the appointment of a committee to determine what British statutes were in force in the Commonwealth and which of these should be made a part of the Pennsylvania statute laws. The committee was appointed, and it reported a bill requiring the judges of the Supreme Court to make the study. This was adopted by the legislature and signed by the Governor.[26]

Even this did not satisfy the legislators. Boileau introduced on April 3, 1807, a resolution which forbade the reading of any precedents or decisions in the Pennsylvania courts except those of courts of the United States. Both houses approved the resolution; but it was sent to the Governor so late in the session that he took no action on it prior to the adjournment of the legislature.[27]

The Democrats again attempted to embarrass the Quids and Federalists by offering an address to Jefferson requesting that he accept another term as President. After a bitter struggle the address was finally adopted; but a number of Federalists entered a protest on the journal of the House. They objected to it on the grounds that the legislature could not constitutionally act in matters of this sort and that it did not comport with its dignity to indulge in party politics. The protest also defended the Federalist record and asserted that under the conditions then existing the national administration was not entitled to eulogies. When the country had "the means of resisting aggression, and of punishing injustice," they would then be willing "as individuals" to praise those responsible.[28]

The Federalists were able to turn the tables in the Cumberland Road dispute. McKean sent to the legislature on December 30, 1806, a message from Jefferson requesting the passage of an act authorizing the building of some 81 miles of the National Road through Pennsylvania. The route proposed did not pass through several important communities in the western part of the State nor did it connect directly with the important State roads leading to Philadelphia.

Horace Binney, a Federalist Representative from the city, aided by Democrats and others moved by local considerations, was able to get through a bill authorizing the road only if it followed a specified route which was different from that contemplated. The Senate amended the measure so as to make the route optional with the President; but the bill was lost when the two houses failed to agree. The Senate then passed its own bill leaving the route to the discretion of Jefferson. This was sent to the House in the last days of the session and was accepted by a large majority.[29]

The legislative session was also the scene of a vindictive fight between Leib and Boileau for control of the Democrats. At bottom this was a contest between Philadelphia and the country for political supremacy, but it was made harsher because of the conflicting ambitions and personalities of these leading antagonists.

Leib was not a person to relish a minor role under any circumstances, and with the next gubernatorial election in view he set about attempting to overthrow Snyder. His first move was to oppose in caucus Snyder's nomination for Speaker of the House. He argued that the Quids were so violently opposed to Snyder that he was sure to be defeated, while Leib believed that some of the Quids could be counted on to support the election of James Engle, his colleague from Philadelphia County. Snyder's friends held that both consistency and honor demanded that Snyder be nominated; and he received the votes of the great majority of the caucus. In the election in the House on December 2, 1806, Snyder defeated Samuel D. Ingham, Quid representative from Bucks County, by a vote of 42-41.[30]

The real fight came over the choice of a United States Senator to succeed George Logan. The Federalists and Quids were determined to back Andrew Gregg, Congressman from Centre County, who had been defeated for re-election in October. At the Democratic caucus on December 4, 1806, John Thompson, a member of the Philadelphia County delegation, warmly supported the nomination of Leib. He praised his services and talents and argued that the commercial interests of Philadelphia were entitled to a representative since the agricultural interest was already represented by Samuel Maclay. At a second caucus on the following day a vote was taken; and John Steele, former State Senator from Lancaster County, was chosen over Leib by 37 votes to nine.[31]

The two houses met in joint session on December 9, 1806, and balloted three times. On each ballot Steele and Gregg were tied with 54 votes apiece. On this occasion two Quid Senators were absent; and a vacancy existed in the Philadelphia County delegation due to the death of George S. Bensell, a Democrat, whose successor had not then been chosen. It seemed that Gregg was assured of victory when the whole membership was present.

Despite this appearance, the Democrats actually outnumbered the Quids and Federalists; but two of them had voted for Gregg for personal reasons. James Poe, Senator from Franklin County, was Gregg's brother-in-law; and William Rankin, Representative from Centre County, was his neighbor. These two were persuaded by the Democrats to vote for a postponement of the election till January. Thus, when the two houses held a second session on December 16, 1806, although the two absent Quids were now present, it was voted 56-54 to adjourn until January 13, 1807.[32]

The Democratic prospects did not look too good at this time even though Bensell's successor would be able to vote on the next ballot. McKean felt confident of Gregg's selection by a margin of one vote.[33] The only apparent way for the Democrats to defeat him was to find a candidate who would be able to gain a few Quid votes and to hold those that had been given to Steele. It was this situation which explained the nomination of Boileau by the Democrats in January.

A Democratic caucus was held on January 12, 1807, to decide on a nominee to be supported for State Treasurer at the election on the following day. The Leib group backed Samuel Bryan; but a large majority chose William Findlay, Representative from Franklin County. Thereupon, Leib hastily moved that the meeting adjourn; and James Engle, who was chairman, declared it so without asking for the nays on the question. When a motion was made to reorganize the meeting to discuss the senatorial nomination, Engle angrily declared that he would not be tricked and left the room. The caucus chose a new chairman and voted 31-9 to support Boileau in place of Steele. A committee was then appointed to inform all those who had not been present at the meeting.[34]

The next morning the members of both houses assembled in the Senate chamber to elect the State Treasurer. William Findlay received 69 votes; and the rest were scattered among four other candidates. Immediately following the Treasurer's election the members went to the House chamber to vote for a United States Senator. Gregg was elected on the first ballot with 55 votes, while Boileau and Steele received forty and fourteen votes respectively. Boileau, Leib, and most of the Philadelphia County delegation were among those voting for Steele.[35]

There were two absentees at the senatorial election—John Orr, a Democratic Representative from Cumberland County who was ill; and John Thompson of Philadelphia County who had voted in the election for State Treasurer. Had Thompson attended and voted for anyone other than Gregg, the latter would have failed of election since he would not have had a majority. There might then have been a chance for a Democratic victory when Orr returned.

An investigation of the circumstances showed that Thompson, a devoted follower of Leib, had come to the Treasurer's election with his head tied in a handkerchief and had complained of a toothache or gumboil. He had voted and then had gone to the House chamber where he sat for a few moments and left. Whether he talked with Leib in the meantime was a disputed point. His absence was noted and a messenger sent after him. Thompson agreed to come; but a member who then went in search of him found him at his lodging roasting figs before the fire. The two started back to the House; but the election was over before they reached there.

The Democrats were much angered by the incident and blamed Leib for Thompson's conduct. They held a caucus at which a committee was appointed to draw up an account of Leib's actions during the session, but they eventually decided not to make it public at that time.[36]

It is fairly certain that Leib was responsible for Gregg's election. He was probably motivated to some extent by chagrin at his own failure to receive the nomination; but it is likely that his chief purpose was to gain control of the party in the legislature. In every caucus he and his followers were greatly outnumbered by the country Democrats, who were led, as Leib professed to believe, by a small clique which sought to monopolize all power in the State. With such a narrow Democratic majority in the legislature, Leib could control enough votes to give him the balance of power; and he apparently hoped to use this as a means of getting control for himself.[37]

However, he was forced to alter his tactics. The senatorial election and his arrogance in other matters were most irritating to the country Democrats. Thus, on January 26, 1807, when he proclaimed that the vote on the second section of his bill to amend the general election law would determine those who were real Democrats, Boileau opposed him; and the House defeated the section by 58 votes to nineteen.[38] Boileau and his friends were also responsible for Duane's failure to be chosen a director of the Bank of Pennsylvania in the elections held on January 29 and 30.[39]

Despite these setbacks, Leib had managed to regain a shaky control by the end of the session. According to the *Lancaster Journal,* he achieved it partly by dropping his dictatorial manner and assuming the garb of a "cringing, smiling sycophant" and partly by his own skill in putting Boileau and his other enemies on the defensive. This was done by attacking Boileau for failing to give hearty support to McKean's impeachment. The *Journal* believed that a compromise had been reached whereby the Snyder-Boileau group backed the impeachment in return for Leib's promise of support of Snyder for Governor.[40]

II

The long and eventful legislative session set the tone for the political campaign of 1807. The movement to impeach McKean and the renewed attack on the judicial system rejuvenated the disintegrating coalition of the Quids and Federalists. The Leib-Boileau struggle in the legislature was but the prelude to an open attack on Leib by the Democratic faction supporting Snyder and Boileau. The prize that each Democratic faction contended for was the gubernatorial nomination in 1808.

While the election of 1807 was dominated by these themes, Burr's conspiracy and the ever more ominous foreign situation were swiftly making national questions the dominant political issues. The suspicious movements of Burr attracted attention as early as July, 1805, when the *United States' Gazette* published a series of questions on Burr's objectives in the west. The *Aurora* had scoffed at the implications in July, but in November it republished an article from a Petersburg, Virginia, paper which also hinted that Burr had evil designs.[41]

In the summer of 1806 the *Aurora* took note of Burr's trip to the west and asked if he were going to prepare the "great flame" which Gideon Granger had predicted in the western country. By the end of November Jefferson had issued his proclamation against the Burr project; and the *Aurora* was filled with articles on Burr and insisting that his plans were closely tied in with Granger and the Yazoo speculation. Referring to Burr as the "Emperor of the Quids," the paper attempted to link him with Dallas, Andrew Ellicott, and McKean.[42] At the same time the Pittsburgh *Commonwealth* accused a number of prominent Federalists of being involved in the scheme; but nothing seems to have come of the incident.[43]

All in all, though the *Aurora* continued to print columns of material on the affair and Duane attended the trial at Richmond in August, 1807, the Burr Conspiracy seems to have had virtually no effect on the politics of the State.[44]

Far more significant was the foreign situation. In April, 1806, Congress had passed a limited nonimportation act to take effect in November of that year. Congress had hardly adjourned before the British frigate *Leander,* in firing a shot across the bow of a vessel near New York, killed John Pearce, who was aboard a coasting sloop which unfortunately happened to be in the line of fire. The incident aroused a tremendous protest; and the Federalists began berating the administration for its failure to put an end to British outrages and for neglecting to build up a strong navy and coastal defenses.[45] The *Aurora* defended the administration and continued to insist on nonimportation and the sequestration of British property as the best means of forcing Great Britain to respect American rights.[46]

However, neutral rights were soon to suffer even worse restrictions. On May 16, 1806, the British declared a blockade of the European coast from Brest to the Elbe River. On November 21 Napoleon responded with his famous Berlin Decree which proclaimed a blockade of the British Isles, made all British property and all merchandise coming from Great Britain prize of war, and barred all ports to vessels coming from Great Britain or her colonies. The British government in retaliation issued an order in council of January 7, 1807, which prohibited all trading by vessels between any two ports lying within territory owned or possessed by France or her allies.[47]

Meanwhile, in December, 1806, James Monroe and William Pinkney had negotiated a treaty with Great Britain which ignored all the chief grievances of the United States. Jefferson was so displeased that he refused even to send the treaty to the Senate. The *Aurora* defended his action; but the *United States' Gazette* wrote darkly that it smacked of French influence.[48]

Despite these things, Congress took no effective action. It suspended the Nonimportation Act and, under the leadership of John Randolph, cut down appropriations, refused to strengthen the army and coastal fortifications, and provided for the building of gunboats rather than frigates and ships of the line.[49]

The Federalists demanded a vigorous policy of strengthening the navy and erecting harbor defenses; but the Republican papers combatted this strongly. In numerous articles the *Aurora* argued that America's true policy was a policy of peace. Huge armies and navies would prove futile and expensive. A great standing debt would be created; the mass of the people would be ground down by financial exactions; and their liberties would be sacrificed to a moneyed aristocracy. One had only to observe England to see the truth of these observations. America must build up its own manufactures and internal trade and thus become truly independent. Great Britain could be brought to terms by a policy of commercial restrictions. The paper supplemented specific discussions of these topics with 24 articles entitled "Politics for Farmers" and seven entitled "Politics for Mechanics." The theme of these was that the farmers and mechanics had interests basically different from those of the commercial classes who were subservient to England. If they would unite in support of a program of domestic manufactures and home markets, the British-inspired schemes of the merchants would be defeated.[50]

In the midst of these debates over foreign policy news came of the attack of the British frigate *Leopard* on the American frigate *Chesapeake*. In Philadelphia Federalists and Republicans united in reprobating the outrage and in demanding restitution. Some 6,000 people attended a meeting at the State House on July 1, 1807, at which Matthew Lawler, a Democrat, was chairman, and Joseph Hopkinson, a Federalist, was secretary. Leib spoke briefly and introduced a set of resolutions which were unanimously adopted. They denounced the attack on the *Chesapeake,* pledged support to the administration in any and every measure to obtain retribution, and agreed to withhold supplies and assistance from British vessels until the government acted. The meeting also chose a committee of correspondence which included both Democrats and Federalists. The *Aurora* and the *United States' Gazette* united in agreeing that party distinctions had disappeared in the universal resentment against the British.[51]

Such was not long to be the case. The *Gazette* began to criticize the administration's inaction and to assert that the defenseless state of the country invited such outrages. By August it was assailing the government for using the flag to cover British deserters in the *Chesapeake* affair.[52]

The *Aurora* had also expected Congress to be called into immediate session, and it demanded that an embargo be passed both to enforce American demands for redress and to protect the country against a refusal. Great Britain, the *Aurora* said, would be ruined by such a measure; and it would not harm the United States because the British would soon capitulate. When Jefferson failed to convene Congress immediately, however, the *Aurora* did not criticize but began to berate the Federalist papers for their attacks. By the end of August unanimity against Great Britain had disappeared.[53]

The most spectacular aspect of the campaign of 1807 in Philadelphia was the fight of the Snyder supporters led by John Binns and the *Democratic Press* to overthrow Leib. Binns was one of the most colorful figures to take part in the politics of that period. Thirty-four years old in the spring of 1807, he had had a crowded and exciting life. The son of a Dublin hardware merchant, he left Ireland as a young man and went to London where he became a close associate of William Godwin and other radical leaders. An active member of the London Corresponding Society, he also served as its president. Several times imprisoned for his activities, he was tried for treason in 1798 but was acquitted.

Leaving England in 1801 he migrated to Northumberland, Pennsylvania, where Joseph Priestley and Thomas Cooper had also come for refuge. Duane, who had known Binns in London in 1795, urged him to take the editorship of a paper he intended to establish in Washington and even offered to send his son, William J. Duane, there and make Binns editor of the *Aurora*. However, Binns had become much involved in the politics of Northumberland County, and in December, 1802, he began the publication of the Northumberland *Republican Argus*, a paper which drew high praise from the *Aurora*. He continued to publish this until he began the *Democratic Press*.[54]

Binns was to prove a worthy antagonist of Duane in the years that followed. Alike in their ardent love of Ireland and hatred of the British government, the two men held almost identical views on other political questions; and both were characterized by boldness and a tendency toward self-righteousness. Binns was somewhat less capable than Duane as a writer; but this deficiency was more than offset by the latter's defects of temperament. Duane alienated many by his dogmatism and dictatorial manner, while his vindictiveness almost precluded reconciliation. Binns was more affable and preferred compromise to destruction of his opponents, although he would not run from a fight when no agreement was possible.

The exact persons responsible for the establishment of the *Democratic Press* are unknown. Duane's friends later charged that it had been created for the express purpose of "writing down" Dr. Leib and the *Aurora*. According to them, the project was begun by Boileau and other members of the legislature because Duane had refused to denounce Leib's conduct in the senatorial election. They also asserted that Dallas and the McKean group had co-operated in the venture; but this appears to have little foundation.[55]

Binns stated that an unnamed friend in Philadelphia had written him in January, 1807, and urged the need of another Democratic paper in Philadelphia to aid the *Aurora*. He had then journeyed to the city by way of Lancaster, where the project was approved by some of his friends in the legislature. In Philadelphia he had discussed the matter with Duane, who at first tried to dissuade him and then promised his support.[56]

Whoever was chiefly responsible, the establishment of the *Democratic Press* was a sound political move for the supporters of Snyder. The *Aurora* had for years been accepted as a sort of Democratic Bible; and its denunciations had destroyed politically any Republicans who had opposed its edicts. Considering the coolness of Duane and Leib toward Snyder's nomination in 1805 and the maneuvers against him in the legislature, it was apparent that his friends must have a press of statewide power and influence located in Philadelphia to prevent the *Aurora* from defeating his nomination in 1808.

Another consideration which may have had some influence was the position of the Quids. With McKean ineligible for another term in 1808 and with national issues making union with the Federalists less and less palatable, the great majority of Constitutional Republicans wished to return to Republican ranks. However, they had no desire to submit to the leadership of Leib and Duane after the many indignities they had suffered at their hands. An alliance with the country Republicans, who were also seeking to rid the party of the domination of Leib and Duane, seemed a logical and natural arrangement.[57]

Binns at first experienced some difficulties in obtaining subscriptions for his new paper because of the opposition of Leib and young William J. Duane. However, William Duane had promised his support; and through his influence a Democratic meeting in March adopted resolutions favorable to the establishment of the *Democratic Press* and appointed a committee to solicit subscriptions. These efforts were successful; and the first issue appeared on March 27, 1807. Beginning as a triweekly, the paper was issued daily after June 29, 1807.[58]

For a time matters ran along smoothly, and there were no quarrels among the Democrats. Binns was even asked to make the "long talk" before the Tammany Society at its anniversary celebration of May 12, 1807. This was a significant distinction since the organization was headed by Leib as "grand sachem" and formed the very core of the political faction led by him and Duane. Binns's address was a lengthy review of the blessings of republican government and an exposition of the basic principles of democracy as he saw them. It also pled for moderation toward the Quids who wished to return to the party. The talk was apparently well received and was unanimously ordered to be printed.[59]

Such harmony was not long to prevail. In May the *Freeman's Journal* reported a rumor that the "Junto faction" had recently held a caucus in which it was decided to support Leib for Governor and George Clinton for President.[60] Whether occasioned by this or not, in the same month a pamphlet attacking Leib began to circulate in the city. The greater portion of it was the report of Leib's conduct in the legislature which had been prepared by a committee appointed by a caucus of the Democratic members shortly after the senatorial election. It was largely the work of Abner Lacock, representative from Beaver County. This report related the circumstances surrounding Snyder's choice as Speaker, Findlay's selection as State Treasurer, and Gregg's victory in the senatorial election. To it was added an introduction which stated that the legislative report had not been published in January because of Leib's part in the impeachment of McKean and because he was believed to have repented of his conduct. However, since his return to Philadelphia he had denounced those who disapproved of his actions and had attempted to injure Snyder. It was therefore necessary to expose him to the public.[61]

The pamphlet was first noticed in the *Aurora* on June 3, 1807, when it and its author were denounced in an unsigned communication. The next day the *Freeman's Journal* reprinted most of the pamphlet; and on June 5 the *Democratic Press* published a letter from Joseph Lloyd admitting that he had been responsible for the publication and denying the *Aurora's* charge that he was a tool of McKean.[62]

For a time there was no further evidence of disagreement; but in August the storm broke in full fury. The controversy was renewed by a Democratic meeting at Germantown on August 1, 1807, which adopted resolutions and an address favoring the use of the district delegate system of nominations in Philadelphia County. The proceedings were printed in the *Democratic Press* and were followed by a number of articles on the subject. These publications argued that the delegate plan would eliminate the intrigue accompanying the general county meeting and would strengthen the party.[63]

The Leib faction responded by calling a general county meeting at the Northern Liberties on August 17, 1807, at which Leib presided. It chose conferees, renominated the previous assembly ticket, and adopted a strong address in support of nominations by a general county meeting. Their proceedings were censured by the *Democratic Press;* and the Snyderites continued with their district meetings and eventually drew up a separate ticket for the members of the assembly.[64]

The *Democratic Press* now began an open assault on Leib by publishing six letters signed "Veritas." Introducing the first letter, Binns wrote that he had been led to print them because Leib had been denouncing him as an apostate. He was also convinced that Leib had organized a plot against Snyder and three-fourths of the Democrats in the last legislature. He proposed therefore to publish the facts and let the party judge which was the real apostate.[65]

Ignoring Leib's private conduct, the letters concerned themselves wholly with political affairs. The first three dealt with Leib's opposition to Snyder. He was accused of having tried to defeat Snyder after his nomination in 1805, first by supporting the proposed Carlisle convention and then by secretly discouraging strong efforts in his behalf. He was likewise charged with attempting to prevent Snyder's nomination for Speaker in 1806 and also with having dickered with the Quids to oppose it even after the caucus had made its decision. Lastly, Leib was asserted to have plotted with Daniel Rose, a Quid representative from Berks County, to support Joseph Hiester for Governor in 1808. The last three letters minutely reviewed Leib's conduct in the senatorial election in January. They sought to prove that Leib had resigned from Congress in order to become Senator; that being disappointed in his plans he had determined to defeat the Democratic nominee; and that he had achieved his aim by prevailing upon John Thompson to leave the election.[66]

Leib never made any direct reply to, or denial of, these charges; but his friends soon began a strong attack on Binns and Boileau. The first notice taken of the publications was at a meeting at the Wheat Sheaf Tavern in Philadelphia County on August 29, 1807. The district delegate system was denounced; and a resolution was adopted expressing complete approval of Leib's conduct and avowing that they would feel him unworthy of their support "if he should descend to enter the list with a vagabond scribbler, or mushroom patriot of doubtful character."[67]

The *Aurora* entered the squabble on September 3, 1807, with an attack on the "Quadroons," which it described as a new party deriving its name from a *"Creole* epithet" because of its leader. Such a name was appropriate, it thought, because the party was also the successor to the Quids of the third party and had the same objects in view. The *Democratic Press* retorted by asking if this were the group formed by Leib's intrigues and if Leib had truly become the agent of Dallas.[68] The next day the *Aurora* publicly denounced Binns and the *Democratic Press*. At the same time it announced that Leib needed no defense from the calumnies of his enemies and that the whole thing was at bottom an attempt to serve McKean.[69]

During September and early October the *Aurora* lashed out savagely at Boileau and Binns. It laid the chief responsibility for the Democratic troubles on Boileau and made a scathing review of his intrigues. He was accused of bartering his vote in the legislature for personal ends and of being the cause, along with Dallas, of the split electoral votes in the election of 1800. He was charged with having offered to support Robert Whitehill for the gubernatorial nomination in 1805 in return for the appointment as Secretary of the Commonwealth and of having dropped Whitehill to support Snyder when the offer was refused.

In the senatorial election of the previous session Boileau was stated to have approached Leib on the day following Steele's nomination and to have proposed that Steele be dropped and Boileau supported as the senatorial candidate—a proposition which Leib virtuously refused. The monstrousness of such a proposal was enhanced by the fact that Steele was being sued by McKean for $50,000 for signing the purported address of the legislative caucus in 1805, while Boileau, its author, escaped prosecution.

Boileau was also asserted to have shown ingratitude to Samuel Bryan because he had backed William Findlay for State Treasurer after he had promised to support Bryan. Boileau's objective in this instance, according to the *Aurora*, was to remove Findlay from the legislature because he feared that he might become a rival. The paper attributed the attack on Leib to the same jealous ambition.[70]

Binns was assailed for duplicity and lack of principles. It was asserted that before the *Democratic Press* was established Binns had vehemently avowed his friendliness toward Leib and the *Aurora* while he had intended to attack them from the very beginning. As for the charges of "Veritas" against Leib, they were ridiculous. Leib was the "Vital Spirit" of Democracy in the State, and his record was proof against the slanders of Binns.

The *Aurora* admitted that Duane and Leib had opposed Snyder's nomination in 1805, but it pointed out that they had done yeoman work in supporting him after the nomination was made and the choice was found to be acceptable to the majority. They were willing to do the same again "whenever the choice is made in a manner free from the baleful influence of legislative intrigue and the huxtering of offices." Snyder would do well, however, to restrain the professed friends who were using him to cover a "monstrous heresy." It was an exceedingly strange thing to find Boileau and Dallas so close and to see Snyder's name used to proscribe Leib and the *Aurora*. The paper also printed letters from Daniel Rose and John Thompson to refute the charges that Leib had intrigued with Rose on the gubernatorial nomination or had had anything to do with Thompson's absence at the senatorial election.[71]

Answering these attacks Boileau disclaimed any special agency in establishing the *Democratic Press* and denied having any dealings with Dallas. He had never made proposals to Whitehill, Snyder, or anyone else offering to back them for Governor in return for the appointment as Secretary of the Commonwealth. He had had no conversations with Leib on the senatorial nomination. He had supported Findlay for Treasurer because he found that Bryan could not be elected. He owed Steele nothing in the matter of the caucus address since the *Aurora* had already admitted that Duane and Leib had altered it so that it was a far different thing from his original production. Furthermore, Duane had published it of his own volition and not from any pressure put on him by Boileau. Finally, Boileau pointed out that mere denunciations of him did not clear Leib of the charges made by the *Democratic Press*.[72]

There was one other significant development in the fight between the two Democratic factions. At a meeting of the Delaware County Democratic Republicans on August 29, 1807, a resolution was adopted asking that the nominee for Governor be chosen by a State convention because counties without Republicans in the legislature were without a voice in the caucus. Since the same meeting also denounced the *Democratic Press*, it seems certain that the resolution was inspired from Philadelphia.[73]

At any rate the suggestion received warm support from the Philadelphia town meeting on September 21, 1807. Young William J. Duane, making his first prominent appearance in politics, introduced the proposal for a convention; and, although the Snyderites argued against it, the sentiment in its favor was so strong that it was adopted without resistance. Beginning with the premise that nominations should be made by the people themselves or by delegates expressly chosen for the purpose, the resolution denounced nominations by legislative caucuses as unwarranted usurpations of power. It proposed that, during years when a Governor was to be chosen, county or district meetings should be held to select delegates in a number equal to the representation in the assembly and that these delegates should meet in convention to choose the gubernatorial candidate. To avoid the baleful influence of executive patronage, no person should be elected a delegate who held any office under the Governor and who would not pledge himself to refuse any office from the Governor for the three years following the election. The plan was to go into effect when it was adopted by a majority of the counties.[74]

Although there were certainly valid objections to caucus nominations, the introduction of the scheme at this time was unquestionably a move to defeat the nomination of Snyder. The country Democrats were predominant in the legislature, and almost all of them were supporters of Snyder. However, there was a possibility that a convention whose members were elected under a heavy propaganda barrage from the *Aurora* might follow the paper's lead in selecting a candidate. Whether the plan would have defeated Snyder's nomination is uncertain because it was not used.

The quarrel with McKean was forced into the background by the fight with the *Democratic Press,* but it was by no means forgotten. Leib was arrested in April on charges of conspiring against the Governor; and he retaliated by obtaining an indictment against Thomas McKean, Jr., for sending him a challenge in the previous October.[75]

Such personal disputes were less important than the contests for Sheriff and State Senator. The Democrats renominated Wolbert for Sheriff and chose Duane as their candidate for the Senate. The latter's candidacy brought a storm of protest from the *Freeman's Journal.* It pointed out that Duane had been the originator of the movement to impeach the Governor and that he was seeking to be chosen a Senator where he would vote on McKean's guilt if the impeachment were continued at the next session. The *Journal* also charged that Duane hoped to get himself chosen Speaker of the Senate so that he would become Governor in case of McKean's conviction.[76]

Such dangers led the Quids to co-operate even more closely with the Federalists. Donaldson was renominated for sheriff; and a mixed ticket representing both groups was supported for the other offices.[77]

The election brought the largest vote Philadelphia had ever known. The total vote in the city was more than 4,200, compared with 3,500 in 1805 and 3,900 in 1806. In the county more than 4,500 votes were cast, compared with 3,900 in 1805 and 4,000 in 1806. The Federalist-Quid majority in the city was more than 450; while the Democratic majority in the county was only 500 votes, about half of what it had been in 1806.

In the sheriff's election Wolbert polled 4,437 votes, 532 votes more than in 1806; but Donaldson amassed 4,575 votes, an increase of 764. In the senatorial election Duane ran far behind the rest of the Democratic ticket. His total of 4,546 was 281 votes less than the Democratic candidate had polled in 1806; while his Quid opponent received 5,786, which was 1,580 more votes than was given to the Federalist-Quid candidate in 1806. Leib was re-elected to the assembly, but he polled 175 votes less than the highest man on the county Democratic ticket; and he was only 359 votes ahead of Jacob Holgate who was supported by both Quids and Quadroons. The latter had approved the whole Democratic ticket except for three county candidates for assembly; and two of their nominees for these places were also on the Quid ticket. Their other candidate received only 76 votes according to the *Aurora*.[78]

Duane was apparently much disgruntled by the election results. The *Aurora* did not mention the preliminary ward elections and printed none of the returns for the general election. An article in the paper afterward blamed the Democratic losses on Binns, saying that his attacks had encouraged the Federalists and disheartened the Democrats. On the other hand, the *Democratic Press* attributed Wolbert's defeat to Duane's unpopularity. The popular rebuke to his ambitions led Duane to turn the editorship of the *Aurora* over to his son, William J. Duane, although he himself unquestionably continued to direct its policies.[79]

The results of the elections in the rest of the State were also somewhat unfavorable to the Democrats. The Constitutionalists elected four out of seven State Senators, but they were still outnumbered in the Senate by three votes. In the election of Representatives each party won 43 seats. Although this amounted to a Democratic gain of one member when compared with what the Constitutionalists had claimed in 1806, it was really a loss since the Democrats in the last session had had a working majority of about three votes in the House. The

Constitutionalists made gains in Fayette and York counties, but they lost ground in Franklin and Chester. The other counties remained unchanged.[80]

The year 1807 had been one of great political strife in Pennsylvania. The renewed attack on the judiciary and the attempt to impeach McKean had revived the strength of the Federalist-Quid coalition. The Philadelphia Democrats led by Leib had attempted to overthrow control of the party by the country areas, but they had only succeeded in creating a new menace to the Leib-Duane supremacy in Philadelphia in the form of John Binns's *Democratic Press*. At the same time the foreign situation had worsened to a point where war with Great Britain seemed a distinct possibility. The impact of this issue was in the following year to counteract the State's political trends in 1807 by breaking up the alliance of the Federalists and Constitutional Republicans and by enforcing unity on the quarreling Democratic factions.

CHAPTER VII

THE ELECTION OF 1808

THE ELECTION of 1808 was a crucial one in American politics. On the national scene, Jefferson, the founder and idol of the Republicans, was retiring. His mantle had fallen on James Madison, whose lot was to be a difficult one. Inheriting all of Jefferson's enemies, he did not fall heir to his personal magnetism and overwhelming prestige. Personal and sectional jealousies combined with the transcendent issue of the embargo to make Madison's election doubtful. His eventual triumph was due in large measure to the staunchness of the Republicans in Pennsylvania.

In that State the presidential and congressional elections coincided with the choice of a Governor. For the first time since 1800 national questions completely dominated State politics. The embargo became the central issue; and party alignments, responding to this touchstone, once more fell into the traditional and sharp divisions of Federalists and Republicans. McKean and constitutional revision lost their significance; and the Constitutional Republicans were no longer able to maintain themselves as a third party but were compelled to make a definite choice of allegiance.

The pressure of the struggle revived Republican unity and forced the city and country factions among the Democrats to suppress their disputes. The same tradition of unity and party regularity induced the Pennsylvania Republicans to overcome their antipathy to Madison and to work wholeheartedly and successfully for his triumph. The election returns proved decisively that there was no hope for Federalism in the State so long as the Republicans were united.

I

The legislative session which began on December 1, 1807, was fated to accomplish little in the way of constructive legislation. The Democrats had a working majority in the Senate with fourteen members to seven for the Quids and four for the Federalists. In the House the Democrats held 43 seats, which exactly equalled the combined strength of the Quids with 21 seats and the Federalists with 22.[1] However, Snyder was again chosen Speaker by a margin of two votes, because of the death of one Constitutionalist and the absence of another.[2]

The close division in the House resulted in excessive parliamentary maneuvering and prevented the passage of controversial measures except on those occasions when absences gave one side or the other a temporary advantage. The greater part of the session was spent in debate over McKean's impeachment and in political maneuvering on the nomination of candidates for Governor.

One of the chief questions to be settled by the legislature was the impeachment of McKean. On December 3, 1807, the Governor delivered his annual address and also returned two measures of the previous session to the House with his vetoes. Conciliatory in tone, the address touched on the foreign situation, militia reform, revision of the judicial system, and a number of other topics. It omitted any reference to the explosive matter of libels which had caused such an uproar in the previous session.[3] One of the vetoes applied to a bill which vested almost complete financial control in the State Treasurer. It was an ill-considered measure, and the Governor pointed out its limitations and questioned its constitutionality; but his language was temperate and lacked the acerbity it had formerly displayed on such occasions.[4]

Most striking, however, was his veto of the resolution forbidding the reading of foreign precedents and cases in the Pennsylvania courts. Probably McKean's outstanding state paper as Governor, it began with an expression of deference to the views of the legislature. Differences of opinion, the Governor said, were natural in both public and private life and should never cause "passion, prejudice or reproach." He had never arraigned the purity of the legislature's motives when there had been differences of opinion, though he had often been led to question his own judgment. In exercising his veto upon this resolution he was not condemning others but was simply assigning reasons to vindicate himself.

With this introduction, he began a dispassionate and persuasive review of the deficiencies of the resolution. It would, in the first place, prevent access to the accustomed sources of legal information and would result in "more partiality, uncertainty, and delay in the administration of justice." Secondly, the right to read American precedents did not furnish an adequate substitute. The states differed in their legal systems; and the decisions in one state were not necessarily apposite in another, nor were these decisions well reported. The jurisdiction of the Federal courts was so limited that they could furnish little guidance in broad areas of jurisprudence. In medicine, theology, navigation, agriculture, and all other pursuits, Americans took advantage of foreign experience and knowledge; and it hardly seemed prudent to deprive them of these sources in the administration of justice.

Finally, in many cases foreign sources were the best and only information of the law of the land. The English statutes and the common law as they existed in March, 1776, were specifically made a part of the law of Pennsylvania; the civil law was the guide of the orphans' and registers' courts; the law of merchants governed in questions of navigation, trade, insurance, and matters of that sort; and the municipal law of a foreign country determined the decisions upon foreign contracts. Unless foreign precedents and decisions could be used in such matters the courts of the State would in many instances be completely unable to administer justice with wisdom.[5]

The unusual humility of the Governor was not without its effect. A motion to draft an answer to the address was defeated; but there was no jeering reply such as Leib had sponsored in the last session. A majority of the House sustained the veto of the bill to broaden the powers of the State Treasurer; and, although the vote was delayed until March 25, 1808, a majority also upheld the veto of the resolution against the reading of foreign precedents.[6] One wonders how different the politics of the State would have been had McKean displayed such temperateness in 1802 and the years that followed.

Despite the Governor's mildness, the Democrats showed no disposition to dismiss the impeachment. It was introduced as unfinished business on December 7, 1807; and a motion was offered the following day to postpone consideration until January 11. This proposal was defeated by a tie vote. On January 15 the Constitutionalists moved to consider the matter; but the Democrats prevented it by a vote of 43-43. On January 27, 1808, however, with one Democrat missing and with one voting with the Constitutionalists, the impeachment was taken up and killed by a general postponement. McKean's friends made use of their temporary supremacy to insert on the House Journal the

Governor's replication to the charges of the committee of inquiry, while the Democrats entered on the journal the report of the committee and the evidence which supported it. They also added a bitter protest against the printing of McKean's replication.[7] Thus ended the attempt to impeach the Governor.

With controversial legislation blocked by the equal division in the House, the most important fights, apart from McKean's impeachment, took place over national issues. One of these was a projected revision of the Federal Constitution. John Marshall's decision in the Burr trial had given much dissatisfaction to the Republicans; and they felt that it gave a new proof of the necessity of bringing the national judiciary under better control by the people.

Accordingly, on December 15, 1807, Leib, seconded by Lacock, introduced a resolution to instruct the Senators and request the Representatives of Pennsylvania in Congress to use their influence to have the Constitution so amended that Federal judges should hold office for a term of years, should be removable by the President on the address of a majority of both houses of Congress, and should be subject to conviction on an impeachment by a simple majority of the Senate. The resolution came up for consideration on January 9, 1808, and, despite frantic attempts by the Democrats to adjourn, it was defeated by the tie vote of 43-43. On February 11, 1808, a similar resolution from the Senate was received by the House; and the Democrats, having a majority on that day, rushed through an immediate approval in spite of the Constitutionalist attempts at delay.[8]

A more significant fight developed over the adoption of an address to the President expressing support and approval of the conduct of foreign affairs. The Senate adopted a resolution requesting that a joint committee of the two houses prepare such an address. The Federalists attempted to forestall this in the House by introducing a resolution making a simple pledge of support to the Federal government in case of war and providing for a program of readying the State's military forces for such an occasion. Though the greater part of the Federalist program was adopted, the House appointed the joint committee, and it made its report on December 31, 1807.

The proposed address reprobated the conduct of Great Britain and pledged the legislature to sustain all measures of the administration to obtain reparation for the injuries suffered at her hands. It closed with a tribute to Jefferson's wisdom and patriotism. The Federalists tried desperately to add a clause condemning the conduct of France and to strike out the paragraph praising the administration. The Quids supported them in attempts to avoid a vote; but when the Democrats forced a decision on the address all but a very few deserted the Federalists and voted in its favor.[9] In the words of the *Aurora*, "the moment they were chased from their cover, they went *helter skelter*, the *new* and *old* feds flying in opposite directions."[10]

The Constitutionalists were more fortunate on the resolution approving of the embargo. This was introduced by Leib on January 29, 1808; and John Sergeant, a Constitutional Republican from Philadelphia, immediately moved that it be postponed generally. Since the Quids stood firm and three Democrats were absent, the resolution was thus killed by a vote of 43-40.[11]

The greatest interest in the legislative session centered about the choice of gubernatorial candidates. Among the Democrats the basic question was whether Snyder would be renominated without opposition or whether the quarrels of the previous session and the past campaign would cause a new division. Eventually, there was unanimous support of Snyder; and this result was largely due to the effective work of his adherents in the various counties over the State.

Snyder's friends intended to take no chances with a group as resourceful as the Leib-Duane faction. The resolutions of the Philadelphia town meeting in September, 1807, in favor of a State nominating convention alarmed them; and they immediately set about to destroy its chances of success. Meetings, apparently inspired by some unknown central committee, were held in counties all over the State during late November and December, and they adopted resolutions which showed considerable uniformity. All contained an endorsement of Snyder for Governor and an expression of confidence in caucus nominations as the best and fairest system of choice. Most of them denounced the convention scheme as inexpedient, unnecessary, and likely to cause a division in the party. The *Aurora* disapproved the holding of these meetings but to no avail. It was clear that Snyder's supporters had executed a shrewd political maneuver which had not only strengthened his chances of nomination but had also effectively scuttled the projected nominating convention.[12]

When the legislature assembled on December 1, 1807, Leib held a very strategic position. With a Democratic majority of only one in the House at that time, his vote and those of the rest of the Philadelphia County delegation could defeat Snyder's choice as Speaker.

Leib was still smarting over the attacks of Binns and, according to his own story, had determined to oppose Snyder as Speaker unless he could be satisfied that the latter had had nothing to do with the establishment of the *Democratic Press*. Snyder gave such assurances to one of the Philadelphia County representatives, and Leib accordingly supported his election. While the story seems plausible in its main outlines, it should be observed that Leib would have been politically ruined if he had caused the success of a Constitutionalist; and his assertion that the Federalists and Quids had promised to support his colleague, James Engle, for the speakership if he would abandon Snyder sounds highly improbable. Leib's conduct in this instance would appear to be as much the result of prudence as of Snyder's assurances.[13]

A similar deference to expediency seems to have had much to do with the understanding that Leib reached with Snyder sometime in the middle of December. Though Leib and Duane were never adherents of Snyder, they had never dared to attack him directly even in the midst of the assaults on Binns and Boileau in the preceding election. This probably indicates that Snyder's popularity was so great that it would have been politically unwise to assail him openly.

Such a view is supported by the illuminating commentary on Snyder and his relations with Leib made by Jonathan Roberts, Jr., then Senator from Montgomery County. It was written just prior to the conference between the two men and by a man who disclaimed adherence to either faction.

> I hope that Snyder will be the republican candidate for governor without opposition & even without any latent dissatisfaction— Since I have been here I have not been inattentive to his character as specially relating to his fitness for governor the result has been satisfactory— He appears incapable of intrigue it even appears he is more candid & less solicitous to appear what he is not than when I knew him before if such a thing be possible from aught that I have seen he will not be a German governor nor the governor of a faction but the governor of the people of pennsylvania— He does not appear to want confidence in himself but that confidence sits easy on him it is the confidence of virtue

of an uncorrupt heart—the confidence of a farmer of man—During the heats & intrigues of the last session he seems to have acted with such consummate prudence & discretion that while he acted with the friends of Boileau Leib has brought no charge against him either public or private & that he will support him now if he can satisfy him that he did not assist in setting up Binns to put down the Aurora this I believe he can do for in anything he appears to have done in that measure he did it with his usual candor & prudence—[14]

After his talk with Snyder, Leib professed to be convinced that the former had had no agency in establishing the *Democratic Press* and that he disapproved of Binns's attacks on Leib.[15] Commenting on the conference, a Quid writer asserted that Snyder had allied himself with Leib and had deserted Boileau and his faction.[16] Such an interpretation was unquestionably pleasing to Leib; but a different one seems to have greater plausibility.

On the whole, it is more probable that Leib had found opposition to Snyder futile and that he sought some device whereby he might support him without loss of face. Snyder had never been a blind follower of Boileau as his votes in the previous session proved;[17] and, as Roberts indicated, his conduct had been such that Leib had found nothing to criticize. The latter was certainly aware of all this; and it is therefore likely that his conditions and the well-publicized talk with Snyder were elaborate mummeries intended to give the impression that Snyder had disavowed Boileau and Binns as the price of Leib's support, while they actually represented nothing more than a capitulation on Leib's part to forces he could not control.

The renewed harmony in the party was demonstrated at a caucus on January 6, 1808. It was here agreed that counties without Democratic representatives should be called upon to elect delegates who should meet in Lancaster on March 7, 1808, with the Democratic members. This mixed group would then make the nominations for Governor and presidential electors. To give a further evidence that the members were acting in accordance with the will of the people, it was also recommended that all the counties hold meetings to advise their representatives of their sentiments respecting the candidates to be chosen.[18] Thus the Democrats in 1808 introduced a hybrid caucus-convention system for nominations, usually referred to today as the mixed legislative caucus, although it was then generally called a convention or conference.[19]

Such an accommodating spirit did not continue to prevail, however. By the latter part of January the feud between Boileau and Leib had once more become open as the result of the defeat of Leib and Duane for bank directors. Lacock was also blamed for this situation. A coolness likewise seemed to be developing between Leib and Snyder, and there were hints of plans to nominate someone else for Governor. The candidates most generally mentioned were Joseph Hiester and Presley Carr Lane, the Speaker of the Senate. However, such schemes came to nothing. Samuel Maclay, viewing affairs from Washington, thought that, even though harmony could be gained by another nomination, Snyder was so closely identified with principle that one could not be sacrificed without the other.[20]

At the caucus-convention held on March 7 and 8, 1808, the supporters of Snyder were apparently determined that the Leib-Duane group should be so intimately associated with Snyder's nomination that they should have no possible way to evade supporting him. Thomas Leiper, a close friend of Duane and a delegate from the city, was chosen to preside over the sessions; and Leib was made one of the secretaries. On the first day the convention unanimously nominated Snyder for Governor, chose a ticket of 20 electors of President and Vice President, selected a state correspondence committee, and appointed Leib and two other members to draw up an address. The State committee was composed of Leiper, Leib, Duane, and four other Philadelphians of the same faction, while Leiper and Leib were also included on the electoral ticket.

The address, which was adopted on the second day, referred to Snyder as a man whose nomination was desired by the people and depicted him as the embodiment of Democratic principles and a staunch supporter of the national administration. It also recommended the electoral ticket with the brief assertion that it was made up of "friends of Jefferson, and of democratic principles," but it made no reference to the presidential candidate to be supported. The Pennsylvania Democrats were irrevocably committed to the election of Snyder; but their course in the presidential contest was by no means certain.[21]

The Federalists and Quids were unable to reach any agreement. In a Constitutionalist caucus at Lancaster on January 29, 1808, the Quids proposed Joseph Hiester and John Spayd as candidates for Governor. The former's name was later withdrawn; and they united behind Spayd, who was Hiester's son-in-law and president judge of the judicial district which included Berks County. The Federalists for the most part backed James Ross, their candidate in 1799 and 1802; but a portion of them supported William Tilghman, the Federalist Chief Justice of the State Supreme Court, as a compromise candidate. Since the Quids would not agree to accept any Federalist candidate and since Tilghman had no desire to contest the nomination with Ross, he withdrew his name from consideration.[22]

While this deadlock existed, Ross seems to have made something of an electioneering tour in his own behalf. Taking two months to make the one-week journey from Pittsburgh to Philadelphia, he arrived in Lancaster during the latter part of February and after spending several days there proceeded on to Philadelphia. At that place, according to his opponents, he promised that he would make no removals from office if elected Governor. On March 7, 1808, a few days after his arrival, the Philadelphia Federalists held a meeting, nominated Ross for Governor, and appointed a corresponding committee to work for his election.[23]

Some of the more moderate Federalists deplored this action as certain to insure the election of Snyder. However, such men as Joseph Hopkinson gave it their decided approval. They were determined not to be dominated by the Quids; they thought that the anxiety of the latter to retain their offices would force them to support Ross; and they counted heavily on the continuance of the embargo to weaken the Democrats.[24]

Ross's nomination ended any possibilities of a compromise among the Constitutionalists in the legislature. The Federalists and Quids met twice in March to discuss the subject, but it was to no avail. The Quids refused the Federalist proposal for a nominating convention, and the latter walked out of the caucus rather than be bound by the nomination of Spayd. The Quids then adjourned their meeting to March 23, 1808, when they made formal announcement of their nominees. They included Spayd as candidate for Governor and a list of presidential electors pledged to support Madison for President and George Clinton for Vice President.[25]

By the time the legislature adjourned on March 28, 1808, its members had settled the matter of McKean's impeachment, had given stress to the national issues which were to dominate the campaign of that year, and had nominated gubernatorial and electoral candidates. The Democratic members, however, had not indicated their preferences for President nor had the Federalists disclosed their intentions on the presidential election.

II

The spring and summer of 1808 witnessed a great deal of maneuvering on the subject of the presidential election. The Democrats were wavering between the support of Madison or Clinton; and the Federalists were undecided as to whether they should nominate a ticket of their own or co-operate with a portion of the Democrats in the election of Clinton. For a time the issue was doubtful; but eventually Clinton was dropped by both Democrats and Federalists.

Whatever differences Binns and Duane had in State politics, they were united in their desire for the nomination of George Clinton for President and in their antipathy toward James Madison. After it was known that Jefferson would not accept a third term, almost every Democratic dinner in 1807 was the occasion of a toast to Clinton as the next President.[26] To a large extent this was owing to his own popularity, but it also represented a strong aversion to Madison.

Lacking personal magnetism, Madison had a public career little calculated to appeal to the average Pennsylvania Democrat. Without a military record, he was also considered too moderate in his Republicanism. A member of the Federal convention in 1787, he had led the fight for ratification of the Constitution and had been a Federalist leader in Congress for a short period. Though he had later joined the Republicans, he had not been active during Adams's "reign of terror." Furthermore, as Secretary of State, he had retained many extreme Federalists in office, and he had favored the Yazoo compromise. Finally, there was some objection to Madison because many felt that Virginia had too long held the presidency.[27]

Despite Madison's unpopularity, a congressional caucus on January 23, 1808, nominated him for President and designated Clinton as his running mate.[28] Its proceedings received a most unfavorable reception in Philadelphia. The *Democratic Press* had violently opposed the caucus even before it was called. After it had met the paper assailed the constitutionality of the proceedings and printed frequent articles praising Clinton and abusing Madison.[29]

Duane was much less forthright. The *Aurora* displayed little interest in the congressional caucus and recorded its nominations with the comment that it was not a time to argue over men. The main thing was to ensure a continuance of Jefferson's policies. "The democracy will not divide—they will support the choice made in the usual manner, since no other or better manner has been provided by the constitution."[30] While this indicated an acquiescence in the choice of Madison, it was certainly devoid of all enthusiasm; and there were many who felt that Duane sought only a plausible excuse to back someone else.

A good portion of the Pennsylvania congressional delegation was also strongly opposed to Madison. The most important of these was Senator Samuel Maclay, who worked untiringly for the nomination of Clinton. According to William Findley, Maclay and a number of Pennsylvania Congressmen who lodged with him were members of a "flying squad who called themselves republicans," but who could never be depended upon to vote with the party. Those following Maclay's lead were William Hoge of Washington County, Samuel Smith of Erie County, Daniel Montgomery, Jr., of Northumberland County, and John Rea of Franklin County. Findley also suspected the Republicanism of William Milnor of Bucks County, Robert Jenkins of Lancaster County, and Joseph Clay of the city of Philadelphia.[31]

Republican congressional opposition to Madison did not content itself with subdued mutterings. On February 27, 1808, seventeen members, including John Randolph, published a protest against the caucus and the nomination of Madison. Five of the signers were Pennsylvanians—Maclay, Clay, Hoge, Montgomery, and Smith. The protest denounced caucus nominations as unconstitutional and as open to corruption through the use of executive patronage. It admitted that the practice had been sanctioned by previous use, but it excused this on the ground that it had arisen in a time of strong Federalist opposition. The Federalists were now impotent, and such devices were no longer required. The protest then assailed Madison as unsuited for the presidency because of his lack of Revolutionary service, his retirement from politics during Adams's administration, his support of the Yazoo compromise, and his alleged partiality for France.[32]

It was against this background that the Pennsylvania Democrats held their caucus-convention at Lancaster on March 7 and 8, 1808.

Sentiments were also divided here. Some members, such as Thomas Leiper, were strong supporters of Madison. Others were equally determined in backing Clinton. Unable to come to any agreement, the meeting finally chose a ticket of electors pledged simply to support Jeffersonian principles.[33]

With great plausibility, the Quids charged that this course was a demonstration of the prudence of "discreet politicians" who were doubtful as to which would be the successful candidate. They also asserted that a majority of the convention was favorable to Clinton, and this view was supported by a number of other observers.[34]

Duane's position at this time was still somewhat equivocal. Thomas Truxtun, a former naval commander, reported in March that Duane had assured him of his intention of working for Madison's election, but Truxtun believed that he had lately become "luke warm." His fears on this score were further excited by a letter from Duane to Samuel Pleasants, Jr., editor of the Richmond *Virginia Argus*, which had been published in that paper on March 11, 1808.

Duane's letter was dated February 23 at Philadelphia and was written in answer to charges made by a writer in the *Argus* who signed himself "Hortensius." Duane stated flatly that he preferred Clinton first and Monroe next for the presidency, but he added that it was no time to quibble over men. He indicated that there was a great necessity for unity and implied that he would support Madison. However, he left himself a door for retreat by asserting that he would abide by the will of the majority.[35]

Truxtun believed that the talk of majority will was all camouflage and that Duane's letter should be interpreted to read: "Make it My Interest, and I will go to work first and Make a Strong Side, and then support that Side through thick & thin." Truxtun urged that the administration do something to win over Duane because there was a strong party for Monroe in the city, while the country districts were balancing between Clinton and Madison. Under such circumstances, the aid of the *Aurora* was vital because of its great influence and wide circulation in Pennsylvania and the other states.[36]

There is some support for the belief that Duane was motivated by personal interest. In February he wrote Madison that he and John Bioren were publishing a new edition of the Federal laws. He did not directly ask patronage, but he observed cryptically that association with Bioren enabled him to engage in a business which his "activity in the best interests of the country has hitherto *prevented*, rather than promoted as might in justice have been expected." Whatever success he may have had in the matter of printing contracts, in July Duane received a commission as lieutenant colonel of a rifle regiment; and this appointment certainly gave plausibility to the charge that his conduct was guided by personal considerations.[37]

However, there were other factors which probably had even greater weight with Duane. Binns had unequivocally opposed Madison and supported Clinton, and his course had in effect aligned the Snyderites on that side. On the other hand, since Madison had been nominated in the accepted fashion, his supporters could claim party orthodoxy with better grace than his opponents. Thus, there was a possibility that if the Duane group supported Madison, the control of State politics by the Snyderites might be broken by damning them as apostates. There was the further consideration that if Samuel Maclay could be ruined because of his support of Clinton, he would probably be dropped as United States Senator by the legislature when he came up for re-election in December. In such case, Leib or another person of similar connections might be chosen in his stead.

Duane may also have been considerably influenced by Thomas Leiper, his close ally and a fellow-member of the Democratic State correspondence committee, who was working hard for the election of Madison. Finally, he was led to support Madison because Gideon Granger, Timothy Pickering, and others who had aroused Duane's ire were known to be opposed to him.[38]

Whatever the exact reasons, in early May the *Aurora* came out strongly for Madison; and the State committee of correspondence, composed of Duane, Leib, and their adherents, began active measures to promote his success in Pennsylvania. The committee on April 30, 1808, issued a call for a town meeting on May 16; and a few days later the *Aurora* proclaimed itself in Madison's favor because of his talents and knowledge and because he would be most likely to continue Jefferson's policies. Under such circumstances, the actions of the town meeting were a foregone conclusion. Despite the attempts of Binns's followers to postpone action until October, the gathering adopted resolutions to support the caucus ticket of Madison and Clinton.[39]

Having decided upon its policy, the State committee began to make great exertions to carry it out. Its first public address, dated June 4, 1808, limited itself to recommending that meetings be held to indicate the public sentiment so that the electors might be guided by the will of the people in making their choice.[40] Privately, however, the committee seems to have sent out circular letters arguing for the support of Madison. In any case, a considerable number of county meetings in May and June began to declare themselves for Madison, and most of these made some reference to a circular letter from the committee.[41]

Not every county proved so complaisant. On June 28, 1808, a meeting of the Democratic delegates of Northumberland County was held in Sunbury. Samuel Maclay spoke at great length, and the meeting then adopted resolutions in favor of Clinton for President and Monroe for Vice President. The resolutions also denounced reports that some of the Lancaster electoral ticket would support Madison. In their opinion, this was a malicious rumor circulated for the purpose of weakening Republican unity. Finally, the meeting adopted a lengthy address filled with praise for Clinton and Monroe and with strong denunciations of Madison.[42]

The State committee now dropped all pretenses and issued a second public address on July 25, 1808. It assailed Maclay without reserve and denied categorically that the Lancaster convention had ever discussed any of the presidential candidates. While the committee paid full honor to the talents and services of Clinton and Monroe, it called for the support of Madison "because the choice has been made in the usual manner, and because the choice itself is good; because not to accord with that choice would subject us to the reproach of being *veering politicians* and faithless to our country and our principles."[43]

The work of the State committee soon bore fruit. On May 2, 1808, the *Democratic Press* had favored meetings to get the people's view on a presidential candidate, but when such meetings were recommended by the State committee the paper began to reverse itself and began to argue that such decisions should be postponed until after the gubernatorial election to avoid Democratic splits. During May and June the *Press* continued its attacks on Madison, and as late as July 14, 1808, it published the address of the Sunbury meeting.[44]

Four days later, however, Binns switched his support to Madison. He claimed to have reached this decision because Republican meetings and Republican toasts on the Fourth of July were overwhelmingly in favor of Madison, while but few were for Clinton. He had also found the same thing to be true of the Republican press. Binns avowed that he had become convinced that Clinton could only be elected with Federalist aid, and added that he would be "infatuated, criminally obstinate or corrupt" if he did not oppose such a connection, even though he retained his former opinions on the respective merits of Madison and Clinton.[45]

Binns's capitulation ended all hope for the Democratic supporters of Clinton in Pennsylvania. The Democrats in Northumberland County denied any intention of opposing the will of the majority and at a meeting on August 20, 1808, recommended the election of Madison.[46]

A similar change appeared in the westernmost tier of counties. Both the Congressmen from this section, William Hoge and Samuel Smith, had signed the protest against the caucus and against the nomination of Madison; and their sentiments seemed to be shared by their constituents. Except for a meeting in Mercer County in July, the Democrats in that region had studiously avoided declaring themselves in favor of Madison. The Fourth of July toasts had uniformly included Clinton and omitted Madison. In September, 1808, however, almost all the Democratic meetings in these counties adopted resolutions in support of the latter.[47] The State committee had won its victory.

During the course of the campaign the Democrats had continually laid stress upon Madison's retention of Federalists in his office, and they had demanded their removal and also a cleaning out of the Federalists and Quids holding Federal offices in Philadelphia.[48] These demands were not fully acceded to; but the Duane-Leib group did receive one appointment which unquestionably gave energy to their support of Madison. This was the lucrative position of Collector of the Port.

Peter Muhlenberg had died in October, 1807, after a long illness. Duane's friends had sought the appointment of John Steele as his successor, partly because his selection would irritate McKean. Jefferson had felt obligated to give the position to John Shee; and this was satisfactory to the Duane faction because Shee had been removed as flour inspector by McKean and Jefferson's favor to him had the appearance of a rebuke for the removal.[49]

When Shee died in August, 1808, Leiper and Duane once more sought the appointment of Steele as his successor. Gallatin favored William Jones for the position, but he recognized that the affair was so closely connected with the life of the party in the State that he only advised Jefferson not to be hasty. Nevertheless, Jefferson appointed Steele to the vacancy less than three weeks after Shee's death. Such a policy was warmly applauded by the *Aurora*, which asserted in October that "The appointments by the general government had no small share on the present occasion in *rousing, uniting,* and restoring confidence among the republican family."[50]

The Democratic decision to support the caucus ticket of Madison and Clinton had a decisive influence on the Federalists both in Pennsylvania and the country at large. Since the Federalists in Congress had made no choice of candidates, there was considerable doubt as to what should be done. Hearing reports that there was some talk of Federalist support of Clinton, Charles Willing Hare, a Federalist Representative from Philadelphia, wrote Harrison Gray Otis on June 2, 1808, and inquired what the Massachusetts Federalists intended to do. Those in Pennsylvania would follow their lead, but they had to know definitely so that they could either prepare their own electoral ticket or make arrangements with the Clinton Democrats.[51]

Hare's letter galvanized the Massachusetts leaders into action; and on June 10, 1808, their correspondence committee sent out letters recommending that a meeting of the Federalist leaders from the various states be held in New York to decide upon a course of action. In Philadelphia about a dozen of the Federalist leaders met, approved this suggestion, and appointed a correspondence committee composed of Hare, Thomas Fitzsimons, Robert Waln, George Latimer, and Benjamin R. Morgan. The Philadelphia group also suggested that the meeting be deferred until the middle of August.[52]

By the time the Federalists convened in New York in the third week of August, the political situation in Pennsylvania had greatly changed. Binns had given up Clinton, and the Northumberland group had also recanted. There was no longer any body of Clintonians in Pennsylvania with whom the Federalists could ally. Although Otis and other Massachusetts leaders still favored support of Clinton, most of the delegates felt that the defection of Pennsylvania made his cause hopeless. Accordingly, they decided to cleave to their principles and chose

Charles Cotesworth Pinckney and Rufus King as their candidates for President and Vice President.[53]

The decision was not made public for some time because the meeting had been secret; and there was a likelihood that it might arouse considerable objections. A writer in the *Aurora,* however, reported that the meeting had been held; but he was in error when he asserted that it had nominated Clinton for President and Pinckney for Vice President.[54]

With the decision made, the Federalist corresponding committees from Philadelphia and a number of counties, including Bucks and Delaware, met on August 27, 1808, and sent out letters to the various congressional districts requesting that they make recommendations for presidential electors. In this fashion the Federalist ticket was formed, but it was not published until October 26.[55]

The Pennsylvania Democrats had begun the year with a distaste for Madison and an inclination to support Clinton. By the end of August they were united in support of Madison. This metamorphosis was the result of many factors, but it was probably due chiefly to the influence of party traditions of regularity, unity, and majority rule. The *Aurora* and the Duane-dominated State correspondence committee had done effective work in achieving this change; and their activities resulted from complex considerations of personal interest, patronage, and party control as well as from party traditions and a distrust of Clinton's supporters. The Democratic support of Madison had in turn caused the Federalists to decide to offer their own electoral ticket.

III

Contrary to the trends of the seven preceding years, the campaign of 1808 was wholly dominated by a national issue—the continuance of the embargo. This revived the old questions of French and British partialities, of a strong navy and coastal defenses, of commercial and agrarian interests which had divided parties in the days of John Adams. It also introduced a new factor in the attempt to substitute commercial restrictions for war as a means of international coercion.

Pennsylvania Federalism had always been more concerned with national than with State or local issues. The party had declined to almost nothing by 1804, but it had been brought into a limited activity in 1805 by the attack on the Pennsylvania Constitution. The period of rejuvenation coincided with the growing tension in foreign affairs, and Pennsylvania Federalism once more began to play an active role in the politics of the State. With the retirement of Jefferson and the imposition of the embargo, which brought hardships to farmers as well as merchants, the party felt that its great opportunity to regain power had come, and it fought strenuously in 1808 to restore its ascendancy in the State.

During the latter part of 1807 the infringements of Great Britain and France on American neutral rights were still further increased. In October the British navy began to enforce its impressment policy to its full extent; and in November the government issued a new order in council which in effect required that all American commerce except to Sweden and the West Indies must go through a British port and receive a British license. Napoleon responded in December with his Milan Decree. Under its terms any neutral vessel which had been searched by a British vessel or had paid duties to the British government or which was sailing to or from a British port was liable to capture.[56]

Even before these new measures were known in America the policy of commercial restrictions had been inaugurated. On December 14, 1807, the Nonimportation Act of April, 1806, was put into operation; and eight days later the Embargo Act, without limit as to time, became law. The provisions of the latter were made more stringent by supplementary acts passed in January and March, 1808.[57]

The economic effects of the embargo in Pennsylvania cannot be precisely determined; but contemporary observers agreed that, although it caused hardships, it did not bring ruin to the State. John Howe, an emissary of Sir George Prevost, the British Lieutenant Governor at Halifax, visited Philadelphia in June, 1808, and reported that "The Embargo has produced no failures here of any consequence, though great injury is sustained, and many of its inhabitants subjected to much suffering."[58] Nicholas Biddle in the following September noted that the measure pressed heavily on the people but that it had been put into operation without difficulty.[59]

The merchants, of course, fared worst under the embargo. The renewal of the European wars in 1803 had brought them great prosperity. In the fiscal year ending September 30, 1803, the total American exports had dropped to less than $56,000,000. During the next four years they nearly doubled, reaching a total of more than $108,000,000 in the year ending September 30, 1807. In the succeeding fiscal year, with the embargo in effect for nine months, they dropped by nearly 80 per cent to less than $23,000,000.[60] Under such conditions the merchants could not avoid severe hardships, and the same difficulties applied to the mariners and others directly affected by the state of foreign commerce.

Important as the merchants were, they were far less numerous than the farmers in Pennsylvania; and the farmers were also sufferers from the embargo. American exports of domestic origin, most of which were farm products, declined from nearly $49,000,000 in the fiscal year 1807 to less than $10,000,000 in the succeeding year, a drop of nearly 84 per cent.[61] Even the Democrats, who supported the embargo, made no attempt to deny that it hurt the farmers, but defended it on the ground that it was the only alternative to war and even worse hardships.[62] Its opponents claimed that the farmer could not "sell his grain for what it cost in raising, gathering, and taking it to market."[63]

The saving feature of the embargo in Pennsylvania was the tremendous impetus given to manufactures. No other city enjoyed this to a greater degree than Philadelphia. Despite the sufferings of the mercantile interests, the city experienced considerable prosperity. Capital turned from foreign trade to manufacturing and began to exploit the great market afforded by the cessation of imports from abroad. The volume of production greatly increased, and new products of domestic manufacture made their appearance. This activity furnished employment to thousands and created a domestic demand for farm products which to some extent offset the loss of foreign markets.[64]

While the embargo had far-reaching economic effects, these were but incidental to its purpose as an instrument of coercion in foreign relations. Hence, although men were influenced by economic considerations in their attitudes, other factors were perhaps of more significance in determining their overall reactions to the embargo.

One of these factors was the international situation. Between the orders in council and decrees of the two belligerents, American commerce was apparently doomed to destruction in any case. Therefore, many felt that the embargo was the only sensible course until some new arrangement could be worked out. If no accommodation could be reached with Great Britain and France, war seemed inevitable; and an embargo was a wise precautionary measure to get American property safe at home and to give time to arm American vessels before hostilities began. Implicit in this view was the assumption that the measure was purely temporary until a different course was decided upon.

Thomas Truxtun, who could hardly be considered an enemy to commerce, saw the matter in this light, and he reported that "all Sensible and discerning Men" with whom he had talked thought the same way regardless of their political opinions.[65]

On the other hand, many of the Democrats wholeheartedly supported the embargo as a substitute for war. Duane had long favored such a measure as an easy way to prostrate Great Britain while avoiding the dangers to liberty inherent in a standing army, a large navy, and a permanent debt.[66] John Binns shared these sentiments and highly praised the policy in the *Democratic Press*.[67] The Pittsburgh *Commonwealth* was less hearty in its endorsement and indicated that it expected Congress to make considerable modifications.[68]

Although the Pennsylvania Democrats adopted the thesis expounded by Duane, it is likely that they did so only out of party loyalty. Most of them felt that the *Chesapeake* attack, impressments, and seizures of American ships demanded immediate retribution from Great Britain; and it is probable that the embargo impressed them as a temporizing expedient rather than as a forceful way to settle the nation's difficulties. A correspondent of the Pittsburgh *Commonwealth* in February, 1808, was highly critical because Congress had failed to declare war. At the other end of the State, William Jones, who had given much public support to the embargo, also called for more decisive measures.[69]

The factor which probably clinched Democratic loyalty to the embargo was the Federalist determination to make this the chief issue of the gubernatorial campaign. Although Truxtun's letter indicates that most Federalists did not question the wisdom of the embargo as a temporary measure, the *United States' Gazette* immediately attacked it as evidence of the administration's complete subservience to France.[70] At the same time such Federalist leaders as Joseph Hopkinson saw in the embargo a chance for their party to win control of the State.[71]

As the campaign continued the Federalists dwelt more and more heavily on the theme that Ross's election was "absolutely essential to the restoration of those COMMERCIAL HABITS which have been *unconstitutionally* and flagrantly infringed upon."[72] The Democrats were not loath to accept the gage thus thrown to them. The *Aurora* defiantly proclaimed its willingness to make this the issue and to determine for all time whether the Americans preferred "baseness and servitude" or were "Worthy of Independence and Liberty."[73] The same forthrightness in support of the embargo characterized the Democratic addresses and resolutions throughout the campaign.[74]

Though neither Ross nor Snyder could have done anything directly about the embargo, a Federalist victory in the State would have had a great influence on the national election. The Republican victory in Pennsylvania in 1799 had been the prelude to national victory in the following year. According to Jesse Higgins, a Delaware Republican, Ross's election would likewise be "a sure passage to change in the Union."[75] John Howe, the British emissary, also believed that the results in Pennsylvania would determine the course of the neighboring states.[76]

The Pennsylvania Republicans were thus called upon to play once more their role as the keystone in the Democratic arch. The issue was the national question of the embargo. The opposition was the traditional antagonist, Federalism. If they remained firm, Madison's election was a virtual certainty. If they faltered, a Federalist national victory was not only possible but even probable.

IV

Apart from the central issues of the presidential election and the embargo, the next most important question was the part to be played by the Constitutional Republicans. The bitter contest was also filled with personalities and factional strife.

The Democrats in their addresses and articles furiously assailed Ross. Most of the attacks dwelt chiefly on his support of the Federalist program during Adams's administration—the funding system, the excise taxes, a standing army, a large navy, the Alien and Sedition Acts. He was denounced as a lawyer, an aristocrat, a British partisan, a friend to land speculators, and an enemy to Christianity. It was proclaimed that his election would once more bring all the evils of the Federalist "terror" and destroy the liberties of the people.[77]

The most slanderous attack accused Ross of having obtained his home in Pittsburgh through illegal and violent means. This was the famous case of Jane Marie. The story was briefly as follows: In January, 1803, Ross purchased from John Marie, a French tavern-keeper in Pittsburgh, a house and lot on Grant's Hill; and in the same month Marie left to go to France. In selling this property Marie directly violated a legally registered agreement with his wife, Jane, not to dispose of it without her consent. She refused to give up possession and finally was forcibly ejected in August, 1803, by agents of her husband, with Ross taking possession from them. A few months later she visited the house and apparently created such a scene that Ross beat her with a whip. Matters rested thus until 1806 when Marie returned from France and began divorce proceedings against his wife. The divorce was granted in August, 1807; and in the same month Ross obtained full title to the property from John Marie.

The details of the story were much disputed. The *Aurora* gave full publicity to it, and a pamphlet detailing Jane Marie's version was also printed and circulated. She charged that Ross had no legal right to the property but that his influence in Pittsburgh prevented her from obtaining justice. She also asserted that the power of attorney used by Marie's agents in expelling her from Grant's Hill was a forgery. Finally, she accused Ross and his friends of taking advantage of the senility of Marie, who was over eighty years of age, to persuade him to divorce her and to issue a statement favorable to Ross.

The Federalist papers carried defenses of Ross's conduct; and the *Aurora* published statements from John Wilkins, Jr., and from John Marie, exonerating Ross from the charge of dishonest conduct. Generally, Ross's defense covered the following points: He had purchased in good faith and had punctually carried out his part of the bargain. The agreement between Marie and his wife was a private one and did not alter his rights to the property. He had not taken part in ejecting her from the house, and his beating her was the result of her having abused Mrs. Ross. Finally, the defenders of Ross attacked Jane Marie as an unfaithful wife and a drunkard.[78]

Such a sensational story was certainly damaging to Ross, but it is doubtful that it played any significant part in determining the course of the election. It does, however, indicate the bitterness with which the campaign was waged.

The Federalists and Quids assailed Snyder as an uncouth and ignorant man unfitted to discharge the office of Governor. He was denounced as the enemy of the Constitution and the judiciary, as the advocate of a perpetual embargo, as the leader of a French party, and as the tool of scheming politicians. The Quakers were told that Snyder wished to take away the vote of all who would not bear arms, and poor men were warned that he had said that they should not be allowed to vote. His private conduct was also attacked. He was accused of having deprived his brother's orphans of a portion of their inheritance, of having collected debts twice, and of having sold screenings from his flour mill to the poor at an exorbitant price. These tales were denied by the Democratic papers, and they probably had no influence on the voters.[79]

The *Aurora* and the Democratic State correspondence committee worked hard for Snyder's election. The *Aurora* gave him unstinted support throughout the campaign; and the correspondence committee issued three addresses, all of which praised Snyder highly and warmly advocated his election on his own merits as well as because of the unsuitability of Ross and the dangers resulting from a Federalist victory.[80]

Binns and his followers, however, took no chances and conducted a separate campaign. In Philadelphia at the beginning of the year, they had already organized the "Society of Independent Democrats"; and in May they formed the "Associated Friends of Democracy and Simon Snyder" for the sole purpose of electing Snyder to office. These two organizations issued their own addresses during the campaign and completely ignored the regularly designated State committee of correspondence. This was carried to such an extent that the *Democratic Press* did not publish any of the addresses issued by the regular State committee. The *Aurora*, in turn, denounced these groups as mere office-seekers and refused to print the proceedings of their meetings.[81]

The two factions differed little in their propaganda for Snyder, however, except on one occasion. With the disastrous results of the attack on the Constitution in 1805 fresh in their minds, the Snyderites steadily avoided the subject in their addresses. At the same time the *Democratic Press* published articles addressed to the Constitutional Republicans in which it was avowed that Snyder and his friends believed that the vote in 1805 had shown conclusively that the people did not desire constitutional reform and that they therefore considered the matter closed.[82]

Nevertheless, the State committee of correspondence in its first address, dated June 4, 1808, devoted a full column to a discussion of the shortcomings of the Constitution and the judiciary.[83] This was certainly unwise at a time when the Democrats were seeking to gain the Quid votes for Snyder, and it gave rise to charges that the Duane group was trying to prevent Snyder's election. A writer in the *Freeman's Journal*, noting that Snyder was reported to have considered the issue of constitutional revision settled, inquired whether there was discord among the Democrats or whether there was a secret plot to revise the Constitution if Snyder were elected.[84]

Whatever may have been the reasons for discussion of the subject by the State committee, the address apparently met with a cold reception and was published in none of the Democratic papers in the State other than the *Aurora*.[85] This mark of disapproval seems to have been effective because the matter of constitutional reform was given no further attention either in the addresses of the committee or in the columns of the *Aurora*.

Apart from this aberration, both factions assiduously attempted to woo the Quid voters; and their efforts had a great deal of success. One of the most astounding evidences of change was the presence of William T. Donaldson, the Quid sheriff, at the Fourth of July dinner given by the Society of Friends of the People and presided over by Leib.[86] In truth, it seemed that the lion had laid down with the lamb. Nevertheless, the matter was not to be settled without difficulties.

The Quid position became more and more untenable as the campaign developed. Except in the counties of Berks and Northampton support of Spayd almost completely disappeared as the Federalists united behind Ross. It was soon obvious that a vote for Spayd was wasted; and the Quids had to make the hard choice of voting for Snyder, whom they had opposed so bitterly in 1805, or of backing Ross and Federalism at a time when national issues imperatively demanded party regularity.

In the midst of their tribulations the Quids suffered from the defection of their most influential newspaper. As early as February, 1807, William McCorkle, editor of the *Freeman's Journal*, had announced that he would devote more space to commercial and less to political affairs in his future issues. He professed to expect a "liberal mercantile support" in return.[87] This announcement was rather significant since the mercantile interest was largely Federalist.

In March, 1808, prior to Ross's nomination, the *Journal* had hailed the nomination of Spayd as certain to bring success over Snyder. After the Federalists had put Ross forward the paper was for a time discreetly silent as to the relative merits of the two men. In May it derided reports that the Quids would vote for Snyder, but it did not indicate whom they would support. In June it began to print rumors that French funds were being used to promote the election of Snyder, and in July the editor openly avowed his support of Ross. At the same time the *Journal* began to attack administration favoritism toward France and to denounce the embargo, though it had approved of the latter in April.[88]

If the Quids were to continue their claims to being Republicans such conduct could not be permitted to go unchallenged. Accordingly, a Constitutional Republican meeting was held at the Rising Sun Tavern on August 13, 1808, at which Edward Heston was chairman and Mathew Carey was secretary. Resolutions were adopted which approved of Madison's nomination, the conduct of the national administration, and the wisdom of the embargo. It was also resolved that they would not support Ross for Governor. A final resolution dissented from the recent articles in the *Freeman's Journal* and asserted that the paper had abandoned its principles, forfeited their support, and could "no longer be considered as speaking the language of the constitutional party, or as having any remaining claims to republican confidence."[89]

The reaction of McCorkle was a ridiculous attempt to picture himself as the victim of a "terrible proscription." Here, he asserted, were men professing Republicanism who were attempting to deprive his family of subsistence solely because he exercised his privilege of thinking and speaking freely. This was *"coercion and tyranny, equalled only by Napoleon."* He even had the presumption to compare himself with Johann Philipp Palm, the Nuremburg bookseller who had been summarily executed by the French emperor for circulating an unfavorable pamphlet.[90]

Although some Constitutionalist meetings adopted resolutions favorable to McCorkle,[91] it is unlikely that anyone was seriously impressed by his absurd rantings. A party editor losing his support because of his renunciation of the candidates and measures of his party could not in good faith claim to have been the victim of an unjust proscription.

The disintegration of the Constitutional Republicans in Philadelphia now proceeded swiftly. A second meeting at the Rising Sun Tavern on August 24, 1808, agreed to back Snyder on the ground that a vote for

Spayd could only serve to assist Ross. A portion of those who attended, however, withdrew and held a separate meeting which proclaimed their continued adherence to Spayd. It also disapproved of the denunciation of McCorkle.[92]

No Quid meeting in the city came out openly for Ross; but the *Democratic Press* reported that a secret meeting at the White Horse Tavern on September 13, 1808, attended by Moses Levy and Joseph B. McKean, adopted resolutions in his favor. A number of Quids, including McCorkle, Levy, and McKean, were also prominent in drawing up a ticket for the "Friends of the Constitution." Such a designation for the group was a pure euphemism. Although no mention was made of the gubernatorial race, the candidates for the other offices were all Federalists.[93]

As the campaign went into its final stages the Federalists began to do everything possible to strengthen their position. They were probably responsible for the call of a meeting of the captains and officers of ships at the White Horse Tavern on September 17, 1808. However, their plans went awry when William Jones, Quid merchant and mariner, attended the meeting and persuaded it to adopt a set of very temperate resolutions. These resolutions renounced political measures, agreed that the embargo was a wise policy in the face of foreign aggressions and preferable to war *"in an unprepared state,"* and announced that since no changes had taken place in the foreign situation, it was the duty of good citizens to await the decision of Congress as to "whether the dispositions of the belligerent powers are such as to ensure safety to our trade, and whether a temporary embargo is more intolerable than an appeal to arms."[94]

Jones's action rather effectively crippled the Federalist hopes for a unanimous endorsement of their program by the maritime groups. However, they were able to arrange a second meeting at the Merchants' Coffee House on September 22, 1808, where more than ninety masters and mates of vessels endorsed Ross and denounced the embargo.[95]

Jones now took another decisive step when he, along with Richard Bache and John Sergeant, issued a call for a Constitutional Republican meeting to be held at the White Horse Tavern on September 24, 1808, to consider the question of promoting Madison's election. According to Federalist charges, however, the real instigator of the meeting was Dallas.[96]

In July Dallas had written Gallatin expressing his disgust at the way things were going. He believed that "one year more of writing, speaking, and appointing would render Mr. Jefferson a more odious President, even to the Democrats, than John Adams." He only hoped that it would not affect Madison's election. As for himself he had abandoned politics.[97] Such idleness by a prominent Federal official in a crucial campaign was not likely to be viewed kindly; and the Federalists asserted that Samuel Smith, United States Senator from Maryland, had spurred Dallas into action by reminding him of this fact during an interview in the middle of September.[98]

At any rate, Dallas took a prominent part in the meeting at the White Horse Tavern, although Jones served as chairman. It was quickly agreed that Madison's election must not be imperiled by splitting the Republican vote between two sets of electors. A committee appointed for the purpose then reported an electoral ticket identical with that of the Democrats except that Isaac Worrell was substituted for Leib. Dallas argued for the inclusion of Leib, but he finally gave way; and the ticket reported by the committee was adopted. The *Democratic Press* printed the proceedings, but it specifically disapproved the dropping of Leib and called for *"unanimous* and *undivided* support" of the official Democratic ticket.[99]

The rapprochement between the Quids and the Democrats was made much easier by the existence of the Snyderites and the *Democratic Press*. The *Aurora,* of course, had made appeals for Quid reunion with the Democrats; but it was pretty generally understood that such unity meant Quid subservience and the proscription of such leaders as Dallas. The Snyderites were less harsh in their terms, and the Quids were able to co-operate with them without the disagreeable necessity of submitting themselves to the tender mercies of Duane and Leib.[100]

All over the State Spayd was virtually dropped from consideration as a candidate, and there were numerous reports of his complete withdrawal from the contest. Even in his home county of Berks he was called upon by a committee from a Quid meeting to state definitely whether or not he was still a candidate. According to the *Democratic Press,* John S. Hiester, son of Joseph Hiester and brother-in-law of Spayd, who headed the committee, announced that Spayd had declined giving any answer and that he believed that he should no longer be considered a candidate. There was opposition to this view, and nothing further seems to have come of the incident.[101]

With Spayd's course doubtful, the Democratic State committee decided to take action. Having previously ignored his candidacy, it came out on August 31, 1808, with an address attacking him sharply for failing to withdraw and asserting that a vote for him was in effect a vote for Ross and Federalism. A few weeks later the *Aurora* announced that Spayd had publicly withdrawn; but there was no supporting evidence; and it is uncertain whether he ever formally declined to be a candidate. The vote he received in Berks County, however, would indicate that he did not.[102]

The Democratic disputes were subordinated in the face of the strong Federalist campaign. Despite their independent efforts in the gubernatorial campaign and their slighting of the State committee, the Snyderites made no attempt to contest the Leib-Duane control of Philadelphia city and county. No "Quadroon" ticket was offered, and Binns served without disturbance on the general ward committee.[103]

The effects of Democratic unity and a revival of a clear-cut division between Federalists and Republicans was clearly shown in the results of the general election on October 11, 1808, when the Republicans carried the city for the first time since 1804. The total vote for Governor exceeded 5,600 votes, which surpassed by more than 1,300 the total in 1807. Snyder polled 2,897 votes to Ross's 2,737; and the rest of the Democratic ticket was carried by like majorities.

In Philadelphia County the total vote also increased by better than 1,300, amounting to 5,907 in the Governor's race. Snyder received 3,860 votes to Ross's 2,047. The Democratic assembly ticket, with the exception of Leib, did even better, amassing a majority of nearly 3,000 votes. Leib defeated William Duncan by only 1,241 votes. Exactly what caused this situation is unknown. Duncan had previously taken part in the Leibite county meetings and then, presumably out of personal pique, ran as a candidate on the opposition ticket. The Snyderites do not appear to have been involved in the affair.[104]

The Democrats made a similar sweep in the State as a whole. In the Governor's race 111,564 ballots were cast, an increase of 39,042 over the total in 1805. Of these, Snyder polled 67,975, Ross 39,575, Spayd 4,006, and eight votes were scattered. Ross carried only Luzerne, Bucks, Delaware, Chester, Lancaster, and Adams counties; and his margin of victory was very narrow in Bucks and Chester. Every other county cast a majority for Snyder. Spayd's vote was negligible except in Berks and

The Election of 1808

Northampton counties where Joseph Hiester's influence was paramount. Here he ran second to Snyder, but he polled only 3,154 votes to Snyder's 6,375 and Ross's 2,506.[105]

In its previous session the legislature had adopted a new apportionment act which raised the membership of the House to 95 and the Senate to 31.[106] None of the papers of the time made any compilation of the political affiliations of the legislature elected in 1808; but a comparison with the affiliations of members in other years indicates that the Democrats won 74 seats in the House to 21 for their opponents. These last were elected from the same counties which furnished majorities to Ross; and it is probable that they were all Federalists, though there may have been one or two Quids. A similar study shows that the Democrats elected ten out of thirteen new State Senators and that they had a majority of 19-12 in that branch of the legislature.

In the congressional election the Democrats won twelve out of eighteen seats. Federalist-Quid coalitions were successful in William Findley's district centering about Westmoreland County and in the three-member Lancaster-Berks-Chester district. They also won two out of the three seats in the district which included Montgomery, Bucks, Northampton, Wayne, and Luzerne counties. Their successful candidates, however, were all Quids; and James Kelly, the only avowedly Federalist member, was defeated for re-election in the York-Adams district. Of the six Quid Congressmen, the *Aurora* felt that only William Milnor, John Ross, Robert Jenkins, and William Findley could not be depended upon to support the administration. Though the others were probably doubtful, it seems that Duane included Findley more out of personal dislike than for any justifiable reason.[107]

With such an overwhelming victory in the State elections, the Democrats immediately began to organize for the presidential election on November 4, 1808. Although the Federalists in Philadelphia promulgated an electoral ticket and held ward meetings for its support, their efforts were obviously futile. The *Lancaster Journal* printed the ticket but asserted that it saw no reason for the Federalists to take the trouble to vote since the Democrats had "gotten the *people* compleatly hoodwinked."[108]

The election returns showed how utterly dispirited the Federalists were. They even failed to carry their strongholds in Luzerne and Adams counties, and their ticket received a majority only in Delaware

County. With the total vote less than half that cast in the gubernatorial election, the Republican electors polled 42,318 votes to 11,649 for the Federalists.[109]

The election of 1808 was a significant demonstration of the depth and strength of Pennsylvania Republicanism. The Federalists had been favored by many circumstances—Republican disunity over presidential candidates; the Leib-Boileau quarrel among the Democrats; Quid cooperation with them in the three preceding elections; and, most important, the economic hardships of the embargo. Yet they had lost by an overwhelming majority.

Republican unity reappeared under the stimulus of a revived Federalism campaigning on national issues. Internal divisions were suppressed, and the Republicans gave undivided support to Madison and Snyder. The stresses of the campaign destroyed the Constitutional Republicans as a third party, though there were vestiges in a few counties. The election was fought squarely on the issues of the embargo and the policies of Jefferson; and the result demonstrated that in a crisis Pennsylvania was indeed the keystone in the Democratic arch.

CHAPTER VIII

THE OLMSTED AFFAIR: STATE RIGHTS AND FACTIONAL POLITICS: 1809

THE EIGHT YEARS which followed the election of 1808 differed greatly from the eight which preceded it. There was a new orientation in the politics of Pennsylvania. The earlier period had been chiefly concerned with State and local issues—judicial and constitutional reform, the personality of McKean, and the feuds over patronage and political control. The Federalists had dwindled into insignificance by 1804 and then had begun to revive as partners in coalition with the Constitutional Republicans. Until 1808, however, the party battles had not been clear-cut struggles between Federalism and Republicanism.

The new era was dominated by two themes. The first of these was the national issue of supporting the administration's foreign policy, including the War of 1812. Party lines were sharply drawn, and a strong Federalist minority took an active part in politics. The second was the bitter feud between the Leib-Duane faction and the followers of Snyder. This persisted in full rancor throughout the period and was only partially subdued by the compulsion for Democratic unity exerted by the War of 1812. Although at times it affected the results of party conflicts with the Federalists, it proceeded independently for the most part and will therefore be considered separately.

The separate development of these two themes in State politics is illustrative of the conflicting trends which were manifesting themselves not only in Pennsylvania but in the country at large. There was in the first place a tendency toward the disintegration of the old parties and the formation of new alignments. Counteracting this was the pressure to maintain existing divisions exerted by the hotly debated question of foreign policy.

Republican and Federalist differences were being obliterated on many of the key issues which had divided them. In the matter of popular government, the Federalists for the most part had discovered that it was impossible to gain political control on the frankly avowed principle of the rule of "the wealthy, the wise, and the good." Most of them were now willing to accede to the necessity of paying deference to the principle of popular sovereignty.

On the other hand, it had become obvious to most Republicans that there was no danger of the establishment of monarchy or hereditary aristocracy in the country. Furthermore, a considerable number of them had begun to fear the results of unrestricted popular rule and to desire to put a halt to changes calculated to disturb property rights and existing institutions. Their views were closely akin to those of the less extreme Federalists.

Similarly, there had been a change in party attitudes on economic matters. Many Republicans began to see great virtues in the formerly obnoxious Bank of the United States; and their handling of government finances since they had been in control of the national government had done little to justify the excessive fears of the Federalists in 1800. The economic changes during Madison's regime also had a powerful effect on parties. The restrictions on commerce tended to weaken the power of the commercial interests and led many merchants to invest their idle capital in manufacturing enterprises. They were thus brought into sympathy with the views of a sizable portion of the Republicans who were supporting the twin theses of domestic manufactures and development of the home market. The end of the European wars closed the golden era of foreign commerce and further strengthened the trend to the creation of parties more attuned to the changing economic balance of the country.

Federalist and Republican divergences over state rights and national power were also largely eliminated. After the Republicans took office, it became increasingly clear that one's views on these issues were for the most part determined by whether one were in or out of office—that state rights were minority defenses against the majority rather than matters of basic principle. The Republicans in office came eventually to support a strong army and navy, a protective tariff, a national bank, and other policies characteristic of a strong government; while the Federalist stronghold of New England in the same period gave to state rights a more ominous cast than they had known even in the days of the Virginia and Kentucky Resolutions.

Other factors which contributed to the disintegration of the old parties were the retirement of Jefferson, the development of congressional and cabinet divisions among the Republicans, and the sectional jealousy inspired by the continued dominance of Virginia in the national councils.

Opposing these disruptive trends was the continued vitality of the issue of foreign policy which imperatively demanded allegiance to old shibboleths. Federalists and Republicans continued to maintain opposing views on the questions of French and British partialities, the doctrine of neutral rights, and the merits of commercial restrictions and passive defense as opposed to a strong navy aggressively protecting commercial rights. The strength of this appeal to old loyalties was forcefully demonstrated in Pennsylvania where it inhibited the coalition of Federalists and dissident Democratic factions until after the close of the War of 1812.

I

The legislative session of 1808-1809 began the new era in Pennsylvania politics. The old friction between the legislature and the Governor disappeared; many items in the Democratic program of judicial reform were enacted as laws; and the suppressed struggle between the Duane-Leib faction and the country Democrats was renewed with great virulence over the question of the Olmsted Case.

When the legislature convened on December 6, 1808, the Democrats in the House displayed commendable unanimity in the election of a speaker. With five members absent, Boileau received 71 votes; and John Hulme, a Federalist from Bucks County, polled nineteen.[1]

A like unanimity was shown in the election for United States Senator which took place a week later. There were ninety votes cast for Leib, 24 for Joseph Hemphill, a Federalist, and eleven for John D. Coxe. Most of those who supported Coxe were Quids; but one of his votes came from Leib and another from Elisha Gordon, a Democrat from the city of Philadelphia.[2]

Behind this apparent unity lay a clever design on the part of the Snyderites. Boileau had long been intended as Snyder's Secretary of the Commonwealth; but his appointment was felt to be doubtful because of the old charges that he had originally made a bargain to support Snyder in return for the position. On the other hand, Thomas Leiper had written Snyder and recommended Leib for the office.[3] Their respective choices as Speaker and Senator seemed to indicate that neither would be appointed; but the truth was far different. In voting for Boileau for Speaker his opponents had been tricked into a tacit certification of his good character. Therefore, they could hardly bring up the old charges against him as an objection to his being appointed Secretary of the Commonwealth. Thus, they were silent on December 20, 1808, when Snyder made the appointment as the first official act of his administration. However, the Leib faction did receive some recognition when James Engle was selected to succeed Boileau as Speaker.[4]

Soon afterward, the resignation of Samuel Maclay as United States Senator gave the Snyderites the opportunity to remove Leib from the legislature immediately. Maclay had opposed the embargo and had strongly supported Clinton in preference to Madison as President. His failure to be re-elected seemed to mark the legislature's disapproval of this conduct. Therefore, on January 4, 1809, he resigned, stating that it was his duty to give the legislature the privilege of electing someone more in accord with its views.[5]

Apart from such becoming deference to the theory of representation, Maclay also seems to have been motivated by the expectation of receiving the appointment as Surveyor General. His hopes did not appear to be groundless, for it had been Snyder's intention to offer him the office. However, something seems to have gone awry; and the *Aurora* reported on January 12, 1809, that Snyder had refused to commission him. A year later it was asserted by Snyder's opponents that Boileau and other State officials had feared Maclay's influence on the Governor and that Boileau had drafted a memorial against the appointment and had informed Snyder that it would be signed by every Democrat in the General Assembly unless the Maclay appointment was given up.[6]

Even before Maclay's resignation, Leib's supporters had foreseen the move that was planned. A meeting of the Democrats in the Northern Liberties on December 21, 1808, referring to rumors that Leib might be chosen to fill the vacancy occasioned by Maclay's resignation, protested against it on the grounds that they did not wish to be put to the expense of another election and that they wished him to continue in the legislature to push through certain reforms in the common law. They accordingly instructed the Philadelphia County delegation to oppose Leib's choice.[7]

Despite their plea, Leib was elected on January 9, 1809, to fill Maclay's unexpired term, and he resigned from the House two days later. Even this brief delay occasioned complaint from a correspondent in the *Democratic Press*. The Snyderites were evidently most anxious to get him out of the way.[8]

Although these events gave evidence that the Democratic division had not been eliminated by the campaign of 1808, there was on the surface no sign of any disunity. The new regime apparently began under the most auspicious circumstances.

Shortly after Snyder's election, William Findlay, the State Treasurer, wrote him and suggested that he be met by a military troop and be escorted by it into Lancaster on the occasion of his inauguration. Snyder refused the offer and wrote Boileau that he had done so "because I hate and despise all ostentation- pomp & parade, as anti democratic, my habits of life- the circle I have moved in unfit me for such an exhibition. I should feel extreemly [*sic*] awkward nay in pain during such a Cavalcade."[9] When his refusal became public, the *Aurora* praised him highly, asserting that perseverance in such principles would place him "upon an eminence, such as no man who has occupied the executive chair has yet obtained."[10]

The same simplicity was evident in his inaugural address. Dropping McKean's use of the term "gentlemen," he addressed the legislators as "fellow citizens." He approached his new duties, he said, with "diffidence and solicitude" and with the determination to promote the "Freedom, Honor, and Happiness of our Country." Voicing his gratitude for the confidence shown him in the election, he appealed for the "friendly aid" of the legislators, upon whose "wisdom, patriotism, and information" he felt he should heavily rely; and he expressed his hope of having "a perfect good understanding and harmonious intercourse" with them. He concluded by referring to the necessity of united support of the Federal government in the existing crisis in foreign affairs.[11]

Controlling the legislature and assured of a favorable reaction from the Governor, the Democrats set about enacting into law some of the objects they had sought unsuccessfully during McKean's administration. In this work Leib took a prominent part during the time that he was a member of the House.

One of the first measures sought was a revision of the libel law. Leib's resolution to appoint a committee to prepare a bill on the subject was adopted on December 21, 1808. He reported the bill as head of the committee on January 3, 1809, but it was not finally passed until March. The act forbade criminal prosecutions for publications respecting the official conduct of public officers or proceedings of the legislature, and it also directed that the truth might be pleaded in justification or given in evidence in any civil or criminal actions for libel. The act was limited to a term of three years.[12]

Another measure introduced by Leib was a bill defining contempts of court. Bearing on the matters in dispute in the Passmore Case, this act limited the summary power of judges in cases of contempt to misconduct of the officers of the court, negligence of or disobedience to its process, and misbehavior in the presence of the court. Publications on the conduct of the judges or of parties to any cause were not to be considered contempts; but any person feeling injured by such a publication might seek an indictment or bring a civil suit against the author or publisher, and a jury should decide in such cases. No contempts except those in open court were to be punished by imprisonment. The act was limited to a period of two years.[13]

Leib also offered a bill to prohibit the reading or quoting of foreign precedents or adjudications in the Pennsylvania courts. Sentiment was more divided on this measure; and after Leib's resignation the bill languished and was not passed.[14]

Two other important judicial measures were adopted during the session. The first of these was a further revision of the court system of the Commonwealth. The number of Supreme Court justices was reduced from four to three, and two additional districts for sessions of the court were established. At the same time the judges were relieved from the onerous duty of holding circuit courts in the counties. The second was an amendment to the arbitration act of 1806, making it and a supplement passed in 1808 perpetual and providing that arbitration would be used as a method of trial when demanded by either of the parties rather than both as had formerly been the case.[15]

The legislature also passed resolutions expressing support of the national administration and approval of the embargo. There was considerable debate in the House over the exact phrasing, but the resolutions gave unequivocal approbation to both. They were adopted in the House by a vote of 72-20 and in the Senate by a vote of 20-5. In each house the Federalist minority entered a protest which denounced the embargo as an ineffective method of coercion in international affairs and as an abandonment of American rights to free navigation of the seas. They also asserted a lack of confidence in the national administration.[16]

A further set of resolutions in support of the embargo and Jefferson's policies failed of adoption under peculiar circumstances. The evasions of the embargo had led to the passage of the Enforcement Act of January 9, 1809, which gave wide discretionary powers to customs officials to seize goods which they considered intended for export in violation of the law. The act had raised a storm of protest in New England, where town meetings adopted resolutions demanding that the enforcement of the embargo be resisted. The legislature of Massachusetts also made a strong report on the situation and recommended the passage of a law to protect the people of the state from unreasonable and arbitrary searches. Implicit in these resolutions was a threat of disunion and of forcible resistance to the embargo and its collateral acts.[17]

The occurrences in Massachusetts caused the Pennsylvania Senate on March 4, 1809, to adopt resolutions strongly supporting the Union and denouncing as "enemies and traitors" any who sought to dissolve it. Even before these were received by the House, there had been introduced in that body a still stronger set of resolutions. These reprobated the actions of the Massachusetts legislature, provided for the furnishing of troops to the Federal government to enforce the national laws, and opposed the repeal of the embargo. The House gave the resolutions a second reading on March 1, 1809; but there was no further action on them or on the Senate resolutions.[18]

The repeal of the embargo on March 1, 1809, may have been one reason for the dropping of the resolutions. However, it was probably due in greater measure to the fact that at this juncture Pennsylvania had herself become involved in open resistance to the enforcement of the decisions of the national judiciary.

II

The most important question before the legislature in the session of 1808-1809 was the Olmsted Case. It climaxed a dispute of thirty years over claims to a prize captured in the Revolution, and it also brought to a head long standing grievances between the State and the Federal judiciary over the alleged encroachments of the latter on the rights of the State. The affair was marked by dramatic circumstances involving armed resistance to the service of Federal court writs, and it ended with the ignominious defeat of the State. In politics the Olmsted Case served as the occasion for an open break between the Leib-Duane and the Snyder factions among the Democrats.

The Continental Congress on November 25, 1775, adopted resolutions recommending to the colonies that they establish admiralty courts and that such courts should try all cases by jury. It was also provided that appeals should be allowed to Congress in all such cases. On September 9, 1778, the Pennsylvania legislature passed an act establishing a court of admiralty and providing that the trials of all causes should be by jury, whose determination of facts should not be subject to appeal. Apart from this limitation, appeals were to be allowed to Congress in all cases.[19]

The act had hardly been passed before the admiralty court was faced with a trial on the case of the sloop *Active*. This was a British vessel which had sailed from Jamaica on August 1, 1778, with a cargo for New York. Included among those on board were four American seamen, prisoners of war—Gideon Olmsted, Artemas White, David Clarke, and Aquila Rumstead. Off the New Jersey coast on the night of September 6, these men, led by Olmsted, seized the vessel and drove the captain, crew, and passengers below. However, the captain wedged the rudder so that they were unable to sail the vessel into Egg Harbor as they had planned. Consequently, they remained off the coast until the morning of September 8.

At that time the Pennsylvania state brigantine *Convention,* commanded by Captain Thomas Houston, boarded the *Active*. Over the protests of Olmsted and his companions, who claimed they needed no assistance, Houston took charge of the vessel and sent it into Philadelphia as a prize. A Philadelphia privateer, *Le Gerard,* was also in sight at the time of the capture and thus had a claim to a share in the capture.

The cause was tried before the Pennsylvania admiralty court on November 4, 1778. The jury decided that Olmsted had not completely subdued the vessel and decreed that he and his companions should receive only a quarter of the proceeds. The remainder was awarded to Houston and Captain Josiah, who had commanded *Le Gerard*. Eventually, this was divided so that a quarter went to the State as owner of the *Convention,* a quarter went to Houston and the crew, and a quarter was given to Josiah.

Olmsted appealed the decision to Congress, which referred the matter to a committee. After reviewing the case, the committee on December 15, 1778, annulled the award of the Pennsylvania court and decreed that all the proceeds should go to Olmsted and his companions. However, George Ross, judge of the admiralty court, felt that he was bound by the Pennsylvania law and refused to obey the directive of the committee of appeals because it reversed the finding of the jury.

The committee then referred the question to Congress. That body on March 6, 1779, upheld the committee's decision. It averred that Congress had the sovereign power of war and peace; that the execution of the law of nations was an incident of such power; that questions of capture must be decided by the law of nations; that control by appeal was necessary to insure uniformity of decision; and that decisions on appeals must necessarily extend to both law and fact.

The Pennsylvania legislature saw the matter differently. It was perfectly willing to concede that a decision by a jury might not be desirable in admiralty cases, and it cheerfully recognized the right of Congress under the Articles of Confederation to decide finally on all appeals in such matters. However, it held that this had no bearing on the case of the *Active*. The Articles of Confederation had not been adopted at that time; and the case was governed by the Pennsylvania act of September 9, 1778, and the congressional resolution of November 25, 1775, upon which the act was based. Under these, Congress had no authority to reverse the findings of a jury; and Pennsylvania absolutely refused to comply with the decision of the committee of appeals. Matters were thus deadlocked, since Congress was unable to enforce its view.

Meanwhile, a new complication had been added. Judge Ross had insisted that he be given a bond of indemnity by those to whom he paid the proceeds of the sale of the *Active* and its cargo. David Rittenhouse, the Pennsylvania State Treasurer, made such a bond on May 1, 1779, for the quarter-share belonging to the Commonwealth. When he left office, however, Rittenhouse retained the loan certificates in which the share had been paid and refused to turn them over to the State until he was released from his bond.

Olmsted then began to seek the money through the State courts and won a judgment against the administrators of Ross's estate. The administrators in turn entered suit against Rittenhouse to recover on the bond of indemnity. The case was argued before the State Supreme Court and decided in April, 1792. The court unanimously ruled that Olmsted's action against Ross and the subsequent case against Rittenhouse could not be sustained because neither the State courts of common pleas nor the Supreme Court had jurisdiction in admiralty matters.

The justices differed, however, in their views on the merits of Olmsted's claims. McKean, then Chief Justice, upheld the State's view. He asserted that Congress and the State had the power to alter the law of nations and that they had done so in providing for jury trial in cases of capture. With jury trial established, both the common law and the Pennsylvania statute forbade a change in the findings of fact by a jury. However unwise this change to jury trial may have been, it had been made; and the decree of the committee of appeals was therefore "extrajudicial, erroneous and void." On the other hand, the associate judges, Jasper Yeates and Edward Shippen, were inclined to adopt the views of Congress.[20]

In 1795 the United States Supreme Court gave its decision in the case of *Penhallow* et al. v. *Doane's Administrators*. The circumstances were similar to those in the Olmsted matter. A capture decided in the New Hampshire courts had been appealed to Congress in violation of the state law. The congressional committee of appeals reversed the decision of the state courts; but New Hampshire would not abide by the decree. After the adoption of the Articles of Confederation, the case was brought before the Court of Appeals established under it; and in 1783 that court also ruled against the state and upheld the jurisdiction of the committee of appeals. New Hampshire still refused to conform to the decision.

After the adoption of the new constitution the case was brought before the Federal courts and reached the Supreme Court on appeal. In deciding upon the matter, the justices unanimously agreed that the decision of the Court of Appeals under the Confederation was final, since that was a court of last resort and competent to determine its own jurisdiction. The majority of the justices were also inclined to support the authority of the committee of appeals, although they made no unequivocal ruling on the matter. However, the question had been decided by the Court of Appeals, so that the decision in *Penhallow* v. *Doane* amounted to a tacit recognition of the authority of the committee of appeals.[21]

For several years there were no new developments in the Olmsted affair. Rittenhouse died in 1796, and his heirs continued to hold the certificates. In February, 1801, the Pennsylvania legislature passed an act authorizing the State Treasurer to receive these funds from the heirs and after receipt to furnish them with a bond of indemnity. Although the preamble stated that Rittenhouse's heirs had declared their willingness to do so since Rittenhouse's bond to Ross was reported to be lost, the transfer did not take place, possibly because the bond of indemnity was not in fact lost.[22]

Olmsted and his associates now entered suit in the United States District Court in Philadelphia against Elizabeth Sergeant and Esther Waters, Rittenhouse's executrices. The case was decided by Judge Richard Peters on January 14, 1803. His opinion ignored the question of the validity of the original decision. In his view that had been determined by the Court of Appeals. The main question as he saw it was the ownership of the funds; and he ruled that Rittenhouse, and later his heirs, were in the position of stakeholders "liable to pay over the deposit to those lawfully entitled thereto." He therefore decreed that the certificates with accumulated interest should be paid over to Olmsted.[23]

The decision immediately aroused opposition. Governor McKean transmitted it to the legislature on January 31, 1803, with the following remarks:

> Having had knowledge of the cause and all the circumstances attending it twenty-four years ago, I cannot in duty to the commonwealth, silently acquiesce in some of the former or late proceedings therein. By the ingenuity exercised in this business, an act of Congress, an act of the General Assembly of the state, and a verdict of a jury, are held for nought; by a strained construction, the Treasurer of the state is converted into a stake-holder, a sentence given in favor of the libellants, without any summons, notice to, or hearing of the commonwealth of Pennsylvania, the other real party whose interest may be thereby affected to the amount of near fifteen thousand dollars.

The Governor went on to say that the Commonwealth could not appeal since it had not been made a party to the suit; and if it had been made a party the case would have been thrown out since under the Eleventh Amendment a state could not be sued by citizens of another state. He felt that resistance would be "extremely disagreeable," but he thought it his duty to lay the matter before the legislature "for advice and direction."[24]

In response to McKean's message, the House appointed a committee to consider the matter. On March 23, 1803, it reported a bill. The preamble reviewed the circumstances in the case and proclaimed that the decree of the committee of appeals was illegal and void. Likewise, it asserted that Rittenhouse had not been a stakeholder but had been an agent of the State. Hence, the State was the real party to the suit; but since it could not be sued, Peters had illegally usurped and exercised jurisdiction in the affair.

The first section of the act required the Governor to direct the Attorney General to apply to Mrs. Sergeant and Mrs. Waters for the funds and to enter legal proceedings to recover them if they should refuse. The second section provided that the executrices should receive a bond of indemnity if they complied with the requisition. It also required the Governor

> to protect the just rights of the state in the premises, by any further means and measures that he may deem necessary for the purpose, and also to protect the persons and properties of the said Elizabeth Sergeant and Esther Waters from any process whatever issued out of any federal court in consequence of their obedience to the requisition. . . .

In the House the second section was adopted by a record vote of 64-6; and the whole bill was finally passed by a vote of 66-6. In all, 67 Republicans and one Federalist voted for the bill and six Federalists voted against it. In the Senate the measure was adopted 19-2, with seventeen Republicans and two Federalists for it and two Federalists against it. The act was signed by McKean on April 2, 1803.[25]

This action met the entire approbation of the *Aurora*. In its view, Peters had usurped jurisdiction since the State was the real defendant. It applauded the efforts of the legislature to prevent "incipient encroachments of the federal judiciary" and avowed that the "spiritt [*sic*] of the union" and the "liberties of the people" would be destroyed if the courts "under the insidious cover of legal forms and technical decisions, can legislate for the separate states, or set aside their legislative acts, or bring state independency under the controul of jurisdiction."[26]

The forthright opposition of Pennsylvania had its effect. The heirs of Rittenhouse turned the money over to the State; and the district court forbore to take further action in the matter. It seemed that the encroachments of the judiciary on the rights of the State had been effectively stopped. However, there were other areas of conflict.

One of these concerned disputed land titles in northwestern Pennsylvania under the State law of April 3, 1792. The matter was a complex one, but the full details need not be considered here. Essentially, it was a quarrel over the titles of the Holland Land Company, the Pennsylvania Population Company, and other speculators to certain tracts which they claimed under warrants issued by the State. These tracts had been entered upon by "actual settlers" or "intruders," who claimed that the rights of the warrantees had lapsed because they had not carried out the provisions of the act with respect to settlement and residence within the specified time.[27]

The warrantees argued that because of an Indian uprising these requirements had been superseded by the proviso in the ninth section of the act. This stated that if settlement had been prevented "by force of arms of the enemies of the *United States*," referring to the Indians, and the settler or warrantee had persisted in his efforts to make the settlement that "he and his heirs shall be entitled to have and to hold such lands, in the same manner, as if the actual settlement had been made and continued."[28]

The disputes over these lands were bitter and had an important effect upon politics in that section of the State. The matter was also agitated in the legislature, which was inclined to sympathize with the views of the actual settlers. The Pennsylvania Supreme Court, while holding that the title to each tract must be decided upon its merits, ruled that mere prevention of settlement did not give title but simply extended the period within which the required settlement and residence might be made. In all cases, the court held, these requirements must be met before the title was valid.[29]

This ruling would have been decisive except that the Holland Land Company, being owned by foreigners, could bring the question before the Federal courts; and it did so in the case of *Huidekoper's Lessee* v. *Douglass,* an action to eject an intruder from lands claimed by the company. On February 27, 1805, John Marshall delivered the opinion of the United States Supreme Court and ruled that prevention did operate to give title and dispensed with the requirements for settle ment and residence.[30]

A modern historian of the Supreme Court has concluded that Marshall's construction of the law in this case was "exceedingly strained." The Pennsylvania legislature at the time felt the same way. In March 1805, it adopted resolutions giving approval to a constitutional amendment proposed by Kentucky to prevent the Federal courts from taking jurisdiction in disputes over land claims within the states. It prefaced the resolutions with a preamble which noted the necessity for uniformity of decisions in suits involving land titles, pointed out that not all claimants were able to avail themselves of the Federal courts and asserted that the judges of the State courts had more knowledge of and were better able to decide questions on land titles within the State.[32]

These resolutions were mild compared to those adopted in March 1807. The latter were reported in the House of Representatives by committee headed by Abner Lacock, a resident of Beaver County, which lay within the region affected by the decision. The preamble avowed that the lands in question really belonged to the State; that the State was therefore a party to any suits concerning them; and that consequently under the Constitution as amended the Federal courts had no jurisdiction. It went on to assert that if the State could not dispose of its own lands and enforce its own contracts in its own courts but must submit to the Federal courts it was "no longer sovereign and independent."

In harmony with the preamble, the resolutions then declared flatly that the Federal courts could exercise no jurisdiction in any case arising under the act of April 3, 1792, and directed that copies of the resolutions be sent to the judges of the United States Supreme Court and to the Federal marshal and judge of the district of Pennsylvania. These resolutions were adopted by both houses, but, as previously noted, they were vetoed by McKean.[33]

While the State was thus aroused over the encroachments of the Federal judiciary in the matter of the northwestern lands, a new dispute arose between the State and the national government over their respective claims to the property of a bankrupt. William Nicholl, who served as clerk of the mayor's court in Philadelphia from 1788 to 1794, was found to be delinquent in his accounts by nearly $8,00 when they were settled by the Comptroller General in 1797. He appealed the settlement to the Supreme Court; but in September, 1802, the court awarded the Commonwealth the amount claimed with accrued interest.

In the meantime, Nicholls had become United States Collector of Internal Revenue and became delinquent to the amount of more than $29,000. In June, 1798, he executed a mortgage for the sum to William Miller for the use of the United States; and in March, 1802, the State Supreme Court awarded Miller a judgment on the mortgage. The property of Nicholls was subsequently sold; and the proceeds, amounting to $14,530, were deposited with the Prothonotary of the Supreme Court. In May, 1802, Nicholls made a voluntary assignment of all his property to his creditors and thus became a bankrupt.

Both Pennsylvania and the United States claimed the money deposited with the Supreme Court. The State asserted that under the terms of an act of February 18, 1785, a lien on Nicholl's property was created from the moment that the Comptroller General found him in default in 1797 and that this lien existed prior to the execution of the mortgage to Miller and the subsequent assignment of his property to his creditors. In March, 1805, Joseph B. McKean, the Attorney General, moved before the Supreme Court that cause be shown why the sum due to the State should not be paid.

Dallas, as United States District Attorney, filed an objection, citing an act of Congress of March 3, 1797, which provided that claims of the United States should have priority of settlement in cases of insolvency. The court took the matter under consideration and in September, 1805, ruled in favor of the State. The money stayed in the court, however, because the case was appealed to the High Court of Errors and Appeals; but this appeal was quashed in July, 1808. Dallas then appealed the matter to the United States Supreme Court in December, 1808; and a citation was issued to the Governor and Attorney General of Pennsylvania to appear in the case. Snyder sent these documents to the legislature on January 14, 1809.[34]

On the same day the House referred the message to a committee headed by Charles Smith, a Federalist attorney from Lancaster. Three days later Smith offered the report of the committee. After reviewing the facts in the case, the report asserted that a precedent dangerous to the sovereignty of the State might be established by taking part in the suit. The committee felt that the State's right to the money was unquestionable; that it was inexpedient to take any notice of the writ of error; and that the Federal act of March 3, 1797, could not impair the rights of the State. It concluded by offering a resolution to appoint a committee to prepare a bill directing that the money be paid into the State Treasury.

This resolution was adopted on January 19, 1809, by a vote of 82-6; and the matter was referred to the same committee. Smith, for the committee, reported a bill on January 21. The first of its three sections directed that the Prothonotary of the Supreme Court pay the money into the State Treasury; the second, like the provision in the act of April 2, 1803, in the Olmsted Case, instructed the Governor to protect the rights of the State by such means as he deemed necessary and also to protect the Prothonotary from any judicial process issued by the Federal courts; and the third provided that copies of the act should be sent to the judges of the United States Supreme Court.

The House adopted the first section on January 25 by a vote of 78-11. Two Democrats from Fayette County then offered a substitute for the second section providing that the State should indemnify the Prothonotary in any suit and directing the Governor to pay such claims from the Treasury. This was defeated by 75 votes to thirteen. The section was then amended by striking out the more bellicose portions and adopted. The third section was also approved. On the following day the measure passed its third reading by a vote of 77-13 and was sent to the Senate. The opposition to its passage came from seven Federalists and six Democrats.

The Senate adopted the first section by a vote of 17-11, but it struck out the other two. The amended bill was then passed on February 1 1809, and returned to the House, which concurred in the changes made by the Senate. In its final form the act asserted flatly that the State had never given up to the Federal government its right to enforce collection of its own revenues and that it was not "willing to ascribe to the federal court, by mere implication and in destruction of such preexisting right of the state government, a power which would involve such a consequence."[35]

While the Nicholls affair was occupying the attention of the legislature, there were new developments taking place in the Olmsted Case. In March, 1808, the United States Supreme Court, acting upon a request of Olmsted, ordered Judge Peters to show cause why a writ of mandamus should not issue to compel the enforcement of his decree of January, 1803, against the heirs of Rittenhouse. Peters replied in a letter that "an act of the legislature of Pennsylvania had commanded the governor of that state to call out an armed force to prevent the execution of any process to enforce the performance of the sentence." He would not, therefore, do anything further in the matter unless directed to do so by the Supreme Court.[36]

Marshall delivered the decision of the Supreme Court on the Olmsted Case on February 20, 1809, at a time when the Federal government was being defied on the enforcement of the embargo by the New England states. Noting that Peters had cited the act of the legislature as his reason for not enforcing the decree, Marshall observed that the Constitution would become a "solemn mockery" if the legislatures were able at will to annul the judgments of the Federal courts. He also reprobated the attempt of Pennsylvania to decide upon the jurisdiction of the national courts. That power, he said, rested only with the Supreme Court.

Turning to the matter of Federal jurisdiction in the case, he ruled that the State had no title to the funds because the Court of Appeals had reversed the decision of the Pennsylvania admiralty court. Furthermore, the State had never had possession of the funds. Rittenhouse had retained them in his own name until the State should indemnify him for the personal bond he had executed to Ross. On his death, the funds had passed to his descendants just like any other property. Since Pennsylvania neither possessed nor had a right to the funds and since it was not a party to the suit, Marshall held that the Eleventh Amendment did not apply and that Pennsylvania had "no constitutional right to resist the legal process which may be directed in this cause." He therefore ordered that a peremptory mandamus be issued to Judge Peters to enforce his sentence of January, 1803.[37]

The Olmsted affair now began to move to a climax. John Sergeant, stepson of Elizabeth Sergeant, wrote Snyder on February 24, 1809, informing him of the decision and stating that it was necessary that the Governor take steps to protect the executrices from the process of the Federal court. Three days later Snyder reported the situation to the General Assembly and announced that it was his duty to protect the ladies under the terms of the act of April 2, 1803. Since he had no other means at his disposal, he was making arrangements to call out a portion of the militia, though the necessity was "painful" to him. On the same day he issued orders to Brigadier General Michael Bright to place in readiness enough of the Philadelphia militia to carry out the mission.[38]

The House immediately referred the message to a committee headed by Jacob Mitchell, a Democrat from the city of Philadelphia. Charles Smith, the Federalist who had taken such a prominent part in the Nicholls affair, was also a member. On March 1, 1809, after some dispute over whether the request should be sent to the Governor or the Secretary of the Commonwealth, the House unanimously adopted a resolution requesting the Secretary to furnish it with full information on the calling out of the militia. Snyder's orders to Bright were accordingly sent to the House the next day.

The committee on March 10, 1809, reported a preamble and six resolutions. The preamble gave a detailed review of the Olmsted Case and defended the State's position in the matter. The resolutions dealt with the wider problem of Federal and State relations. The legislature expressed a perfect willingness to submit to national authority exercised under the delegated powers of the general government, but it asserted that it could not permit the Federal courts to infringe upon the rights of the State.

The resolutions recognized that it was difficult to set precise limits to the powers of the State and Federal governments and "lamented" that "an impartial tribunal" to decide such disputes did not exist. Under the circumstances the states were left with the undesirable alternatives of resisting judicial encroachments by force or of submitting in all cases. Such submission could only result in the eventual destruction of state independence and sovereignty and a consequent loss of liberty by the people. To remedy this situation, the fifth resolution instructed the Pennsylvania delegation in Congress to sponsor a constitutional amendment providing for the creation of a tribunal to decide conflicts between the state and federal governments.

The sixth resolution directed the Governor to send a copy of the resolutions to the President to be laid before Congress. It also required him to correspond with the President on the existing dispute "and to agree to such arrangements as may be in the power of the Executive to make, or that Congress may make, either by the appoint ment of commissioners or otherwise, for settling the difficulties between the two governments."

The report was given its second reading on March 16, 1809; and a bitter struggle over its provisions was begun. The opponents of the measure first introduced a substitute requiring the Governor to draw money from the Treasury and pay it to settle the claim of Olmsted. This was defeated by a vote of 68-15. The minority was made up of thirteen Federalists and two Democrats, one each from the city and county of Philadelphia. The majority comprised five Federalists and 63 Democrats, including two from the city and four from the county of Philadelphia.

The opposition then offered a resolution to repeal the act of April 2, 1803, to indemnify Mrs. Sergeant and Mrs. Waters, and to bring the whole question before the United States Supreme Court. This was defeated without a record vote. Disgusted at the way matters were proceeding, Charles Miner, a Federalist from Luzerne County, then offered a resolution stating that Pennsylvania would resist the execution of the court's decree "at every hazard." This was defeated 82-1, with Richard O'Brien, a Democrat from the city of Philadelphia making up the minority. His vote was hardly sincere, since he had favored payment of the claim and opposed adoption of the committee's report.

The Senate had appointed its own committee on the matter; and the committee on March 6, 1809, had reported a preamble and resolutions essentially the same as those in the House. There was no further action, however, until the House resolutions were received on March 17, 1809. After being amended in committee of the whole, the resolutions were considered on March 23. The opposition here also tried to push through a resolution directing the Governor to pay the claim. It was defeated 19-11. The minority included seven Federalists, two Quids, and two Democrats. The majority was made up of three Quids and sixteen Democrats. An attempt to repeal the act of 1803 failed by a similar majority. On the same day the Senate approved all the resolutions and returned them to the House with two amendments, the first of which was the inclusion of a long preamble and the second was an instruction to the Governor to send copies of the resolutions to all the states. The House concurred on March 28; and the Governor approved the resolutions on April 3, 1809.[39]

While the legislature was occupied with these matters, the affair was arousing considerable interest in Philadelphia. The *Aurora* late in December had given some attention to the Olmsted claim and had favored payment as a matter of justice.[40] While this view may have been entirely sincere, it is odd that a similar conviction had not been manifested earlier when the Olmsted affair was under discussion; and it may have been a clever maneuver on the part of Duane to justify a break with Snyder when the case was decided by the Supreme Court.

When Snyder's message was sent to the legislature, the *Aurora* remarked that "infatuation and folly" had spread from Boston to Lancaster. The Governor, it said, was sworn to obey the State law which authorized the calling out of the militia, but he was also sworn to obey the national laws. Then, in blithe disregard of its views in 1803, the paper described the act of April 2, 1803, as "an *ex post facto* law, produced by intrigue to cover injustice." It went on to argue for the validity of Olmsted's claim.[41]

The *Democratic Press* asserted that the law compelled Snyder to adopt the course he had taken, but it expressed a belief that the legislature would take such action that Pennsylvania would not "in the present crisis" be found among "the disorganizing states." It concluded, however, by supporting the State's view of its right to the prize money.[42]

The *United States' Gazette* felt that Snyder was doing what the law required but believed that the Federal decree would be enforced and that there would be "serious consequences." Two weeks later it asserted that resistance to the decree was treason. However, it showed considerable inconsistency on the following day by praising the report of the House committee, which it attributed to Charles Smith.[43]

There was really no important development in the affair until March 24, 1809, when Judge Peters issued writs against Mrs. Sergeant and Mrs. Waters. On the same day Bright called into service a detachment of fourteen men to protect them. The next day Marshal John Smith attempted to serve the process and was prevented from doing so by the drawn bayonets of the guard. Smith took down the names of the guards for the purpose of charging them with treason, and he began to make preparations for calling out a posse to help enforce the court's decree.[44]

The *Democratic Press* was alarmed by these developments and deplored that such a situation had arisen. It avowed that it would have been pleased if the legislature could have adopted some method of settling the matter, but it doubted that anything would be done since three-fourths of the members felt that it was a question of principle.[45]

The events in Philadelphia seem to have had a chastening effect on the legislature. Charles Smith, on March 28, 1809, introduced a bill appropriating $18,000 for the use of the Governor in carrying out the provisions of the act of April 2, 1803, or of the resolutions just adopted by the legislature. When it came up for consideration on April 1, 1809, attempts were made to amend it so as to provide specifically for the payment of the money to settle Olmsted's claim, but these were defeated. The bill passed both houses on April 3, the day before adjournment; and the Governor signed it on April 4, 1809.[46]

The responsibility for the affair now rested wholly with Snyder. Although the legislature had not instructed him to pay the claim, it had made it possible for him to do so. John Sergeant wrote him and complained that the methods thus far used for the protection of the two ladies had caused them considerable annoyance. They had been kept virtual prisoners and had been forced to witness considerable disorder and turmoil. Sergeant went on to hint strongly that the legislature had now provided a means by which the matter could be settled more satisfactorily.[47]

Snyder had Boileau reply to this letter. He regretted that the ladies had been inconvenienced, but he was not yet convinced that the course he had adopted was incorrect. He felt that it would be premature to use the discretionary power to pay the claim at this time, as he had hopes that a settlement could be arrived at through negotiations with the President.[48]

Snyder wrote Madison on April 7, 1809, and sent him copies of the legislature's resolutions and of the act of April 4, 1809. In the letter Snyder averred that Madison with his knowledge of the Constitution and his desire to protect the sovereignty of the states would "justly discriminate" between opposition to the Constitution and laws and resistance to "the decree of a judge, founded, as it is conceived, in an usurpation of power and jurisdiction." He also suggested that he and Madison might settle the matter in a manner "equally honorable to them both."[49]

Madison's reply quickly dissipated Snyder's hopes of aid from that quarter. He pointed out that the President had no authority to prevent the execution of a court decree but was specifically enjoined to enforce it where resistance was made. On the other hand, Madison felt it was a "propitious circumstance" that the act of the legislature made it possible for Snyder to remove the "existing difficulty."[50]

In Philadelphia the "Fort Rittenhouse" affair moved seriocomically to its conclusion. A near riot resulted on March 26, 1809, when one of a mob who were insulting the guards was wounded by a bayonet. Two weeks later Marshal Smith gained entrance into Mrs. Sergeant's house only to have her escape while he attempted to pacify the children who were frightened by his appearance. A grand jury on April 12, 1809, indicted Bright and eight of his men and bound them over to appear before the United States Circuit Court. Meanwhile, Marshal Smith was busily engaged in serving summonses for a posse to assemble on April 18, 1809. These summonses were issued to more than 2,000 people; and Smith seems to have taken care to serve them on the same persons that Bright would have called for duty in the militia.[51]

An open collision was avoided, however, when the Marshal managed to serve the writs on the morning of April 15, 1809, by going through alleys and over fences to effect an entrance from the rear of the houses. The *Aurora* hinted that this had been arranged by collusion between Smith and the guards, but Dallas later denied this. On the other hand, there does seem to be some reason to suspect that there may have been some co-operation from members of Mrs. Sergeant's family.[52]

After the arrest of Mrs. Sergeant and Mrs. Waters, the State Attorney General, Walter Franklin, applied to William Tilghman of the State Supreme Court for a writ of habeas corpus. When the writ was denied, the money was paid over by the State; and the ladies were freed from arrest.[53] The affair was concluded on May 2, 1809, by the trial and conviction of Bright and his men for resisting the service of the writs. The former was sentenced to three months in prison and fined $200, while the latter escaped with one month's imprisonment and a fine of $50. All, however, were pardoned by Madison within a week.[54]

This ended Pennsylvania's most determined struggle for state rights. Her attempts to resist the alleged encroachments of the Federal judiciary had only brought humiliation, and she was forced to give a grudging acquiescence. The affair was concluded so far as it involved the State and Federal governments, but it was to remain a live issue in State politics for another year.

III

State politics in 1809 centered largely about the fight in Philadelphia between the Leib-Duane group and the followers of Snyder led by Binns. The avowed issue was the Olmsted Case; but personal resentments and patronage were probably of equal or greater importance in causing the split.

From the very beginning the *Aurora* had opposed Snyder's course in the Olmsted affair. At first it had shown a disposition to spare him and to blame his advisors, who, it claimed, had connived with Charles Smith to deceive the Governor on the legal aspects of the case. However, on April 11, 1809, the paper, in an article headed "Put the Saddle on the Right Horse," laid the responsibility squarely on Snyder and exonerated the legislature. According to the *Aurora*, Snyder had acted without informing the legislature; and the members were reluctant to disavow his actions after they were taken. Though Snyder was perhaps ill-advised, he had selected his own advisors and could not shift the blame. The same theme was developed at greater length six days later. From this time on the paper assailed Snyder and his supporters without reserve.[55]

Duane's reasons for this course were probably very mixed. For one thing, he was sincerely interested in the success of the embargo and had been excoriating the Massachusetts legislature for opposition to its enforcement. Sheer consistency demanded that he uphold the Federal government against the State in a similar question in Pennsylvania. Despite the inconsistency of his views on the Olmsted Case in 1803 and 1809, he must, therefore, be credited with a large measure of sincerity.

On the other hand, he was much interested in the political advantages to be gained from such a course. His strategy was easily apparent. In order not to alienate the great body of the legislature and the Democratic Party, he constantly insisted that the affair could not be blamed upon them but only upon a small clique consisting of Snyder and his advisors. At the same time, he hoped that his support of the Federal government would enable his faction to make a strong alliance with the national administration in opposition to the Snyderites.

Duane's official thesis that the legislature and the body of the Democrats opposed Snyder's course did not really square with the facts; and there was considerable danger that his opposition to the State's view in the Olmsted Case might result in the isolation of his faction rather than in its gaining control of the party. He therefore asked Madison to pardon Bright and his men quickly in order to frustrate those "seeking to engender feuds and divisions" out of the case. He also hinted that he would like to deliver the pardon himself.[56] The hint was ignored; but it is obvious that Duane would have benefited greatly if it had been successful. He would have received credit for the pardoning; he would have appeared as the particular favorite of the administration; and Dallas would have been discredited because the administration had not sent the pardon through him.

Duane also had personal reasons for coming out in open opposition to Snyder. In the first place, the Governor had refused to quash the libel suits instituted by Yrujo in 1806. Snyder claimed that he did not have the authority to do so; but Duane's friends doubted that he would have held the same view if Binns had been involved. Besides this matter, Duane was probably disgruntled because Snyder had chosen Boileau rather than Leib as Secretary of the Commonwealth and had generally failed to conduct affairs in the way Duane desired.[57]

Leib's opposition to Snyder was apparently based purely on political and personal considerations. In two letters to Jonathan Roberts, Jr., he denounced Snyder savagely but did not so much as mention the Olmsted Case. Instead, he castigated the Governor for his appointments in Philadelphia, his failure to quash Duane's libel suits, and his alleged dishonesty to Leib in denying responsibility for the establishment of the *Democratic Press*.[58]

Whatever political advantage Duane and Leib expected to gain from the Olmsted affair, Snyder and his supporters were not disposed to retreat from their position. The *Democratic Press* took its stand by calling upon the people and the legislature to continue their fight against such usurpations until the rights of the States were secured against such "daring bare-faced attacks."[59]

Public support was reflected by the dinner given in honor of Bright and his men on May 25, 1809. Although it was organized largely by the Snyderites, there were among the 300 present such stalwart supporters of Leib as William Binder and Frederick Wolbert. Snyder did not attend but sent a letter praising highly the efforts of Bright and the militiamen to uphold the rights of the State.[60] The Snyderites were apparently more than willing to wage the campaign on the issue of state rights.

As a matter of fact, although the *Aurora* continued to stress the issue and announced that it was the sole issue in the election, it really seems to have been given little consideration. None of the public meetings made any declaration on the subject; and a number of the candidates supported by the *Aurora* had certainly favored Snyder's actions by their votes in the legislature or by attending the dinner to Bright. On the whole, the campaign appears to have been waged almost entirely on a factional and personal basis.

In the city the "Patent Democrats," as the *Aurora* dubbed the Snyderites, made a determined effort to win control of the general ward committee. They were soundly defeated, however, by the Leib-Duane group, who now began to call themselves the "Old School Democrats." Despite their lack of success, the Snyderites did not run an opposition ticket in the city.[61]

No such mildness marked the campaign in the county. Because the *Aurora* was spending so much time on national affairs, Leib's supporters decided to establish their own newspaper to carry on the fight against the Snyderites with more intensity. This new organ was a weekly called the *Pennsylvania Democrat,* which began publication on August 11, 1809. Oddly enough, its editor was Joseph Lloyd, the man who had published the pamphlet denouncing Leib in 1807 and who had publicly refused to obey the summons to serve in the marshal's posse in the Olmsted Case.[62]

The objectives of the paper were stated clearly in its prospectus. Its principal object was to be an attack on Snyder and his administration. In particular, Lloyd avowed the intention of unmasking Boileau and the other "silly, unprincipled, intriguing sycophants who govern the governor: the little squad into whose hands Simon Snyder, from consciousness of his own incapacity, has surrendered the reins of the government of Pennsylvania." He hoped for the support of the people because, excepting for the *Aurora,* Snyder and his clique had bribed the Democratic papers through patronage. In evidence of this premise, he referred to the appointments given to the editors of the Pittsburgh *Commonwealth,* the Easton *Northampton Farmer,* the *Carlisle Gazette,* and the German Democratic paper in Philadelphia.[63]

Avowing such an object, the paper maintained a running fire of scurrility against Snyder and his supporters. The Harrisburg *Dauphin Guardian* censured it for *"venom* and *envy";* and the *Commonwealth* said its prospectus was filled with "shameful & gross libels." To the *Democratic Press* it was a "filthy sewer . . . created to carry off the dregs and dirty water of the *Aurora."* In one instance, Leib's followers altered a letter taken from a pamphlet on Binns's treason trial in 1798 in such fashion as to make it appear that Binns had betrayed James Coigley, a Catholic priest, in order to save his own neck. Though Lloyd was not himself aware of the deception when he published the letter, the incident is indicative of the character of the material printed in the paper.[64]

The Democratic general county meeting was held on September 4, 1809, and seems to have been marked by considerable violence. Leib's supporters put him in the chair; but his right to the seat was challenged by Jacob Holgate on the ground that Leib was no longer a resident of the county but lived in the city. This occasioned a disturbance, in the course of which Leib and the speaker's platform were upset. However, he finally gained recognition as the presiding officer and, according to the *Democratic Press,* pushed through his program without regard to the opposition. The *Aurora* denied these charges and also the accusation that Leib had been forced to flee from the meeting after adjournment in order to avoid insult and injury.[65]

Defeated in their attempt to gain control of the general county meeting, the Snyderites fell back on the district delegate system. A meeting at Germantown on September 16, 1809, presided over by Jacob Holgate, issued a call for the election of district delegates and published an address to the electors of the county. The address denounced the continuance of the general county meeting plan and particularly the intrigues which had taken place under it. It excoriated the Old School for the attempt to put down Snyder and announced their own loyalty to him. Finally, it assailed the meeting on September 4 because Leib, a nonresident of the county, presided and because as chairman he had selected the committees which nominated the assembly candidates and the conferees.[66] Other Snyderite district meetings were held, and their delegates met on September 27. They adopted a ticket which differed from that of the Old School only in two candidates for assembly and in one of the senatorial nominations.[67]

While these Democratic squabbles were taking place, the Federalists were beginning to show an unwonted skill in political organization. Taking a page out of Dallas's book in 1805, they formed an "American Republican Society" with branches in each ward of the city and in the election districts of the county. Using this title, they adopted nearly all the Democratic machinery. In the city they held ward meetings and chose a general ward committee, which they called the "ward conferees." In the county they used the district delegate system to make nominations. The conferee plan was also used to select candidates for Congress and the State Senate. The only Democratic device they ignored was the town meeting to approve the ticket adopted by the general ward committee.[68]

Because the Federalist senatorial ticket contained one name backed by the Snyderites, the *Aurora* insinuated that the two had made a deal whereby the Federalists would back a senatorial candidate favorable to Snyder in return for Snyderite opposition to the rest of the Democratic ticket. The *Democratic Press* quickly pointed out that the Federalist ticket also had a senatorial candidate supported by the Old School and went on to note that two of the Old School candidates for the Senate had favored Snyder in the Olmsted Case.[69]

The election returns failed to support the charges of the *Aurora*. The total vote in the city was about 900 less than 1808; but the Democratic ticket won in every instance, though by narrower majorities. In the county the vote dropped even more sharply, being nearly 2,000 less than in the preceding year. The relative strength of the parties and factions in the county was shown in the assembly race. Democratic candidates supported by both Snyderites and the Old School averaged about 2,860 votes, over 1,500 votes less than in 1808. The Federalist candidates polled an average of 1,016 votes, 400 fewer than in the previous election. The two Old School nominees received 1,729 and 1,724 votes compared to 1,230 and 1,176 by the opposing Snyderites. Despite its victory, the Old School had won by a comparatively small margin, and it was apparently losing its dominance in county politics.[70]

Although the *Aurora* hailed the results of the election as a repudiation of Snyder's conduct in the Olmsted Case, such a conclusion was unwarranted in Philadelphia; and it was certainly untrue in the rest of the State. Other papers in the State gave very little prominence to the matter, and it apparently did not figure in the various local splits which appeared. There were factional quarrels in Dauphin and Allegheny counties based upon personalities; but the only issue of any importance in the State outside Philadelphia was the renewed demand for constitutional revision which appeared in Washington and Greene counties. This does not seem to have had any significant support elsewhere.[71]

The election left the Democratic strength in the legislature virtually unchanged. The party elected all nine of the new Senators and 73 of the 95 Representatives. The Federalists carried Luzerne, Adams, and Delaware counties and won a few seats from Bucks, Lancaster, and Erie. The Quids showed revived local strength in Berks, Westmoreland, Armstrong, Indiana, and Lancaster counties and captured eleven seats in the House.[72]

Snyder's first year in office had not been a happy one. The fight he had waged for state rights in the Olmsted Case had resulted only in an ignominious defeat, which damaged his prestige. At the same time, it had furnished an opportunity for a renewed attack by the Leib-Duane faction. Led by the *Aurora*, that faction had solemnly vowed that Snyder should "never again be the candidate of the democracy of Pennsylvania."[73] The events of the next two years were to prove this a very poor prophecy.

GOVERNOR SIMON SNYDER

CHAPTER IX
SNYDER HONEYMOON: 1810-1811

THE TWO YEARS which followed the election of 1809 saw the decline into complete impotence of the Old School Democrats led by Leib and Duane. Lacking allies in the rest of the State, the group even lost its control in the city and county of Philadelphia. State politics in these years, except for a few local quarrels and the clamors of the Old School, lapsed almost into somnolence. Although American foreign relations were steadily worsening and the disagreements between the Federalists and Republicans were becoming more virulent, these developments affected State politics very little except as they prevented coalition between the Federalists and the Republican opponents of Snyder.

I

The opening of the legislative session on December 5, 1809, began a determined attack by the Old School faction to overthrow Snyder and his supporters. Though they concentrated on the Olmsted affair, they extended their assaults to all phases of Snyder's administration. Their efforts were abetted by newspaper articles more scurrilous even than those directed against McKean. However, the excessive vindictiveness of the group boomeranged, and their attacks served only to strengthen Snyder.

Jonathan Roberts, Senator from Montgomery County, who professed neutrality as between the Old School and the "cabinet" party, made an interesting analysis of the situation at the beginning of the session. The Senate, he thought, had a few adherents of the cabinet but none wholeheartedly devoted to the Old School. In the House, however, the lines were sharply drawn, with young William J. Duane leading Snyder's opponents and Richard T. Leech, Boileau's brother-in-law, heading the Governor's partisans. Nevertheless, Roberts believed that a good portion of the Representatives belonged to neither group and were "disposed to an independent course."[1]

Young Duane's faction was victorious in organizing the House. They elected James Engle as Speaker and James Thackara, one of their adherents in Philadelphia, as Clerk. The Snyderites made no opposition to either of these men, although they had previously considered backing other candidates. Observing these events, Roberts concluded that the cabinet party was "utterly unfit to cope with their opponents."[2] The Old School had made an auspicious beginning.

The chief interest in the session was the struggle over the Olmsted Case. In his message on December 7, 1809, Snyder gave a brief review of the matter and expressed his alarm over the "dreadful consequences" likely to result from continued usurpations by the Federal judiciary. If the situation were not remedied by a constitutional amendment, he feared further clashes of jurisdiction, particularly in the western part of the State where the Federal decisions in land cases had already caused much oppression.[3]

The House on December 12, 1809, appointed a grand committee, consisting of one member from the city and one from each county, to consider the Olmsted affair. William J. Duane was chosen as the member from the city and thus became the chairman. On December 16, Snyder's special message containing the correspondence and other documents relating to the matter was sent to the legislature. These were corrected on January 13, 1810, by a communication from Boileau, which stated that a letter from him to Bright dated March 29, 1809, in the documents should have been dated April 14. Five days later Boileau sent a copy of a personal letter from him to Bright, dated March 29, 1809, to explain the discrepancies occasioned by the previous change of dates.

In the meantime, young Duane, as head of the grand committee, had submitted its report on January 15, 1810. The preamble began with a general assertion of the sanctity of state rights, reprobated judicial encroachments, and reiterated the State's position on the validity of its claim to the Olmsted money. It then turned to a review of the conduct of Snyder in the matter. In the opinion of the committee, the act of April 2, 1803, did require the Governor to call on the militia; and he had correctly interpreted the views of the legislature in doing so. It pointed out that nearly a month elapsed between the time Snyder notified the legislature of his intentions and the actual calling out of the troops to prevent the service of the writs. In that period the legislature had had ample time to decide on the matter, and it had overwhelmingly opposed payment of the money. The committee felt, therefore, that Snyder was "not only *exempt from all censure*" but merited "*the approbation of every friend of the just rights of the state.*"

The committee then offered six resolutions. The first disapproved the conduct of the Federal courts in the Olmsted Case. The second was a general statement of support of state rights and of opposition to a consolidated government. The third expressed "highest approbation" of the conduct of Snyder. The fourth approved Madison's pardon of Bright and the eight militiamen. The fifth approved the constitutional amendment proposed at the last session. The last directed that copies of the resolutions be sent to the Pennsylvania delegation in Congress.

The spirit of these resolutions is noteworthy. While they maintained the correctness of Pennsylvania's views on the Olmsted affair, they showed a disposition to let bygones be bygones so far as the national administration was concerned by praising Madison for his pardons. On the whole, it appears that the Snyderites sought only a chance to save face and then to let the matter drop. However, they were not to escape so easily.

The committee's report lay on the table for two weeks before it was taken up for consideration. Except for the receipt of Boileau's private letter to Bright, the only incident of significance in this interval was an attempt by young William J. Duane to prove collusion between the State and the Federal officials in the affair. This took the form of a request to the Governor to submit all correspondence between Walter Franklin, the Attorney General, and the United States officers. The object was to some extent an attempt to show that Snyder had been guilty of duplicity, but perhaps more important was a desire to discredit Marshal John Smith or Dallas, the Federal District Attorney. After considerable debate the resolution was passed; and Franklin sent a letter stating that he had had neither verbal nor written communication with either Smith or Dallas.

The committee's report was considered in committee of the whole on January 30 and 31, 1810, and reported favorably with minor amendments to the preamble. The debate on adoption by the House began on February 2. With the first resolution under consideration, it was moved to postpone all resolutions generally. This motion was defeated 58-33. The minority was made up of ten Federalists, eleven Quids, and twelve Democrats. Of the Democrats, four were from the city of Philadelphia, two from Philadelphia County, two from Chester County, and one each from Northumberland, Bedford, York, and Lancaster counties. The majority was made up entirely of Democrats and included one member from the city and three from the county of Philadelphia.[4] James Engle, the sixth member of the Philadelphia County delegation, was absent.

The attempt to kill the resolutions failing, young Duane, who was bitterly opposed to the report he had been forced to submit as head of the grand committee, moved to postpone to introduce a substitute. Couched in arrogant terms, the substitute announced that it was necessary to give a summary of the background of the case because previous reviews on the legislative journals contained "so much sophistry and so many appearances of a desire to conceal the whole truth." It then launched into an extended discussion, upholding the justice of Olmsted's claim, the power of the congressional committee of appeals to reverse the decision of the admiralty court, and the jurisdiction of the Federal courts in the matter. It assailed the objections of Pennsylvania to the decision and held that Snyder had acted unconstitutionally and contrary to his oath in calling out the militia.

The substitute closed with a series of resolutions. Proclaiming the supremacy of the Federal laws and courts, the resolutions asserted that armed resistance to the enforcement of judicial decisions warranted the most extreme punishment provided by the laws. Opposition by those sworn to uphold the Constitution (meaning Snyder) called for impeachment. It was ridiculous to continue to seek amendment to the Constitution in view of the replies received from other states. Finally, the resolutions held that the legislature would be guilty of "duplicity and falsehood" if it made declarations of submission to the Constitution and laws when such declarations were contradicted by its own acts and statements.

This vindictive tirade was hardly calculated to receive much support, and it was defeated by an even greater majority than the motion to postpone generally the committee's report. Only 25 voted in its favor, with 67 opposed. The minority was composed of eleven Federalists, eight Quids, and six Democrats. The Democrats included four from the city and two from the county of Philadelphia. The majority was made up of three Quids and 64 Democrats, including one from the city and three from the county of Philadelphia. After some further debate the House then adopted the first resolution reported by the committee by a vote of 59-33.

Further consideration was deferred until the next day. At that time all the remaining resolutions except one were adopted by a vote substantially the same as on the previous day. The resolution approving Madison's conduct was defeated by a vote of 58-36, the majority being a mixture of Federalists, Quids, Snyderites, and Old School Democrats, while the minority was made up largely of Snyder's supporters. The resolutions were then sent to the Senate.[5]

The situation in that house was less favorable to the Snyderites. Jonathan Roberts estimated that fifteen members were inclined to support the resolutions, thirteen definitely opposed, and three doubtful. In his opinion, they would not pass the Senate. His judgment was verified when the resolutions were laid on the table and not given any further consideration.[6]

However, the Senate did adopt a measure to pay fifty dollars to each of those who had been imprisoned in the Olmsted affair. This passed on March 16, 1810, by a vote of 15-11. The minority was made up of four Federalists, two Quids, and five Democrats. With only four days remaining in the session, the House took no action on the bill and it was lost.[7]

The complete defeat of the Old School in their opposition to the Olmsted resolutions was indicative of their great loss of influence in the legislature. Though they had been able to rout their opponents in the early days of the session, their vindictiveness and arrogant conduct in the months that followed completely ruined their hopes of defeating Snyder. One of the factors in their decline was the abusive newspaper war carried on by the *Aurora*.

Although there had been a great deal of material against Snyder and his advisors all along, the *Aurora* began its most vengeful assaults on January 8, 1810, with the publication of the first of the articles by "Conrad Weiser." These continued at intervals until the middle of February and were supplemented by the effusions of "Jacob Fulmer," "Stophel Funk," "One of the People," and other pseudonymous contributors. From the point of view of the legislature, they were made even more objectionable because there was good reason to believe that young William J. Duane was "Conrad Weiser," even though the anonymous author denied it.[8]

The general theme of the articles was the complete corruption of the Snyder regime. Proclaiming that Snyder's actions in the Olmsted Case were unconstitutional and deserving of impeachment, they asserted that he had acted thus because of the influence of Abner Lacock, Senator from Beaver County, who hoped to prevent enforcement of the Federal decisions in the land disputes of northwestern Pennsylvania. This idea was developed at great length; and on February 10, 1810, it was flatly stated that Lacock was the "prime mover" of the Olmsted "rebellion" and that his object was to produce *"another rebellion* in the western counties" for the benefit of "a set of intruders against law and against every principle of equity and morality." In addition, Lacock was charged with being motivated by an expectation of personal profit.[9]

A second important type of attack in the articles asserted that the Governor and his advisors were using patronage to corrupt the legislature. Boileau and William Findlay, the State Treasurer, were alleged to hold nightly caucuses with the members and to be using considerable pressure on the House committee on the Olmsted Case. Furthermore, on one occasion Snyder was stated to have given appointments to more than forty members of the preceding legislature, though this was later reduced to the assertion that that number had sought such appointments. From this, the articles drew the conclusion that Snyder had forced the last legislature to approve his action by corrupt use of his patronage.[10] Apart from the development of these two main lines of attack, the articles devoted a great deal of space to Boileau's blunders with respect to the correspondence with Bright and to extremely scurrilous personal attacks on Snyder and his close associates.[11]

The intemperateness of the Old School was further displayed in the elder William Duane's actions with respect to a mass meeting held in Philadelphia on February 14, 1810, to express the popular sentiment on national affairs. The *Aurora* not only reprobated the preliminary ward meetings because none of them had denounced Snyder's conduct in the Olmsted affair, but it also claimed that a denunciatory resolution had actually been adopted at the general mass meeting and continued to insist upon this in the face of denials by the chairman and secretary of the meeting. Furthermore, the paper refused to publish one of the addresses adopted by the meeting on the ground that it was filled with "*blunders* and *false constructions.*"[12]

The *Democratic Press* replied to these attacks by the *Aurora* as well as it could. Much space was necessarily devoted to refuting or denying assertions made by the Old School writers; but there were also strong articles assailing William J. Duane both for the pieces by "Conrad Weiser" and for his conduct in the legislature.

One of the charges against young Duane was that he had been elected to office under false pretenses. According to the *Press*, he had in the previous summer expressed warm approbation of Snyder's actions and had denounced Leib and the control he exercised over the *Aurora*. The Snyderites laid the subsequent change in his attitude to his disappointment at failing to receive the office of recorder of Philadelphia for which he had applied.[13]

The *Press* also assailed him for his arrogant and insolent course in the legislature. In the middle of January William Piper, a Representative from Bedford County, offered to the House a communication from Andrew Porter, the Surveyor General. As such messages were usually sent to the Speaker of the House, young Duane opposed receiving the documents and indulged in a long tirade about "back stairs influence." One of the members remarked that such charges came with ill grace from a disappointed officeseeker, and Duane flatly denied that such a reference applied to him. As it was generally known that he had asked for an office, his denial was regarded as a complete falsehood. Duane went on to declare that any person who voted to receive Porter's message from Piper was unworthy to be a member of the House. Such effrontery naturally outraged the Representatives, and they voted 76-17 to receive the papers.[14]

Though young Duane later made apologies for his actions in this instance, he behaved in a somewhat similar fashion on January 31, 1810, during the debate on the report of the Olmsted committee. At that time one of the members read a number of excerpts from the *Aurora's* issues in March and April, 1809, and pointed out several inconsistencies. Turning from this, he referred to young Duane's conduct and asserted that he had prevented the introduction of a resolution for his expulsion from the House. To this Duane replied by expressing regret that the member had interfered and avowed that he would have considered expulsion an honor.[15]

With such conduct inside and outside the legislature, it was little wonder that the Old School lost all influence. Though their object was to regain supremacy in the Democratic Party, the members of the faction became so overcome by their desire to ruin Snyder and his advisors that they lost all discretion and acted in a manner calculated only to ruin themselves. Seldom, if ever, has there been an example of such inept bungling.

In the first place, it was politically unwise to attack Snyder's conduct in the Olmsted Case, because, as Roberts observed, the Governor was "propd round by the Legislative acts & votes" and was "invulnerable except thro them."[16] It was bad enough to assail such a popular position in any case, but it was sheer madness to impugn the good faith of the legislators upholding state rights by charging that they had been corrupted by the Governor.

In like manner, it was very imprudent to have dragged in gratuitously the question of the northwestern lands. The Democrats had traditionally been sympathetic toward the actual settlers and unfavorable to the big land companies. They were unlikely to reverse these opinions overnight at the behest of the *Aurora*. The attack, therefore, served only to alienate another section of the legislature and of the party generally.

These factors, combined with disgust at the arrogance of young Duane, soon had their effect. The changing sentiment can be followed in the attitude of Jonathan Roberts, who was none too sympathetic with the "cabinet" party. In the middle of January Roberts believed that the Old School had been exceedingly skillful in maneuvering the Snyderites into a resolution of direct approval of Snyder's conduct. In his opinion, this left them vulnerable to the damning charge of supporting men rather than principles.[17] By February 4, 1810, he had altered his views sharply and wrote as follows:

> The resolutions in Olmsteds case has occupied the house for several days— Duane Thompson and Todd have gone as great length in violence & invective against Snyder as Leib & his partizans did against M'Kean on the question of impeachment— No charge of weakness intrigue & corruption was left unmade— It does not appear however these denunciations had any effect except to unite the democrats more closely.... Duane & Thom[p]son are so completely in discredit with the house that their usefulness is destroyd I am sorry for it— The guise was completely thrown off in the substitute offerd by Duane who declard the governor ought to be impeached— *It has become necessary for the country democrats to assert their independence or give themselves up to be governed by a few men in the city*— After much conversation Duane & I have taken our stations on opposite sides there can be no more

confidence tho' there may be civility— I have all along declar'd I would adhere to Snyder as long as he adhered to principle but Duane has calld every man corrupt who will not denounce him it is not possible we can be confidential after this[.][18]

A similar change was occurring in public sentiment in Philadelphia. The excessive violence of the *Aurora* and its arrogance in the matter of the proceedings of the town meeting was ruining the Old School even in its citadel. One observer wrote that they were "destroying themselves by their violence and passions," while Snyder was "daily regaining his popularity in the City & County of Phila."[19] Thus, the Leib-Duane faction by its vindictiveness had spoiled its best opportunity to recover supremacy among the Pennsylvania Democrats.

II

The campaign of 1810 was an important one since it was a congressional election year and since the legislature then elected would probably nominate the gubernatorial candidate for 1811. Despite its crucial nature, little interest was shown in the election outside Philadelphia, where the Old School and Snyderites fought with extreme bitterness.

Determined to avoid defeat in the ensuing campaign, the Snyderites in Philadelphia began to organize their forces early. The first evidence of their activity was the formation in late April and early May of the "Democratic Society of the City and County of Philadelphia." Michael Bright was chosen president, and John Binns was made a member of the corresponding committee. Its evident, though not avowed, object was the re-election of Snyder; and it thus became the successor of the Associated Friends of Democracy and Simon Snyder which had been disbanded in December, 1808.[20]

The Old School Democrats were not to be outdone in the matter of organizing societies. They held a meeting on July 14, 1810, and appointed a committee, including Leib, Thomas Leiper, and young William J. Duane, to draw up a constitution. The *Aurora* did not publish the proceedings; but the *Democratic Press* reported that the "Society of Friends of the Constitution of the United States, and Enemies of State Rebellion" had assembled and pointed out that the man who had called the meeting had served as paymaster under Bright in the Olmsted affair.[21]

The next meeting of the group on July 24, 1810, formally announced the creation of the "Whig Society of Pennsylvania," which was intended to be a statewide organization with separate meetings for each county. Its principles were those of the Declaration of Independence; and its two chief purposes were the support of the Constitution and laws of the United States and the exposure of corruption. A subsequent meeting on August 6, 1810, elected Thomas Leiper as president and established a corresponding committee, which included Leib, James Engle, and young William J. Duane.[22]

The Whig Society was as obviously intended to defeat Snyder as the Democratic Society was to elect him. One of the Snyderites believed that the chief purpose of the organization was to establish branches, however small, in each county to elect delegates to a State nominating convention in 1811 to oppose the expected caucus nomination of Snyder. This analysis seems to have had much validity.[23]

Meanwhile, the Snyderites were taking early measures to establish the district delegate system in Philadelphia County. Preliminary gatherings were held in April; and in late July and August the district meetings convened for the choice of delegates. These delegates met on August 13, 1810, and drew up an assembly ticket for the county. The three members in the last session who had supported Snyder were renominated, but the others were dropped. An address was then drawn up explaining why these men were dropped and announcing that as the district nominations were the first submitted to the Democratic voters, the ticket to be adopted at the subsequent general county meeting could only be considered that of a faction.[24]

The Old School was not silent in such a situation. Writers in the *Aurora* denounced the district system and called for adherence to the old reliable general county meeting. They also censured the purported activity of State officeholders in seeking to organize support for the district elections. Despite these articles, the Old School Democrats in Southwark seemed disposed to accede to the demand for district meetings. However, they were overruled by their compatriots in the Northern Liberties; and a call was issued for a general county meeting to be held on August 20, 1810.[25]

Prior to the meeting, "Democritus," in the newly established Old School daily paper, the *Evening Star,* appealed to the Old School to expel the Snyderites from the party at their meeting. The whole election, he avowed, turned upon the question of the gubernatorial nomination in 1811; and the line should be drawn at once without further procrastination. The Snyderites should be proscribed until their actions accorded with their principles—until they were willing to "renounce rebellion against the union, and recognize the will of the majority."[26]

All those in attendance at the meeting were first pledged to support its nominations. The assemblage then nominated its conferees and drew up the assembly ticket. The latter included those who had been dropped by the Snyderites and omitted those they had retained. The meeting next adopted a long address submitted by Leib. It assailed the district plan of nominations and the candidates on the Snyderite ticket, who were charged with being the pliant tools of executive influence. It closed with resolutions denouncing legislative caucus nominations and approving a plan for the establishment of a gubernatorial nominating convention.[27]

The two factions also engaged in a fierce struggle in the city. The Snyderites were again unsuccessful in their attempts to capture the general ward committee, but they showed no disposition to accept the situation passively. The Old School won control of most of the ward meetings and influenced them to adopt severe resolutions against caucus nominations. However, in a number of meetings there was strong opposition and even open violence. In Chestnut Ward the elder Duane and Binns were narrowly restrained from coming to blows.[28]

The relations between the two men had steadily worsened since their break in 1807. In the previous August Duane had suffered a severe blow to his pride when the *Democratic Press* had displaced the *Aurora* in its old offices in Franklin Court.[29] Another incident had been the issuance of a Supreme Court mandamus in March, 1810, which forced Duane as president of the St. Patrick's Benevolent Society to reinstate Binns to membership on the grounds that his expulsion in 1807 had been illegal.[30] Personal scurrilities had also been exchanged; and in June, 1810, Binns had jeered cruelly at Duane's military pretensions by writing that "The only ground for the rumor which is so general this morning, that a war is probable, is predicated upon the annunciation of Wm. Duane, that he has resigned his commission in the army." Binns went on to say that though Duane was more like Thersites than Achilles, it was only justice to say that he did not resign from choice, but because of hints from the government.[31]

At the Chestnut Ward meeting on July 26, 1810, the two met face to face. Binns referred to Duane as a poltroon, and the latter picked up two candlesticks with burning candles and hurled them at him. In relating the incident, Binns also alleged that Duane had tried to draw a dagger but was restrained by those present.[32]

The Snyderites continued to make charges of chicanery and intimidation at the ward meetings and thus laid the ground for their bolt late in August. The split took place when the general ward committee refused to recognize the Snyderite county conferees. This action caused the Democratic Society to meet and issue a call for new ward meetings to be held, with one delegate to be chosen from each ward. The fourteen thus selected were to meet, elect five other members, and then confer with the delegates from Philadelphia and Delaware counties.[33]

The plan was followed; and the conferees held their meeting on September 5, 1810. Four of the five conferees chosen by Delaware County met with this group. At the meeting William Anderson, Adam Seybert, and Dr. John Porter were approved for re-election to Congress. A subsequent meeting of the conferees from the city and county of Philadelphia made nominations for State Senators and Sheriff.[34] However, it should be noted that the Snyderites did not offer an opposition ticket for offices within the city of Philadelphia.

The Old School conferees did not hold their meeting until September 12, 1810. The congressional ticket was the same as the Snyderite except that Robert McMullin was substituted for Porter. They also made separate nominations for State Senators, Sheriff, and the other city-county offices. The dropping of Porter, long a Democratic stalwart, occasioned quite a storm; but it was explained by a writer in the *Aurora* on the grounds that he had become attached to a faction, that as a friend to Snyder he could not be a true supporter of the general government, and that his deafness prevented him from discharging his duties adequately.[35]

The Old School now began to proceed with its plans to oust Snyder in 1811. On August 30, 1810, the general ward committee issued a long address demanding that a convention be called to make the gubernatorial nomination and that the delegates be pledged not to accept any office from the candidate nominated. The address contained a lengthy review of the importance of nominations under the existing system of political organization and explained that they should only be made by the people themselves or by those specially delegated for that purpose. It then attacked legislative caucus nominations generally and charged that Snyder was using patronage to obtain his renomination. It closed with an expression of willingness to support any candidate chosen by a majority of the people or their delegates, but it announced that the Philadelphia Democrats would not be bound by a caucus nomination.[36]

While the *Aurora* was filled with denunciations of the Snyderites as officeholders and officeseekers and as enemies to the Constitution and the general government, the *Democratic Press* and the Snyderites were replying with charges of their own. They asserted that the Old School was run principally by disappointed officeseekers. Among these they listed Leib, who had wanted to be Secretary of the Commonwealth; young William J. Duane, who had sought the position of recorder of the city and county of Philadelphia; and Joseph Lloyd, who had applied for the appointment of clerk of the mayor's court. William Duane was accused of being disgruntled because Snyder had not quashed the libel suits against him.[37]

The *Press* also asserted that Leib and the Old School were intriguing for Federalist aid and were intending to support William Tilghman for Governor in 1811. In the case of Leib, the paper even detailed when and where such alleged proposals to the Federalists were made. Whether these charges were true or not, they were given some semblance of verity when the Federalist *United States' Gazette* took the unusual step of publishing the Old School tickets for that year.[38]

The Federalists, meanwhile, under the name of American Republicans, continued to display the political skill of the preceding year. Using the ward committee system in the city and the delegate system in the county, they nominated a full ticket for all offices and worked effectively for the support of their candidates.[39]

The desperate position of the Old School in the county was shown by the fight at the preliminary election for assessors and inspectors of elections at the Northern Liberties on September 28, 1810. The *Aurora* avowed that the Old School had been in the majority and had placed their judges in the townhouse, but that the Snyderites had thrown them out. In the ensuing turmoil, it said, the Snyderites had managed to win a partial victory in the election.[40] A different story was given by the *Democratic Press*. It said that the Snyderites had slightly outnumbered the Old School, with the Federalists holding the balance of power. Despite this, Leib urged on his followers to take possession. The Snyderites then threw them out. After some dispute, the matter was finally settled by taking two judges from each Democratic faction and one from the Federalists. In the subsequent election the Snyderites won.[41]

At the general election on October 9, 1810, the Old School failed to carry a single office. In Philadelphia County their nominees for assembly polled the average of 1,561 votes, while the Federalists averaged 1,079, and the Snyderites (or "New School," as they were beginning to be called) averaged 1,947. The Old School was in the minority in the Northern Liberties and in every other district in the county except Southwark. In the city the Old School made a better showing, polling about 1,500 votes to 700 for the Snyderites for offices where both ran candidates. However, the Federalists carried every city candidate by a majority of more than 700 votes. They also elected both State Senators, the Sheriff, and one of the three members of Congress.

It should be noted that these Federalist gains did not mark any real increase in their strength. Their victory in the city was entirely due to the Democratic split. The Snyderites do not seem to have voted for the Federalist candidates, but they likewise appear to have withheld their support from the Old School nominees. The election of James Milnor to Congress arose solely out of the split between McMullin and Porter. The other Democratic congressional candidates won by a majority of nearly 1,400 votes.[42]

While these fierce contests were being waged in Philadelphia, the rest of the State was fairly quiet. The only notable incidents occurred in Allegheny and Berks counties in connection with the congressional elections.

The Congressman from the district including Allegheny, Beaver, Butler, Mercer, Crawford, Venango, Warren, and Erie counties was Samuel Smith. He had been given to following a somewhat independent course, opposing the adoption of the embargo and the caucus nomination of Madison in 1808. These irregularities had been overlooked, and he had been re-elected in that year. However, when he opposed the adoption of resolutions censuring the conduct of the British minister, Francis James Jackson, in the session of 1809-1810, public meetings in the district had adopted resolutions of disapproval. Though Smith subsequently made explanations of his actions, it was obvious that he would not be renominated.[43]

A warm dispute developed, however, on the question of his successor. The Allegheny County conferees insisted upon the nomination of Adamson Tannehill of Pittsburgh; and those from Beaver, Butler, and Mercer counties supported Abner Lacock or David Mead. The Allegheny delegation then withdrew, and a Pittsburgh meeting chose Tannehill without any reference to the rest of the district. They defended this action on the ground that as Allegheny County had the greater population it was entitled to a larger voice in the nominating conference than it had at that time when all counties had an equal representation.[44]

The other counties accused the Allegheny Democrats of attempted dictation and responded by backing Lacock. They argued that they represented the majority in the party since their counties cast a greater proportion of the Democratic vote. In such a conflict of local jealousies, there could be no arbiter except the voters. Tannehill carried Allegheny County by more than 1,000 votes and Crawford County by nearly 300; but Lacock received majorities in every other county and had a total of 2,897 to Tannehill's 2,455. The Federalists did not bother to put up a candidate.[45]

In Berks County Matthias Richards, who had served two terms as Quid Representative in Congress, was again nominated by the Quids. However, the Federalists in the county in 1810 offered their own man, Marks John Biddle. Richards on September 19, 1810, publicly withdrew his name, stating that in the three-county district of Chester, Berks, and Lancaster a split in the Democratic vote might result in the election of three Federalists, which he believed bad for the country. Since all Democrats voted the same on national issues, he felt that he should prevent a split by dropping out of the race.[46]

This action gave the appearance of unselfish sacrifice for the benefit of the party and the country in response to the existing crisis in foreign affairs; and it may have been so. However, Richards's letter closed by observing that the Republicans were divided only in State politics and that the division would remain as long as Snyder was in office. In his opinion, reunion would come only if "another republican, of respectability and talents," should be nominated in 1811. With such a conclusion, it was little wonder that the *Democratic Press* ridiculed Richards' professions of disinterestedness. It attributed his actions solely to the fact that the Federalist decision to run Biddle had made his own chances of election negligible.[47]

The incident is significant in two ways. For one thing, even if Richards were not wholly sincere in his protestations, his claim of resignation in the interests of party harmony indicated that public sentiment was turning in that direction. It therefore illustrates the compulsion for Democratic unity exerted by national issues. In the second place, the opposition to Snyder showed that an alliance between the Old School and the Berks County Quids was being formed. In 1806 the *Aurora* had assailed Richards for alleged corruption in a county election; and it had constantly attacked the Snyderites for political dereliction because they welcomed the aid of the Quids. Now in 1810 the *Aurora* was proclaiming Richards to be a sterling example of Republican virtue. This change was a prime demonstration of the fact that the Democratic feuds in the State had little relation to anything but personalities.

In the State as a whole the Democratic supremacy was overwhelming. Except for James Milnor, elected as a result of the Democratic split in Philadelphia, all the new Congressmen were Republicans; and, with the exception of William Findley, none were Quids. In the legislature the only significant change was the election of a Federalist delegation from the city of Philadelphia. In the House the *Democratic Press* counted 72 Democrats, seventeen Federalists, and six "nondescripts" or Quids. In the Senate it listed 21 Democrats, seven Federalists, one Quid, and two Old School Democrats. The election of 1810 was a resounding victory for the Snyderites.[48]

III

The gubernatorial election of 1811 took place in a condition of almost complete political calm. The storms which had shaken the State so violently in 1809 and 1810 were long past. The interest of the people seemed in large measure to have turned to objects other than politics. The legislative session of 1810-1811 proceeded without notable incident, and the Democratic opposition to Snyder lapsed into impotence.

The years after 1808 were prosperous ones for the State. In his first annual message to the legislature in December, 1809, Snyder had remarked upon the great prosperity which prevailed, the increased population, the building of new houses and barns, the clearing of additional lands, and the progress in the construction of bridges and turnpikes. He laid particular stress upon the development of home manufactures:

> Our mills and furnaces are greatly multiplied; new beds of ore have been discovered, and the industry and enterprize of our citizens are turning them to the most useful purposes. Many new and highly valuable manufactories have been established, and we now make in Pennsylvania, various articles of domestic use, for which, two years since, we were wholly dependent upon foreign nations.
>
> We have lately had established in Philadelphia large shot manufactories; floor-cloth manufactories; and a queens' ware pottery, upon an extensive scale. These are all in successful operation, independent of immense quantities of cotton and wool, flax and hemp, leather and iron, which are annually manufactured in our state, and which save to our country the annual export of millions of dollars.[49]

Pennsylvania, in fact, was in the midst of a boom. The *Aurora* in February, 1810, decried the infatuation for new banks which had seized the State. It averred that five new banks had been agitated for Philadelphia in the course of a single day and that new banks were mushrooming in the inland towns of Lancaster, Harrisburg, York, Reading, Easton, Washington, and Pittsburgh. It predicted that all the property of the State was "about to be sunk into the *den of sordid* speculation" with consequent ruin to many innocent persons, while the "cunning and profligate" would flourish.[50]

William Tilghman made similar observations a few days later. Philadelphia, he asserted, had become *"Bank mad"*; and he expected that the mania would spread to the rest of the State. He was inclined to avoid dealing in the stocks of banks and insurance companies until business went back to normal. He also believed that the continued rise in Philadelphia real estate prices was unsound. In his opinion, it was a good time to sell such holdings.[51]

These conditions inevitably affected the legislature. New projects for the creation of banks and companies for the construction of bridges and turnpikes or for the improvement of river navigation were continually brought before it. The mania for banks was so extensive that it was the subject of comment by observers in 1812; and one of them observed that it had been "the secret spring of action these two years."[52] However powerful the influence of such schemes may have been, it operated upon the level of local and personal interests and did not follow partisan or factional lines. The chief effect was to lessen interest in old issues and in political contests generally. The new economic forces were beginning to be reflected in politics, but their first effects were largely negative.

When the legislature convened on December 4, 1810, the two houses organized with a minimum of friction. Snyder's message was long and well-written. It spoke hopefully of a possible improvement in foreign relations and then suggested a number of matters for the consideration of the legislature. First in importance was militia reform. Snyder warmly praised the republican virtues of a militia as opposed to mercenary armies, but he insisted that the continuance of the system depended upon better discipline and equipment. The institution of these reforms, he felt, was the most pressing problem before the legislature.

Next in importance was the development of the State's internal resources through improvements in roads and water communications and the stimulation of industry. In many of these projects, he believed that private capital was inadequate and required the assistance of State funds. Alluding to the constitutional provisions for the establishment of free schools for the poor, he emphasized the importance of education in a republican government and asked that the legislators take effective measures to establish the contemplated system. The message closed by listing a number of other matters needing the attention of the lawmakers.[53]

The document drew praise from unexpected quarters. The editor of the *United States' Gazette* declared that he had no intention of disputing Snyder's claim to the title of "King of Ignorance," which had been bestowed upon him by some of the Democrats, but he would say that the message compared favorably with Madison's to Congress, "considered with reference either to its literary merits, or to the depth and solidity of the political disquisitions which it contains."[54]

Even the *Aurora* grudgingly characterized it as "one of the best . . . that has been presented from the chair of this State for several years." However, the paper tempered its praise by observing that the message was only words and that it would be necessary to observe the performance. After all, it said, in 1804 and 1805 the Snyderites had been devoted to constitutional reform, but they did not even mention it now. It would be well to see if the same fate overtook the proposals in the message.[55]

The legislative session was unusually quiet; and this was chiefly due to the absence of the brawling Philadelphia Representatives of the Old School. One of the new Federalist members from the city was Nicholas Biddle, who had assumed his duties with a feeling of lofty indifference. He was both surprised and pleased to find that he took a real interest in the proceedings, and he discovered a genuine liking for many of his fellow members. He felt particular pride in the leadership that he and the other Philadelphia Federalists were able to exercise; and his remarks on this matter are illuminating as to the reasons for the loss of party control by the Philadelphia Democrats:

> The fact is that we members from Phila have succeeded to a number of very noisy people who quarreled with every body till they brought the City into disgrace from which it is now our business to retrieve it. This can only be done by gentleness and mildness, and as fortunately all my associates are of a pleasant temper & manners, ... we are flattered by the unanimous approbation of the house .... The universal sentiment is that for the last twenty five years there has not been so harmonious a session, & the value of this compliment is enhanced by considering that the effect is universally ascribed to the City members who generally take the lead. Hitherto, those members, feeling that they possessed a superiority of information have been too ambitious of shewing it—and when any thing occurred in which they could display their own knowledge, too often employed it to ridicule their adversaries. ... Our endeavor is to obtain political good—to conciliate these well meaning misdirected people—and therefore instead of making their projects appear ludicrously before the house, we tell them privately what we think the defects of their plan and suggest a remedy which they are always willing to adopt. This has obtained us a large share of good will. ...[56]

The Olmsted Case was again presented to the legislature as the result of the petition of Olmsted, averring that the State Treasury had in it the quarter-share of the proceeds of the *Active* awarded to Captain Houston and the crew of the *Convention* and requesting that such proceeds be paid to him. The petition was referred to a House committee in December, and it made its report on February 6, 1811. This report insisted that Olmsted had not completely captured the *Active*, that he was therefore not entitled to all the money, and that he had already been sufficiently compensated for what he had done. The committee recommended that the petition be denied, and its report was accepted without a record vote on March 5.[57]

The Olmsted affair was also involved in the revival of the measure to compensate Bright and the militiamen who had been imprisoned. A bill for this purpose was introduced in the House in March and passed its second reading by a vote of 64-23. After dropping Bright from the list of beneficiaries, it was approved on the third reading and sent to the Senate, where it passed by a vote of 15-12. It provided for the payment of $50 to each of the men concerned.[58]

Another legislative measure passed at this session did much to help bring to an end the dispute over land titles in the northwestern section of the State. The act sought to encourage compromises between the actual settlers and the warrantees over disputed tracts by promising that the State would validate titles under certain circumstances provided the settlement and residence requirements were met. It set forth a number of contingencies, but in general it tried to foster arrangements whereby the warrantee would give the actual settler 150 acres of the 400-acre tracts. The bill was adopted unanimously by the House and approved by a vote of 19-7 in the Senate.[59]

This measure did not immediately resolve all the land disputes in the northwest, but it ended the political significance of the question. The tendency toward compromise had already made great progress. By February, 1810, the Holland Land Company had no intruders upon its lands. In July of the same year a resident of Meadville reported that land disputes were subsiding and that the country was beginning to take a great interest in internal improvements. However, the best reflection of the changed situation was shown by the fact that the Supreme Court at its September session in Pittsburgh in 1810 had only enough business to occupy half the allotted time.[60] Thus, the struggles over land titles in the region were already in process of solution when the act of March 20, 1811, was adopted; and it served only to accelerate rather than initiate final settlement of the matter.

Another issue which arose in this session of the legislature was the rechartering of the Bank of the United States. The bank's original charter expired by limitation on March 4, 1811; but a bill to extend the life of the institution had died without final action in the congressional session which ended in May, 1810. In the next session another bill was introduced, but it was defeated in the Senate on February 20, 1811, by the casting vote of Vice President George Clinton.[61]

The question aroused considerable interest in Pennsylvania. The *Democratic Press* in March, 1810, indicated its opposition to the renewal of the national charter, but it was favorably inclined toward giving the existing bank a Pennsylvania charter. The *Aurora* was opposed to renewing the bank in any form; and it used the issue as an excuse for attacking Gallatin, whom it blamed for alleged intrigue in favor of the bank.[62]

Beginning in November, 1810, the *Aurora* ran articles on the bank in almost every issue until the latter part of February. A good portion of the material was given to a nasty personal assault on Matthew Carey because of two pamphlets he had written in favor of the continuance of the bank. Carey's replies were published in the *Democratic Press,* although that paper did not agree with his views on the issue.[63]

In addition to newspaper opposition to the bank, the Democrats in Philadelphia organized ward meetings to remonstrate against the renewal of the charter. By the time the remonstrance was prepared the bank bill had been defeated, and it was never sent. It should be noted, however, that a number of prominent Philadelphia Democrats, including Thomas Leiper, supported the renewal of the bank's charter.[64]

In the legislature the matter first came up with the introduction of resolutions in the House instructing the Pennsylvania delegation in Congress to oppose the chartering of any bank authorized to operate outside the District of Columbia. The resolutions passed the House on January 4, 1811, by a vote of 68-20, the minority comprising fourteen Federalists, five Quids, and one Democrat. The Senate modified them by inserting a new preamble and by changing the phrasing so that opposition was expressed to the creation of a bank to operate within the states without the prior consent of their legislatures. The preamble made a concise statement of the compact theory of the union and the doctrine of strict construction of the Constitution, and it then avowed that Congress did not have the power to charter corporations within the states without their consent. In this form the resolutions were adopted by a vote of 20-8 in the Senate on January 10, 1811. The House concurred on the following day.[65]

The directors of the defunct bank petitioned the legislature for a State charter on March 18, 1811. The petition was referred to a House committee which reported a bill for the purpose two days later. The committee of the whole ruled unfavorably on the measure on March 25;

and the House sustained it by a vote of 51-35. It was thus lost for the session.[66]

Meanwhile, the Democrats in the legislature proceeded with the nomination of a gubernatorial candidate. A caucus on December 17, 1810, presided over by Presley Carr Lane, speaker of the Senate, had adopted a resolution asking counties not having Democratic members in the legislature or those partially represented by Federalists or Quids to choose delegates in a number equal to their authorized membership. These delegates were to meet with the Democratic legislators in Lancaster on February 18 to select a candidate for Governor.[67]

A Democratic meeting in Pittsburgh announced its opposition to such caucus nominations. This action probably resulted from the split over the congressional election in the past October. Tannehill was strong in the Pittsburgh organization, and his supporters believed that the Snyderites had used official influence to aid in the election of Lacock. In any case, there does not appear to have been any close connection with the Old School group in Philadelphia.[68]

Despite this sour note, the caucus-convention met on February 18, 1811, with Lane as chairman. The seventeen Senators, 68 Representatives, and seventeen elected delegates unanimously renominated Snyder as the Democratic candidate for Governor.[69]

Just as in 1805 and 1808, there was an abortive movement for a nominating convention to oppose Snyder. One suggestion for such a convention was made by the Federalist *Lancaster Journal*. Strongly attacking Snyder for incompetence and favoritism, it called for a union of all virtuous men without regard to party to oppose his re-election. Specifically, it suggested that a meeting of Snyder's opponents be held in June at Lancaster, Harrisburg, or Carlisle to unite on a suitable candidate.[70] It is doubtful that this proposal from a Federalist, with its reminiscences of the "union of all honest men," made much appeal to dissident Democrats.

A convention was also sponsored by a source much more acceptable to the Democrats. Joseph Hiester presided over a meeting at Reading on April 3, 1811, which adopted resolutions opposing caucus nominations and calling for a nominating convention to meet at Carlisle on May 27, 1811. The meeting also chose delegates to attend from Berks County. However, even this effort was fruitless. The *Democratic Press* asserted that only 25 attended the Reading meeting and that the greater part of the Quid leaders in the county refused to take part. Although there were apparently some futile attempts in Lancaster and Chester counties to select delegates, the projected Carlisle convention was never held.[71]

Surprisingly enough, there was little agitation in Philadelphia by the Old School. That faction had long taken the lead in opposing Snyder; and the *Aurora* in October, 1809, had announced that he would never again be the Democratic candidate. The general ward committee had made a strong demand in August, 1810, for a nominating convention and had proclaimed that a caucus nomination would not be supported. Furthermore, the Whig Society in November had issued a long address, which had denounced Snyder and his associates in unmeasured terms and had asserted that the next gubernatorial election would decide whether republican government should be ruined by corruption or whether it should be restored to its former virtue. Despite all these things, ward meetings had been held; and delegates instructed to support Snyder had been sent from the city to take part in the caucus-convention. The Old School apparently did not oppose this nor did it foster a convention against Snyder after his nomination.[72]

The reason for this passive conduct was that the Old School had been virtually destroyed as an effective political organization. The *Pennsylvania Democrat* ceased publication in November, 1810; and the rather pallid *Evening Star* followed suit in January, 1811.[73] Leib was thus deprived of their services at a time when Duane was devoting the *Aurora* almost wholly to national politics.

The extent of the demoralization of the Old School is well described in an anonymous document, which was probably written in mid-January by a Federal officeholder in Philadelphia as a letter to Leib. The writer gave the following picture:

> It is to be hoped there are yet a few that have not put their principles to sleep but I fear they are too few to be able to effect any thing a strange stupor seems to prevail if not a total indifference to events— I have conversed with a great many on the subject & have not met with a single person but Thompson that appeared willing to engage in any opposition they say all attempts to remove Snyder is hopeless as the whole country appears to be drawn into the views of the Faction indeed it too much looks like it when you see such men as P. C. Lane at the head of a Caucus to support Snyder. I did hope the Whig Society might do something but they are dwindled to

nothing seldom more than 12 or 15 attends their meetings and they are composed of those who generally resort to [John] Millers [Green Tree Tavern] I was there last night we could not muster more than 10 to form the Society & adjourn and the most influential person among them was Cochran and not a single Officer when such is the apathy of the Whigs I must confess things look rather squally It seems to me when you are away the Life & Spirit of the party is gone too— It must be admitted that there are some difficulties in the way that is not easily got over scarcely a Man can be found among [us] fit to write any thing for the press and if there was we have no paper of influence to publish in Duane will do nothing in State politicks and as for the Star it has become too contemptible to effect any thing.[74]

The plight of the Leib-Duane faction was largely due to their own shortcomings. Arbitrary and dictatorial, they had exercised their power with great arrogance for a number of years and had gradually alienated more and more of the Democrats in their own Philadelphia district. In State politics, eschewing the excellent opportunity for leadership by persuasion, they had sought to rule or ruin. The violence of their attacks on Snyder in the Olmsted Case, the exaggerated claims of executive and legislative corruption, the denunciation of influential country Democratic leaders and editors, and the assaults on the actual settlers in the northwest had destroyed their chance to gain control of the party. The country Democrats had become convinced that the city sought domination of the State for purely personal and selfish reasons, and they closed ranks in support of Snyder.

On the other hand, Leib and Duane had for the first time met really worthy antagonists. Against the Quids, they had been able to claim a desertion of principle and to point to co-operation with the Federalists. With the Snyderites, no differences in principle existed; and there had been no alliance with Federalism. Also the Quids had formed only a small faction, which, even with the aid of patronage and the support of the Federalists, never achieved any solid control of the government. The Snyderites, on the contrary, represented the country Democrats, who formed the great bulk of the party in an overwhelmingly Democratic State. Coupling all this with a shrewd use of the patronage, a conciliatory attitude toward former opponents, and the effective efforts of John Binns and the *Democratic Press,* the Snyderites were virtually impregnable to external attack.

The position of the Old School at this time was also weakened by a growing alienation from Madison's administration and by Duane's own personal difficulties. The latter had apparently hoped to gain great credit with the Federal government in the Olmsted affair and correspondingly to weaken the Snyderites. However, such a plan was doomed from the start because of Duane's bitter hatred of Gallatin.

The break between the two men had begun in 1804, and the *Aurora* in the years that followed had often castigated Gallatin severely. However, these attacks were infrequent after 1808 until they were vigorously resumed in January, 1810, and they continued throughout the year. The charges against him were various; the betrayal of cabinet secrets, intrigues with Congress to get the bank rechartered, secret enmity to Jefferson and friendship with John Randolph, use of his official position to speculate in lands, secret association with the Snyderites, and a number of others.[75]

The attacks were renewed with even greater violence in February, 1811, and they now began to strike obliquely at Madison himself. The old charges were reiterated; and Gallatin was continually pictured as a malevolent intriguer, who, by devious methods, had come to be the true power behind the throne.[76] Evidently seeking to drive him from the cabinet, the *Aurora* asserted in February that "if Mr. Madison suffers *this man* to lord it over the nation—Mr. Gallatin will *drag him down;* for no honest man in the country can support an administration of which he is a member." In April the paper bluntly stated that if Madison expected to be renominated "he must convince the people that *he* is in *reality* the *president.*"[77]

Such intemperate attacks resulted in great difficulties for Duane. Joseph Clay and Thomas Leiper, his steadfast allies for many years, refused in March, 1811, to renew their endorsements to Duane's notes in the amount of $8,000. Clay withdrew his support because of the strictures against John Randolph. Leiper's exact reasons are unknown; but he was presumably irritated by the threats against Madison, since he was unfriendly to Gallatin.[78]

Under these circumstances, Duane sought financial assistance from Jefferson. The latter attempted to raise funds through friends in Richmond; but the *Aurora's* censure of Madison in April caused much resentment, and the Virginians refused to give aid. Jefferson also reproved Duane mildly for his course and hinted strongly that it would lead to his being read out of the party since he was going against the will of the majority and verging toward an alliance with the Federalists in opposition to the administration.[79]

Delicately phrased though Jefferson's reproof was, Duane was offended. Far from revising his opinions, he later wrote with characteristic self-righteousness that he was "perfectly satisfied" with his own integrity and was "indifferent to the frowns and favors of mankind." In August, 1811, he stated in the *Aurora* that he had become the victim of administration proscription and referred in a veiled fashion to the refusal of Leiper and Clay to extend him assistance and to the failure of the attempt to raise money in Virginia as evidences of the fact.[80]

It was hardly to be expected that the Old School should be favored with Federal patronage under such conditions; and the Snyderites began to woo the general government on their own account. These matters reached a climax in the early months of 1811.

In January Leib had apparently interposed objections to the reappointment of John Smith as Federal Marshal, largely on the ground that he had secretly collaborated with the Snyderites in avoiding an open clash in the Olmsted affair. Leib's attack failed, but it occasioned a considerable stir. Dallas wrote Gallatin in defense of Smith; and Thomas Leiper, a stalwart of the Old School, wrote Madison and asserted that Leib was seeking the office for himself. Such charges were so damaging that Leib went to the extent of writing Madison and requesting him to say whether he or his friends had sought the office.[81]

A new incident took place in April, when the office of Commissioner of Loans in Pennsylvania became vacant. Leib made a confidential application for the position for himself; but the Snyderites apparently believed that the Old School was trying to get the place for Frederick Wolbert. Since Snyder had just removed the latter as prothonotary of the court of common pleas in Philadelphia and had appointed Dr. John Porter in his stead, the Snyderites were anxious to prevent the appointment of Wolbert at all costs.[82]

The *Democratic Press* had long complained that the Federal patronage had been exercised by John Steele, the Collector of the Port, for the benefit of the Old School; and the Snyderites were anxious to make an alliance for themselves with the national administration.[83] With the *Aurora* engaged in an unrestrained attack upon Gallatin and in threats against Madison, the time certainly seemed propitious to make the approach. Binns accordingly wrote a long letter to Gallatin.

Immediately concerned with protesting against the rumored appointment of Wolbert, it also discussed the general situation in State politics at great length. Binns pointed out that Snyder was supported by the great body of the Democrats and that the Old School had become a minority even in Philadelphia. He argued that Leib and Duane were seeking to prevent an alliance between the national administration and the Snyderites with a view to defeating Madison in the next election. He went on to say that although it was now becoming clear that the faction was not really friendly to Madison, the way in which the Federal patronage was exercised in the State aroused suspicions of the administration in the minds of many Republicans. He then referred to Steele's actions in the customhouse and to the fact that William Dickson, editor of the Lancaster *Intelligencer* and nephew of Steele, had been given the contract to publish the Federal laws in his paper immediately after he had begun to oppose Snyder.[84]

The chief significance of Binns's letter does not lie in the matter of patronage, since the administration would hardly have favored Duane's friends at that time in any case. Rather, it is important because it indicates a shift in political alignments. The Snyderites had been reluctant supporters of Madison in 1808, and they had been somewhat estranged by the outcome of the Olmsted Case. On the other hand, the Old School had affected to be the special friends of the administration. Now the scene was changing—the Snyderites were Madison's backers; the Old School was in the opposition.

Fallen to such a low state in both State and national politics, it was little wonder that the Old School could do nothing effective to prevent the nomination of Snyder. Led by Leib, however, a portion of them began to intrigue with the Federalists and Quids to run McKean for Governor. According to a writer in the *Democratic Press*, this scheme arose out of negotiations between Leib and Joseph Hiester in July, 1811, and it involved a number of McKean's old supporters in Lancaster and Philadelphia.[85] Despite his 77 years, McKean was transparently eager for the nomination.[86]

The success of the plan depended upon Federalist co-operation; but the Federalists were convinced of the futility of opposition to Snyder and had decided not to offer any candidate.[87] Their most influential leaders were cold to the projected alliance with the Quids and the Old School to back McKean; but there was so much agitation that a number of meetings were held in August to decide the question. At the first two it was agreed not to run a candidate; but the supporters of McKean were dissatisfied and refused to abide by the decision.[88]

They called a meeting for August 19, 1811; but the final settlement of the question was deferred until August 22. At that time James Milnor, Federalist Congressman-elect, opposed making a nomination but was overruled. He then argued successfully against the choice of McKean and proposed that William Tilghman be selected. This was done; and a committee was appointed to notify Tilghman, who was then attending the Supreme Court session in Pittsburgh.[89]

Tilghman declined the nomination with expressions of gratitude for the honor. Privately, he wrote Milnor saying that the State was "not prepared for a change of Governor" and that it was too late to begin opposition. Even the Federalists he had seen throughout the State had "made up their minds to submit to the re-election of the present Governor." Tilghman thought that there might have been a chance if the nomination had been made earlier, but under the circumstances he felt it would only hurt the Federalists to campaign against Snyder at such a late date before the election.[90] These facts were as obvious to the committee as to Tilghman; and it seems that his nomination was made solely for the purpose of stopping the coalition movement in favor of McKean.

Blocked in this last desperate attempt to oppose Snyder, the Old School was also outmaneuvered in the city and county of Philadelphia. The Snyderites won a majority of the general ward committee despite the vociferous protests of some of the Old School group. The latter charged that the meetings had been called on short notice and in such a fashion as to preclude the attendance of a majority of the Democrats. They also pointed out that the Old School had polled by far the greater portion of the Democratic votes in the city and excoriated the Snyderites for refusing to submit to new ward elections. The Governor's supporters were unmoved by these strictures and went on with their business. In keeping with their professions of a desire for Democratic harmony, they did, however, place two Old School men on the city assembly ticket.[91]

The Snyderites proceeded with equal disregard of their opponents in the county. Announcing that the results of the last election had conclusively settled the question of county and district meetings, they held their meetings and elected delegates, who met on August 26, 1811, and drew up a ticket. The delegates then met with the conferees from the city to nominate candidates for State Senator and other joint offices.[92]

The Old School, in an attempt to stem the Snyderite tide, held a meeting on August 5, 1811, at which it was agreed to use the district delegate system; but it was specified that the nominations by the delegates must be submitted to a general county meeting for approval. Although the Snyderites ignored this call, the Old School held its district meetings and adopted a county assembly ticket at a general meeting on September 2. The delegates were then instructed to make nominations for State Senator and other joint offices if the general ward committee refused to meet with them.[93]

Accordingly, the Old School county delegates joined by a few men from the city met on September 18, 1811, and adopted a ticket as they had been instructed. They also published a long address which reviewed the course of events in the city and county. Castigating the Snyderites for rejecting the proffered compromise on the delegate system, it proclaimed that the Old School alone was adhering to the Democratic principle of popular rule, because it submitted the delegate nominations to the people for approval. It then spent a great deal of space denouncing the dictation exercised by Binns and the State officeholders and assailing the Snyderites for their shady manuevers in the city.[94]

The *Aurora* held itself aloof from all these disputes. It printed the proceedings of both Snyderite and Old School meetings and even published resolutions adopted by the Democratic Society. However, Duane announced that this did not indicate either approval or disapproval of what was printed in the paper. He had decided to *"stand neutral."*[95] The *Aurora's* apathy was so pronounced that the paper published no election returns and even failed to announce the re-election of Snyder.

The Federalists in Philadelphia continued the political methods of the two preceding years and likewise the use of the name of American Republicans. The only noteworthy development in their activities was the formation of the "Washington Association," a body of young men organized for the purpose of furthering Federalist principles and used to aid the vigilance committees during the election.[96]

The election on October 8, 1811, was marked by great apathy. The Federalists carried the city by more than 700 votes, though they polled nearly 200 votes less than in 1810. Snyder received only 1,382 votes, while the Democratic assembly ticket averaged 1,498. The greater part of the city Democrats apparently refrained from voting. In the county the Old School assembly candidates averaged 1,380 votes to 2,007 for the Snyderites. The Federalists in the county did not run an assembly ticket, but they gave 817 votes to the senatorial candidate. Snyder received 2,326 votes in the county.[97]

In the State at large Snyder had virtually no opposition. He carried every county and had 52,319 votes out of 57,603. Tilghman received 3,609 votes, the majority of them coming from Chester, Adams, and Luzerne counties. There were 1,675 scattered votes, most of them in Lancaster County.[98]

The Democratic victory was equally impressive in the election of legislators. They won all nine of the senatorial races and captured 84 out of the 95 seats in the House of Representatives. The Federalist delegation in the House was reduced to eleven, and that in the Senate to five. The Federalists won majorities only in Adams and Delaware counties and in the city of Philadelphia, while they elected one member each from Luzerne and Lancaster counties.[99]

Outside Philadelphia the only significant incident was the split in Pittsburgh and the senatorial district of Allegheny, Beaver, and Butler counties. This was partially a continuation of the schism over the congressional nomination in 1810, but it was also due to a fight over the establishment of a new bank in Pittsburgh.

In February a public meeting in Pittsburgh adopted resolutions favoring the creation of a Bank of Pittsburgh and forwarded a copy of the proceedings to the legislature. This meeting was denounced violently by writers in the *Commonwealth;* and feeling ran so high that Dennis S. Scully, an opponent of the bank, was assaulted by Ephraim Pentland and James Riddle, who were supporting it.[100]

After the adjournment of the legislature, the bank question was subordinated; and the Democrats of Allegheny County proceeded to choose their district delegates. The delegates met on August 12, 1811, made their nominations, and recommended Thomas Baird as senatorial candidate. At the same time they appointed delegates to confer with those from Beaver and Butler counties on the nomination of a Senator, and they instructed them to seek a revision of the delegate ratio between the counties so that Allegheny would be represented in proportion to its population.[101]

Such a proposition was not likely to appeal to the other counties, and the delegate meeting broke up without altering the ratio or nominating a candidate. The Allegheny Democrats went on to support Baird, but the Beaver County group dissented. They pointed out that Allegheny already had one of the two Senators to which the district was entitled and that it should not be permitted to have both. While agreeing that the nomination properly belonged to Butler County, the Beaver Democrats refused to recognize the withdrawal of the Butler candidate in favor of Baird. Instead, they nominated Robert Moore as their candidate for Senator.[102]

Meanwhile, a committee of fourteen Democrats in Pittsburgh, including Pentland and Riddle, published a brief address which attacked the regular Democratic ticket as the product of "the machinations of a few designing and ambitious individuals, for sinister purposes." They offered instead a completely new ticket.[103] The regular Democratic correspondence committee replied with a defense of their nominations and asserted that the aim of the bolters was to secure legislators who would forward the bank project. They warned that a bank would benefit only the speculators and stockholders and that it contained the "germ of aristocracy." The bolters answered by pointing out that one member of the regular correspondence committee was a director of the Pittsburgh branch of the Bank of Pennsylvania and that the others had shown little disposition to shun that institution. They went on to argue strongly the advantages of creating another bank.[104]

With the Federalists offering no candidates, the election was fought wholly between the two Democratic factions. In Allegheny County the regular assembly ticket carried by a majority of only 60 votes, although Baird defeated Moore by 180. Butler County furnished a majority of more than 200 votes for Baird and of 300 votes for the assembly ticket. These margins were sufficient to elect the assembly ticket and to override the Beaver County vote for Moore.[105]

The split is significant for its indication of the centrifugal tendencies beginning to reappear among the Democrats and also because it demonstrates the impact of new economic forces which were beginning to disrupt old political alignments.

In the two years from 1809 to 1811, the country Democrats had achieved complete and almost unchallenged mastery of State politics. Yet there were many disaffected elements which awaited only a favorable opportunity to seek to overthrow the Snyder regime. The Quids were still strong in Berks, Westmoreland, and Armstrong counties; and the Old School was still potentially powerful in Philadelphia. Apart from these main foci of Republican discontent, there were signs of restlessness in Allegheny County. Altogether these dissidents amounted to very little in comparison with the Snyderites, but with Federalist aid they would have formed a powerful coalition. That such an alignment did not take place was due principally to the demand for unity imposed by the War of 1812.

CHAPTER X

FOREIGN AFFAIRS, WAR AND THE PRESIDENTIAL ELECTION: 1809-1812

AMERICAN POLITICS since 1805 had been increasingly influenced by the Napoleonic wars in Europe. Despite the Republican success in 1808, the embargo was repealed in the following year; and the expedients adopted in its stead proved no more successful in achieving a relaxation of belligerent restraints on neutral trade. By the time the Twelfth Congress convened in November, 1811, the country felt that it had only the alternatives of submission or war; and war was declared against Great Britain in June, 1812.

Coming as it did in a presidential election year, the war became the prime issue in the political campaign. The Federalists exerted themselves to the utmost; and, aided by the candidacy of the dissident Republican, DeWitt Clinton, and the inept conduct of the war by the administration, they came very near to defeating Madison. That they failed was due principally to the staunchness of Pennsylvania. Overcoming for the most part their internal divisions, the Democrats of that State rallied once more to oppose the Federalists and demonstrated again their claim to the title of the keystone in the Democratic arch.

I

Although the struggle between the Snyderites and the Duane-Leib faction was the chief concern of Pennsylvania politics in the three years which followed the election of 1808, the people of the State continued to manifest a lively interest in the course of foreign affairs. In keeping with their traditional party regularity, the Democrats gave loyal support to the policies of the Madison administration; but their real sentiments appear to have favored more aggressive actions in support of national rights.

With the Federalists making the embargo the chief issue, the Democrats had rallied warmly to its support in 1808. Some had viewed the measure as a wise precaution taken in preparation for war; Duane and others had seen it as a substitute for war; and many had probably regarded it as only a temporizing expedient. All, however, had backed it as a party policy.

With the election ended, many Democrats began to seek a change in the policy. In September, 1808, William Jones had used his very considerable influence to dissuade a meeting of Philadelphia ship captains from condemning the embargo. Two months later he expressed his views more freely in a letter to his close friend Nathaniel Macon, a leading Republican Congressman from North Carolina. He demanded that the embargo be continued only for the duration of the next session of Congress and that preparations be made for war at that time. If American rights were still ignored, he favored an open declaration of war on either France or Great Britain. He proclaimed his abhorrence of war but added that it was "possible for a free peaceful & virtuous people to prize the blessings of peace & deprecate the horrors of war [with] too much sensibility."[1]

A similar tone appeared less openly in the resolutions offered in the State House of Representatives on December 8, 1808, by Jacob Mitchell of the city of Philadelphia. Although the embargo was approved, the fourth resolution referred to the privations it caused and concluded by stating that if the country were forced into war that it would be waged "with all our hearts and with all our strength." Leib offered substitute resolutions which described the embargo as "a wise, pacific, and patriotic measure, . . . calculated to exact an observance of our national rights, without a resort to the horrors and desolations of war"; and his views appeared in the resolutions finally adopted. However, the incident demonstrates that at least some of the Democratic legislators preferred war to a continuance of the embargo, although they continued to support the latter out of party loyalty.[2]

While these doubts were assailing the Pennsylvania Democrats, the embargo was undergoing a fierce assault in New England and in Congress which eventually forced its repeal. This strident opposition to the law led the Democrats in Philadelphia to take measures for its support. A public meeting was called at the State House for January 23, 1809; and the wards appointed vigilance committees charged with insuring a full attendance.[3]

According to the *Aurora*, there were at least ten thousand present when the meeting was called to order. William Jones, a former Quid, served as chairman, and Robert McMullin, a follower of Leib, was secretary. Jones opened the proceedings with a brief address which stated that the purpose was to give evidence of support to the national government and the enforcement of national laws. Referring to the embargo, he stated that it was evidently a temporary measure and within a few months "must be superceded, either by the peaceful enjoyments of our commercial rights and independence, or their maintenance at the point of the sword."

He was followed by Walter Franklin, Attorney General of the State and a prominent Snyderite leader, who offered the resolutions adopted by the meeting. These resolutions denounced the actions taken in New England against the enforcement of the embargo, approved that law and its supplements, and proclaimed a willingness to assist in the enforcement of these laws. They also gave evidence that war was soon expected to follow. The resolutions approved preparations for war and asserted that if the embargo had been rigidly observed "it would have . . . prevented the necessity of a recurrence to any other means to ensure justice from the belligerent nations."[4]

The Federalists were determined not to let this meeting go unchallenged and began preparations to hold one of their own at the State House on January 31, 1809. To counteract this, the Democrats immediately began to organize to oppose them and called a second meeting to be held at the same time and place. A number of the Federalists, such as William Tilghman, were doubtful of the expediency of the meeting because of the Quaker aversion to such proceedings and believed that the Federalists would do better by circulating memorials against the embargo. However, a number of others, led by Thomas Truxtun, felt that it would destroy the party if they receded in the face of Democratic opposition; and they prevailed upon the rest to continue with the plans for the meeting.[5]

Federalist and Democratic sources differ widely as to what took place at the meeting. With both groups scheduled to appear at eleven o'clock, the Federalists arrived an hour early and began their proceedings. Thomas Truxtun was made chairman, and George Clymer secretary. In anticipation of possible disturbances, a sizable squad of husky seamen was placed around the platform.

Thus organized, the meeting adopted a number of fairly temperate resolutions. They began by asserting loyal support to the union "whatever may be the errours of the administration, and however severe the pressure which those errours may have occasioned." They denounced as Democratic artifices the reports that opponents of the embargo were disaffected to the union. They declared a longer continuance of the embargo to be "unjust, oppressive, and impolitick." They excoriated the Enforcement Act as an invasion of civil liberties and as contrary to the provisions of the Constitution. They announced a determination to maintain their rights but called upon all citizens to resist violations of the embargo laws. Finally, they provided for the appointment of a committee to circulate a memorial to Congress in conformity with these opinions.[6]

The meeting did not proceed without violence, but the exact circumstances are disputed. According to the Federalists, several hundred Democrats attempted to break up the meeting but were forced off until the proceedings were completed. The *Aurora* told a different story. It said that the Federalists had hardly begun when the Democrats began to arrive in great numbers. Unable to proceed further, the Federalists had attempted to break up the platform and chairs. This caused a fight to break out; but by the intervention of William Jones and others the Federalists were permitted to retreat under a shower of snowballs.[7]

After the Federalists were gone, the Democrats, who numbered eighteen thousand according to the *Aurora,* selected William Jones and Robert McMullin as chairman and secretary, respectively. Jones and Alexander J. Dallas addressed the crowd; and the meeting declared its adherence to the resolutions adopted on January 23, 1809, and appointed a corresponding committee to work for the objectives expressed therein.[8]

With party spirit running so high, tempers became even more inflamed when a number of Democrats in the Northern Liberties on February 6, 1809, burned an effigy of Senator Timothy Pickering of Massachusetts, one of the leaders in the fight against the embargo in Congress. The Federalists were already enraged because they felt that the Democrats had unwarrantedly interfered with their meeting on January 31; and the *United States' Gazette* had made particularly vicious attacks on Dallas as a result. The burning of the effigy led Truxtun to call on Dallas and inform him that the Democratic leaders would be held personally responsible if any Federalist were injured by mob action. Dallas' denial of any connection with the affair satisfied Truxtun; and he used his influence to prevent the more hot-headed

Federalists from openly insulting Dallas at the Washington's Birthday ball.[9]

Despite the support given by the Democrats in Philadelphia and by other meetings in the State,[10] the embargo was repealed by the Nonintercourse Act of March 1, 1809.[11] The *Aurora* was much downcast by this turn of events. Wholeheartedly in favor of the embargo, the paper believed that the repeal was the result of an artificial panic created by Massachusetts and Connecticut which enabled the minority to triumph over the majority. In its opinion, Great Britain would thereby be encouraged to even greater arrogance and war would thus become inevitable.[12]

The proceedings of Congress also brought despair to William Jones, though for different reasons. Writing to William B. Giles, Senator from Virginia, he said that he had taken a prominent part in the recent meetings with a confidence that the embargo would soon be "superceded by measures of dignity and energy" which would "arouse the people from present torpitude to future hope and enthusiasm." However, the course of Congress foreshadowed a Federalist triumph; and Jones bitterly requested that he and his friends be told what Congress proposed to do in order that they might be prepared for their humiliation as "objects of derision for our credulity."[13]

Congress had thus failed to satisfy either section of the Democrats by its actions. Duane, of course, favored the embargo policy for its own sake. Jones backed it as a party measure, but he hoped to see it ended in favor of war. There is no way of measuring the strength of these opposing views; but the evidence indicates that Jones's sentiments were those of the great majority of Democrats and that the latter favored war if the belligerents did not accord full respect to the neutral rights of the country.[14]

A new turn was given to foreign affairs by the Erskine agreement in April, 1809. Ignoring specific conditions laid down in his instructions, David M. Erskine, the British minister, conducted a correspondence with Secretary of State Robert Smith and eventually announced that the British orders in council would be withdrawn on June 10, 1809, in return for the withdrawal of nonintercourse against Great Britain. Using the authority granted by the Nonintercourse Act, Madison accordingly proclaimed that the restrictions on trade with Great Britain were withdrawn.[15]

The *United States' Gazette* at first hailed this arrangement with delight and heaped praise on Madison for thus daring to resist the French decrees. In the face of Democratic skepticism, the paper insisted that there was no trick in the matter and that the British government would carry out "with good faith, the contract which has been made with their minister here."[16] It was therefore stunned in late July when it learned that the British foreign secretary, George Canning, had in fact repudiated the agreement because Erskine had exceeded his instructions. For several days the editor refrained from comment, although he published pseudonymous contributions which were highly critical of the British government. By the middle of August, however, the paper had sufficiently recovered from its chagrin to resume its criticisms of the Madison administration.[17]

The Democratic reaction was far different. The *Aurora* in a long article announced complacently that the repudiation was just what it had predicted. It believed that Erskine had acted in good faith but described him as the "dupe of his own government." The paper then excoriated the Tenth Congress for its "infatuation" in repealing the embargo under a panic inspired by Timothy Pickering. As for the future course to be followed, the *Aurora* decried talk of war except in case of actual invasion. Instead, it proposed the passage of strict navigation laws and a program of domestic manufactures and commerce. If this did not succeed, a total nonintercourse should be tried; and if that failed the country must go to war.[18]

Such staid advice was not welcomed by the Democrats of Lower Delaware Ward. They adopted resolutions on August 14, 1809, which denounced the actions of the British government and proclaimed

> that we conceive open war preferable to such a degraded state of suspence; and unless customary insult has rendered us callous to national honor, it cannot be avoided, without suffering our rights to be trampled upon by every petty tyrant. . . .[19]

Matters were made still worse by the mission of Francis James Jackson, whom Canning sent to replace Erskine as British minister. Jackson, who had achieved considerable notoriety for his arrogant actions at Copenhagen, arrived in September and began negotiations with Secretary Smith in October. During their interviews and in their correspondence, Jackson insisted that the American government had concluded the arrangement with Erskine with full knowledge that it was contrary to Canning's instructions. Despite warnings, Jackson persisted in his statements; and on November 8, 1809, the Secretary of State refused to have further correspondence with him.[20]

The *United States' Gazette* at first gave a cautious approval to the breaking off of relations with Jackson. Within a week, however, it was expressing its belief that the administration had known of Erskine's instructions; and by the early part of December the paper could find nothing in Jackson's conduct to warrant dismissal.[21]

The Democrats were outraged by Jackson's attitude, but they seemed to be seized with a strange lassitude. In the Pennsylvania House of Representatives resolutions on the subject were introduced as early as December 7, 1809; and twelve days later a committee reported revised resolutions censuring Jackson and proclaiming that the rejection of Erskine's agreement and other British abuses "ought to nerve the arm and invigorate the spirit of every freeman in the country." They also pledged support of war whenever the national government thought it necessary. Despite this high tone, the House did not adopt the resolutions until January 5, 1810, while the Senate did not approve them until March 6.[22]

A like languor had taken possession of Congress. It had adopted after lengthy debate Senator Giles's resolutions excoriating Jackson, but it did not follow this action by preparations for war. Instead, it began the discussion of a bill introduced in the House by a committee headed by Nathaniel Macon. This measure, known as Macon's Bill No. 1, proposed to substitute for nonintercourse a system excluding British and French vessels from American ports while permitting the importation of the products of those countries in American vessels. It amounted to a form of navigation act, and it was certainly far from being an aggressive defense of American rights.[23]

The *Democratic Press* decried the bill as "most contemptible and most unworthy an American Congress" and suggested that the people hold a meeting to denounce it.[24] Responding to this proposal, the Democratic machinery in the Philadelphia area was set in motion; and the members of the city general ward committee met on February 7, 1810, with the conferees of Philadelphia and Delaware counties. This group drew up a memorial to Congress recommending the passage of a nonimportation law and the adoption of measures for defense in anticipation of what was regarded as an inevitable war. The conferees also issued a call for a public meeting of the congressional district to be held at the State House on February 14.[25]

The resolutions adopted by the gathering at the State House were unequivocal in their demands for effective action. Approving Madison's conduct, they professed to see no possibility of diplomatic redress for the wrongs committed by Great Britain and asserted that these constituted acts of war "calling for immediate atonement or immediate retaliation." They expressed their willingness "to rally under the national standard whenever congress shall respond to the feelings and spirit of the people"; and they called upon the government either to declare war or to enter into an armed neutrality to maintain the freedom of the seas. Deprecating the weak measures proposed by Macon, they insisted that British hostages be seized in a number equal to the impressed American seamen and that these hostages be put to work until the seamen should be released. The meeting also adopted strong addresses to Madison and to the American people.[26]

The effect of the resolutions was spoiled by the attempt of the Old School faction to gain approval of a resolution denouncing Snyder's conduct in the Olmsted affair. The *Aurora* insisted that this censure had been adopted, although the officers of the meeting denied it. The *Aurora* also aroused protest by its refusal to publish the address to the people of the United States on the ground that it was filled with "*blunders* and *false constructions.*"[27]

Congress was unmoved by the sentiments of the Philadelphians and adopted the measure known as Macon's Bill No. 2, which repealed the Nonintercourse Act of the previous year and left trade open with both belligerents. However, it provided that if either France or Great Britain should cease its violations of American rights the President would renew nonintercourse against the other power.[28]

Such a retreat from any real resistance to the belligerent aggressions brought condemnation from both the *Democratic Press* and the *Aurora*. The *Press* asserted that the Tenth Congress would be "little less than execrated" for its repeal of the embargo; and it complained bitterly of the indecision of the Eleventh Congress in the session just closed. The paper believed, however, that the country's true policy was to maintain "*a rigid and conscientious neutrality*" and to "preserve peace at every risk short of National Independence." It then excoriated Macon's Bill as an abandonment of the policy of commercial restric-

FOREIGN AFFAIRS AND THE PRESIDENTIAL ELECTION 245

tions begun by the embargo and asserted that such a policy was the only means the country had of forcing Great Britain to accord it justice.[29]

The *Aurora* condemned Macon's bills as the *"resolution* of congressional folly" resulting from the abandonment of the embargo by the Tenth Congress. In its opinion, with the possible exception of the senate of Carthage, the world had never known "degeneracy so extreme in such a short course of years, as has been shewn in the congress of the United States of America."[30]

Despite such castigations of Congress and the evident dissatisfaction of those who wished for war, the congressional campaign in 1810 was not marked by great excitement. Even the Federalists, with the exception of those in Philadelphia, showed little concern. In Allegheny County, where there was a considerable latent Federalist vote, the party did not offer a ticket, although there were desultory suggestions that the Federalists should support Samuel Smith, the Democratic incumbent who had been dropped because of his failure to vote for Giles's resolutions censuring Jackson. Nothing came of this proposal; and the chief interest in the congressional race in this district centered about the claims of Adamson Tannehill and Abner Lacock, the opposing Democratic candidates.[31]

In the congressional district of York and Adams counties, the total congressional vote amounted to only 4,122, although it had reached 7,656 in 1808. Staunchly Federalist Adams County in 1810 mustered only 664 votes for the candidate of that party as compared with 1,454 in 1808.[32] A similar lassitude was displayed in the Lancaster-Berks-Chester district, where the total vote in 1810 amounted to only 12,000 as compared to nearly 21,000 in 1808. The only notable incident in this district was the withdrawal of Matthias Richards as the Quid candidate from Berks County.[33]

Even in the first congressional district, comprising Philadelphia city and county and Delaware County, the total average congressional vote in 1810 amounted to only 10,579, a drop of more than 3,000 from the vote in 1808. In spite of the activities of the American Republican Society, the Federalist vote in this district declined by more than 1,700, while the Democrats lost only 1,300. It was solely because of the split between the Old School and the Snyderite factions that the Federalist James Milnor was chosen as one of the district's three

Congressmen. He was the single successful Federalist congressional candidate in the state.[34]

The concluding weeks of this lackadaisical campaign coincided with a revival of American hopes that the European nations might be induced to recognize American rights. It was announced in August that France had revoked her decrees so far as they affected the United States. Although this changed policy was communicated in an equivocal fashion by means of a letter from the French foreign minister to the American envoy at Paris, Madison proclaimed in November that under the terms of Macon's Bill No. 2 nonintercourse would be revived against Great Britain in the following February.[35]

The *United States' Gazette* condemned this action upon a bare promise of the French to lift their restrictions; but the Democrats viewed matters more hopefully.[36] Governor Snyder, in his annual message to the legislature in December, saw "more flattering prospects" in foreign relations and believed that the belligerents had shown a disposition to end their unjust measures.[37] The legislators apparently shared his sentiments, since they refrained from adopting any resolutions on foreign affairs for the first time in four years.

In the two years which followed 1808 Pennsylvania had shown a convincing loyalty to the foreign policy of the national administration. The Democrats had upheld the embargo and nonintercourse laws, although the general sentiment of the party in the State seemed to favor war. The Federalists had fought stoutly against the policy of commercial restrictions and had given evidences of a disposition to oppose anything which might lead to a war with Great Britain. Despite their newspaper diatribes and their efforts to build up an effective organization in Philadelphia, however, the party had made little progress and actually seemed to decline in strength during this period. By the close of 1810 Pennsylvania had reached a condition of relative calm and was waiting to see what further developments would take place in foreign affairs.

II

The events of 1811 crushed the hopes of an improvement in foreign relations; and there was a general expectation that the Twelfth Congress would declare war when it convened in its first session in November,

1811. Such eventually proved to be the case; but the declaration was deferred until June, 1812, and in the intervening months there was much uncertainty as to what action Congress would take. During this period the Pennsylvania Democrats consistently supported the policy of war.

In the early months of 1811 even the *Aurora* had come to feel that there was no other course than war with Great Britain. It hailed the naval action of the *President* and the *Little Belt* in May with approval and asserted that the popular reaction to the affair gave convincing proof that the people would support the government if it would take firm action to protect the flag from insult and American citizens from impressment. In August the paper made a lengthy review of British-American relations and concluded that there existed no other alternatives than war or submission.[38]

President Madison's message to Congress on November 5, 1811, indicated that he had come to the same conclusions. He outlined the existing situation in foreign affairs, spoke of the continued aggression of Great Britain and the unsatisfactory nature of relations with France, and recommended that Congress put the country "into an armor and an attitude demanded by the crisis, and corresponding with the national spirit and expectations."[39]

The *Aurora* applauded the message and proclaimed that it had put an end to the apathy into which the country had fallen as a result of the repeal of the embargo and the equivocation of the Eleventh Congress. It particularly welcomed the recommendations for military preparations.[40]

Other Democrats were also pleased with the message; but their approval was tempered with a caution induced by the disappointments of the preceding years. Their attitude was well expressed in a letter to Jonathan Roberts from one of his constituents, asking that Roberts, now a Congressman, keep him informed of the progress of affairs in Washington:

> The Presidents message which I have just receivd & read makes me still more anxious to solicit the favour. By that I perceive that strong measures are expected to be pursued. and so far as I am able to see, it is right—my feelings all say it is right. The indignation of the people has been so often rous'd by the insults & injuries offer'd by the British Govt. and so often allay'd again by the glimmering prospects of

amicable adjustment, that, I fear a continuance of a policy *too amicable* (so to speak) may have a tendancy to break and destroy that *honest* spirit of indignation so necessary to preserve the honour of the nation & redress its wrongs. Our policy, therefore, now, if ever, ought to be mark'd by a decision that Cannot be mistaken by our enemies either at home or abroad.[41]

Even the Federalists affected to welcome the message and the subsequent report of the House committee on foreign relations. The *United States' Gazette* disapproved of the relative lenity shown France, but it professed to see the measures of defense as evidence that the Republicans were being forced to adopt the principles of the Federalists and to abandon the attempt to coerce foreign powers by commercial restrictions. The *Pittsburgh Gazette* expressed similar views and hoped that the country would return to the policies of Washington and abandon the proclamations and gunboats which had disgraced and almost ruined it.[42]

The government of Pennsylvania likewise indicated its approval. Snyder gave high praise to the conduct of the President and recommended that the militia be reformed to prepare it for the war which seemed imminent.[43] His program was not carried out by the members, but they left no doubt as to their warlike sentiments. In the Senate, John Gemmil, a minister from Chester County, introduced a set of strong resolutions on December 5, 1811. They denounced British aggressions on American commerce, the impressment of American seamen, and the unreasonable demands made upon the American government. Proclaiming that such injustices must be forcibly resisted, they pledged the legislators to give zealous aid to the military preparations of the Federal government. They favored the use of State funds to promote domestic manufactures and recommended that the legislators wear only American-made clothing. Most radical of all was the proposal that British property be sequestered to indemnify those whose ships and property had been seized and that British subjects in America be imprisoned and forced to labor under conditions similar to those imposed upon impressed American seamen.

Making only minor amendments, the Senate adopted these resolutions on December 14, 1811, without a record vote and sent them to the House. In that chamber an attempt to include a denunciation of the French government was defeated 80-14, with eleven Federalists and three Democrats making up the minority. The resolution for retaliation upon British property and British subjects was adopted by a vote of 72-23, the opposition being composed of twelve Federalists and eleven Democrats. The only change made in the resolutions by the House was the inclusion of a clause pledging support to the general government in case of war. This was adopted with only four dissenting votes, all Democratic. In this form the resolutions were approved and returned to the Senate on December 21, 1811; and that body concurred with the amendment on the same day.[44]

The legislature gave further proof of its support of the administration by two other measures during the session. One of these authorized State banks in which the Commonwealth held stock to make loans to the general government with the approval of the Governor.[45] The second gave the Governor authority to make immediate payment of any direct tax apportioned to the State during the recess of the legislature.[46] Neither of these acts aroused any opposition.

Three other matters of interest occupied the attention of the legislature during this session. The first of these was its final refusal to give a State charter to the stockholders of the late Bank of the United States. Even though a bonus of a half million dollars was offered for the charter, the House voted 69-22 against the bill on January 20, 1812.[47]

The session also witnessed the revival of the movement for a revision of the State Constitution. This began on January 9, 1812, when Isaac Weaver, Jr., of Greene County, introduced resolutions in the Senate providing that the people should vote at the next election on whether or not a convention should be called to amend the Constitution in certain specified particulars. The changes proposed were as follows: reduction of the term of State Senators to one year; fixing the opening of the legislative session in January rather than December; modification of the Governor's veto power so that it might be overridden by a simple majority in each branch of the legislature; appointment of judges of the Supreme Court and the courts of common pleas for terms of seven years; election of justices of the peace for terms of five years; and provision for a system of future constitutional amendments by the legislature.

Weaver's proposal was rejected by the committee of the whole on February 12, 1812; and the Senate approved the report of the committee by a vote of 16-12 on the same day. Most of the votes in favor of the convention came from the extreme western and the central sections of the State, while the bulk of those opposing it were from the southeastern counties.[48]

Two days later Robert Anderson, a member from Washington County, introduced identical resolutions in the House. In that chamber the committee of the whole considered the matter on March 5, 1812, and reported a substitute resolution which provided for a vote by the people on the question of holding a convention but omitted any reference to the subjects which the convention should consider. The House voted on the report that day and rejected it by the narrow margin of 45-43. The extreme western and the central counties were almost unanimously in favor of the convention, and the southeastern section mustered more than a dozen votes in its support. The Federalist counties of Luzerne, Adams, and Delaware, the normally Quid counties of Westmoreland, Armstrong, Indiana, Jefferson, and Berks, and the Democratic counties of Montgomery and Philadelphia were solidly opposed as was the Federalist delegation from the city of Philadelphia.[49]

On the whole, it seems likely that the movement would have succeeded had it not been for the imminence of war. The Snyderite Harrisburg *Pennsylvania Republican* agreed that the Constitution was defective in a number of respects, but it stated flatly that the time was not proper to enter into attempts to revise these shortcomings.[50] Its views were probably representative of those of many of the legislators.

The third important measure passed in the session was a new apportionment act for Congressmen. Under the act of Congress of December 21, 1811, Pennsylvania was allowed 23 Congressmen, an increase of five members above its previous representation. The legislature in March, 1812, redistricted the State to take care of the new members. It made several changes calculated to strengthen the Democrats; but none were of a sort likely to arouse much opposition.[51]

While the legislature was engaged with these matters, the country had once more fallen into a state of apathy. The initial energy of Congress had been succeeded by a period of indecision, which led the *Democratic Press* in February to say that Congress had chilled "the noblest spirits in the Union." The paper demanded that there be an end to such "shilly-shally, he-would-and-he-would-not" conduct. The *Aurora* also scored Congress for falling so far behind the people in spirit. A Democratic editor in Montgomery County wrote privately to Jonathan Roberts in March and reported that the people were apathetic because of the "contrariety of opinions in Congress" and because of a doubt that the administration seriously intended going to war.[52]

The *Aurora* did not confine its criticism to Congress. It fulminated against the incompetence of Secretary of War William Eustis and renewed its intemperate attacks on Gallatin when he recommended a program of internal taxation for carrying on the contemplated war. It said that such taxes were unnecessary, that money could be raised in ample amounts by loans secured by the public lands, and that Gallatin's intention was to prevent a declaration of war by asking for the levying of the very taxes which the Republicans had reprobated so strongly in 1798 and 1799.[53]

The administration's blunder in the matter of the Henry Letters added further to Democratic discomfiture.[54] The Federalist press unanimously condemned the attempt to brand their party as traitorous and asserted that the letters had been published in order to influence the Massachusetts elections in the spring. They also noted that Henry's reports had not only failed to show any Federalist treachery but proved the exact contrary. Their most effective answer was the publication of proof that the administration had paid $50,000 to purchase Henry's correspondence. They were thus enabled to accuse the government of having wasted public money for purely partisan purposes.[55]

The Democratic papers could make no adequate reply to the Federalist attacks. The *Aurora* maintained weakly that Henry's failure to mention names did not constitute proof that the Federalists had not dealt with him, and it also attempted to make much of the similarity of views expressed by the New England leaders and the Henry Letters. The editor of the Harrisburg *Pennsylvania Republican* refused to make any defense. He asserted that the letters amounted to very little, and he specifically disapproved their purchase with government funds. Other Democratic editors in the State wished to make a defense but were uncertain as to how it could be done.[56]

The Federalist papers kept up a constant criticism of all aspects of the Democratic program. Countering the administration's claim that the French decrees had been rescinded, they published frequent accounts of the seizure and burning of American ships by French vessels.[57] They deplored the Democratic favoritism to France and decried the association with such a tyrant as Napoleon.[58] The more extreme Federalists viewed the latter as an antichrist and conversely pictured Great Britain as God's chosen instrument. To such people, those who wished war with the British were "warring with their own existence, with the purpose of the MOST HIGH, and with the whole kingdom of the REDEEMER throughout the world."[59]

The main Federalist theme was that sustained by the *United States' Gazette*. It gave hearty support to the program of preparedness on the ground that it coincided with the true Washingtonian principles, but it disapproved of war with Great Britain because in its opinion the grievances against France were of equal or greater seriousness. At the same time, it professed to disbelieve in the good faith of the administration and charged that its bold words were subterfuges intended to conceal its real intention of returning to the system of commercial restrictions. The delays in Congress gave much force to this reasoning; and when a three-month's embargo was laid in April the *Gazette* avowed that the charges were proved conclusively.[60]

The Democrats reacted differently to the embargo. It revived their hopes of a more active policy. Both the *Aurora* and the Pittsburgh *Commonwealth* regarded it as a prelude to war; and the latter rejoiced to see Congress throw off its lethargy.[61]

Others were less pleased with the prospect. Paschal Hollingsworth, a Philadelphia flour merchant, drew up a letter for the millers of Easton and sent it to Robert Brown, William Rodman, and Jonathan Roberts, the Congressmen for the Easton district. The letter was written in a most indiscreet fashion. It said that the embargo was injurious to the millers and that a war would be ruinous to them. They would therefore hold the Congressmen responsible for their actions in these matters. Hollingsworth went on to insinuate that the administration was governed by French influence and declared that the millers would not consider the British orders in council a sufficient cause of war since the orders did not diminish either "their profits or their happiness."[62]

Jonathan Roberts replied in a public letter dated April 13, 1812. He observed sarcastically that the government could hardly be accused of precipitancy in its measures and asserted that any miller who was not forewarned of the possibility of a temporary embargo and a succeeding declaration of war must be afflicted with a "strange blindness." He listed the American grievances against Great Britain and expressed confidence that the people were incapable of choosing profit in preference to virtue. Denying the charge of French influence, he countered by accusing Hollingsworth of partiality not for one foreign nation over another but for a foreign government over that of the United States.[63]

Roberts's letter greatly discomfited Hollingsworth and even amused some Federalists,[64] but it failed to allay Democratic dissatisfaction. The Harrisburg *Pennsylvania Republican* took issue with Roberts's statement that the millers had been sufficiently warned. On the contrary, it said, the delays in Congress might reasonably lead one to the opposite conclusion. The paper believed that there were ample reasons for going to war; but the procrastination of the government had led many to fear that there would be a similar sluggishness in the prosecution of the war. The editor therefore doubted that a majority of the people would approve a declaration of war at that time.[65]

His views seemed to be substantiated in May by the failure of the Eleven Million Loan. The Federalist gibes on this occasion made the Democrats writhe. John Binns found them insupportable and wrote Roberts that war was now a necessity. To his mind, "The honor of the Nation and that of the party are bound up together and both will be sacrificed if war be not declared."[66]

Other Philadelphia Democrats were likewise convinced that the time had come to take effective action. Meeting upon the request of a group headed by Thomas Leiper, all Republican factions co-operated in choosing delegates, who met and issued a call for a public meeting of the congressional district at the State House on May 20, 1812.[67] William Jones, who had long desired war, acted as chairman of the meeting and was author of the resolutions which it adopted. Another prominent figure was Charles J. Ingersoll, Philadelphia Congressman and erstwhile Federalist, who delivered a long address which recapitulated the grievances against the British, laying particular stress upon impressment, the seizures of American ships, and the Indian depredations in the Northwest. The meeting then adopted resolutions demanding war as the only effective remedy for such outrages.[68]

The *United States' Gazette* derided the meeting, claiming that hardly two thousand attended and that few real Americans and "respectable"

254   THE KEYSTONE IN THE DEMOCRATIC ARCH

Democrats were present. Its charges seem to have been captious, however. A good number of the most conservative Democrats took part in the meeting, and one of them described it privately as the largest he had ever attended. The Democratic papers naturally took the same view and set the attendance at from ten to twelve thousand.[69]

Democratic unity on this occasion was somewhat marred by the refractory conduct of Duane. Apparently disgruntled by the active part taken by the Snyderites, he did not attend the meeting. Furthermore, he refused to publish its proceedings because they had been given first to Binns, and he would not take them at second hand. Even war could not overcome the personal antipathies of the two Democratic editors.[70]

Though the Federalists had jeered the Democratic meeting, they were beginning to be alarmed. The *United States' Gazette* lost its blithe confidence that the administration could not be kicked into a war and began to cry loudly at the heinousness of war against the British in league with such a bloody tyrant as Napoleon. The editor on June 6, 1812, went so far as to accuse Madison of a double diplomacy, asserting that he was deceiving both Congress and the country with the object of bringing the United States under the rule of the French emperor.[71] The Federalists in Philadelphia now began a belated movement to circulate antiwar memorials and send them to Congress. They began to arrive in Washington early in June, but they did not receive much attention. However, Jonathan Roberts rejoiced that the memorials had not arrived earlier as he thought they might have proved "exceedingly embarrassing."[72]

Meanwhile, the Democrats continued to insist upon war. A meeting at Easton on May 23, 1812, demanded action by Congress; and an observer reported that the people both wished and expected a declaration of war against Great Britain.[73] The *Aurora* added to this cry. Deploring the incompetence of Eustis and the inadequate preparations that had been made, it insisted that war was a necessity, that the people were prepared for it, and that military reform would be forced upon the government after the war had begun.[74]

Such clamor was probably unnecessary so far as the Pennsylvania Congressmen were concerned. They were all present on June 4, 1812, when the House voted secretly on Madison's recommendation for war, and they approved the measure by 16-2. The dissentients were James

Milnor, Federalist representative from Philadelphia, and William Rodman, a Democrat from Bucks County, who had also opposed the passage of the embargo act in the preceding March.[75]

Much uncertainty prevailed with regard to the attitudes of the two Senators, Andrew Gregg and Michael Leib. The former wrote to a friend in Carlisle on June 4, 1812, and expressed the opinion that the Senate would not approve war but would substitute a measure for the issuance of letters of marque and reprisal against both France and Great Britain. He continued by saying that he favored adjourning Congress until the fall when the country would be better prepared. He added that *"To declare a war now is . . . tantamount to a paper blockade, for we are* TOTALLY UNPREPARED *as yet to carry such a declaration into effect."* Gregg's correspondent made this letter public, and it appeared in the newspapers to the evident chagrin of the Democrats.[76]

Leib's opposition to the war did not receive as much publicity, but it was generally known and caused much unfavorable Democratic comment. In private letters he argued that there was no greater cause for war in 1812 than there had been for the preceding five years and stressed the lack of preparations by the country. Jonathan Roberts and other Pennsylvania Democrats believed that Leib was chiefly motivated by hatred of Madison and by a desire to see De Witt Clinton elected President. One person even wrote Roberts that if Madison had not persevered in seeking war Leib and the Clintonians would have come out strongly for it and would have denounced the administration for its weakness.[77]

Despite their opposition to war, neither Leib nor Gregg dared oppose what was apparently the overwhelming sentiment of the people of the State. Both voted favorably for the declaration of war in the Senate on June 18, 1812. Gregg's views on the matter were not made public; but Leib was later quoted by the Snyderites as saying that he had voted for war " 'because my constituents, *and be damned to them,* would have made a noise if I had not.' "[78]

The coming of the war ended a wearisome period of indecision for the people of Pennsylvania. Although the Federalists in the State had been solidly opposed to the declaration of war, most of them were apparently willing to give it loyal support once it had been determined upon.[79] Nevertheless, there were some intransigents whose attitude boded ill for the administration and the nation at large. The editor of the *United States' Gazette* expressed the views of this group when he declared that it was "a war of the *administration*—a war of a *party*, and not of the country." All citizens should give such aid as could be constitutionally demanded; but there was no obligation which should deter the opponents of the war from exposing the motives and conduct of the government and from seeking to restore peace by removing the administration from office.[80]

On the other hand there is little doubt that the war was overwhelmingly approved by the Democrats; and they were at least twice as numerous as the Federalists in Pennsylvania. The Democrats in the State had given loyal support to the administration policy of commercial restrictions; but their public meetings and legislative declarations indicated that they much preferred war. They had persevered in these sentiments in the face of congressional ineptitude; and their attitude had been sufficiently powerful in 1812 to force the State's recalcitrant Senators into voting for a war which they opposed. However important the role of the frontier west may have been in bringing on the war of 1812, a good share of the credit or blame must be given to the Democrats of Pennsylvania.

III

Inevitably, the war and its conduct were the central issues in the presidential campaign of 1812. The Federalists attacked the administration vigorously on both scores and displayed an energy they had not shown since the repeal of the embargo. They would have made slight progress, however, had it not been for the appearance of a serious schism among their opponents.

Ambitious Republican leaders in New York had long been resentful of Virginia domination of the party. They had sought unsuccessfully in 1808 to elect George Clinton President; and they nominated De Witt Clinton, his nephew, as Madison's opponent in 1812. There was no possibility of winning over the South and the West to the support of their candidate, but there were excellent prospects of victory if a coalition of Middle States Republicans and New England Federalists could be formed to back Clinton. The tacit assistance of the Federalists was won without great difficulty; but the success of the plan was thwarted by the loyalty of Pennsylvania to the administration.

FOREIGN AFFAIRS AND THE PRESIDENTIAL ELECTION   257

Although Madison aroused no great personal enthusiasm among the Pennsylvania Democrats, he had been nominated in the regular way by a congressional caucus, and he was identified with the continuance of the war which they had so long demanded. With the Federalists clamoring for his defeat as the only way to restore peace, the Democrats of the State for the most part eschewed their personal and local quarrels and united strongly in his support. Many of them were dissatisfied with the inept conduct of the war, and the Clintonians laid great stress upon this issue; but the tradition of party unity and regularity coupled with evidences of an understanding between Clinton and the Federalists effectively overcame this feeling. In the end Pennsylvania gave Madison a substantial majority, and its electoral votes saved him from defeat.

By the early months of 1812 a complete metamorphosis had taken place with respect to the views of the Snyderites and the Old School toward the Madison administration. While it was true that Duane had been notably reluctant to support Madison in the early stages of the campaign in 1808, he and his associates had finally taken hold of affairs and had led a successful fight to crush the strong sentiment for George Clinton evinced by the *Democratic Press* and such Snyderites as Samuel Maclay. In the Olmsted affair which followed, the *Aurora* and the Old School had been the champions of the Federal government and Madison against Snyder.[81]

The harmony between the administration and the Old School did not long survive. The alliance with Madison had been one of convenience, and it had failed to produce the expected benefits. Furthermore, Duane's inveterate antipathy to Gallatin made it impossible for him long to remain at peace with a government of which Gallatin formed an important part. In 1810 and 1811 the *Aurora* began a savage onslaught against the Secretary of the Treasury and went to the extent of declaring that Madison should not again be President unless he dismissed Gallatin.[82] These sentiments underwent no change in the succeeding year. Replying to an article in the New York *Public Advertiser* in March, 1812, the paper announced that it would support George Clinton if he were nominated and stated categorically that it would never give its aid to any administration of which Gallatin was a member.[83]

The Snyderites had also reversed their attitude. Binns, who until late in the summer of 1808, had written for George Clinton and against

Madison, was now a devoted partisan of the latter. Getting wind of a rumor that there were plans to include Snyder as a vice presidential candidate on a ticket opposed to Madison, he wrote in the *Democratic Press* that there was no need for a change in the administration and asserted that Snyder was too patriotic to listen for a moment to intrigues against "the distinguished statesman who fills the chief magistracy."[84] Other articles in the paper criticized the reported ambitions of De Witt Clinton, defended Madison and the cabinet, and derided the opposition of Duane and the *Aurora*.[85]

The same feeling animated the Democratic members of the legislature. Meeting in a caucus on March 7, 1812, before any congressional caucus had been held, they prepared an electoral ticket and unanimously pledged support to Madison for President and George Clinton for Vice President. Despite the sarcasm of the *Aurora*, the Snyderites by this step had done much to commit the party to the nomination of Madison.[86]

As it soon appeared that Clinton would retire as Vice President, there was much speculation as to his successor. Among those mentioned was William Jones. Binns was violently opposed to his choice, ostensibly on the ground that Jones was dominated by Dallas. However, his main interest seems to have been in preventing the selection of anyone who might be renominated in 1816 as he hoped to gain the nomination for Snyder at that time.[87]

Binns was also vigilant to prevent the development of an opposition to Madison within the city of Philadelphia. When an announcement in the *Aurora* called for a meeting of all parties upon the death of George Clinton in April, he ignored the matter in his paper but worked successfully in private to oppose it. Few attended this meeting; but Binns was convinced that its object was to form a "Union of all honest men" to oppose the Democrats. He continued to be suspicious of the Old School and believed that they were working with the Federalists to offer an electoral ticket in opposition to that adopted by the legislative caucus in March.[88]

The actions of the Pennsylvania congressional delegation were calculated to relieve Binns of some anxiety. Fourteen of that group attended the nominating caucus on May 18, 1812, and they all gave their votes to Madison, who was chosen without opposition. Even Leib, who was known to favor De Witt Clinton, lacked the courage to oppose the

FOREIGN AFFAIRS AND THE PRESIDENTIAL ELECTION   259

evident feeling of the State and added his voice to the rest. Of the five Democratic Congressmen from Pennsylvania who were absent, two were known to be favorable to Madison, one unfavorable, and the others were expected to follow the will of the majority.[89]

The *Aurora* greeted the news of the caucus cautiously. In spite of its previous tirades against the administration, it made only a bare mention of Madison's nomination and accompanied it with the noncommittal statement that there would apparently be two Republican candidates since the New Yorkers intended to make their own nomination.[90]

This prediction was speedily justified by a legislative caucus at Albany on May 29, 1812. Although many of the State's Republican leaders were opposed to the action, 91 of the 95 members of the party in the legislature attended the caucus; and ninety of them voted to support De Witt Clinton as candidate for President.[91] The long-anticipated Republican schism was now a reality.

The Clintonians made strenuous efforts to win over the Democrats of Pennsylvania. Apparently possessing ample funds, they kept the State deluged with addresses in behalf of their candidate, and they supplemented these with visits by emissaries seeking the co-operation of prominent Democratic leaders. These "boring committees," as they were termed, were reported in all sections of the State, but they failed for the most part to enlist the support of men possessing any real influence.[92] They did, however, succeed in creating the semblance of a Republican political organization devoted to the promotion of Clinton's election.

This body had its inception in a secret meeting held at Lancaster on August 26, 1812, and presided over by Joseph Lefever, Democratic Congressman from that district. Although the proceedings issued by the group described it as "a very numerous highly respectable meeting," it seems to have been attended by less than a dozen people, most of them from Lancaster. They unanimously agreed to support Clinton for President and then adopted an address to be printed and distributed over the State.

The address opened with a caustic attack on the corruption of congressional caucus nominations, went on to denounce the administration for incompetent conduct of the war, and demanded that Pennsylvania assume the position of leadership to which she was justly entitled by her talents, wealth, and population. It closed by recommending that county meetings be held to make nominations for presidential electors and for a Pennsylvanian as Vice President. Such nominations were to be sent to Lefever at Lancaster before September 24, 1812, in order that he might publish the ticket.[93]

Not all the counties responded to this invitation, although meetings of Clinton Democrats were held in York, Lancaster, Nazareth, and Pittsburgh. The meeting at York nominated Jared Ingersoll, Attorney General of the State, for Vice President, and all the rest except that at Pittsburgh approved this course. No public meetings seem to have been held in Philadelphia; but the *Democratic Press* charged that Leib had persuaded some of his Old School friends to permit the use of their names on the Clintonian ticket.[94]

While thus engaged in rallying Democratic support, the Clintonians did not neglect to make overtures to the Pennsylvania Federalists. When a group of his associates journeyed to Philadelphia late in July, De Witt Clinton personally requested that a New York Federalist furnish them with a letter of introduction to Charles Willing Hare. At the same time Clinton apparently informed the Federalists that he was an "American Federalist" and that he would make an immediate peace with England if elected.[95]

It seems unquestionable that approaches were made to the Pennsylvania Federalists by the Clinton emissaries; but such contacts were not calculated to have a decisive effect. Inclined to follow the lead of Boston and New York in such matters, the Pennsylvanians showed a cautious reserve until they were assured what course would be pursued by their associates in those localities. Although articles favoring coalition behind Clinton appeared in the Federalist papers in Philadelphia, they were not written in such fashion as to commit the party.[96]

In trying to determine what the Federalists generally would do, the Pennsylvanians found diverse opinions. Gouverneur Morris was so enamored of the project for a northern confederacy that his views in regard to Clinton and the election were of little value.[97] Rufus King believed that the Federalists should adhere strictly to their own principles and opposed support of Clinton.[98] Timothy Pickering would have preferred John Marshall to Clinton but asserted his willingness to vote for anyone in preference to Madison.[99]

A different attitude was taken by such men as Harrison Gray Otis. Motivated, in the opinion of some Federalists, by a desire for office and power, they early sought assurances as to Clinton's views and gave to him their strongest support. A number of this group held a meeting in Connecticut in June and decided to call a secret convention of the party leaders in New York in September to decide upon the policy to be adopted. A correspondence committee in Philadelphia was delegated to make this decision known to Federalists in the South. Meanwhile, in Massachusetts Otis made it clear that he would not attend the gathering unless it was understood that the state's delegates would promote the election of Clinton.[100]

The Federalist leaders in New York were given positive assurances of Clinton's position. In a conversation on August 5, 1812, with John Jay, Rufus King, and Gouverneur Morris he expressed his complete agreement with the Federalist views of the war but said that it was politically inexpedient to give publicity to the matter because his Republican friends were divided on the subject. He went on to pledge his honor that the break with the Madison administration was irrevocable.[101]

With this background Federalist leaders from South Carolina and the states north of the Potomac met in New York on September 15, 1812, in a convention which lasted three days. Over the opposition of Rufus King, the delegates decided that it was impracticable and inexpedient to nominate a candidate of their own; that the party should support candidates likely to follow a policy different from that of the Madison administration; and that five Pennsylvanians should be appointed as a committee to learn the views of the electors chosen in each state and to communicate those views to the electors of other states. The convention had thus agreed in effect to give its support to Clinton but had felt it best to keep this decision secret in order not to alienate the Democrats who might otherwise vote for him.[102]

The Federalist hope for secrecy was vain so far as it concerned Pennsylvania. The *Democratic Press* took notice on September 14, 1812, that Horace Binney, John B. Wallace, Joseph Hopkinson, and a number of others had gone to New York that morning to attend a Federalist caucus on the question of the presidential election. Soon after the convention adjourned the *Press* reported that the Federalists had decided not to run a candidate of their own. At the end of the month the paper published a copy of a circular letter signed by Binney for the correspondence committee appointed in New York and declared that this furnished positive proof of Federalist support of Clinton.[103]

The *United States' Gazette* quibbled in answering the publication of the letter. While not admitting the genuineness of the document, the *Gazette* stated that it showed only that the Federalists would support Clinton if he had a reasonable chance of success and that it clearly demonstrated the absence of any understanding between the party and Clinton.[104]

When the *National Intelligencer* in October printed a remarkably accurate description of the proceedings of the New York convention, the *Gazette* was equally evasive. It avoided a direct denial of the account, but it published a letter from Otis which declared the story to be "entirely false."[105] These Federalist equivocations did not alter the fact that their hopes of secrecy had been effectively destroyed.

The Pennsylvania Federalists fared somewhat better in concealing their movements. They held a conference at Carlisle on September 25, 1812, presided over by James Riddle. They adopted resolutions paralleling those of the New York convention; but there was no notice of these proceedings until they were published in a Federalist address a few days prior to the presidential election.[106]

Cogent reasons existed for the great efforts of the Pennsylvania Federalists to mask their support of Clinton. There was always the important consideration of Democratic antipathy to any of their number who co-operated with the Federalists. Even more important at this time was the very real difference existing between the Federalists and the Pennsylvania Clintonians on the issues in the campaign.

The position of the regular Democrats was consistent and easily stated. They wholeheartedly endorsed the declaration of war and called upon all citizens to make every effort in its support. All Democratic factions were expected to subordinate local and personal quarrels and to unite behind the regularly chosen candidates for every office as the surest means of indicating approval of the war and of bringing it to a speedy and successful conclusion. Viewed in the most charitable light, the candidacy of Clinton was a regrettable breach of Democratic unity calculated to give comfort to the opponents of the war, and it was therefore anathema. Subsequent evidences of Clintonian co-operation with the Federalists only served to strengthen a position already taken so far as the Democrats were concerned.[107]

The Federalists also maintained a fairly consistent attitude. Having opposed the declaration of the war, they now denounced it as unjust, unnecessary, and inexpedient. They argued strongly that the ostensible reasons for waging the war were either specious or futile, and they coupled this with the obvious unpreparedness of the country to draw the conclusion that the sole purpose of the war was to effect Madison's re-election. Proclaiming themselves the friends to peace, union, and commerce, they asserted that the Madisonian policies were destructive to all three. Finally, they denounced a war against Great Britain in conjunction with the tyrannical Napoleon as destructive to American liberties. In supporting this thesis, they pointed to the Baltimore riots in June and July and either charged or insinuated that they had been instigated by the administration.[108]

While the Federalists made scathing attacks on the administration's conduct of the war, this was only an ancillary theme to them; but to the Clintonians in the State it was the chief point of attack. Nothing, perhaps, offers more conclusive evidence of the Democratic enthusiasm for the war than the manner in which the Clintonians avoided denouncing it for itself. Some of their addresses made oblique denunciations of the administration's alleged enmity to commerce and presumed subservience to France; but none had the hardihood to decry the war with Great Britain. Instead, they censured Madison for forcing a declaration of war without adequate preparation and asserted that the blunders and inefficiency in the conduct of the war furnished proof of Madison's incapacity to bring it to a successful conclusion.

Although the course of the war in 1812 gave the Clinton Democrats ample support for this thesis of administrative incompetence, their propaganda seems to indicate that they would have preferred to ignore the war altogether and wage the campaign on other issues. They laid heavy stress on the unconstitutionality and corruption of the congressional nominating caucus and attempted to appeal to sectional prejudice by excoriating Virginia domination of the national government. In Pennsylvania this was buttressed by an attempt to arouse a sense of injustice and injured pride. The Clintonians asserted that the State had not received its fair proportion of high Federal offices and reminded the citizens that a Virginia Congressman had openly declared that this was due to the State's lack of talents. It was in the exploitation of this theme that the Clintonians nominated Jared Ingersoll as their vice presidential candidate in the State.[109]

Meanwhile, the Democrats were making strenuous efforts to achieve harmony and to bring to bear the full force of their numbers in the coming elections. In Berks County, where the Quids remained strongly intrenched, John Spayd, the Quid gubernatorial candidate in 1808, participated actively in a meeting designed to unite Quids and Democrats in support of the war, the administration, and a common ticket for State and local offices. The recommendations adopted at this time were subsequently carried out in a joint meeting of the two factions held in September.[110]

In Philadelphia the ward and district meetings in the city and county gave warm support to party reunion. Young William J. Duane worked earnestly to combat the activities of the Clintonians and Federalists; Alexander J. Dallas emerged sufficiently from his political retirement to advise the State Democratic committee and to help draft an address for it; and all factions participated in drawing up the local tickets. In all this William Duane and the *Aurora* remained curiously detached. The paper called for unity in support of the war, but it maintained a baffling silence on the subject of Madison's candidacy. Despite this situation, Thomas Leiper was elated by the evidences of party harmony and informed Madison that he believed that neither Duane, Binns, nor Leib would ever again be able to cause dissension.[111]

Events soon proved that Leiper had underestimated the capacities of Leib. The district delegates for Philadelphia County, chosen by both the Old School and the Snyderite factions, met at Spring Garden on September 5, 1812, and nominated the Democratic assembly ticket. Even though James Engle, one of the staunchest of Leib's supporters, served as secretary of the meeting, a number of the Old School faction in the Northern Liberties met four days later and called for a general county meeting to reconsider these nominations.[112]

The Old School county meeting on September 21, 1812, struck off four of the six nominations made by the district delegates and substituted others in their stead. The ostensible reason for this action was that the four nominees had supported in the last session of the legislature an insolvency act for Philadelphia which had resulted in great injustices. The Snyderites, however, pointed out that one of the men dropped had been a strong opponent of the law in question; and other portions of the address adopted by the meeting make it clear that the motives of those concerned were purely factious. Delegate nominations were once more denounced as usurpations, and the cry for party harmony was depicted as an attempt to subdue principles to expediency. Denouncing expedients as the "nostrums of political empirics," the address virtuously proclaimed that honorable men could not make a union in support of wrong.[113]

Although Leib did not take part publicly in these proceedings, he unquestionably was a moving spirit in them. The *Democratic Press* pointed out that he was working for Clinton and noted that two of his lieutenants in the county had been placed on the Clinton electoral ticket. It further asserted that his friends had sought to bargain for Federalist support of the Old School assembly ticket in the county by offering to give their votes to the Federalist congressional nominees. While none of these charges were substantiated, there is very little doubt that Leib was working steadily for his own objectives without regard to the pleas for party harmony.[114]

Democratic unity was also nonexistent in Pittsburgh. The leaders of the bank faction in the previous year now proclaimed themselves the friends of western prosperity and manufactures, and, ignoring the district meetings called by the regular Democratic committee, they organized their own delegate system and adopted a complete opposition ticket. In this revolt they sought to give themselves the stamp of orthodoxy by announcing wholehearted support of the war, of Madison and Gerry, and of Snyder. Such efforts had some weight because of the studied failure of the regular Democrats to indicate their position on the presidential issue and because of the subsequent leadership of the Clinton Democrats taken by Thomas Baird, who also led the regular Democratic organization in local politics. Baird's position on the national election, however, did not receive the unanimous approval of those who supported his local ticket.[115]

The Federalists, meanwhile, were exerting themselves to the utmost. In Philadelphia they held their ward and district meetings early and made strenuous preparations for the coming contest. No item of political organization was overlooked as they sought to muster their full strength. Even the moribund Federalists in Pittsburgh roused themselves and offered a ticket for the first time since 1808, although they differed from their Philadelphia brethren by avoiding a denunciation of the war itself and by confining themselves to strictures on its conduct by the administration.[116]

Despite the lack of complete Democratic harmony, the zealousness of the Federalists, and the disastrous surrender of General William Hull at Detroit in August, the result of the general election on October 13, 1812, was a resounding Democratic triumph.

In the legislature the Federalists showed minor gains. They carried their full assembly tickets in Luzerne, Delaware, Chester, and Adams counties and elected one out of four representatives from Bucks County. This gave them seven additional seats in the House; but they still held only eighteen out of a total of 95. They also managed to maintain their strength in the Senate at five members by electing three out of the nine Senators chosen in the election. Such meager gains had little practical significance.[117]

A schism in Dauphin County prevented the Democrats from carrying all the 23 congressional contests. The Federalists however, could derive little pleasure from the victory of John Gloninger in that district since his party affiliations were at least doubtful, while it was confidently averred by the Democrats that he was a strong supporter of the war.[118]

The results in Philadelphia gave proof of the great efforts made by both sides. In the city the total vote reached nearly 5,800, about 150 greater than in the election of 1808. The average Democratic majority amounted to more than 160 votes in the congressional election and to nearly 220 in the contests for State Representatives.[119] The total vote in the county was nearly 6,250, an increase of 300 over the total in 1808. The average Democratic majority for Congress was more than 1,700 votes. In the election for assembly the four Old School candidates averaged about 900 votes with the greater part of them coming from the Northern Liberties. Their regular Democratic opponents amassed an average of more than 3,000 votes, while the Federalist candidates polled about 2,200 votes. The Old School had failed to achieve its objectives; but its strength at a time of great pressure for Democratic unity was an ominous portent of continued factionalism in the party.[120]

Considerable factional strength was also shown in the returns from Allegheny and Berks counties. In the first, the bolting ticket polled from 300 to 400 votes, enough to give the Federalist candidates a plurality. However, since Allegheny was joined with Butler County for assembly and congressional elections, the regular Democratic ticket managed to triumph over both the Federalists and the bolters. In Berks County the united ticket of Quids and Democrats was triumphant, but it was not unopposed. Dissident Quids were candidates for a number of offices, and, apparently with Federalist support, they polled up to 1,700 votes out of a total of nearly 3,800. In no instance, however, did they succeed of election.[121]

Foreign Affairs and the Presidential Election 267

The Federalist defeat was a severe disappointment to the editor of the *United States' Gazette,* and he charged that the Democratic victory in Philadelphia had been obtained through intimidation and fraud. Although he devoted much space to this matter and asserted that the results would be contested, the subject was soon dropped.[122]

With the presidential election taking place on October 30, 1812, few people were disposed to waste time on the cavilling of the *Gazette.* The Clinton electoral ticket was published just prior to the general State election. It was headed by ex-Governor Thomas McKean and contained the names of a number of prominent Republicans, including that of Joseph Hiester. The latter and a number of others refused to serve on the ticket, and the Clintonians were forced constantly to revise their list of nominees right up to the time of the election.[123]

The Federalists now dropped all pretenses of neutrality. The party conferees of the city met on October 17, 1812, and announced support of the Clintonian ticket. They defended this action by publishing the proceedings of the Federalist meeting at Carlisle on September 25 which had resolved not to put a Federalist ticket in nomination but to support any other ticket opposed to Madison. With this declaration of policy the Federalist press and organizations in Philadelphia began to work energetically for Clinton's success.[124]

The Philadelphia Democrats were also active in preparing for the election. Ward and district meetings adopted resolutions for Madison and Gerry and excoriated the candidacy of Clinton; and the Democratic Young Men published a long address of the same tenor. Even William Duane and the *Aurora* were forced to drop their neutrality. On October 13, 1812, the paper had replied to criticisms of its inactivity by reminding its critics of the adage *"Let very well alone";* but eleven days later it carried a long letter signed by Duane declaring his support of Madison because of the necessity of a united front against Great Britain.[125]

Leib, however, did not respond to such reasoning. Although he had avoided open support of Clinton in the weeks preceding the general election on October 13, 1812, he now made manifest his opposition to Madison. The day after the election a triweekly paper called the *Whig Chronicle* appeared and began to make strong appeals in behalf of Clinton. Published by Leib's friends and evidently under his control, the paper was derisively labeled "Michael's Chronicle" by the *Democratic*

Press. It had a short life, ceasing publication in the following January.[126]

The vote in the previous presidential elections in the State had usually been very light as compared with the preceding general elections. The results of the latter had generally indicated such overwhelming Democratic strength as to make the contest futile. Thus in 1808 more than 111,000 votes had been cast for Governor, but only 53,967 for the presidential electors. Though the presidential vote in 1812 was lighter than in the general election, the usual apathy was missing; and the vote was greater than in any previous contest. More than 78,000 ballots were given the opposing tickets. The Madisonian electors averaged 48,946 votes to 29,056 for the Clintonians. The latter received majorities only in Luzerne, Bucks, Delaware, Chester, Lancaster, and Adams counties. Madison's majority was more than 10,000 votes less than in 1808, but it was still substantial and convincing.[127]

The significance of the Pennsylvania election at this time can hardly be overstated. Madison received all the electoral votes of the southern and western states except Maryland, which gave Clinton five of its eleven votes. North of Maryland Madison carried only Vermont with eight votes and Pennsylvania with 25. The final count gave Madison 128 votes to 89 for De Witt Clinton. Had Pennsylvania supported the latter, he would have won by 11 votes. The staunchness of the State had saved the administration.[128]

The regular Democratic victory was due to two main factors. The first of these was the impulsion for unity in support of the war. The Pennsylvania Democracy had for years favored the adoption of energetic measures of opposition to British maritime restrictions and the practice of impressment; and it had played an active part in forcing action from a reluctant Congress in 1812. Madison and the administration were identified with the war policy; and the Pennsylvania Democrats did not intend to weaken the latter by a failure to support the former.

The second important factor was the influence of the party tradition of loyalty and unity in time of stress. Madison was the regular nominee; his re-election was bitterly opposed by the Federalists, who also opposed the declaration of war; and Clinton's candidacy, therefore, placed him in alliance with the Federalists. Whatever misgivings the Pennsylvania Democrats may have had as to Madison's abilities and however strong may have been their liking for the Clinton family, the great majority of them could not and would not condone an action so contrary to their political principles. In quieter times the party might dispute over men; but in a crisis there must be unity and the submergence of personalities.

In the face of such considerations, minor Democratic defections, the strenuous exertions of the Federalists, and the military fiascos in the conduct of the war were alike powerless to move the keystone in the Democratic arch.

CHAPTER XI
WAR, POLITICS, AND SCHISM: 1813-1814

THE DEMOCRATIC ASCENDANCY in Pennsylvania continued unshaken in the two years after the election of 1812. The successes and reverses of the war were reflected in the election returns, with the Democrats benefiting in 1813 and suffering a setback in 1814. The attitude of the Federalists toward the war was somewhat mixed—a portion of them tending toward its support and the extremist minority becoming more and more embittered. The State also experienced during this time a manufacturing boom, a continuing mania for additional banks, wartime speculation and profiteering, and the threat of invasion by the British forces. In this complex situation Democratic factionalism in Philadelphia grew in boldness and significance despite the evident need for party harmony.

I

When the legislature convened on December 1, 1812, for its first session in the new capital at Harrisburg, the military situation was gloomy. The high hopes of a quick success in Canada had been doomed. The military disasters at Detroit and Queenston Heights were succeeded by the abandonment of the projected expedition against Montreal; and even as the legislators were assembling the bombastic Alexander Smyth was displaying more discretion than wisdom as he countermanded his orders for the invasion of Canada from Buffalo. Pennsylvania felt a special mortification over the events at Buffalo since less than a third of the State's volunteer brigade serving with Smyth under Adamson Tannehill had been willing to invade Canadian soil. Furthermore, the unit had compiled a humiliating record in the matter of desertions. While the brigade attached to William Henry Harrison's forces in the Northwest was acting much better, it made constant complaints about inadequate supplies of food and clothing.[1]

Despite these unfavorable developments the legislature remained firm in its support of the war and the administration. It adopted with little change several strong resolutions which appealed for wholehearted efforts to continue the war until American wrongs had been redressed and which denounced the refusal of Massachusetts and Connecticut to supply their quotas of militia. It also passed legislation of a more substantial sort. The Governor was authorized to subscribe a million dollars to the new government loan; and he was required to see that the Pennsylvania troops with Harrison were adequately supplied with winter clothing. A bonus of twenty dollars was offered to any of these volunteers who would agree to serve for an additional two months. Finally, the legislature established a system to permit Pennsylvanians in service to vote in the general elections. It failed, however, to make the sweeping revisions in the militia law which Governor Snyder had requested.[2]

In matters concerning the war the Democrats were almost wholly of one sentiment, while the weak Federalist minority was impotent. On other matters the majority was less in agreement. One of the first instances of friction appeared in the election of a United States Senator to succeed Andrew Gregg, whose term was to expire in March, 1813.

The leading aspirant for the position was Abner Lacock, then serving as Congressman from Beaver County. Of Virginia descent, he had lived in western Pennsylvania from early youth. Operating an inn at Beaver, he had become prominent in local politics and had served for a number of years in the State legislature where he had achieved recognition as a leader. He had been one of the House managers at the impeachment trial of the Supreme Court judges in 1805 and had been active in the attempt to impeach McKean. After Snyder's election he had energetically backed resistance to the Federal courts in the Olmsted Case and had become one of the chief objects of wrath to the Old School group. He had been elected to Congress in 1810 in opposition to Adamson Tannehill, who was the choice of the Pittsburgh Democratic leaders. As an outstanding adherent of Snyder and the war, he was the logical choice as Gregg's successor; and his availability was enhanced since he came from the western part of the State and would thus balance the representation in the Senate.[3]

While assured of strong support for the senatorship, Lacock had to encounter a good deal of opposition. Much of this came from young William J. Duane, whose choice as a Representative from the city had been one of the heaviest prices the Snyderites had paid for unity in the past election. Aided by legislators from Centre and Mifflin counties, he attended the Democratic caucus on December 7, 1812, denounced its proceedings, and persuaded more than thirty of those attending to walk out. The remainder voted overwhelmingly to support Lacock.[4]

At the election on the following day Lacock was chosen with 63 votes. The Federalists, aided by two Democrats, gave 22 votes to James Brady, Quid Senator from Westmoreland County, who was later to be considered one of their number. Most of the dissident Democrats united behind Daniel Montgomery, Jr., of Northumberland County, who in 1808 had joined Samuel Maclay and John Randolph in the congressional protest against the nomination of Madison. The greater part of the 26 votes he received came from Lacock's Pittsburgh opponents and Representatives of Northumberland and other counties in the central part of the State. A few anti-Snyderite Senators voted for Isaac Weaver, Jr., Senator from Greene County.[5]

Young Duane and the other opponents of the Snyder regime had more success in preventing the choice of John Binns as a director of the Bank of Pennsylvania. Their victory was short-lived, however, as the man chosen in his place was discovered to be ineligible, and a second election resulted in a triumph for Binns.[6]

The bitterest struggle in the session was on the question of incorporating additional banks. The mania for new institutions which had been so pronounced in 1810 continued unabated, and the legislature was under constant pressure from the promoters of such projects. In his annual message on December 3, 1812, Snyder had taken note of this situation and had sought to discourage the movement by showing that the existing banks had patriotically made liberal subscriptions to the government loans and that they had ample funds to take care of all legitimate requirements for capital in the State. He also noted the difficulties which had plagued the promoters of new banks in New York.[7]

The legislature was not disposed to listen to such warnings, however. Less than three weeks after the session had begun, the supporters of the new banks made a shrewd maneuver to aid their projects. Recognizing that individual measures for the incorporation of single banks had little chance of success, they induced the House to appoint a committee to draw up a bill for a "general banking system." By providing for several new institutions, such a measure would offer excellent opportunities for vote trading by local groups and thus enhance the possibilities of passage by the legislature.

The bill was reported in the House on January 20, 1813, and after a great deal of debate and logrolling was approved on February 10 by a vote of 43-42. Ten members were absent or abstained from voting. In the Senate the measure went through a similar process and was adopted with amendments on March 2 by a majority of 14-13. Four Senators did not participate in the vote. The House concurred with the amendments; and the bill, now providing for the incorporation of 25 new banks, was sent to the Governor on March 9, 1813.[8]

The passage of the measure was a sore trial to Snyder. As a strong adherent of Republican principles, he had a great distaste for banks generally. On the other hand, he was also inclined to favor executive deference to the legislature. Less than two months earlier he had apologetically vetoed the first measure since his inauguration in 1808, and he was now most reluctant to challenge again the wisdom of the legislators.[9]

Nevertheless, he determined to disapprove the bill and returned it to the House on March 19, 1813, with an extremely able message setting forth his objections. Expressing himself in the most respectful terms, Snyder began by pointing out that corporations in general were privileged orders which should never be created except when clearly demanded by the people or when obviously essential for the public good. Such caution was particularly necessary in the case of banks, whose influence had long been complained of and feared.

From these general considerations, he turned to list the evils which might flow from the bill. The creation of additional banks would tend to drive specie out of circulation and to reduce confidence in bank notes. The existing banks were more than capable of supplying the capital requirements of legitimate enterprises. Further supplies of bank credit could only serve to demoralize the community by encouraging dangerous speculative schemes, aiding counterfeiters, and bringing on the disasters of a worthless paper currency. Financial experiments were unwise in time of war, particularly when the State government derived such a large part of its revenue from investments in the existing banks.

Snyder also noted that there had been no public demand for many of the banks created by the measure and called attention to the fact that it had not been passed by a majority of the members in either house. Finally, he noted that there would be no harm done by deferring the matter to the next legislature, while if it passed and were found evil the damage would be irreparable since there was no provision for modification or repeal by subsequent legislatures and under such conditions the act would partake of the nature of a contract protected by the Constitution.[10]

The House reconsidered the bill on March 24, 1813. The veto was sustained, with 36 Democrats and two Federalists voting to pass the measure and 28 Democrats and twelve Federalists voting against it. Most of the favorable votes came from the western and central counties, although the measure received strong support from the Bucks and Northampton delegations as well.[11]

The vote on the banking act was the most politically significant event of the session. It indicated a changing sentiment among the Democrats, who had traditionally been opposed to such measures; and it also marked the first time when an important difference of opinion had existed between Snyder and a great portion of the country Democrats who had been his most dependable supporters.

II

During the year 1813 the Pennsylvania Democrats remained staunchly in favor of the continuance of the war. News of the massacre at the River Raisin, Cockburn's raids in Chesapeake Bay, and the sacking of Hampton, Virginia, only served to arouse their fierce resentment and to lead them to demand increased vigor in the prosecution of hostilities.[12] Many of the more ardent even decried the passage of the act to bar the use of alien seamen on American vessels and the prompt acceptance of the Russian offer of mediation as concessions to Federalist pressure and evidences of a weakening of the administration's will to wage a vigorous war until its objectives had been attained.[13]

There were some instances of despondency and dissatisfaction among the Democrats. In March a Philadelphia merchant despaired so much because of Federalist obstructionism and the tendency of the people to talk rather than act that he favored making peace on any terms short of a surrender of territory; and in April the citizens of Huntingdon County were so disgusted by the experiences of the last campaign that they failed to fill their militia quota; while in August Alexander J. Dallas openly expressed his lack of confidence in the ability of Madison's administration to carry on the war effectively.[14]

With Dallas expressing himself in this fashion, it was hardly surprising to find William Duane criticizing the conduct of the war. Writing to Jefferson in February he commented at length on the military disasters and attributed them to the political intrigues which had raised incompetent men to commands while such virtuous and able patriots as James Wilkinson were persecuted. He also hinted that Gallatin had been the source of information leaks to the enemy which had resulted in the fall of Michilimackinac and the capture of Hull's supplies.[15]

The following month Duane was appointed Adjutant General of the Pennsylvania military district by John Armstrong, who had succeeded Eustis as Secretary of War. Subsequently, the War Department adopted certain military handbooks published by Duane and gave additional appointments to some of his Old School associates. Despite these marks of favor Duane continued to be highly critical of the way affairs were handled and wrote Jefferson in September railing against the generals and Madison's policy of *"courting enemies* and *sacrificing friends."*[16]

Without the captious overtones of Duane's remarks, John M. Snowden, the able Democratic editor of the Pittsburgh *Mercury,* made trenchant criticisms of the lack of progress by Harrison and the northwestern army. Taken to task for his articles, he refused to back down or to discuss the matter further. In his opinion, it was time that words should be displaced by deeds, and his criticisms had been well worthwhile if they reminded the generals that military honors lasted only when they were earned.[17]

These critical attitudes among the Democrats were only normal reactions toward a war in which American successes had thus far been scanty indeed. Basically, the people were still convinced of the wisdom of the war and determined to carry it on until victory was won. This spirit was well expressed by a young politician at Harrisburg, who, in the midst of a denunciation of incompetent generals, announced that his zeal was greater than ever and that one must never despair of the republic. Such sentiments seemed to have their reward in September and October when news came of Perry's victory on Lake Erie and of Harrison's success at the Battle of the Thames. The Democrats at last had important victories to celebrate, and they made the most of their opportunities.[18]

It was not to be expected that the Federalists who had strenuously opposed the declaration of war would ever do more than give it a reluctant support. If the attitude of the *United States' Gazette* was representative, they would not even accord that. The *Gazette* had been extremely violent in 1812 and became even more so in 1813. While the Democrats were outraged at the reports of British atrocities at the River Raisin and in the Chesapeake area, the *Gazette* either ignored or scoffed at such stories as mere rumors. It even attempted to offset them with reports of army bestialities in the execution of deserters and of western offers of bounties for Indian scalps in 1791. It also denounced American use of torpedoes against British warships as barbarism.[19]

Along with such defenses of British humanity, the *Gazette* maintained an incessant carping criticism of the administration, the war, and everything Democratic. It opposed militia reform and increases in the strength of the army as moves to foster domestic despotism. It printed rumors of slave rebellions in the South and stories of inadequate shelter and clothing for American troops in the field. It devoted columns of discussion to the presumed administration alliance with France and to the double diplomacy which it considered to be proved by the publication of Napoleon's spurious St. Cloud Decree. It bitterly assailed government opening of foreign mail and maliciously caricatured Madison in the role of the nation's chief letter-breaker. It took keen delight in ridiculing Secretary of the Navy William Jones for refusing to accept the challenge of a disgruntled officer and for other alleged shortcomings. It even went to the extent of chiding a writer in the *Edinburgh Review* who took the British ministry to task for its failure to prevent the American war and asserted that the responsibility lay wholly with the government of the United States.[20]

The most glaring instances of the growing intransigence of the *Gazette* and of the political motivation of its opposition to the war appeared in its reactions to the foreign seamen's bill and the Russian mediation. The previous attitude of the paper had been that its main objective was the restoration of peace, which it professed to believe easy to obtain if the administration sincerely desired it. In November, 1812, the editor asserted that if an act to bar aliens from serving as seamen on American ships were passed and adequate pledges given for its enforcement—and if peace did not then result—, he believed that the people should give the administration their hearty support.

However, when such an act was passed, the *Gazette* chose to ignore this earlier declaration and by May had even come to refer to the act as an insult to the British Parliament.[21]

Similar caviling appeared in its reaction to the appointment of a commission to make peace through Russian mediation, even though one of the three commissioners was James A. Bayard, a prominent Federalist from Delaware. At first the *Gazette* pretended to believe that no offer of mediation had been made and that the whole thing was a hoax designed to aid in floating the new loan. Later it attacked the administration for having begun the war in the first place and averred that it would be entitled to no gratitude if peace resulted from the mediation. Finally, it denounced the administration policy as degrading to the national character since the commissioners had been appointed without learning whether or not the British would also accept Russia's good offices.[22]

The outlook would have been most gloomy if all the Federalists had shared the extreme sentiments of the *United States' Gazette*. There were evidences, however, that the paper was far in advance of the party as a whole. One indication of this appeared in toasts offered at dinners in which the Federalists participated. In February, 1813, at a dinner given in honor of Stephen Decatur, the set toasts were prepared by a committee which included Alexander J. Dallas, Horace Binney, and Joseph Hopkinson. These were patriotic and somewhat innocuous; but an observer reported that the whole group present at the dinner showed much enthusiasm for a number of *"stiff volunteers,"* including one to the freeing of impressed sailors.[23]

At a similar entertainment in honor of Commodore William Bainbridge in December, the toasts were somewhat warmer in support of the war; and the breach between the extreme Federalists and their compatriots became even more pronounced. In an unprecedented action, the editor of the *Gazette* presumed to criticize bitterly some of the leading Federalists for attending a dinner in which William Duane had occupied a seat of honor. The paper felt that there had been a triumph over principle when "respectable and distinguished federalists" were to be found "huggermugger" with such Democrats.[24]

Other criticisms in the *Gazette* indicated that patriotic enthusiasm and the lure of profits in war contracts were enlisting Federalists in support of the war;[25] but the heaviest grievance to the extreme

Federalists was the substantial amount subscribed by their fellow party members to the two government loans in 1813.

The *United States' Gazette* had been delighted by the dismal failure of the Eleven Million Loan in May, 1812.[26] When the announcement was made of the Sixteen Million Loan in March, 1813, the paper attacked it savagely and looked forward rather expectantly to its defeat. After the ignominious response to the first two offerings in March the paper was jubilant. It was then stunned by the announcement in early April that John Jacob Astor, David Parish, and Stephen Girard had taken up the balance, amounting to more than ten million dollars. While the *Aurora* was exultant over this proof of Democratic capacity to finance the war, it was generally known that the bulk of the funds subscribed came from Federalists attracted by the favorable terms but averse to buying the stock publicly under their own names.[27]

The loan for $7,500,000 offered in September was even more successful. It was oversubscribed by five millions on terms more favorable to the government than those of the previous loan. Federalists from Pennsylvania and New York again contributed their money; and the *Gazette* was reduced to making bitter reflections on the turpitude of those who denounced the war as wicked while furnishing the means for its continuance.[28]

On the whole, it seems safe to conclude that the extreme Federalists represented a small, though extremely vocal, minority in Pennsylvania. The majority were not inclined to factious opposition to the conduct of the war and were not averse to making a profit by supporting it with their money. With the Democrats almost unanimously in favor of the war, the administration had little need to be concerned over the attitude of Pennsylvania.

III

With only legislative seats and local offices at stake for the most part, the Democrats made extensive gains in the campaign of 1813. The Federalists waged a bitter fight, particularly in Philadelphia, but they lost ground. In view of the already existing Democratic preponderance in the State, however, these Federalist losses were not nearly so significant as the growing return to Democratic factionalism in Philadelphia.

One notable development of the year was the evidence of increased political wisdom among the Federalists. Abandoning still further their early disdain for Democratic electioneering devices, they sought to gain support from the ranks of those whom they had previously considered to be a mob unworthy of the attentions of "the wealthy, the wise, and the good." Following the example previously set in New York and New England, a group of Philadelphia Federalists, which included General Robert Wharton and Enos Bronson, editor of the *United States' Gazette,* organized late in January, 1813, the "Washington Benevolent Society." With the dual purposes of strengthening Federalist principles among the members of the party and of offering fraternity to the lower classes as a substitute for Democratic equality, it was calculated to enable the party to meet more effectively the challenge of its opponents.[29]

At the same time the party began to make better use of the Washington Association, an organization of young Federalists founded in 1811. This group issued and distributed long political addresses in support of the Federalist cause and served actively with the vigilance committees during the elections.[30]

The Democrats made savage attacks on the Washington Benevolent Society as a secret organization of British adherents which sought to cloak its political aims by a hypocritical mask of charity; and they accused it of distributing funds and supplies only when and where they might be expected to produce Federalist votes. Nevertheless, the Democrats hastened to establish their own "American Patriotic Fund Society" to provide aid for needy soldiers and sailors and their dependents. They also increased the activities of the "Association of Democratic Young Men" to combat the work of the Washington Association.[31]

In March the war and politics became closely associated as the result of the appearance of a British blockading squadron in Delaware Bay. Its presence led the editor of the *United States' Gazette* to berate the government for its failure to prepare adequate defenses for the coastal cities and to suggest that the administration was neglecting this deliberately in order that the war might become a defensive one. With Duane serving as Adjutant General, the *Aurora* did not keep silent under these strictures. It denounced the alarmist rumors of the Federalists and pointed out that the government must use the regular troops at the points of conflict. As for Philadelphia the defenses of the city were in good order and required only the aid of volunteers to man them. Since nearly four thousand men had offered their services within a few days, the *Aurora* averred that the city was in no danger.[32]

Political division was also apparent in the dispute between the two city councils. When the absence of a quorum in the Select Council on two successive occasions prevented action on the defense of the city, the Common Council in March called a meeting of the citizens to consider the subject. The town meeting denounced the Select Council and appointed a committee to investigate the condition of the city's defenses. At a second meeting the committee reported that preparations were well advanced and offered certain recommendations which the meeting adopted along with specific instructions to the councils to be active in advancing the military readiness of the city.[33]

Since the majority of the Select Council were Federalists and all the members of the Common Council were Democratic, the Federalists claimed that the whole affair was simply an attempt to discredit them. They were quick to point out that more Democratic than Federalist members of the Select Council had been absent at the two meetings when there had been no quorum; and they asserted that the real purpose of the maneuver was to get an alteration of the city charter so as to do away with the Select Council.[34]

For a time matters quieted down; but the British raids in Chesapeake Bay and the seizures of small craft in Delaware Bay and River led to the calling of a meeting of the more substantial citizens at the Merchants' Coffee House on May 6, 1813. Charles Biddle, a Federalist, presided; but the meeting was attended by men of both parties. Committees were appointed to collect funds from the wards and districts for the purpose of building and manning small sloops to protect shipping in the bay and river. Additional meetings were held in Southwark, the Northern Liberties, and Delaware County. The project was also helped by an appropriation from the city councils. At the same time a detachment of militia was called out by General Joseph Bloomfield, who commanded the military district, and sent to Delaware to prevent British depredations.[35]

Despite the co-operation of both parties in these activities, political bickering continued. The *United States' Gazette* denied that the appearance of a British fleet made it essential for the Federalists to unite with the Democrats in support of the war. It went on to assail the administration for leaving the great cities defenseless and added that if local regions were expected to provide for their own protection they might exercise other sovereign prerogatives and "enter into stipulations and compacts with the enemy, for their own local security."[36]

As these questions passed into the background the Federalists began to prepare for the elections in October. They made much of the incompetence of the administration, berated its failure to establish adequate protection for the city, and claimed great credit for having shown the Democrats how to act rather than talk in a time of stress. At the same time they held their ward and district meetings, chose their committees, drew up their tickets, published addresses, and even formed a committee to aid in the naturalization of foreigners, a Democratic custom which they had long denounced.[37]

The Democrats were equally zealous; but the principal question which faced them was the increasing difficulty of maintaining unity in their own ranks. The feud of the Snyderites and the Old School had been exceedingly bitter prior to the war, and it had only been partially suppressed in the previous year. The rebellion of the Leib faction was to be even bolder in 1813.

The ostensible occasion for the bolt at this time was the nomination of a Democratic candidate for Sheriff. Due to the lucrative fees attached to the office it was one of the most desirable of political plums. For that reason it had been difficult for the Democratic leaders to enforce party discipline whenever the office was at stake. Another factor which made the matter more difficult was the fact that this was one of the few offices where the candidates had adopted the practice of advertising and working in their own interests. Thus, when the city and county conferees on September 2, 1813, gave their approval to the candidacy of Jacob Fitler, they precipitated the incipient revolt.[38]

Richard Palmer, a self-announced aspirant from Southwark and an electoral candidate on the Clinton ticket in 1812, replied to this action with a long letter of denunciation. Proclaiming that the conferees were under the control of a faction dominated by Binns, he announced that he would not submit his pretensions to them but would refer them to Democrats who still cherished *"principles and not men."* He also made a wordy attack on the county district delegate system and excoriated the delegates for the nominations they had made.[39]

The *Democratic Press* was quick to reply. Denouncing Palmer as a Federalist and a trimmer, it denied his charges and pointed out his inconsistent behavior with respect to some of the men mentioned in the letter. In general, however, the paper was inclined to attribute the authorship of the letter to Leib and responded with vituperative attacks upon him.[40]

Following up Palmer's letter, a number of Old School followers of Leib drew up their own ticket and organized machinery for the campaign. Their addresses ignored the existence of the war, while they excused their departure from party unity by acclaiming their adherence to principle and by denouncing the Snyderite debauching of the party.[41]

As the movement developed, the *Aurora* began to break away from the neutral position it had previously professed. Although Duane had ostensibly given up the editorship to James Wilson in May, the paper was still under his influence and control.[42] Despite his interest in the war and his insistence upon unity in its support, the columns of the *Aurora* in September began to lean heavily in favor of the Old School bolters.

The first signs appeared in the publication of Palmer's letter and the proceedings of the dissident meetings. This was followed by an arrogant refusal to publish an address adopted by the Democratic town meeting on the grounds that it was verbose, trite, and unsuitable. In spite of the criticisms of the *Democratic Press,* the *Aurora* went further and refused to publish ward resolutions denouncing the bolters, while it continued to print denunciations of the regular ticket by the latter. The paper did not oppose the regular candidates openly, but it gave them no assistance, and it clearly indicated its real sympathies with the Leib group.[43]

While plagued with this factional fight the Democrats were maintaining a stiff campaign against the Federalists. In contrast to the previous year, they were favored by the course of the war. News of Perry's victory on Lake Erie arrived in Philadelphia on September 21, 1813. The editor of the *United States' Gazette* immediately proclaimed Perry's Federalism and pretended to believe that the news would aid the Federalists in the election. Such claims deceived no one. Then news of a victory on Lake Ontario and of Harrison's capture of Malden arrived on the day of the general election to give added assistance to the Democratic cause.[44]

Under such circumstances the results of the election on October 12, 1813, were a foregone conclusion. The Democrats made a clean sweep of all offices in the city and county. In the city, with a total vote almost as much as in 1812, the Democratic majority averaged nearly 470 votes in the assembly race as compared with less than 220 in the previous year. In the county the total average vote for assembly was more than 800 less than in 1812. The Federalists declined to an average of 1,700 votes, while the regular Democratic ticket averaged a little better than 3,100, and the Old School a little more than 800. Where the Old School and the regular Democrats had opposing candidates for assembly, the latter polled majorities of nearly 2,000 votes over the former. As in the city the regular Democrats appeared to be more firmly in the saddle than ever.[45]

The Democrats showed similar gains in the State as a whole. The Federalists lost eight seats in the House and carried only Delaware, Lancaster, and Adams counties, which gave them a total representation of only ten as compared with 85 for the Democrats. They captured only one of the seven contests for the State Senate, giving them six members to 25 for their opponents.[46] A year of war had strengthened rather than weakened Democratic control of Pennsylvania.

IV

The legislative session of 1813-1814 was almost completely dominated by politics. Hearty support was again given to the war; but the legislators were more concerned with their own pay, the Federal patronage in Philadelphia, the passage of a general banking act, and the nomination of a candidate for Governor.

The legislature gave several indications of continued support of the administration and the war. Early in the session both houses adopted resolutions approving the retaliatory seizure of British hostages to offset threatened British executions of naturalized Americans they had captured. Later resolutions forthrightly denounced resistance to presidential control of the militia by Vermont and Massachusetts and expressed the willingness of Pennsylvania to aid in the enforcement of Federal laws and the punishment of those who disobeyed them. More substantial support was proved by the passage of an act for State assumption of the direct tax assessed by a recent act of Congress and by the adoption of a new militia law, which was better than the previous one although it fell far short of answering the desires of the Governor.[47]

The character of the legislature was more clearly revealed, however, by the adoption of a measure to raise the pay of its members from three to four dollars a day. Introduced in the Senate with the support of both parties, it was passed without a record vote and sent to the House. Young William J. Duane and a few others made a strong fight against the bill in that chamber. One attempt was made to amend it so that the pay raise would not be retroactive to the beginning of the session and another to make it effective only in the next session. Both were defeated by overwhelming majorities. The first section of the bill was then adopted by a vote of 53-34, with four Federalists voting yea and two nay. The entire Philadelphia County delegation supported the bill, while the city members divided evenly with one absent. An almost identical vote was given on its final passage.[48]

Far from being apologetic for this action, the supporters of the measure were most brazen. A Harrisburg correspondent of the *Democratic Press*, probably one of the Philadelphia County Representatives, with considerable cynicism and an astonishing absence of political wisdom, reported that the friends of the bill had said that the people would not be concerned about the measure " 'as they had sense enough to know *that legislators who were not wise enough to take care of themselves could never be wise enough to take care of the commonwealth.*' "[49]

As the legislators were thus pleasantly engaged in increasing their own emoluments, they became immersed in a political storm over the question of Federal patronage. Robert Patton, the postmaster at Philadelphia, had recently died; and a considerable furore had developed over the question of his successor. The leading contender for the position was Richard Bache, Jr., son-in-law of Dallas and a close associate of Binns and his clique in Philadelphia. His candidacy was supported by almost the entire Pennsylvania delegation in Congress and by a sizable proportion of the members of the legislature.[50]

The other person chiefly considered was none other than Michael Leib. His appointment was warmly backed by Duane, but it was anathema to the many political enemies he had accumulated. Dallas protested loudly against the choice of Leib and avowed that he could have no confidence that his mail would not be tampered with in such a case.[51]

Had the appointment rested with Madison, it is likely that Bache would have received the position without much ado. Certainly, it would hardly have been given to Leib who had displayed a fractious opposition to the administration in the Senate and who had worked for the election of Clinton in 1812. However, the decision lay with Postmaster General Gideon Granger; and he appointed Leib in early February, ostensibly because his pride had been affronted by the offensive pressure exerted by Congressman Charles J. Ingersoll for the appointment of Bache.[52]

The Snyderites harshly denounced this action, and the *Democratic Press* charged that Granger had made the appointment in return for Leib's suppression of attacks upon the Postmaster General in the *Aurora*. Binns and his followers immediately began to seek the removal of Granger with the ultimate objective of removing Leib as well. Eighty-six members of the legislature signed a memorial for the dismissal of the Postmaster General, and Binns's henchmen circulated similar petitions in Philadelphia. The friends of Leib were naturally opposed to this proceeding; but many who disliked him also disapproved of the memorials because they resented the dictatorial tactics of Binns.[53]

Madison removed Granger even before he had received the memorial from the legislators; but, much to the chagrin of Binns, the new Postmaster General, Return J. Meigs, permitted Leib to remain in office. Although matters had quieted down somewhat by March, Leib's enemies were far from contented, and they did not rest in their efforts to be rid of him.[54]

So far as the Snyderites were concerned the Leib appointment had only one favorable aspect. It made necessary his resignation as United States Senator. In an unusual departure from custom, occasioned perhaps by the criticisms of the *Aurora* or simply by the existence of a Democratic preponderance in the legislature of nearly eight to one, no caucus was held before the selection of his successor. Nevertheless, a convincing majority was given to Jonathan Roberts, Congressman from Montgomery County. He received 82 votes out of 116 cast. Of the remaining votes, 23 went to Thomas Sergeant, a Democratic Representative from Philadelphia; eight were given to Horace Binney, a Federalist lawyer; and three others were scattered among as many nominees.[55]

The major interest of the legislators in this session as in the preceding one was the passage of a general banking act. A bill for this purpose was introduced in the House during the second week of the session. Improving upon the technique developed in the previous legislature, the friends of the measure had provided for still further banks in order to gain more votes. These tactics were successful. Unfriendly amendments were beaten down; and on January 19, 1814, the bill was ordered to the third reading by a vote of 62-30. On the following day it was sent to the Senate without another vote being taken.[56]

After considerable discussion, the Senate on February 9 negatived the first section of the bill by a vote of 17-13, one member being absent. Four days later a motion to reconsider was defeated 16-14. However, the supporters of the measure took advantage of the absence of a number of its opponents and on February 15 by a vote of 14-9 revived it. After two weeks of additional debate, the Senate on February 28 passed the bill by a majority of 19-10. It was then returned to the House with a long series of amendments which, among other things, provided for eleven banks more than the original measure. These amendments furnished a good clue to the reasons why six Senators had changed their votes from nay to yea. After a brief dispute between the two chambers, the bill was finally approved by both on March 5 and was sent to the Governor four days later.[57]

Fearing Snyder's disapproval, the legislators delayed adjournment until he should act. Their fears were confirmed when the bill was returned on March 19, 1814. The Governor referred to his previous veto and asserted that the objections stated therein gained added strength when applied to a measure to create 41 new banks. He pointed out the drain of specie from the State into New England and warned of the consequences to be feared by the government if the new banks added to the pressure on the inadequate supply of hard money. Alluding briefly to the lack of public demand for such a bill and to the "fluctuations of opinions" among the legislators while it was being considered, he closed with a respectful statement that he believed it a duty he owed to the people, the State and the country to return it.[58]

Receiving the bill on a Saturday, the House overrode the veto on the following Monday by a vote of 66-24. On the same day with one opponent of the measure ill and another changing his vote, the Senate passed it by a margin of 20-10, exactly the majority necessary to override. Thus, the legislature had its way.[59]

Snyder's courage and devotion to duty can better be appreciated in view of the fact that he delivered his veto while a legislative caucus was considering his nomination for re-election. Holding its first session on March 17, 1814, the caucus had unanimously chosen Snyder and had then adjourned until March 19 to receive the report of a committee appointed to prepare an address. On that day the Governor's veto message was received, and the caucus postponed the meeting until March 23. By that time the Forty Banks Bill had become law; and the caucus concluded its business by approving and directing the publication of a brief address recommending Snyder's re-election. What would have been its course if the banking act had failed is a matter of speculation.[60]

This concluded a session devoted principally to politics, logrolling for special interests, and a legislative raid on the public purse.

V

One of the favorite arguments of the extreme Federalists against the war was that it would bring economic disasters. They envisioned in dark terms the plight of the farmer deprived of a market for his produce, the poverty of the seamen and mechanics thrown out of work by the stoppage of commerce, and the ruin awaiting the merchants as their ships rotted at the quays. The growth of a heavy overland traffic by wagons served only to furnish them with an opportunity to ridicule it in derisive paragraphs under the heading of "Horse Marine Intelligence." Significantly enough, however, most of these Federalist tales of economic ruin were in the form of predictions and seldom purported to describe actual conditions.[61]

The truth was that few of these forebodings were realized in fact. Far from lacking markets for his products, the Pennsylvania farmer found the demand heavier than ever. In November, 1813, it was reported in Pittsburgh that a hundredweight of flour was selling for as much as a barrel had brought before the war. Potatoes were priced at 75 cents per bushel; hay was quoted at 20 dollars per ton; and other prices were similarly high. While these figures reflect only a local and perhaps temporary situation, statistics of the wholesale prices of domestic commodities in Philadelphia show a fairly steady rise from the beginning of the war until its close. In February, 1815, they were nearly 35 per cent higher than in June, 1812. War had not brought disaster to the Pennsylvania farmer.[62]

Even more spectacular was the growth of domestic manufacturing. At the western edge of the State Pittsburgh was enjoying an unprecedented prosperity and increase in population. Commerce was heavy; steamboats were rapidly being built and launched; and all manufacturing enterprises were being expanded. It was estimated that the value of manufactured products for 1814 would be two million dollars, double that of 1810. Other communities in that section of the State were showing similar progress.[63]

Manufacturing was also making great strides in the Philadelphia area. Wide varieties of goods of domestic manufacture were offered for sale, and the papers were filled with advertisements of manufacturers seeking skilled workmen. There were also many notices of suitable factory sites for sale and proposals for the establishment of new ventures.[64] The existence of a war boom was confirmed by the bitter comments of the editor of the *United States' Gazette,* who wrote in October, 1813:

> The war hawks are thriving and fattening upon the hard earnings of the industrious and peaceable part of the community. Many who eighteen months since were starving with their families in rags and indolence, have already become sleek and fat with pay and rations, and strut in blue broadcloth, instead of lounging in drab homespun with their elbows out. The whole host of army contractors, &c. &c. drink in full bumpers "duration of the war." It is to them *meat, drink, washing and lodging.*[65]

Such sentiments were not, however, exclusively Democratic as the *Gazette* implied. In December, 1813, Congress had laid a new embargo, but for various reasons had repealed it in April, 1814. Consistency would have demanded Federalist approval of the repeal, but such was not the case. Some New England representatives denounced it in

Congress, and their sentiments were shared by many of their brethren in Philadelphia. Dallas predicted that the repeal would produce a mixed reaction there:

> The Federal Capital, and the republican industry and talents, were thrown into the direction of manufactures; and you will hear more opposition to the repeal, than you did to the enactment of the non-importation laws &c. The truth is, that the *monied interest* was every day becoming more and more, favorable to the war, and to the Administration, and nothing remained to be encountered, but the alarum of Party Leaders.[66]

Dallas' predictions were verified. The *United States' Gazette*, which had so strongly denounced the passage of the embargo and had clamored against its provisions, also opposed its repeal and accused the administration of attempting to ruin New England industry. Correspondents in the *Aurora* were likewise critical of the abandonment of the measure.[67]

The economic effects of the war were not all beneficial. Among the trials which plagued the people was commodity speculation, particularly in items such as coffee, sugar, and cotton. In December, 1813, speculation reached almost unprecedented heights in Philadelphia and resulted in the formation of consumers associations whose members pledged themselves not to buy coffee and sugar at prices in excess of 25 and 30 cents per pound, respectively. While it is doubtful that such groups could have exerted effective pressure on the speculators, the rumors of an early peace quickly achieved the same objective. Prices dropped spectacularly and were brought, at least temporarily, to the levels specified by the associations.[68]

The war also seemed to increase the demands for charity, particularly from the dependents of soldiers. Independent efforts to alleviate their sufferings were made in the winter of 1812-1813 in the Northern Liberties; but the contributions were meager and insufficient. The American Patriotic Fund Society apparently had little more success and in January, 1814, was denounced by Duane, probably for political reasons, as an imposture. Inadequate funds were also complained of by the Philadelphia Female Hospitable Society and the president of the Board of Guardians of the Poor. The relative lack of interest in local charity was made more glaring by the fact that an appeal for funds for this purpose by the Committee of Defense in the fall of 1814 brought only $5,000, while more than $13,000 had been raised in the preceding January and February for the relief of victims of a disastrous fire in Portsmouth, New Hampshire.[69]

The hardships of the indigent were not sufficiently great to give verity to Federalist predictions of economic ruin; but in 1814 the growing shortage of specie and the near bankruptcy of the government at last brought partial fulfillment to their dire prophecies.

The dissolution of the Bank of the United States in 1811 had made the problem of war finance particularly difficult. The country lost its only national circulating medium apart from specie; and the specie supply was greatly reduced by the withdrawal of more than seven million dollars by foreigners who had held stock in the bank. State bank notes replaced the notes of the national bank, but they fluctuated widely in value away from the place of issue, and as their volume increased they exerted a correspondingly heavier pressure on the limited supply of specie.

The war by its interruption of commerce drastically cut the revenue of the government and at the same time prevented the replenishment of American supplies of specie by the sale of products abroad. These difficulties were accentuated by certain regional dislocations produced by the war. For nearly a year the British did not extend their blockade of the American coast to the greater part of New England. This fact, together with the growth of manufacturing in that section, made New England abnormally important as a source of goods for other sections; and specie flowed into the region, since the normal methods of exchange of commodities were upset. This was particularly unfortunate for the government because New England disaffection toward the war prevented it from taking its fair share of the loans; and without a national currency the taxes collected in other sections of the country could not be spent in New England after the specie was exhausted.

Matters were made still worse by the deliberate efforts of the New Englanders to embarrass the financial conduct of the war. They went out of their way to draw specie from the other regions by presenting huge quantities of notes for redemption. At the same time they traded heavily with the British forces in Canada and purchased large amounts of British government bills at a discount. The bills were also offered for sale at attractive prices in New York, Philadelphia, and Baltimore.

This not only amounted to a loan to the national enemy, but it also contributed substantially to the drain of specie.

As the specie shortage became more and more acute the banks were forced to curtail their discounts; distress appeared among the borrowers; and the banks outside New England were finally compelled to suspend specie payments. Washington and Baltimore began the movement in August; Philadelphia followed suit on the last day of that month; and the New York banks ceased making specie payments on September 1. The government thus had no alternatives except to depend upon irredeemable State bank notes and its own treasury notes for conducting the war.[70]

Such a situation boded ill for the government loans in 1814. The extreme Federalists saw almost within their grasp the chance to end the war by forcing the government into bankruptcy, and they redoubled their efforts to prevent the success of the loans.

The *United States' Gazette* began a strenuous campaign for this purpose. As the government sought to borrow ten million dollars in April, the paper warned would-be subscribers that previous purchasers stood to lose as the price of government stocks declined and that future lenders might suffer a similar fate. Furthermore, it pointed out that a Federalist administration might not feel obligated to pay the war loans. Knowing that many might be inclined to subscribe on the theory that peace was imminent, it argued that such a hope was delusive and that peace rumors were deliberately begun by the administration to aid in floating the loan. It excoriated Federalists who deserted their principles by lending money to the government and intimated that God would hold subscribers responsible for the continuance of a wicked war since a failure of the loan would bring hostilities to a close.[71]

Hopes of large profits and the expectation of an early peace nevertheless led even Federalists of the "Boston stamp" to scheme to participate in the loans. Harrison Gray Otis of Boston worked with Charles Willing Hare, a staunch Federalist of Philadelphia, to conclude a deal in co-operation with David Parish, who had played such an important part in the Sixteen Million Loan in 1813. The project fell through, but its mere existence is indicative of the lure of profits on even the hardiest of Federalists.[72]

Due to the desire of George W. Campbell, the Secretary of the Treasury, to conclude the loan on terms as good as in the Sixteen

Million Loan, only nine millions of the offers made in April, 1814, were accepted; and more than half this amount was subscribed by Jacob Barker of New York, whose credit was somewhat shaky and who had difficulty in paying his installments. Following this, the Secretary negotiated with Astor, Parish, Girard, and a Baltimore banker for the sale of seven millions more. With the specie situation worsening daily, the bankers refused in July to conclude the contract even at a price of 85. In August the government met a partial failure in the Six Million Loan even though it sold at 80. By November it was no longer able to meet its obligations and was in effect bankrupt.[73]

Federalist predictions of economic ruin were thus far verified.

VI

The election of 1814 took place in the midst of stirring events occasioned by the British invasion of the Chesapeake area. Extreme Federalists found conditions all in their favor, and they increased their efforts to overthrow the administration, convinced that at last the crisis had arrived when the country would be forced to turn to their party to save it from the chaos of democracy. Under such circumstances politics prevented complete unity even in the face of invasion. However, the Federalists would have achieved little in Pennsylvania even under these conditions had it not been for the Democratic division in Philadelphia. The Old School co-operated with the Federalists in the county; and a large portion of the Democratic voters in the city boycotted the election. These things jarred the Democratic keystone; but the staunchness of the rural districts held it firm in its place.

American morale had reached a high point in September and October, 1813, as news came of the victories of Perry and Harrison. Such elation was soon dissipated. In November Wilkinson began and abandoned his disgraceful campaign against Montreal. In December the Canadian town of Newark was wantonly burned by American forces abandoning Ft. George. This was followed by the British capture of Ft. Niagara and by punishing raids on the New York frontier. The year closed with the report of "blue lights" at New London, Connecticut, allegedly used by British sympathizers to signal the British blockading squadron and prevent the escape of Stephen Decatur with the American war vessels stationed there.[74]

Matters seemed to improve little in the early months of 1814. In March Wilkinson again proved his incapacity at La Colle; in May Oswego was raided and partially destroyed; and in August George Croghan was repulsed in an attempt to regain Michilimackinac. Although Jacob Brown had achieved gratifying successes in July and August at Ft. Erie, Lundy's Lane, and Chippewa, they were more than overbalanced by British advances in Maine and by the initiation of large-scale attacks in New York and the Chesapeake region.[75]

Great Britain's increased energy in the war was due to the developments in Europe. Since the failure of the Russian invasion in 1812, Napoleon had been continually losing ground and had finally been forced to abdicate in April, 1814. This released large numbers of seasoned British troops to take part in the war against the United States.

Though this situation was fraught with great danger for the country, the more radical Federalists refused to see it in this light. Extolling British magnanimity and insisting that peace could be made on honorable terms at any moment when the administration abandoned its unwarranted demands, they hailed with delight the news of Napoleon's defeats in Europe. In Philadelphia they even went to the extent of celebrating with a dinner in honor of Czar Alexander. The news of Napoleon's abdication led them to extravagant perorations on the Bourbons and the blessings of a people restored to the rule of their legitimate monarch.[76]

Democratic editors did not share the illusion that peace in America would automatically follow the end of the conflict in Europe. They warned of a continued and harsher struggle. The *United States' Gazette*, however, refused to see that the threat of invasion had made any change in the nature of the war. It announced that if a factional war resulted in a disgraceful peace that only the responsible faction would be thereby dishonored. It clamored for the resignation of Madison and asserted that it would be futile for Federalists to co-operate with the administration "in supporting any rights whatever *by force of arms.*" Its position was made indelibly clear by an anonymous correspondent who wrote: "Federalists must direct the councils, or Federalists cannot wield the sword."[77]

Not all Federalists partook of these extreme sentiments. Some of the toasts given at dinners of the Federalist Washington Guards in Philadelphia were staunchly loyal to the nation and opposed to division in the face of foreign attack. In New York Oliver Wolcott, who had succeeded Hamilton as Secretary of the Treasury, believing the character of the war to have changed, sought to organize the "Washington Federalists" to oppose the disunionists among his party. The *Gazette* heaped recriminations upon such political apostates and continued to seek party advantage in the national woe. Yet even its deluded editor was momentarily shaken by the vindictive British peace terms and by the British disposition to draw no distinction between Federalists and other Americans.[78]

Academic arguments over British intentions soon gave way to practical considerations of defense. The knowledge that the British were planning an active campaign spurred the Pennsylvanians to energetic measures. In the early part of July both Federalists and Democrats in Philadelphia were busily engaged in forming companies for the protection of the city; and on July 22, 1814, Governor Snyder issued general orders detaching 14,000 militia to be called into service at the discretion of the national government.[79]

Snyder was considerably embarrassed by this requisition from the Secretary of War because of the peculiar status of the Pennsylvania militia at this time. The act passed by the legislature in March had repealed the old militia law and its supplements as of August 1, but it had not provided for the completion of reorganization under the new system until late in October. Therefore, when the War Department late in August directed that 5,000 militia be sent to Washington, the Governor had no real authority to compel the militiamen to obey; and his general orders of August 26 curiously blended military directives and appeals to patriotism. His faith in the people was vindicated when 7,500 men reported at York in September in response to these orders.[80]

In the meantime, news of the capture and burning of Washington had reached Philadelphia and galvanized its citizens into feverish action. A public meeting was held at the State House on August 26, 1814, with ex-Governor McKean as chairman and Joseph Reed as secretary. It chose a "Committee of Defence," headed by Charles Biddle and composed of members of all parties, to take measures to defend the city. The committee immediately set to work at its appointed task. The Philadelphia city councils and the corporations of Southwark and Northern Liberties furnished funds amounting to a half million dollars; numerous volunteers devoted days of labor to the preparation of fortifications; and new military units were formed daily. All parties seemed united against the common foe.[81]

Such appearances were deceptive. From the beginning the committee tended to try to engross all power and to ignore both the city government and General Bloomfield, the commandant of the United States military district. It also developed a somewhat localized point of view on the overall military situation. Matters were still further complicated by the introduction of a fourth authority when Governor Snyder moved his headquarters to Philadelphia.

Political jealousies muddled the situation even more, particularly after news of the British repulses at Lake Champlain and Baltimore had relieved the tension. Duane, as Adjutant General and proponent of the government's military views, privately and through the columns of the *Aurora* denounced the committee for officiousness and accused it of deliberately attempting to sabotage the administration. Snyder was also resentful of its grasping for authority, and dubbed it the "Committee of Offence." Binns, in the *Democratic Press*, assailed it for allegedly drawing up articles of impeachment against Snyder and Madison.[82]

Relations between the Governor and the district commandant were also strained to the breaking point. There were many causes of friction; but the chief one was the question of the organization of volunteer militia units in the Federal service. The volunteer groups were established under the old State law which provided for proportionately more officers and proportionately fewer privates than the army regulations. Under the peculiar situation then existing Snyder felt unable to compel the volunteer units to conform to the regular organization and in ordering them to service under General Bloomfield had specified that no changes in organization were to be made.

No difficulties arose until Bloomfield was succeeded by Major General Edmund P. Gaines on October 7, 1814. Probably taking advantage of the latter's ignorance of the previous understanding, Duane a week later arbitrarily directed the reorganization of Lieutenant Colonel Louis Bache's regiment. As the officers successively refused to obey his commands, Duane ordered them arrested and held for court martial. Bache was found guilty on a number of charges and was cashiered. The remaining officers were never tried.

The Governor was thoroughly angered by this procedure and considered withdrawing the Pennsylvania militia from service under General Gaines. This could not be done, however, without giving the appearance of distrust of the national administration, an action which would have given much aid and comfort to the Federalists of New England who were then talking loudly of disunion. He was therefore forced to content himself with protesting. He was somewhat mollified by Bache's unanimous re-election to command of the same regiment.[83]

With politics running so high in the matter of public safety, it was natural that the political campaign being conducted simultaneously should be severely contested. The Federalist papers assailed Snyder for failing to provide effectively for the troops in camp and generally denounced him for incompetence. They also sharply attacked the national administration and even printed a memorial requesting Madison to resign, asserting that the country could be saved in no other way. Meanwhile, a meeting of Philadelphia Federalists in late September had nominated Isaac Wayne, former Senator from Chester County, for Governor and had refused to accede to his request that his name be withdrawn.[84]

More significant was the widening breach among the Democrats. The *Democratic Press* and the Snyderites continued to denounce Leib and to call for his removal as postmaster; while the adherents of the Old School began to organize their forces more closely, assail Snyderite proscription, and defend Leib as the virtuous and unoffending public servant whose devotion to principle had brought upon him the persecution of the corrupt.[85]

It was inevitable that another split should follow. No breach at first appeared. The Old School participated in the county delegate elections and succeeded in capturing the Northern Liberties district. This gave them eight votes out of a total of nineteen, which was not enough to dominate the committee of delegates. After being voted down, the Northern Liberties group issued an address denouncing the other delegates and attacking the regular assembly ticket because it contained men who had voted to raise their own pay, supported the Forty Banks Bill, and signed the memorial for the removal of Granger. They called a general county meeting, which made new nominations and appointed its own conferees for the congressional and other joint nominations.[86]

The *Aurora* abandoned any pretense of neutrality. It published communications highly critical of Snyder and his military advisors and also attacked the domination of the general ward committee by officeholders and officeseekers. While it omitted the tickets adopted by the regular Democratic organizations, it gave much space to the proceedings and addresses of the Old School group. Early in October it denounced both the regular city and county nominees as being with few exceptions unworthy of the title of Democrats. Some had voted to raise their own pay; others had attempted to dictate the appointments of the United States government; and still others had been political trimmers. It closed by stating that it would "never support any *knave* or *ideot* for any office" whatever his party.[87]

In the face of the Old School schism and the attacks of the *Aurora*, the *Democratic Press* was unusually silent. Not only did it fail to denounce its opponents with its usual vigor, but it hardly bothered even to defend Snyder and his followers against the charges leveled at them. Such a departure from its normal policy was probably due to Binns's preoccupation with his duties as Snyder's aide-de-camp.[88]

The effect of these things was clearly shown in the election returns. In the city the most noticeable feature was a spectacular drop in the Democratic vote. Even after the ballots of the militia in camp were counted, the Democratic assembly ticket received an average of only 2,022 votes, which was 1,070 less than in the previous year. Federalist candidates for the same office averaged 2,921 votes, an increase of nearly 300 over 1813. Thus, nearly 800 Democrats in the city apparently refrained from voting. Needless to say, the Federalists made a clean sweep of the city election.

In the county the drop in the regular Democratic vote was not so significant. The interesting fact here was that there was clear evidence that the Old School had abandoned the Democratic tickets for Governor, Congressmen, and State Senators to vote for Federalists. All three groups had run tickets for the assembly; and the average vote had been 1,726 for the Federalists, 2,663 for the regular Democrats, and 725 for the Old School. These figures may be assumed to reflect the approximate voting strength of each group. Nevertheless, Isaac Wayne received 2,521 votes for Governor; Nicholas Biddle amassed 2,563 for State Senator; and the Federalist congressional candidates averaged 2,286. Binns's charges of Leibite co-operation with the Federalists seem well substantiated.

Under these circumstances the Federalists in Philadelphia not only won all the city offices and most of the joint city-county positions, but they elected five Representatives, two State Senators, and four Congressmen. The principal Democratic success was the election of the county assembly delegation.[89]

The Democrats also suffered setbacks in the rest of the State. The Federalists elected five out of nine State Senators, giving them ten out of 31; and they also won 24 out of the 95 seats in the House, fourteen more than in the previous legislature. Even the overwhelmingly Democratic counties of Dauphin and Lebanon returned a Federalist Senator because of a local schism.[90]

The Federalists also succeeded in electing a Congressman in the district composed of Allegheny and Butler counties. Adamson Tannehill, the Democratic incumbent, lost by 28 votes out of nearly 2,800 to John Woods. Since the same counties gave the Democratic assembly ticket an average majority of 245 votes, it appears that Tannehill's defeat was attributable to local circumstances. Most probably it was the result of his dismal record as commander of the volunteer brigade at Buffalo in 1812, although there may have been other less apparent reasons.[91]

The gubernatorial race was hardly a contest in view of the delayed nomination of Wayne and the uncertainty as to his acceptance of the office if elected. Despite these handicaps, he polled 29,566 votes and carried the city of Philadelphia and the counties of Delaware, Chester, Lancaster, and Adams. Snyder garnered 51,099 votes and carried the remaining counties, but he won in Philadelphia County by only seven votes out of a total of 5,049. George Latimer, another Federalist, received 910 votes, nearly two-thirds of which came from Huntingdon County. There were eighteen additional scattered votes. Snyder's majority was thus only 20,605 as compared with 24,386 in 1808 and 47,035 in 1811.[92]

A number of factors contributed to the Democratic losses. One of the most important was the failure of the administration to conduct successfully the military and financial affairs of the government. Even before the fall of Washington, Dallas had informed William Jones that while Pennsylvania was as staunchly Republican as ever, it was losing faith in the administration.[93] The British destruction of Washington and the ensuing military plight combined with the virtual bankruptcy of the government to give added weight to the Federalist charges of administrative incompetency. At the same time Federalist co-operation in home defense made that party a somewhat more palatable alternative than it had previously been.

State and local issues were also of great significance. The *Aurora* was not at a loss to name such causes. The election results, in its opinion, were attributable to the proscription and denunciation of the "democrats of '98, '99, and 1800." They were due to Snyder's own unpopularity, his bad appointments, and the "execrable character" of his advisors. They were also assignable to the venality of a legislature which raised its own pay, flooded the State with banks, and stepped out of its proper sphere to demand the removal of Granger because of Leib's appointment as postmaster. The Democratic losses were, therefore, simply the result of the desertion of principle by those who controlled the party.[94]

The *Democratic Press* blamed Leib and Duane. The former and his henchmen were accused of having co-operated with the Federalists; and the *Press* was able to make out a good case for this accusation so far as Philadelphia County was concerned. Duane was guilty on two counts. In the first place he had aroused alarm by speaking of moving the *Aurora* to a place of safety just prior to the election. The people became panicky and were led to believe that the administration had neglected its duties because Duane as Adjutant General might be expected to know what the true situation was. Secondly, the *Aurora* had openly denounced the Democratic ticket just prior to the election; and the Federalists had circulated this castigation as proof of their charges of the party's "corruption, wickedness, and folly."[95]

To the *United States' Gazette* the election returns were proof that the people were beginning to do their own thinking. It believed that they saw the incompetence of the administration; that they were indignant at the type of appointments made to Federal and State offices; that they were resentful of the domination of Binns and his associates; and that they had by their votes condemned the venality of both Snyder and Madison.[96]

So far as the results in Philadelphia were concerned, all three views seem to be correct in some degree. Certainly, the incompetence of the government had some influence on the voters. Equally certain is the effect of Leibite co-operation with the Federalists. Duane's denunciation of the party also had some weight, but it probably would not have amounted to much except for the disgust occasioned by the highhanded conduct of Binns and his cohorts in the Leib appointment and in other matters. The actions of the legislature likewise seem to have been of some importance.

Outside Philadelphia it is even more difficult to determine exactly what and how important were the various causes of the Democratic losses. In general, however, it would appear that the principal ones were the discouraging financial and military situation of the government and the recreant conduct of the legislature. There seems to be some correlation between the lists of legislators who failed to return to the House and those who voted for the salary grab and the bank bill. In 1813 there had been 42 new members elected to the House; but in 1814 the number had increased to 63. Of the members not re-elected in 1814, there were 45 who had voted for raising their own pay and 44 who had supported the passage of the bank bill over Snyder's veto. The people had apparently rebuked their representatives.[97]

In the two years which followed Madison's re-election Pennsylvania remained staunch in its support of the war, but at the end of the period the State had lost much confidence in the ability of the administration to conduct it properly. At the same time centrifugal forces in the Democratic Party, encouraged by the appearance of venality among the legislators, officeholders, and party leaders, were threatening the tradition of party harmony. The restoration of peace was soon to quiet questions on the conduct of the war, but it was only to increase party tensions which had refused to be downed even in the face of threatened foreign invasion.

CHAPTER XII
PEACE AND DEMOCRATIC DISINTEGRATION: 1815-1816

By February, 1815, the close of the war had brought to an end the gloomy prospects which the country faced in the waning months of 1814. The dangers of invasion and disunion were dissipated; and the nation was able to turn its attention to the problems of internal expansion and development. An era in American history had closed.

Such a change in the national outlook was reflected in party politics. Except for the questions of foreign policy attendant upon the Napoleonic wars, the old alignments of Federalists and Republicans had long since been outmoded. The restoration of peace removed this issue and made such distinctions wholly unrealistic.

Jeffersonian successes had proved the untenability of a political platform frankly emphasizing the rule of "the wealthy, the wise, and the good"; and the more sagacious of the Federalists had already begun to adopt the Republican political techniques and to couch their appeals in such fashion as to attract the support of a broader section of the voters. A change was also taking place in the Federalist views on Federal and State relations. As a party in control of the general government, it had developed the philosophy of loose construction and a strong government dedicated to a positive program of action for the benefit of the propertied classes, particularly the mercantile and banking groups. As a minority party, the Federalists became aware of the inconveniences of a strong government carrying out measures to the detriment of their particular interests, and they fell back upon the state-rights defenses erected by their opponents.

The Republicans had also undergone a metamorphosis. Some of their number had developed serious qualms as to the desirability of unrestricted popular rule. They were disturbed by attacks upon such a cherished institution as the judiciary, and as political machinery grew in effectiveness they became increasingly alarmed at the efficacy of demagogic appeals and the rise of machine politics.

Republicans had likewise altered their views on the powers and policies of the Federal government. Mindful of their experiences in the period of commercial restrictions and war, they no longer laid such emphasis upon the power of the states; they ceased their insistence upon a strict construction of the Constitution; and they abandoned their negative views of the functions and powers of the general government. They became the exponents of a strong navy, an efficient army, and the second Bank of the United States. They even sponsored economic legislation along Hamiltonian lines by adopting the first avowedly protective tariff in 1816.

A realignment of parties was evidently in the making, but it was not immediately forthcoming. Parties as institutions tend to outlive the issues which gave them birth. Furthermore, new alignments depended upon the appearance of new issues, and it was not apparent just what these would be in the closing years of Madison's administration. Until Jeffersonian Republicanism was disintegrated by factionalism, and men had resolved upon their attitudes toward such new developments as manufacturing and western expansion, party politics degenerated into a mere question of personalities—the perennial battle of the "ins" and the "outs."

Nowhere was this more true than in Pennsylvania in 1815 and 1816. With the Federalists reduced to an impotent minority, the story of that State's politics had been for many years a tale of the struggles of Democratic factions for power. Not even the coming of the war had completely obliterated internecine strife. The restoration of peace removed all restraints and made it politically feasible for discontented Democratic factions to ally themselves with the Federalists.

The political warfare of these years was basically a matter of personalities, but it took the form of an attack upon party machinery. Such machinery had been an important factor in achieving Democratic ascendancy in the State; but Federalist impotence seemed to offer little reason for its continued functioning. Moreover, through the effective distribution of patronage, it was being used to perpetuate in office the groups then holding power. The dissident factions, finding it virtually impossible to capture control of the party machinery, therefore concentrated their assaults upon it, particularly upon the congressional and legislative nominating caucuses. While they did not completely succeed in their objectives, they made much progress. Disintegration of the Pennsylvania Democracy, the proud keystone in the Democratic arch, had begun.

I

For four months after the election in October, 1814, the citizens of Pennsylvania were much concerned over matters connected with the war and the disunion movement in New England. The first weeks of February brought news of Jackson's victory at New Orleans and of the signing of the Treaty of Ghent. Public rejoicing was great as the people turned their thoughts to other things.

The excessive conditions of peace offered by the British at the opening of the negotiations at Ghent served to convince many Federalists that there had been a change in the nature of the war and that they must rally to its support regardless of their feelings toward the Madison administration. Such were the views of James A. Bayard, Rufus King, and John Jay; and their sentiments were echoed in the conversation of Joseph Hopkinson, one of Philadelphia's firmest Federalists.[1]

Some of the more extreme members of the party saw things differently. The editor of the *United States' Gazette* scoffed at appeals for unity behind the administration. He believed that Madison and his followers were simply seeking to maintain themselves in positions of power and that they were not concerned with the honor and interests of the country. Federalists could never support such men; but he had his own prescription to save the country:

> The whole system must be revised— These men must be told by the people in a tone which they dare not disobey that they must give way to abler and better men— Let the talents, the integrity and the honour of the country be brought into power, and you will quickly see credit restored, disgrace effaced, apprehension banished— The enemy will perceive the change as soon as we. The negotiations at Ghent, will assume a different aspect, and ere long will produce, what will never be effected under present auspices, an HONOURABLE PEACE.[2]

If the editor of the *Gazette* expected such a change to come about through the resignation of Madison, he seems to have stood almost alone. A full month after the printing of the memorial for the President's resignation, the *Aurora* reported that there had been no attempt made to circulate it. Some, perhaps, may have expected to achieve the same object through the appointment of Federalists to the cabinet. At any rate, this was one of the proposals to restore national harmony advanced in Mathew Careys' *Olive Branch*. Democratic writers, however, were opposed to the scheme.[3]

In the meantime, the Federalists in Massachusetts had issued their call for a convention of the New England states at Hartford on December 15, 1814. The project drew both denunciation and derision from the *Aurora,* while the Federalist reaction was somewhat mixed. The *Pittsburgh Gazette* considered the Massachusetts resolutions which initiated the project as "dignified and patriotic"; but the *United States' Gazette* avoided comment and did not give approval to the movement.[4]

Charles Willing Hare was inclined to support the project, but he warned Harrison Gray Otis that disunion must be avoided. In his opinion, the object of the convention should be to revise the Federal Constitution and to provide a means for changing the national administration more quickly than was possible under normal circumstances. What attitude Hare would have taken if these objectives could not be gained is not made clear.[5]

Not many of the Philadelphia Federalists seemed to share such ideas. William Tilghman did not believe that the New Englanders intended to break up the Union, but he disliked the convention. In his opinion, they would, by seeking revision of the Constitution, cause such confusion that the British would be encouraged to continue the war. His views seem to have been those of the leading members of the party in the State.[6]

In the midst of these circumstances, the legislature convened on December 4, 1814. The Governor's message was long and emphasized the necessity for a thorough reform of the militia laws in order to prepare the State for the expected renewal of the war in the spring. Among other things, Snyder recommended the establishment of a permanent body of State troops for defense against invasion. Such a project based upon a modified plan of conscription was sponsored by Nicholas Biddle, Federalist Senator from Philadelphia, but it failed to gain a majority in the House. A new militia bill was finally adopted shortly before the close of the session; but the Governor vetoed it after the coming of peace had made it possible to give the matter more leisurely consideration.[7]

Meanwhile, the legislature took heed of other matters. On December 13, 1814, it held an election for United States Senator. Jonathan Roberts won an easy re-election, receiving 84 Democratic votes. His Federalist opponents, Samuel Sitgreaves and Jared Ingersoll, received 32 votes and one vote, respectively, all but two of which came from members of their own party.[8] The legislators also took note of public disapproval of the pay raise voted in the previous session. The Senate passed a bill for reducing the pay of the members; but it was lost when the two houses failed to agree on the measure.[9] A greater spirit of compromise was shown in the adoption of an act reapportioning representation in the legislature. Apart from making provision for a number of new counties which had recently been established, it made few significant changes.[10]

While the legislature was thus engaged, events of great significance had been occurring. The Hartford Convention had assembled on December 15, 1814, and remained in secret session until the following January 5. The result of its deliberations was a report which recommended that the Federal government be required to assign to the New England states a portion of the revenue collected therein to be used for directing their own defense. Should this proposition not be acceded to, a second convention should be called to determine what further steps should be taken. In addition, the convention recommended that seven amendments to the Constitution should be adopted in order to protect New England from a recurrence of the evils of which she complained.[11]

The *Aurora* was most scornful of the report. It summarized its contents, derided its recommendations, and asserted that the mountain in labor had delivered a mouse. At Pittsburgh the *Mercury* reached identical conclusions, while the Federalist *Pittsburgh Gazette* contented itself with printing the report without comment of any sort.[12]

The events of the next few weeks were soon to increase the jeers of the Democrats at those who had assembled at Hartford. By February 6, 1815, Philadelphia had news of Jackson's victory at New Orleans; and a week later it was known that a peace had been signed by the commissioners at Ghent. The *Aurora* was moved to even greater heights of ridicule; and the legislature, which had received the suggested amendments to the Constitution, adopted a lengthy report prepared by Nicholas Biddle which examined the proposals in detail and denied both their wisdom and their desirability.[13]

Jackson's victory and the news of the peace were both celebrated with great joy; but the Federalist papers did not fail to note that the administration had not achieved a single objective for which the war was declared. Though such a peace was a blessing to the country, they insisted that it was without honor for the government. The war had brought no fruits except the loss of thousands of lives, a huge debt, heavy taxes, and a nearly bankrupt treasury. In the words of the *Pittsburgh Gazette,* the country had " 'gained a loss.' "[14]

Democrats viewed matters differently. A Congressman-elect from Dauphin County was ecstatic over the coming of a peace "so happy for our country & so opportune for us democrats." He was certain that there was no dishonor. After all, he wrote, the war had been declared only against the remnant of the British forces not used against France; but, contrary to plans, the country had had to face the whole of the British might. To have done so and escaped "in statu quo" was, to his mind, "honor."[15]

The Pittsburgh *Mercury* in a thoughtful article discussed the causes of the war and the conditions under which peace was made and concluded that the government had gained all that it had sought in declaring it. Peace was made "at a time when peace was truly desirable— when all obstructions to a free trade and all pretence for the impressment of our people had ceased to operate."[16]

The *Aurora* was also convinced that the war had been of great benefit. It had taught many valuable lessons in military affairs to the American people, but, most important, it had demonstrated that a free representative government was the strongest government on earth. The country had been raised to a position of respect in the eyes of other nations.[17]

Thus ended the turmoil over foreign affairs, which had plagued the country almost continuously for more than two decades. Its passing permitted politics to assume a new direction.

II

The post-war pattern of politics in Pennsylvania began to be evident in the political struggles of 1815. The Snyderites cemented a close alliance with the national administration and controlled the patronage in their mutual interests. The Federalists and the reviving Old School Democrats in Philadelphia united in attacking this combination, and they also showed a growing disposition to co-operate in other respects. Elsewhere in the State there were indications of restiveness and of opposition to the existing conduct of party affairs. The disintegration of the Pennsylvania Democracy was under way.

One result of the financial crisis which had engulfed the administration in the summer of 1814 had been to bring Alexander J. Dallas back into political prominence. Madison had considered offering Dallas the post of Secretary of the Treasury as early as January, 1814; but there had been opposition from some of the Pennsylvania delegation in Congress; and Dallas himself had been reluctant to give up his lucrative legal practice in Philadelphia. In September, however, after Secretary Campbell had resigned, Dallas indicated his willingness to take the office. Madison made the appointment, and it was confirmed by the Senate on October 6.[18]

Three months after Dallas joined the cabinet Leib was removed as postmaster of Philadelphia. Richard Bache, his successor, was an intimate political associate of Binns and Dallas' son-in-law. The *Democratic Press* was elated over Leib's dismissal, while the *Aurora* indulged in melancholy reflections on the decline of Democratic virtue. The *United States' Gazette* contented itself with sarcastic references to Bache's talents and his connection with Dallas.[19]

Additional evidence of the growing liaison between the national administration, acting through Dallas, and the Snyderites, represented by Binns, appeared in the appointment of Charles J. Ingersoll to succeed Dallas as United States Attorney for Pennsylvania. Ingersoll had warmly supported Bache for postmaster in 1814, and he was likewise a close political ally of Binns.[20] It was clear that control of Federal and State patronage had been united in the hands of a small clique and that it would be used to promote their own projects and those of the existing Federal and State administrations.

Sharing a mutual antipathy to Dallas, Binns, and the Madison and Snyder regimes, it was almost inevitable that the Federalists and the Old School should begin to co-operate. Significant indications of this growing cordiality appeared even before the political campaign of 1815 began. In May the *United States' Gazette,* hitherto violently opposed to Leib, published a communication vigorously defending his election as president of the Board of Prison Inspectors. A month later young William J. Duane was admitted to the Philadelphia bar under the sponsorship of Joseph Hopkinson, a man whom the *Aurora* had for years denounced as one of the worst of the Federalists. Of minor importance in themselves, these incidents showed the change in the political atmosphere.[21]

Meanwhile, the Old School began to make vigorous preparations to regain its former supremacy. Beginning at the lowest level, it organized its forces for the corporation elections in the Northern Liberties in May. Its ticket for commissioners was completely victorious, and the party was jubilant when Leib was unanimously selected as president of the board. Though the election was a minor one, the Old School had won its first victory in years, and it seemed an omen of better times to come.[22]

Of greater importance was Duane's resumption of active editorship of the *Aurora* in June. Professing himself to be greatly dissatisfied with the conduct of the State and national governments, he announced his intention of attacking them without reserve. In the months that followed the columns of the paper were filled with denunciations of Snyderite corruption, of the control of the nominating machinery by officeholders, and of the failure of the Snyderites to carry out the constitutional reform which the *Aurora* alleged to have been their program when they came into office.[23]

More interesting was Duane's revival of one of his oldest feuds. With the Snyderites closely allied with Dallas, he renewed his old charges that the politics of the State had for years been dominated by the behind-the-scenes intrigues of Dallas and Gallatin. The *Aurora* asserted that a bargain had been made whereby the latter had been allowed full power to wield Pennsylvania's influence in national affairs in return for giving the Snyderites unmolested control of the State government and the distribution of local patronage. Such an understanding fully accounted for the great activity of the officeholders in the election of 1815. With the State's influence vital in the presidential nominating caucus, the clique was seeking to tighten its grip on the legislature and the congressional delegation. Although many of the *Aurora's* statements were extreme, there seems to be much truth in its analysis of the existing political arrangements in Pennsylvania.[24]

Though the Federalists did not participate in this Democratic family quarrel, the *United States' Gazette* savagely attacked Dallas for his conduct as Secretary of the Treasury. Among other things, it asserted that he had given to his son-in-law, Richard Bache, exclusive rights to subscribe to a new issue of government stock at a price of 95 when the market price for similar stock was 97 or 98. The *Gazette* continued to publish these charges despite denials in the *Democratic Press*.[25]

The Philadelphia election of that year was soon to give more tangible evidences of co-operation between the Old School and the Federalists. In the city the Old School at first sought to capture the ward machinery. As the time for the choice of ward committeemen approached, a writer in the *Aurora* published a number of articles savagely attacking the political depravity of the Snyderites. He asserted that their ascendancy had been gained through control of the nominating machinery and detailed the methods by which the officeholders dominated the ward meetings. Reform must therefore begin on that level; and he urged the people to attend these meetings and prevent the continuance of such shameful abuses of the right of free election.[26]

Against this background, the wards began holding their meetings early in August. For a time, it seemed that the ostensible unity of the preceding years would be maintained; but when the Old School found itself unable to overthrow the domination of Binns and his satellites, it broke away and held meetings of its own in Upper Delaware, Locust, and Walnut wards. No rival general ward committee was formed; but a number of Old School Democrats from the city did act with the county conferees in drawing up a ticket for joint offices.[27]

In the county the break between the two factions developed more quickly. Both adopted the district delegate system and held their separate meetings; but the Old School, as usual, made the nominations by the delegates subject to the confirmation of a general county meeting. Each group nominated a full ticket for the General Assembly.[28]

Since the Federalists had proceeded with their own organization for the election in both the city and county,[29] it seemed that there would be no coalition between them and the Old School. However, signs of such a coalition soon began to appear. Late in August a writer in the *Aurora* questioned whether Federalism had ever disgraced "honest democrats" so much as Snyderite *"jacobinism."* He saw only a choice of evils between the two. Eleven days later the *Aurora* printed communications denying the charge that Leib had sought to bargain with the Federalists for support of the Old School ticket in the county. The Old School, asserted these correspondents, adhered to the "principles of '76"; the Quids and Federalists found their refuge with the New School.[30]

Such statements contrasted grotesquely with the events which soon followed. The *United States' Gazette* on September 9, 1815, urged strongly the formation of a "union of honest men" on a permanent basis in order to restore the prosperity and glory of the country and to end the misrule of the "poor, ignorant and imbecile faction" which had abused it. Less than two weeks later the Federalist conferees nominated John Sergeant, a prominent Quid, as their candidate for Congress to fill the vacancy caused by the death of Jonathan Williams. Three days after the announcement of this nomination, the *Aurora* published an address by the Old School conferees putting forward Sergeant as their candidate for Congress.[31]

The *Democratic Press* immediately saw this as proof of its charges of co-operation between the Old School and the Federalists. It recalled Sergeant's quiddism and reprinted some of the violent denunciations which the *Aurora* had made of him in earlier days. The *Aurora* refused to be concerned by such inconsistencies. It found nothing criminal in the fact that the Federalists had decided to support the Old School choice for Congressman. Sergeant, said the paper, was a man of superior abilities and a firm adherent of old Whig principles who had differed with his fellow Republicans at one time by refusing to support Snyder. His election would be of great benefit to the people.[32]

The election returns gave evidence of an even broader co-operation between the Old School and the Federalists. The latter made a clean sweep of the contests in the city and also carried their ticket for Congressman, State Senator, County Commissioner, and Auditor. In the county, however, the Snyderites were victorious. Their assembly ticket polled an average of 2,342 votes to averages of 1,753 for the Old School and 292 for the Federalists. Such figures did not represent the true strength of the three groups, since there were much different results in the votes for State Senator, County Commissioner, and Auditor. In these contests, the vote for the Snyderites varied from 2,303 to 2,310; for the Old School, from 1,497 to 1,543; and for the Federalists, from 729 to 762. This indicates that nearly 400 Federalists supported the Old School assembly ticket and is convincing proof of an understanding between the two groups.[33]

Following the election, the editor of the *United States' Gazette* attributed the Federalist victory to an uprising of the people to crush a "venal and corrupt faction" and added that if Binns would only move to

Northampton that county would likewise become Federalist. The *Democratic Press* regarded this as a substantiation of its charges of a growing rapprochement between the Old School and the Federalists; but even clearer evidences of this new relationship were given by the articles of "Codrus" in the *Aurora*. With arguments much similar to those so scathingly denounced by the same paper when they had been advanced by the Quids in 1805, this writer asserted that all who loved their country were really Democrats and all who supported the Union were really Federalists. The mass of the people in both parties thus desired the same things and supported the same principles. Why, asked "Codrus," should they be divided into two parties? The publication of such arguments in the *Aurora* was a witness of the changing times and a symptom of the crumbling of party traditions.[34]

Signs of restlessness and change began to appear elsewhere in the State. In Pittsburgh the regular Democratic nominee for State Senator was soundly defeated by a candidate from Beaver County.[35] In Berks County the attempt of the Democratic organization to quiet criticism by nominating two candidates for each position nearly resulted in a Federalist victory for one of the assembly seats.[36] In Dauphin County dissident Democrats made a determined attack on the delegate system of nominations and co-operated with the Federalists in an unsuccessful attempt to defeat the regular ticket.[37] In Lancaster County there was dissatisfaction with both the regular Democratic and Federalist tickets on the ground that they discriminated against the upper districts of the county; and an attempt was made to unite members of both parties in opposition to them.[38]

The effect of local unrest was shown to some extent in the election returns for the State as a whole. The Federalists lost five assembly seats in Montgomery, Lancaster, and Luzerne counties, but they picked up six new ones from Bucks, Indiana, Armstrong, Jefferson, Erie, Crawford, Warren, Mercer, and Venango counties. Overall, they elected 25 out of 97 members of the House and three out of seven Senators, giving them one additional seat in each branch of the legislature.[39]

The election of 1815 made no significant changes in the existing political status; but the unrest and local quarrels which accompanied it evidently presaged the disruption of old party alignments, though without giving any clear indication of what would replace them.

III

The Democratic disintegration which had begun to be apparent in 1815 was sharply accelerated in the succeeding year. The process would have gained some momentum in the natural course of events, but it was greatly stimulated by the presidential election of 1816 and the approaching gubernatorial election of the following year.

With both Madison and Snyder leaving office, Pennsylvania politicians of all varieties were keenly concerned over the question of their successors. The Snyderites co-operated in the support of Monroe for President; and a few, led by Binns, sought Snyder's nomination as Vice President. They were developing much internal friction, however, as to the nominee for Governor. The Old School was opposed to the ruling cliques of both the Federal and State administrations and attempted to overthrow them by attacking the nominating caucuses through which they perpetuated their power. With Federalist aid, it gained a surprisingly large vote for a ticket of presidential electors nominated by a convention at Carlisle. Such success augured well for a gubernatorial nominating convention in 1817 and forced the Snyderites to abandon the legislative caucus for a convention of their own. The old order was giving place to the new.

The polls had barely closed in 1815 before the Old School was hard at work to unseat their opponents in the Federal and State governments. The *Aurora* made vigorous attacks on Snyderite corruption of the press and assailed the evils of caucus nominations. It asserted that Snyder, through his control of the legislature, was able to choose his own successor and that he had fixed upon William Findlay, the State Treasurer, as the next Governor.[40]

The *Democratic Press* averred that these attacks were not made in good faith. It charged the Old School and the Federalists with having come to a secret understanding that the next candidate for Governor should be a lawyer and a resident of Philadelphia. The paper alleged further that the Federalists had agreed to furnish funds for the creation of newspapers and the sending of emissaries to gain adherents throughout the State. Meanwhile, all caucus nominations were to be denounced as the vile work of officeseekers.[41]

Succeeding events were to give every semblance of verity to this analysis. Late in October, 1815, Leib made a trip to New York, presumably to consult with De Witt Clinton. In any case, he journeyed through the State to Pittsburgh in the following December, talking with politicians in the various towns, arguing the merits of Clinton as a presidential candidate, and seeking to arouse opposition to caucus nominations of any sort. The tour was quite evidently intended for building political fences; and there was little reason to doubt that it had been sponsored jointly by the Federalists and the Old School as the *Democratic Press* charged.[42]

The two groups were also co-operating in seeking to promote John Sergeant as their candidate for Governor in 1817. Benjamin R. Morgan, Federalist Senator from Philadelphia, assured Sergeant in December, 1815, that divisions among the Snyderites offered excellent prospects for his success through a union of the Old School and Federalists. Hugh Hamilton, erstwhile Quid and then editor of the Old School Harrisburg *Chronicle,* was also sanguine as to Sergeant's chances and enthusiastic in his support. The *Aurora* did not commit itself on the matter of Sergeant's candidacy, but in February, 1816, it went out of its way to bestow high praise on his conduct in Congress.[43]

By the middle of March the project seems to have fallen to the ground. Hamilton disgustedly wrote Sergeant that the superciliousness of the city members in the legislature had completely alienated those from the country. The former had created such a stir over a proposal to sell the State House in Philadelphia that they had ruined Sergeant's prospects. He also felt that the *Aurora* by its inaccurate and intemperate attacks on the Snyderites had caused a revulsion of feeling against the Old School. Hamilton's views were probably accurate; but there was another factor which hurt Sergeant's availability. He had probably become unacceptable to Duane because of his support of the bill to charter the second Bank of the United States—a measure which the *Aurora* had opposed vociferously. At any rate, the paper no longer published encomiums on his ability and devotion to Democratic principles.[44]

The Snyderites likewise experienced difficulties in maintaining unity during the session. At its beginning a caucus intrigue resulted in the displacement of Jacob Holgate, Representative from Philadelphia County, as Speaker of the House. Explanations of this action varied. Some attributed it to the presumptuous ambition of Dr. Joel B. Sutherland, his colleague; others to the jockeying for position of William Findlay's supporters for Governor; and still others to the influence of the banking question. Whatever the reason, the incident was symptomatic of the ill-concealed dissensions among the formerly united backers of Governor Snyder.[45]

A similar divergence was displayed in the matter of the presidential election. Binns was exerting all his influence to obtain united support for a ticket of Monroe and Snyder, but his efforts were to no avail. He was greatly shocked by the failure of a public dinner in Harrisburg to include a toast to the Governor and exhorted his friends to renew efforts in behalf of Snyder for the vice presidency. Possibly because Snyder himself displayed little interest in the matter, a secret caucus in February refused to instruct the Pennsylvania delegation in Congress to back such a ticket, although some 60 members later signed a circular to that effect.[46]

The nominating caucus on March 11, 1815, was equally refractory. It chose a ticket of presidential electors, designated Binns and four others to act as a State committee of correspondence, and appointed county committees to assist in the work. It declined, however, to pledge the electors to Monroe and Snyder, despite the best efforts of Richard Bache, who came from Philadelphia to persuade it to do so. Though this may have been due in large part to a feeling that it was inexpedient to make nominations until the congressional caucus had acted, it was a great disappointment to Binns and was another sign that factions among the Snyderites were working at cross-purposes.[47]

In the congressional caucus at Washington on March 16, 1816, Monroe was nominated for President by the narrow margin of 65-54 over William Crawford of Georgia. Governor Daniel D. Tompkins of New York defeated Snyder for the vice presidential nomination by 85 votes to thirty. The *Democratic Press* at first indulged in vain hopes that Tompkins would refuse to run, but it soon gave these up and began to assert that Snyder had favored the nomination of the New Yorker.[48]

The circumstances under which the congressional caucus met were such as to give considerable aid and comfort to the opponents of caucus nominations. The House of Representatives on March 4, 1816, had appointed a committee to consider the matter of congressional pay. A bill was reported two days later and passed the House on March 8. It was approved by the Senate on March 14 and signed by Madison on March 19. The measure thus hastily adopted purported to be an act changing the mode of compensation from a per-diem-and-mileage basis to a fixed salary of $1,500 a year. According to the opposition, this virtually doubled the pay of the members; and the precipitate manner of its passage coupled with the convening of the nominating caucus at just that time apparently gave substance to the cries of those who accused the administration of using corrupt means to bring about the nomination of Monroe. In Pennsylvania the Compensation Act was to play a prominent part in the congressional elections of 1816 as well as to give impetus to the anticaucus movement.[49]

Despite the very evident opportunity presented by this occurrence and the continuous barrage of criticism and charges of corruption which the *Aurora* had leveled at both State and Federal administrations, organized opposition to the caucus ticket of electors was slow in developing. The *Aurora* had published a series of articles detailing the evils of caucus nominations in February; and two months later it had spoken disparagingly of the electoral ticket chosen by the legislature in March and had reported a "strong disposition" in the State to form a new one. Yet, late in July it could do no more than assert that "a silent apathy, a cold discontent everywhere prevails—the corrupt tremble and the virtuous are looking only for an occasion to call forth their united voices."[50]

Such an occasion presented itself early the following month. The *Aurora* on August 2, 1816, printed a communication from "I. C.," who reported that Charles Thomson, former Secretary of the Continental Congress, had stated that he was opposed to having another President from Virginia and would vote for De Witt Clinton. "I. C." proposed that a new electoral ticket headed by Thomson be drawn up. The *Aurora* countered by suggesting that its correspondent offer such a ticket or that a meeting of "respectable men" be held "to devise such constitutional means as may lead to a full and fair assertion of the people's rights, in opposition to factious usurpation and official corruption." It promised to give such a movement its complete support.[51]

Matters now moved swiftly. At Lancaster on August 12, 1816, a Republican meeting, presided over by George Hoffman, adopted resolutions denouncing caucus nominations and calling upon their "democratic republican brethren" to hold county meetings and select delegates to attend a convention at Carlisle on September 19 to prepare another ticket. Those counties which could not send delegates were requested to make nominations for electors from their districts and forward them to Thompson Brown, a lawyer, at Carlisle.[52]

The Snyderite papers ridiculed the meeting, asking how a secret gathering of six or seven persons, whose chairman was not a qualified voter, could seriously and in good faith complain of the evils of a caucus. The Snyderites also asserted that the meeting had been called as a gathering of persons "friendly to De Witt Clinton as president of the United States." The *Aurora* had denied that the movement favored either Clinton or Monroe; and this pose of support of a principle rather than a man was maintained for the remainder of the campaign.[53]

In this instance, political expediency seems to have superseded candor, as there are good reasons to believe that the new electoral ticket was intended to support Clinton. For one thing, the original communication by "I. C." indicated such a connection. Secondly, a number of the personnel associated with the project had been prominent in the Clinton movement in 1812. Among these was Joseph Lefever of Lancaster and Thompson Brown of Carlisle. Brown had been secretary of the Lancaster meeting on August 26, 1812, at which Lefever had presided, had been a Clinton elector in that year, and, according to the *Democratic Press*, was the promoter of the Lancaster meeting which called the Carlisle convention. Finally, such an interpretation appears justified in view of Leib's trips to New York and western Pennsylvania and the purported alliance of the Old School and the Federalists in support of Clinton.[54]

In the latter part of August the *Aurora* printed a mass of material in favor of the proposed convention. The strongest denunciations of caucus corruption were the work of young William J. Duane, who, writing under the name of "Bryan," demanded that officeholders and officeseekers should be prohibited from participating in the convention. This led to the revival of Snyderite charges that he and his father had turned against Snyder because the latter had not accorded them all that they had desired in the way of political favors. Young Duane responded in September with two long articles over his own name defending both his father and himself against these accusations.[55]

In the midst of such bickering, meetings in Philadelphia, Lancaster, Dauphin, Berks, and Cumberland counties met and chose delegates to attend the convention. Other meetings in Allegheny, Mifflin, Northampton, and perhaps other counties gave their approval and forwarded nominations for electors. Eventually, a total of eleven delegates assembled at Carlisle, met secretly on September 19 and 20, 1816, and departed without publishing their proceedings. This silence was maintained until the day after the general election.[56]

State politics were meanwhile displaying further evidences of Democratic disintegration. The Snyderites not only had to contend with the Old School and the Federalists, but also with the centrifugal effect of gubernatorial ambitions among their own leaders. The most likely choices to succeed Snyder were William Findlay and Boileau; and their supporters were maneuvering for a favorable position in nearly every county. Findlay was particularly active and sought to turn the antipathy between Philadelphia and the rest of the State to his own advantage. Newspaper articles depicting him as the "country candidate" were frequent, while Boileau was pictured as the candidate of the arrogant metropolis. His unabashed electioneering moved Snyder to express a mild disgust, and it certainly laid the basis for a major split in the Snyderite ranks.[57]

Political confusion was also apparent on the local level. In Philadelphia the Old School once more set up its own organizations in the city and county, loudly denounced Snyderite proscription and the domination of Democratic political machinery by officeholders indebted to Dallas or Binns, and called for those who were faithful to the sterling principles of '98 and '99 to rally and overthrow the corrupt politicians who had seized control of the party.[58]

The Snyderites had proceeded with their own organization, but they showed a disposition to compromise and seek a reunion of the party. These efforts at first appeared to promise success; but the antagonism between the two groups was too great. The Old School was not willing to accept anything less than complete control; and the Snyderites would agree to co-operation only on terms which would have eliminated such Old School leaders as Leib and young William J. Duane. The attempted union was therefore a failure. A number of the party were dissatisfied with both sides; and a group in the Northern Liberties, describing themselves as "Independent Democrats," proposed candidates of their own. Party lines were becoming more and more blurred.[59]

In the Philadelphia election on October 8, 1816, the Snyderites were soundly defeated. The Federalists carried the city by a wide margin and also won the contests for Sheriff, County Commissioner, and Auditor. In the county they gave their votes to the Old School assembly ticket, which triumphed by a convincing majority over the Snyderites, who polled fewer votes than in 1815. In the congressional election, Adam Seybert and William Anderson, Democrats supported by both factions, were elected; but John Sergeant and Joseph Hopkinson, Federalists, captured the other two seats because of the split between the Old School and the Snyderites.[60]

The political confusion in Philadelphia was worse confounded in Pittsburgh. Without any previous notice in the newspapers, the Democratic delegates of Allegheny County met on August 12, 1816, and drew up a ticket which contained no residents of Pittsburgh as candidates for the State House of Representatives and which included Walter Lowrie of Butler County as candidate for Congress. It also adopted resolutions denouncing the Compensation Act and the system of caucus nominations. The Pittsburgh *Mercury* assailed these proceedings and reflected bitterly upon those who prated of caucus evils while they used similar methods to gain party control for themselves. The *Commonwealth* defended the meeting and asserted that there had been ample publicity; but matters were not to be settled so simply.[61]

The nature of the discontent with the ticket was soon evident. Correspondents in the *Mercury* denounced it as unrepresentative of the growing importance of Pittsburgh as a manufacturing center, suggested the nomination of Henry Baldwin for Congress, and called for a new meeting to consider the matter. Such a gathering, representing only the city, was held on August 24, 1816. It prepared a new ticket headed by Baldwin and adopted resolutions proclaiming that representation on any future county nominating committees must be apportioned on the basis of taxable population in order to give Pittsburgh its proper weight. The Federalists also supported Baldwin, though they nominated their own candidates for the other offices.[62]

The *Commonwealth* made caustic denunciations of this union with the Federalists, but it gave its support to an attempted fusion of the Democratic factions. The corresponding committees of the two groups met on September 5, 1816, and prepared a ticket which backed Baldwin and proposed assembly candidates not on either of the previous tickets. This try at harmony was disrupted when the Butler County

Peace and Democratic Disintegration

conferees backed Lowrie and the ticket adopted on August 12. The ultimate in confusion was reached when a Mifflin Township meeting denounced all that had been done previously and proposed a ticket made up of all those who had been nominated by the earlier meetings, including the Federalists.[63]

The voters seemed to be much impressed by this suggestion. At any rate, they cast their ballots for all those listed. Baldwin won handily, as did two of the Democrats placed on the compromise ticket for assembly. The other two assembly seats and the county offices fell to the Federalists. Party divisions had become almost meaningless in Pittsburgh.[64]

Similar situations apparently existed in other counties. The Federalists and Old School combined elected 40 out of 97 members of the House and four out of nine Senators. In the congressional election, the *Democratic Press* credited the Federalists with four seats and the Democrats with seventeen. It classified Baldwin and Joseph Hiester as "nondescripts."[65] These results, though apparently reflecting Federalist gains, were rather a measure of Democratic disintegration. Unity was departing from the Pennsylvania Democracy.

The extent of the party's decline was made apparent in the presidential election on November 1. With the completion of the State elections, the silence as to the actions of the Carlisle convention was ended. On October 9, 1816, the *Aurora* published a long address approved by that gathering on September 19. Indited in the solemn tones and using some of the phraseology of the Declaration of Independence and the Constitution, it declared that the members of the convention would resist caucus usurpation and corruption during their lives and impose it as a duty upon their children if that were necessary. It denounced categorically the congressional caucus nominations of Monroe and Tompkins and the legislative nomination of an electoral ticket. It closed by offering an electoral ticket "composed of men, who are not pledged to any vote or act."[66]

Three days later the *Aurora* printed a second address which had been adopted by the convention on September 20, 1816. It spoke with horror of the corruption of popular government in Pennsylvania brought about through the baleful influence of executive patronage in combination with a caucus selection of gubernatorial candidates. As a remedy, it proposed the holding of a nominating convention at Carlisle in June, 1817, to select a candidate for Governor. A corresponding committee to promote the success of the venture was likewise appointed.[67] Such was the work of the Carlisle convention of 1816.

The Snyderites quickly assailed the convention as an unexampled instance of effrontery. It was astounding to see eleven men, chosen by no more than 500 others and not even daring to publish their own names, presuming to brand the elected representatives of more than four million people as usurpers. These men pretended extraordinary devotion to principle, yet they sought only the benefits of office and aligned themselves with Federalists to achieve their aims. They attempted to delude the people by asserting that none of the electors they had nominated were pledged to any candidate, yet four of these men were on the regular ticket and had specifically promised to support Monroe and Tompkins. The citizens of Pennsylvania must stand fast and avoid the seductions of such self-seeking men.[68]

The *Aurora* was filled with articles in support of the Carlisle ticket, and it was joined by the Pittsburgh *Mercury* and the Harrisburg *Chronicle*. The Philadelphia Federalists announced their backing of the movement; and the *United States' Gazette* soon added its voice to those denouncing caucus usurpations.[69]

Despite this frantic activity, the results of the election must have come as a surprise to the supporters of the Carlisle convention. With a total vote of less than 43,000, the regular ticket polled only 25,473 to 17,492 for the convention ticket. Monroe thus had a majority of 7,981, nearly 12,000 less than Madison had received in the closely contested election of 1812.[70] The Democratic keystone had begun to crumble ominously.

The significance of the election was not lost on the Snyderites. With good reason, they had felt that the Carlisle convention in 1816 was concerned primarily with preparing the way for a gubernatorial nominating convention in 1817, and they had discounted its importance in the presidential contest. The vote given the Carlisle electors proved that they had grossly underestimated the growing dissatisfaction with the existing regime and the political machinery by which it had maintained itself. They now moved quickly to remedy that error. Late in November the *Democratic Press* suggested that the presidential electors and the Democratic members of the legislature meet together and propose a method of selecting the candidate for Governor. At a meeting in Harrisburg on December 4, 1816, the electors issued an address recommending that the counties select delegates to attend a convention in Harrisburg on the following March 4 to make the gubernatorial nomination.[71] King Caucus was breathing his last in Pennsylvania.

The once-united Democracy of Pennsylvania had experienced a rapid disintegration in the two years following the election of 1814. Primarily, this was the result of the need for a realignment of parties after the return of peace in Europe had removed the last significant differences between the Federalists and Republicans. It was also due to the fact that the same people had too long controlled both the State and Federal governments and had become more concerned with perpetuating their own ascendancy than with serving the people. The political machinery through which they dominated thus became the logical point of attack. Finally, the collapse of the party was hastened by personal feuds and the restless ambitions of disappointed politicians. These last furnished the driving force in the movement for change and would continue to do so until new issues had created new parties to succeed those now outmoded.

CHAPTER XIII

PENNSYLVANIA POLITICS IN RETROSPECT: 1800-1816

THE VICISSITUDES of the Democratic Republicans constitute the major portion of the history of the politics of Pennsylvania from 1800 to 1816. Although the Federalists survived throughout the period and, paradoxically, appeared to gain strength at its close, they were never able seriously to challenge Democratic predominance following their defeat in the gubernatorial election of 1799. Their continued existence, therefore, was chiefly important because of the latent threat of their cooperation with discontented Republican factions to overthrow the supremacy of the majority of that party in the State.

The low position of Federalism in Pennsylvania was due principally to the unpopular nature of its principles, its inept political organization, its close identification with the commercial classes, its pro-British attitude, and the imprudent excesses of the party in Adams' administration.

Federalist principles had originated as the expression of the views of a conservative minority, which, in the formative years of the national government, sought to create a strong government, dedicated principally to the preservation of life and property and the maintenance of conditions favorable to the prosperity of the commercial classes. While such objectives were not unworthy ones, this minority associated with them a strong distrust of popular rule and a conviction that only those of birth, wealth, and education should have the direction of public affairs.

Such principles were ill calculated to appeal to the people of Pennsylvania, where the restrictions on suffrage were minor and where democratic modes of government had become an established tradition. They also hampered the Federalists by inhibiting the creation of political machinery and techniques designed to muster large masses of voters in support of their program at the polls; and this occurred at a time when the Republicans were perfecting such devices.

Federalism also suffered from the narrowness of its economic objectives. In a predominantly rural and agricultural State, its program for the most part embodied the views of the commercial elements. With the passage of time, the party became relatively insignificant except in New England, where commercial interests were predominant; and as the geographical basis of the party narrowed, so likewise did the breadth of its conceptions. Federalism in its later years thus became to a great degree the expression of the sectional interests of New England and, therefore, something alien to the majority of the people in Pennsylvania. Some, of course, continued to cleave to the broader aspects of its principles; but leadership naturally fell to those areas where the party had local vitality; and the bulk of the Federalists accepted the interpretations imposed by New England.

The party's aversion to government by the masses and its commercial outlook caused it to favor the British in the wars of the French Revolution and Napoleon. This ran counter to the prevailing Anglophobia and in some cases left the Federalists open to the accusation of being willing to subordinate American rights to anti-French prejudices and a greed for profits.

Finally, the high-handed methods of Federalism in 1798 and 1799, the Alien and Sedition Acts, the direct taxes, and the suppression of Fries's Rebellion were exploited by an alert Republican Party to create a tradition of terrorism. The memory of these things faded slowly, and the Federalists in Pennsylvania were never able to obliterate it.

Despite such disadvantages, Federalism persisted as a latent force, which mustered nearly 40,000 votes, better than a third of the whole, for its gubernatorial candidate in 1808. The greatest proportion of its votes came from the areas surrounding Philadelphia and Lancaster, the largest urban centers; and the leadership of the party seemed to rest principally with merchants and lawyers. However, in Philadelphia small shopkeepers, mechanics, and artisans constituted a sizable fraction of the active party workers; and such agricultural counties as Luzerne, Delaware, and Adams returned almost unbroken Federalist majorities throughout the period. It is generally true that Federalism was the political faith of the wealthy, commercial elements in the cities; but such a generalization is subject to demonstrable exceptions.[1]

Republican hegemony in Pennsylvania resulted from a course virtually the reverse of the Federalist. Their principles stressed the doctrine of popular rule and sought to make it more effective by reserving the bulk of power to local and state governments which would be more responsive to the people's wishes. They developed political machinery to organize and discipline masses of voters in support of their candidates. They appealed to the farmers and the urban working classes. They catered to the widespread anti-British sentiment, stressed freedom of speech and press, and avoided the more distasteful forms of taxation. Given opponents such as the Federalists, it was little wonder that they triumphed.

Party alignments in the State were thus basically determined by the political question of popular as opposed to oligarchic government and by the economic conflict of agrarian and commercial interests. The last is subject to much qualification. York County, which lies between Lancaster and Adams, differed little from its neighbors in any respect— all were primarily agricultural. Yet Adams and Lancaster counties were consistently Federalist, while York was consistently Republican. These differences can be explained in part by such imponderables as tradition and the quality of local leadership, but they certainly prove that economic considerations were not all-powerful in determining party preferences.

Geographical, racial, and religious factors appear to have had little influence on party allegiances. Western and other frontier regions seem to have been no more staunchly Democratic than other rural areas of older settlement in the eastern part of the State, nor even than Philadelphia County, which was largely urban. Whatever effect the frontier may have had on political views stemmed principally from its characteristic economic activities and interests rather than from location *per se*.

The most homogeneous of the State's diverse racial elements were the Germans, who formed a significant proportion of the population, sharply differentiated from other groups by their language. Yet there is no indication that cultural factors had any effect on their political leanings. Politicians, naturally, saw to it that German candidates were offered in German counties; but this was a practice of both parties. The only instance where the Germans as such figured prominently was in 1805 when Joseph Hiester and Peter Muhlenberg apparently turned the gubernatorial election in favor of McKean. Yet, even in this case, heavily German Dauphin County voted for Snyder, and Snyder was himself a German. It would, therefore, seem to be more an example of the influence of personal leadership than of cultural unity.[2]

The only religious group to which specific political appeals were directed was the Quakers. This was particularly true at the time of the embargo and the War of 1812. Their pacifist principles may have led many of them to vote with the Federalists during the war; but they constituted a significant element in only a very few counties, and, even if they tipped the balance in some of these, they made no appreciable impression on politics in the State at large.

Continued Republican predominance in Pennsylvania created problems of its own. Party machinery and discipline had been instituted as a means of achieving victory over Federalism through unity. In the absence of the impelling force of a strong opposition, factionalism began to threaten the cohesiveness of the party.

The strength and nature of this factionalism varied, but it never entirely disappeared. The first stage lasted from 1800 to 1805. Personal and local differences appeared almost immediately as the Federalists virtually abandoned politics. The struggle between Governor McKean and the country Democrats in the legislature over judicial reform and the failure of the attack on the judiciary culminated in the movement for a constitutional convention. Duane and Leib, whose arbitrary control of the party in Philadelphia had produced a violent schism, took sides against the Governor. Aided by the Federalists, the Constitutional Republicans, generally called Quids, were able to defeat the project for a convention and to re-elect McKean.

The second period, which ended with the election of 1808, was characterized by two main questions—whether the Federalist-Quid coalition was to form the basis of a permanent new party; and whether the city Democrats, led by Leib and Duane, or the country Democrats, controlled by the adherents of Snyder, should dominate the party. The growing importance of foreign relations arising out of American neutrality in the Napoleonic wars settled the first question in the negative and forced the postponement of a decision of the second. In the face of a resurgent Federalism, Pennsylvania Republicans suppressed their differences and united in a successful support of Snyder, Madison, and the embargo.

Foreign affairs continued to be important for the next three years; but congressional vacillation and the relaxing of Federalist efforts within the State permitted the Snyderites and the Duane-Leib faction, now known as the Old School, to fight out their battle for control of the party. The Olmsted affair offered the occasion, and for a time it appeared that the Old School might be victorious. However, its own intemperate violence and political blundering redounded to the benefit of the Governor and his adherents; and by 1811 Duane had forsworn State politics, and the Old School consisted only of Leib and a few hangers-on. The Snyderites not only dominated the State as a whole, but, acting through Binns, had achieved supremacy in Philadelphia.

National issues again predominated during the War of 1812. The Federalists once more exerted themselves to the utmost; and the Democrats subordinated their factional differences to unite in support of the administration. Inept conduct of military affairs, Madison's own unpopularity, and Democratic internal feuds combined with Federalist aid, however, to furnish a sizable vote for the Clinton ticket in the presidential election of 1812. Democratic divisions, particularly in Philadelphia, were too irreconcilable to be suppressed even by the pressure of war, and, strengthened by military defeats and financial collapse in 1814, they enabled the Federalists to make substantial gains in that year.

Factionalism acquired new strength in the era inaugurated by the restoration of peace. Democratic unity, which had previously been able to sustain itself against such assaults with fair success, now began to crumble rapidly. This was principally a result of the outmoding of old issues which had divided Federalists and Republicans. The quest for office now became the prime factor in political contests, with the "outs" combining against the "ins," and attacking the party machinery which gave an advantage to the latter. Cohesion disappeared when the motives prompting it no longer existed.

The disintegration of the Republicans in Pennsylvania after the Peace of Ghent was a reflection of the crumbling of Jeffersonian Republicanism on the national scene, and it emphasized the curious interrelation between national and State politics in party matters.

It has long been a truism that national parties in the United States represent at best no more than loose federations of State parties, adhering to vaguely defined principles and cemented by patronage. Certainly, in the Jeffersonian period there existed no continuing party organizations on the national level, nor even within the states. Furthermore, the course of politics in Pennsylvania was principally concerned with State and local rather than national issues. Nevertheless, the State's political behavior was conditioned by, and responsive to, developments in national politics.

The Federalist Party was created by Alexander Hamilton and his associates when they controlled the general government; and its program outlined a policy of national action but did not concern itself with State and local questions. Jeffersonian Republicanism, as originally conceived, repudiated both the philosophy and conduct of Federalism. It also propounded a set of general principles, which emphasized decentralization and popular control of government. Though these last bore some relationship to State and local issues, the primary distinctions between the parties rested on national issues.

The effect of such issues in determining political conduct within the states was effectively demonstrated in Pennsylvania from 1800 to 1816. The mildness and success of Jefferson's first administration resulted in the virtual disappearance of the Federalist Party. This coincided with the rise of schism in Pennsylvania. Lacking Federalist opposition, personal cliques among the Republicans began to fight for party control; and the issues of constitutional and judicial reform emerged to furnish another source of differences in the party. Despite the fact that Federalist aid was sought and obtained by the Constitutional Republicans, Jefferson steadfastly refused to favor either faction. Though this resulted in severe, albeit private, criticisms by such men as Dallas, the national party was soon to profit by Jefferson's shrewdness.

During the early years of his second administration the Republican schism in the State became worse. Not only did the supporters of McKean appear to be merging with the Federalists; but a sharp struggle arose between the Duane-Leib and Snyderite factions for dominance over the regular Republicans. At this juncture, the emergence of the national issue of foreign affairs redrew party lines clearly and reversed the trend toward disintegration of the Pennsylvania Republicans.

So long as questions of neutrality and war continued in Madison's administrations, the forces for unity overbalanced those of factionalism in the State, but the latter began to gain strength with the passage of time. The end of the war removed any real justification for continuing the distinction between Federalists and Republicans, and factionalism made rapid strides. The Republican State organization could not survive the decline of the national party.

The benefits which Pennsylvania Republicans received from the national party were principally fortuitous; but the assistance they gave to it was direct and vital. The most obvious instances were the presidential elections of 1808 and 1812. In the first, the staunch Republicanism of the State had discouraged a projected union of Federalists and eastern Republicans in support of George Clinton; and the influence of its example had probably held wavering New Jersey in the Republican column. In the second, the coalition of Federalists and Clintonians was formed and won the votes of New Jersey and every state to the north and east except Vermont; but Pennsylvania was unmoved by their strenuous efforts and furnished the margin by which Madison was re-elected. The Republicans in the State might well boast that they formed the keystone in the Democratic arch.

Jeffersonian Republicanism was likewise indebted to Pennsylvania for preventing it from becoming a sectional party centered in the South and West. This was of primary importance because the New England Federalists during this period sponsored projects of disunion and generally sought to expand on the basis of sectional appeals. They emphasized the anticommercial attitude of the Republicans and attributed their supremacy to the baleful effects of slave representation. Enjoying a large commerce and without slavery, Pennsylvania hardly fitted this picture; and her continued loyalty to Republicanism was an important cause of the ill-success of these New England schemes.

One of the primary factors in Republican predominance in Pennsylvania was the existence of an effective party organization. This had been developed as a means of giving reality to the potential Republican majority in the State, and it had proved most efficacious in the overthrow of Federalism. As factionalism grew, this organization became the main object of attack since it was the chief means of preserving the political supremacy of the group in office.

The best organization existed at the local level. Most counties had adopted the district delegate system, with townships or other units holding meetings of the voters to select representatives to a county committee which formed the tickets. In many cases, these committees were permanent bodies holding power until new ones were chosen.

The delegate system was open to much criticism. Its opponents pointed out that meetings for the choice of delegates were ill-attended and were dominated by officeholders. Since nomination by the committee was equivalent to election, the State administration through patronage virtually controlled the politics of the entire Commonwealth. This was largely true; but no acceptable alternatives were offered. Mass meetings of the citizens of most counties were impracticable; and nominations by self-created cliques were subject to much the same objections as the delegate system.

On the State level party organization was less stable and less permanent. The legislative nominating caucus appeared in a half-hearted form in 1802; but not until 1804 did it assume the responsibility of making nominations and co-ordinating the Statewide elections of the party. An improvement over the former system, it was liable to charges of executive domination achieved through the Governor's appointive power.

For this reason the nominating caucus was under constant attack and was never fully accepted. A proposal for a nominating convention in 1805 failed; but a similar movement two years later resulted in the use of the mixed caucus-convention in 1808 and also in 1811. The pure legislative caucus was used in 1812, 1814, and 1816, but increasing opposition led to its abandonment in favor of the nominating convention for the gubernatorial election of 1817. The movement against the legislative caucus was paralleled by the growing protest against the congressional caucus which began in 1808. In both cases, the opposition was directly traceable to dissenting factions, whose motives were as selfish as those of the men they opposed. Schism was thus an important factor in party reform.

The political machinery established in this early period of the national existence had already created in Pennsylvania a class of professional politicians. These men, though responsive to popular opinion and economic pressures, were primarily concerned with the winning of elections. They made a career of marshalling voters at the polls and reaped their rewards in the patronage of government. To achieve success in their objectives demanded unceasing work and a keen analysis of the social and economic conditions and trends of the time. Those who contested for political control in the years after the War of 1812 found their tasks most difficult.

Politics in Retrospect, 1800-1816

The sixteen years in which the politics of Pennsylvania had undergone such fundamental transformations were years of far-reaching social and economic changes both for the State and the country as a whole. With the return of peace in Europe the nation had weathered its most severe foreign peril, had reaffirmed its nationalism, and had rid itself of the last vestiges of colonialism. The day of the gentleman and of aristocratic government had passed beyond recall. Far less dramatically and much more irrevocably than in France, the wearers of knee breeches had been overthrown by the *sans-culottes;* and all Americans gave lip service at least to the Jeffersonian principles of popular government.

After 1815 an ever-increasing tide of European immigrants swelled the working classes of the eastern cities and contributed to the accelerated westward migration of the American people. Within a few years these urban immigrants and western frontiersmen were to combine in a Jacksonian interpretation of popular government which was to repeat the Jeffersonian rout of its conservative opponents. A dynamic and restless society was launched upon the conquest of a continent and had but small patience with those who clung to the old patterns of existence.

The end of the Napoleonic wars not only resulted in a decline of public interest in foreign affairs. It likewise reduced foreign trade to its normal proportions and channeled American energy and capital into the creation of manufacturing enterprises and the building of a great domestic market. The first of these gave a strong stimulus to urban growth; and the second combined with the process of westward expansion to quicken the construction of turnpikes, canals, and railroads, and the improvement of rivers and creeks for steam navigation. The politics of the coming era had to respond to these new forces; and, until sectional conflict over slavery distorted the picture, the chief political issues were the tariff, internal improvements, cheap banking capital, the removal of Indians from western lands, homestead and pre-emption laws, and the acquisition of additional territory.

The processes writ large on the national stage were faithfully reproduced within Pennsylvania. The population of the State's 35 counties in 1800 had been 602,365. By 1820 it had increased nearly 75 per cent, with 1,049,398 people living in 51 counties. The city of Philadelphia had not kept pace with the rest of the State. It had experienced an increase of only 55 per cent, from 41,220 to 63,802, in the same period. The center of gravity in the State was being shifted westward and northward. The city and thirteen counties in the southeastern corner of the State had accounted for nearly 65 per cent of the inhabitants in 1800; but the same area in 1820, consisting of the city and seventeen counties, furnished only 58 per cent.[3]

The migration of the State capital to Lancaster in 1799 and to Harrisburg in 1812 was a reflection of the changing balance of population in the State. Sentiment for the removal of the State capital westward had had a long existence. Attempts to move it from Philadelphia had failed in 1784 and 1787, but had been successful in April, 1799, when the legislature had voted in favor of Lancaster.[4]

Local interests and Democratic antipathies to the Federalist-Quid stronghold of Lancaster insured continued agitation for removing from that place. William Maclay served as a Representative from Dauphin County in the session of 1803-1804; and his chief purpose, according to Nathaniel B. Boileau, was to obtain the capital for Harrisburg. Maclay's devotion to this object was so intense that he was accused by Jasper Yeates of having brought about the impeachment of the Supreme Court judges in an effort to gain support for his pet project.[5]

The legislature, however, did not approve the change until February, 1810, when it passed a measure providing for the removal of the capital to Harrisburg in 1812. This occurred during and immediately after the bitter legislative fight over approval of Snyder's conduct in the Olmsted affair, but the change provoked no comments even in hostile newspapers despite the wholesale recriminations then being hurled at the Snyderites. The voting on the issue appears to have been motivated largely by local rather than partisan or factional political considerations.[6]

The westward movement of the capital was symbolic of the fall of Philadelphia from political leadership. The city, which had dominated politics until 1800, had by 1816 become a lucrative satrapy where the victorious politicians of the interior of the State satisfied the cravings of their patronage-hungry followers.

Such politicians, however, were not without their problems. Population changes, the dynamic forces of industrialism and expansion, and the disintegration of the party structure of Jeffersonian Republicanism outmoded the methods of the McKean and Snyder eras and introduced complexities hitherto unknown. At the same time the growing wealth of the nation increased the rewards of office and sharpened personal and factional conflicts for their possession. By 1816 the politicians of Pennsylvania were just embarking upon the search for techniques to master these new circumstances. It is little wonder that the State's politics in the succeeding era have been described as "a game without rules."[7]

FOOTNOTES FOR CHAPTER I

[1] From an address "To the Democratic Citizens of Philadelphia County," in *Aurora*, October 8, 1803. William H. Egle, *History of the Commonwealth of Pennsylvania* (Philadelphia, 1883), 235, cites this as probably the first use of the term "keystone" in connection with Pennsylvania. However, a similar idea is expressed in a Republican toast printed in the *Aurora*, October 19, 1802. In any case the expression was used frequently in the years that followed. See, for example, *ibid.*, October 29, 1804; July 9, 1808; July 8, 1813.

[2] Paul L. Ford (ed.), *The Works of Thomas Jefferson*, 12 vols. (New York, 1904-1905), IV, 82-86.

[3] *Ibid.*, 18-30, 80-81.

[4] Henry Adams, *History of the United States of America* [during the Administrations of Jefferson and Madison], 9 vols. (New York, 1889-1891), I, 114-15.

[5] Solon J. Buck and Elizabeth H. Buck, *The Planting of Civilization in Western Pennsylvania* (Pittsburgh, 1939), 1-5; Wayland F. Dunaway, *A History of Pennsylvania* (New York, 1944), 3-5.

[6] *Return of the Whole Number of Persons within the Several Districts of the United States* (Washington, 1801), 2A-2G.

[7] *Aggregate Amount of Persons within the United States in the Year 1810* (Washington, 1811), 51a.

[8] *Ibid.*, 33-51, *passim*.

[9] Dunaway, *History of Pennsylvania*, 76-78

[10] *Ibid.*, 78-83.

[11] *Ibid.*, 78, 84-87.

[12] *Ibid.*, 89-95.

[13] Adam Seybert, *Statistical Annals . . . of the United States of America . . .* (Philadelphia, 1818), 11-12.

[14] *Ibid.*

[15] Dunaway, *History of Pennsylvania*, 305-306, 693-94.

[16] Seybert, *Statistical Annals*, 11-12.

[17] Dunaway, *History of Pennsylvania*, 333-54, *passim*.

[18] The text of the Constitution of 1776 may be found in Francis N. Thorpe (comp.), *The Federal and State Constitutions . . . and Other Organic Laws . . . of the United States*, 7 vols. (Washington, 1909), V, 3081-92.

[19] The political struggles which culminated in the adoption of the Constitution of 1790 are described in Robert L. Brunhouse, *The Counter-Revolution in Pennsylvania, 1776-1790* (Harrisburg, 1942).

[20] The Constitution of 1790 appears in Thorpe (comp.), *Federal and State Constitutions*, V, 3092-3103.

[21] George D. Luetscher, *Early Political Machinery in the United States* (Philadelphia, 1903), 13. The statements respecting suffrage qualifications in other states are based on a comparison made by the author.

[22] The principal election laws for this period may be found in James T. Mitchell *et al.* (comps.), *The Statutes at Large of Pennsylvania from 1682 to 1809*, 18 vols. (Harrisburg, 1896-1915), XVI, 163-81; XVII, 50-53.

[23] Emory R. Johnson *et al.*, *History of the Domestic and Foreign Commerce of the United States*, 2 vols. (Washington, 1915), II, 15-19.

[24] *Ibid.*, 14-15.

[25] Charles A. Beard, *Economic Origins of Jeffersonian Democracy* (New York, 1915), 464-67.

[26] The impact of national issues on the politics of Pennsylvania and the formation of parties in the State has been well developed in Harry M. Tinkcom, *The Republicans and Federalists in Pennsylvania, 1790-1801: A Study in National Stimulus and Local Response* (Harrisburg, 1950).

[27] *Ibid.*, 271-72.
[28] Gallatin to Thomas Jefferson, September 14, 1801, in Henry Adams (ed.), *Writings of Albert Gallatin*, 3 vols. (Philadelphia, 1879), I, 50; "Pennsylvania Politics, November, 1803," in *Aurora*, August 7, 1805; *Democratic Press*, October 26, 1812.
[29] *Ibid.*, July 14, 1808; *Aurora*, May 14, 1807. See also, *ibid.*, November 4, 1800; September 18, 1802.
[30] The principles listed in the foregoing discussion were extracted from a wide variety of sources but principally from the following: *Democratic Press*, March 27, 1807; *Aurora*, April 11, 1803; Jefferson to William Duane, March 28, 1811, in Ford (ed.), *Works of Jefferson*, XI, 193-94; Jasper Yeates to William Tilghman, February 23, 1809, in Hampton L. Carson Collection (Historical Society of Pennsylvania).
[31] See the views of Binns in the *Aurora*, May 14, 1807.
[32] See, for example, Jefferson to Duane, March 28, 1811, in Ford (ed.), *Works of Jefferson*, XI, 193; *Aurora*, September 27, 1802.
[33] "Proclus," in *U. S. Gazette*, December 10, 1813.
[34] See, for example, election returns headed "Democratic" and "Republican", *ibid.*, October 14, 1801. See also, *Aurora*, November 4, 1800; September 18, 1802; April 11, 1803. In this work the terms Democratic and Republican are often used interchangeably, although the former is seldom used except when referring to political affairs within the State. The term Federalist will be used when speaking of their opponents.
[35] *Ibid.*, March 1, 1802.
[36] *Gazette of the U. S.*, March 5, 1801.
[37] *Ibid; Pittsburgh Gazette*, September 10, 1802.
[38] "Judaeus Appella," in *Gazette of the U. S.*, September 22, 1801, asserted that the chief distinctions between the two parties rested on differences in constitutional views and attitudes toward the French Revolution. The *Aurora*, March 1, 1802, emphasized the dispute over centralization of governmental power as the main factor in party divisions.
[39] *Democratic Press*, October 26, 1812; Gallatin to Jefferson, September 14, 1801, in Adams (ed.), *Writings of Gallatin*, I, 50; "Pennsylvania Politics, November, 1803," in *Aurora*, August 7, 1805.
[40] James A. Peeling, "Thomas McKean," in *Dictionary of American Biography*, 20 vols. and index (New York, 1928-1937), XII, 79-81; *id.*, "The Public Life of Thomas McKean, 1734-1817" (Unpublished dissertation, University of Chicago, 1929), *passim*; *id.*, "Governor McKean and the Pennsylvania Jacobins (1799-1808)," in *Pennsylvania Magazine of History and Biography*, LIV (1930), 320-21. The *Dictionary of American Biography* will hereafter be cited as *DAB*. The *Pennsylvania Magazine of History and Biography* will hereafter be cited as *PMHB*.
[41] J. Harold Ennis, "Alexander James Dallas," in *DAB*, V, 36-38. See also, Raymond Walters, Jr., *Alexander James Dallas: Lawyer-Politician-Financier, 1759-1817* (Philadelphia, 1943).
[42] Claud G. Bowers, "William Duane," in *DAB*, V, 467-68; J. T. Scharf and Thompson Westcott, *History of Philadelphia, 1609-1884*, 3 vols. (Philadelphia, 1884), I, 496-97, 505; *Gazette of the U. S.*, August 20, 1801; *Aurora*, July 17, 1801; November 17, 1802; October 30, 31, November 1, 1806.
[43] James H. Peeling, "Michael Leib," in *DAB*, XI, 149-50; *Biographical Directory of the American Congress, 1774-1927* (Washington, 1928), 1218; Jonathan Roberts, Jr., to Jonathan Roberts, January 8, 1808, in Jonathan Roberts Papers (Historical Society of Pennsylvania).
[44] "Pennsylvania Politics, November, 1803," in *Aurora*, August 7, 1805; *Democratic Press*, October 26, 1812.
[45] James H. Peeling, "James Ross," in *DAB*, XVI, 178; Russell J. Ferguson, *Early Western Pennsylvania Politics* (Pittsburgh, 1938), 113-16, 164.
[46] Albert C. Flick (ed.), *History of the State of New York*, 10 vols. (New York, 1933-1937), VI, 10; Luetscher, *Political Machinery*, 151-52.
[47] This analysis of political organization rests principally upon a study of Pennsylvania political meetings during the period 1800-1816, but it is also derived from the following secondary accounts: Luetscher, *Political Machinery*, 2-4, 66-67, 75-83, 125-35;

M. Ostrogorski, "The Rise and Fall of the Nominating Caucus, Legislative and Congressional," in *American Historical Review*, V (1900), 253-83; Joseph S. Walton, "Nominating Conventions in Pennsylvania," *ibid.*, II (1897), 262-78; Tinkcom, *Republicans and Federalists*, 24-25. The *American Historical Review* will hereafter be cited as *AHR*.

[48] *Aurora*, May 14, 1808.

[49] "Pennsylvania Politics, November, 1803," *ibid.*, August 7, 1805; *Democratic Press*, October 26, 1812.

FOOTNOTES FOR CHAPTER II

[1] John Quincy Adams to Rufus King, October 8, 1802, in Charles R. King (ed.), *The Life and Correspondence of Rufus King*, 6 vols. (New York, 1894-1900), IV, 176.

[2] John B. McMaster, *A History of the People of the United States, from the Revolution to the Civil War*, 8 vols. (Philadelphia, 1885-1913), II, 308-467, *passim*.

[3] The official results are printed in *Senate Journal, 1799-1800*, pp. 29-30. Due to a technicality McKean's official vote in Chester County was 792 less than the actual count. *Ibid.*, 30.

[4] [Alexander Graydon], *Memoirs of a Life, Chiefly Passed in Pennsylvania* . . . (Harrisburg, 1811), 358-59, 361. Graydon was a Federalist who had been removed as prothonotary of Dauphin County by McKean.

[5] John Adams to James Lloyd, February 14, 1815, in Charles F. Adams (ed.), *The Works of John Adams*, 10 vols. (Boston, 1850-1856), X, 120-22.

[6] Tinkcom, *Republicans and Federalists*, 271-72; Peeling. "Public Life of Thomas McKean," 190-97; [Graydon], *Memoirs*, 358-59; William Findley to I. [J.?] Israel, February 25, 1801, in Ferdinand J. Dreer Collection (Historical Society of Pennsylvania).

[7] *Aurora*, November 6, 8, 1799, cited in Peeling, "Public Life of Thomas McKean," 211.

[8] *Pennsylvania Archives*, 4th Series, 12 vols. (Harrisburg, 1900-1902), IV, 444-49. See also, Peeling, "Public Life of Thomas McKean," 213-19; Charles Biddle, *Autobiography, 1745-1821* (Philadelphia, 1883), 282-83; *Aurora*, November 6, 1800. William Findley believed that McKean had in general dismissed only incompetent or dishonest men and that he had retained good men who had voted against him unless they had been too violent. Findley to Jefferson, March 15, 1804, in Jefferson Papers (Library of Congress).

[9] Tinkcom, *Republicans and Federalists*, 243-45; Glenn A. Lehman, "Gerrymandering in Pennsylvania prior to the Civil War" (Master's thesis, University of Pennsylvania, 1932), 69-70.

[10] McKean to Jefferson, March 7, 1800, in Jefferson Papers; Tinkcom, *Republicans and Federalists*, 245.

[11] Luetscher, *Political Machinery*, 155.

[12] Election results are given in *Aurora*, November 4, 18, 1800. For McKean's proclamation, see *Pennsylvania Archives*, 4th Series, IV, 452-53.

[13] *Aurora*, November 1, 6, 1800.

[14] *Ibid.*, November 4, 1800.

[15] *Lancaster Journal*, extra, November 5, 1800.

[16] *Gazette of the U. S.*, November 6, 1800; *Aurora*, November 19, 1800.

[17] *Ibid.*, November 19, 22, 1800.

[18] *Gazette of the U. S.*, November 14, 1800.

[19] The dispute is covered in detail in Tinkcom, *Republicans and Federalists*, 247-53. See also the issues of the *Aurora* from November 12 to December 6, 1800.

[20] McKean to Jefferson, December 15, 1800, draft copy, in Thomas McKean Papers (Historical Society of Pennsylvania).

[21] Jasper Yeates to Edward Burd, January 5, 1801, in Shippen Family Papers (Historical Society of Pennsylvania).

[22] *Pittsburgh Gazette*, January 23, 1801.

[23] Edward Stanwood, *A History of the Presidency from 1788 to 1897* (Boston and New York, 1898), 54-73; McMaster, *History*, II, 523-26.

[24] *Aurora*, January 10, 1801; McKean to Jefferson, January 10, 1801, in Jefferson Papers; *id.* to *id.*, February 20, 1801, *ibid.*; *id.* to *id.*, March 21, 1801, *ibid.*

[25] *Lancaster Journal*, February 21, 1801; Jacob Alter to Mathew Carey, February 18, 1801, in Lea and Febiger Collection (Historical Society of Pennsylvania).

[26] Jonathan Roberts, Jr., to Jonathan Roberts, Sr., December 10, 1800, in Roberts

Papers; *id.* to John Roberts, February 23, 1801, *ibid.; Aurora*, February 23, 24, 25, 27, 1801.

[27] Anna Lane Lingelbach, "George Logan," in *DAB*, XI, 359-60.
[28] George H. Gensmer, "John Peter Gabriel Muhlenberg," *ibid.*, XIII, 311-13; "Pennsylvania Politics, November, 1803," in *Aurora*, August 7, 1805.
[29] *Ibid.*, February 23, 24, 25, 27, 1801.
[30] *Lancaster Journal*, March 21, 1801; *Gazette of the U. S.*, March 24, 1801.
[31] *Aurora*, April 6, 1801.
[32] Findley to I. [J.?] Israel, February 25, 1801, in Dreer Collection. Due to the similar characters used for "I" and "J" in the writing of the time, it is not possible to determine the exact addressee. It could have been and probably was, Israel Israel, a long-time Republican and the sheriff of Philadelphia County. With almost equal plausibility it might have been John Israel, his son, editor of the Pittsburgh *Tree of Liberty* and the Washington *Herald of Liberty*, both of which circulated in Findley's senatorial district.
[33] Duane to Jefferson, June 10, 1801, in "Letters of William Duane," in *Massachusetts Historical Society Proceedings*, 2d Series, XX (1907), 265. This collection of letters will hereafter be cited as "Letters of Duane."
[34] *Aurora*, October 16, 1802; "Pennsylvania Politics, November, 1803, *ibid.*, August 7, 1805.
[35] Findley to Israel, February 25, 1801, in Dreer Collection; McKean to Jefferson, February 20, 1801, in Jefferson Papers; *id.* to *id.*, March 21, 1801, *ibid.; Pennsylvania Archives*, 9th Series, 10 vols. (Harrisburg, 1931-1935), III, 1756-57.
[36] *Lancaster Journal*, extra, March 10, 1801. The motto was first used in the issue of April 25, 1801.
[37] For the changing tone of the Federalist papers, see *Gazette of the U. S.*, March-August, 1801. On Tom Paine, see *ibid.*, July 14, 21, 22, 1801; *Pittsburgh Gazette*, August 21, 28, September 11, 1801.
[38] For Duane's legal difficulties, see *Aurora*, April 11, 27, 28, 30, May 7, 8, 12, 14, 19, 20, 21, 22, 25, June 2, 1801; *Gazette of the U. S.*, May 30, June 19, 1801.
[39] *Aurora*, July 10, 1801.
[40] *Ibid.*, August 5, 8, 10, 13, 14, 17, 19, 22, September 4, 18, 24, 25, 28, October 1, 2, 1801.
[41] *Ibid.*, June 23, September 8, 22, 1801.
[42] *Gazette of the U. S.*, September 28, 30, 1801; *Aurora*, October 1, 1801.
[43] *Ibid.*, October 6, 15, 1801.
[44] *Gazette of the U. S.*, October 5, 29, 31, November 3, 4, 5, 6, 1801.
[45] *Aurora*, October 21, November 16, 1801; *Poulson's American Daily Advertiser*, November 14, 1801.
[46] Pittsburgh *Tree of Liberty*, July 4, August 22, 1801.
[47] *Ibid.*, July 4, August 15, 1801.
[48] *Pittsburgh Gazette*, August 21, 1801.
[49] *Ibid.*, July 31, September 4, 11, 25, October 2, 1801; Pittsburgh *Tree of Liberty*, August 29, 1801.
[50] *Ibid.*, July 18, August 8, 15, 22, 29, September 5, 12, 26, October 10, 1801; *Pittsburgh Gazette*, September 11, October 2, 1801.
[51] *Ibid.*, October 23, 1801; Pittsburgh *Tree of Liberty*, October 24, 1801.
[52] On the Bucks County schism, see *Aurora*, May 11, July 1, 9, 22, August 5, 10, 25, 29, September 1, 15, 16, 19, 24, 28, October 1, 3, 6, 16, 1801.
[53] William Findley to Dallas, December 8, 1801, in Dallas Papers (Historical Society of Pennsylvania).
[54] *House Journal, 1801-1802*, pp. 60-63.
[55] See Chapter III below.
[56] 4 *Dallas* 229.
[57] *House Journal, 1801-1802*, pp. 91-92, 94, 112, 115, 124, 174-75, 185, 216-18, 238, 251; *Senate Journal, 1801-1802*, pp. 86, 88, 95, 101, 106-107, 110-11, 125, 142-44, 166, 169-70. Dallas accepted the verdict in good spirit and immediately resigned as recorder. If Leib was the "gentleman in Washington" whose letter was published in the *Aurora*,

he was considerably less gracious, attacking both the constitutionality and the policy of the Incompatibility Act. *Aurora*, February 19, April 8, 1802.

[58] See comments of the *Lancaster Journal*, May 1, 1802.

[59] McKean to Joseph Hiester, February 5, 1802, in Gregg Collection (Library of Congress).

[60] Findley to Dallas, February 4, 1802, in Dallas Papers; *Lancaster Journal*, April 10, 1802; *Gazette of the U. S.*, April 19, 1802.

[61] *Aurora*, January 14, July 29, 1802; *Gazette of the U. S.*, August 5, 1802; *Lancaster Journal*, January 30, 1802.

[62] *Ibid.*, May 1, 1802.

[63] *Ibid.*; *Poulson's American Daily Advertiser*, April 15, 1802; *Aurora*, April 16, 1802.

[64] *Ibid.*, August 3, 1802; "A Pennsylvania Elector," in *Gazette of the U. S.*, August 5, 1802. See also, "A German Clodpole," in *Aurora*, September 21, 1805. The latter asserts that Muhlenberg listened to the Federalist overtures, but delayed giving a final answer until he was assured of the collectorship.

[65] For the fight in Congress over repeal of the Judiciary Act of 1801, see Adams, *History*, I, 274-98.

[66] *Aurora*, February 1, 3, 1802; *House Journal, 1801-1802*, pp. 218, 221-23, 234; *Senate Journal, 1801-1802*, pp. 149, 152, 154-55, 160.

[67] *Gazette of the U. S.*, January 30, February 1, 3, 1802; *Aurora*, February 6, 1802.

[68] *Ibid.*, February 6, 8, 9, 10, 1802.

[69] *Ibid.*, February 12, 1802.

[70] *Ibid.*, August 8, 1801; Duane to Butler, November 12, 1801, in "Letters of Duane," 271-73.

[71] See his views expressed in Jefferson to William Findley, March 24, 1801, in Ford (ed.), *Works of Jefferson*, IX, 224-26; and *id.* to McKean, July 24, 1801, *ibid.*, 282-85.

[72] Gallatin to Jefferson, August 17, 1801, in Adams (ed.), *Writings of Gallatin*, I, 39; Duane to *id.*, June 10, 1801, in "Letters of Duane," 266-68.

[73] Gallatin to *id.*, [December 15, 1801], *ibid.*, 258-59; *id.* to *id.*, [February 9, 1802], in Jefferson Papers; Duane to Thomas M. Thompson, March 26, 1802, in Dreer Collection; *Gazette of the U. S.*, June 5, July 19, 1802; *Aurora*, June 18, 19, 1802.

[74] *Ibid.*, June 30, 1802; Thomas Leiper to Jefferson, August 26, 1802, in Jefferson Papers.

[75] *Aurora*, July 26, September 8, 11, 1802.

[76] *Gazette of the U. S.*, April 17, 18, 20, 21, 23, 24, 1801. An explanation of the affair favorable to Leib appears in the *Aurora*, October 16, 1802. The story was briefly this: Leib had served as physician to a personal friend, Joseph Penrose, who died in his home. He had received from Penrose certain depreciated certificates which he regarded as a gift or payment for his services. After the funding of the Federal debt, these certificates increased greatly in value; and Leib had written the executors of Penrose in May, 1790, offering them the amount of the legacy. They had countered by entering suit against him. The suit had never been pressed; and in 1799 Leib's counsel demanded that it be tried or thrown out of court. The matter was eventually settled by a compromise in which Leib turned over the funds but refused to pay interest, alleging that he had made a tender of the principal in 1790 which had been refused. The five heirs presented Leib with an acknowledgment expressing their belief in his good faith and rectitude. According to the story in the *Aurora*, this testimonial had been unsolicited.

[77] *Ibid.*, September 17, 1802.

[78] *Ibid.*, August 7, September 3, 4, 15, 17, 18, 20, 1802.

[79] *Ibid.*, September 22, 23, 24, 1802.

[80] *Ibid.*, September 15, 17, 18, 20, 21, 22, 23, 27, October 2, 4, 6, 7, 8, 9, 12, 1802; *Poulson's American Daily Advertiser*, September 17, 18, 20, 21, October 2, 4, 7, 9, 11, 1802; *Gazette of the U. S.*, September 17, 18, 22, 1802; *Philadelphia Gazette*, September 17, 23, 1802.

[81] Duane to Jefferson, October 18, 1802, in "Letters of Duane," 276-78; Leiper to *id.*, September 19, 1802, in Jefferson Papers; *id.* to *id.*, September 22, 1802, *ibid.*; Jones to Joseph H. Nicholson, October 20, 1804, draft copy, in Euselma C. Smith Collection

(Historical Society of Pennsylvania). Leib's views of Logan's motives are supported in "Pennsylvania Politics, November, 1803," in *Aurora*, August 7, 1805.

[82] *Ibid.*, June 18, 21, 22, 23, 25, 26, August 5, 11, 17, September 11, 25, 28, 29, October 2, 9, 22, 1802.

[83] *Ibid.*, September 27, 1802; Leiper to Jefferson, September 22, 1802, in Jefferson Papers.

[84] *Gazette of the U. S.*, September 29, October 4, 5, 6, 7, 8, 16, 1802; *Lancaster Journal*, August 7, 1802.

[85] *Gazette of the U. S.*, August 2, 1802; *Aurora*, August 27, 1802.

[86] Pittsburgh *Tree of Liberty*, August 21, 28, September 4, 11, 18, 25, October 23, 30, 1802; *Pittsburgh Gazette*, August 27, September 17, 24, October 8, 1802.

[87] The Montgomery County split can be followed in the *Aurora*, September 9, 10, 28, October 5, 6, 7, 9, 11, 20, 27, 1802.

[88] *Ibid.*, October 15, 30, 1802; *Gazette of the U. S.*, November 17, 1802; *Senate Journal, 1802-1803*, p. 54.

FOOTNOTES FOR CHAPTER III

[1] *House Journal, 1802-1803*, pp. 24, 40-45.
[2] Julian P. Boyd, "Samuel Maclay," in *DAB*, XII, 122-23; "Pennsylvania Politics, November, 1803," in *Aurora*, August 7, 1805. In regard to the special conditions involved in Duane's publication of this essay, see footnote 52 in this chapter.
[3] *House Journal, 1802-1803*, pp. 387, 388, 401-405; Boileau to Mathew Carey, February 15, 1803, in Lea and Febiger Collection; *id.* to *id.*, February 18, 1803, *ibid.*; William Wilson to *id.*, February 16, 1803, *ibid.*; Lancaster *Intelligencer*, March 1, 1803.
[4] *House Journal, 1802-1803*, p. 401; James H. Peeling, "Simon Snyder," in *DAB*, XVII, 389-90; Snyder's own memoir of his life in John Binns, *Recollections of the Life of John Binns* (Philadelphia, 1854), 347-49.
[5] *Pennsylvania Archives*, 4th Series, IV, 461, 478.
[6] Mitchell et al. (comps.), *Statutes at Large*, XVI, 187-91; *House Journal, 1801-1802*, pp. 102-103, 125-26, 196, 231, 351-52, 430-33; *Senate Journal, 1801-1802*, p. 308.
[7] *Ibid.*, 250, 292, 320, 326-27, 337, 365-67, 369; *House Journal, 1801-1802*, pp. 466, 469, 475-77, 479, 482-83, 489.
[8] *Pennsylvania Archives*, 4th Series, IV, 496-500.
[9] *Senate Journal, 1802-1803*, pp. 8-13, 63, 78.
[10] McKean's veto messages are in *Pennsylvania Archives*, 4th Series, IV, 519-22. The proceedings of the legislature on the bills in question are in *Senate Journal, 1802-1803*, pp. 80, 91, 107, 119-20, 122, 181, 200, 209-11, 219-27, 230-32, 237, 342, 373-75, 379-80, 396-97, 425-28, 429, 529, 557-58; *House Journal, 1802-1803*, pp. 320, 413, 419-24, 429-30, 482, 527-29.
[11] *Ibid.*, 227, 269, 559, 598, 616, 619, 643.
[12] McKean to Jefferson, February 7, 1803; in Jefferson Papers.
[13] Ferguson, *Western Pennsylvania Politics*, 115-16; William H. Loyd, *The Early Courts of Pennsylvania* (Boston, 1910), 141-42.
[14] Melvin J. White, "John Baptiste Charles Lucas," in *DAB*, XI, 485-86.
[15] Pittsburgh *Tree of Liberty*, December 27, 1800; 4 *Dallas* 225. See also, Hugh Henry Brackenridge to Dallas, May 25, 1805, in Dallas Papers.
[16] Pittsburgh *Tree of Liberty*, December 27, 1801.
[17] *House Journal, 1801-1802*, pp. 113, 157, 179, 262, 283-84, 298, 346-47, 358, 390-91, 394, 416, 423-26, 468-69; *Senate Journal, 1801-1802*, pp. 280, 284-86, 313-14, 321, 339-40.
[18] *House Journal, 1802-1803*, pp. 18-20, 38, 52-57, 67-68.
[19] *Senate Journal, 1802-1803*, pp. 16, 30, 32, 40, 55-68, 145, 152-75. The full proceedings of the trial are given in Thomas Lloyd, *The Trial of Alexander Addison* (Lancaster, 1803). See also the issues of the *Aurora* from January 19 to January 31, 1803.
[20] For criticisms of Addison's conviction, see Loyd, *Early Courts*, 141-43; J. W. F. White, "The Judiciary of Allegheny County," in *PMHB*, VII (1883), 158; Elizabeth K. Henderson, "The Attack on the Judiciary in Pennsylvania, 1800-1810," *ibid.*, LXI (1937), 118. The last article cited is based upon the author's broader work, "Some Aspects of Sectionalism in Pennsylvania, 1790-1812" (Unpublished dissertation in history, Bryn Mawr College, 1935). McKean's views are expressed in McKean to Jefferson, February 7, 1803, in Jefferson Papers. For comments of the Federalist press, see *Poulson's American Daily Advertiser*, January 31, February 1, 26, June 17, 1803; *Gazette of the U. S.*, January 31, February 1, 1803; *Pittsburgh Gazette*, February 3, 11, 18, 25, March 4, 25, 1803.
[21] *Aurora*, December 15, 1802; January 4, March 15, 24, 25, 1803; *Lancaster Journal*, April 2, 1803.
[22] *House Journal, 1801-1802*, pp. 475-76; *ibid., 1802-1803*, pp. 429-30.
[23] Loyd, *Early Courts*, 143-45; *House Journal, 1803-1804*, pp. 468-76; Edward Shippen to Jasper Yeates, February 13, 1804, in Legal Men of Pennsylvania Collection (Historical Society of Pennsylvania).

NOTES—CHAPTER III

[24] *House Journal, 1802-1803,* pp. 393-94, 456, 492-93, 513-14, 518-19, 525, 583, 592, 597.
[25] See pp. 35-36 above.
[26] *Aurora,* March 31, 1803. Comments on the proceedings in the legislature appear frequently during March and the first week of April.
[27] *Ibid.,* April 1, 1803.
[28] *House Journal, 1802-1803,* p. 597.
[29] *Aurora,* December 1, 22, 24, 1802; Leib to Carey, December 13, 1802, in Lea and Febiger Collection.
[30] The draft copies of the letters to Jefferson are in the Smith Collection. See also, Andrew Gregg to William Jones, March 1, 1803, *ibid.;* Jones to John Randolph, March 19, 1803, *ibid.;* Randolph to Jones, April 20, [1803], *ibid.* The letters intended to be sent to Jefferson are printed in the *Aurora,* August 6, 1805.
[31] *Ibid.,* March 7, 11, 16, 17, 23, 31, April 5, 7, 11, 13, 15, May 4, 6, 21, 31, 1803; August 6, 1805; *Gazette of the U. S.,* May 3, July 6, 1803. See also, Jones to Randolph, March 19, 1803, in Smith Collection; Dallas to Gallatin, March 30, 1803, in Gallatin Papers (New-York Historical Society).
[32] *Aurora,* August 6, 1805; "Pennsylvania Politics, November, 1803," *ibid.,* August 7, 8, 1805; Jones to Randolph, March 19, 1803, in Smith Collection; *id.* to Joseph H. Nicholson, October 20, 1804, draft copy, *ibid.*
[33] McMaster, *History,* II, 410-14.
[34] *Aurora,* July 16, 17, 19, 20, 21, 22, 23, 31, August 4, 6, 7, 10, September 6, 30, 1802; *Gazette of the U. S.,* July 15, August 9, 1802; Stephen Girard to Duane, August 11, 1802, copy, in Stephen Girard Collection (Girard College); Duane to Girard, August 12, 1802, *ibid.*
[35] On the yellow fever and Donaldson, see *Aurora,* April 16, May 24, 31, June 1, 3, 4, 6, 7, 8, 9, 10, 11, 13, 14, 15, 16, 28, September 13, 16, 17, 19, 20, October 3, 5, 1803; *Gazette of the U. S.,* June 6, 7, 9, 14, 17, August 26, September 16, 19, October 11, 12, 1803.
[36] *Aurora,* June 11, 13, 17, 18, 20, 21, 22, 24, August 13, 22, 1803.
[37] On the proceedings of this meeting, see *ibid.,* July 7, 9, 13, 14, 1803.
[38] *Poulson's American Daily Advertiser,* July 9, 12, 16, 19, 23, 1803; *Aurora,* July 22, 1803.
[39] *Ibid.,* July 25, 29, 30, 1803; *Freeman's Journal,* September 6, 1804.
[40] *Poulson's American Daily Advertiser,* August 17, September 3, 6, 7, 9, 16, 1803; *Aurora,* September 2, 1803.
[41] *Ibid.,* September 3, 5, 1803.
[42] *Ibid.,* October 8, 1803.
[43] *Ibid.,* October 5, 10, 11, 13, 14, 18, 19, 1803; *Relf's Philadelphia Gazette,* October 12, 1803.
[44] *Aurora,* April 22, 27, 1803; Adams, *History,* I, 282.
[45] *Aurora,* June 22, 1803. Coxe is identified as the author in *ibid.,* August 17, 1804.
[46] *Ibid.,* June 25, 1803.
[47] James Hopkins to Dallas, May 28, 1803, in Dallas Papers. Duane believed that both Dallas and McKean were involved; but there is some reason to doubt this. See, "Pennsylvania Politics, November, 1803," in *Aurora,* August 7, 8, 1805; Dallas to McKean, October 27, 1803, in McKean Papers.
[48] *Lancaster Journal,* July 25, 30, August 6, September 17, 24, October 1, 5, 1803; Lancaster *Intelligencer,* July 19, 26, August 2, 9, 16, 23, 30, September 13, 20, 27, October 4, 11, 18, 1803.
[49] For the splits in Chester and Allegheny counties, see *Aurora,* September 22, 30, October 1, 3, 4, 19, 1803; *Gazette of the U. S.,* September 28, 1803; Pittsburgh *Tree of Liberty,* August 20, October 8, 22, 1803; *Pittsburgh Gazette,* October 14, 1803.
[50] See issues of the *Gazette of the U. S.* for 1803.
[51] *Aurora,* November 6, 1803.
[52] Veiled insinuations against the Governor are made in *ibid.,* October 3, 21, 1803, but they are so phrased as to leave room for retreat. However, there are no such equivocations in Duane's essay on State politics in November, 1803. This was pub-

lished in two issues of the *Aurora* in August, 1805. Neither the author nor the person for whom it was prepared are given; but the latter is easily identified as Gideon Granger, Jefferson's Postmaster General, while other evidence and the charges of the opposition make it practically certain that Duane wrote it. See "Pennsylvania Politics, November, 1803," *ibid.*, August 7, 8, 1805; "Inimicus Mendacus," in *Freeman's Journal,* August 10, 1805; McKean to Jefferson, February 18, 1805, in Jefferson Papers. On the rumor of McKean's supposed hopes of the presidential nomination in 1804, see Nathaniel B. Boileau to Jonathan Roberts, Jr., December 10, 1803, in Roberts Papers.

[53] *Pennsylvania Archives,* 4th Series, IV, 527-28.

[54] *Senate Journal, 1803-1804,* p. 26. The Republicans in general felt that the practice of opening the legislative session with a personal address by the executive and the complimentary replies by the two houses were relics of monarchy and should be abolished. It was characteristic of McKean's conservatism and love of pomp that he should continue the custom despite this prejudice. See Boileau to Mathew Carey, December 7, 1803, in Lea and Febiger Collection.

[55] *Pennsylvania Archives,* 4th Series, IV, 522-24; *House Journal, 1803-1804,* pp. 17-20, 100; *Senate Journal, 1803-1804,* pp. 68-69, 81-82.

[56] Lancaster *Intelligencer,* December 20, 27, 1803; January 3, 10, 1804; *Aurora,* January 21, 23, 1804.

[57] *House Journal, 1803-1804,* pp. 233, 276-77, 294-95, 330, 405, 410-11, 465-71, 474-77, 479-81, 498-99, 568-70, 576-78, 587-89, 702; *Senate Journal, 1803-1804,* pp. 315, 350, 354, 360-65, 370-74, 378, 389-90, 396, 509; *Aurora,* March 22, 1804; McKean to Thomas McKean, Jr., March 15, 1804, in McKean Papers.

[58] *House Journal, 1803-1804,* pp. 231, 281-82, 583-87, 629-30, 633-35, 646-56, 658-59, 662, 682, 685, 692, 712-13, appendix; *Senate Journal, 1803-1804,* pp. 465-79, 488, 490-91, 497-99, 556, 558.

[59] *House Journal, 1803-1804,* pp. 670, 676-78, 687-88, 705-706, 724, 735-37; *Senate Journal, 1803-1804,* pp. 543, 548, 550-51.

[60] McKean to Caesar A. Rodney, February 25, 1814, in McKean Papers.

[61] *Aurora,* February 6, 7, April 6, 1804.

[62] *Philadelphia Evening Post,* February 20, 1804; Clarence S. Brigham, "Bibliography of American Newspapers, 1690-1820," in *American Antiquarian Society Proceedings,* New Series, XXX (1920), 112. These *Proceedings* will hereafter be cited simply as *AAS Proceedings* together with the appropriate volume number. Duane, if his summary of politics for Granger was not altered to fit subsequent events, knew of the plan to found the paper in November, 1803, but he is vague as to its exact promoters. See "Pennsylvania Politics, November, 1803," in *Aurora,* August 8, 1805.

[63] *Philadelphia Evening Post,* March 10, 1804.

[64] *Ibid.,* March 22, April 14, 1804.

[65] *Aurora,* May 14, 15, 16, 18, 19, 1804; *Philadelphia Evening Post,* May 15, 16, 17, 19, 1804; *U. S. Gazette,* May 17, 1804.

[66] *Freeman's Journal,* June 12, 1804. The change was made because the *Aurora* had adopted the practice of quoting the *New York Evening Post,* a leading Federalist journal, without designating the city and thus giving the impression that the *Philadelphia Evening Post* was printing Federalist material.

[67] The attacks on Leib began in May, but they reached their height in June and were continued until the election in October. The articles against Duane also began in earnest in June and lasted throughout the campaign. See issues of *Philadelphia Evening Post,* May 15-June 11, 1804; *Freeman's Journal,* June 12-October 10, 1804.

[68] During May and June, 1804, the *Aurora* published a series of nine articles with documents explaining the Penrose affair from Leib's point of view. See *ibid.,* May 25, 26, 28, 29, June 15, 16, 19, 20, 22, 1804. Consistent use of the term "Tertium Quid" began in *ibid.,* May 19, 1804.

[69] *Ibid.,* November 7, 1800. See also, Duane to Jefferson, October 18, 1802, in "Letters of Duane," 276-78; Gideon Granger to *id.,* May 6, 1803, in Jefferson Papers.

[70] [Graydon], *Memoirs,* 108-10; Broadus Mitchell, "Tench Coxe," in *DAB,* IV, 488-89; *Gazette of the U. S.,* November 4, 1800; July 6, 1803; *Aurora,* November 7, 1800.

NOTES—CHAPTER III

[71] The *Aurora* began attacking Coxe in the issue of June 12, 1804. The Federalist attitude is expressed in the *U. S. Gazette*, June 16, 19, 1804.

[72] *Philadelphia Evening Post*, May 12, 1804; *Aurora*, May 18, June 22, September 8, 1804; *Freeman's Journal*, June 11, 18, 19, 20, 21, 23, 1804.

[73] *Aurora*, June 16, 22, 23, September 8, 1804; *Philadelphia Evening Post*, May 22, 1804; *Freeman's Journal*, June 16, 25, 26, 28, 30, 1804.

[74] *Aurora*, September 8, 1804; *Freeman's Journal*, July 3, 10, 11, 1804. The protest of the minority of the general ward committee is printed in *ibid.*, July 10, 1804.

[75] On the Delaware County quarrel, see *ibid.*, August 11, 13, 14, 15, 16, 17, 18, 21, 25, 27, September 10, 11, 13, 24, 27, 29, October 1, 2, 3, 4, 1804; *Aurora*, August 10, 14, 16, 18, September 10, 11 25, October 1, 3, 6, 8, 1804.

[76] *Ibid.*, August 17, 1804. In his letter Leib asserted that he had announced his intention of retiring to a number of friends in Congress during the preceding session. This is substantiated by a letter to the President of the United States from Joseph Clay, Jacob Richards, and Frederick Conrad, dated January 23, 1804, which spoke of Leib's intention to retire and asked that he be given an appointment to office. The letter is in the Gallatin Papers and is endorsed: "Leib Michael. to be in Customs Phila." What prevented his retirement is unknown.

[77] *Freeman's Journal*, September 3, 4, 7, 8, 11, 12, 1804; *Aurora*, September 4, 5, 6, 7, 8, 10, 1804.

[78] *Ibid.*, October 11, November 2, 1804.

[79] *Ibid.*, September 4, 1804.

[80] *Freeman's Journal*, August 17, 18, 1804.

[81] *Aurora*, August 18, October 8, 9, 1804; Dallas to Duane, August 20, 1804, draft copy, in Dallas Papers; *id.* to Gallatin, October 16, 1804, cited in Adams, *History*, II, 197; Jones to Nicholson, October 20, 1804, draft copy, in Smith Collection.

[82] Duane to Gallatin, August 12, 1802, in Gallatin Papers.

[83] Duane printed his version of the story in the *Aurora*, August 30, 1816. The matter was also mentioned, but without details, by "Clonensis," in *Freeman's Journal*, July 7, 1804.

[84] "Hutchinson," in *Aurora*, October 9, 1804; toasts at dinner held on October 27, 1804, *ibid.*, October 29, 1804.

[85] *Ibid.*, August 26, September 1, 6, 22, 29, October 13, 26, 1804; *U. S. Gazette*, September 11, 1804; *Freeman's Journal*, September 7, 14, 21, October 12, 19, 1804.

[86] *Aurora*, October 13, 22, 1804; *Freeman's Journal*, November 10, 1804; *Pittsburgh Commonwealth*, August 7, 1805.

[87] *Lancaster Journal*, October 26, 1804; *Aurora*, November 16, 1804.

[88] *Ibid.*, November 2, 1804.

[89] Timothy Pickering to McKean, December 19, 1803, in McKean Papers; Uriah Tracy to *id.*, December 19, 1803, *ibid.*; McKean to Jefferson, January 8, 1804, *ibid.*; *id.* to Pickering, January 14, 1804, *ibid.*; *id.* to Tracy, January 14, 1804, *ibid.*

[90] *Aurora*, April 4, 1804.

[91] *Philadelphia Evening Post*, April 6, 1804; *Freeman's Journal*, October 27, 29, 30, November 1, 1804; *Aurora*, September 4, 1804.

[92] *Ibid.*, March 1, 6, 1804. Stanwood, *History of the Presidency*, 83, asserts Pinckney and King were the Federalist candidates but does not know how the nominations were made. King (ed.), *Rufus King*, IV, 350, reports that the two were nominated at a Federalist dinner in Washington on February 22, 1804, and that at a later meeting Pinckney was designated the candidate for President. The *Aurora* discussed the great uncertainty as to the identity of the Federalist candidates in the issue of November 6, 1804.

[93] *Ibid.*, October 25, November 29, 1804; *Lancaster Journal*, November 2, 1804.

[94] Jefferson to the Secretary of the Navy [Robert Smith], August 28, 1804, in Ford (ed.), *Works of Jefferson*, X, 99.

FOOTNOTES FOR CHAPTER IV

[1] *House Journal, 1804-1805,* pp. 49-50.
[2] *U. S. Gazette,* December 17, 22, 1804; *Aurora,* December 18, 1804.
[3] *U. S. Gazette,* December 22, 1804; Adams, *History,* II, 219-20.
[4] *Senate Journal, 1803-1804,* pp. 468-76.
[5] The full proceedings of the trial are given in William Hamilton, *Report of the Trial of E. Shippen, J. Yeates, and T. Smith . . . on an Impeachment before the Senate of the Commonwealth . . .* (n.p., 1805). See also, Loyd, *Early Courts,* 143-46; *Senate Journal, 1804-1805,* appendix; *Aurora,* January 9-30, 1805; Dallas to Gallatin, January 26, 1805, in Gallatin Papers.
[6] *Aurora,* January 30, 1805.
[7] *Ibid.,* February 12, 1802.
[8] "Dialogue No. IV—A Lawyer and a Parson," *ibid.,* December 28, 1804.
[9] "Amicus," *ibid.,* February 9, 1805.
[10] *Ibid.,* February 28, 1805.
[11] *Freeman's Journal,* February 28, March 2, 1805; *Aurora,* March 2, 1805.
[12] Moses Auge, *Lives of the Eminent Dead . . . of Montgomery County, Pa.* (Norristown, Pa., 1879), 43-51; *Aurora,* December 27, 1800; January 11, 12, 22, 1805; *House Journal, 1801-1802,* pp. 91-92, 320, 358, 454; Jonathan Roberts, Jr., to Mathew Roberts, January 28, 1808, in Roberts Papers.
[13] *Freeman's Journal,* July 5, 1805; Boileau to Jonathan Roberts, Jr., March 1, 1805, in Roberts Papers. On Boileau's authorship of the memorial, see *Aurora,* June 15, 1805; "Jacob Fulmer," *ibid.,* January 31, 1810.
[14] *House Journal, 1804-1805,* pp. 473-74.
[15] Dallas to Gallatin, January 26, 1805, in Gallatin Papers.
[16] *Freeman's Journal,* March 5, 7, 15, 1805.
[17] *Ibid.,* March 18, 23, 1805; *U. S. Gazette,* March 19, 1805.
[18] *House Journal, 1804-1805,* pp. 473-74, 527, 535, 547, 568, 569, 584-85, 588, 595-96, 606-607, 615-16, 633-39, 658-61.
[19] Dallas to McKean, January 14, 1805, in McKean Papers.
[20] McKean to Dallas, May 25, 1805, printed in *Aurora,* June 3, 1805.
[21] *Ibid.,* March 29, 1805.
[22] *Pennsylvania Archives,* 4th Series, IV, 560-64.
[23] *House Journal, 1804-1805,* pp. 574-84, 603-604; *Senate Journal, 1804-1805,* pp. 363-68, 388, 392-93.
[24] *Pennsylvania Archives,* 4th Series, IV, 564-66; *House Journal, 1804-1805,* pp. 612-14, 643.
[25] *Aurora,* April 5, 1805. See also, *ibid.,* April 17, May 20, 1805; *Freeman's Journal,* April 6, 17, 1805.
[26] *Aurora,* March 4, 1805; *Lancaster Journal,* March 15, 22, 1805; *U. S. Gazette,* March 19, 1805; John Kean to Dallas, March 20, 1805, in Dallas Papers; Jasper Yeates to Edward Burd, April 2, 1805, in Shippen Family Papers.
[27] "Pennsylvania Politics, November, 1803," in *Aurora,* August 7, 1805.
[28] James H. Peeling, "Joseph Hiester," in *DAB,* IX, 10; "Pennsylvania Politics, November, 1803," in *Aurora,* August 7, 1805. On Hiester's refusal to be a candidate in 1805, see Daniel Udree to Hiester, March 30, 1805, *ibid.,* September 23, 1805; Hiester to Udree, March 31, 1805, *ibid.*
[29] *Ibid.,* April 1, 4, 12, 1805.
[30] *Ibid.,* April 12, 1805; September 29, October 3, 1807. Boileau denied these charges in the *Democratic Press,* October 8, 1807.
[31] "Honestus," *ibid.,* September 24, 1807.
[32] *Aurora,* May 11, 20, July 1, 15, August 19, 1805; October 7, 1807; *Freeman's Journal,* July 11, 15, August 14, September 3, 1805. Leib was later accused of giving strong support to the movement. See "Veritas," in the *Democratic Press,* August 27, 1807.
[33] *Lancaster Journal,* April 6, 1805.
[34] *Freeman's Journal,* March 23, 29, 1805.

Notes—Chapter IV

[35] *Ibid.*, March 25, 1805.
[36] *Ibid.*, April 13, 1805.
[37] *Aurora*, March 25, 28, 29, April 3, 1805.
[38] "A Constitutionalist," in *Freeman's Journal*, March 13, 1805.
[39] Attacks on McKean first appear in *Aurora*, February 7, 1805. In the latter part of March they became more frequent, and by April they were appearing almost daily. A good summary of the charges relating to Yrujo and Cabrera appears in the issue of September 6, 1805.
[40] Serious attacks on Dallas began in March and were almost continuous after that time. The gist of them may be found in *ibid.*, June 5, August 5, 6, 1805.
[41] *Freeman's Journal*, March 21, 1805.
[42] *Ibid.*, August 27, September 7, 1805.
[43] *Aurora*, May 20, 1805.
[44] *Freeman's Journal*, June 11, 12, 1805.
[45] On the authenticity of the caucus address, see *Lancaster Journal*, July 5, August 16, 1805; *Aurora*, September 30, October 3, 1807; *Democratic Press*, October 8, 13, 1807; December 6, 1810.
[46] Jefferson to George Logan, May 11, 1805, in Andrew A. Lipscomb (ed.), *The Writings of Thomas Jefferson*, 20 vols. (Washington, 1903-1904), XI, 71-72; *id.* to Michael Leib, August 12, 1805, in Ford (ed.), *Works of Jefferson*, X, 143-44; Logan to Jefferson, June 10, 1805, in Jefferson Papers; Leib to *id.*, July 22, 1805, *ibid.*
[47] The proceedings of the various meetings were published in the *Aurora* from May to September. A good idea of the way in which most were conducted can be gained from the proceedings of the Northumberland County delegates, *ibid.*, June 26, 1805.
[48] Accounts of these meetings appear in the *Freeman's Journal* from March to September. A typical meeting was that in Chester County, *ibid.*, June 5, 1805.
[49] *Ibid.*, July 11, 1805.
[50] Resolutions of a Washington County meeting on August 28, 1805, in Pittsburgh *Commonwealth*, September 4, 1805; address of Berks County Democratic Republican Committee, August 28, 1805, in *Aurora*, September 7, 1805.
[51] *Ibid.*, September 28, 1805.
[52] Jasper Yeates to Edward Burd, April 2, 1805, in Shippen Family Papers; *Lancaster Journal*, April 6, July 19, 1805.
[53] See *Freeman's Journal*, March 15, 25, April 15, June 12, 1805.
[54] *U. S. Gazette*, May 28, June 3, 1805.
[55] *Lancaster Journal*, July 19, August 23, 1805.
[56] *U. S. Gazette*, August 17, 1805.
[57] *Freeman's Journal*, September 17, 1805.
[58] *Ibid.*, September 21, October 3, 4, 1805; *U. S. Gazette*, September 21, 23, 24, 25, 26, 30, 1805.
[59] *Freeman's Journal*, August 28, 29, September 5, 1805.
[60] "One of the People," reprinted from the Northumberland *Republican Argus* in Lancaster *Intelligencer*, December 3, 1805.
[61] *Aurora*, September 25, October 1, 1805.
[62] *Ibid.*, September 20, 21, 23, 24, 25, 26, 28, 30, 1805. The toast in question had been given at Meadville on July 4, 1805. As originally given it read: *"The Judiciary of Pennsylvania—May it be confined within constitutional bounds and exercised only for the equitable distribution of property."* When printed in the *Crawford Weekly Messenger*, "equal" had inadvertently been substituted for "equitable." In the next issue a correction was made, changing the toast to read the "equal distribution of justice." This version was adopted upon the suggestion of Thomas Atkinson, editor of the *Messenger*, in place of the form in which it had been delivered. The first printed version was seized upon by the Pittsburgh *Tree of Liberty*, which took no notice of the subsequent correction, and was circulated in this form by the Quid papers. See *Freeman's Journal*, August 9, 10, September 24, 1805; October 11, 1806; Pittsburgh *Commonwealth*, August 7, 1805; *Aurora*, August 5, September 5, 1806.
[63] *Ibid.*, May 25, 27, 28, June 11, July 18, August 22, September 4, 6, 1805.
[64] *Freeman's Journal*, May 21, 23, June 4, August 13, 28, September 13, 17, 1805; *U. S. Gazette*, October 3, 1805.

[65] For Bucks County, see *Aurora,* May 10, July 23, 26, September 9, October 12, 1805; *Freeman's Journal,* April 18, May 8, July 24, 30, September 2, 18, 1805. For Chester County, see *Aurora,* May 24, 28, June 20, August 17, 30, September 18, 19, 25, October 1, 1805; *Freeman's Journal,* June 5, August 28, September 19, 1805. For Montgomery County, see *Aurora,* May 17, 21, June 8, July 30, August 24, September 14, 1805; *Freeman's Journal,* May 18, 27, July 29, August 31, September 28, 1805.
[66] *Aurora,* August 28, September 7, 23, 25, October 2, 19, 1805; *Freeman's Journal,* May 25, August 28, 29, 1805.
[67] *Ibid.,* April 8, 16, 22, May 7, 13, 22, June 3, 4, 17, 19, 24, July 2, October 5, 1805; *Aurora,* September 16, 1805; William Findley to Gallatin May 20, 1805, in Gallatin Papers; *id.* to McKean, December 24, 1805 in McKean Papers.
[68] Pittsburgh *Commonwealth,* September 18, 28, October 5, 1805.
[69] For the campaign in Pittsburgh and the establishment of the *Commonwealth,* see *Aurora,* June 22, July 4, August 9, September 16, 27, 1805; *Freeman's Journal,* June 11, 17, July 6, September 19, 23, 1805; Pittsburgh *Commonwealth,* July 24, 31, August 7, 14, 21, 28, 31, September 4, 7, 11, 14, 18, 21, 28, October 5, 9, 16, 19, 23, 1805; Hugh Henry Brackenridge to Dallas, May 25, 1805, in Dallas Papers; Joseph P. Norris to Charles Thomson, July 1, 1805; in Simon Gratz Collection (Historical Society of Pennsylvania).
[70] *Aurora,* August 8, 1805.
[71] Election returns for 1799 are taken from *Senate Journal, 1799-1800,* pp. 29-30. The 1805 returns are from *House Journal, 1805-1806,* pp. 69-70. On the disputed returns from Bucks County, see *Aurora,* October 15, 21, December 24, 1805. McKean carried the city of Philadelphia and the counties of Luzerne, Lycoming, Northampton, Berks, Bucks, Montgomery, Delaware, Chester, Lancaster, York, Adams, Bedford, Somerset, Westmoreland, Fayette, Allegheny, and Beaver. Snyder carried the counties of Philadelphia, Wayne, Northumberland, Dauphin, Cumberland, Franklin, Mifflin, Huntingdon, Centre, Washington, Greene, Erie, Crawford, Mercer, Venango, Warren, and Butler.
[72] *U. S. Gazette,* November 4, 1805. The *Gazette* gives the Constitutionalists 54 seats in the House, but it erroneously lists Francis McClure of Allegheny County as a Constitutionalist, when McClure was run on the regular Democratic ticket. See *Aurora,* September 27, 1805.
[73] Based upon an analysis by John Binns under the pseudonym, "One of the People," and reprinted from the Northumberland *Republican Argus* in the *Aurora,* November 21, December 7, 1805.
[74] Gallatin to Jean Badollet, October 25, 1805, in Henry Adams, *The Life of Albert Gallatin* (Philadelphia, 1879), 331. Hereafter cited as Adams, *Gallatin.*

FOOTNOTES FOR CHAPTER V

[1] Gallatin to Jean Badollet, October 25, 1805, in Adams, *Gallatin*, 331.
[2] Peeling, "Public Life of Thomas McKean," 266; *Aurora*, October 21, 22, November 1, 5, 6, 7, 8, 9, 14, 16, 25, December 9, 10, 1805; *Pennsylvania Archives*, 9th Series, III, 2168 ff.
[3] Barton to Dallas, November 19, 1805, in Dallas Papers.
[4] *Pennsylvania Archives*, 9th Series, III, 2173; *Aurora*, November 9, 1805.
[5] *Ibid.*, November 20, 28, 1805; *Freeman's Journal*, November 19, 21, 23, 25, 27, 1805.
[6] *Aurora*, October 16, 1805.
[7] *Freeman's Journal*, November 26, December 13, 1805.
[8] *Aurora*, November 15, 20, 21, 22, 26, 27, 28, December 3, 1805; *Freeman's Journal*, November 26, 27, 1805; McKean to John Dickinson, November 28, 1805, in McKean Papers.
[9] *Aurora*, July 16, August 15, 1803.
[10] *Gazette of the U. S.*, August 13, 1803.
[11] See *ibid.*, August-September, 1803; *Aurora*, August-September, 1803.
[12] Adams, *History*, II, 396; III, 44-46, 91-96.
[13] *Aurora*, December 14, 1805.
[14] *Ibid.*, January 18, 1806; *U. S. Gazette*, January 8, 1806.
[15] *House Journal, 1805-1806*, pp. 29-31, 51-53, 56-60.
[16] *Ibid.*, 108, 144, 150-51, 153, 155, 174-76, 178-82, 184-91, 195-202, 204-205, 290-93, 302-303, 325, 329-30, 367-68; *Senate Journal, 1805-1806*, pp. 120, 144-45, 151, 155, 158, 161-65, 167-75, 183, 185-86, 192-93; Mitchell *et al.* (comps.), *Statutes at Large*, XVIII, 229-38.
[17] *House Journal, 1805-1806*, pp. 361, 437, 442-43, 451-56, 470-71, 537-39, 542-44, 550; *Senate Journal, 1805-1806*, pp. 283, 320, 325-26, 331-33, 335-37; Mitchell *et al.* (comps.), *Statutes at Large*, XVIII, 229-38.
[18] Quoted in Lancaster *Intelligencer*, December 25, 1805.
[19] *House Journal, 1805-1806*, pp. 69-70, 80, 86-88.
[20] *Ibid.*, 101, 110, 154-55, 157, 166-70, 307-24, 327, 381, 387-88, 414-17, 420-21; *Aurora*, January 14, 15, 17, 20, 27, 1806; *Freeman's Journal*, January 14, 15, 16, 20, 21, 1806.
[21] For the Senate election of bank directors and subsequent events in the affair, see *Senate Journal, 1805-1806*, pp. 139-42; *Aurora*, January 29, 31, February 3, 4, 7, 15, 20, 22, March 4, 7, 14, 29, May 3, June 4, 1806.
[22] Articles and other material on the Yazoo question are particularly frequent in the *Aurora* in October, November, and December, 1804, and in February, March, June, July, August, September, and October, 1805. See particularly the issues of September 17, 1804; February 15, March 26, October 14, November 10, 1805.
[23] Randolph's attack on the Yazoo compromise in 1804 is described in Adams, *History*, II, 211-17.
[24] For Randolph's actions in the session of 1805-1806, see *ibid.*, III, 126-84.
[25] *Aurora*, January 20, 28, February 5, 1806.
[26] Leib to Rodney, February 8, 1806, in Gratz Collection.
[27] *Aurora*, February 19, March 28, April 1, 2, 3, 4, 5, 7, 8, 12, 16, 28, May 3, 8, 10, 12, 13, 15, 16, 17, July 12, 1806.
[28] Leib to Rodney, April 1, 1806, in Gratz Collection.
[29] *Freeman's Journal*, March 17, 1806; *Aurora*, April 12, 1806.
[30] *Freeman's Journal*, March 28, 1806.
[31] Attacks on the Governor appeared almost daily, but material on the points mentioned in the text may be found in *Aurora*, April 30, May 2, 5, July 11, 12, August 13, October 13, 1806.

[32] The impeachment of McKean was common talk in August, 1806. See Peter Stephen DuPonceau to Robert R. Livingston, August 20, 1806, in Gratz Collection.

[33] On the events surrounding Duane's arrest and release, see *Aurora,* August 9, 12, 13, 16, 19, 1806; *U. S. Gazette,* August 12, 1806. On McKean and Cobbett, see Peeling, "Public Life of Thomas McKean," 183-85.

[34] *Freeman's Journal,* August 18, 30, 1806.

[35] *Aurora,* August 6, 29, September 10, 1806.

[36] "One of the Libelled," *ibid.,* September 8, 1806.

[37] *Ibid.,* September 11, 16, 17, 18, 19, 20, 22, 25, October 3, 6, 7, 1806.

[38] *Freeman's Journal,* October 9, 1806.

[39] *Ibid.,* August 14, 15, 19, 20, 21, 22, 25, 26, 29, 30, September 1, 4, 18, 20, 22, 23, 24, 25, 27, 30, 1806.

[40] *Aurora,* September 9, 10, 23, 24, 25, 26, 30, October 1, 10, 1806.

[41] *Ibid.,* August 23, 28, 29, September 3, 4, 5, 6, 9, 30, October 13, 1806.

[42] *Freeman's Journal,* October 3, 1806; *Aurora,* October 10, 1806.

[43] *Ibid.,* September 13, 20, 23, 24, 25, October 3, 8, 13, 1806.

[44] *Freeman's Journal,* September 10, 11, 1806; *Aurora,* September 25, 27, October 7, 8, 9, 1806.

[45] The election returns are printed in *ibid.,* October 15, 16, 1806; *Poulson's American Daily Advertiser,* October 16, 18, 1806.

[46] Pittsburgh *Commonwealth,* December 4, 25, January 8, 15, 22, February 5, 1806; *Freeman's Journal,* January 16, 18, 1806; *Aurora,* January 20, 21, 1806.

[47] On the campaign in Pittsburgh and the surrounding area, see Pittsburgh *Commonwealth,* July 23, August 13, 20, 27, September 3, 24, October 1, 8, 14, 1806.

[48] *Ibid.,* October 22, November 5, 1806.

[49] *Poulson's American Daily Advertiser,* November 14, 1806; *Aurora,* November 7, 1806; Northumberland *Republican Argus* quoted in *ibid.,* November 19, 1806.

[50] *Ibid.*

[51] *Poulson's American Daily Advertiser,* November 14, 1806.

[52] Pittsburgh *Commonwealth,* November 5, 1806; *Aurora,* October 29, 1806; William Findley to Joseph Hiester, April 9, 1808, in Gregg Collection.

[53] See the views expressed in DuPonceau to Livingston, August 20, 1806, in Gratz Collection.

FOOTNOTES FOR CHAPTER VI

[1] *U. S. Gazette,* October 14, 15, 1806; *Aurora,* October 15, 17, 1806. A copy of the pamphlet is in the Historical Society of Pennsylvania. It bears the following title: *The Quid Mirror. The First Part.* A foreword dated at New York on August 30, 1806, states that the manuscript came from Philadelphia. The exact author is still uncertain, although one writer claims that the pamphlet was the work of William Dickson, editor of the Lancaster *Intelligencer.* See Walters, *Dallas,* 142.

[2] Leib later presented this challenge to the grand jury. See p. 143 below. Papers dealing with the matter are in McKean Papers, IV, 2-7 (Historical Society of Pennsylvania).

[3] Pennsylvania Constitution of 1790, Article VI, Section 1, in Thorpe (comp.), *Federal and State Constitutions,* V, 3098-99; Mitchell *et al.* (comps.), *Statutes at Large,* XVI, 177.

[4] *Aurora,* October 16, 1806.

[5] *Pennsylvania Archives,* 9th Series, III, 2293-94.

[6] Testimony of John Barker before the House committee of inquiry on March 24, 1807, in *House Journal, 1807-1808,* I, 348-49.

[7] *Ibid.,* 347-48.

[8] *U. S. Gazette,* November 3, 1806; *Freeman's Journal,* November 7, 11, 12, 20, 27, 1806.

[9] *Poulson's American Daily Advertiser,* December 5, 6, 1806.

[10] *Pennsylvania Archives,* 4th Series, IV, 579-85.

[11] *House Journal, 1806-1807,* pp. 22, 34-36, 64-68, 130-31.

[12] *Ibid.,* 30, 175-90.

[13] *Ibid.,* 58, 75, 133, 155, 213, 215-16, 246-47, 433-36, 438-40, 443, 532-33, 629, 682-84, 747-48; *Senate Journal, 1806-1807,* pp. 230, 267, 274-75; *Aurora,* August 13, 1806; March 31, April 1, 4, 1807.

[14] *House Journal, 1806-1807,* pp. 46, 153, 234, 255-60, 261, 265-66, 317, 401-402, 406, 415, 516-17, 662; *Senate Journal, 1806-1807,* pp. 213, 243-44, 247, 256, 259, 265.

[15] *Pennsylvania Archives,* 9th Series, III, 2328-30.

[16] *Aurora,* January 12, 29, February 7, 28, 1807; *House Journal, 1806-1807,* pp. 309-13, 499, 513-14.

[17] *Ibid.,* 727-38.

[18] *Ibid.,* 738, 746, 821-24, 832-33. The report and the evidence are printed in *House Journal, 1807-1808,* I, 324-407. The progress of the attempted impeachment and the documents relating to it are printed in the *Aurora,* March 3, 5, 9, 21, 24, 26, 27, April 3, 6, 7, 8, 10, 11, 13, 17, 1807.

[19] *Ibid.,* March 20, 21, 1807.

[20] *Ibid.,* April 11, 1807.

[21] *Senate Journal, 1806-1807,* pp. 29, 31, 72-73, 104-105, 159-60, 176, 205-206, 218, 259-60, 339, 351, 371, 525-26; *House Journal, 1806-1807,* pp. 212, 231, 405; *Pennsylvania Archives,* 4th Series, IV, 601-602.

[22] 3 *Cranch* 1.

[23] *House Journal, 1806-1807,* pp. 321, 338, 383, 418, 448-50, 490, 515-16, 637, 751-54; *Senate Journal, 1806-1807,* pp. 275, 281, 312, 323, 327, 329, 334-37, 357, 436-38; *Pennsylvania Archives,* 4th Series, IV, 604-606.

[24] *Senate Journal, 1806-1807,* pp. 235, 281, 298, 309, 313-14, 317, 349-50, 493-94, 501; *House Journal, 1806-1807,* pp. 592, 614, 618, 650, 713, 798-99; *Pennsylvania Archives,* 4th Series, IV, 606-607.

[25] *House Journal, 1806-1807,* pp. 335, 478, 506, 621-28, 631, 632-33, 698-99, 701-702, 704-705, 708, 709, 714, 764-75, 830, 859-60; *Senate Journal, 1806-1807,* pp. 338, 355, 360, 369-70, 381-82, 387-88, 394-95, 399, 400, 408, 438, 440.

[26] *House Journal, 1806-1807,* pp. 389-90, 515, 657, 717, 739-40, 779, 792, 818; *Senate Journal, 1806-1807,* pp. 419, 452, 465.

[27] *House Journal, 1806-1807*, pp. 790, 805-806, 825; *Senate Journal, 1806-1807*, pp. 502, 516-17.
[28] *House Journal, 1806-1807*, pp. 196, 226, 411-13, 488, 506, 540-46, 701-703, 807-809, 812, 815-17; *Senate Journal, 1806-1807*, 301, 312, 355, 361-62; 384-85, 503, 507.
[29] *House Journal, 1806-1807*, pp. 93-94, 225, 262, 493, 520, 553, 574-76, 581-82, 646-47, 662, 704, 711, 719-20, 768-69, 781-82, 785, 829, 834; *Senate Journal, 1806-1807*, pp. 53-56, 58-59, 66, 168, 177-78, 202, 208-209, 213-14, 221-22, 225, 231, 240-41, 248, 314, 322-23, 325-26, 341-42, 345, 348, 355-56, 360, 394, 403-404, 413, 417, 449, 481-82, 512; Horace Binney to John B. Wallace, March 13, 1807, in John William Wallace Papers (Historical Society of Pennsylvania); Joseph Huston to Gallatin, April 6, 1807, in Gallatin Papers.
[30] *Freeman's Journal*, June 4, 1807; *Aurora*, December 4, 1806.
[31] *Freeman's Journal*, June 4, October 6, 1807; *Aurora*, September 30, October 1, 1807; *Democratic Press*, October 13, 1807.
[32] *House Journal, 1806-1807*, pp. 27, 28, 37-38, 70; *Democratic Press*, September 19, 1807; *Freeman's Journal*, June 4, 1807.
[33] McKean to George Logan, December 20, 1806, in McKean Papers.
[34] *Freeman's Journal*, June 4, October 6, 1807.
[35] *House Journal, 1806-1807*, pp. 175, 191-93.
[36] *Freeman's Journal*, June 4, 1807; *Democratic Press*, September 19, 1807.
[37] Leib's views are given in Leib to George Bartram, January 18, 1807, in *Freeman's Journal*, October 6, 1807.
[38] *Ibid.*, January 29, 1807; *House Journal, 1806-1807*, pp. 255-57.
[39] *Ibid.*, 273, 299-304; *Senate Journal, 1806-1807*, pp. 151-52; *Lancaster Journal*, January 30, February 6, 1807.
[40] *Ibid.*, extra, April 13, 1807.
[41] *U. S. Gazette*, July 27, 1805; *Aurora*, July 30, November 13, 1805.
[42] References appear almost daily during late November and December, 1806, and in January, February, and March, 1807. See particularly, *ibid.*, August 23, October 13, November 5, 22, December 5, 13, 1806; January 12, 13, 31, 1807.
[43] Pittsburgh *Commonwealth*, December 24, 31, 1806; January 14, 21, 1807.
[44] Accounts of the Burr trial begin in the *Aurora* in April and continue through December, 1807.
[45] Adams, *History*, III, 155, 175, 199-200; *Aurora*, April 28, 29, 30, May 1, 2, 5, 9, 1806; *U. S. Gazette*, April 29, 1806.
[46] *Aurora*, January 24, March 21, May 8, 1806.
[47] Adams, *History*, III, 389-90, 397-99, 416.
[48] *Ibid.*, 408-13, 429-40; *Aurora*, March 7, 9, 25, 1807; "A.B.," in *U. S. Gazette*, March 26, 1807.
[49] Adams, *History*, III, 349-55.
[50] *Aurora*, January 1-May 26, 1807. See particularly, issues of February 3, 5, 7, 10, 12, May 1, 2, 26, 1807.
[51] *Ibid.*, June 29, 30, July 1, 2, 4, 1807; *U. S. Gazette*, July 1, 1807.
[52] *Ibid.*, July 2, 11, August 8, 13, 1807.
[53] *Aurora*, July 3, 6, 22, 23, 24, August 21, 1807.
[54] John D. Wade, "John Binns," in *DAB*, II, 282-83; Binns, *Recollections*, 78-139, 176-77; *Democratic Press*, March 27, 1810; *Aurora*, August 8, 1805; Brigham, "Bibliography of American Newspapers," in *AAS Proceedings*, XXX (1920), 148-49.
[55] *Aurora*, September 25, 28, October 1, 3, 1807. See also, *Lancaster Journal*, extra, April 13, 1807.
[56] *Democratic Press*, March 27, 1810.
[57] Binns, *Recollections*, 192-93.
[58] *Democratic Press*, March 27, June 29, 1807; March 27, 1810; *Aurora*, March 17, 1807; Binns, *Recollections*, 196-97.
[59] *Aurora*, May 14, 1807; Binns, *Recollections*, 197.
[60] *Freeman's Journal*, May 11, 13, 1807.
[61] *A Narrative of Facts relative to the Conduct of Some of the Members of the Legislature of Pennsylvania, Professing to be Democrats, at the Election of a Senator to*

Represent this State in the Senate of the United States, on the 13th of January, 1807 (Philadelphia, May, 1807). A second edition in June states that the first had been circulated free, but that the second was to be sold to pay printing expenses. Both editions may be found in the Historical Society of Pennsylvania.

[62] *Aurora*, June 3, 1807; *Freeman's Journal*, June 4, 1807; *Democratic Press*, June 5, 1807.
[63] *Ibid.*, August 4, 7, 10, 11, 12, 15, 1807.
[64] *Aurora*, August 19, 21, 1807; *Democratic Press*, August 18, 19, 20, 21, 24, 25, 28, 29, September 21, 23, 1807.
[65] *Ibid.*, August 26, 1807.
[66] *Ibid.*, August 26, 28, September 2, 10, 19, 28, 1807.
[67] *Aurora*, September 1, 1807.
[68] *Ibid.*, September 3, 1807; *Democratic Press*, September 3, 1807.
[69] *Aurora*, September 4, 1807.
[70] For the attacks on Boileau, see *ibid.*, September 24, 28, 29, 30, October 1, 5, 7, 1807.
[71] For the attacks on Binns, see *ibid.*, September 25, 26, October 3, 5, 9, 10, 1807.
[72] *Democratic Press*, October 5, 6, 8, 13, 1807.
[73] *Aurora*, September 4, 1807.
[74] *Ibid.*, September 23, 1807; *Freeman's Journal*, September 23, 1807. William J. Duane, son of the editor of the *Aurora* and Catharine Corcoran, was born in Clonmel, County Tipperary, Ireland, May 9, 1780. He came to Philadelphia with his father in 1796 and worked with him on the *True American* and the *Aurora* before becoming a partner of William Levis, a paper merchant, in 1806. He served three terms in the State House of Representatives (1809-1810, 1812-1813, 1819-1820) and became one of the leading members of the Philadelphia bar. He is best known for his refusal as Secretary of the Treasury in 1833 to obey President Jackson's orders to discontinue the depositing of government funds in the Second Bank of the United States. H. W. Howard Knott, "William John Duane," in *DAB*, V, 468-69. He is to be distinguished from his father by the addition of the middle initial "J.," and in this study will, where necessary, be referred to as "young William J. Duane" or "young Duane." Unless apparent from the context, the unadorned term "Duane" will always refer to his father.
[75] *Aurora*, May 7, 8, 1807.
[76] *Ibid.*, September 4, 11, 1807; *Freeman's Journal*, September 11, 18, 22, 26, 1807.
[77] *Ibid.*, August 25, September 1, 7, 8, 9, 15, 17, 24, 1807.
[78] *Poulson's American Daily Advertiser*, October 15, 17, 1807; *Aurora*, October 20, 1807. Election returns for 1805 and 1806 are given in *ibid.*, October 10, 11, 1805; October 16, 1806; *Poulson's American Daily Advertiser*, October 16, 18, 1806.
[79] *Aurora*, October 15, 20, 1807; *Democratic Press*, October 22, 1807; *Freeman's Journal*, November 2, 1807; Duane to Jefferson, October 16, 1807, in "Letters of Duane," 304.
[80] *Aurora*, October 31, November 16, 1807; *Democratic Press*, November 20, 1807.

FOOTNOTES FOR CHAPTER VII

[1] *Democratic Press,* November 20, 1807. Samuel Carver, Constitutional Republican from the city of Philadelphia, died before the opening of the session. His successor was Thomas P. Cope, a Federalist, elected on December 22, 1807. *Freeman's Journal,* December 12, 23, 1807.

[2] *Aurora,* December 3, 1807; *Democratic Press,* November 20, 1807.

[3] *Pennsylvania Archives,* 4th Series, IV, 621-27.

[4] *Ibid.,* 619-21.

[5] *Ibid.,* 612-19.

[6] *House Journal, 1807-1808,* I, 14-22, 35, 52-53; II, 402.

[7] *Ibid.,* I, 43, 44, 50-51, 113-14, 226, 307-308, 321-434.

[8] *Ibid.,* I, 64, 115, 148, 154, 161-62, 163, 170-72, 173-74, 178-84, 242; II, 78-85; *Senate Journal, 1807-1808,* pp. 105-107, 113-14, 163-70, 218, 220-24, 232.

[9] *Ibid.,* 5-11, 52, 73, 81-82, 89-91, 119; *House Journal, 1807-1808,* I, 49-50, 57, 74, 82, 86-91, 121-23, 187-88, 210-14, 217, 225.

[10] *Aurora,* January 16, 1808.

[11] *House Journal, 1807-1808,* II, 6-7.

[12] See proceedings of meetings in Berks, Centre, Lycoming, Lancaster, Mifflin, Cumberland, and Montgomery counties in *Democratic Press,* November 24, December 9, 16, 24, 1807; Harrisburg *Dauphin Guardian,* January 19, 1808; *Aurora,* November 24, 1807. See also, *ibid.,* December 26, 1807; Thomas J. Rogers to Jonathan Roberts, Jr., December 6, 1807, in Roberts Papers.

[13] Leib to *id.,* December 16, 1809, *ibid.*

[14] Jonathan Roberts, Jr., to Jonathan Roberts, Sr., December 13, 1807, *ibid.*

[15] Leib to Roberts, December 16, 1809, *ibid.; Aurora,* January 11, 1808.

[16] *Freeman's Journal,* December 21, 1807.

[17] For example, in January, 1807, after the senatorial election, Snyder voted with Leib and against Boileau in support of the second section of Leib's bill to amend the general election law and also sided with him in the election of bank directors. See *House Journal, 1806-1807,* pp. 255-57, 277-304.

[18] *Aurora,* January 11, 1808; Jonathan Roberts, Jr., to Jonathan Roberts, Sr., January 8, 1808, in Roberts Papers.

[19] Luetscher, *Political Machinery,* 135; Ostrogorski, "The Rise and Fall of the Nominating Caucus, Legislative and Congressional," in *AHR,* V, 278; *Aurora,* March 10, 1808.

[20] *Senate Journal, 1807-1808,* pp. 159-61; *House Journal, 1807-1808,* I, 306-307, 434-42; *Lancaster Journal,* January 29, 1808; Lancaster *Intelligencer,* February 2, 1808; *Pittsburgh Gazette,* February 23, 1808; *Democratic Press,* February 2, 1808; *Freeman's Journal,* July 28, 1808; Jonathan Roberts, Jr., to Jonathan Roberts, Sr., January 22, 1808, in Roberts Papers; *id.* to Mathew Roberts, January 28, 1808, *ibid.;* Samuel Maclay to Jonathan Roberts, Jr., February 2, 1808, *ibid.*

[21] *Aurora,* March 10, 1808. See also, *Freeman's Journal,* July 28, 1808.

[22] Charles W. Hare to William Tilghman, February 1, 1808, in William Tilghman Correspondence (Historical Society of Pennsylvania); Tilghman to Hare, February 3, 1808, *ibid.*

[23] Pittsburgh *Commonwealth,* March 9, 1808; *Democratic Press,* July 28, 1808; *U. S. Gazette,* March 7, 8, 1808.

[24] Richard Peters to Timothy Pickering, March 15, 1808, typed copy, in Pickering Collection (Library of Congress); Joseph Hopkinson to [?], March 22, 1808, in Dreer Collection.

[25] Hare to Tilghman, March 21, 1808, in Society Collection (Historical Society of Pennsylvania); Boileau to Andrew Porter, March 19, 1808, in W. W. Porter Collection (Historical Society of Pennsylvania); *Freeman's Journal,* March 28, 1808; *Lancaster Journal,* April 1, 1808.

[26] See, for example, *Aurora,* April 21, May 9, 14, July 7, 1807.

[27] See, for example, *Democratic Press,* February 24, 26, March 1, 2, 3, 1808.

NOTES—CHAPTER VII

[28] *Aurora*, January 26, 28, February 1, March 22, 1808.
[29] *Democratic Press*, January 1, February 9, 10, 24, 26, 27, 1808. See also the issues for March, April, May, and June.
[30] *Aurora*, January 28, 1808.
[31] William Findley to Joseph Hiester, April 9, 1808, in Gregg Collection.
[32] *Democratic Press*, March 9, 1808.
[33] Views of Thomas Leiper given in letter of Thomas Truxtun to Thomas Tingey, March 17, 1808, in Madison Papers (Library of Congress).
[34] "Troilus," in *Freeman's Journal*, July 28, 1808. On the matter of convention sentiment for Clinton, see *ibid.*, March 10, 1808; *Lancaster Journal*, March 11, 1808; *Democratic Press*, March 9, July 14, 1808.
[35] Truxtun to Tingey, March 17, 1808, in Madison Papers. Duane's letter to Pleasants is reprinted from the Richmond *Virginia Argus* in the *Aurora*, March 28, 1808.
[36] Truxtun to Tingey, March 17, 1808, in Madison Papers.
[37] Duane to Madison, February 8, 1808, in "Letters of Duane," 308-309; *id.* to R. C. Weightman, December 20, 1808, *ibid.*, 312; "Publius Gavius Cosanus," in *Freeman's Journal*, August 2, 1808.
[38] Truxtun to Tingey, March 17, 1808, in Madison Papers; *Aurora*, May 5, June 27, 1808.
[39] *Ibid.*, May 4, 5, 17, 1808; *Democratic Press*, May 17, 1808.
[40] *Aurora*, June 7, 1808.
[41] *Ibid.*, May 7, June 1, 2, 22, July 16, 1808.
[42] *Democratic Press*, July 14, 1808.
[43] *Aurora*, August 8, 1808.
[44] *Democratic Press*, May 2, 6, 9, 12, 13, 19, June 23, 1808.
[45] *Ibid.*, July 18, 1808.
[46] *Ibid.*, August 9, September 7, 1808; *Aurora*, August 17, 1808.
[47] Pittsburgh *Commonwealth*, June 8, 22, 29, July 6, 13, 20, 27, August 3, 31, September 14, 21, 1808.
[48] Leib to Caesar A. Rodney, May 19, 1808, in Gratz Collection; Duane to Jefferson, August 9, 1808, in "Letters of Duane," 310-11; Leiper to Madison, August 9, 1808, in Madison Papers; *id.* to Jefferson, August 18, 1808, in Jefferson Papers.
[49] Jefferson to Leiper, August 21, 1807, in Ford (ed.), *Works of Jefferson*, X, 482-83; *Aurora*, October 2, 13, 1807.
[50] *Ibid.*, August 6, September 2, October 13, 1808; *Democratic Press*, September 2, 1808; Duane to Jefferson, August 9, 1808, in "Letters of Duane," 310-11; Leiper to Madison, August 9, 1808, in Madison Papers; *id.* to Jefferson, August 18, 1808, in Jefferson Papers; Gallatin to *id.*, August 6, 1808, in Adams (ed.), *Writings of Gallatin*, I, 402.
[51] Hare to Otis, June 2, 1808, quoted in Samuel E. Morison, "The First National Nominating Convention, 1808," in *AHR*, XVII (1912), 748.
[52] *Ibid.*, 748-51; Christopher Gore to Rufus King, June 16, 1808, in King (ed.), *Rufus King*, V, 101-102.
[53] Morison, "The First National Nominating Convention, 1808," in *AHR*, XVII, 753-58.
[54] *Ibid.*, 759-61; "Thraso," in *Aurora*, August 31, 1808.
[55] Samuel Sitgreaves to Benjamin R. Morgan, September 8, 1808, in Gratz Collection; Alexander Graydon to *id.*, September 23, 1808, *ibid.*; *U. S. Gazette*, October 26, 1808.
[56] Adams, *History*, IV, 101-103, 126-27, 166.
[57] *Ibid.*, 165-75, 178, 200-204.
[58] David W. Parker (ed.), "Secret Reports of John Howe, 1808," in *AHR*, XVII (1912), 96.
[59] Nicholas Biddle to J. M. de la Grange, September 26, 1808, quoted in Louis M. Sears, "Philadelphia and the Embargo of 1808," in American Historical Association *Annual Report for 1920* (Washington, 1925), 261.
[60] Seybert, *Statistical Annals*, 93.
[61] *Ibid.*

[62] Cumberland County Democratic address, August 3, 1808, in *Aurora,* August 16, 1808.
[63] Printed circular issued by Abraham Horn at Easton, September 30, 1808, in Northampton County Papers (Historical Society of Pennsylvania).
[64] Sears, "Philadelphia and the Embargo of 1808," in American Historical Association *Annual Report for 1920,* 253-63. See also, "Ne Quid Nimis," in *Aurora,* July 20, 1808.
[65] Truxtun to Tingey, March 17, 1808, in Madison Papers.
[66] *Aurora,* December 14, 1805; May 26, July 3, 1807.
[67] *Democratic Press,* December 26, 1807; August 13, 1808.
[68] Pittsburgh *Commonwealth,* February 17, 1808.
[69] "Arion," *ibid.,* February 3, 1808; *Aurora,* September 20, 1808; William Jones to Nathaniel Macon, November 16, 1808, in Jones and Clark Papers (Historical Society of Pennsylvania).
[70] *U. S. Gazette,* December 20, 1807; January 14, 1808.
[71] Hopkinson to [?], March 22, 1808, in Dreer Collection.
[72] "Fabius," in *U. S. Gazette,* August 8, 1808. See also, "An Old Republican," reprinted from *Huntingdon Gazette* in *Freeman's Journal,* July 20, 1808.
[73] *Aurora,* July 13, 1808.
[74] See, for example, *ibid.,* June 7, July 16, 20, August 11, September 8, 1808; Pittsburgh *Commonwealth,* August 3, September 14, 1808.
[75] Higgins to Jonathan Roberts, Jr., June 28, 1808, in Roberts Papers.
[76] Parker (ed.), "Secret Reports of John Howe, 1808," in *AHR,* XVII, 96. See also, Adams, *History,* IV, 286.
[77] See, for example, *Aurora,* June 7, July 20, 23, August 11, 22, September 8, 1808; Pittsburgh *Commonwealth,* August 3, 31, 1808.
[78] For the Jane Marie case, see *Aurora,* August 22, 23, 24, 26, September 22, 24, 26, 27, 28, October 5, 6, 1808; *U. S. Gazette,* September 10, 21, October 4, 7, 1808; *Democratic Press,* September 1, 1808; Harrisburg *Oracle of Dauphin,* October 8, 1808; James I. Brownson, *The Life and Times of Senator James Ross* (Washington, Pa., 1910), 37-45.
[79] *Freeman's Journal,* July 16, 20, 21, 1808; *U. S. Gazette,* September 16, 30, 1808; Harrisburg *Oracle of Dauphin,* October 8, 1808; Stephen Balliet, Jr., to John Arndt, July 30, 1808, in Northampton County Papers; *Democratic Press,* July 20, September 27, 1808; Pittsburgh *Commonwealth,* August 24, September 28, 1808; *Aurora,* September 26-October 8, 1808.
[80] The State committee published addresses dated June 4, July 25, and August 31, 1808. These are printed in *ibid.,* June 7, August 8, September 2, 1808.
[81] *Democratic Press,* January 5, May 12, 17, June 3, August 3, 1808; *Aurora,* May 17, June 7, 1808.
[82] *Democratic Press,* May 17, June 3, August 3, 1808.
[83] *Aurora,* June 7, 1808.
[84] "Troilus," in *Freeman's Journal,* July 7, 1808.
[85] "Troilus," *ibid.,* July 11, 1808; "Secta," in *Democratic Press,* May 1, 1809.
[86] *Aurora,* July 6, 1808.
[87] *Freeman's Journal,* February 20, 1807.
[88] *Ibid.,* March 2, April 6, May 26, June 14, July 22, 25, 26, 29, August 9, 1808.
[89] *Democratic Press,* August 15, 1808.
[90] *Freeman's Journal,* August 15, 16, 1808.
[91] *U. S. Gazette,* August 24, 27, 1808.
[92] *Democratic Press,* August 25, 29, 1808; *U. S. Gazette,* August 25, 1808.
[93] *Democratic Press,* September 16, 1808; *U. S. Gazette,* September 15, 23, 1808.
[94] *Aurora,* September 20, 1808.
[95] *U. S. Gazette,* September 24, 1808.
[96] *Aurora,* September 22, 1808; *U. S. Gazette,* October 1, 1808.
[97] Dallas to Gallatin, July 30, 1808, in Adams, *Gallatin,* 372-73.
[98] *U. S. Gazette,* October 1, 1808.
[99] *Ibid.; Democratic Press,* September 28, 1808.

Notes—Chapter VII

[100] On this subject, see *Aurora*, July 6, 20, 1808; *Democratic Press*, July 28, 29, 30, August 3, 1808; May 1, 1809; *Freeman's Journal*, June 4, 1808; Leib to Rodney, May 19, 1808, in Gratz Collection.
[101] *Democratic Press*, August 5, 1808.
[102] *Aurora*, September 2, October 1, 8, 10, 1808.
[103] *Ibid.*, July 25, 1808.
[104] Election returns for the city and county are given in *Poulson's American Daily Advertiser*, October 19, 1808; *Aurora*, October 13, 14, 17, 20, 1808. On the Duncan affair, see *ibid.*, October 11, 22, November 2, 9, 1808.
[105] *House Journal, 1808-1809*, pp. 86-87.
[106] Mitchell *et al.* (comps.) *Statutes at Large*, XVIII, 796-99.
[107] *Aurora*, October 22, November 7, 10, 1808; May 17, 1809; *Poulson's American Daily Advertiser*, October 22, 1808.
[108] *Aurora*, October 22, 25, 27, 28, 29, 31, November 1, 2, 3, 1808; *U. S. Gazette*, October 26, 1808; *Lancaster Journal*, October 28, 1808.
[109] *Aurora*, December 16, 1808.

FOOTNOTES FOR CHAPTER VIII

[1] *Democratic Press,* December 8, 1808.
[2] *House Journal, 1808-1809,* pp. 31-32, 38-39, 44-45, 48-49.
[3] *Democratic Press,* August 3, 1810; *Aurora,* September 28, 1810.
[4] Binns, *Recollections,* 205-206; *Pennsylvania Archives,* 9th Series, IV, 2587; *House Journal, 1808-1809,* pp. 122-23.
[5] *Pennsylvania Archives,* 4th Series, IV, 664.
[6] Snyder to Boileau, October 31, 1808, in Simon Snyder Correspondence (Historical Society of Pennsylvania); *Aurora,* January 12, 1809; "Jacob Fulmer," *ibid.,* February 2, 1810.
[7] *Ibid.,* January 7, 1809.
[8] *House Journal, 1808-1809,* pp. 145-46, 153, 174-76, 193; *Democratic Press,* January 12, 1809.
[9] Snyder to Boileau, October 31, 1808, in Snyder Correspondence.
[10] *Aurora,* December 1, 1808.
[11] *Pennsylvania Archives,* 4th Series, IV, 660-61.
[12] *House Journal, 1808-1809,* pp. 29, 59-60, 125-26, 137, 186-87, 221, 320-22, 327, 582-83, 646-47; *Senate Journal, 1808-1809,* pp. 172, 185, 196, 285-86, 288-90, 349; Mitchell *et al.* (comps.), *Statutes at Large,* XVIII, 985-86.
[13] *House Journal, 1808-1809,* pp. 33, 60, 150, 337, 346-47, 352, 871-72; *Senate Journal, 1808-1809,* pp. 183, 198, 241, 245-46, 489-90, 492-93, 499-500; Mitchell *et al.* (comps.), *Statutes at Large,* XVIII, 1110-11.
[14] *House Journal, 1808-1809,* pp. 69, 154, 162, 163, 209, 834, 846-48.
[15] Mitchell *et al.* (comps.), *Statutes at Large,* XVIII, 962-67, 1082-89.
[16] *House Journal, 1808-1809,* pp. 14-16, 37-38, 54-55, 57-58, 70-76, 132-33; *Senate Journal, 1808-1809,* pp. 82, 87-89, 90.
[17] Adams, *History,* IV, 398-400, 408-17.
[18] *Senate Journal, 1808-1809,* pp. 236-37, 292-94; *House Journal, 1808-1809,* pp. 530-32, 551-52, 583.
[19] The account of the Olmsted affair is based upon a wide variety of sources. The fullest account is contained in Richard Peters, Jr., *The Whole Proceedings in the Case of Olmsted et al. vs. Rittenhouse's Executrices* (Philadelphia, 1809). See also the following articles: Hampton L. Carson, "The Case of the Sloop 'Active,' " in *PMHB,* XVI (1892), 385-98; Mary E. Cunningham, "The Case of the Active," in *Pennsylvania History,* XII (1946), 229-47. Good summaries are also to be found in *House Journal, 1808-1809,* pp. 787-98; *ibid., 1809-1810,* pp. 404-23.
[20] 2 *Dallas* 160.
[21] 3 *Dallas* 54.
[22] Mitchell *et al.* (comps.), *Statutes at Large,* XVI, 578-79.
[23] Peters's decision is quoted in the report of *The United States* v. *Judge Peters,* 5 *Cranch* 115.
[24] *Pennsylvania Archives,* 4th Series, IV, 511-12. Carson asserts that McKean acted from irritation at the flaunting of his decision in 1792. Carson, "The Case of the Sloop 'Active,' " in *PMHB,* XVI, 334.
[25] *House Journal, 1802-1803,* pp. 245-46, 514, 559, 600, 613, 619-20, 629; *Senate Journal, 1802-1803,* pp. 189-90, 507, 510, 520-21; Mitchell *et al.* (comps.), *Statutes at Large,* XVII, 472-80.
[26] *Aurora,* April 11, 1803.
[27] The question of the northwestern lands is considered in detail in Elizabeth K. Henderson, "The Northwestern Lands of Pennsylvania, 1790-1812," in *PMHB,* LX (1936), 131-60. See also, Paul D. Evans, *The Holland Land Company* (Buffalo, 1924), 107-69; Buck and Buck, *Planting of Civilization,* 206-12, 486; Ferguson, *Western Pennsylvania Politics,* 182-85, 196-99.
[28] Quoted in report of *The Commonwealth* v. *Tench Coxe,* 4 *Dallas* 170.

NOTES—CHAPTER VIII

[29] See Ferguson, *Western Pennsylvania Politics*, 182-85, 196-99; Henderson, "The Northwestern Lands of Pennsylvania, 1790-1812," in *PMHB*, LX, 131-49; 4 *Dallas* 170; 4 *Dallas* 237.
[30] 3 *Cranch* 1.
[31] Charles Warren, *The Supreme Court in United States History*, 3 vols. (Boston, 1923), I, 370.
[32] *House Journal, 1804-1805*, pp. 452-54, 536-37; *Senate Journal, 1804-1805*, pp. 352, 361, 369-70, 374, 411.
[33] *House Journal, 1806-1807*, pp. 448-50, 515-16, 637, 751-54; *Senate Journal, 1806-1807*, pp. 275, 281, 312, 323, 327, 329, 334-37, 357, 436-38; *Pennsylvania Archives*, 4th Series, IV, 604-606. See pp. 128-29 above.
[34] The account of the background of the Nicholls affair is based upon *House Journal, 1808-1809*, pp. 224-26; Warren, *Supreme Court*, I, 370-72.
[35] *House Journal, 1808-1809*, pp. 218, 224-28, 249-51, 265, 273, 282, 288-90, 292-93, 338; *Senate Journal, 1808-1809*, pp. 120-26, 162, 169, 170-72, 174, 183; Warren, *Supreme Court*, I, 372-74; Mitchell *et al.* (comps.), *Statutes at Large*, XVIII, 327-30.
[36] Footnote to report of case of *The United States* v. *Judge Peters*, 3 *Cranch* 115.
[37] *Ibid.*
[38] Sergeant to Snyder, February 24, 1809, in *Pennsylvania Archives*, 4th Series, IV, 691-92; *ibid.*, 667-68; *ibid.*, 9th Series, IV, 2616.
[39] *House Journal, 1808-1809*, pp. 533-34, 547-51, 554-57, 615-29, 693-97, 786-98, 843; *Senate Journal, 1808-1809*, pp. 269, 294-307, 379, 407, 411-30, 433, 474.
[40] *Aurora*, December 29, 1808.
[41] *Ibid.*, March 2, 1809.
[42] *Democratic Press*, March 2, 1809.
[43] *U. S. Gazette*, March 1, 15, 16, 1809.
[44] *Ibid.*, March 27, 1809; Michael Bright to Boileau, March 24, 1809, in *Pennsylvania Archives*, 4th Series, IV, 693; *id.* to *id.*, March 25, 1809, *ibid.*, 694; *id.* to *id.*, March 31, 1809, *ibid.*, 695-96.
[45] *Democratic Press*, March 27, 1809.
[46] *House Journal, 1808-1809*, pp. 841, 891, 897-902, 904, 915-16; *Senate Journal, 1808-1809*, pp. 523, 526-27, 529; Mitchell *et al.* (comps.), *Statutes at Large*, XVIII, 1163-64.
[47] Sergeant to Snyder, April 5, 1809, in *Pennsylvania Archives*, 4th Series, IV, 696-97.
[48] Boileau to Sergeant, April 7, 1809, *ibid.*, 699-700.
[49] Snyder to Madison, April 7, 1809, *ibid.*, 698-99.
[50] Madison to Snyder, April 15, 1809, *ibid.*, 702. The date of the letter is given as April 13 in *Letters and Other Writings of James Madison*, 4 vols. (New York, 1884), II, 438-39.
[51] Richard Bache, Jr., to Walter Franklin, March 27, 1809, in Society Collection (Historical Society of Pennsylvania); Bright to Snyder, April 13, 1809, in *Pennsylvania Archives*, 4th Series, IV, 703-704; William Tilghman to Jasper Yeates, April 11, 1809, in Yeates Papers (Historical Society of Pennsylvania); *U. S. Gazette*, April 10, 1809; *Aurora*, April 11, 13, 1809.
[52] *Ibid.*, April 17, 1809; *U. S. Gazette*, April 15, 1809; *Pennsylvania Archives*, 4th Series, IV, 704-705; Dallas to Gallatin, January 13, 1811, in Gallatin Papers.
[53] Franklin to Snyder, April 15, 1809, in *Pennsylvania Archives*, 4th Series, IV, 706; *id.* to *id.*, April 26, 1809, *ibid.*, 709-10; *Aurora*, April 27, 1809; *Democratic Press*, April 26, 27, 1809.
[54] *Aurora*, May 3, 4, 6, 9, 1809.
[55] *Ibid.*, March 2, 3, 30, April 6, 11, 17, 18, 1809.
[56] Duane to Madison, May 3, 1809, in "Letters of Duane," 320-21.
[57] *Id.* to Jefferson, February 4, 1809, *ibid.*, 319; *Democratic Press*, April 17, 1809; Leib to Jonathan Roberts, Jr., December 16, 1809, in Roberts Papers.
[58] *Id.* to *id.*, August 6, 1809, *ibid.*; *id.* to *id.*, December 16, 1809, *ibid.*
[59] *Democratic Press*, April 27, 1809.
[60] *Ibid.*, May 11, 26, 1809.
[61] *Aurora*, July 21, 31, August 9, 1809; *Democratic Press*, July 29, 31, August 9, 1809.

[62] *Aurora*, August 2, 30, 1809; *Democratic Press*, April 15, 1809. See also p. 139 above.
[63] *Aurora*, August 2, 1809. The German paper referred to was John Geyer's *Neue Philadelphische Correspondenz*. See Brigham, "Bibliography of American Newspapers, 1690-1820," in *AAS Proceedings*, XXXII (1922), 148-50.
[64] Harrisburg *Dauphin Guardian*, August 29, 1809; Pittsburgh *Commonwealth*, August 2, 1809; *Democratic Press*, August 21, 1809; Binns, *Recollections*, 311-15.
[65] *Aurora*, September 6, 12, 1809; *Democratic Press*, September 7, 1809.
[66] *Ibid.*, September 18, 1809.
[67] *Ibid.*, September 18, 19, 21, 22, 26, 29, 30, 1809.
[68] *U. S. Gazette*, June 14, 30, July 6, August 18, 19, 21, 22, 23, 24, 29, 31, September 1, 22, 23, 26, 1809; *Aurora*, September 27, 1809.
[69] *Ibid.*, September 30, 1809; *Democratic Press*, September 30, 1809.
[70] *Aurora*, October 12, 14, 1809.
[71] *Ibid.*, October 18, 1809; Harrisburg *Dauphin Guardian*, September 13, 19, 26, October 3, 17, 1809; Pittsburgh *Commonwealth*, July 19, 26, August 2, 9, 16, 30, September 13, October 4, 18, 1809; Pittsburgh *Gazette*, September 20, 27, 1809.
[72] *Democratic Press*, November 14, 1809.
[73] *Aurora*, October 18, 1809.

FOOTNOTES FOR CHAPTER IX

[1] Jonathan Roberts to Mathew Roberts, December 7, 1809, in Roberts Papers. Since Jonathan Roberts, Sr., died shortly after the close of the legislative session of 1808-1809, Jonathan Roberts, Jr., will hereafter be designated simply as Jonathan Roberts, which was the way he referred to himself. On his father's death, see Philip S. Klein (ed.), "Memoirs of a Senator from Pennsylvania: Jonathan Roberts, 1771-1854," in *PMHB*, LXII (1938), 96.

[2] Roberts to Mathew Roberts, December 7, 1809, in Roberts Papers; *id.* to *id.*, December 16, 1809, *ibid.*; *Aurora*, December 7, 11, 1809.

[3] *Pennsylvania Archives*, 4th Series, IV, 678-80.

[4] The vote appears in *House Journal, 1809-1810*, pp. 402-403. The analysis according to political affiliations is based upon the list given in the *Democratic Press*, November 14, 1809, which is used in this study for the analysis of other votes in the session. It differs from the vote analysis in the same paper on February 8, 1810, which stated that the minority was made up of eleven Federalists, eleven Quids, and eleven Democrats. Jonathan Roberts broke it down in still another fashion, stating that the minority was composed of seventeen Federalists and Quids and sixteen Old School Democrats. Roberts to Mathew Roberts, February 4, 1810, in Roberts Papers. This indicates how uncertain party lines were in some instances.

[5] The House proceedings on the Olmsted affair appear in *House Journal, 1809-1810*, pp. 32, 46-47, 84-97, 118-19, 134, 142-46, 238-39, 250-54, 281-82, 296-97, 310, 315-18, 332, 382, 389, 402-26, 433-36. The report of the committee appears on pp. 250-54; and Duane's substitute resolutions are printed on pp. 403-23.

[6] Roberts to Mathew Roberts, February 4, 1810, in Roberts Papers; *Senate Journal, 1809-1810*, pp. 226-33.

[7] *Ibid.*, 304-305, 308-13, 376-82, 454, 461-63, 467, 474-77, 485-86; *House Journal, 1809-1810*, pp. 824-25.

[8] See "Conrad Weiser," in *Aurora*, January 25, 1810; *Democratic Press*, January 15, 17, 20, 1810; Roberts to Mathew Roberts, January 13, 1810 in Roberts Papers. See also n. 9 below.

[9] "Conrad Weiser," in *Aurora*, January 12, 13, 29, February 10, 14, 1810. The last two articles give additional reason to believe that "Conrad Weiser" was William J. Duane because their statements on the northwestern lands dispute follow so closely the views of Callender Irvine given in his letter to Duane, January 22, 1810, in Northern, Interior, and Western Counties Papers (Historical Society of Pennsylvania).

[10] "Conrad Weiser," in *Aurora*, January 8, 9, 10, 12, 17, 18, 20, 1810.

[11] "Conrad Weiser," *ibid.*, January 16, 17, 22, 1810; "Truth," *ibid.*, January 18, 1810; "One of the People," *ibid.*, January 19, 22, 23, 30, 1810; "Stophel Funk," *ibid.*, January 20, 25, 27, February 1, 1810; "Philo-Veritas," *ibid.*, January 30, 1810; "Jacob Fulmer," *ibid.*, January 31, February 1, 2, 8, 1810.

[12] *Ibid.*, January 19, February 7, 13, 15, 16, 17, 1810; *Democratic Press*, February 16, 1810.

[13] *Ibid.*, December 20, 1809; January 18, 19, 20, 1810.

[14] *Ibid.*, January 19, 20, 1810. William J. Duane later asserted that he had not denied applying for the office, but that he had only denied that his application had been turned down. His explanation is given at length in his letter in the *Aurora*, September 2, 1816.

[15] *Democratic Press*, February 5, 1810.

[16] Roberts to Mathew Roberts, January 13, 1810, in Roberts Papers.

[17] *Ibid.*

[18] *Id.* to *id.*, February 4, 1810, *ibid.* Italics mine. John Thompson was the Representative from Philadelphia County whose gumboil played such an important part in the senatorial election in January, 1807. John Tod was a Representative from Bedford County who had opposed Snyder's actions in the previous session. Although he often voted with the Old School, he was not properly one of that group and followed an independent course.

[19] Robert Porter to General Andrew Porter, February 15, 1810, in Porter Collection.
[20] *Democratic Press,* January 6, 1809; April 26, May 3, 7, 10, 23, 1810.
[21] *Ibid.,* July 16, 1810; *Aurora,* July 26, 1810.
[22] *Ibid.,* July 26, August 9, 1810; *Democratic Press,* July 25, 1810.
[23] *Ibid.,* August 15, 1810.
[24] *Ibid.,* April 28, May 12, 21, June 14, 15, 18, July 17, 24, 26, 27, August 7, 11, 14, 1810.
[25] *Aurora,* April 19, June 5, 12, July 21, 24, 1810.
[26] "Democritus," in *Evening Star,* quoted in *Aurora,* August 17, 1810. The *Evening Star* began publication on July 4, 1810. See Brigham, "Bibliography of American Newspapers, 1690-1820," in *AAS Proceedings,* XXXII (1922), 112.
[27] *Aurora,* August 22, 1810.
[28] For proceedings of the ward meetings, see *ibid.,* July 25, 27, 28, 30, August 1, 3, 4, 11, 15, 17, 1810; *Democratic Press,* July 26, 27, 28, August 1, 2, 3, 1810.
[29] *Ibid.,* May 20, August 14, 1809.
[30] *Ibid.,* April 2, 1810.
[31] *Ibid.,* June 6, 1810.
[32] *Ibid.,* July 27, 1810.
[33] *Ibid.,* August 30, 1810.
[34] *Ibid.,* September 1, 3, 4, 5, 6, 8, 1810.
[35] *Aurora,* September 14, 17, 1810; *Democratic Press,* September 17, 21, 1810.
[36] *Aurora,* September 3, 1810.
[37] *Democratic Press,* August 3, 1810.
[38] *Ibid.,* July 25, August 15, 18, 23, 1810; *U. S. Gazette,* July 6, August 30, September 11, 1810.
[39] *Ibid.,* August 22, 23, 24, 25, 28, 29, September 1, 11, 12, 13, 15, 18, 1810.
[40] *Aurora,* October 1, 1810.
[41] *Democratic Press,* September 29, 1810.
[42] Election returns are printed in *ibid.,* October 16, 1810; *Aurora,* October 12, 15, 1810.
[43] Pittsburgh *Commonwealth,* January 24, February 21, June 11, July 23, 30, August 13, 20, 1810; *Pittsburgh Gazette,* February 2, 1810.
[44] Pittsburgh *Commonwealth,* July 2, September 3, 10, 17, 24, October 19, 1810.
[45] *Ibid.,* September 3, 17, 24, October 1, 1810; *Pittsburgh Gazette,* October 19, 1810.
[46] *Aurora,* September 22, 1810.
[47] *Ibid., Democratic Press,* September 28, 1810.
[48] *Ibid.,* November 14, 1810.
[49] *Pennsylvania Archives,* 4th Series, IV, 677.
[50] *Aurora,* February 7, 1810.
[51] Tilghman to Jasper Yeates, February 18, 1810, in Yeates Papers.
[52] George Bryan to Jonathan Roberts, February 26, 1812, in Roberts Papers; John Connelly to *id.,* April 3, 1812, *ibid.* The quotation is from Connelly's letter.
[53] *Pennsylvania Archives,* 4th Series, IV, 728-36.
[54] *U. S. Gazette,* December 8, 1810.
[55] *Aurora,* December 11, 1810.
[56] Biddle to Mrs. Margaret Craig, December 19, 1810, in Biddle-Craig Papers (Historical Society of Pennsylvania).
[57] *House Journal, 1810-1811,* pp. 25, 405-409, 588.
[58] *Ibid.,* 585, 595-96, 631-32, 640-41, 698; *Senate Journal, 1810-1811,* pp. 415, 427-30, 471-72, 474; *Acts of the General Assembly of the Commonwealth of Pennsylvania . . .* [1810-1811] (Lancaster, 1811), 113.
[59] *House Journal, 1810-1811,* pp. 286, 486-87, 521, 532, 543-44, 632-34, 642; *Senate Journal, 1810-1811.* pp. 326, 379, 386, 401-404, 406-407, 422; *Acts of the General Assembly* [1810-1811], 78-83.
[60] Ferguson, *Western Pennsylvania Politics,* 198-99; Buck and Buck, *Planting of Civilization,* 486; Evans, *Holland Land Company,* 160-69; Jacob Herrington to General Andrew Porter, July 20, 1810, in Porter Collection; *Pittsburgh Gazette,* September 21, 1810.
[61] Adams, *History,* V, 207-209, 327-37.

NOTES—CHAPTER IX

[62] *Democratic Press*, March 29, 1810; *Aurora*, January 8, May 8, 1810.
[63] *Ibid.*, November 8, 1810-February 23, 1811; *Democratic Press*, January 14, 17, 24, February 19, 1811.
[64] *Aurora*, February 13, 15, 16, 25, 1811; *Democratic Press*, February 20, 1811.
[65] *House Journal, 1810-1811*, pp. 65-70, 129, 153, 159-60, 168-69, 172, 183-84, 211-13, 217-18; *Senate Journal, 1810-1811*, pp. 92-93, 94, 98, 101, 103-105, 107.
[66] *House Journal, 1810-1811*, pp. 665-66, 681, 716-17.
[67] *Democratic Press*, December 26, 1810.
[68] *Aurora*, January 25, 1811; Pittsburgh *Commonwealth*, October 1, 1810.
[69] *Democratic Press*, February 20, 21, 1811.
[70] *Lancaster Journal*, quoted in *Pittsburgh Gazette*, May 3, 1811.
[71] *Aurora*, April 6, 1811; *Democratic Press*, April 13, May 31, 1811.
[72] *Aurora*, October 18, 1809; September 3, November 14, 1810; *Democratic Press*, January 21, 22, 23, 24, February 7, 1811.
[73] *Ibid.*, November 28, 1810; January 25, 1811.
[74] The document quoted in the text is apparently the rough draft of a letter. Without date, addressee, signature or other identifying marks, it is filed under "Simon Snyder" in the Society Collection of the Historical Society of Pennsylvania. The contents, however, give a reasonably clear notion of its date, addressee, and author. It was written sometime after December 17, 1810, when the first legislative caucus took place, and before January 25, 1811, when the *Democratic Press* reported the discontinuance of the *Evening Star*. As the Whig Society meetings were held on the second Thursday of each month, which would have been January 10, the letter was therefore probably written on January 11, 1811. The addressee was almost certainly Michael Leib, who was attending the United States Senate in Washington and who had long been the "Life & Spirit" of the Old School faction. The writer of the letter appears from the portion not quoted in the text to have been a Federal officeholder in Philadelphia under whom Leib proposed (in an act he was sponsoring) to place the functions then performed by Tench Coxe, the Purveyor of Public Supplies. Exactly who this was is uncertain; but it was probably either John Steele, Collector of the Port, or William Linnard, Military Agent, both of whom were supporters of the Old School.
[75] See, for example, *Aurora*, January 1, 2, 4, 8, May 8, June 6, 14, 16, July 20, 21, 23, 24, 25, 27, 28, 30, 31, August 1, 6, 8, September 18, December 18, 20, 21, 24, 25, 27, 28, 29, 31, 1810. See also, Duane to Henry Dearborn, July 3, 1810, in "Letters of Duane," 334-38.
[76] These attacks began in the issue of February 11 and continued almost without pause until the end of August. A good portion of the later articles were concerned with the dismissal of Robert Smith as Secretary of State. On the damaging nature of the attacks upon Gallatin as "an irresistible magician," see Adams, *Gallatin*, 437-39.
[77] *Aurora*, February 11, April 8, 1811.
[78] Duane to Jefferson, March 15, 1811, in "Letters of Duane," 345-48.
[79] *Ibid.*; Jefferson to Duane, March 28, 1811, in Ford (ed.), *Works of Jefferson*, XI, 189-95; *id.* to Madison, April 24, 1811, *ibid.*, 201-203; *id.* to Duane, April 30, 1811, *ibid.*, 195-97; *id.* to William Wirt, May 3, 1811, *ibid.*, 198-201; Madison to Jefferson, May 3, 1811, in Gaillard Hunt (ed.), *The Writings of James Madison*, 9 vols. (New York, 1900-1910), VIII, 150-51; *id.* to *id.*, June 7, 1811, *ibid.*, 156.
[80] Duane to *id.*, July 5, 1811, in "Letters of Duane," 348-49; *Aurora*, August 7, 1811.
[81] Dallas to Gallatin, January 13, 1811, in Gallatin Papers; Leiper to Madison, January 14, 1811, in Madison Papers; Leib to *id.*, February 7, 1811, *ibid.*
[82] *Id.* to *id.*, April 18, 1811, *ibid.*; *Democratic Press*, April 26, 1811; Binns to Gallatin, April 27, 1811, in Gallatin Papers.
[83] *Democratic Press*, November 3, 1810; February 19, 1811.
[84] Binns to Gallatin, April 27, 1811, in Gallatin Papers. The appointment at Commissioner of Loans went to Blair McClenachan, who had been recommended by Dallas. Dallas to *id.*, April 26, 1811, *ibid.*
[85] "Franklin," in *Democratic Press*, August 19, 1811.
[86] McKean to John Way, July 16, 1811, in Dreer Collection. In this letter McKean wrote that he had been besought to run by "*Individuals* of all parties," but that he

would not relinquish his comfortable retirement "without it was the desire of a majority of my fellow citizens; and I have heard nothing from the Western counties."

[87] *Democratic Press,* May 20, 1811; Nicholas Biddle to James Monroe, June 6, 1811, in Monroe Papers (Library of Congress).

[88] *Democratic Press,* August 14, 19, 20, 28, 1811.

[89] *Ibid.,* August 20, 24, 1811; *U. S. Gazette,* August 20, 1811.

[90] James Milnor *et al.* to William Tilghman, August 24, 1811, in Tilghman Correspondence; Tilghman to Milnor *et al.,* September 2, 1811, copy, *ibid.; id.* to Milnor, September 2, 1811, copy, *ibid.*

[91] *Democratic Press,* August 2, 3, 6, 8, 9, 13, 17, September 3, 19, 1811; *Aurora,* August 1, 3, 5, 6, 7, 8, 10, 13, 1811. For an Old School view of the Snyderite tactics, see their address in *ibid.,* September 20, 1811.

[92] *Democratic Press,* August 6, 7, 12, 28, September 9, 1811; *Aurora,* August 7, 13, 28, 1811.

[93] *Ibid.,* July 20, August 7, 21, September 3, 1811.

[94] *Ibid.,* September 20, 1811.

[95] *Ibid.,* August 20, 1811.

[96] *U. S. Gazette,* July 31, August 16, 17, 19, 20, 21, 22, 23, 24, 26, 29, September 17, 23, October 5, 1811.

[97] *Democratic Press,* October 11, 12, 1811.

[98] *House Journal, 1811-1812,* pp. 82-83. The official returns for some unexplained reason omit the returns from Allegheny County. This county gave Snyder 1,652 votes, so that his total vote should have been 53,971. See Pittsburgh *Commonwealth,* October 14, 1811.

[99] *Democratic Press,* November 5, 1811.

[100] Pittsburgh *Commonwealth,* February 25, March 18, 25, 1811.

[101] *Ibid.,* July 15, 22, August 19, 1811.

[102] *Ibid.,* September 2, 23, 30, 1811.

[103] *Ibid.,* September 23, 1811.

[104] *Ibid.,* September 23, 30, 1811; *Pittsburgh Gazette,* September 27, 1811.

[105] Pittsburgh *Commonwealth,* October 14, 21, 1811.

FOOTNOTES FOR CHAPTER X

[1] Jones to Macon, November 16, 1808, in Jones and Clarke Papers.
[2] The House proceedings on the resolutions appear in *House Journal, 1808-1809*, pp. 14-16, 37-38, 54-55, 58, 70-76, 132-33. Portions quoted appear on pp. 15, 71.
[3] *Aurora*, January 18, 23, 1809.
[4] *Ibid.*, January 25, 1809.
[5] *U. S. Gazette*, January 24, 27, 30, 1809; *Aurora*, January 28, 30, 31, 1809; Tilghman to Jasper Yeates, January 31, 1809, in Society Collection (Historical Society of Pennsylvania); Truxtun to Jonathan Dayton, February 18, 1809, in Gratz Collection.
[6] *U. S. Gazette*, January 31, 1809.
[7] *Ibid.*, February 1, 1809; Truxtun to Dayton, February 18, 1809, in Gratz Collection; *Aurora*, February 1, 2, 1809.
[8] *Ibid.*, February 1, 1809.
[9] *U. S. Gazette*, February 2, 10, 11, 13, 1809; Truxtun to Dayton, February 18, 1809, in Gratz Collection.
[10] A meeting in Pittsburgh on February 18 gave somewhat equivocal approval to the embargo while announcing hearty support of war if that were deemed expedient. Pittsburgh *Commonwealth*, February 22, 1809. A meeting in Harrisburg on February 22 also approved the embargo and pledged support to any measures including war which might be adopted to uphold American rights. Harrisburg *Dauphin Guardian*, February 28, 1809.
[11] Adams, *History*, IV, 454.
[12] *Aurora*, February 9, 10, March 1, 4, 1809.
[13] Jones to Giles, February 4, 1809, copy, in Smith Collection.
[14] An interesting example of war sentiment and of Democratic antipathy toward Great Britain appeared in the *Aurora*, January 25, 1809. The article in question was a speech intended to have been delivered at the meeting on January 23. Thomas Leiper was the author although the *Aurora* does not mention his name. See his letter to Jefferson, January 26, 1809, in Jefferson Papers. In the proposed speech, Leiper said in part: "For certainly we are arrived to that period that either the orders of [*sic*] council of the 11th of November, and the acts of parliament that are bottomed on them must be repealed, as to us, or we must *do what?* — For my part I see no alternative, we must *fight them* once more, as we fought before, and I believe we can give now as good an account of them as we did then, and in a shorter time too." As for France, Leiper believed that Napoleon was only following the British example, and that her decrees would be repealed when the orders in council were rescinded.
[15] Adams, *History*, V, 71-73.
[16] *U. S. Gazette*, April 24, June 10, 1809.
[17] *Ibid.*, July 20, 21, 26, August 12, 15, 1809.
[18] *Aurora*, July 21, 1809.
[19] *Democratic Press*, August 16, 1809.
[20] Adams, *History*, V, 96-105, 115-32.
[21] *U. S. Gazette*, November 16, 23, December 5, 1809.
[22] *House Journal, 1809-1810*, pp. 12-15, 46, 49, 64-65, 104-105, 180-81, 730-31; *Senate Journal, 1809-1810*, pp. 104-105, 133, 264-66, 402-403, 418.
[23] On Giles's resolutions, see Adams, *History*, V, 178-79, 181-83. On Macon's Bill No. 1, see *ibid.*, 183-84.
[24] *Democratic Press*, December 22, 1809.
[25] *Ibid.*, January 10, 11, 18, 19, 20, February 9, 16, 1810; *Aurora*, January 10, 17, 18, 19, 20, 23, 24, 1810.
[26] *Ibid.*, February 16, 1810; *Democratic Press*, February 14, 1810.
[27] *Ibid.*, February 16, 1810; *Aurora*, February 15, 16, 17, 1810.
[28] Adams, *History*, V, 194-97.
[29] *Democratic Press*, May 10, 1810.

[30] *Aurora*, May 26, 1810.
[31] See *Pittsburgh Gazette,* September 28, 1810.
[32] *Aurora,* October 25, 1808; *Democratic Press,* October 29, 1810.
[33] *Poulson's American Daily Advertiser,* October 22, 1808; *Democratic Press,* October 16, 1810. On Richards's withdrawal, see pp. 219-20 above.
[34] *Poulson's American Daily Advertiser,* October 19, 1808; *Democratic Press,* October 16, 1810.
[35] *Aurora,* September 25, 1810; Adams, *History,* V, 253-56, 302-304.
[36] *U. S. Gazette,* December 13, 1810.
[37] *Pennsylvania Archives,* 4th Series, IV, 728-29.
[38] *Aurora,* May 27, August 8, 1811.
[39] Adams, *History,* VI, 124-26.
[40] *Aurora,* November 7, 8, 9, 1811.
[41] Richard T. Leech to Roberts, November 8, 1811, in Roberts Papers.
[42] *U. S. Gazette,* November 12, December 6, 1811; *Pittsburgh Gazette,* December 13, 1811.
[43] *Pennsylvania Archives,* 4th Series, IV, 746-49.
[44] *Senate Journal, 1811-1812,* pp. 9-12, 29, 32, 39, 40, 43, 61, 63; *House Journal, 1811-1812,* pp. 81, 101, 104-10, 115.
[45] *Ibid.,* 422, 430, 452-53, 497, 500, 718; *Senate Journal, 1811-1812,* pp. 325, 376, 400, 403-404, 519, 557.
[46] *House Journal, 1811-1812,* pp. 584, 593-94, 629, 637, 656, 705-706; *Senate Journal, 1811-1812,* pp. 478, 515.
[47] *House Journal, 1811-1812,* pp. 69, 103, 260-61, 271, 302-304. The stockholders of the bank did a great deal of lobbying to obtain the charter. See the correspondence between Stephen Girard and Thomas Willing Francis in December, 1811, and January, 1812, in the Girard Collection.
[48] *Senate Journal, 1811-1812,* pp. 88-92, 103-104, 222-23, 242-44. The proposed system for amendments would have worked as follows: the third legislature after the adoption of the proposed changes and every tenth legislature thereafterward was to be authorized to adopt amendments to the Constitution. If these were approved by the succeeding legislature, they were to become effective.
[49] *House Journal, 1811-1812,* pp. 412-14, 532-35.
[50] Harrisburg *Pennsylvania Republican,* January 21, March 3, 1812.
[51] *Acts of the General Assembly of the Commonwealth of Pennsylvania* . . . [1811-1812], (Lancaster, 1812), 127-30. See also, Lehman, "Gerrymandering," 84-86. The most important changes were the following: Chester and Montgomery counties were linked to form a two-member district, as were Lancaster and Dauphin. The representation of the first district, consisting of Philadelphia and Delaware counties and the city of Philadelphia, was increased from three to four. Allegheny and Butler counties were formed into a single-member district, while Beaver and the other northwestern counties made up another. York County was given one representative; and Adams was grouped with Cumberland and Franklin counties in a two-member district. The changes made with respect to Lancaster, Chester, and Adams counties were intended to offset their Federalist vote by a greater Democratic strength.
[52] *Democratic Press,* February 18, 1812; *Aurora,* February 24, 1812; J. Swaine to Jonathan Roberts, March 20, 1812, in Roberts Papers. Swaine was editor of the *Norristown Register.*
[53] For the attacks on Eustis, see *Aurora,* December 24, 31, 1811; January 9, 1812. For those on Gallatin, see *ibid.,* January 25, 28, February 1, 11, March 7, 11, 1812.
[54] John Henry was a British agent who had been sent from Canada into New England in 1808 and 1809 to determine what attitude that section would take in case of war with Great Britain. He was also instructed to serve as a link with the British government for any Federalists who might desire to correspond with it. Although Henry had social relations with a number of prominent members of that party, none made overtures to him; and he returned to Canada without having disclosed his true status. Disgruntled because he thought the British had not sufficiently rewarded him, Henry sold his letters through an intermediary to Secretary of State James Monroe

for $50,000. They were sent to Congress in a special message by Madison on March 9, 1812. Adams, *History*, IV, 243-48, 460-61; VI, 176-84.

[55] See comments in *Poulson's American Daily Advertiser*, March 13, 14, 16, 17, 18, 1812; *Pittsburgh Gazette*, March 20, 27, April 3, 1812; *U. S. Gazette*, March 11, 12, 13, 14, 16, 17, 19, 20, 24, 1812.

[56] *Aurora*, March 13, 14, 15, 18, 1812; Harrisburg *Pennsylvania Republican*, March 31, 1812; Swaine to Roberts, March 20, 1812, in Roberts Papers; Samuel Maffet to *id.*, March 28, 1812, *ibid.* Maffet was editor of the Wilkes-Barre *Susquehanna Democrat*.

[57] See *U. S. Gazette*, November 12, 18, 23, 1811; March 10, 1812; *Poulson's American Daily Advertiser*, March 11, 1812.

[58] See, for example, *U. S. Gazette*, November 12, 1811.

[59] "Christian Politician," in *Trenton Gazette*, quoted in *Poulson's American Daily Advertiser*, February 1, 1812.

[60] For the development of the theme, see *U. S. Gazette*, November 12, December 6, 12, 1811; February 5, March 16, 19, April 2, 3, 7, 8, 9, 14, 16, 1812.

[61] *Aurora*, April 2, 7, 16, 1812; Pittsburgh *Commonwealth*, April 14, 1812.

[62] *Aurora*, April 20, 1812. The original letter, dated April 6, 1812, is in the Roberts Papers.

[63] *Aurora*, April 20, 1812. A draft copy of Roberts's reply is in the Roberts Papers.

[64] See Edward Fox to Roberts, April 20, 1812, in Roberts Papers; Charles Biddle to *id.*, June 27, 1812, *ibid.*

[65] Harrisburg *Pennsylvania Republican*, April 28, 1812.

[66] Binns to Roberts, May 5, 1812, in Roberts Papers.

[67] *Aurora*, May 11, 15, 16, 1812.

[68] Manuel Eyre to Roberts, May 18, 1812, in Roberts Papers; *Democratic Press*, May 21, 1812.

[69] *U. S. Gazette*, May 21, 1812; *Aurora*, May 21, 1812; *Democratic Press*, May 21, 1812; John Connelly to Roberts, May 21, 1812, in Roberts Papers.

[70] *Aurora*, May 21, 1812; *U. S. Gazette*, May 23, 1812; *Democratic Press*, May 22, 1812; Edward Fox to Roberts, May 20, 1812, in Roberts Papers; Binns to *id.*, May 24, 1812, *ibid.*

[71] *U. S. Gazette*, May 20, 23, 30, June 4, 6, 1812.

[72] *Ibid.*, May 27, 1812; Roberts to William Jones, June 7, 1812, in Smith Collection.

[73] Thomas J. Rogers to Roberts, May 24, 1812, in Roberts Papers. Rogers was editor of the Easton *Northampton Farmer*.

[74] *Aurora*, June 18, 1812.

[75] Adams, *History*, VI, 221-28; *Democratic Press*, June 22, 1812.

[76] *Aurora*, June 16, 1812.

[77] Rogers to Jonathan Roberts, June 14, 1812, in Roberts Papers; Jonathan Roberts to Mathew Roberts, June 7, 1812, *ibid.*; *id* to *id.*, June 17, 1812, *ibid.*; Edward Fox to Jonathan Roberts, June 24, 1812, *ibid.* It was Fox who believed that Leib would have supported the war if the administration had been against it.

[78] *Democratic Press*, June 22, 1812. Leib's statement is quoted from an article signed "One of the Conferees," *ibid.*, September 13, 1813.

[79] In Harrisburg the Federalists were reported to be determined "to go every length to support the Measure, and that no Man should be permitted to remain in our country, who dare oppose the measures we have adopted." General Andrew Porter to George B. Porter, June 26, 1812, in Porter Collection. Charles Biddle, a prominent Federalist in Philadelphia, wrote that he was opposed to war at that time but since it had been declared he felt it the duty of all good citizens to support the government to the utmost. Biddle to Roberts, June 27, 1812, in Roberts Papers.

[80] *U. S. Gazette*, June 23, 1812.

[81] See Chapters VII and VIII above.

[82] *Aurora*, April 8, 1811.

[83] *Ibid.*, March 9, 1812.

[84] *Democratic Press*, January 28, 1812.

[85] *Ibid.*, January 29, March 5, 9, 1812.

[86] *Niles' Weekly Register*, II (1812), 32; *Aurora*, March 28, 1812.

[87] Binns to Abner Lacock, April 2, 1812, in James M. Swank Papers (Historical Society of Pennsylvania).
[88] *Id.* to Roberts, April 26, 1812, in Roberts Papers; *id.* to *id.*, May 3, 1812, *ibid.*
[89] The proceedings of the caucus together with a list of those present appear in *Niles' Weekly Register*, II, 192-93. The caucus chose John Langdon of New Hampshire as candidate for Vice President. After he declined, a second caucus on June 8 nominated Elbridge Gerry of Massachusetts. At this second caucus William Crawford of Pennsylvania announced his support of the nomination of Madison. *Ibid.*, 276. Leib's attitude is described by Jonathan Roberts in a letter to Mathew Roberts, May 20, 1812, in Roberts Papers. In the same letter Roberts expressed his opinion on the probable course of the absent members. He erred in assuming that Joseph Lefever of Lancaster would concur in the nomination. See pp. 259-60 below.
[90] *Aurora*, May 20, 1812.
[91] *Niles' Weekly Register*, II, 235; De Alva S. Alexander, *A Political History of the State of New York*, 2 vols. (New York, 1906), I, 201-202.
[92] For the activities of the Clintonians in the State, see *Democratic Press*, August 1, 31, September 5, October 10, 1812; Pittsburgh *Commonwealth*, September 15, October 13, 27, 1812; Pittsburgh *Mercury*, September 17, 1812; Harrisburg *Pennsylvania Republican*, September 8, 1812; James M. Porter to General Andrew Porter, August 8, 1812, in Porter Collection; James Hamilton to Gallatin, September 9, 1812, in Gallatin Papers.
[93] The proceeding and address are printed in *Poulson's American Daily Advertiser*, September 1, 1812. The *Democratic Press*, September 5, 1812, prints a letter from Lancaster which describes the machinations which lay behind the meeting.
[94] *U. S. Gazette*, September 9, 26, 28, 1812; Pittsburgh *Commonwealth*, September 29, 1812; *Democratic Press*, October 9, 1812. The first ticket of electors included Richard Palmer and Samuel Castor, staunch Old School men of Philadelphia County. See list in *U. S. Gazette*, October 8, 1812. Jared Ingersoll was a Philadelphia lawyer of great distinction, then serving as Attorney General of the State by appointment of Governor Snyder. He had never been active in politics but was generally considered a Federalist. His son, Charles J. Ingersoll, was an ardent supporter of Madison and the war and was running for re-election to Congress on the Democratic ticket in 1812. See Witt Bowden, "Jared Ingersoll," in *DAB*, IX, 468-69.
[95] King (ed.), *Rufus King*, V, 265-66.
[96] See *U. S. Gazette*, April 27, June 5, July 17, 22, 1812.
[97] Morris to Mr. [Charles Willing?] Hare, June 30, 1812, in Anne C. Morris (ed.), *The Diary and Letters of Gouverneur Morris*, 2 vols. (New York, 1888), II, 542-43; *id.* to Benjamin R. Morgan, August 20, 1812, in Jared Sparks, *The Life of Gouverneur Morris, with Selections from his Correspondence and Miscellaneous Papers*, 3 vols. (Boston, 1832), III, 273-74.
[98] King to Christopher Gore, September 19, 1812, in King (ed.), *Rufus King*, V, 276-80.
[99] Pickering to Edward Pennington, July 12, 1812, in Henry Adams (ed.), *Documents Relating to New-England Federalism, 1800-1815* (Boston, 1877), 389.
[100] On the views of Otis, see Josiah Ogden Hoffman to Otis, July 17, 1812, in Samuel E. Morison, *The Life and Letters of Harrison Gray Otis, Federalist, 1765-1848*, 2 vols. (Boston and New York, 1913), I, 316-17; Otis to William Sullivan, August 17, [1812]. *ibid.*, 318. On the motives of Federalist supporters of Clinton, see Oliver Wolcott to George Gibbs, November 7, 1812, in Oliver Wolcott Letters (Library of Congress); and Gore to King, October 5, 1812, in King (ed.), *Rufus King*, V, 281-84. On the meeting in Connecticut, see *ibid.*, 272; Morison, *Otis*, I, 308. For a sample letter of the Philadelphia correspondence committee soliciting attendance at the New York convention, see Horace Binney to Charles F. Mercer, August 13, 1812, in Personal Papers, Miscellaneous (Library of Congress).
[101] Notes of King, in King (ed.), *Rufus King*, V, 268-70.
[102] The best account of the convention is given in King to Gore, September 19, 1812, *ibid.*, 276-80; and in King's notes of the proceedings printed as a note in *ibid.*, 280-81. An account from the point of view of a delegate who favored support of Clinton is given by Robert G. Harper to Colonel John Lynn, September 25, 1812, in Bernard C.

Steiner, *The Life and Correspondence of James McHenry* (Cleveland, 1907), 583-86. John S. Murdock, "The First National Nominating Convention," in *AHR*, I (1896), 680-83, is not trustworthy since it appeared before the publication of King's correspondence and relied upon the recollections of William Sullivan made a considerable period after the event.

[103] *Democratic Press,* September 14, 25, 30, 1812. The *Press* listed John B. Wallace, Joseph Hopkinson, Horace Binney, and Robert Wharton as the Philadelphia delegates and "Lawyers Watts and Duncan" of Carlisle as the others. Binney's circular letter does not mention Watts but includes Samuel Sitgreaves of Easton. The last was certainly present as he was mentioned by Harper as one of those who opposed supporting a non-Federalist candidate. Harper to Lynn, September 25, 1812, in Steiner, *McHenry*, 584.

[104] *U. S. Gazette,* October 2, 1812.

[105] *National Intelligencer* (triweekly), October 15, 1812; *U. S. Gazette,* October 24, 1812. The account in the *Intelligencer* includes statements made by Clinton to Morris, Jay, and King in the conference on August 5, although it is written in such fashion as to give the impression that this discussion took place at the time of the convention in September. This was one point on which Otis attacked it most strongly. However, Harper stated that Clinton's assurances to the Federalists were repeated while he was in New York; and Otis must have had knowledge of this. Harper to Lynn, September 25, 1812, in Steiner, *McHenry*, 584. Otis's letter is filled with quibbles and in some particulars contains demonstrable lies.

[106] Address of the Federal Republican conferees of the city of Philadelphia, October 17, 1812, in *U. S. Gazette,* October 20, 1812.

[107] A good sampling of the Democratic attitude may be found in the ward resolutions in July. *Aurora,* July 22, 23, 25, 27, 28, 29, 1812. See also the address of the Philadelphia Democratic general ward committee, *ibid.,* September 5, 1812.

[108] These opinions with variations in emphasis appear in Federalist articles throughout the campaign. Their essence is conveniently expressed in an address adopted by the Federalist Young Men of the City and County of Philadelphia which appeared in the *U. S. Gazette,* August 24, 1812.

[109] The foregoing discussion is based upon an analysis of Clintonian addresses issued by meetings at York, Lancaster, and Pittsburgh which were published in *U. S. Gazette,* September 9, 28, 1812; Pittsburgh *Mercury,* October 8, 1812. The Pittsburgh address was unequivocal in support of the war and devoted most of its attention to the incompetence of the administration. The York and Lancaster addresses appeared to avoid the subject as much as possible in favor of other issues.

[110] *Aurora,* August 12, 1812; *Democratic Press,* September 25, 1812.

[111] The proceedings of the ward and district meetings are given in the *Aurora,* July 22, 23, 25, 27, 28, 29, August 3, 4, 6, 8, 11, 12, 1812. See also, William J. Duane to Joseph Hiester, August 16, 1812, in Gregg Collection; Dallas to Gallatin, October 5, 1812, in Gallatin Papers; Leiper to Madison, August 16, 1812, in Madison Papers.

[112] *Aurora,* September 7, 11, 1812.

[113] For the proceedings and address of the meeting, see *ibid.,* September 23, 1812. For Snyderite comments, *Democratic Press,* September 28, 1812.

[114] *Ibid.,* October 9, 1812.

[115] The situation in Pittsburgh was exceedingly complex. It can be followed in Pittsburgh *Commonwealth,* August 18, 25, September 8, 15, 22, 29, October 6, 1812; Pittsburgh *Mercury,* August 27, September 17, October 1, 8, 1812.

[116] For the activities of the Philadelphia Federalists, see the issues of the *U. S. Gazette,* July 8-October 13, 1812. For those in Pittsburgh, see *Pittsburgh Gazette,* September 11, 18, 25, October 2, 1812.

[117] A list of Federalists elected to the legislature is given in Harrisburg *Pennsylvania Republican,* November 17, 1812. The Federalist margin in Chester County, which had five representatives, was a very narrow one, amounting to slightly more than 100 votes out of a total of nearly 6,300. *Democratic Press,* October 21, 1812.

[118] On the results of the congressional election, see *ibid.,* October 26, 1812. Jacob Bucher was the regular Democratic nominee for Congress for Dauphin County; but some Democrats asserted that he had been nominated by intrigue at the expense

of Edward Crouch. Bucher lost about 700 Democratic votes in the election; and the Federalist majority for Gloninger in Lancaster County gave the latter a majority in the district. See Harrisburg *Pennsylvania Republican,* September 15, 22, October 6, 20, 1812. On Gloninger's political sentiments and attitude toward the war, see *ibid.,* October 6, 20, 1812; General Andrew Porter to George B. Porter, October 28, 1812, in Porter Collection.

[119] *Aurora,* October 16, 1812.

[120] *Ibid.,* October 19, 1812; *Democratic Press,* October 17, 1812.

[121] Pittsburgh *Commonwealth,* October 21, 1812; *Democratic Press,* October 19, 1812.

[122] *U. S. Gazette,* October 14, 16, 17, 20, 21, 22, 23, 26, 28, 30, 1812. See also, Biddle, *Autobiography,* 338-40; *Aurora,* October 21, 1812.

[123] The first version of the ticket appeared in the *U. S. Gazette,* October 8, 1812, being reprinted from the Lancaster *Pennsylvania Farmer.* In addition to McKean and Hiester, it included such well-known figures as William Hoge of Washington County, Charles Porter of Fayette County, James Mountain and James Martin of Allegheny County, and John Sergeant of the city of Philadelphia. This first ticket included three followers of Leib—James Sharswood from the city and Richard Palmer and Samuel Castor from the county of Philadelphia. A second version, printed in the *Gazette,* October 21, 1812, omitted Castor and included Joseph Sansom, a Federalist. For later changes in the ticket, see *ibid.,* October 23, 29, 1812; Pittsburgh *Mercury,* October 29, 1812.

[124] Proceedings of the meeting appear in *U. S. Gazette,* October 20, 1812. See also, *ibid.,* October 23, 29, 1812.

[125] *Aurora,* October 13, 21, 24, 28, 29, 30, 1812.

[126] *Democratic Press,* October 17, 1812. On January 4, 1813, the *Press* published a letter from Carlisle stating that the *Whig Chronicle* was edited by Leib and financed by William Binder and that it had been established primarily to promote the election of Clinton. On January 12, 1813, the *Press* asserted that the *Chronicle* was established by Leib in the Northern Liberties on October 14, 1812, and was last published on January 8, 1813. George F. Goodman, an associate of Leib, is listed as publisher in Brigham, "Bibliography of American Newspapers, 1690-1820," in *AAS Proceedings,* XXXII (1922), 212.

[127] Election returns for 1808 are taken from *House Journal, 1808-1809,* pp. 86-87; *Aurora,* December 16, 1808. Election returns for 1812 are taken from *ibid.,* November 20, 1812; *Democratic Press,* November 21, 1816. The account of the presidential vote for 1812 in the *Aurora* does not give the total vote but lists the majorities by counties. It claims a Madison majority of 20,133, although the figures listed show a total majority of 20,211. Due to this and other discrepancies, the account in the *Democratic Press* has been used in the text. It states that Madison's majority was 19,890 out of a total of 78,004 votes. An attempt to find the actual vote by counties in the State Archives was unsuccessful.

[128] The electoral vote is printed in Stanwood, *History of the Presidency,* 104. On the importance of Pennsylvania in the election, see also, Adams, *History,* VI, 412.

FOOTNOTES FOR CHAPTER XI

[1] For comments on the behavior of Tannehill's brigade, see *Aurora*, October 13, December 25, 1812; January 11, 28, February 4, 9, 1813; *U. S. Gazette*, November 24, December 24, 1812; *Pittsburgh Gazette,* December 18, 1812; Pittsburgh *Mercury,* January 7, 1813. For comments on the volunteers with Harrison's army, see *Aurora*, October 22, November 4, 1812; January 11, February 12, 13, 1813.

[2] On the war resolutions, see *Senate Journal, 1812-1813,* pp. 29-31, 35, 44-49, 76, 79; *House Journal, 1812-1813,* pp. 73, 89, 95-97, 120. On the subscription to the loan, see *Senate Journal, 1812-1813,* pp. 183, 202, 209, 212, 217, 265, 268, 337, 343, 347-48, 413, 414, 417, 549, 563, 579-80, 599; *House Journal, 1812-1813,* pp. 459, 490 493-97, 502, 510, 643-44, 646, 652, 661, 683, 684. The subscription was never made as the loan was completely taken up before it was arranged. See *Pennsylvania Archives*, 4th Series, IV, 828. On the clothing of Pennsylvania troops with Harrison, see *ibid.,* 9th Series, V, 3289-90, 3295. On the bonus, see *ibid.,* 3348, 3365-66. On voting by militia and volunteers, see *House Journal, 1812-1813,* pp. 36-37, 623-24, 634-35, 662; *Senate Journal, 1812-1813,* pp. 539, 547, 554, 558.

[3] For biographical sketches of Lacock, see James H. Peeling, "Abner Lacock," in *DAB*, X, 521-22; J[ames]. M. S[wank]., "General Abner Lacock. United States Senator from Pennsylvania from 1813 to 1819," in *PMHB*, IV (1880), 202-208; *Biographical Directory of the American Congress,* 1196. See also, John Binns to Jonathan Roberts, November 13, 1812, in Roberts Papers; Roberts to Thomas J. Rogers, November 16, 1812, in Dreer Collection.

[4] On the caucus proceedings, see Jesse Bean to Archibald Darrah, December 7, 1812, in Roberts Papers. Bean was a Representative from Montgomery County who attended the caucus.

[5] *House Journal, 1812-1813,* pp. 40-41, 54-55. See also, Jonathan Roberts to Mathew Roberts, December 16, 1812, in Roberts Papers; *id.* to Rogers, December 17, 1812, in Dreer Collection.

[6] *Senate Journal, 1812-1813,* pp. 169-72; *House Journal, 1812-1813,* pp. 247, 256-59, 287, 291-92, 299, 305-307.

[7] *Pennsylvania Archives*, 4th Series, IV, 788-89.

[8] *House Journal, 1812-1813,* pp. 103, 107, 227, 273, 278, 294, 310, 317, 326-29, 334-38, 354, 474-76, 500; *Senate Journal, 1812-1813,* pp. 271, 273, 323, 327, 331, 340, 352, 355-60, 363-68, 404.

[9] On January 23 Snyder vetoed on constitutional grounds a bill to incorporate Orwigsburg as a borough. In the House 50 members sustained him and only 33 voted to override. The legislature subsequently adopted a modified act which he signed. *House Journal, 1812-1813,* pp. 254-56, 319-20, 338, 444, 450, 463, 468.

[10] *Pennsylvania Archives,* 4th Series, IV, 805-809. Jonathan Roberts asserted years later in his memoirs that he had been sent to Harrisburg by Gallatin to persuade Snyder to veto the bill but that Snyder had done so prior to his arrival. Roberts confused the bill with the Forty Banks Bill of 1814, but since Gallatin was not in Washington in 1814, it is evidently this measure to which he refers. Klein (ed.), "Memoirs of a Senator from Pennsylvania," in *PMHB*, LXII (1938), 361.

[11] *House Journal, 1812-1813,* pp. 578-82, 625.

[12] *Aurora*, March 8, 9, 11, May 13, June 15, 22, July 7, 10, 17, 1813. The British actions at Hampton even drew the unmeasured reprobation of the Federalist *Lancaster Journal,* July 13, 1813.

[13] Pittsburgh *Commonwealth,* February 24, April 21, 1813; *Aurora,* March 31, April 22, May 4, 1813.

[14] Chandler Price to William Jones, March 19, 1813, in Smith Collection; David R. Porter to General Andrew Porter, April 23, 1813, in Porter Collection; Dallas to Jones, August 2, 1813, in Smith Collection; Samuel Clarke to *id.,* August 14, 1813, *ibid.*

[15] Duane to Jefferson, February 14, 1813, in "Letters of Duane," 359-61.

373

[16] Adams, *History,* VII, 41; *Aurora,* March 23, 1813; *U. S. Gazette,* March 27, 30, 1813; Edward Fox to Jones, May 14, 1813, in Smith Collection; Clarke to *id.,* August 14, 1813, *ibid.;* Duane to Jefferson, September 26, 1813, in "Letters of Duane," 361-65. Armstrong, who had presidential ambitions and was in high favor with the Old School faction in Philadelphia, was appointed on January 8, 1813, to succeed Eustis. On the same day William Jones of Philadelphia was made Secretary of the Navy to succeed Paul Hamilton. Adams, *History,* VI, 426-29. There were no Democratic criticisms of Jones's appointment; but his close association with Dallas must have made it unwelcome to the latter's enemies.

[17] Pittsburgh *Mercury,* September 2, 1813.

[18] Amos Ellmaker to John Tod, July 18, 1813, in Gratz Collection; *U. S. Gazette,* September 25, 27, October 19, 20, 26, 1813; *Aurora,* September 24, 27, 28, October 19, 23, 1813; Clarke to Jones, September 25, 1813, in Smith Collection; George B. Porter to General Andrew Porter, September 30, 1813, in Porter Collection.

[19] *U. S. Gazette,* February 12, March 2, 4, 26, April 8, 30, May 1, 3, 4, 5, 7, 13, 21, June 23, July 3, 1813.

[20] On the militia and the army, see *ibid.,* January 1, 2, February 24, 1813. On slave rebellions and the conditions of troops, see *ibid.,* December 1, 1812; January 8, February 23, April 6, 1813. On the administration's relations with France, see *ibid.,* March 13, 15, 16, 18, 20, 23, 30, June 18, 23, July 8, 14, 15, 16, 17, 20, 21, 23, August 20, September 2, 8, 11, 15, 17, October 12, 1813. On the opening of the mails, see *ibid.,* May 17, 19, August 9, 12, September 7, 8, 10, 15, 22, October 2, 5, 1813. On the *Edinburgh Review,* see *ibid.,* December 14, 1813.

[21] *Ibid.,* November 11, 1812; February 9, May 4, 1813.

[22] *Ibid.,* March 12, 13, 24, April 6, 9, 10, 12, 13, 19, May 4, 27, June 5, 30, 1813.

[23] *Aurora,* February 8, 1813; Edward Gray to Jones, February 5, 1813, in Smith Collection.

[24] *U. S. Gazette,* December 4, 7, 1813.

[25] See "Anti-Fourbe," *ibid.,* July 22, 1813; "Proclus," *ibid.,* November 18, 1813; editorial comment, *ibid.,* October 11, 1813.

[26] Adams, *History,* VI, 207; *U. S. Gazette,* May 4, 5, 6, 1812.

[27] *Ibid.,* March 6, 11, 15, 19, 22, 23, April 14, 1813; *Aurora,* April 10, 1813. On the part played by Astor, Parish, and Girard, see Adams, *History,* VII, 44-45; *id., Gallatin,* 477; Gallatin to Madison, April 19, 1816, in Adams (ed.), *Writings of Gallatin,* I, 696; Kenneth L. Brown, "Stephen Girard's Bank," in *PMHB,* LXVI (1942), 41-43; Walters, *Dallas,* 179-81. On Federalist purchasing of the stock, see Ellis P. Oberholtzer, *Philadelphia, A History of the City and Its People, A Record of 225 Years,* 4 vols. (Philadelphia, [1912]), II, 26; *Niles' Weekly Register,* IV (1813), 131; Timothy Pickering to Samuel Hodgdon, December 25, 1814, in Adams (ed.), *Documents Relating to New-England Federalism,* 419. See also the bitter comments of "Proclus," in *U. S. Gazette,* October 27, 28, 1813.

[28] *Ibid.,* September 30, October 27, 28, 1813; *Niles' Weekly Register,* V (1813-1814), 76; [Jacob Barker], *Incidents in the Life of Jacob Barker of New Orleans, Louisiana.* . . . (Washington, 1855), 39-44.

[29] On the origin and purposes of the Washington Benevolent Society, see Flick (ed.), *History of the State of New York,* VI, 10; William Sullivan, *Familiar Letters on Public Characters, and Public Events, from the Peace of 1783, to the Peace of 1815.* . . . (Boston, 1834), 279. On the organization of the Philadelphia Society, see *Democratic Press,* January 29, 1813; *Aurora,* February 15, 1813; *U. S. Gazette,* February 23, 24, July 8, 1813.

[30] On the activities of the Washington Association, see *ibid.,* February 25, August 10, 14, September 22, October 11, 1813.

[31] For Democratic criticisms of the Washington Benevolent Society, see *Democratic Press,* January 29, 1813; *Aurora,* February 15, July 21, 29, August 13, December 10, 1813. On the American Patriotic Fund Society, see *ibid.,* March 11, June 25, 29, July 19, 24, 1813. On the activities of the Association of Democratic Young Men, see *ibid.,* January 6, August 6, 16, 31, October 4, 1813.

[32] *U. S. Gazette,* March 19, 1813; *Aurora,* March 22, 1813. On the formation of the volunteer companies, see Manuel Eyre to Jones, March 23, 1813, in Smith Collection;

NOTES—CHAPTER XI

James M. Porter to General Andrew Porter, April 3, 1813, in Porter Collection; *id.* to George B. Porter, April 27, 1813, *ibid.; U. S. Gazette,* March 22, 23, 24, 1813; *Aurora,* March 23, 25, April 7, 1813; Scharf and Westcott, *History of Philadelphia,* I, 563.

[33] *Aurora,* March 22, 24, 26, 1813.
[34] *U. S. Gazette,* March 22, 25, 30, 1813.
[35] Biddle, *Autobiography,* 343-44; *Aurora,* May 8, 10, 11, 24, June 4, 1813; Eyre to Jones, May 9, 1813, in Smith Collection.
[36] *U. S. Gazette,* May 11, 1813.
[37] *Ibid.,* July 16, 20, 21, 22, 24, 29, August 7, 10, 12, 18, 31, September 1, 11, 14, 15, 18, 22, 23, 24, 28, 29, October 11, 1813.
[38] *Aurora,* September 10, 1813.
[39] *Ibid.,* September 8, 1813.
[40] *Democratic Press,* September 8, 10, 16, 1813.
[41] For the proceedings of the bolters and their writings, see *ibid.,* September 11, 22, 24, 28, 1813; *Aurora,* September 13, 21, 28, 29, October 6, 8, 9, 1813.
[42] Presumably Duane gave up the editorship because of his duties as Adjutant General. Wilson took over the paper on May 4, 1813. The *Democratic Press* and the *United States' Gazette* ignored the change and credited Duane with responsibility for anything appearing in the paper.
[43] See *Aurora,* September 8, 13, 16, 21, 30, October 6, 1813; *Democratic Press,* September 14, 16, 24, 29, 1813.
[44] *U. S. Gazette,* September 21, 23, 24, 25, 1813; *Aurora,* October 14, 1813.
[45] Election returns are taken from *ibid.,* October 16, 1812; October 14, 15, 18, 1813; *Democratic Press,* October 17, 1812; October 16, 1813.
[46] *Aurora,* November 17, 1813. The Democrats also managed to rid the congressional delegation of John Gloninger, the lone Federalist member from the State. He resigned in September, 1813, to accept an appointment as associate judge of Lebanon County from Governor Snyder. Edward Crouch, a Democrat, was chosen as his successor. See *Pennsylvania Archives,* 9th Series, V, 3403; Harrisburg *Pennsylvania Republican,* October 19, 1813.
[47] On the resolutions regarding hostages, see *House Journal, 1813-1814,* pp. 45-46, 77, 170; *Senate Journal, 1813-1814,* pp. 54, 97-99, 115, 121. On the resolutions regarding Vermont and Massachusetts (the states were not mentioned by name), see *House Journal, 1813-1814,* pp. 251-54, 294-96, 438, 463; *Senate Journal, 1813-1814,* pp. 212, 348, 350-51, 361, 372. On the assumption of the direct tax, see *House Journal, 1813-1814,* pp. 10, 37, 51, 55-56, 69; *Senate Journal, 1813-1814,* pp. 34, 38-39, 44. On the new militia law, see *Pennsylvania Archives,* 9th Series, V, 3503; *Aurora,* February 18, 1814.
[48] *Senate Journal, 1813-1814,* pp. 49, 52, 94, 112-13, 117, 163; *House Journal, 1813-1814,* pp. 170, 227, 232, 238-40, 245.
[49] *Democratic Press,* February 2, 1814.
[50] C. J. Ingersoll to Madison, January 5, 1814, in Madison Papers; Chandler Price to Jones, February 28, 1814, in Smith Collection; *U. S. Gazette,* March 14, 1814; Harrisburg *Pennsylvania Republican,* February 15, 17, 1814.
[51] Duane to Madison, June [January] 22, 1814, in "Letters of Duane," 367-68; Price to Jones, February 14, 1814, in Smith Collection; Dallas to *id.,* January 3, 1814, *ibid.*
[52] Adams, *History,* VII, 48-49, 399-400; Granger to John Todd [*sic*], February 7, 1814, in Gratz Collection.
[53] *Democratic Press,* February 14, 16, 17, 18, 19, 25, 26, 28, March 3, 9, 1814; Harrisburg *Pennsylvania Republican,* February 15, 22, March 1, 1814; *Aurora,* February 19, 1814; *U. S. Gazette,* March 4, 10, 14, 29, 1814; Clarke to Jones, February 14, 1814, in Smith Collection; Price to *id.,* February 28, 1814, *ibid.;* Duane to Madison, February 22, 1814, in "Letters of Duane," 365-67; Thomas Leiper to *id.,* February 22, 1814, in Madison Papers.
[54] Adams, *History,* VII, 401; *Democratic Press,* March 22, April 25, 1814; Binns to Madison, July 11, 1814, in Madison Papers.
[55] *House Journal, 1813-1814,* pp. 341, 345, 347, 358, 375, 376-77; *Aurora,* February 23, 28, 1814; *Democratic Press,* February 26, 28, 1814; Harrisburg *Pennsylvania Republican,* March 1, 1814; Jonathan Roberts to Mathew Roberts, February 28, 1814,

in Roberts Papers. Sketches of Roberts's career may be found in Jeannette P. Nichols, "Jonathan Roberts," in *DAB*, XVI, 9-10; *Biographical Directory of the American Congress,* 1468.

[56] *House Journal, 1813-1814,* pp. 69, 116-17, 119-20, 122-23, 125, 141-45, 147-48, 151-54, 161-62, 171-72, 177, 181-85, 190.

[57] *Senate Journal, 1813-1814,* pp. 137, 196, 200, 202, 203-204, 207-11, 213-17, 228-29, 240-42, 280-82, 292-96, 298-99, 301-305, 308-13, 342-44, 346-49; *House Journal, 1813-1814,* pp. 402-403, 413-20, 423-25, 432, 451.

[58] Thomas Burnside to William Norris, March 10, 1814, in Gratz Collection; *Pennsylvania Archives,* 4th Series, IV, 836-38.

[59] *House Journal, 1813-1814,* pp. 524-27, 534, 537; *Senate Journal, 1813-1814,* pp. 449-52, 458-59. On the fight for the banks, see also *Aurora,* February 19, March 23, 25, 1814; *Democratic Press,* March 16, 23, 1814; Biddle, *Autobiography,* 344-45. There are a number of letters on the subject from Charles Biddle, Benjamin R. Morgan, and John Connelly, members of the legislature, to Stephen Girard during January, February, and March, 1814, in Girard Collection.

[60] *Democratic Press,* March 21, 23, 28, 1814; *Aurora,* March 22, 23, 25, 1814.

[61] See *U. S. Gazette,* April 1, November 6, 18, December 22, 1813; January 25, June 28, 1814.

[62] Pittsburgh *Commonwealth,* November 3, 1813; Arthur H. Cole, *Wholesale Commodity Prices in the United States, 1700-1861* (Cambridge, 1938), 146. For other comments on agricultural prices, see Thomas J. Rogers to Jonathan Roberts, November 1, 1812, in Roberts Papers; *Niles' Weekly Register,* VI (1814), 210.

[63] On conditions in Pittsburgh and western Pennsylvania, see *ibid.,* 184, 197-98, 199, 207, 208, 320; *U. S. Gazette,* December 13, 1813; *Aurora,* December 10, 1813.

[64] See, for example, *U. S. Gazette,* October 12, 13, 16, November 13, 1813; January 29, February 15, 16, 18, 22, 1814.

[65] *Ibid.,* October 11, 1813.

[66] Adams, *History,* VII, 369, 372-79; Dallas to Jones, April 8, 1814, in Smith Collection.

[67] *U. S. Gazette,* December 27, 31, 1813; January 1, March 7, 9, April 2, 4, 5, May 4, 1814; *Aurora,* April 14, 1814.

[68] On speculation, see *U. S. Gazette,* December 31, 1813; *Niles' Weekly Register,* V (1813-1814), 280, 309-10; William Young to Jones, December 16, 1813, in Smith Collection; Manuel Eyre to *id.,* January 5, 1814, *ibid.;* Clarke to *id.,* January 8, 1814, *ibid.* On the consumers associations, see *Aurora,* December 23, 25, 1813; January 7, 1814; *U. S. Gazette,* January 25, 1814.

[69] On charity in the Northern Liberties, see *Aurora,* December 10, 24, 30, 1812; January 30, 1813. On the American Patriotic Fund Society, see *ibid.,* March 11, June 25, 29, July 19, 29, 1813; *U. S. Gazette,* October 13, 1813; January 15, 1814. For appeals by the Hospitable Society and the Board of Guardians, see *ibid.,* October 30, November 26, December 17, 1813. On aid to Portsmouth and the response to the appeal of the Committee of Defence, see *ibid.,* January 15, March 1, 1814; Mathew Carey, *The Olive Branch: or Faults on Both Sides,* 2d ed. (Philadelphia, 1815), 323.

[70] On the financial and currency situation, see Adams, *History,* VII, 385-90; VIII, 213-15; *id.* (ed.), *Writings of Gallatin,* III, 283-87; Carey, *Olive Branch,* 298-305; Rufus King to Christopher Gore, July 11, 1814, in King (ed.), *Rufus King,* V, 397-99; *id.* to *id.,* July 15, 1814, *ibid.,* 400-401; Gore to King, July 28, 1814, *ibid.,* 402-403; John Savage to Jones, July 30, 1814, in Smith Collection; *Pennsylvania Archives,* 4th Series, IV, 837, 854; *Niles' Weekly Register,* VI (1814), 66-67, 353; VII (1814-1815), 10; VII (Supplement), 176-77; *U. S. Gazette,* February 16, 28, March 2, 8, 1814; *Aurora,* June 9, August 31, 1814.

[71] *U. S. Gazette,* January 29, February 5, March 8, 12, 14, 31, April 7, 9, 12, 21, 28, 1814.

[72] Morison, *Otis,* II, 65-67; note of James Lloyd, April, 1814, *ibid.,* 72-73; Hare to Otis, April 13, 1814, *ibid.,* 74; *id.* to *id.,* April 26, 1814, *ibid.,* 74-75.

[73] Adams, *History,* VIII, 17-18, 213, 244-45; Walters, *Dallas,* 183-84; King to Gore, July 11, 1814, in King (ed.), *Rufus King,* V, 398; *U. S. Gazette,* May 27, June 15, July 15, 16, 19, 1814. On Jacob Barker and the Ten Million Loan, see [Barker], *Incidents,* 46 ff.

NOTES—CHAPTER XI

[74] Adams, *History*, VII, 184-90, 199, 201-202, 203-204, 279-80; *Niles' Weekly Register*, V (1813-1814), 299-300, 352; *U. S. Gazette*, December 1, 6, 30, 1813; January 4, 8, 14, 1814; *Aurora*, January 20, 1814. The British invasion of New York caused alarms for the safety of the fleet at Erie and led to the calling out of militia and volunteers for its defense. See *Pennsylvania Archives*, 9th Series, V, 3449, 3451, 3465-66, 3470, 3472; *U. S. Gazette*, January 13, 14, 22, February 21, March 7, 15, 18, 1814; *Aurora*, January 18, 20, February 7, 21, 1814.

[75] Adams, *History*, VIII, 25-26, 29-30, 32, 39-81, 94-97.

[76] *U. S. Gazette*, January 3, 8, 11, 18, 22, 24, February 1, 8, 17, 19, March 2, May 16, 17, 18, 19, 20, 21, 23, June 7, 8, 22, 23, July 2, 1814.

[77] *Aurora*, June 8, 17, 21, 1814; Pittsburgh *Mercury*, June 22, 1814; *U. S. Gazette*, May 23, June 1, 16, 24, 25, 28, 30, July 1, 12, 14, 1814. The quotations are from *ibid.*, June 25, July 12, 1814, respectively.

[78] See toasts 7 and 14 at Washington's Birthday dinner and Captain Condy Raguet's volunteer toast at the Fourth of July dinner, *ibid.*, February 24, July 7, 1814. On Oliver Wolcott and Federalist apostasy, see *Aurora*, April 29, 1814; *U. S. Gazette*, May 4, 5, 7, 12, 1814. For the *Gazette's* surprised protest at British vindictiveness, see *ibid.*, July 22, 1814.

[79] *Ibid.*, July 13, 14, 16, 18, 1814; *Aurora*, July 15, 19, 28, 1814; *Pennsylvania Archives*, 9th Series, V, 3921-22, 3924-27.

[80] Nathaniel B. Boileau to John Armstrong, July 25, 1814, in *Pennsylvania Archives*, 2d Series, 19 vols. (Harrisburg, 1873-1890), XII, 669; *ibid.*, 9th Series, V, 3927-28, 4038; VI, 4042-44; *Aurora*, September 13, 16, 1814.

[81] *Ibid.*, August 27, 29, 30, 31, September 3, 5, 8, 12, 15, 16, 17, 22, October 7, 1814; *U. S. Gazette*, August 29, 1814; *Niles' Weekly Register*, VII (1814-1815), 9. A complete summary of the activities of the Committee of Defence appears in *Minutes of the Committee of Defence of Philadelphia, 1814-1815* (Philadelphia, 1867). This comprises the eighth volume of the *Memoirs of the Historical Society of Pennsylvania*.

[82] *Aurora*, August 31, September 20, 23, 1814; *Democratic Press*, September 20, 1814; Duane to Major Daniel Parker, August 31, 1814, in Daniel Parker Papers (Historical Society of Pennsylvania); Dallas to Jones, September 18, 1814, in Smith Collection; Snyder to Boileau, October 31, 1814, in Snyder Correspondence.

[83] On the Bache affair, see *Aurora*, October 11, 27, November 15, 1814; *Democratic Press*, November 12, 19, 21, 1814; Duane to Parker, October 26, 1814, in Parker Papers; *id.* to *id.*, November 2, 1814, *ibid.*; *id.* to *id.*, November 15, 1814, *ibid.*; Snyder to James Monroe, September 10, 1814, in *Pennsylvania Archives*, 2d Series, XII, 741-42; *id.* to Bloomfield, September 14, 1814, *ibid.*, 750; *id.* to Gaines, November 3, 1814, *ibid.*, 9th Series, VI, 4171; *id.* to Boileau, October 21, 1814, in Snyder Correspondence; *id.* to *id.*, October 26, 1814, *ibid.*; *id.* to *id.*, August [October] 27, 1814, *ibid.*; *id.* to *id.*, November 1, 1814, *ibid.*; *id.* to *id.*, November 3, 1814, *ibid.*; John W. Harpster (ed.), "Major William Darlington's Diary of Service in the War of 1812," in *Western Pennsylvania Historical Magazine*, XX (1937), 197-214. Darlington was a physician in Chester County and was one of the officers arrested along with Bache. He was elected to Congress just prior to his arrest. He later acquired considerable reputation as a botanist. See Donald C. Peattie, "William Darlington," in *DAB*, V, 78-79.

[84] On Federalist meetings and propaganda during the campaign see *U. S. Gazette*, July 26, 27, 28, 29, 30, August 2, 4, 6, 26, September 14, 20, 23, 26, 28, 29, October 1, 3, 4, 10, 1814; *Aurora*, October 7, 1814.

[85] *Democratic Press*, April 26, 27, May 14, 31, June 6, July 13, 14, 15, 1814; Binns to Madison, July 11, 1814, in Madison Papers; *Aurora*, May 14, 19, 21, July 6, 1814.

[86] *Ibid.*, August 3, 9, 11, 15, September 13, 20, 1814; *Democratic Press*, August 1, 6, 17, September 5, 1814.

[87] *Aurora*, August 25, 26, September 17, 19, 20, 29, October 3, 1814. The quotation is from the issue of October 3.

[88] *Democratic Press*, October 13, 1814. See also, the other issues for September and October. Binns performed a number of military errands for the governor at this time. See, for example, *Pennsylvania Archives*, 9th Series, VI, 4085, 4089.

[89] Election returns for both the city and county together with an analysis appear in the *Democratic Press,* November 17, 1814. See also, *Poulson's American Daily Advertiser,* October 13, 14, 17, 1814.

[90] On the composition of the legislature, see *Aurora,* December 10, 1814. On the situation in Dauphin and Lebanon counties, see Harrisburg *Pennsylvania Republican,* September 20, 27, October 4, 11, 18, November 15, 1814. Another factor which favored the Federalist candidate, John Forster, was that he commanded a militia detachment at Baltimore during the election and probably received a larger percentage of the camp vote than he otherwise might have received.

[91] On the results in Allegheny and Butler counties, see Pittsburgh *Mercury,* July 13, August 17, 24, September 28, October 19, 1814; *Pittsburgh Gazette,* October 5, 1814.

[92] *House Journal, 1808-1809,* pp. 86-87; *ibid., 1811-1812,* pp. 82-83; *ibid., 1814-1815,* pp. 69-71. A total of 6,107 votes was cast by Pennsylvanians in military camps. *Democratic Press,* December 10, 1814.

[93] Dallas to Jones, August 13, 1814, in Smith Collection.

[94] *Aurora,* October 21, 1814. See also, *ibid.,* October 15, 19, 1814.

[95] *Democratic Press,* October 12, 1814. See also, *ibid.,* October 21, November 17, 1814. On the alarmist publications in the *Aurora,* see the issues of August 31 and September 5, 1814.

[96] *U. S. Gazette,* October 13, 1814.

[97] The figures on the new members are based upon a comparison of the membership of the House in 1812, 1813, and 1814. See *House Journal, 1812-1813,* pp. 3-5; *ibid., 1813-1814,* pp. 3-5; *ibid., 1814-1815,* pp. 3-6. On the votes on the pay raise and the bank bill, see *ibid., 1813-1814,* pp. 239-40, 534.

FOOTNOTES FOR CHAPTER XII

[1] Bayard to Robert G. Harper, August 19, 1814, in "Letters Relating to the Negotiations at Ghent, 1812-1814," in *AHR,* XX (1915), 115-16; King to Gouverneur Morris, October 13, 1814, in King (ed.), *Rufus King,* V, 419; *id.* to Sir William Scott, December 11, 1814, *ibid.,* 443; Jay to Timothy Pickering, November 1, 1814, in Henry P. Johnston (ed.), *The Correspondence and Public Papers of John Jay,* 4 vols. (New York, 1890-1893), IV, 377-79; Peter S. Du Ponceau to Dallas, December 14, 1814, in Dallas Papers.

[2] *U. S. Gazette,* October 20, 1814.

[3] *Aurora,* November 3, 1814; Carey, *Olive Branch,* 23; *Aurora,* November 19, 1814. On the memorial for Madison's resignation, see p. 297 above.

[4] On the initiation of the movement for the Hartford Convention, see Adams, *History,* VIII, 222-27. For comments, see *Aurora,* November 10, 11, 14, December 3, 13, 15, 1814; *Pittsburgh Gazette,* October 26, 1814. The *U. S. Gazette* published excerpts on the subject from the New England papers in October, November, and December, but refrained from editorial comment so that its attitude cannot be determined. Peter S. Du Ponceau reported that the paper feared that the convention would go too far. Du Ponceau to Dallas, December 14, 1814, in Dallas Papers.

[5] Hare to Otis, October 1, 1814, in Morison, *Otis,* II, 176-78; *id.* to *id.,* October 15, 1814, *ibid.,* 178-80.

[6] Tilghman to Jasper Yeates, November 8, 1814, in Yeates Papers; Du Ponceau to Dallas, December 14, 1814, in Dallas Papers.

[7] *Pennsylvania Archives,* 4th Series, IV, 845-56, 893-94; *Aurora,* January 21, 27, February 3, 8, 1815; Bernard Henry to Nicholas Biddle, January 10, 1815, in Nicholas Biddle Papers (Library of Congress); *id.* to *id.,* January 30, 1815, *ibid.;* Biddle to James Monroe, January 17, 1815, *ibid.*

[8] *House Journal, 1814-1815,* pp. 21, 44, 46, 48-49.

[9] *Senate Journal, 1814-1815,* pp. 9, 33-34, 36-37, 41-46, 52, 54, 60-62, 66, 72-74, 76, 149-50, 151-53, 162-63, 363; *House Journal, 1814-1815,* pp. 50, 102, 140, 158, 162-63, 169-70, 207-10, 220, 224-25, 302, 526.

[10] *Ibid.,* 311-14, 407-408, 413, 443, 451, 458, 515, 523, 544; *Senate Journal, 1814-1815,* pp. 311, 312, 328, 334-35, 341-43, 349-50, 369-70, 371.

[11] Adams, *History,* VIII, 292-98.

[12] *Aurora,* January 10, 1815; Pittsburgh *Mercury,* January 25, 1815; *Pittsburgh Gazette,* January 17, 1815.

[13] *Aurora,* February 6, 8, 13, 14, 1815; *Senate Journal, 1814-1815,* pp. 249, 288, 373, 381-97, 408, 430-32, 455-56; *House Journal, 1814-1815,* pp. 368-71, 389, 403-404, 429-33, 511-12, 562, 609, 611.

[14] *U. S. Gazette,* February 13, 14, 15, 1815; *Lancaster Journal,* March 31, 1815; *Pittsburgh Gazette,* July 8, 1815.

[15] Amos Ellmaker to William Norris, February 21, 1815, in Gratz Collection.

[16] Pittsburgh *Mercury,* March 21, 1815.

[17] *Aurora,* February 20, 1815.

[18] Walters, *Dallas,* 182, 186-87; Dallas to William Jones, February 3, 1814, in Smith Collection; *id.* to *id.,* October 2, 1814, *ibid.;* *id.* to *id.,* October 7, 1814, *ibid.*

[19] *Democratic Press,* January 10, 1815; *Aurora,* January 10, 1815; *U. S. Gazette,* January 10, 1815.

[20] *Democratic Press,* March 3, 1815. On Ingersoll's importunities in behalf of Bache, see Gideon Granger to John Todd [sic], February 7, 1814, in Gratz Collection.

[21] *U. S. Gazette,* May 6, 10, 1815; *Aurora,* June 16, 1815.

[22] *Ibid.,* May 4, 11, 1815.

[23] *Ibid.,* June 17, August 5, 9, 28, September 19, 23, 25, 26, 29, 1815.

[24] *Ibid.,* September 23, 30, October 3, 4, 5, 17, 1815.

[25] *U. S. Gazette,* June 27, 29, 30, July 3, 12, 13, 19, 1815. A partial defense of Dallas appears in the *Democratic Press,* July 3, 1815. There were undoubtedly others, but the issues from July 7-30 were missing from the files used by the author in the Historical Society of Pennsylvania.

[26] "One of the People," in *Aurora,* August 5, 9, 1815.

[27] *Ibid.,* August 11, 12, 15, 16, 17, 21, 24, September 25, 1815; *Democratic Press,* August 4, 5, 8, 9, 10, 11, 12 15, 16, 28, 1815.

[28] *Ibid.,* August 8, 14, 17, 23, September 2, 22, 1815; *Aurora,* August 14, 17, 22, 24, 28, October 2, 1815.

[29] *U. S. Gazette,* July 21, August 5, 8, 9, 11, 12, 14, 16, 18, 23, 28, 1815.

[30] *Aurora,* August 28, September 8, 1815.

[31] *U. S. Gazette,* September 9, 22, 1815; *Aurora,* September 25, 1815.

[32] For the Snyderite denunciations, see particularly, *Democratic Press,* September 28, 1815. For the Old School defense, see *Aurora,* September 22, 29, October 2, 1815.

[33] *Poulson's American Daily Advertiser,* October 12, 1815; *Democratic Press,* October 14, 1815. The *Press* claimed that the bargain was for the Old School to support the Federalist senatorial candidate. In further evidence of the existence of an understanding between the two, the *Press* pointed out that the Federalist papers in printing the election returns ignored the votes cast for the Federalist assembly ticket in the county. *Ibid.*

[34] *U. S. Gazette,* October 11, 1815; *Democratic Press,* October 12, 1815; *Aurora,* October 13, 16, 1815.

[35] Pittsburgh *Mercury,* July 15, August 12, 26, September 23, October 21, 1815; *Pittsburgh Gazette,* September 16, 23, 1815; Pittsburgh *Commonwealth,* October 21, 1815.

[36] *Aurora,* September 15, 1815; *Democratic Press,* October 16, 1815.

[37] Harrisburg *Pennsylvania Republican,* August 29, September 12, 19, 26, October 10, 17, 1815; Harrisburg *Oracle of Dauphin,* September 2, 16, 30, October 7, 1815; Harrisburg *Chronicle,* October 2, 1815.

[38] *Lancaster Journal,* August 30, September 15, October 11, 16, 1815; *Lancaster Intelligencer,* September 2, 1815; Philip S. Klein, "Early Lancaster County Politics," in *Pennsylvania History,* III (1936), 101.

[39] The analysis of political affiliations in the legislature is based upon the following: *Democratic Press,* November 6, 7, 1815; *Lancaster Journal,* November 29, 1815; *House Journal, 1815-1816,* pp. 10, 14, 75-76.

[40] *Aurora,* October 18, 24, 1815.

[41] *Democratic Press,* October 27, 1815.

[42] *Ibid.,* October 31, December 9, 12, 1815; January 1, 1816; *Aurora,* December 27, 1815; Pittsburgh *Commonwealth,* May 29, 1816.

[43] Morgan to Sergeant, December 18, 1815, in John Sergeant Papers (Historical Society of Pennsylvania); Hamilton to *id.,* January 4, 1816, *ibid.; id.* to *id.,* March 11, 1816, *ibid.; Aurora,* February 9, 13, 1816.

[44] Hamilton to Sergeant, March 11, 1816, in Sergeant Papers; *id.* to *id.,* March 12, 1816, *ibid.* The *Aurora* began attacking the projected bank in December. Articles on the subject appeared in almost every issue during March and April.

[45] On the Speaker's contest, see Morgan to Sergeant, December 18, 1815, in Sergeant Papers; Hamilton to *id.,* January 4, 1816, *ibid.; Aurora,* December 27, 1815; *House Journal, 1815-1816,* p. 5. For a characterization of Sutherland, see Philip S. Klein, *Pennsylvania Politics, 1817-1832; A Game without Rules* (Philadelphia, 1940), 79, n. 11. Evidence of his vanity is clearly shown in Sutherland to Charles Cist, December 10, 1814, in Gratz Papers. The influence of gubernatorial politics on actions of House committees is described in John M. Scott to William Tilghman, January 13, 1816, in Tilghman Correspondence.

[46] *Democratic Press,* March 4, 1815; January 29, 1816; Harrisburg *Pennsylvania Republican,* February 20, 1816; *Aurora,* February 19, 26, 1816; Binns to Thomas J. Rogers, February 5, 1816, in Dreer Collection. In the Pennsylvania Miscellaneous Papers in the Historical Society of Pennsylvania there is an undated and unsigned memorandum in Snyder's handwriting, asserting that he lacked the proper background to preside over the United States Senate. He refused in his person "to dishonor Penna by exposing the self taught plebian [sic] to the torturing scoffs & sneers of the fashionable literati proud of his superabundant acquirements—" Whether it was intended that this should be taken at face value is impossible to say; but such diffidence was characteristic of Snyder.

Notes—Chapter XII

[47] *Democratic Press,* March 15, 21, 1816; Hamilton to Sergeant, March 12, 1816, in Sergeant Papers.

[48] *Aurora,* March 20, 1816; *U. S. Gazette,* March 20, 1816; *Democratic Press,* March 18, 21, 1816; Adams, *History,* IX, 122-24. Accounts of the caucus list those who attended but do not indicate how they voted. All but two Republican members of the Pennsylvania delegation attended the caucus but not all of them voted for Monroe. See *ibid.,* October 28, 1816.

[49] On the passage of the Compensation Act and its effect on politics in the country at large, see Adams, *History,* IX, 119-22, 134-38. For the reaction in Pennsylvania, see *Aurora,* March 14, 21, June 19, August 3, 10, 13, 14, 20, 23, 26, 28, September 20, 23, 1816; Pittsburgh *Mercury,* August 10, 1816; *Democratic Press,* October 2, 28, 1816; [John Binns] to [Thomas J.] Rogers, [December, 1816], in Dreer Collection; *id.* to *id.,* December 7, 1816, *ibid.*

[50] *Aurora,* February 17, 28, April 24, July 23, 1816.

[51] *Ibid.,* August 2, 1816.

[52] *Ibid.,* August 15, 1816; *Lancaster Journal,* August 21, 1816.

[53] Harrisburg *Pennsylvania Republican,* September 10, 1816; *Democratic Press,* October 15, 24, 1816; *Aurora,* August 5, September 24, 1816. This author has not seen any notice calling the Lancaster meeting nor any report of its proceedings referring to it as a meeting of persons "friendly to De Witt Clinton as president of the United States." However, it is so charged in the two issues of the *Democratic Press* cited above and is so stated in Klein, *Pennsylvania Politics,* 79.

[54] On Lefever and Brown, see *Democratic Press,* September 5, 1812; October 24, 1816; *Poulson's American Daily Advertiser,* September 1, 1812; *U. S. Gazette,* October 8, 21, 1812; *Aurora,* August 15, 1816. On Leib's trips and the alliance of the Old School and Federalists, see pp. 314-15 above.

[55] *Aurora,* August 22, 23, 24, 26, 27, September 2, 4, 1816.

[56] *Ibid.,* August 26, 28, September 2, 18, 20, 23, 24, October 9, 12, 1816; *Democratic Press,* October 15, 1816; Harrisburg *Chronicle,* September 16, 1816; Harrisburg *Pennsylvania Republican,* September 17, 24, 1816; Pittsburgh *Mercury,* September 7, 1816.

[57] Pittsburgh *Commonwealth,* July 30, August 6, 27, 1816; Harrisburg *Chronicle,* September 2, 1816; *Aurora,* August 9, September 11, 24, 1816; Snyder to Boileau, September 3, 1816, in Snyder Correspondence.

[58] *Aurora,* July 27, August 8, 14, 17, 27, September 7, 9, 21, 24, 28, 1816.

[59] *Ibid.,* September 7, 17, 18, 19, 21, 23, 24, 25, 28, 1816; *Democratic Press,* October 1, 2, 4, 1816.

[60] *Ibid.,* October 11, 17, 1816. It should be observed that the Old School did not support Sergeant, who had been their candidate in 1815.

[61] Pittsburgh *Mercury,* August 17, 1816; Pittsburgh *Commonwealth,* August 13, 20, 1816.

[62] Pittsburgh *Mercury,* August 17, 24, 31, 1816; *Pittsburgh Gazette,* August 27, September 10, 1816.

[63] Pittsburgh *Commonwealth,* August 20, 27, September 3, October 1, 1816; Pittsburgh *Mercury,* September 14, 21, 28, 1816.

[64] *Ibid.,* October 19, 1816.

[65] *Democratic Press,* October 28, 1816. The *Press* lists Joshua Lewis, representative from Armstrong, Indiana, and Jefferson counties, as a Democrat. The *Greensburg Gazette,* quoted in the *Lancaster Journal,* November 29, 1815, described him as a Federalist; and he has been so considered in giving the figures in the text.

[66] *Aurora,* October 9, 1816.

[67] *Ibid.,* October 12, 1816.

[68] *Democratic Press,* October 15, 18, 23, 24, 31, 1816.

[69] See particularly, *Aurora,* October 15, 18, 19, 1816; Pittsburgh *Mercury,* October 19, 26, November 2, 1816; Harrisburg *Chronicle,* October 14, 21, 28, 1816; *U. S. Gazette,* October 19, 22, 24, 25, 31, 1816; *Democratic Press,* November 2, 1816.

[70] *Ibid.,* November 19, 1816. On the results in 1812, see p. 268 above.

[71] *Democratic Press,* November 25, December 12, 1816.

FOOTNOTES FOR CHAPTER XIII

[1] The statements regarding Federalist leadership are based upon an analysis of the occupations of seventy Federalist ward delegates in 1811. Of these, 27 were merchants, four were manufacturers, nine were lawyers, two were editors, and one each were doctors and stockbrokers. There were fifteen mechanics and artisans, including tailors, hatters, tanners, shoemakers, saddlers, coachmakers, carpenters, masons, painters, tinplate workers, and watchmakers. Four were small shopkeepers. Other occupations represented were collector, notary public, stablekeeper, boardinghouse keeper, accountant, and gentleman. The occupations of two persons could not be found. In the same year the Democratic general ward committee, of the same membership, included the following: ten merchants, three manufacturers, two lawyers, one editor, one doctor, one stockbroker, nineteen mechanics and artisans, seven small shopkeepers, eight officeholders, one stablekeeper, one sea captain, two accountants, two gentlemen, one laborer, and one artist. The occupations of ten committeemen either could not be found or could not be identified with certainty. Thus, merchants and lawyers constituted 51 per cent of the Federalist committee and 17 per cent of the Democratic. Small shopkeepers, artisans, and mechanics made up 27 per cent of the Federalists and 37 per cent of the Democrats. See *U. S. Gazette,* August 16, 17, 19, 20, 21, 23, 24, 26, 29, 1811; *Freeman's Journal,* September 3, 11, 1811; *Democratic Press,* August 9, 1811; James Robinson (comp.), *The Philadelphia Directory for 1811* . . . . ([Philadelphia, 1811]).

[2] These conclusions agree with those of Andreas Dorpalen, "The German Element in Early Pennsylvania Politics, 1789-1800: A Study in Americanization," in *Pennsylvania History,* IX (1942), 176-90.

[3] The population statistics are based upon the following census returns: *Return of the Whole Number of Persons within the Several Districts of the United States,* 2A-2G; *Aggregate Amount of Persons within the United States in the Year 1810,* pp. 33-51; *Census for 1820* (Washington, 1821), 15-21.

[4] See Brunhouse, *Counter-Revolution in Pennsylvania,* 115, 149, 197; Tinkcom, *Republicans and Federalists,* 272-73.

[5] Boileau to Jonathan Roberts, December 10, 1803, in Roberts Papers; Yeates to Edward Shippen, April 4, 1804, in Shippen Family Papers.

[6] The votes on the adoption of the bill for the removal of the capital show little consistency except to local interests, the most notable being the bitter antipathy and solid opposition of the Berks County delegation to the location of the capital at Harrisburg. The main struggle in the Senate took place on January 25, 1810, on the second reading of the favorable report of the committee of the whole on the bill. Opponents of the measure attempted to substitute other locations. They were defeated by the following votes: Northumberland, 23-8; Philadelphia, 19-12; Reading, 22-9; Carlisle, 25-6; Columbia, 24-7; and Lancaster, 22-9. The report of the committee was then approved by 22-9, and on the following day the bill passed its third reading by a vote of 20-9 and was sent to the House. A similar fight took place there. The committee of the whole reported unfavorably on February 5, but it was overruled on the next day by a vote of 59-29. Towns other than Harrisburg were rejected by the following votes: Northumberland, 48-39; Bellefonte, 70-19; Columbia, 54-34; and Reading, 61-27. The bill was then returned to the committee of the whole on February 7, where it was amended in several particulars, the most important change being to defer the removal until 1812. The bill was then reported on February 8 with the second reading the following day. An attempt to substitute Sunbury was defeated 62-25, and another to leave the capital at Lancaster was voted down 55-36. The third reading took place on February 12, when the measure was passed 57-28 and returned to the Senate. It was approved by Governor Snyder on February 21; and the capital was actually moved in April, 1812. *Senate Journal, 1809-1810,* pp. 179-84, 189; *House Journal, 1809-1810,* pp. 351, 443, 445, 465-66, 472-74, 482-84, 491-92, 498; *Pennsylvania Archives,* 9th Series, IV, 2827; *Niles' Weekly Register,* II (1812), 119.

[7] The phrase is taken from Klein, *Pennsylvania Politics, 1817-1832; a Game without Rules.*

BIBLIOGRAPHY
MANUSCRIPT COLLECTIONS
Girard College, Philadelphia.
  The Stephen Girard Collection.
The Historical Society of Pennsylvania, Philadelphia.
  Biddle-Craig Papers.
  Hampton L. Carson Collection.
  Dallas Papers.
  Ferdinand J. Dreer Collection.
  Simon Gratz Collection.
  Jones and Clark Papers.
  Lea and Febiger Collection.
  Legal Men of Pennsylvania Collection.
  Thomas McKean Papers.
  Northampton County Papers.
  Northern, Interior, and Western Counties Papers.
  Daniel Parker Papers.
  Pennsylvania Miscellaneous Collection.
  W. W. Porter Collection.
  Jonathan Roberts Papers.
  John Sergeant Papers.
  Shippen Family Papers.
  Uselma Clarke Smith Collection.
  Simon Snyder Correspondence.
  Society Collection.
  James M. Swank Papers.
  William Tilghman Correspondence.
  John William Wallace Papers.
  Yeates Papers.
The Library of Congress, Washington, D. C
  Nicholas Biddle Papers.
  Gregg Collection.
  Jefferson Papers.
  Madison Papers.
  Monroe Papers.
  Personal Papers, Miscellaneous.
  Timothy Pickering Collection.
  Oliver Wolcott Letters.
The New-York Historical Society, New York City.
  Gallatin Papers.

NEWSPAPERS
Harrisburg:
  Chronicle. 1813-1816.
  Dauphin Guardian. 1805-1811
  Oracle of Dauphin. 1802-1816.
  Pennsylvania Republican. 1811-1816.
Lancaster:
  Lancaster Journal. 1800-1816.
  Intelligencer. 1800-1808, 1814-1816.
Philadelphia:
  Aurora. 1800-1816.
  Democratic Press. 1807-1816.
  Freeman's Journal. 1804-1808.

Gazette of the United States. 1800-1804.
Philadelphia Evening Post. February-June, 1804.
Philadelphia Gazette. 1802.
Poulson's American Daily Advertiser. 1800-1816.
Relf's Philadelphia Gazette. 1803.
United States' Gazette. 1804-1816.

Pittsburgh:
  Commonwealth. 1805-1816.
  Mercury. 1812-1816.
  Pittsburgh Gazette. 1800-1804, 1807-1809, 1810-1816.
  Tree of Liberty. 1800-1804, 1807-1808.

Baltimore:
  Niles' Weekly Register. I-VII. 1811-1815.

Washington, D. C.:
  National Intelligencer (triweekly). October 24, 1812.

OTHER PUBLISHED SOURCES

Acts of the General Assembly of the Commonwealth of Pennsylvania . . . [1809-1816]. Lancaster and Harrisburg, 1810-1816.
Adams, Charles F., ed. *The Works of John Adams.* 10 vols. Boston, 1856.
Adams, Henry, ed. *Documents Relating to New-England Federalism, 1800-1815.* Boston, 1877.
————, ed. *Writings of Albert Gallatin.* 3 vols. Philadelphia, 1879.
Aggregate Amount of Persons within the United States in the Year 1810. Washington, 1811.
[Barker, Jacob]. *Incidents in the Life of Jacob Barker of New Orleans, Louisiana.* . . . Washington, 1855.
Biddle, Charles. *Autobiography, 1745-1821.* Philadelphia, 1883.
Binns, John. *Recollections of the Life of John Binns.* Philadelphia, 1854.
Carey, Mathew. *The Olive Branch: or, Faults on Both Sides.* 2d ed. Philadelphia, 1815.
Census for 1820. Washington, 1821.
Cranch, William. *Reports of Cases Argued and Adjudged in the Supreme Court of the United States.* . . . III, V. New York, 1807, 1812.
Dallas, Alexander J. *Report of Cases Ruled and Adjudged in the Several Courts of the United States, and of Pennsylvania, Held at the Seat of the Federal Government,* II, III, IV. Philadelphia, 1798, 1799, 1807.
Ford, Paul L., ed. *The Works of Thomas Jefferson.* 12 vols. New York, 1904-1905.
[Graydon, Alexander]. *Memoirs of a Life, Chiefly Passed in Pennsylvania.* . . . Harrisburg, 1811.
Hamilton, William, ed. *Report of the Trial of E. Shippen, J. Yeates, and T. Smith . . . on an Impeachment before the Senate of the Commonwealth.* . . . n. p., 1805.
Harpster, John W., ed. "Major William Darlington's Diary of Service in the War of 1812," in *Western Pennsylvania Historical Magazine,* XX (1937), 197-214.
Hunt, Gaillard, ed. *The Writings of James Madison.* 9 vols. New York, 1900-1910.
Johnston, Henry P., ed. *The Correspondence and Public Papers of John Jay.* 4 vols. New York, 1890-1893.
King, Charles R., ed. *The Life and Correspondence of Rufus King.* 6 vols. New York, 1894-1900.
Klein, Philip S., ed. "Memoirs of a Senator from Pennsylvania: Jonathan Roberts, 1771-1854," in *Pennsylvania Magazine of History and Biography,* LXI (1937), 446-74; LXII (1938), 64-97, 213-48, 361-409, 502-51.
Letters and Other Writings of James Madison. 4 vols. New York, 1884.
"Letters of William Duane," in *Massachusetts Historical Society Proceedings,* 2d Series, XX (1907), 257-394.
"Letters Relating to the Negotiations at Ghent, 1812-1814," in *American Historical Review,* XX (1915), 108-29.

Lipscomb, Andrew A., ed. *The Writings of Thomas Jefferson.* 20 vols. Washington, 1903-1904.
Lloyd, Thomas. *The Trial of Alexander Addison.* Lancaster, 1803.
Minutes of the Committee of Defence of Philadelphia, 1814-1815. Philadelphia, 1867. Volume VIII of the *Memoirs of the Historical Society of Pennsylvania.*
Mitchell, James T., et al., comps. *The Statutes at Large of Pennsylvania.* . . . 18 vols. Harrisburg, 1896-1915.
Morris, Anne C., ed. *The Diary and Letters of Gouverneur Morris.* 2 vols. New York, 1888.
A Narrative of Facts relative to the Conduct of Some of the Members of the Legislature, Professing to be Democrats, at the Election of a Senator to Represent this State in the Senate of the United States, on the 13th of January, 1807. 2d ed. Philadelphia, 1807.
Parker, David W., ed. "Secret Reports of John Howe, 1808," in *American Historical Review,* XVII (1912), 70-102, 332-54.
Pennsylvania Archives. 2d Series. 19 vols. Harrisburg, 1873-1890.
―――――. 4th Series. 12 vols. Harrisburg, 1900-1902.
―――――. 9th Series. 10 vols. Harrisburg, 1931-1935.
Pennsylvania. *Journal of the . . . House of Representatives of the Commonwealth of Pennsylvania,* 1799-1800, 1801-1802 to 1816-1817. Lancaster and Harrisburg, 1800, 1802-1817.
―――――. *Journal of the . . . Senate of the Commonwealth of Pennsylvania,* 1799-1800, 1801-1802 to 1816-1817. Lancaster and Harrisburg, 1800, 1802-1817.
Peters, Richard, Jr. *The Whole Proceedings in the Case of Olmsted et al. vs. Rittenhouse's Executrices.* Philadelphia, 1809.
The Quid Mirror. The First Part. [New York, 1806].
Return of the Whole Number of Persons within the Several Districts of the United States. Washington, 1801.
Robinson, James, comp. *The Philadelphia Directory for 1811.* . . . [Philadelphia, 1811].
Sullivan, William. *Familiar Letters on Public Characters, and Public Events, from the Peace of 1783, to the Peace of 1815.* . . . Boston, 1834.
Thorpe, Francis N., comp. *The Federal and State Constitutions . . . and Other Organic Laws . . . of the United States.* 7 vols. Washington, 1907.

SECONDARY WORKS

Adams, Henry. *History of the United States of America* [during the Administrations of Jefferson and Madison]. 9 vols. New York, 1889-1891.
―――――. *The Life of Albert Gallatin.* Philadelphia, 1879.
Alexander, De Alva S. *A Political History of the State of New York.* 2 vols. New York, 1906.
Auge, Moses. *Lives of the Eminent Dead, and Biographical Notices of Prominent Living Citizens of Montgomery County, Pa.* Norristown, Pa., 1879.
Beard, Charles A. *Economic Origins of Jeffersonian Democracy.* New York, 1915.
Biographical Directory of the American Congress, 1774-1927. Washington, 1928.
Brigham, Clarence S., comp. "Bibliography of American Newspapers, 1690-1820," in *American Antiquarian Society Proceedings,* New Series, XXX (1920), 81-150; XXXII (1922), 81-214, 346-79. The citations are only to the sections on Philadelphia and other Pennsylvania papers.
Brown, Kenneth L. "Stephen Girard's Bank," in *Pennsylvania Magazine of History and Biography,* LXVI (1942), 29-55.
Brownson, James I. *The Life and Times of Senator James Ross.* Washington, Pa., 1910.
Brunhouse, Robert L. *The Counter-Revolution in Pennsylvania, 1776-1790.* Harrisburg, 1942.
Buck, Solon J., and Elizabeth H. Buck. *The Planting of Civilization in Western Pennsylvania.* Pittsburgh, 1939.

Carson, Hampton L. "The Case of the Sloop 'Active,'" in *Pennsylvania Magazine of History and Biography*, XVI (1892), 385-98.
Cole, Arthur H. *Wholesale Commodity Prices in the United States, 1700-1861.* Cambridge, 1938.
Cunningham, Mary E. "The Case of the Active," in *Pennsylvania History*, XII (1946), 229-47.
Dorpalen, Andreas. "The German Element in Early Pennsylvania Politics, 1789-1800: A Study in Americanization," *ibid.*, IX (1942), 176-90.
Dunaway, Wayland F. *A History of Pennsylvania.* New York, 1935.
Egle, William H. *History of the Commonwealth of Pennsylvania.* Philadelphia, 1883.
Evans, Paul D. *The Holland Land Company.* Buffalo, 1924.
Ferguson, Russell J. *Early Western Pennsylvania Politics.* Pittsburgh, 1938.
Flick, Albert C., ed. *History of the State of New York.* 10 vols. New York, 1933-1937.
Henderson, Elizabeth K. "The Attack on the Judiciary in Pennsylvania, 1800-1810," in *Pennsylvania Magazine of History and Biography*, LXI (1937), 117-36.
——————. "The Northwestern Lands of Pennsylvania, 1790-1812," *ibid.*, LX (1936), 131-60.
——————. "Some Aspects of Sectionalism in Pennsylvania, 1790-1812." Unpublished dissertation in history, Bryn Mawr College, 1935.
Johnson, Allen, and Dumas Malone, eds. *Dictionary of American Biography.* 20 vols. and index. New York, 1928-1937.
Johnson, Emory R., et al. *History of the Domestic and Foreign Commerce of the United States.* 2 vols. Washington, 1915.
Klein, Philip S. "Early Lancaster County Politics," in *Pennsylvania History*, III (1936), 98-114.
——————. *Pennsylvania Politics, 1817-1832; A Game without Rules.* Philadelphia, 1940.
Lehman, Glenn A. "Gerrymandering in Pennsylvania prior to the Civil War." Unpublished master's thesis, University of Pennsylvania, 1932.
Loyd, William H. *The Early Courts of Pennsylvania.* Boston, 1910.
Luetscher, George D. *Early Political Machinery in the United States.* Philadelphia, 1903.
McMaster, John B. *A History of the People of the United States, from the Revolution to the Civil War.* 8 vols. Philadelphia, 1885-1913.
Meigs, William M. "Pennsylvania Politics Early in This Century," in *Pennsylvania Magazine of History and Biography*, XVII (1893), 462-90.
Morison, Samuel E. "The First National Nominating Convention, 1808," in *American Historical Review*, XVII (1912), 744-63.
——————. *The Life and Letters of Harrison Gray Otis, Federalist, 1765-1848.* 2 vols. New York, 1913.
Murdock, John S. "The First National Nominating Convention," in *American Historical Review*, I (1896), 680-83.
Oberholtzer, Ellis P. *Philadelphia, a History of the City and Its People, a Record of 225 Years.* 4 vols. Philadelphia, [1912].
Ostrogorski, M. "The Rise and Fall of the Nominating Caucus, Legislative and Congressional," in *American Historical Review*, V (1900), 253-83.
Peeling, James H. "Governor McKean and the Pennsylvania Jacobins (1799-1808)," in *Pennsylvania Magazine of History and Biography*, LIV (1930), 320-54.
——————. "The Public Life of Thomas McKean, 1734-1817." Unpublished dissertation in history, University of Chicago, 1929.
Scharf, J. T., and Thompson Westcott. *History of Philadelphia, 1609-1884.* 3 vols. Philadelphia, 1884.
Sears, Louis M. "Philadelphia and the Embargo of 1808," in American Historical Association *Annual Report for 1920* (Washington, 1925), 251-63.
Seybert, Adam. *Statistical Annals . . . of the United States of America. . . .* Philadelphia, 1818.

Sparks, Jared. *The Life of Gouverneur Morris, with Selections from His Correspondence and Miscellaneous Papers.* 3 vols. Boston, 1832.
Stanwood, Edward. *A History of the Presidency from 1788 to 1897.* Boston, 1898.
Steiner, Bernard C. *The life and Correspondence of James McHenry.* Cleveland, 1907.
S[wank], J[ames] M. "General Abner Lacock. United States Senator from Pennsylvania from 1813 to 1819," in *Pennsylvania Magazine of History and Biography,* IV (1880), 202-208.
Tinkcom, Harry M. *The Republicans and Federalists in Pennsylvania, 1790-1801: A Study in National Stimulus and Local Response.* Harrisburg, 1950.
Walters, Raymond, Jr. *Alexander James Dallas: Lawyer-Politician-Financier, 1759-1817.* Philadelphia, 1943.
Walton, Joseph S. "Nominating Conventions in Pennsylvania," in *American Historical Review,* II (1897), 262-78.
Warren, Charles. *The Supreme Court in United States History.* 3 vols. Boston, 1923.
White, J. W. F. "The Judiciary of Allegheny County," in *Pennsylvania Magazine of History and Biography,* VII (1883), 143-93.

INDEX

A

Aberdeen University, 53
Active, British sloop, case of, 184-185, 223, 360. *See also* Olmsted case.
"Actual settlers," 118, 128, 189
Adams, Henry, on Pennsylvania as "ideal American State," 2
Adams, John, 16, 25, 27, 31, 46, 69, 156, 163, 167, 173, 325; on McKean's election, 1799, 26
Adams, John Quincy, on collapse of Federalism, 25
Adams County, 73, 85, 119, 250, 368; in election of 1800, 28; of 1801, 37; of 1802, 46; of 1804, 75; of 1805, 350; of 1808, 174; of 1809, 204; of 1810, 245; of 1811, 234; of 1812, 268; of 1813, 284; of 1814, 299; Federalists in, 65, 74, 266, 326-327
Addison, Alexander, 19, 78; impeachment of, 40, 49, 53-55, 344; sketch of, 53
Admiralty court, Pennsylvania, and Olmsted case, 184-185, 193, 208
Agriculture, 1-2, 5, 9; effect of embargo, 165; of war, 289, 376
Albany, New York, 259
Aldermen, 51-52, 129
Alexander, Czar of Russia, 294
Alien and Sedition Acts, 12, 16-17, 25, 27, 167, 326
Allegheny County, 37-38, 53, 99, 368, 372; in election of 1799, 26; of 1801, 37, 38; of 1803, 64, 345; of 1805, 99, 350; of 1806, 118; of 1809, 203-204; of 1810, 218-219, 245; of 1811, 234-236, 366; of 1812, 266; of 1814, 299, 378; of 1816, 319, 320-321
Allegheny Mountains, 2, 3
Allegheny River, 2, 3, 4, 118
American Patriotic Fund Society, 280, 290, 376
American Republicans, *see* Federalists
American Republican Society, and election of 1810, 245; formed by Federalists, 1809, 203
Amiens, Peace of, 106
Anderson, Robert, 250
Anderson, William, candidate for Congress, 1810, 216; re-elected, 1816, 320
Annapolis Convention, 1786, 69
Anti-Constitutionalists, *see* Republicans
Anti-Federalists, 22, 69. *See also* Republicans.
Apportionment, Congressional, 250; 368; Legislative, 175
Arbitration: advocated by Snyder, 51; bill, 53, 55; McKean vetoes, 86-87; temporary act, 108, 182
Armstrong, John, 374; appoints Duane Adjutant General, 276
Armstrong County, 250; 381; in election of 1809, 204; of 1815, 313; Quids in, 236
Articles of Confederation, 185, 186
Associated Friends of Democracy and Simon Snyder, in campaign of 1808, 169, 213
Association of Democratic Young Men, 1813, 280
Astor, John Jacob, and war loans, 279, 293, 374
Atkinson, Thomas, editor of *Crawford Weekly Messenger*, 349

INDEX

Aurora, 12, 16, 22, 34, 60-62, 65, 73-74, 80-81, 90, 92-93, 99, 110, 122-123, 137-138, 141, 143, 151, 153, 180, 202-203, 211-213, 215, 264, 286, 315, 337, 355, 367; approves Steele's appointment as Collector of Port, 162; Bache, B. F., editor, 12, his death, 17, 59; on banks, 221, 225; on Burr, 134, 354; on Carlisle convention, 1816, 318, 321; on Carlisle ticket, 322; on caucuses, 92-93, 151, 157, 259, 314; on Chesapeake affair, 136; on constitutional revision, 80-81; on contempts of court, 57; defends Jefferson, 35; defines Democrat and Federalist, 313; denies attack on McKean, 1803, 63-64; denounces Committee of Defense, 296; on district delegate system, 214; Duane, William, editor, 17-18, 230, 310; Duane, William J., editor, 144; on election of bank directors, 110; and election of 1801, 31-32; of 1804, 71, 72-74; of 1805, 88-89; of 1806, 116, 118; of 1808, 144, 175; of 1809, 201-204; of 1810, 216-217; of 1811, 233; of 1812, 267; of 1813, 283; of 1814, 298; of 1815, 309-313; on embargo, 136, 167, 238-241, 244-245, 252, 290; on Erskine agreement, 242; on Federal patronage, 43, 58; on Federalist meeting in New York, 1808, 163; on Florida purchase, 112; on foreign affairs, 106-107, 134-135; and Gallatin, 229; on government loans, 279; on Hartford convention, 306-307; on Henry Letters, 251; on Hundred Dollar act, 66; on impeachment of McKean, 126; on impeachment of Supreme Court judges, 78-79; influence of, 158; on judicial reforms, 55, 57; on Judiciary act of 1801, 42-43; and Leib affair, 139-142; on Leib's dismissal as Philadelphia postmaster, 309; on Leib's nomination for Congress, 44; on libel charges against Duane, 114; on Logan's defeat for United States Senator, 33; on Macon bills, 245; on Madison, 1808, 159; on Madison, 1811-1812, 230-231, 258, 305; on Madison's foreign affairs message, 247; on McKean, 85-86, 91-92, 113, 349, 351; on Muhlenberg and "trout letter," 98; on national politics, 29, 44, 135, 227, 250-251; on nomination of George Clinton, 257; on Olmsted case, 188, 195-196, 198-199, 257; opposes nomination of Van Horne for Congress, 39; on opposition to Randolph, 111-112; on Passmore case, 66-67; political affiliations of, 68-69, 94, 163; and quarantine regulations, 59-60; and Quid opposition to Jefferson, 116; and Quid-Democrat reunion, 173; on *Quid Mirror*, 121; refuses to print Barker statement, 122-123; refuses to publish Democratic address, 244; on reprisals against British, 107; on results of war, 308; and Rising Sun movement, 45, 63; on Ross and Jane Marie case, 168; and Snyder administration, 169-170, 181, 204, 209-213, 222, 227, 310-311, 314; and Spayd's withdrawal, 174; and split among Republicans, 283; on State and Federal administrations, 317; on State and local issues, 1814, 300; on State patronage, 104-105; on State rights, 201; on Tench Coxe, 70; on ward meetings, 61; on war policy, 247, 254, 280-281; Wilson, James, editor, 283, 375; on withdrawal of Richards as Congressional candidate, 220; on Yazoo land speculation, 110-111

B

Bache, Benjamin Franklin, editor of *Aurora*, 12; death, 17, 59

Bache, Lt. Col. Louis, court martial of, 296, 377; re-elected to command, 297

Bache, Richard, Jr., 172, 310; candidate for postmaster in Philadelphia, 285-286, 309, 379; and Monroe-Snyder ticket, 316

Bainbridge, Commodore William, 278

Baird, Thomas, 265; candidate for State Senator, 234-235

Baldwin, Henry: Congressional candidate, 1816, 320-321; and Pittsburgh politics, 117

Baltimore, 263, 378; British government bills on sale, 291; British repulse at, 296; suspension of specie payment, 292; as trade competitor, 3, 5; and war loans, 1814, 293

Bank of North America, 5.

Bank of Pennsylvania, 5; election of directors, 1806, 109-110, 351, 356; 1807, 133; John Binns elected director, 273; Pittsburgh branch, 235

Bank of Pittsburgh, proposed, 234-235

Bank of the United States, 5, 178; *Aurora* opposes re-chartering, 315; effect of dissolution, 291; and foreign trade, 9; refused State charter, 224-226, 249, 368; and Republicans, 304

Index

Banking, 234-235, 303, 315, 316, 333, 376; bankers refuse war loans, 293; fluctuation of bank notes, 291-292; legislation, 1813-1814, 273-275, 284, 287-288, 301, 373; and Philadelphia's financial leadership, 5; promotion of, 221, 271, 300; Republican attitude, 13, 304; State banks and Federal loans, 249
Baptists, 6
Barker, Jacob, and war loans, 293
Barker, John, 90; elected sheriff in Philadelphia, 1803, 63, 116; and election for sheriff, 1806, 122-123; interview with McKean, 122; remains in office, 126
Barton, William, 104; and third party, 64
Bartram, George, 90
Bates, Tarleton: and Pittsburgh politics, 117; supports McKean, 1805, 99; and *Tree of Liberty*, 117
Bayard, Andrew, and Passmore affair, 56, 78
Bayard, James A.: on peace commission, 278; and peace terms, 305
Beaver, 272
Beaver County, 128, 139, 190, 210, 272, 368; delegates to Pittsburgh meeting, 37-38; in election of 1805, 350; of 1806, 118; of 1810, 218-219; of 1811, 234-235; of 1815, 313
Bedford County, 3, 109-110, 207, 211; in election of 1805, 350
Bellefonte, 382
Bengal Journal, 17
Bensell, George S., 131
Berks County, 4, 19, 25, 88, 89, 140, 155, 173, 226, 250, 349, 356; delegate meetings in, 318-319; in election of 1799, 26-27; of 1805, 99-100, 350; of 1808, 170, 174; of 1809, 204; of 1810, 218-220, 245; of 1812, 264, 266; of 1815, 313; German vote in, 93; legislators from, 97; opposes moving capital to Harrisburg, 382; Quids in, 236
Berlin Decree, 135
Bethlehem, 26
Biddle, Charles, 369; heads investigation of board of health, 60; heads Committee of Defense, 281, 295
Biddle, Marks John, candidate for Congress, 1810, 219
Biddle, Nicholas: and conscription, 306; on embargo, 164; on Philadelphia Democrats, 223; report on Hartford Convention, 307; in State Senatorial election, 1814, 298
Bill of rights, 7, 17
Binder, William, 200, 372
Bingham, William, 30, 32
Binney, Horace, 130, 261, 278, 371; candidate for U. S. Senate, 287
Binns, John, 152, 153, 174, 200, 202, 213, 254, 264, 282, 285-286, 377; *Aurora* denounces, 141, 144; denounces Committee of Defense, 296; dominates Democratic party, 300-301, 311-312, 319; editor of *Democratic Press*, 137, 145; editor of Northumberland *Republican Argus*, 99; elected director of Bank of Pennsylvania, 273; in election of 1808, 156, 159, 169; of 1814, 298; on embargo, 166; favors war policy, 253; on Federalists, 19, 23; Federalists and Old School Democrats oppose, 309; leads Snyderites, 136, 145, 199, 228, 233, 329; and Leib affair, 140-141; on Leibite cooperation with Federalists, 298; letter to Gallatin on State politics, 231; and nominating caucus, 1815, 316; opposed by Leib and young Duane, 138; and patronage, 309; quarrel with Duane, 215-216; renounces Clinton, 162; on Republicanism, 13, 15; sketch of, 136-137; supports Madison, 1808, 160-161; 1812, 257-258; supports Monroe-Snyder ticket, 314, 316; supports Richard Bache for postmaster of Philadelphia, 285-286, 309
Bioren, John, 158-159
Bleakley, John, 32

Blockade: of American ports, 107, 280, 291; European, 135

Bloomfield, General Joseph: Committee of Defense ignores, 296; sends militia to Delaware, 281; succeeded by Gaines, 296

Blue Mountains, 2, 97

Board of Guardians of the Poor, 290

Boileau, Nathaniel B., 93, 115, 181, 205, 210, 319, 334, 356; *Aurora* attacks, 140-142, 152; on common law, 127; and *Democratic Press*, 137, 142; and Duane, 133, 200; elected Speaker, 179; and election of 1802, 46; and election of State Treasurer, 1803, 50; of U. S. Senator, 1801, 40; 1807, 131-132; feud with Leib, 130, 140-142, 152-153, 154, 176; and impeachment of McKean, 126-127, 133; of Supreme Court judges, 77; and Incompatibility Act, 40; and Olmsted case, 197, 206-207; opposes Samuel Maclay, 180; *Pennsylvania Democrat* attacks, 201-202; sketch of, 81-82; and Snyder nomination, 88; Snyder appoints, Secretary of the Commonwealth, 180

Boston, 196, 260, 292

Bourbons, 294

Brackenridge, Hugh Henry, 54, 56, 92; and impeachment of Supreme Court judges, 67; Republican leader in western Pennsylvania, 19, 53

Brady, James, in election of U. S. Senator, 1812, 273

Brest, 135

Bright, Brig. Gen. Michael, 210, 213; and Olmsted affair, 194, 196, 198, 200, 201, 206-207, 224

British, 9, 10, 17, 31, 33, 69, 79, 80, 85, 106, 111, 112, 127, 137, 145, 150, 165, 166, 179, 241, 243, 244, 245, 260, 267, 280, 281, 282, 284, 306, 308, 367, 368; bills purchased by Americans, 291; blockade, 107, 135, 280, 291; court precedents, 57, 129; destroy Washington, 299; Erskine agreement, 241; grievances against, 134, 135, 136, 164, 253, 268; impressment of Americans, 107; Nonintercourse Act applied against, 246; party attitudes toward, 11, 106-107, 179, 238, 242, 244, 247, 252-255, 277-278, 327; peace terms, 295, 305; repudiate Erskine agreement, 242; retaliation against, proposed, 107, 244, 248-249, 284; seize American ships, 11, 107, 253; withdraw troops from Northwest posts, 10; and War of 1812, 237, 247, 271, 283, 293, 294, 295, 296

Bronson, Enos: editor of *United States' Gazette*, 60; and Washington Benevolent Society, 280

Brooke, Major William, 71

Brown, Jacob, military successes, 294

Brown, Robert, 58, 73, 252

Brown, Thompson, promotes Clinton campaign, 1816, 318

Bryan, Samuel, 89; candidate for State Treasurer, 131, 141-142; Comptroller General, 41; investigation of, 109; removal from office, 103, 108

Buchanan, Dr. George, appointed Lazaretto physician, 113, 126

Bucher, Jacob, 371; and impeachment of Supreme Court judges, 77

Bucks County, 4, 25, 130, 157, 179, 255, 341; and banking bill, 275; in election of 1799, 26; of 1802, 46; of 1805, 99, 350; of 1808, 163, 174-175; of 1809, 204; of 1812, 268; of 1815, 313; Federalists in, 266; Republican committee in, 39

Buffalo, New York, 271, 299

Buffalo Valley, 50

Burr, Aaron, 28, 30-31, 63, 116, 354; called "Emperor of the Quids," 134; trial of, 134, 150

Butler, Pierce, 43

Butler County, 368; in election of 1805, 350; of 1806, 118; of 1810, 218-219; of 1811, 234-235; of 1812, 266; of 1814, 299, 378; of 1816, 320-321; elects delegates to Pittsburgh meeting, 37-38

C

Cabrera, Joseph, 91, 126, 349
Caen, University of, 53
Calcutta, 17
Cambria County, in election of 1806, 119
Campbell, George W., U. S. Secretary of the Treasury: resigns, 1814, 309; and war loans, 292-293
Canada, 368; invasion of, 271, 293; trade with New England, 291
Canning, George, British foreign secretary, repudiates Erskine agreement, 242
Canonsburg, 19
Capital, movement of State, 334
Carey, Matthew, 45, 58, 171; and Bank of the United States, 225; proposals for national harmony, 305
Carlisle, 4, 89, 140, 226-227, 255, 314, 371, 382; Federalist meeting at, 262, 267; Republican nominating convention at, 1816, 317-318, 319, 321, 322
Carlisle Gazette, 201
Carpenter, Jacob, State Treasurer, death of, 50
Carson, James, 90
Carver, Samuel, 356; on Passmore affair, 66
Castor, Samuel, 370, 372
Caucus-conventions: and gubernatorial nomination, 1808, 153-154, 157-158; 1811, 226-227; use of, 332
Caucuses, 70, 316; end in Pennsylvania, 323; opposition to, 143, 215, 226, 259-260, 263, 304, 314-316, 317, 320, 332; replaced by nominating convention, 332
Caucuses, Congressional, 310; and presidential nomination, 1808, 156-157; 1812, 257, 258, 370; 1816, 316, 321, 381
Caucuses, legislative, 98, 217, 226, 272, 286, 315, 332, 373; at Albany, 259; and gubernatorial nomination, 1802, 41; 1805, 77, 87, 92, 93, 141; 1808, 288; and nomination of State Treasurer, 1807, 131-132; and presidential nomination, 1804, 74; and U. S. Senatorial election, 1806, 131; 1812, 272
Centre County, 131, 272, 356; in election of 1805, 350
Chase, Samuel, U. S. Supreme Court Justice, 78, 81
Chesapeake affair: reaction in Philadelphia, 136; retribution demanded for, 166
Chesapeake Bay, 3; British raid, 275, 277, 281, 293-294
Chester County, 4, 207, 227, 248, 297, 340, 349, 368, 377; in election of 1800, 28; of 1801, 37; of 1803, 64, 345; of 1804, 73; of 1805, 99, 350; of 1807, 145; of 1808, 174; of 1810, 219, 245; of 1811, 234; of 1812, 268, 371; of 1814, 299; Federalists in, 64, 266
Chestnut Ridge, 3
Chippewa, 294
Chronicle, Harrisburg; on John Sergeant, 1817, 315; supports Carlisle ticket, 322
City Tavern, 56, 78
"Clapboard Row junto," 38
Clarke, David, 184
Clay, Joseph, 90, 92, 157; breaks with Duane, 229-230; candidate for Congress, 70, 115; supports Randolph, 113
Clinton, De Witt, 286; Leib favors, 255, 315; in presidential campaign, 1812, 237, 256-258, 260, 261-262, 265, 267-268, 282, 329; 1816, 317, 318, 381
Clinton, George, 257, 258; death of, 258; in election of 1804, 74; of 1808, 139, 155-163, 180, 256, 331; vote on re-chartering Bank of United States, 224

Clintonians, or Clinton Democrats, 255, 265, 269, 370; and administration policies, 263; and election of 1812, 257, 259, 264, 267-268; electors, 260, 370, 372; and Federalists, 162, 260, 262, 331. *See also* Democrats.
"Clodpole affair," 85-86, 88, 92
Clunn, Joseph, 39
Clymer, Joseph, 239
Cobbett, William, editor of *Peter Porcupine's Gazette,* 12; libel case, 1797, 114
Cochran, 228
Cockburn's raids, 275
Coigley, James, 202
Columbia, Pennsylvania, 382
Commerce, 288-290, 331; British aggressions on, denounced, 248; and end of Napoleonic wars, 333; Federalists demand protection for, 107; fluctuation in foreign, 9, 165; government revenue and, 291; restrictions on, 164, 165, 178-179. *See also* Embargo.
Committee of Defense: appeals for relief funds, 290-291, 376; and military situation, 296; Philadelphia appoints, 295
Common law, 129, 149, 180, 186
Commonwealth, Pittsburgh: and Burr, 134; and election of 1806, 118; on embargo, 166, 252; and new bank, 234; and Pittsburgh politics, 99, 117, 201-202, 320
Compensation Act of 1816, 316-317, 320, 381
Comptroller General, 86, 89, 108; and Nicholls case, 191
Congress, 22, 25, 33, 38, 39, 40, 42, 44, 150, 172, 185, 186, 187, 194, 222, 237, 240, 247, 251, 268, 285, 316, 320, 377; adopts Macon's Bill No. 2, 244, 245; and embargo, 238, 241-242, 252, 289-290; and foreign affairs, 166, 246-247; on Francis James Jackson, 243; Pennsylvania delegation in, 207; favors war, 254-255; opposes Dallas's appointment, 309; and re-charter of Bank of the United States, 224, 229; reapportionment of, 250. *See also* Caucuses, congressional.
Connecticut, 74, 261, 293; claim of, 4; and embargo, 241; refuses militia for war, 272
Conrad, Frederick, 34, 46, 81
Constitution, Federal, 7, 83, 87, 156-157, 190, 193-194, 197, 208, 214, 217, 225, 240, 304, 321; amendment of, 150, 190; Hartford Convention and, 306-307
Constitution, Pennsylvania, 1, 6; of 1776, 6, 337; of 1790, 6-8, 16, 19, 83-84, 87, 88, 93-98, 126-127, 170, 275, 337; amendment of, 77, 79-83, 119, 147, 169-170, 204, 207, 249-250, 368; attack on, influences McKean vote, 100; defended by McKean, 85; and election of sheriff, 117, 121; and Federalists, 164; and restriction of press, 124; Snyder called enemy of, 169
Constitutional convention, Federal, 10, 156
Constitutional convention, State: of 1776, 6; of 1789-1790, 33, 51; movement for new, 81-83, 84, 88-90, 92-95, 97-98, 328
Constitutional Democrat, Lancaster, Quids found, 108
Constitutional Republicans, 82-83, 90-91, 95, 104, 110, 138, 145, 147, 151, 152, 167, 169, 177; and administration policy, 107; adopt Democratic electoral ticket, 172-173; coalition with Federalists, 96, 103; on constitutional convention, 1805, 94; disavow *Freeman's Journal,* 171; disintegration of, 171, 176; in election of 1805, 89; and foreign affairs, 106; and Jefferson's administration, 330; policies of, 118-119; support McKean's reelection, 77, 328. *See also* Quids.
Constitutional Society, *see* Society of Constitutional Republicans
Constitutionalists (c. 1776-1790), 6
Constitutionalists, 104, 110, 152, 155; and amendment of Federal Constitution, 150; in election of 1805, 99-100; of 1806, 117-119; of 1808, 144-145; and embargo, 151; and judicial reform, 107-108; and McKean impeachment, 149
Contempts of court, 36, 42; legislation on, 57, 182; and Passmore affair, 56, 66-67
Continental Army, 33

Continental Congress, 16, 184, 317
Convention, State brigantine, 184-185, 223
Conventions, nominating, 89, 151, 153-154, 226, 314; agitation for, 142-143; at Carlisle, 1817, 321-322; failure of proposal for, 1805, 332; in Harrisburg, 1788, 22; Quids refuse Federalist proposal for, 155; use of, 332
Cooper, Thomas, 137
Cope, Thomas P., 356
Copenhagen, 242
Corcoran, Catharine, 355
Cornwallis, Lord, 17
Corresponding committees: on embargo, 240; in Philadelphia, 261, 370; of Pittsburgh area, 320; to promote Carlisle convention, 322
Council of Censors, 6, 7
County committees, 21-22
Court of appeals, State, 186-187, 193
Courts, Federal, *see* Federal courts
Courts, Pennsylvania, 82, 108, 190; circuit, 108, 182; foreign precedents in, 148-149
Cox, Paul, 90
Coxe, John D., 179
Coxe, Tench, 63, 72; appointed Purveyor of Public Supplies, 59, 365; Philadelphia Republican leader, 19, 71; sketch of, 69-70; as writer for *Freeman's Journal,* 70, 347
Crawford County: in election of 1805, 350; of 1806, 118; of 1810, 218-219; of 1815, 313
Crawford Weekly Messenger, and "Meadville toast," 349
Crawford, William, Congressman from Pennsylvania, 370
Crawford, William, defeated by Monroe for presidential nomination, 1816, 316
Croghan, George, 294
Crouch, Edward, 372, 375
Cumberland County, 57, 132, 356, 368; delegate meetings in, 318-319; in election of 1805, 350
Cumberland Road, 130
Cumberland Valley, 4

D

Dallas, Alexander J., 46, 56, 58, 64, 101, 104, 134, 137, 198, 203, 258, 278, 285, 299, 319, 374, 379; and Addison impeachment, 55; advises McKean, 84; antipathy of Federalists and Old School Democrats to, 309; appointed recorder of Philadelphia, 40, 341; appointed U. S. Secretary of the Treasury, 309; *Aurora* attacks, 72, 91, 110, 116, 141, 142, 349; on conduct of war, 275-276; and Constitutional Republicans, 82, 83, 88, 90, 92, 95, 104, 105, 172-173; criticizes Jefferson, 173, 330; defends John Smith, 230; and Duane, 42, 43, 59, 65, 72, 200, 310; and Federal patronage, 43, 309; and Federalists, 95, 96, 104, 105, 240-241; and Madison's election, 173, 264; and Nicholls case, 191; and Olmsted case, 207; opposes Leib for postmaster of Philadelphia, 286; and presidential election, 1800, 30; and repeal of embargo, 290; and Rising Sun group, 45; sketch of, 16; supports McKean, 16, 92-93; supports Snyder, 310; and trial of Supreme Court judges, 78, 79
Danton, 92
Darlington, William, 377
Dauphin County, 19, 308, 334, 340, 368; in election of 1799, 26; of 1805, 327, 350; of 1809, 203-204; of 1812, 266, 371; of 1814, 299, 378; of 1815, 313; of 1816, 318-319
Dauphin Guardian, Harrisburg, 202
Decatur, Stephen, 278, 293
Declaration of Independence, 16, 91, 321

396   INDEX

Delaware, 2, 16, 78, 167, 278; militia sent to defend, 281
Delaware Bay, British blockade, 280-281
Delaware County, 126, 142, 163, 216, 243, 250, 281, 368; in election of 1800, 28; of
   1801, 36, 37; of 1802, 44, 46; of 1804, 70, 71, 72; of 1805, 98, 350; of 1808, 174-176;
   of 1809, 204; of 1810, 245; of 1811, 234; of 1812, 268; of 1813, 284; of 1814, 299;
   Federalists in, 65, 266, 326; meeting with Philadelphia delegates, 115-116
Democratic newspapers: defend Snyder, 169-170; on Henry Letters, 251; protest
   Bryan's removal, 108; and State patronage, 201. See also Aurora, Democratic
   Press, Pennsylvania Democrat, etc.
Democratic Press, 172, 173, 213, 219, 226, 231, 260, 283, 321; on Committee of Defense,
   296; criticizes Congress, 250; on district delegate system, 139; and election of
   1808, 169; of 1809, 202-203; of 1810, 217; of 1813, 283; of 1814, 298; of 1815,
   311-313; on embargo, 166, 244; establishment of, 137, 138; on Federal patronage,
   230; on Federalists, 261, 314; feud with Leib-Duane group, 139, 141-142, 144,
   145, 152, 153, 300; on gubernatorial nominations, 322; on Lancaster and Carlisle
   meetings, 318; on legislative pay increase, 285; on Leib, 136, 140-141, 143, 181,
   265, 267-268, 286, 297, 309, 315; on Macon's Bill, 243-245; on nominations for
   Vice President, 1816, 316; on Olmsted case, 196-197, 200; opposes Madison, 1808,
   156-157, 160; on *Pennsylvania Democrat,* 202; on re-chartering of Bank of the
   United States, 225; rivalry with *Aurora,* 139, 210-211, 215; supports Madison,
   1812, 257-258; supports Snyder, 137-138, 210, 228
Democratic Republicans, *see* Democrats
Democratic Societies, 18, 213-214, 216, 233, 267
Democrats or Democratic Republicans, 61, 90, 91-92, 94, 95, 105, 108, 109, 110, 116,
   130, 133-134, 138, 141, 150, 156, 162-163, 173, 174, 180, 192, 194, 199, 202, 211-
   212, 213-214, 220, 222, 223, 225-228, 245, 250, 252-255, 259, 261, 262, 272, 275-
   276, 278-279, 282, 301, 307, 325, 327-328, 334; and banking bill, 275; and
   Clintonians, 160-162, 259; on defenses of Philadelphia, 281-282, 295; definitions,
   14, 91, 313, 338; and district delegate system, 139; in election of 1805, 98-99;
   of 1806, 114-115, 117-119, 131; of 1808, 129, 143-144, 154-156, 157-158, 162-163,
   174-176; of 1809, 203-204; of 1810, 218-220, 245; of 1811, 232, 234-235; of 1812,
   237, 256-269, 273; of 1813, 279-284; of 1814, 293, 298-301; of 1815, 310-313;
   of 1816, 320-321; of 1817, 322; and embargo, 151, 165-167, 237-238, 239-241, 252;
   factionalism among, 121, 142, 145, 147, 304, 309, 314, 319, 321; factions, *see* Constitutional Republicans, Leib-Duane group, Old School Democrats, Quids, Rising
   Sun movement, Snyderites; and foreign affairs, 103, 107, 151, 238, 242-243,
   246-249, 251, 253-256, 262-263, 272, 275; and judicial reform, 119, 179, 181-182;
   and Leib-Duane group, 115, 130-131, 179, 297, 309, 328; and McKean impeachment, 149-150; on Olmsted case, 179, 184, 195, 207-209; relations with Madison,
   159-160, 161-163, 237, 268-269; and Snyder, 151, 154, 169-170, 226, 236; and
   "trout letter," 97-98; and War of 1812, 177, 267-268, 271, 275-276, 308, 329. *See
   also* Republicans.
Detroit, 265, 271
Dickson, William, 110, 231, 353
District of Columbia, 225
District delegate system, 139, 331; in Philadelphia County, 214; use by Federalists, 217
Donaldson, William T., 60, 63, 125-126, 170; as candidate for sheriff, 1806, 116-117,
   121; 1808, 143-144
Duane, William, 22, 33, 34, 35, 42, 45, 49, 50, 65, 68, 69, 79, 90, 93, 123, 152, 154,
   163, 173-175, 205, 231, 278, 290, 355; abandons State politics, 227-228, 233, 264,
   329; as Adjutant General, 276, 280, 296, 375; attacks on, 81, 92; and Binns,
   137-138, 215-216, 254; and Committee of Defense, 296; on conduct of war, 276;
   defeated for directorship of Bank of Pennsylvania, 109-110, 133, 154; and election
   of 1804, 70-72; of 1805, 87-89, 100; of 1806, 113-115, 121-122; of 1807, 144-145;
   of 1808, 154, 156-158, 159, 175; of 1812, 267; of 1814, 300; and embargo, 166, 237,
   241; and Fries's Rebellion, 26; hostility to Gallatin, 72, 73, 229; Jefferson re-
   proves, 229-230; legal battles, 35-36, 113-114, 124, 125, 127, 217, 341, 352; and

INDEX 397

Leib, 105, 112, 141-142, 286; loses election for State Senator, 1807, 143-144; and Madison administration, 231, 257-258; makes James Wilson editor of *Aurora*, 283, 375; makes son editor, 144; and Olmsted affair, 179, 196, 199-200, 210; opposition to McKean, 65, 67, 103, 113, 121-128, 328, 345-346; and Passmore memorial, 55, 57-58; and patronage, 43, 58-59, 158-159, 162; and Pittsburgh *Commonwealth*, 99; on politics in Pennsylvania, 13-15, 19, 310; on Republicanism, 13-15; resumes editorship of *Aurora*, 1815, 310; sketch of, 16-18; and Snyder, 170, 199-200; succeeds Bache as editor, 12; supports Madison, 159, 267; supports Randolph, 110-113; at trial of Burr, 134; withdraws support of John Sergeant, 315; and yellow fever, 59-60. *See also Aurora*, Leib-Duane group.
Duane, William J., 81, 137, 142, 209, 212-214, 217; admitted to bar, 309; on caucuses, 318; criticized by *Democratic Press*, 211, 363; as editor of *Aurora*, 144; and election of 1812, 264; as legislator, 211-213; and Olmsted affair, 206-208; opposes Lacock for U. S. Senator, 272; opposes legislative pay increase, 285; opposes Snyder, 205, 273; sketch of, 355; Snyderites oppose, 319; supposed pseudonym "Conrad Weiser," 209, 211, 263; and Whig Society, 213-214
Dublin, Ireland, 136
Duncan, William, 174, 359
Dunkers, 6
Dunwoody's Tavern, 29
Du Ponceau, Peter Stephen, 42
Dutch, 5

E

East India Company, 17
Easton, 221, 252, 254, 371
Economic conditions, after 1808, 221-222
Edinburgh Review, 277
Education, 123, 222
Egg Harbor, 184
Elbe River, 135
Elections, 7-8; of 1802, 43-47; of 1806, 113, 117-119, 121, 125-126, 352; of 1807, 121; of 1808, 174-177, 328, 359, 372; of 1810, 364; of 1814, 293, 299-301, 377, 378; of 1815, 309-313
Elections, Congressional: of 1804, 73; of 1808, 175; of 1810, 213, 216, 218-220, 245-246; of 1812, 266, 371-372; of 1816, 317, 320-321
Elections, Gubernatorial: of 1799, 26-27, 167, 325, 340, 350; of 1802, 41-42, 45-46; of 1805, 77, 87-89, 98-100, 103, 327, 350; of 1808, 121, 134, 151, 153-156, 160, 174-176, 326, 328; of 1811, 220, 234, 366; of 1814, 288, 297-300; of 1817, 314, 332
Elections, Legislative: of 1800, 28, 340; of 1803, 61-65; of 1804, 73; of 1807, 133-134, 140, 144-145; of 1808, 174-175; of 1809, 201-204; of 1810, 213-220; of 1811, 233-235; of 1812, 265-266; of 1813, 279-284; of 1814, 378
Elections, Presidential: of 1796, 28; of 1800, 12, 17, 27, 28-31; of 1804, 73-75; of 1808, 153-157, 167, 175-176, 331; of 1812, 256-269, 331, 372; of 1816, 314-316, 321, 322
Elections, State Treasurer, 1807, 131-132
Elections, U. S. Senators: of 1802, 49-50; of 1807, 132; of 1808, 179-181; of 1812, 272-273; of 1814, 306
Eleven Million Loan, 1812, 279
Eleventh Amendment, 188
Ellicott, Andrew, 64, 134
Embargo, 107, 151, 169, 171-172, 176, 180, 182-183, 199, 218, 245-247, 252, 256, 328, 367; act of 1807, 164; of 1812, 255; demanded by *Aurora*, 136; economic effects, 164-167; new act, 289-290; New England states defy, 193; Pennsylvania Re-

publicans support, 328; Philadelphia supports, 238-240; repeal of, 183, 237, 241, 244; as State and national issue, 147, 163-164, 167, 176, 237-238

Enforcement Act, 183, 240

England, *see* British

Engle, James, 130, 152, 205, 208, 264; and Democratic caucus, 1807, 132; and impeachment trial, 77; succeeds Boileau as Speaker, 180; and Whig Society, 214

Episcopalians, 6

Erie City, 377

Erie County, 118, 157; in election of 1805, 350; of 1806, 118; of 1809, 204; of 1810, 218; of 1815, 313

Erskine, David M., and agreement of 1809, 241-242, 243

Essex decision, and American commerce, 107

European Wars, 8, 65, 106, 164, 246, 323; economic effect, 8-9, 178, 333; and War of 1812, 294

Eustis, William, Secretary of War, 251, 254, 368, 374

Evening Star, 227, 228; on gubernatorial nomination, 1811, 215; and Old School Democrats, 214

Exports, 5; effect of war on, 164-165

Eyre, Manuel, 61

F

Farmers, *see* Agriculture

Farmers Register, Greensburg, 68

Federal courts, 14, 35, 149, 186, 189-190, 192-194, 198; and Olmsted case, 187-189, 206-207, 272; and Pennsylvania land cases, 128; *see also* Supreme Court, U. S.

Federal Republicans, *see* Federalists

Federalists, 1, 13, 16, 18, 25, 29, 32, 34, 38, 41, 45, 59, 61, 70, 81, 83-84, 97, 98, 104, 133, 134, 147-148, 152, 155-157, 164, 172, 192, 205, 223, 225-226, 228, 269, 285, 287, 294, 306, 309, 319, 329, 334, 342, 368, 371; and Addison's impeachment, 55; attitude toward Democratic policies, 35, 60, 65, 107, 129-130, 136, 168-169, 179, 230, 239-241, 250, 251-252, 262-263, 268, 278, 289, 299-300, 309, 330, 331; and banking act, 275; and British peace terms, 295, 305, 377; coalitions: with Clintonians, 260-262, 267-268, 318, 331, 370; with Constitutional Republicans or Quids, 72, 93, 95, 96, 103, 105, 109, 113, 118-119, 145, 328; with Old School Democrats, 293, 304, 308, 314-315, 318, 380, 381; decline of, 21, 27, 30-31, 37, 58, 74, 325-326; and defense, 135, 281-282, 295, 300; definitions, 13, 313, 338; and election of 1799, 26; of 1800, 28, 69; of 1801, 40; of 1802, 44, 46-47, 50; of 1803, 62-65; of 1804, 72-75, 347; of 1805, 89-90, 99-100; of 1806, 115-119, 131; of 1808, 138, 143-144, 154-156, 162-163, 170-176, 326; of 1809, 203-204; of 1810, 218-220, 245; of 1811, 232-235; of 1812, 256-258, 262, 264-267, 273; of 1813, 279-284; of 1814, 293, 297-300; of 1815, 310-313; of 1816, 320-321; of 1817, 315, 322; and embargo, 166-167, 182-183, 237, 246; and Federal patronage, 43, 161; and foreign affairs, 105, 106, 150-151, 179, 248-249, 252, 323; form American Republican Society, 203; and Fries's Rebellion, 26; and government loans, 253, 279, 292, 374; groups forming, 10-12, 23, 326, 382; McKean and, 27-28, 49, 77, 89, 95-96, 231-232; and Olmsted case, 188, 195, 207-209; party leaders, 19-20: *see also* Addison, Hamilton, Hare, Hollingsworth, Hopkinson, Latimer, Lewis, Milnor, Neville (John and Presley), O'Hara, Rawle, Ross, Smith (Charles), and Wilkins; and Passmore affair, 66; predict economic ruin, 291, 293; press of, 12, 20, 35, 42, 111, 136, 168, 251-252, 260, 297, 307-308, 341; principles of, 10-12, 14-15, 20, 167, 177-178, 303-304, 325-326, 330; use name of American Republicans, 217, 233; of Federal Republicans, 14; and war policies, 254, 255, 271-272, 277, 288, 294-295, 297, 307-308, 369

Fenno, John, publisher of *Gazette of the United States*, 12

INDEX 399

Ferguson, Hugh, 56, 77
Finance, Federal, 10, 178, 373; and Democratic party, 301; loans, 253, 293; State banks and, 249, 272-273, 279, 292; virtual bankruptcy, 291, 293, 299, 376
Findlay, William, 141-142, 210; elected State Treasurer, 132, 139; gubernatorial candidate, 1817, 314, 315, 319; on Snyder's inauguration, 181
Findley, William, 34, 175, 340, 341; Congressman, 119, 157, 220; as Republican leader, 19; supports McKean, 1805, 99
Fitler, Jacob, 282
Fitzsimons, Thomas, 162
Florida, purchase of, 111
Foreign affairs, 8-9, 11, 103, 106, 119, 121, 145, 148, 172, 181, 205, 219, 241-245, 246-248, 252-253, 268, 277-278, 294-295, 301, 308, 328, 330, 333; legislature adopts address on, 1807, 150-151; Snyder comments on, 222; and State politics, 134-136, 163-164, 177, 179, 237
Foreign seamen's bill, 277-278
Forster, John, 378
Fort Erie, 294
Fort George, 293
Fort Niagara, 293
"Fort Rittenhouse" affair, 198. *See also* Olmsted case.
Forty Banks Bill, 288, 297, 373
Forward, Walter, editor of *Tree of Liberty*, 117
Fowler, Alexander, 38
France, 5, 8, 95, 157, 165, 168, 238, 243, 255, 277, 308, 333, 367, 374; decrees restricting trade, 164, 242, 244, 246, 252; party attitudes toward, 11-12, 14, 15, 106, 111, 112, 151, 166, 171, 179, 248, 251-253, 263, 326; revokes decrees, 246, 247; war with, 9, 25, 32
Franklin, Benjamin, 32
Franklin, Walter: and embargo, 239; and Olmsted case, 198, 207
Franklin County, 50, 131-132, 157, 368; in election of 1805, 350; of 1806, 119; of 1807, 145
Franklin Court, 215
Freeman's Journal, 81, 113, 115; and Constitutional Republicans or Quids, 70, 71, 75, 82-83, 91, 92, 94, 171; and Coxe, 69-70; denounces embargo, 171; and election of 1807, 138-139, 143; of 1808, 170, 171; new name of *Philadelphia Evening Post*, 69, 346; on Wolbert affair, 117, 122. *See also Philadelphia Evening Post*.
French, 5
French Revolution, 11, 14, 15, 106, 326, 338
Freneau, Philip, publisher of *National Gazette*, 12
Freytag, Michael, 45
"Friends of the Constitution," 172
Friends, Society of, 6
Fries's Rebellion, 17, 25-27; and election of 1799, 27; as Republican issue, 326

G

Gaines, Major General Edmund P., 296-297
Gallatin, Albert, 13, 15, 118, 173, 373; attacked by *Aurora*, 116, 225, 230, 365; and Duane, 59, 72-73, 82, 229, 257, 276, 310; on election of 1805, 100; on factionalism, 103; and Federal patronage, 43, 162; recommends internal taxation, 251; Republican leader, 19; resigns seat in Congress, 38; and Yazoo lands, 110
Gamble, James, 104-105

Gazette of the United States, 12, 20, 30, 46, 60; defines Federalism, 15. *See also United States' Gazette.*
Gazzam, William, 38
Gemmil, John, 248
General Assembly, 6-7, 185, 311; session of 1799-1800, 28; session of 1800-1801, 187: choice of presidential electors, 29-30, 91, 141; elects Peter Muhlenberg U. S. Senator, 32, 34; session of 1801-2, 40-41: elects Logan U. S. Senator, 40; impeaches Addison, 40, 54; and McKean's vetoes, 40-41; session of 1802-3, 49-55: elects Samuel Maclay U. S. Senator, 49-50; impeaches Addison, 53-55; and judicial reform, 51-53, 56-57; and Olmsted case, 187-188; session of 1803-4, 65-67, 75, 334: and McKean, 66-67; session of 1804-5, 77-79, 80, 83-84, 89, 190: and constitutional reform, 83-84; quarrel with McKean, 84-87; trial of Supreme Court judges, 77-79; session of 1805-6, 105-110; session of 1806-7, 121, 123-133, 139: elects Gregg U. S. Senator, 131-133; and land litigation, 128-129, 190; and McKean, 123-124, 126-129; session of 1807-8, 147-151, 152, 155-156: and impeachment of McKean, 148-150; session of 1808-9, 179-183, 193-197, 238: elects Leib U. S. Senator, 179-180; judicial measures, 181-182; and Olmsted case, 183, 193-195, 197; session of 1809-10, 205-209, 211-213, 243, 334: and Olmsted case, 206-209, 212; session of 1810-11, 220-226: and Bank of the United States, 224-226; and land titles, 224; and Olmsted case, 223-224; session of 1811-12, 248-250; session of 1812-13, 271-275, 378: banking bill, 273-275; elects Lacock U. S. Senator, 272-273; session of 1813-14, 284-288, 301: banking bill, 287-288; elects Jonathan Roberts U. S. Senator, 286-287; legislative pay increase, 285; session of 1814-15, 306-307, 315-316: re-elects Roberts, 306-307
Genêt affair, 9, 12
Georgia, 316
German Reformed Church, 4, 6
German Republican Societies, 18
Germans, 4, 6, 19, 26, 152, 201; election of 1799, 25-27; of 1805, 89, 93; and Peter Muhlenberg, 33, 97; in politics, 59, 100; and Republican party, 327-328; and Snyder, 97-98; and "trout letter," 97-98
Germantown, 45, 115, 139, 202
Germany, 33
Gerry, Elbridge, 265, 267, 370
Gettysburg, 74
Ghent, Treaty of, 307, 329; *United States' Gazette* on, 305
Giles, William B.: and embargo, 241; resolutions on Jackson, 243, 245, 367
Girard, Stephen, 5, 368; and war loans, 279, 293, 374
Gloninger, John, 266, 372, 375
Godwin, William, 136
Gordon, Elisha, 179
Governor, office of, 7-8, 80-82, 86
Granger, Gideon, 111, 297, 300, 346; appoints Leib postmaster in Philadelphia, 286; *Aurora* against, 116; and Burr, 134; opposes Madison, 159; removed as Postmaster General, 286; and Yazoo land speculation, 110
Grant's Hill, 168
Graydon, Alexander, 26-27, 69, 340
Great Britain, *see* British
Greene County, 204, 249, 273; in election of 1805, 350
Green Tree Tavern, 90, 228
Gregg, Andrew, 58, 272; elected U. S. Senator, 1806, 131-133, 139; on war, 255

INDEX 401

H

Halifax, Nova Scotia, 164
Hallowell, John, 104, 105
Hamilton, Alexander, 10-11, 12, 295, 330; economic policies of, 304; proposes Federalist societies, 21
Hamilton, Hugh, 315
Hamilton, John, Congressman, 73
Hamilton, Paul, 374
Hamilton, William, 95-96; editor of *Lancaster Journal*, 19-20
Hampton, Virginia, 275, 373
Hanna, John A., 58
Hare, Charles Willing, 20, 162, 260; on Hartford convention, 306; and Sixteen Million Loan, 292
Harp and Eagle Tavern, 70
Harrisburg, 226, 276, 367, 369; new banks in, 221; nominating convention, 1817, 323; State capital moved to, 271, 334, 382; State convention, 1788, 22
Harrison, John, 109
Harrison, William Henry, 276, 284, 293; Pennsylvania troops with, 271-272, 373
Hartford convention, 306-307, 379
Hastings, John, 110
Havre de Grace, Maryland, 3
Hemphill, Joseph, 179; Federalist nominee for Congress, 1806, 116, 117
Henry, John, 368-369; letters of, 251
Herald of Liberty, Washington, 73, 341
Heston, Edward, 171
Hiester, Gabriel, supports Snyder, 99
Hiester, John S., 119, 173
Hiester, Joseph, 19, 140, 173, 226; and Clinton electoral ticket, 1812, 267, 373; and election of 1801, 40; of 1805, 87, 97, 99, 100, 327, 348; of 1808, 140, 154-155, 175; of 1816, 321; and intrigue to nominate McKean, 1811, 231; sketch of, 87-88; and "trout letter," 97
Higgins, Jesse, 167
High Court of Errors and Appeals: abolished, 108; and Nicholls case, 191
Hoffman, George, 317
Hoge, William, 157, 372; in election of 1804, 73; nominated for Congress, 38; protests Madison nomination, 161
Holgate, Jacob, 115, 202; displaced as Speaker, 315; in election for Assembly, 1808, 144
Holland Land Company, and land litigation, 118, 128, 189, 224
Hollingsworth, Levi, 20; and Rising Sun movement, 45; libel case against Duane, 35-36
Hollingsworth, Paschal, on embargo, 252, 253
Hopkins, James, 64
Hopkinson, Joseph, 20, 278; approves Ross's nomination for governor, 155; attends party caucus in New York, 261, 371; and British peace terms, 305; and *Chesapeake* affair, 136; in Congressional election, 1816, 320; on embargo, 166; opposes warrant for Leib's arrest, 127; sponsors William J. Duane for admission to bar, 309
House of Representatives, Pennsylvania, 7-8, 28-30, 36-37, 40-41, 46, 51-52, 65, 82, 86, 100, 108, 128-130, 133, 147-148, 179, 204-206, 225, 229, 250, 266, 284, 315, 320, 321, 355; address on foreign affairs, 1807, 150; approves constitutional amendment, 190; and arbitration bill, 87; and banking act, 273-275, 287, 288;

on British aggression, 248-249; on contempts of court, 56-57; and election of 1801, 32; of 1808, 175; of 1810, 220; of 1811, 234-235; of 1814, 301, 378; of 1815, 313; impeaches Addison, 54, 55; and impeachment of McKean, 148-150; and impeachment of Supreme Court judges, 66-67, 77-78; and judicial reforms, 51, 52, 66; and militia bill, 306; on national administration, 182-183; and Nicholls case, 191-192; on Olmsted case, 188, 194-196, 209, 211, 223, 363; and Passmore affair, 66, 67; and Philadelphia sheriff's election, 125; refuses State charter for Bank of the United States, 225-226, 249; resolutions on embargo, 238; on restriction of press, 123, 124, 125; Snyder re-elected Speaker, 1806, 130, 148; sustains Snyder veto, 373; on Thompson-Bryan affair, 108, 109; vote on change in capital, 1810, 382. *See also* General Assembly.

Houston, Captain Thomas, 184, 185, 223
Howe, General, 69
Howe, John: on embargo, 164; on election of 1808, 167
Huidekoper's Lessee v. *Douglass,* 189-190, 276
Hull, General William, surrenders Detroit, 265, 276
Hulme, John, 179
Hundred Dollar Act, 52, 53, 66; amended, 129
Huntingdon County: in election of 1799, 26; of 1800, 28; of 1801, 37; of 1805, 350; of 1814, 299; Federalists in, 65; and War of 1812, 275

I

Immigration, 333
Impressment, 107, 164, 166, 244, 248, 253, 268
Incompatibility Act, 40, 41, 82, 341-342
India Gazette, 17
India World, 17
Indiana County, 3, 250, 381; in election of 1809, 204; of 1815, 313
Indians, 189, 253, 277, 333
Ingersoll, Charles J., 370; on foreign affairs, 253; pressure on Philadelphia postoffice appointment, 286, 309, 379; U. S. Attorney for Pennsylvania, 309
Ingersoll, Jared: candidate for Senate, 306; counsel for Supreme Court justices, 78, 79; nominee for Vice President, 260, 263, 370
Ingham, Samuel D., 130
Intelligencer, Lancaster, 22, 353; criticizes Weaver, 50; on election of bank directors, 110; opposes third party, 64; receives contract to publish Federal laws, 231
Internal improvements, 123, 222, 333
Ireland, 17, 355
Irish, 5, 59
Iron manufacturing, 221
Irvine, Callender, 363
Israel, John, 38; editor of Washington *Herald of Liberty,* 73, 341
Israel, Israel, 341; on Quid assembly ticket, 73; and Society of Constitutional Republicans, 90

J

Jackson, Andrew, 333, 355; victory at New Orleans, 305, 307
Jackson, Francis James, British minister, 218; and Erskine agreement, 242-243; resolutions censure, 245
Jacobinism, 15, 35, 95-96, 104, 310; in France, 106; Republicans charged with, 72
Jamaica, 184

INDEX

Jay, John, 261; and British peace terms, 305
Jay's treaty, 9, 12, 16
Jefferson, Thomas, 10-12, 15, 16, 18, 27-29, 31-34, 41, 45-46, 58, 59, 65, 74, 82, 106, 112-113, 124, 136, 150-151, 154, 157, 159, 173, 229, 276, 303; and act for National Road, 130; address to, from General Assembly on third term, 129-130; appoints John Shee Collector of the Port, 161; appoints John Steele to succeed Shee, 162; appoints Peter Muhlenberg Supervisor of Revenue, 34; *Aurora* accuses Quids of opposition to, 116; and Coxe, 69; Democratic leaders waver in allegiance to, 112; Democrats support foreign policy of, 103; foreign policy embarrasses Constitutionalists, 119; disapproves Duane's policies, 229-230; disapproves treaty with Great Britain, 135; on Federal patronage, 43, 342; Inaugural address, 35; on Judiciary act, 42; letter to, from Pennsylvania Congressmen, 58; message against Spain, 111; opposition to policy of, 183; Pennsylvania as ideal polity of, 1; on Pennsylvania political situation, 1804, 75; policies, 1808, 176; and political dissensions, 93; and presidential election of 1800, 30; of 1804, 74, 75; principles, 333; proclamation against Burr, 134; retires, 147, 156, 164, 178; tries to purchase Florida, 111; and party organization, 329, 330
Jefferson County, 250, 381; in election of 1815, 313
Jeffersonian Republicanism, 304; crumbling of, 329, 334; Pennsylvania's influence on, 331
Jeffersonian Republicans, *see* Democrats, Republicans
Jenkins, Robert, Republican Congressman, 119, 156, 175
Jones, Nathan, 45
Jones, William, 32, 43, 58-59, 72, 83, 166, 241, 258, 277, 299; appointed Secretary of the Navy, 374; author of Republican resolutions demanding war, 253; Gallatin favors, 162; and mariners' meeting on maritime rights, 172-173; and Rising Sun movement, 45; supports embargo as party measure, 238-240
Josiah, Captain, 184-185
Judicial reform, 43, 49, 51-52, 55, 68, 75, 80-82, 86-87, 92, 100, 101, 105, 107-108, 119, 129, 133, 145, 148, 177, 179, 182. *See also* Arbitration; Courts, Pennsylvania; Supreme Court, Pennsylvania.
Judiciary Act of 1799, State, 51-53, 66
Judiciary Act of 1801, Federal, 35, 36, 40, 42-43, 342
"Junto faction," 138-139
Justices of the peace, 51-53, 55, 66, 129
Juries, 14, 52, 123, 129

K

Kean, John, 40
Kelly, James, Congressman, 73, 119; defeated for re-election, 175
Kentucky, 8, 10, 190
Kentucky Resolutions, 178
"Keystone," as nickname for Pennsylvania, 1, 2, 22, 167, 176, 237, 269, 293, 304, 322, 331, 337
King, Rufus: and British peace terms, 305; Federalist candidate for Vice President, 74, 163, 347; opposes Clinton's nomination, 260-261

L

Lacock, Abner, 150, 154; attacks Leib, 139; elected U. S. Senator, 272-273; election of 1810, 219, 226, 245; and Olmsted case, 210; and report on land litigation, 128, 190; sketch of, 272, 373; and trial of Supreme Court judges, 77
Lake Champlain, 296
Lake Erie, 2, 276
Lake Ontario, 284

INDEX

Lancaster, 4, 41, 50, 58, 87, 89, 108, 122, 127, 137, 153, 154, 155, 157, 158, 160, 191, 196, 226, 231, 259, 260, 317, 318, 381, 382; Constitutionalists, 64, 96; Federalists, 20, 326; new banks, 221; and State capital, 334, 382

Lancaster - Berks - Chester District, and election of 1808, 175

Lancaster County, 4, 87, 104, 110, 131, 157, 207, 227, 318, 319, 356, 368; in election of 1799, 27; of 1800, 28; of 1801, 37; of 1803, 64; of 1804, 73; of 1805, 350; of 1808, 174; of 1809, 204; of 1810, 219, 245; o f1811, 234; of 1812, 268, 372; of 1813, 284; of 1814, 299; of 1815, 313; Federalists in, 64, 327

Land companies, 212

Land titles, 118, 128, 189, 190, 206, 210, 212, 224

Lane, Presley Carr, 226, 227; and election of 1808, 154

Langdon, John, 370

Latimer, George, 20, 41, 162; in election of 1814, 299; and Rising Sun movement, 45

Latscha, Henry, 85

Laurel Ridge, 3

Lawler, Matthew, 90; and *Chesapeake* affair, 136; in election of 1806, 117, 121

Lazaretto, Philadelphia, 40, 60, 113, 126

Leander incident, 134

Lebanon County, 375; in election of 1814, 299, 378

Leech, Richard T., Snyder leader, 205

Lefever, Joseph, 370; and Clinton campaign, 1816, 318; at Lancaster meeting, 1812, 259-260

Le Gerard, Philadelphia privateer, 184

Leib, Dr. Michael, 34, 46, 73, 90, 145, 149, 176, 205, 211, 238, 348, 369, 381; in Assembly session of 1806-7, 123-127, 131-133; of 1807-8, 150-153; of 1808-9, 179-182; attitude toward War of 1812, 255, 369; candidate for Congress, 1802, 40, 43-44; 1804, 70, 71; challenged by Thomas McKean, Jr., 121, 128, 353; on *Chesapeake* affair, 136; and Clintonian ticket, 1812, 260; Constitutional Republicans and, 92-93, 100, 170, 173; *Democratic Press* attacks, 138, 140, 283, 297, 300; elected U. S. Senator, 179-181; and election of 1804, 70-72, 75, 347; of 1805, 88, 89; of 1806, 115, 121-122; of 1807, 136-142, 144; of 1808, 153-154, 159, 173, 174; of 1809, 200, 202; of 1812, 258-259, 264-265; of 1814, 300; of 1815, 311; and election of U. S. Senator, 1807, 115, 131-133, 140-142; feud with Boileau, 130, 133, 154; with McKean, 121-128, 143, 212, 328; with Snyderites, 136, 137-138, 177, 179, 200, 231, 282, 319; and Incompatibility act, 40, 341-342; and intrigue to nominate McKean, 1811, 231; and Old School Democrats, 213-215, 217, 283, 310; opposes Madison, 267, 370; opposed by Rising Sun group, 40, 44-45, 60-62, 68-69; opposition to, 49, 63, 65, 82, 140-142; and patronage, 58-59, 230, 365; and *Pennsylvania Democrat,* 201-202, 227; and Penrose affair, 44, 69, 342, 346; political tour, 1815, 314, 315, 318, 381; as postmaster of Philadelphia, 286, 297, 300, 301, 309; president of Board of Prison Inspectors, 309-310; and Randolph, 111-113; sketch, 17-18; and Snyder nomination, 1808, 152-154, 356; supports Madison, 1808, 159; and Whig Society, 213-214

Leib-Duane group, 70, 151, 174, 199, 213, 237, 298; controls Democratic party, 1805, 105; controls Philadelphia, 115, 145, 174, 328; country Republicans and, 101; decline of, 227-229; denounces district delegate system, 62; effect of cooperation with Federalists, 300; and Jefferson administration, 330; and legislative opposition, 75; as Old School Democrats, 201; and Olmsted case, 179, 184, 199-200; renews attack on Snyder, 204; supports Madison, 161. *See also* Old School Democrats.

Leiper, Thomas, 45, 90, 109, 154, 159, 162, 179, 213-214, 264; criticizes Leib, 230; favors re-chartering of Bank of the United States, 225; and foreign affairs, 253, 367; supports Madison, 158; and Whig Society, 213, 214; withdraws support from Duane, 229, 230

Leopard, British frigate, 136

Letters of marque and reprisal, 255

INDEX 405

Levis, William, 355
Levy, Moses, 42, 125, 172
Levy, Sampson, 42
Lewis, Joshua, 381
Lewis, William, Philadelphia Federalist, 20, 96
Libels, 113-114, 123-125, 148, 181-182
Linnard, William, 365
Little Belt, 247
Lloyd, Joseph, 217; editor of *Pennsylvania Democrat,* 201; and election of 1809, 202; and pamphlet against Leib, 139
Logan, George, 19, 93, 115, 131; and Constitutional Republicans, 83, 90; and election as U. S. Senator, 32-33, 34, 40; and Rising Sun movement, 45; sketch, 32
Logan Act, 32
London, 136-137
London Corresponding Society, 17, 136
Louisiana, 10
Louisiana Purchase, 65, 68, 91, 106
Lowrie, Walter, candidate for Congress, 320-321
Lucas, John B. C., 38, 118; and impeachment of Addison, 53-54; sketch, 53-54
Ludie, Martin, 44
Lundy's Lane, 294
Lutherans, 4, 6
Luzerne County, 3, 4, 109, 127, 195, 250; in election of 1799, 26; of 1800, 28; of 1801, 37; of 1802, 46; of 1805, 350; of 1808, 174-175; of 1809, 204; of 1811, 234; of 1812, 268; of 1815, 313; Federalists in, 39, 65, 266, 326
Luzerne Federalist, Wilkes-Barre, on election of 1805, 95
Lycoming County, 356; in election of 1799, 26; of 1805, 350; of 1806, 119

M

Maclay, Samuel, 19, 40, 87, 131, 154; elected U. S. Senator, 1802, 49, 50; opposes Madison's nomination, 1808, 157, 159, 160, 273; resigns as Senator, 180, 181; sketch, 50
Maclay, William, 19, 49, 50; and removal of capital to Harrisburg, 334
Macon, Nathaniel, 238, 243-244, 246
Madison, James, 178, 180, 218, 222, 273, 277, 296, 304, 305, 314, 369, 370; appoints Dallas Secretary of the Treasury, 309; *Aurora* opposes, 229-230, 231; Clintonian opposition to, 237, 255, 261, 263, 267; and Erskine agreement, 241-242; Federalist opposition to, 261, 263, 297, 300, 309, 379; and Leib's appointment as postmaster of Philadelphia, 286; message to Congress, 1811, 247-248; Old School Democrats and, 229, 309-310; and Olmsted case, 197-198, 200, 207, 209; Pennsylvania Republicans and, 147, 167, 176, 237, 244; and Presidential election, 1808, 147, 155-163, 173, 176; 1812, 256-269, 322, 331, 372; reaction against, 300-301, 329, 330, 331; revives nonintercourse with Great Britain, 246; signs Compensation Act, 1816, 316; sketch, 156-157; Snyderites and, 230-231; and War of 1812, 254, 275-276
Mail, opening of foreign, 277, 374
Malden, 284
Manufacturing, 9, 221, 289, 333; effect of embargo on, 165, 178; in Pittsburgh, 320
Marie, Jane, case of, 167-168, 358
Marshall, John, Chief Justice of the United States, 150, 260; and Olmsted case, 193; and Pennsylvania land cases, 128, 189-190
Martin, Jacob, 50

INDEX

Martin, James, 372
Maryland, 2, 5, 113, 126, 173; in Presidential election of 1801, 31; of 1812, 268
Massachusetts, 6, 74, 240, 251, 261; and embargo, 183, 198, 241; Federalists in, 162; refuses militia, 272, 284, 375
Mathews, John R., editor of Lancaster *Constitutional Democrat*, 108, 115
McCorkle, William: and *Freeman's Journal*, 170-172; and *Philadelphia Evening Post*, 68
McFerran, Samuel, 45
McKean, Joseph B., Attorney General, 42, 54, 172; attempts to arrest Leib, 127; sues Duane for libel, 114, 125, 127; sued for assault on Duane, 114, 127
McKean, Thomas, 19, 33, 34, 42, 50, 60, 68, 69, 72, 88, 105, 117, 137, 138, 139, 141, 161, 177, 181, 205, 212, 295, 328, 330, 334, 340, 344, 360, 372; and Addison's impeachment, 55; advocates judicial reform, 51, 65; appoints Logan U. S. Senator, 40; attempt to impeach, 114, 126-128, 133, 139, 143, 145, 148-150, 155, 272, 352, 353; *Aurora* on, 63-65, 67, 68, 91, 92, 104, 134, 345, 346, 349, 351; breaks with Republican majority, 77, 84-86; and "clodpole" affair, 84-86; and Constitutional Republicans, 77, 90, 93, 95-96, 100, 119, 147; defends judiciary, 67; dismisses Federalists, 27-28; dismisses Samuel Bryan, 103, 108; and election of 1799, 12, 26-27; of 1802, 40, 41, 43, 45, 46; of 1803, 58, 64; of 1805, 89, 90, 93-101, 103, 327, 350; Federalists and, 27, 35, 89, 95-96; feud with Duane and Leib, 68, 113-114, 121-128, 143; and General Assembly: session of 1801-2, 40-41; of 1802-3, 49, 51-53, 55; of 1803-4, 65-67, 75; of 1804-5, 77, 84, 86-87; of 1805-6, 105-110; of 1806-7, 123-131; of 1807-8, 148-150; heads Clinton ticket, 1812, 267; and Hundred Dollar Act, 52, 66; and Leib affair, 121, 127, 128, 143; Leib's intrigue to nominate, 1811, 231, 232, 366, 367; on libels, 123; Muhlenberg supports, 1805, 97-98; and Olmsted case, 186-188; *Philadelphia Evening Post* and, 68; and Philadelphia sheriff's election, 1806, 121-123, 125-126; and Presidential election of 1800, 28-31; sketch of, 16; and suits against Duane, 113-114, 125; supports Twelfth Amendment, 74; "trout letter" and, 97-98; use of facsimile stamp, 113, 126-127; vetoes, 52, 53, 66, 86-87, 128, 129, 148: of Incompatibility Act, 40-41; of resolution on foreign court precedents, 148-149; of resolution on Pennsylvania land cases, 128-129, 190
McKean, Thomas, Jr., challenges Leib, 121, 353
McKinney, Abraham, 84-85; on "clodpole" incident, 92
McMullin, Robert, 216, 218, 238-240
Mead, David, 219
Meadville, 224, 349
Meigs, Return J., Postmaster General, 286
Mennonites, 6
Mercer County, 161; in election of 1805, 350; of 1806, 118; of 1810, 218-219; of 1815, 313
Merchants' Coffee House, 172, 281
Mercury, Pittsburgh: on Allegheny County politics, 320; on Hartford Convention, 307; supports Carlisle ticket, 1817, 322; on War of 1812, 276, 308
Methodists, 6
"Michael's Chronicle," nickname for *Whig Chronicle*, 267, 268
Michigan Territory, 10
Michilimackinac, 276, 294
Mifflin County, 272, 319, 356; in election of 1799, 26; of 1805, 350
Mifflin, Thomas, Governor, 16
Mifflin Township, 321
Milan Decree, 164, 165
Militia, 14, 22, 50, 123, 194, 224, 373, 374, 377, 378; reform, 148, 222, 248, 272, 277, 285, 306; voting, 272, 298, 378; in War of 1812, 281, 284, 285, 295-297, 306
Miller, John, 90, 228

Miller, William, 191
Milnor, James, 20, 218, 220, 232; denounces Dallas, 104; Federalist Congressional candidate, 1810, 245-246; opposes declaration of war, 254-255
Milnor, William, 157, 175; Republican Congressman, 119
Miner, Charles, on Olmsted case, 195
Mississippi River, 2, 10, 65
Mississippi Territory, 10
Mitchell, David, 57, 93
Mitchell, Jacob, 194, 238
Monongahela River, 4
Monroe, James, 158, 160, 368, 381; Congressional caucus nominates, 321; and treaty with Great Britain, 135; in Presidential election of 1816, 316-318, 322; Snyderites support, 314
Montgomery, Daniel, on "clodpole" incident, 92
Montgomery, Daniel, Jr., 157, 273
Montgomery County, 19, 26, 29, 32-34, 40, 81, 152, 205, 250-251, 287, 356, 368, 373; district delegate system in, 39; in election of 1799, 26; of 1802, 46, 343; of 1805, 99, 350; of 1806, 119; of 1808, 175; of 1815, 313
Montreal, 271, 293
Moore, Robert, 235
Moravians, 6
Morgan, Benjamin R., 162, 315
Morris, Gouverneur, 260-261
Mountain, James, 372
Muhlenberg, Frederick A., 34; and German vote, 26
Muhlenberg, Peter, 32-34, 39-41, 45, 83, 342; appointed Supervisor of Revenue, 34; *Aurora* attacks, 98; as candidate for governor, 1805, 87, 88; death of, 161; elected U. S. Senator, 32-34; and election of 1805, 97-98, 327; and German vote, 19, 26, 100; refuses presidency of Society of Constitutional Republicans, 88, 90; replaces Latimer as Collector of Port of Philadelphia, 41; sketch of, 33; "trout letter," 97-98

N

Napoleon Bonaparte, 8, 106, 111, 171, 252, 254, 263, 277, 326, 328, 367; abdicates, 294; and Berlin Decree, 135; and Milan Decree, 164
Napoleonic Wars, 237, 303; and Pennsylvania politics, 106-107, 333
National Gazette, 12
National Intelligencer, 262
National Road, 130
Nazareth, 260
Negroes, 3
Neutral rights, 107, 135, 164, 179, 241, 328
Neville, John, 19
Neville, Presley, 19
New England, 4, 239, 251, 256, 280, 287, 306, 307, 368; and British blockade, 291; disunionism in, 297, 305, 311, 379; and embargo, 183, 193, 238, 289-290; Federalists in, 13, 178, 326; and Hartford Convention, 306; and war finances, 291-292
New Hampshire, 8, 186, 291
New Jersey, 2, 184, 331
New London, Connecticut, 293
New Orleans, Battle of, 305, 307

408 INDEX

New School Democrats, 311. *See also* Snyderites.
New York City, 10, 17, 69, 87, 134, 184, 261, 293, 314, 318; British bills for sale in, 291; Federalist meeting in, 1808, 162, 163; 1812, 261-262, 370-371; suspends specie payment, 292
New York Morning Chronicle, 63
New York State, 2-4, 74, 256, 279-280, 295; banks in, 273; British raid frontier of, 293-294, 377; manufacturing in, 6; supports De Witt Clinton for President, 259
Newark, Canada, 293
Newspapers, 12, 106; control of libels in, proposed, 123-125. *See also under names of parties and newspapers.*
Nicholls, William: case of, 190-192, 194, 361; conflict of State and Federal claims, 191; legislative action on, 191-192
Nominations, 20, 22; by convention, 89, 214, 216-217; by county meeting, 214-215; by district delegate system, 21, 27-39, 61-63, 98, 115, 139-143, 202-203, 214, 282-283, 311, 331-332; by general county meeting, 62, 98, 151; by general meeting in Washington County, 38; ward meetings, 59-60, 98, 282, 311
Nonimportation Act of 1806, 134-135, 164
Nonimportation and nonintercourse laws, 241, 243, 246, 290; Randolph attacks, 111. *See also* Embargo.
Normandy, 53
North Carolina, 238
Northampton County, 4, 25, 89, 275, 313; county delegate meetings in, 319; district delegate system in, 39; in election of 1799, 26, 27; of 1802, 46; of 1804, 73; of 1805, 100, 350; of 1808, 170, 175; German vote in, 93
Northampton Farmer, Easton, 201
Northern Liberties, 18, 60-62, 214, 264, 266, 372, 376; in county delegate elections, 297; and defense of Philadelphia, 295; Democratic caucus in, 1802, 43; in election of 1810, 217-218; and embargo, 240; general county meetings, and, 36, 139; Independent Democrats in, 319; meeting of Democrats in, 1808, 180; Old School Democrats in, 310; and protection of shipping, 281; war relief in, 290
Northumberland, 13, 382
Northumberland County, 3, 19, 50-51, 84, 137, 157, 207, 273, 349, 350; and election of 1799, 26; of 1808, 160-162
Northwest Territory, 2, 10, 271
Northwestern Pennsylvania, dispute over land titles, 189-190, 210, 360
Nuremberg, 171

O

O'Brien, Richard, 195
O'Hara, James, 19
Ohio, 10
Ohio River, 2, 3, 10, 118
Old School Democrats, 226, 236, 258, 272, 374; alliance with Federalists, 293, 308, 309, 311-313, 314-315, 318, 321, 380, 381; alliance with Quids, 220; attack Snyder, 209-210; and Clintonian ticket, 1812, 260, 370; decline of, 205, 227-231; and election of 1809, 201-202, 203; of 1810, 213-218, 220; of 1811, 227, 232-234; of 1812, 264-265, 266; of 1813, 283, 284, 375; of 1814, 293, 297-298; of 1815, 309-313, 380; of 1816, 318-321; and Federal patronage, 230, 276; intemperateness of, 210-211, 213, 223; and Madison administration, 229-231, 257, 309, 314; name adopted by Leib-Duane group, 201, 329; and Olmsted affair, 209, 244, 257; promote Sergeant for governor, 1817, 315; and Snyderites, 205-206, 210-212, 244, 245, 282, 309, 314, 319; and Whig Society, 213, 214
Olmsted, Gideon, 184, 193

INDEX 409

Olmsted Case, 179, 213, 230, 257, 272, 334, 360, 366; *Aurora* on, 188, 196, 198, 199, 209-210; history of, 183-189, 192-198; legislative action on, 1811, 223-224; legislative inquiry on, 1810, 206-209, 211, 212-213; and politics, 184, 199-201, 203-204, 205, 209-210, 228, 229, 244, 329; Roberts on, 212-213; Snyder and, 197-198, 204, 212-213, 231
Orders in council, 165, 252
Orr, John, 132
Orwigsburg, 373
Oswego, 294
Otis, Harrison Gray, 162, 306; on Federalist caucus in New York, 262; and Sixteen Million Loan, 292; supports Clinton, 260, 261, 370

P

Paine, Tom, and Jefferson, 35, 341
Palatinate, 50
Palm, Johann Philipp, 171
Palmer, Richard, 282-283, 370, 372
Paris, 111, 246
Parish, David, and war loans, 279, 292-293, 374
Passmore, Thomas, 55-56; and contempts of court, 55-58; memorial of, 49, 55-58, 66, 67; and trial of Supreme Court judges, 78
"Patent Democrats," 201. *See also* Snyderites.
Patronage, Federal, 43, 49, 58-59, 75, 157, 158-159, 162, 284, 285-286, 308, 309, 310, 329; and Old School Democrats, 230-231
Patronage, State, 77, 177, 228, 304, 309, 310, 334; criticism of, 80-81, 143, 321, 332; McKean and, 103-104, 128; Snyder and, 201, 210, 217
Patton, Robert, 285
Pearce, John, 134
Pearson, John, 71
Penhallow et al. v. Doane's Administrators, 186-187
Penn, William, 6
Pennell, William, 71-72
Pennsylvania: characteristics, 1-2; commerce, 2, 3, 5, 331; and declaration of war, 255-256; government of, 6-8, 80-81, 85; influence in national affairs, 1, 2, 12, 167, 310, 330, 331, 337; physical aspects, 2-3; political ideals, 1-2, 21; prosperity of, after 1808, 220-221; racial groups, 4, 5; religious groups, 4, 6; social and economic characteristics, 1-2, 5, 333
Pennsylvania Democrat: and election of 1809, 201-202; ceases publication, 227
Pennsylvania Population Company, 118, 189
Pennsylvania Republican, Harrisburg: on constitutional revision, 250; on foreign affairs, 251, 253
Penrose, William, in election of 1804, 71-72
Penrose affair, 44, 69, 342, 346
Pentland, Ephraim, editor of Pittsburgh *Commonwealth*, 99, 117; feud with Bates, 117; opposes regular Democrats, 235; supports Bank of Pittsburgh, 234
Perry's victory on Lake Erie, 276, 283, 293
Peter Porcupine's Gazette, 12
Peters, Judge Richard, and Olmsted Case, 187, 188, 193, 196
Petersburg, Virginia, 134
Pettit, Andrew, 78; and Passmore affair, 56
Philadelphia, 3, 10, 17, 29, 32, 41, 42, 55, 57, 65, 67, 91, 97, 108, 110, 127, 130, 131, 151,

152, 154, 155, 157, 158, 179, 184, 190, 194, 195, 197, 198, 200, 207, 208, 210, 211, 223, 227, 228, 230, 231, 244, 252, 255, 260, 261, 285, 287, 308, 309, 315, 316, 371, 372, 382; banks, 5, 221; and *Chesapeake* affair, 136; Committee of Defense, 281, 290-291, 295, 296; and Constitutional Republicans, 82-83, 171-172; declines in political influence, 18, 77, 334; in election of 1799, 26; of 1800, 28; of 1801, 36-37; of 1802, 40; of 1804, 73; of 1805, 96, 99, 104, 350; of 1806, 116-117; of 1807, 136-139, 142-145, 151, 356; of 1808, 155, 156, 161, 162-163, 169, 174, 359; of 1809, 201-204; of 1810, 213, 216-218, 245-246; of 1811, 234; of 1812, 258, 264, 266; of 1813, 279-280, 282-284; of 1814, 299-301, 378; of 1815, 311-312; of 1816, 318-320; and embargo, 164-165, 238-241; and Federal finance, 292-293; Federalists, 162, 175, 217, 233, 245, 250, 260, 264, 294, 326; and foreign affairs, 243-245, 253, 254; manufacturing in, 221, 289; mercantile interests, 2, 107; as national capital, 12, 18; newspapers, 12, 20, 22, 68, 69, 137-139, 201-202, 227; political leaders, 19, 20; population, 4, 333-334; religious groups, 6; Republicans, 22, 75, 101, 113, 199, 205; Rising Sun movement, 40; sheriff's election, 1806, 116-117, 125, 126; as State capital, 334; war boom, 289-290; and War of 1812, 275, 289-290, 294, 305-307; ward committees, 36-37; yellow fever, 59, 60. *See also* Philadelphia County.

Philadelphia County, 4, 18, 64, 130, 131, 140, 152, 180, 195, 207, 208, 243, 250, 285, 300, 315, 327, 368, 370, 372; district delegate system, 139, 214; in election of 1799, 26; of 1802, 43; of 1803, 58, 60-61, 64; of 1804, 71-72; of 1805, 350; of 1807, 132; of 1808, 174, 359; of 1810, 216, 218; of 1812, 264; of 1814, 299, 378; ward committee system, 36-37, 70. *See also* Philadelphia.

Philadelphia Evening Post, 68, 69, 346. *See also Freeman's Journal.*

Philadelphia Gazette, 20

Pickering, Timothy, 74, 159, 260; and embargo, 240-242

Pinckney, Charles Cotesworth, Federalist candidate for President, 74, 163, 347

Pinkney, William, and treaty with Great Britain, 134

Piper, William, 211

Pitt, William, 113

Pittsburgh, 4, 19, 39, 53-54, 108, 113, 118, 155, 167-168, 219, 224, 232, 260, 273, 315; district delegate system in, 37-38; in election of 1802, 46; of 1805, 99, 350; of 1806, 117, 352; of 1810, 272; of 1811, 226, 234-235; of 1812, 265; of 1815, 313; of 1816, 320-321; manufacturing in, 289, 320, 376; new banks in, 221, 234-235; newspapers, 22, 307

Pittsburgh Gazette, 20; on election of 1801, 31; on foreign affairs, 248; on Hartford convention, 306, 307; supports McKean, 99; on War of 1812, 308

Pleasants, Samuel, Jr., 158

Poe, James, 131

Population, 3-5; growth, 333-334, 382; westward trend of, 10

Porter, Andrew, Surveyor General, 211

Porter, Charles, 372

Porter, Dr. John, 230; as candidate for Congress, 115, 216, 218

Portsmouth, New Hampshire, 291, 376

Potomac River, 261

Potter County, 3

Poulson's American Daily Advertiser, 20, 123; on county meetings, 61

Presbyterians, 6, 19

President, naval action with *Little Belt*, 247

Presidential elections, *see* Elections, Presidential

Press, *see* Newspapers

Prevost, Sir George, 164

Priestley, Joseph, 137

Princeton, 81

Public Advertiser, New York, 257

Q

"Quadroons:" *Aurora's* name for Binns' group, 140; and election of 1808, 144, 174
Quakers, 32, 169, 239, 328
Queenston Heights, 271
Quid Mirror, 121, 353
Quids, 110, 112, 113, 140, 152, 153, 161, 225, 227, 228, 236, 238, 245, 273, 311, 312, 313, 334; *Aurora's* name for McKean group, 69; coalition with Federalists, 93, 95-96, 133, 145; difficulties with Federalists, 103-105; and district delegate system, 98; and election of 1804, 70-72, 73, 74-75; of 1805, 93, 94-100; of 1806, 115-119; of 1807, 143-145; of 1808, 154-155, 158, 172, 175-176; of 1809, 204; of 1810, 219-220; of 1812, 264, 266; and election of U. S. Senator, 1806, 131; 1808, 179; and investigation of Bryan, 108-109; and legislature, 1805-6, 107-109; 1807-8, 147-148; as name for Constitutional Republicans, 91, 328; and national issues, 107, 116, 119, 129, 151; newspapers, 68, 69, 92, 108, 171; and Olmsted case, 195, 207-209; oppose constitutional revision, 81, 92-94, 250; and proposed McKean candidacy, 1811, 231-232; and reunion with Republicans, 138, 147, 170-171; and Snyder, 130, 168-169, 170-171, 226; and "trout letter," 97-98. *See also* Constitutional Republicans.

R

Raguet, Condy, 377
Randolph, John, of Roanoke, 18, 110, 113, 115, 229, 273; break with Jefferson, 103, 111; influence on Duane, 110, 111-112, 113; Leib and, 112-113; and nonimportation, 135; opposes Yazoo claims, 110-111; and protest against Madison's nomination, 157
Rankin, William, 131
Rawle, William, 20
Rea, John, 157
Reading, 4, 26, 97, 226, 382; new banks in, 221
Reapportionment Act, 307
Reed, Joseph, 295
Republican Argus, Northumberland, 68, 69, 137; on election of 1806, 118
Republicans, 50, 59, 66, 101, 112, 150, 188, 251, 312; and Addison's impeachment, 55; attitude toward France, 106; and Clinton campaign, 256, 259, 267; country group, 67, 99, 101, 121, 145, 147; and declaration of war, 253; divisions among, 18, 25, 32-34, 37-38, 41, 42, 49, 58, 62, 65, 67-68, 73, 75, 77, 82-83, 89, 90-93, 99, 103, 110, 116, 119, 142, 178-179, 205, 219, 236, 237, 328-330; and election of 1799, 26, 27; of 1801, 35-37; of 1802, 39-41, 43-45, 46-47; of 1803, 61, 64-65; of 1804, 71-73; of 1805, 77, 89, 99-101; of 1808, 174, 176; of 1810, 219-220; and election of U. S. Senator, 1801, 32-34, 40; and Federal patronage, 40, 42, 58-59, 162, 231; and foreign affairs, 106, 135, 179, 237, 248; groups forming, 10-12, 22-23, 327-328, 382; and Judiciary Act, 42; leaders, 15-19; and Madison, 156; national issues unify, 103, 105, 106, 138, 147, 170, 176, 179, 205, 237, 329; newspapers, 12, 68, 69, 137-138; and nominating conventions, 22, 142-143, 317-318; organization of, 21-23, 36-37, 45, 62, 328, 331-332; Pennsylvania's importance to, 1-2, 12, 167, 331; and Presidential election, 1800, 28, 30, 31; 1804, 74-75; 1808, 147, 160-161, 176; 1812, 259; principles of, 11-14, 40, 93, 177-178, 274, 303-304, 326-327, 330. *See also* Constitutional Republicans; Democrats; Old School Democrats; Quids; Snyderites
Revolution, 18, 33, 50, 51, 53, 63, 69, 79, 87, 106, 183
Reynolds, Dr. James, 127
Richards, Jacob, 70-71
Richards, Matthias, Congressman, 119; and election of 1810, 219, 220, 245
Richardson, Dr. Andrew, 38
Richmond, Virginia, 134, 229

Riddle, James, 235, 262; supports Bank of Pittsburgh, 234
Rising Sun movement, 40, 43-44, 58, 62, 68, 116; and Federalists, 63; opposes Leib, 45, 60-61; and ward committees, 70
Rising Sun Tavern, 44, 171-172
Rittenhouse, David, and Olmsted case, 185-188, 193
River Raisin, 275, 277
Roberts, Jonathan, Jr., 32, 82, 200, 209, 247, 251, 254-255, 363, 370, 373; elected to U. S. Senate, 287, 306; on embargo, 252-253; on legislature, 1809, 205-206; on Olmsted case, 212-213; on Snyder's relations with Leib, 152-153
Roberts, Jonathan, Sr., death of, 363
Robespierre, 92
Rodman, William, 252, 255
Rodney, Caesar A., 112; prosecutor in impeachment of Supreme Court justices, 78
Roman Catholics, 6
Rose, Daniel, and Leib affair, 140, 142
Ross, Judge George, and Olmsted case, 185-187, 193
Ross, James, 55; charges against, 167-168; Federalist candidate for governor, 1799, 26-27; 1802, 46; 1805, 100; 1808, 155, 167-172, 174-175; sketch, 19; as U. S. Senator, 30, 49-50
Ross, John, 73
Rumstead, Aquila, 184
Russia, 294; offers mediation in War of 1812, 275, 277-278

S

St. Cloud Decree, 277
St. Patrick's Benevolent Society, 215
Sansom, Joseph, 372
Schwenkfelders, 6
Scotch, 5
Scotch-Irish, 4, 6, 16, 50
Scotland, 53
Scott, Sir William, and *Essex* case, 107
Scully, Dennis, 234
Sedition Act, 35, 124. *See also* Alien and Sedition Acts.
Selinsgrove, 51
Senate, Pennsylvania, 7, 8, 36, 80, 81, 117, 128, 130, 203, 205, 226, 235, 273, 307; banking legislation, 225, 274, 287-288; and constitutional revision, 249-250; Democrats in, 73, 109, 147, 175, 220, 234; and election of bank directors, 109-110, 351; and Federal constitutional amendment, 150; Federalists in, 27, 28, 37, 100, 147, 220, 234, 266, 284, 313, 321; on foreign affairs, 150, 243, 248-249; impeachment trial of Addison, 54-55; of Supreme Court judges, 78-79; and Incompatibility Act, 40-41; and judicial reform, 51-52, 66; on national affairs, 182-183; on Nicholls case, 192; Old School Democratis in, 220, 321; and Olmsted case, 188, 195, 209, 224; and Presidential election, 1800, 28-30; Quids in, 100, 147, 220; sustains McKean's vetoes, 52, 86; vote on changing capital, 1810, 382. *See also* General Assembly.
Senate, United States, 17, 35, 42, 49-50, 78, 123, 150; approves Compensation Act, 316; confirms Dallas as Secretary of the Treasury, 309; and declaration of war, 255, 256. *See also* Elections, U. S. Senators.
"Senex," on election of U. S. Senator, 1801, 33-34
Sergeant, Mrs. Elizabeth, and Olmsted case, 187-188, 193, 195-196, 198

INDEX 413

Sergeant, John, 172, 372, 381; candidate for Congress, 116, 117, 312, 320; as candidate for governor, 315; on embargo, 151; and Olmsted case, 193, 197
Sergeant, Thomas, 287
Seybert, Adam, 5; candidate for Congress, 216, 320
Sharswood, James, 372
Shee, John, 161, 162
Shenandoah Valley, 3, 33
Shippen, Edward, 114; on Olmsted case, 186; and Passmore affair, 56
Shore, Sir John, 17
Sitgreaves, Samuel, 46, 306, 371
Sixteen Million Loan, 279
Slavery, 1, 3, 277, 374
Smilie, John, 19, 58
Smith, Charles, 20; and Nicholls case, 191-192; and Olmsted case, 194, 196, 197, 199; and third party movement, 64
Smith, John, Federal Marshal: and Olmsted case, 196, 198, 207; reappointment, 230
Smith, Jonathan B., 90
Smith, Robert, U. S. Secretary of State, 365; agreement with Erskine, 241; negotiations with Jackson, 242-243
Smith, Samuel, 157, 173, 245; Democratic candidate for Congress, 118, 218; protests Madison caucus nomination, 161
Smith, Thomas, and Passmore affair, 56
Smyth, Alexander, 271
Snowden, John M., 68; on conduct of war, 276
Society of Constitutional Republicans, 82-83, 98-99; adopts address by Dallas, 92-93; dissolution of, 105; elects officers, 88, 90; opposes constitutional convention, 83, 89-90; principles of, 95; supports McKean, 100. *See also* Constitutional Republicans.
Society of Friends of the People, 94, 170; organization, 90; purpose, 91
Society of Independent Democrats, 169
Society of the Sons of St. George, 113
Somerset County, 3; in election of 1800, 28; of 1801, 37; of 1805, 350; of 1806, 119
Snyder, Simon, 95, 136, 138, 141-143, 155, 219, 230, 257, 265, 272, 309, 312, 314, 328, 334, 375, 382; and defense measures, 295, 296-297; and election of 1809, 201-204; and foreign affairs, 246, 248; and General Assembly: session of 1808-9, 179-181, 193-194; session of 1809-10, 205-210, 211, 212-213, 220-221; session of 1810-11, 222; session of 1811-12, 248-249; session of 1812-13, 272-275; session of 1814-15, 306-307; and gubernatorial election of 1805, 92-94, 98-101, 327, 350; of 1808, 167-169, 170, 171-172, 174-176; of 1811, 231-234; of 1814, 298-301; of 1817, 319; inauguration of, 181; Leib-Duane group opposes, 133, 141, 177; Leib opposes, 130, 140, 152, 200; and militia reforms, 248, 272, 306; Muhlenberg opposes, 97-98; and Nicholls case, 191; nominated for governor, 1805, 77, 87-89, 90; 1808, 151, 154; 1811, 226, 227; 1814, 288; and Old School Democrats, 211-212, 216, 220, 227-228, 244, 309; and Olmsted case, 193-198, 200, 206-208, 244, 334; proposed for Vice President, 258, 316, 380; sketch of, 50-51; as Speaker, 50, 84-85, 130, 139, 148; understanding with Leib, 152-153; vetoes banking bills, 273, 274, 287-288, 373
Snyderites, 108, 205, 209, 211, 226, 236, 239, 254, 255, 272; *Aurora* denounces, 310-311, 315; and Clinton candidacy, 1808, 159; and constitutional reform, 169, 222, 250; and *Democratic Press,* 136-138; and district delegate system, 202, 214, 311; and election of 1807, 139, 142-143; of 1808, 173-175; of 1809, 199-201, 203; of 1810, 213-218, 220; of 1811, 232-233; of 1812, 257-258, 264; of 1816, 320, 322; and election of Leib as U. S. Senator, 179-181; factions among, 315-316; and Federal patronage, 230, 231, 308-309; and Jefferson administration, 330; and Leib-Duane

group, 174, 214-216, 228-229, 237, 328-329; and Old School Democrats, 245, 282, 283, 311, 319; and Olmsted case, 184, 199, 200, 207, 209, 334; oppose Leib's appointment as postmaster in Philadelphia, 286, 297; Quids cooperate with, 173; support Madison, 1812, 231, 257-258; support Monroe, 314, 318, 322. *See also* Democrats; Republicans; Snyder, Simon.

South Carolina, 74, 261

Southwark, 214, 218, 281, 282, 295

Spain, 10, 111

Spayd, John, Quid candidate for governor, 1808, 155, 170, 172, 174, 175, 264

Specie, shortage of, 274, 291-293

Speculation, 221, 274, 290, 376

Spring Garden, 264

State correspondence committee, 154-155, 159-161, 163, 169-170, 174

State rights, 10, 178, 183-184, 189, 190, 303; *Democratic Press* on, 200; end of Pennsylvania's struggle for, 198; as issue in election of 1809, 201; and Nicholls case, 191-192; and Olmsted case, 204, 206-207

State Treasurer, 50, 148, 185, 187

Steele, John, 87, 93, 141-142, 161, 365; and Federal patronage, 162, 230-231; nominated for U. S. Senate, 131-132

Stewart, John, Congressman, 58, 73, 85; and "clodpole incident," 85

Stewart, Thomas, 117

Suffrage, 7, 8, 13, 325, 337

Sunbury, 160, 382

Supreme Court, Pennsylvania, 19, 92, 123, 127, 155, 182, 189, 198, 215, 224, 232, 249, 334; and Addison trial, 54; Brackenridge appointed to, 53; decision in Duane case limits control of press, 114; impeachment of justices, 49, 66, 75, 77-79, 348; judges to report on British common law, 129; jurisdiction restricted, 108; McKean urges increase in, 65; on Olmsted case, 186; and Passmore affair, 56; rules in Nicholls case, 191; Tilghman succeeds Shippen as Chief Justice of, 114

Supreme Court, United States: decision in *Huidekoper's Lessee* v. *Douglass*, 189-190; Nicholls case appealed to, 191; and Olmsted case, 186, 192-193, 195-196

Supreme Executive Council, 6-7, 33

Susquehanna River, 3, 5

Sutherland, Dr. Joel B., 315, 380

Sweden, 164

Swedes, 5

T

Tammany Society of Philadelphia, 13, 22, 68, 138

Tannehill, Adamson, 226, 245, 271, 373; in election of 1810, 219, 272; of 1814, 299

Tariff, protective, 304, *333*

Taxes, 25-27, 249, 285, 375

Tennessee, 8, 10

Thackara, James, Clerk of House of Representatives, 205

Thames, Battle of the, 276

Third party movement, 64, 65, 92, 104, 110, 147; difficulty of, 119. *See also* Constitutional Republicans; Quids.

Thompson, John, 132, 140, 212, 227, 363; and Leib affair, 142; supports Leib for U. S. Senate, 131-132; and Thomas McKean, Jr., 128

Thompson, Thomas McKean, 110; Bryan attacks, 109; Secretary of the Commonwealth, 40

INDEX

Thomson, Charles, 317
Tilghman, William, 35, 217, 239; Federalist candidate for Governor, 1808, 155; and gubernatorial election of 1811, 232, 234; on Hartford Convention, 306; issues writ to free Duane, 114; on new banks, 221; and Olmsted case, 198
Tioga County, 3
Tod, John, 212, 363
Tompkins, Daniel D., 316, 321-322
Tracy, Uriah, 74
Treaty with Great Britain, 1806, 135
Tree of Liberty, Pittsburgh, 22, 38, 73, 341, 349; on Addison's impeachment, 54; and Pittsburgh politics, 117; supports McKean, 99
"Trout letter," of Peter Muhlenberg, 97-98
True American, 20, 355
Truxtun, Thomas, 239-240; on Duane, 158; on embargo, 166
Turnpikes, 221

U

Union County, 50
United States' Gazette, 78, 134, 217, 240, 262, 310, 311, 322; and British peace terms, 295, 305, 377; on *Chesapeake* affair, 136; and Constitutional Republicans, 83, 95, 96; on declaration of war, 256; on defense, 280, 281-282; and election of 1812, 267; of 1814, 300; of 1815, 309, 312-313; on embargo, 166, 252, 290; and foreign affairs, 106-107, 135-136, 242-243, 246, 248, 253-254, 277, 278; and Hartford Convention, 306, 379; on Madison administration, 242-243, 294, 305; on Olmsted case, 196; on *Quid Mirror*, 121; on Snyder, 222; on war loans, 279, 292; on War of 1812, 277-278, 283, 289, 294-295. *See also Gazette of the United States*.
University of Pennsylvania, 18
Upper Delaware Ward, 311

V

Van Horne, Isaac, 39; as candidate for Congress, 39
Venango County: in election of 1805, 350; of 1806, 118; of 1810, 218; of 1815, 313
Vermont, 8; in Presidential election of 1800, 31; of 1812, 268, 331; refuses militia, 284, 375
Vigilance committees, 22
Virginia, 1-3, 156, 230, 241, 263, 272, 275, 317; constitution of, 1; dominance of, 179; 256
Virginia Argus, Richmond, 158
Virginia Resolutions, 178
Virginians: refuse financial aid to Duane, 229, 230; in southwestern Pennsylvania, 4
Volunteers, Pennsylvania, 271, 272, 373, 374. *See also* Militia.

W

Wallace, John B., 261, 371
Waln, Robert, 162
Walnut Ward, 311
War of 1812, 177, 179, 236, 263, 305, 328, 332; declared, 237, 254-255; defeats, 1813, 275; Democrats and, 238, 241, 243-244, 246, 251, 254, 275-276, 367; effects of, 288-293, 308; end of, and politics, 303, 323; events of, 1813-1814, 293-296; Federalists and, 254, 255, 271-272, 277, 288, 294-295, 297, 307-308, 369; legislature supports, 271-272, 284, 373; and politics, 237, 329; Russian mediation, 277-278
War Department, 276, 295

INDEX

Warren County: in election of 1805, 350; of 1806, 118; of 1810, 218; of 1815, 313
Washington, George, 19, 26, 248; birthday ball, 241
Washington, D. C., 42-43, 58, 81, 112, 137, 154, 247, 254, 295, 299, 316; burning of, 295, 299; capital moved to, 18; suspends specie payments, 292
Washington, Pennsylvania, 38, 73; new banks in, 221
Washington Associations, 233; and election of 1813, 280, 374
Washington Benevolent Society, 280, 374
Washington County, 19, 38, 53, 157, 349, 372; in election of 1799, 26; of 1804, 73; of 1805, 350; demand for constitutional revision, 204, 250; Democrats in, 99
Washington Guards, 294
Waters, Esther, 187-188, 195-196, 198
Wayne, Isaac, Federalist candidate for governor, 1814, 297-299
Wayne County, 3; district delegate system in, 39; and election of 1799, 26; of 1802, 46; of 1805, 350; of 1808, 175
Weaver, Isaac, Jr., 40, 49, 273; becomes State Treasurer, 50; and constitutional revision, 249
"Weiser, Conrad," supposed pseudonym of William J. Duane, 209, 211, 363
Welles, Rosewell, 127
Welsh, 5
Wertz, Henry, 109-110
West Florida, 10
West Indies, 164
Western Pennsylvania, in election of 1805, 99
Westmoreland County, 34, 99, 250, 273; and election of 1799, 26; of 1805, 100, 350; of 1808, 175; of 1809, 204; Quids in, 236
Wetherill, Samuel, 90, 104
Wharton, General Robert, 280, 371
Wheat Sheaf Tavern, 140
Whelen, Israel, 59, 69
Whig Chronicle: and Leib, 372; supports Clinton, 267-268
Whig Society of Pennsylvania, 213-214, 227-228, 365
Whiskey Insurrection, 10, 12, 19
White, Artemas, 184
White Horse Tavern, 82, 172, 173
Whitehill, Robert, 141-142
Wilkes-Barre, 95
Wilkins, John, 19
Wilkins, John, Jr., 168; candidate for Congress, 46, 117-118
Wilkinson, James, 276, 293, 294
Williams, Jonathan, 312
Wilson, James, Duane's successor as editor of *Aurora*, 283, 375
Wing Dam Bill, 53
Wolbert, Frederick, 62-63, 90, 123, 126, 200, 230-231; as candidate for sheriff, 1806, 116-117, 121, 122; election investigated, 125; political activities, 60; renominated for sheriff, 143-144
Wolcott, Oliver, 295
Woods, John, 299
Worrell, Isaac, 90, 173
Wray's Tavern, 61
Wyoming Valley, 4

X

XYZ Affair, 9

Y

Yankees, 4
Yazoo affair, 110, 111, 116, 118, 351; Burr and, 134; compromise, 156, 157
Yeates, Jasper, 30, 334; on Olmsted case, 186; and Passmore affair, 56; on re-election of McKean, 95
Yellow fever epidemic, 17, 59, 60
York, 4, 50, 295; Clinton Democrats in, 260; new banks in, 221
York-Adams district, and election of 1808, 175
York County, 4, 19, 73, 85, 119, 207, 368; in election of 1800, 28; of 1805, 350; of 1806, 119; of 1807, 145; of 1810, 245; Republicans in, 327
Yrujo, Don Carlos Martinez, 91, 349; libel suits of, 114, 200